Meaning and Grammar

Meaning and Grammar

An Introduction to Semantics

Gennaro Chierchia and Sally McConnell-Ginet

second edition

The MIT Press
Cambridge, Massachusetts
London, England

Second printing, 2001

This book was set in Melior and Helvetica Condensed by Asco Typesetters, Hong Kong, and was printed and bound in the United States of America.

Second edition, first printing, 2000

Library of Congress Cataloging-in-Publication Data

Chierchia, Gennaro.
Meaning and grammar : an introduction to semantics / Gennaro Chierchia and Sally McConnell-Ginet. — 2nd ed.
p. cm.
Includes bibliographical references and index.
ISBN 0-262-03269-4 (alk. paper). — ISBN 0-262-53164-X (pbk. : alk. paper)
1. Semantics. 2. Semantics (Philosophy) I. McConnell-Ginet, Sally. II. Title.
P325.C384 2000
401'.43—dc21 99-20030
CIP

For Isa and for Carl

Contents

Preface

There are many phenomena that could reasonably be included in the domain of semantic theory. In this book we identify some of them and introduce general tools for semantic analysis that seem promising as components of a framework for doing research in natural language. Rather than discussing the many diverse approaches to meaning that have been proposed and are currently pursued, we focus on what has come to be known as logical, truth-conditional, or model-theoretic semantics. This general approach to meaning was developed originally within the tradition of logic and the philosophy of language and over the last twenty years or so has been applied systematically to the study of meaning in natural languages, due especially to the work of Richard Montague.

As we will see, logical semantics as currently conceived leaves many problems with no solution. The role of semantics in a grammar is the center of much controversy. And the relation between syntax and semantics is still not well understood, especially within some of the research paradigms currently dominant (including the one we adopt in this book). Nevertheless, we think that research in logical semantics has generated enough results to show that there are fundamental empirical properties of language that cannot be properly understood without such an approach to meaning. The present book can be viewed as an attempt to substantiate this claim.

We have tried to keep prerequisites at a minimum. The reader will find helpful some minimal acquaintance with syntactic theory, such as what can be acquired from an elementary introduction like Radford (1988). Basic set-theoretic notions and notational conventions are presented in an appendix. We do not assume any knowledge of formal logic, presenting what is needed directly in the text. Each logical tool is first introduced directly and then applied to relevant areas of natural language semantics. For example, in chapter 2 we present the basic semantic concepts associated with propositional logic without quantification. We then describe the syntax of a small fragment of English and use our logical tools to provide an explicit specification of how this fragment is to be interpreted. As we acquire more logical techniques, our fragments become progressively richer; that is, the range of structures analyzed becomes more varied and comprehensive, with later analyses building on earlier results.

Those with linguistic backgrounds but no logic will find the formal techniques new but will recognize many of the kinds of data and arguments used in application of these new techniques to linguistic phenomena. The syntax of our fragments is designed to employ as far as possible widely shared syntactic assumptions. Those with backgrounds in logic but not linguistics will probably encounter unfamiliar facts about language and ways in which logic can be used in empirical arguments. We also introduce a few of the most accessible and interesting ideas from recent research to give the reader some exposure to current work in semantics. Our hope is that the material presented here will give a fair idea of the nature of semantic inquiry and will equip the reader interested in pursuing these topics with the tools needed to get rapidly into what is now happening in the field.

The fragment technique we have adopted from Dowty, Wall, and Peters (1980), and our presentation, though different in many respects, owes much to their work. We use this technique not because we think it is the only way to do semantics but because it seems to us pedagogically so very useful. Fragments force us to show just how the formal theory will work for a very small part of a natural language. To understand how logical tools can be transferred to linguistic semantics and why they might be useful, some experience with this kind of detailed formulation seems essential. For much the same reasons we also provide exercises throughout the text. Readers need to try out for themselves the techniques we are introducing in order to appreciate what is involved in their application to natural language semantics.

In presenting this material, we have also tried to explore the interaction of meaning with context and use (that is, the semantics-pragmatics interface) and also to address some of the foundational questions that truth-conditional semantics raises, especially in connection with the study of cognition in general. This does not stem from any ambition to be comprehensive. But in our experience we find that the truth-conditional approach can be understood better by trying to set it in a broader perspective.

To put our lecture notes in the present form was no easy task for us. Some of the difficulties lie in the nature of things: we are dealing with a subject matter ridden with controversy and constantly shifting. Some of the difficulties were in us: writing this up just wouldn't fit easily with the rest of our research and lives. There has been a lot of back and forth between us on each chapter, although Sally is primarily responsible for chapters 1, 4, 6, 8, and the appendix and Gennaro for chapters 2, 3, 5, 7, and 9. The organization of the material reflects closely the way we have come to like to teach semantics; we can only hope that others may also find it useful. Teachers may wish to omit parts of the book or to supplement it with readings from some of the classic papers in semantics.

We have been helped in various ways by many people. Erhard Hinrichs put an enormous amount of work into commenting on a previous draft; only our recognition that he should not be held responsible for our mistakes kept us from co-opting him as coauthor. Craige Roberts has also provided us with a wealth of helpful and detailed comments. Leslie Porterfield and Veneeta Srivastav have directly inspired many improvements of substance and form at various stages; Leslie did most of the work involved in preparing the separately available answers to the exercises. Much good advice and help also came from Nirit Kadmon, Fred Landman, Alice ter Meulen, Bill McClure, Steve Moore, Carl Vikner, Adam Wyner, and our students in introductory semantics at Cornell and at the 1987 LSA Summer Institute at Stanford (where Gennaro used a draft of the book in the semantics course he taught). Many other friends and colleagues have encouraged us as we worked on this book. We have each also been supported by our families; our spouses in particular have been very close to us through the ups and downs of this project.

We have written this book for the same reasons we chose this field for a living: we want to be rich and famous.

Preface to the Second Edition

When we wrote the first edition of this book, semantics was already a flourishing field in generative linguistics. Now, almost ten years later, it is nearing full maturity. There are many results providing us not only with descriptively adequate accounts of a broad range of phenomena but also with novel significant insight into them. We are thinking, for example, of all the work on generalized quantifiers, anaphora and binding, tense and aspect, and polarity phenomena, to mention but a few key topics. The current state of semantics continues to be very lively. The frontier of the field is constantly being pushed forward, and one cannot take for granted any notion or practise. A graduate student walks in, and there come new ideas about meaning that raise fundamental questions about previous ways of thinking. We are happy to be living through this process.

In spite of the continuing infusion of new ideas into linguistic semantics, a certain number of fundamental notions, arguments, and techniques seem to keep playing a pivotal role. Because our text deals with many of these, we were persuaded that there was some point in updating it a bit. There is, of course, no one best way of presenting core semantic concepts. Some, for example, like to start from the structure of the clause and introduce semantic techniques needed to interpret various aspects of it. In this textbook we instead opted to walk people into the systematic study of linguistic meaning by matching formal tools with linguistic applications in increasing order of complexity (from propositional connectives and truth conditions, to quantification and binding, intensionality, and so on). With all its limits, we and many other teachers find this to be an effective method of introducing semantic argumentation. It strikes a reasonable balance of user friendliness versus completeness and makes it possible to combine formal thoroughness with exploration of the linguistic significance of basic concepts and techniques. This general approach is retained in this second edition.

Four chapters have been pretty substantially rewritten. We have tried to make chapter 3, on variable binding and quantification, somewhat gentler and more user-friendly, though the notions dealt with there probably still remain the hardest to grasp for a beginner. Chapter 5, on intensionality, has been changed mostly in the part on tense, but also in the presentation of the semantics of embedded clauses. Chapter 7, on abstraction, has been restructured, partly to enhance pedagogical effectiveness and partly in light of recent developments in the understanding of VP anaphora. Finally, chapter 8, on word meaning, has gone through an overhaul that has led to a somewhat different take on questions of lexical decomposition, more on event semantics and aspect, and a new section on adverbs. And we've implemented a few local changes elsewhere. For example, following a suggestion by Veneeta Dayal, we have introduced the notion of implicature in chapter 1. We have added a section on type-driven interpretation to chapter 2. We have also extensionalised the final chapter on generalized quantifiers to allow more flexible access to such notions. In its present form, the book has a modular character. After chapter 3, the remaining material can be covered pretty much in any order. For example, one can easily jump from chapter 3 directly to chapter 9 (after a quick look at sec. 1.1. in chapter 7). Instructors can design their own itinerary.

Revising this book has been like updating an old program that still runs. One touches things in one place, and a new bug pops up in some other place. We hope that we have taken all the little bugs out, but we cannot be sure. The whole process has been complicated not only by what has happened in the field since our first try but also by having to work across the Atlantic. Our basic process was the same as before. Sally was the first drafter on the new versions of chapters 3 and 8 plus the new sections in chapters 1 and 2 and the minor additions to the appendix; Genarro was the first drafter for the revised chapters 5 and 7 and the modified sections of chapter 9. Each of us, however, critiqued the other's drafts. The discussions between us have been not in the least less animated than they were before.

We are grateful to our friends and colleagues and students, who have given us feedback over the years. There are many good suggestions we've gotten that we just could not implement, but many of the improvements we were able to make were inspired by others' comments. We owe a big debt of gratitude to Amy Brand for her encouragement in taking up this task and expert help throughout the process. We also thank Yasuyo Iguchi, who consulted with us on revising the book's design, and Alan Thwaits, who edited our very messy manuscript. And our families gave us June together in Italy and July together in Ithaca, without which we could not have managed the job.

As we mentioned above, part of what made us agree to prepare a second edition was the feeling that in spite of its constant growth, the core of semantics in the generative tradition remains on a fairly solid and stable footing. The death knell has sometimes been sounded in recent years for various semantic notions: possible worlds and types and models and even entailment. But examining current semantic practice in the relevant empirical domains seems to show that the concepts in question (or some more or less trivial variants thereof) are still thriving. This is not to say that there are no foundational disagreements. But in spite of them, semantics is an even more vital and cohesive field of inquiry within generative linguistics than it was when we published the first edition of this text.

Readers of the original preface have probably already guessed the other reason we agreed to prepare a second edition. We still cling to the hope that semantics will some day make us rich and famous.

1 The Empirical Domain of Semantics

1 Introduction

Semantics is the branch of linguistics devoted to the investigation of linguistic meaning, the interpretation of expressions in a language system. We do not attempt a comprehensive survey of the many different approaches to semantics in recent linguistics but choose instead to introduce a particular framework in some detail. Many of the concepts and analytical techniques we introduce have their origins in logic and the philosophy of language; we apply them to the study of actual human languages.

When we say that our focus is on semantics as a branch of linguistics, we are adopting a particular conception of the methods and goals of linguistic inquiry. That conception is rooted in the generative paradigm that began to reshape the field of linguistics in fundamental ways over forty years ago. Noam Chomsky's *Syntactic Structures*, published in 1957, introduced the three key ideas that we take to be definitive of that paradigm.

The first is the idea that a grammar of a language can be viewed as a set of abstract devices, rule systems, and principles that serve to characterize formally various properties of the well-formed sentences of that language. The grammar, in this sense, generates the language. This idea was already established in the study of various artificial languages within logic and the infant field of computer science; what was novel was Chomsky's claim that natural languages—the kind we all learn to speak and understand in early childhood—could also be generated by such formal systems. In a sense, when linguists adopted this view, they adopted the idea that theoretical linguistics is a branch of (applied) mathematics and in this respect like contemporary theoretical physics and chemistry.

Few generative linguists, however, would be completely comfortable with such a characterization of their discipline. A major reason for their finding it inadequate lies in the second key idea Chomsky introduced, namely, that generative grammars are psychologically real in the sense that they constitute accurate models of the (implicit) knowledge that underlies the actual production and interpretation of utterances by native speakers. Chomsky himself has never spoken of linguistics as part of mathematics but has frequently described it as a branch of cognitive psychology. It is the application of mathematical models to the study of the cognitive phenomenon of linguistic knowledge that most generative linguists recognize as their aim. Again, the parallel with a science like physics is clear. To the extent that their interest is in mathematical systems as models of physical phenomena rather than in the formal properties of the systems for their own sake, physicists are not mathematicians. A single individual may, of course, be both a mathematician and a linguist (or a physicist). But as linguists, our focus is on modeling the cognitive systems whose operation in some sense "explains" linguistic phenomena. Linguistics is an empirical science, and in that respect it is like physics and unlike (pure) mathematics.

The third idea we want to draw from the generative paradigm is intimately connected to the first two: linguistics cannot be limited to the documentation of what is said and how it is interpreted—our actual *performance* as speakers and hearers—any more than physics can limit its subject matter to the documentation of measurements and meter readings of directly observable physical phenomena. The linguistic knowledge we seek to model, speakers' *competence*, must be distinguished from their observable linguistic behavior. Both the linguist and the physicist posit abstract theoretical entities that help explain the observed phenomena and predict further observations under specified conditions.

The distinction between competence and performance has sometimes been abused and often misunderstood. We want to emphasize that we are not drawing it in order to claim that linguists should ignore performance, that observations of how people use language are irrelevant to linguistic theory. On the contrary, the distinction is important precisely because observations of naturally occurring linguistic behavior are critical kinds of data against which generative linguists test their theories. They are not, however, the only kinds of data available. For example, linguists often ask native speakers (sometimes themselves) for intuitive judgments as to whether certain strings of words in a given language constitute a well-formed or grammatical sentence of that language. Such judgments are also data, but they seldom come "naturally."

Our approach to semantics lies in the generative tradition in the sense that it adopts the three key ideas sketched above: (1) that generative grammars of formal (artificial) languages are models of the grammars of natural languages, (2) which are realized in human minds as cognitive systems (3) that are distinct from the directly observable human linguistic behavior they help to explain. This tradition started, as we have noted, with important advances in the study of syntax; fairly soon thereafter it bore fruit in phonology. There was important semantic work done by generative grammarians from the early sixties on, but it was not until the end of the sixties that systematic ways of linking the semantic methods developed by logicians to the generative enterprise were found. In our view, this development constitutes a breakthrough of enormous significance, one whose consequences linguists will be exploring for some time. One of our main aims in this book is to introduce the concepts and methods that made the breakthrough possible and to indicate some of the ways logical semantics so conceived contributes to the generative enterprise in linguistics.

We begin by considering some of the linguistic phenomena that one might ask a semantic theory to account for, the range of data that seem at first glance centrally to involve meaning. Our first observation may discourage some readers: there is not total agreement on exactly which facts comprise that range. But this is hardly surprising. Recent discussions of epistemology and the philosophy of science repeatedly claim that there are no "raw" or "pure" data, that abstract principles come into play even in preliminary individuation of a given constellation of facts. Thus, identifying phenomena is itself inescapably theory-laden. We will try, however, to introduce data here that are bound to our particular theoretical hypotheses only weakly. That is, accounting for (most of) these data seems a goal shared by many different approaches to semantics.

A second point to remember is that phenomena that pretheoretically involve meaning may prove not to be homogeneous. This too is unsurprising. Linguists have long recognized the heterogeneity of linguistic phenomena and so have divided the study of linguistic forms minimally into phonology and syntax and have further articulated each of these fields. And, of course, it is recognized that syntax and phonology themselves interact with other cognitive systems and processes in explaining, for example, how people arrange and pronounce words in producing utterances. Similarly, the study of meaning is bound to be parcelled out to a variety of disciplines and perhaps also to different branches of linguistics. A major aim of this book is to explore the question of how linguistic investigations of meaning interact with the study of other cognitive systems and processes in our coming better to understand what is involved in the production and interpretation of utterances by native speakers of a language.

It seems very likely that certain aspects of utterance meaning fall outside the realm of semantic theorizing. It has been argued, for example, that some aspects of meaning are primarily to be explained in terms of theories of action. Several different sorts of pragmatic theory adopt this approach. Speech act theories, for example, focus on what people are doing in producing utterances: asserting, questioning, entreating, and so on. Such theories can help explain how people manage to mean more than they actually say by looking at the socially directed intentional actions of speakers.

Here is an example where what is meant might go beyond the meaning of what is said. Suppose Molly is at a restaurant and says to her waiter, "I'd like a glass of water." In a clear sense Molly has not directly asked the waiter to bring her a glass of water, yet she means much the same thing by her utterance as if she had said, "Bring me a glass of water." But if Molly utters "I'd like a glass of water" to her hiking companions as they ascend the final hundred feet of a long trail from the bottom to the top of the Grand Canyon, the interpretation is different. In the latter case she probably means simply to report on her desires and not to make a request of her fellow hiker. How do we know this? Presumably in part because we know that Molly cannot be expecting her words to move her walking companion to produce a glass of water for her, whereas she might well intend those same words so to move the waiter in the restaurant. This knowledge has to do with our experience of restaurants and hiking trails and with general expectations about people's motives in speaking to one another.

Understanding what Molly means by her utterance to a particular addressee seems, then, to involve at least two different kinds of knowledge. On the one hand, we must know the meaning of what she has explicitly said—in this case, what the English sentence "I'd like a glass of water" means. Roughly, semantics can be thought of as explicating aspects of interpretation that depend only on the language system and not on how people put it to use. In slightly different terms we might say that semantics deals with the interpretation of *linguistic expressions*, of what remains constant whenever a given expression is uttered. On the other hand, we will not understand what Molly means in uttering that sentence unless we also know why she has bothered to utter it in the particular surroundings in which she and her addressee are placed—in this case, whether she is trying to do more than update her addressee on her internal state. Pragmatics is the study of *situated uses* of language, and it addresses such questions as the status of utterances as actions with certain kinds of intended effects. Since direct experience with interpretation of language is experience with interpreting uses, however, we cannot always be sure in advance which phenomena will fall exclusively in the domain of semantics and which will turn out to require attention to pragmatic factors as well.

As our adoption of the generative paradigm implies, we take linguistics to include not only the study of languages and their interpretations as abstract systems but also the study of how such systems are represented in human minds and used by human agents to express their thoughts and communicate with others. Thus we develop our semantic theory with a view to its interaction with a pragmatic theory. We will consider not only what linguistic expressions themselves mean (semantics in the strict sense) but also what speakers mean in using them (pragmatics). In this chapter, unless a distinction is explicitly drawn, semantic(s) should be thought of as shorthand for semantic(s)/pragmatic(s).

For most of our initial discussion we can safely ignore the important theoretical distinction between interpreted linguistic forms on the one hand (what, say, the English sentence "I'd like a glass of water" means) and interpreted utterances on the other (what Molly's utterance of "I'd like a glass of water" means). The issue of just how semantics should be related to more pragmatically oriented theories of information processing is wide open, however, and we will return to it at various points.

What should semantics, broadly construed, take as its subject matter? The rest of this chapter addresses this question. Our discussion is intended not to be exhaustive but only indicative of the range of language-related phenomena relevant to inquiry about meaning.

The third section of this chapter considers implication relations between sentences that speakers seem to recognize on the basis of their knowledge of meaning. The fourth and final section considers a number of other semantic properties and relations that speakers' intuitive judgments reveal, some of which are in some sense parasitic on implication relations. Such judgments are often very subtle, and learning how to tap semantic intuitions reliably and discriminate among the distinct phenomena that give rise to them is an important part of learning to do semantics. In a real sense, such intuitive judgments constitute the core of the empirical data against which semantic theories must be judged.

2 General Constraints on Semantic Theory

Before we can fruitfully consider particular varieties of intuitive judgments of semantic properties and relations, we need to consider some general properties of semantic competence.

2.1 The productivity of linguistic meaning

It is a familiar but no less remarkable fact that indefinitely many syntactically complex linguistic expressions in a language can have linguistic meanings associated with them. This is simply the semantic analogue of the fact that indefinitely many complex linguistic expressions can be classed as syntactically well-formed by the grammar.

We have no trouble whatsoever in grasping the meaning of sentences even if we have never encountered them before. Consider

(1) I saw a pink whale in the parking lot.

Few if any of our readers will have heard or seen this particular sentence before. Yet you can quite easily understand it. How is this feat possible? The experience of understanding a newly encountered sentence like (1) seems much like the experience of adding two numbers we have never summed before, say

(2) $1437.952 + 21.84$

We can do the sum in (2) and come up with 1459.792 because we know something about numbers and have an algorithm or rule for adding them together. For instance, we may break each of the two numbers to be summed into smaller pieces, adding first the digits in the thousandths place (having added a 0 in that place to the second number), moving on to the hundredths place, and so on. All we really have to know are the numbers (on this approach, the significance of the decimal representation of each number in a base ten system) and how to sum single digits, and we are then in business. By the same token, we presumably understand a sentence like (1) because we know what the single words in it mean (what *pink* and *whale* mean, for example) and we have an algorithm of some kind for combining them. Thus part of the task of semantics must be to say something about what word meaning might be and something about the algorithms for combining those word meanings to arrive at phrasal and sentential meanings.

Whatever linguistic meaning is like, there must be some sort of compositional account of the interpretation of complex expressions as composed or constructed from the interpretations of their parts and thus ultimately from the interpretations of the (finitely many) simple expressions contained in them and of the syntactic structures in which they occur. We will speak of the simplest expressions as words, except when we want to recognize semantically relevant morphological structure internal to words. Sentences are complex expressions of special importance, but smaller phrases are also semantically relevant. We also briefly look at interpretive phenomena that go beyond single sentences and involve discourse.

In theory the semantically relevant structure of a complex expression like a sentence might bear little or no relation to the syntactic structure assigned to it on other linguistic grounds (on the basis, for example, of grammaticality judgments and intuitions about syntactic constituency). In practice, many linguists assume that semantics is fed fairly directly by syntax and that surface syntactic constituents will generally be units for purposes of semantic composition. And even more linguists would expect the units of semantic composition to be units at some level of syntactic structure, though perhaps at a more abstract level than the surface.

Logicians used to be notorious among linguists for their pronouncements on the "illogicality" of natural language surface syntax. More recently, however, logical approaches to semantics have proposed that the surface syntactic structure of natural language is a much better guide to semantic constituency than it might at first seem to be. Both syntax and the relevant areas of logic have developed rapidly in recent years, but it is still an open question just how close the correspondence is between the structure needed for constructing sentential meanings (what we might think of as semantic structure) and that needed for constructing sentences as syntactic objects. There is also a vigorous debate about whether more sophisticated approaches to semantics and syntax make it possible to dispense with multiple levels of syntactic structure.[1]

Certainly, however, interpretations of both words and syntactic constructions will play a role in any systematic account of how sentences (and larger discourse texts) are assigned interpretations. An important test of a semantic theory is set by compositionality. Can the theory generate the required interpretations for complex expressions from a specification of interpretations for the basic items? As we will see, explicit specification of how word meanings are combined to produce sentential meanings is not a trivial task.

2.2 Semantic universals

A fundamental concern of generative linguistics is to specify what characteristics seem to be constitutive of the human language capacity. In what ways are languages fundamentally alike? We may also be able to say some very interesting things about the ways in which that linguistic capacity constrains possible differences among languages, about the parameters of variation.

There is rather little that might count as semantic typology or as a direct analogue to the parametric approach in syntax.[2] There has, however, been some attention to semantic universals. In the late sixties and early seventies, quite interesting attempts to get at universal semantic principles came from the so-called generative semanticists. Working in the generative tradition, these linguists claimed that semantics was fundamentally just a very abstract level of syntax where a universally available stock of basic words or concepts were combined. The syntax of this universal semantic base was simple, involving a very few categories and rules for combining them. Getting from these abstract structures to the surface sentences of a natural language involved, among other things, replacing complex structures with single words. It was hypothesized, for example, that something like the structure in (3) is the source of English *kill*; a lexical substitution rule replaces the tree with the single word *kill*. Small capital letters indicate that the words represented are from the universal semantic lexicon. (Generative semanticists used V for simple verbs and for other predicate expressions, including predicate adjectives and the negative particle *not*.)

(3)

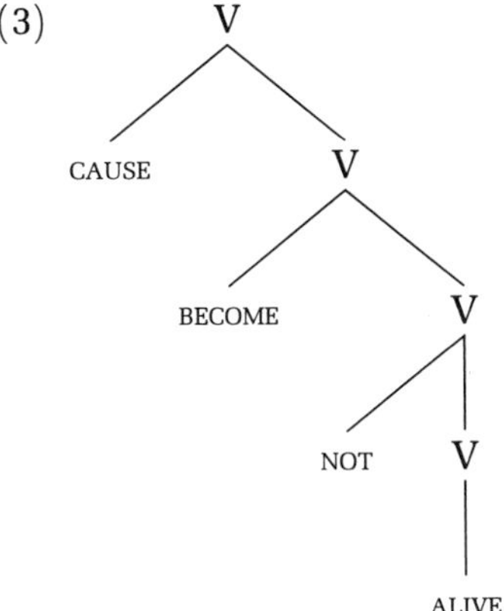

From this standpoint, it is natural to look to syntactic structures for constraints on what might possibly get lexicalized. McCawley (1971), for example, claimed that there could not be a word, say *flimp*, meaning to kiss a girl who is allergic to ..., that is, that no sentence of form (4*a*) could mean what is meant by (4*b*).

(4) *a*. Lee flimped garlic.
b. Lee kissed a girl who is allergic to garlic.

The explanation he offered was that lexical substitution rules have to replace single constituents and *kiss a girl who is allergic to* is not a single constituent. Of course, since the replaced elements come from a universal language that is not spoken by anyone, it is not easy to be sure that something with the meaning in question might not be expressible as a single constituent. The verb *flimp* might be introduced in a group that thinks that kissing a girl allergic to a certain substance in some interesting way affects the kisser's relation to the substance (perhaps allergies can be so transmitted, so flimping puts the flimper in jeopardy of acquiring an allergy). What is interesting, though, is McCawley's attempt to offer a formal account of alleged material universals, such as the absence from all languages of words like *flimp*.[3] We discuss lexical meanings in somewhat more detail in chapter 8.

Even if this particular approach to the kinds of words languages will have may now seem inadequate, the general idea of attempting to find explanations in terms of general linguistic principles for what can and cannot be lexicalized is of considerable interest. For instance, we do not know of any languages that lack a word that is more or less synonymous with *and*, joining expressions from different syntactic (and semantic) categories—sentences, noun phrases, or prepositional phrases—by using what can be seen as the same semantic operation. Nor do we know of a language that uses a single word to mean what is meant by *not all* in English yet uses a syntactically complex expression to mean what *none* means. Although it is often said that comparatives (*taller*) are semantically simpler than the corresponding absolutes (*tall*), no language we know of expresses the comparative notion as a single morpheme and the absolute in a more complex way. Can semantic theory shed light on such observations (on the assumption that they are indeed correct)?

Certain quite abstract semantic notions seem to play an important role in many cross-linguistic generalizations. For example, agent, cause, change, goal, and source have been among the *thematic roles* proposed to link verb meanings with their arguments. Fillmore (1968) suggested a semantic case grammar in which predicates were universally specified in terms of the thematic roles associated with their arguments. Language-specific rules, along with some universal principles ranking the different thematic roles, then mapped the arguments of a verb into appropriate syntactic or morphological structures. The UCLA Syntax Project reported on in Stockwell, Schachter, and Partee (1973) adapted Fillmore's framework in developing a computational implementation of their grammar, and similar ideas have figured in other computational approaches to linguistic analysis. We discuss thematic roles in somewhat more detail in chapter 8.

Are such notions part of universal grammar, or is there another way to think about them? Are they connected more to general cognitive phenomena than to language as such? Perhaps, but in any case, certain empirical generalizations about linguistic phenomena seem linked to these semantic notions. For example, in language after language the words and constructions used to speak about space and spatial relations (including motion) are recycled to speak of more abstract domains, for example, possession. The precise details are not universal: Finnish uses the locative case in many instances where English would use the nonspatial verb *have* ("Minulla on kissa" literally glosses as "At me is a cat" but is equivalent to "I have a cat"). But English does use spatial verbs and prepositions to talk about changes in possession ("The silver tea set went to Mary"). The general claim, however, is that resources for describing perceptual experience and the principles that organize them are universally redeployed to speak of matters that are less concrete. As Jackendoff (1983, 188–189) puts it,

In exploring the organization of concepts that ... lack perceptual counterparts, we do not have to start de novo. Rather, we can constrain the possible hypotheses about such concepts by adapting, insofar as possible, the independently motivated algebra of spatial concepts to our new purposes. The psychological claim behind this methodology is that the mind does not manufacture abstract concepts out of thin air, either. It adapts machinery that is already available, both in the development of the individual organism and in the evolutionary development of the species.

Investigations of the semantic value of words and grammatical particles, especially recurring general patterns of relationships, may help us understand more about human cognition generally.

One area where we find semantic universals is in combinatorial principles and relations; indeed, many investigators assume that it is only at the level of basic expressions that languages differ semantically, and it may well be true that the child need only learn lexical details. For example, languages are never limited to additive semantic principles like that of conjunction; predication, for example, seems to be universally manifested. Logical approaches to semantics have paid more explicit attention to composition than most other approaches and thus suggest more explicit hypotheses about how languages structure meaning. One question has to do with the different kinds of semantic values expressions can have: just as *to* and *number* are of different syntactic categories in English, they are associated with different semantic classes, or *types*, in any logical approach to semantics, and the semantic value associated with sentences is of yet another different type. Universally we need distinctions among types. Semantic theory should provide us with some account of these distinctions and allow us to investigate the empirical question of whether languages differ in the semantic types they encode.

Our discussion will focus primarily on English, since that is the language we and our readers share. Occasionally, however, we draw illustrations from other languages, and we intend our general approach to provide a framework in which to do semantics for human languages generally, not simply for English.

2.3 The significance of language: "aboutness" and representation

Meaning manifests itself in the systematic link between linguistic forms and things, what we speak of or talk about. This "aboutness" of language is so familiar that it may not seem noteworthy. But the fact that our languages carry meaning enables us to use them to express messages, to convey information to one another. As Lewis Carroll observed, we can talk about shoes and ships and sealing wax and whether pigs have wings. We can also speak of South Africa, Ingrid Bergman, birthdays, wearing clothes well, fear of flying, and prime numbers. Were languages not to provide for significance in this sense, the question of meaning would hardly arise. Nonetheless, some semantic theorists have thought that such aboutness is not really part of the domain of semantics. They have focused instead on the cognitive structures that represent meaning, taking the fundamental significance of language to reside in relations between linguistic expressions and what are sometimes called "semantic representations."

On our view, the significance of language, its meaningfulness, can be thought of as involving both aboutness and representational components. Theorists differ in the emphasis they place on these components and in the view they hold of their connections. It will be convenient for the discussion that follows to have labels for these two aspects of significance. *Informational significance* is a matter of aboutness, of connections between language and the world(s) we talk about. Informational significance looks outward to a public world and underlies appraisal of messages in terms of objective nonlinguistic notions like truth. *Cognitive significance* involves the links between language and mental constructs that somehow represent or encode speakers' semantic knowledge. Cognitive significance looks inward to a speaker's mental apparatus and does not confront issues of the public reliability of linguistic communication.

2.3.1 The informational significance of language Language enables us to talk about the world, to convey information to one another about ourselves and our surroundings in a reliable fashion. What properties of language and its uses underlie this remarkable fact? What allows language to serve as a guide to the world and to enable us to learn from what others have perceived (seen, heard, felt, smelled) without having to duplicate their perceptual experience ourselves?

Informational significance does not require that language links to the world in ways that are predetermined by the physical structure of our environment. Nor does it require that environmental information is simply registered or received without active input from perceiving and thinking human minds. Yet it does probably require a regular and systematic correspondence between language and the shared environment, what is publicly accessible to many different human minds.

If you are skeptical about informational significance, consider the use of language in giving directions, warnings, recipes, planning joint activities, describing events. Things occasionally misfire, but by and large such uses of language are remarkably effective. Language could not work at all in such ways were it not imbued with some kind of informational significance, being about matters in a public world.

Let us make this more concrete with a couple of examples. Suppose we utter

(5) This is yellow.

Interpreting *this* and other demonstrative expressions is problematic if the interpreter does not have access to some contextually salient entity to which it refers—perhaps the drapes to which someone is pointing. Since we have provided no picture to accompany (5), readers do not know what *this* refers to and cannot fully understand what its use means. The important points here are (1) that certain expressions seem to be used to refer, to indicate certain nonlinguistic entities, and (2) that knowing how to grasp what such expressions refer to is part of knowing what they mean. Expressions like *this* provide particularly vivid illustrations, but the same point holds of expressions like *the man who is sitting in the third row* and many others.

Now let us consider another example.

(6) The door is closed.

This sentence would accurately describe the situation depicted on the right in (7) but not that depicted on the left.[4]

(7)

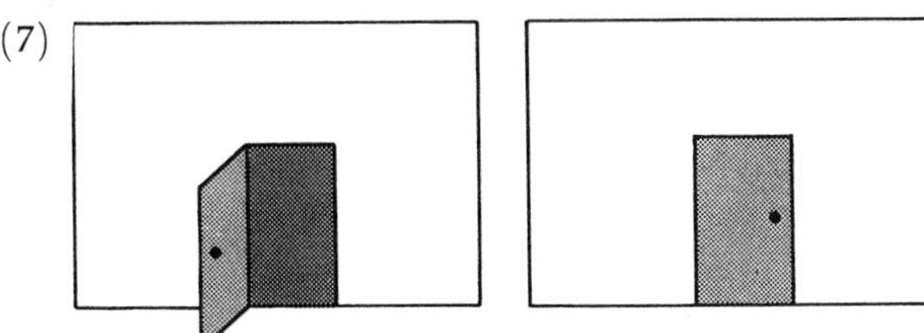

There are quite solid intuitions about the relation of sentence (6) to the two kinds of situations illustrated in (7). This fact is obvious yet nonetheless remarkable.

First, notice that the relation between the sentence and situations seems to be one that is independent of how those situations are presented. Instead of the drawings, we might have included photos or enclosed a videotape. We might even have issued you an invitation to come with us to a place where we could point out to you an open door and one that is closed. If you understand sentence (6), you can discriminate the two sorts of situation, no matter how we present them to you.

Second, observe that (6) can describe not just one or two, but a potential infinity of, different situations. In the picture on the right in (7), there is no cat in front of the closed door. But (6) would apply just as well to a situation like that depicted in (8), which is different from the right side of (7) only in that it contains a cat.

(8)

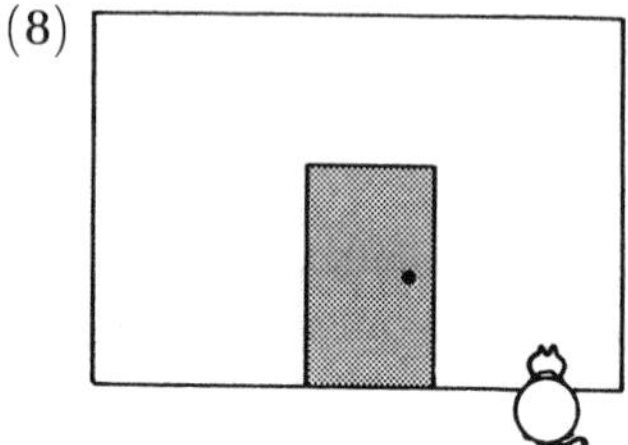

There is no need to stop with one cat or two or three, etc. We know how to keep going. The crucial point is that our knowledge of the relation between sentences and situations is not trivial and cannot consist in just remembering which particular situations are ones that a particular sentence can describe. Understanding what situations a sentence describes or, more generally, what information it conveys is crucial to grasping its meaning. It seems eminently reasonable to expect semantics to provide some account of this phenomenon.

Of course, language also enables us to talk with one another about more private internal worlds, to express our attitudes or mental states: hopes, beliefs, fears, wishes, dreams, fantasies. This too can be thought of as the conveying of information, but information in this case may seem less public or objective because the experiencing subject has some kind of privileged access to it. We cannot draw a picture to illustrate the situations described by sentence (9), but this does not mean that we do not know quite a lot about which situations it does, and which it does not, describe.

(9) Joan wants a tomato sandwich.

It is just that the differences among these situations are not apparent from purely visual signs. We would have equal difficulty using pictures to represent situations described or not described by sentence (10), yet what (10) is about is no less public than what (6) is about.

(10) Joan ate a tomato sandwich yesterday but not today.

What is noteworthy here is that language serves to bring private mental states into the public eye. Joan can speak about her desire to have a tomato sandwich today with the same ease that she speaks about the tomato sandwich that she actually consumed yesterday. Through language we not only inform one another about our external environment; we also manage to inform others of certain aspects of what our internal environment is like, thus externalizing or objectifying that internal experience to some extent. We can (sometimes) tell one another what is on our minds and we can use language to share what we imagine, suppose, or pretend.

Thus, when we speak of informational significance, we include not only links to physical or concrete phenomena but also to mental or abstract phenomena. There are deep philosophical questions that can be raised about the ontological status of different kinds of phenomena, but the important empirical fact for linguistic semantics is that for all of them we do indeed succeed in conveying information to one another by talking about them. It is in this sense that meaning always involves informational significance.

Semantic theories of informational significance are often called *referential* theories. *Truth-conditional semantics* is a particular kind of referential theory, which we will introduce in the next chapter and illustrate in more detail in succeeding chapters.

2.3.2 The cognitive significance of language The whole question of the meaningfulness of language has been approached from the inward-looking perspective of cognitive significance. The general idea is that we have ways of representing mentally what is meant by what we and others say. Perhaps, the suggestion seems to go, your understanding sentence (6), "The door is closed," is a matter of your recovering some internal representation of its meaning. Proponents of representational theories of meaning have usually not paid much attention to informational significance or even more generally to the capacity of people to judge with remarkable uniformity relations between sentences and nonlinguistic situations. Rather, they have focused on understanding as a matter of what interpreters can infer about the cognitive states and processes, the semantic representations, of utterers. You understand us, on this view, to the extent that you are able to reconstruct semantic representations like the ones on which we have based what we say. Communicative success depends only on matching representations and not on making the same links to situations. As we will see in the next chapter, it is not impossible to connect a representational account with a referential one; nonetheless, most representationalists have simply ignored the question of objective significance, of how we manage to judge which of the situations depicted in (7) is described by sentence (6). They have seldom worried about the fact that there is an everyday sense of aboutness in which we take ourselves to be talking about our friends, the weather, or what we just ate for dinner, and not about our representations of them. Even if our impression that we are not just conveying representations but are talking about what is represented might ultimately be illusory, it does deserve explanation.

Some outward looking approaches view the cognitive significance of language as ultimately understood in terms of its informational significance. In such approaches, people may construct representations of what sentences mean, but the question of whether such representations are essentially identical need not arise. Understanding is a matter not of retrieving representations but of achieving consensus on informational significance.

It is almost certainly true that our talk about the world works so well because of fundamental similarities in our mental representations of it. Yet the similar representations required might not be semantic as such but connected to our perceptual experience. Nonetheless, that similar perceptual experience would depend on similar contact with a shared external environment. In this sense, a connection to the represented world is still basic, since it provides the basis for the similarities in perceptual experience, which in turn are somehow linked to linguistic expressions.

The semantic framework developed here emphasizes objective significance and referential connections but does not assume that the meaningfulness of language, its full significance, is exhausted by its informational significance. Indeed, we think that some aspects of how meanings are represented are meaningful even though they do not directly affect informational significance. Our guess is that the aspect of meaningfulness that we have called cognitive significance has important implications for how conveyed information is processed. Chapter 6 discusses approaches to semantics that relate the informational significance of sentences to contextual factors and to the functioning of sentences in discourse, and in chapter 7 and part of chapter 8 we discuss some interesting proposals about the form of semantic representations.

3 Implication Relations

As we noted earlier, native speakers of a language have certain intuitions about what sentences or utterances convey, about the content and wider import of what is said, about what can be inferred on the basis of the sentence uttered, and about what is suggested. We often say that a sentence or utterance *implies* something. What is implied can be expressed by a sentence. For present purposes, we can think of *implication relations* as inferential relations between sentences. If *A* implies *B*, we often say that *A* suggests or conveys *B* or that *B* can be inferred from an utterance of *A*.

Implication relations can be classified on two axes. The first is what *licenses* or underwrites the implication. Where the basis for judging that *A* implies *B* is the informational or truth-conditional content of *A*, we say that *A entails B*. Where what licenses the implication has to do with expectations about the reasons people talk and about their typical strategies in using language, we say that *A implicates* (or *conversationally implicates*) *B*. Philosopher Paul Grice first argued for this distinction and proposed an account of how conversational implicatures work. Although there is still considerable disagreement on the theory of implicature, the need for such a distinction is now widely acknowledged.[5] We will discuss entailments in 3.1 and distinguish them from implicatures, which we discuss briefly in 3.2 (and in somewhat more detail in chapter 4). Formal semantic theories of the kind we develop in this book allow us to characterize entailment relations quite precisely. Distinguishing entailments from implicatures is important in developing semantic analyses, although it is by no means easy to do so (and there are often disagreements on where to draw the line).

The second axis of classification is the *discourse status* of the implication. The primary distinction here is between *assertions* (and various other things we might intend to accomplish when we say something: *questions*, *suppositions*, *orders*) and *presupposi-*

tions. An assertion aims to add content to the ongoing discourse, to effect some kind of change in what the conversationalists assume, whereas a presupposition presents its content as already assumed or taken for granted. Section 3.3 introduces presupposition and empirical tests to distinguish it from assertion and assertion-based implications. We will discuss assertion along with other kinds of speech acts in more detail in chapter 4 and again in chapter 6, where we return to presupposition. On this way of thinking of things, classifying an implication as a presupposition is neutral as to whether the implication might also be an entailment or some kind of conversational implicature (or licensed in some other way); *A* can, e.g., both entail *B* and presuppose *B*.

3.1 Entailment

Consider the following examples.

(11) *a.* This is yellow.
b. This is a fountain pen.
c. This is a yellow fountain pen.

(12) *a.* This is big.
b. This is a sperm whale.
c. This is a big sperm whale.

Imagine yourself uttering the sentences in (11) with reference to a particular object, perhaps a pen, perhaps something else. In such a situation you know that if your assertions of (11*a*) and (11*b*) are true (if the object is indeed yellow and indeed a fountain pen), then your assertion of (11*c*) is also true. It would be contradictory to assert the first two sentences and then deny the third; we discuss contradiction below. Any native speaker of English knows that the information conveyed by uttering (11*c*) is somehow already included in the information conveyed by uttering (11*a*) and (11*b*). This knowledge seems to be part of knowing what these sentences mean: we need know nothing about the object indicated by *this* beyond the fact that it is the same object for all three utterances. We say that the pair of sentences (11*a*) and (11*b*) *entails* sentence (11*c*).

Now imagine yourself uttering the sentences in (12), again keeping fixed what *this* refers to in all three utterances. Matters become very different. Suppose you take yourself to be pointing at a sperm whale. Sperm whales are pretty big creatures, so you might well assert that (12*a*) and (12*b*) are true. Suppose in addition that you judge that this particular specimen is not especially distinguished in size among its fellow sperm whales, that it's one of the smaller ones. In such circumstances it would be quite reasonable to deny (12*c*). In this case the *a* and *b* sentences do not entail the *c* sentence.

We would find the same difference in the two sets of sentences if we used *automobile* instead of *fountain pen* and used *galaxy* instead of *sperm whale*. *Yellow* (along with other adjectives like *round*, *featherless*, *dead*) behaves differently from *big* (and other adjectives like *strong*, *good*, *intelligent*), and this difference seems semantic in nature. (See chapter 8, section 3.1, for discussion of this difference.)

As we have noted, the relation between the pair (11*a*, *b*) and (11*c*) is usually called *entailment*. Together (11*a*) and (11*b*) entail (11*c*), whereas (12*a*) and (12*b*) do not entail (12*c*).

An entailment can be thought of as a relation between one sentence or set of sentences, the entailing expressions, and another sentence, what is entailed. For simplicity we equate a set of entailing sentences with a single sentence, their conjunction, which we get by joining the sentences using *and*. The conjunction is true just in case each individual sentence in the set is true, and it describes exactly those situations that can also be described by each one of the individual sentences. We could, for example, simply look at the English sentences "This is yellow, and this is a fountain pen" and "This is big, and this is a sperm whale" in cases (11) and (12) above.

Theoretically, entailment relations might depend solely on the syntactic structure of sentences. However, the contrast between (11) and (12) (and a host of other such sentences) demonstrates that they cannot be simply a matter of surface syntax. Entailments seem to involve the information conveyed by sentences: if English sentence *A* entails English sentence *B*, then translating *A* and *B* into Finnish sentences *A′* and *B′* with the same informational significance will preserve the entailment relation.

Asked to define entailment, you might come up with any of the following:

(13) *A entails B* $=_{\text{df}}$
- whenever *A* is true, *B* is true
- the information that *B* conveys is contained in the information that *A* conveys

- a situation describable by *A* must also be a situation describable by *B*
- *A and not B* is contradictory (can't be true in any situation)

We will later discuss more formal characterizations of the entailment relation, but for the time being you can adopt any of the preceding definitions.

We can find countless examples where entailment relations hold between sentences and countless where they do not. The English sentence (14) is normally interpreted so that it entails the sentences in (15) but does not entail those in (16).

(14) Lee kissed Kim passionately.

(15) *a.* Lee kissed Kim.
b. Kim was kissed by Lee.
c. Kim was kissed.
d. Lee touched Kim with her lips.

(16) *a.* Lee married Kim.
b. Kim kissed Lee.
c. Lee kissed Kim many times.
d. Lee did not kiss Kim.

Looking at entailments shows, by the way, that what are conventionally treated as translation equivalents are not always informationally equivalent. The English sentence (17*a*) entails (17*b*), but the Finnish sentence (18), which most texts would offer as a translation of (17*a*), does not entail anything about the femaleness of the person or animal said to be big, the Finnish third-person pronoun *hän* being completely neutral as to the sex of its referent.

(17) *a.* She is big.
b. Some female is big.

(18) Hän on iso.

Thus, although sentence (18) can be used to describe any situation (17*a*) describes, the Finnish can also be used to describe situations not describable by (17*a*), for example, to say of some man that he is big. That is, (18) is also a translation of (19*a*), but unlike (19*a*) it does not entail the information conveyed by (19*b*).

(19) *a.* He is big.
b. Some male is big.

In particular contexts, the use of translations that are not informationally equivalent, translations where entailments are not preserved, may be unproblematic, since other information is available to ensure that only the desired information is actually conveyed. But neither (17*a*) nor (19*a*) is an informationally equivalent translation of the Finnish sentence (18), which is informationally equivalent to something like (20).

(20) She or he is big.

You might object to our claim that (14), "Lee kissed Kim passionately," entails (15*d*), "Lee touched Kim with her lips," by pointing out that sentence (21) can be true in a situation where (15*d*) is false.

(21) In her imagination Lee kissed Kim passionately.

Does your example defeat the claim that (14) entails (15*d*)? No. We could counter by claiming that if (15*d*) is false in the situation in which (21) is true then (14) is false in that same situation, and we might further claim that (21) entails (22).

(22) In her imagination Lee touched Kim with her lips.

On the other hand, if you manage to persuade us that Lee's mouthing of a kiss in Kim's direction from a distance of ten feet counts as her kissing him, then we have no good defense of our claim that (14) entails (15*d*) (since we agree that she is unable actually to touch him from that distance). Or your scenario might be romance via computer where Lee types in "I am kissing you passionately," addressing herself to Kim's computer. If we agree to accept either of your cases as real kissing, then our only possible line of defense is that there are different interpretations of *kiss* involved, only one of which requires that the kisser touch the kissee with her lips. In other words, we could accept one of your cases and continue to maintain that (14) entails (15*d*) only if we also argue that (14) is ambiguous, that it has more than one meaning. In this case, the string (14) could entail (15*d*) on one interpretation of *kiss* but not have that entailment on the interpretation your cases involve. We discuss later what considerations support claims of ambiguity.

Similarly, we claim that (14), "Lee kissed Kim passionately," does not entail (16*c*), "Lee kissed Kim many times." You might deny this by noting that the passionate kisser is unlikely to stop with a single kiss. We can agree with that observation and may even agree with you that assertion of (14) does strongly suggest or imply the truth of (16*c*) but nonetheless disagree that the implication is an entailment. For example, we might want to maintain that a situation with one or a few kisses can nonetheless involve passionate kissing, perhaps persuading you by showing a film of a single kiss which you will agree is a passionate one. You might still maintain that Lee herself would never stop short of many kisses once she succumbs to passion, and thus that (14) would never be true without (16*c*) also being true. We must now take a slightly different tack, noting that this is a matter of what Lee happens to be like rather than a matter of what the sentences mean. Or perhaps we would remind you of the possibility that Lee could begin her round of passionate kissing but be allowed only one passionate kiss before Kim breaks free and runs away.

What we should not do in the face of your objections is simply to reiterate our initial claims. Judgments about entailment relations can be defended and supported by evidence. As in the case of any linguistic phenomenon, there may be areas of real diversity within the community of language users, dialectal and even idiolectal differences. This complication must not, however, obscure the important fact that judgments about semantic phenomena are interconnected, and thus that there is relevant evidence to be offered in support of such judgments. In learning to do semantics as a linguist, one must learn to develop semantic arguments and explore semantic intuitions systematically. And one must learn to discriminate between the strict notion of the entailment relation and looser varieties of implication. Test yourself on the following examples. Sentences (23*a*) and (24*a*) imply (23*b*) and (24*b*) respectively, but only one of the implications is an entailment. Try to discover for yourself which is which and why before reading the discussion that follows the examples.

(23) *a*. Mary used to swim a mile daily.
b. Mary no longer swims a mile daily.

(24) *a*. After Hans painted the walls, Pete installed the cabinets.
b. Hans painted the walls.

Sentence (23*a*) implies but does not entail (23*b*). Although in many contexts we would infer from an utterance of (23*a*) that (23*b*) is true, notice that (23*a*) could be used by someone familiar with Mary's routine last year but no longer in contact with her. It might be true that Mary still swims a mile daily, and the speaker we've imagined could make clear that (23*b*) should not be inferred by continuing with something like (25).

(25) I wonder whether she still does [swim a mile daily].

In contrast, (24*a*) not only implies but entails (24*b*). Suppose that Hans did not paint the walls. Then even if Pete did install the cabinets, he did not do so after Hans painted the walls. That is, sentence (26) is contradictory.

(26) After Hans painted the walls, Pete installed the cabinets, but Hans did not paint the walls.

There is one further preliminary point that it is important to make about entailments; namely, that there are infinitely many of them. That is, there are infinitely many pairs of sentences *A*, *B* such that *A* entails *B*. Here are a couple of ways to construct indefinitely many such pairs. Intuitions are fairly sharp, for example, that (27*a*) entails (27*c*) and also that (27*b*) entails (27*c*).

(27) *a.* Lee and Kim smoke.
b. Lee smokes and drinks.
c. Lee smokes.

We can easily keep conjoining noun phrases (*Lee and Kim and Mike and Susan and* . . .), adding descriptions like *the other Lee* or *the woman I love* should our stock of distinct proper names be exhausted. We can also, of course, just keep conjoining verb phrases: *smokes and drinks and has bad breath and lives in Dubuque and* . . .). Either way we get more sentences that entail (27*c*), and we need never stop. That is, we have intuitions that seem to involve the meanings of indefinitely many sentences, a potential infinity. Only finitely many such intuitions could possibly be stored in memory. How, then, are such judgments possible? Here we see again the general issue of the productivity of meaning, which we introduced in 2.1.

Exercise 1 For each pair of sentences, say whether the *a* sentence entails the *b* sentence and justify your answers as well as you can. Where proper names or pronouns or similar expressions are repeated in *a* and *b*, assume that the same individual is referred to in each case; assume also that temporal expressions (like *today* and the present tense) receive a constant interpretation.

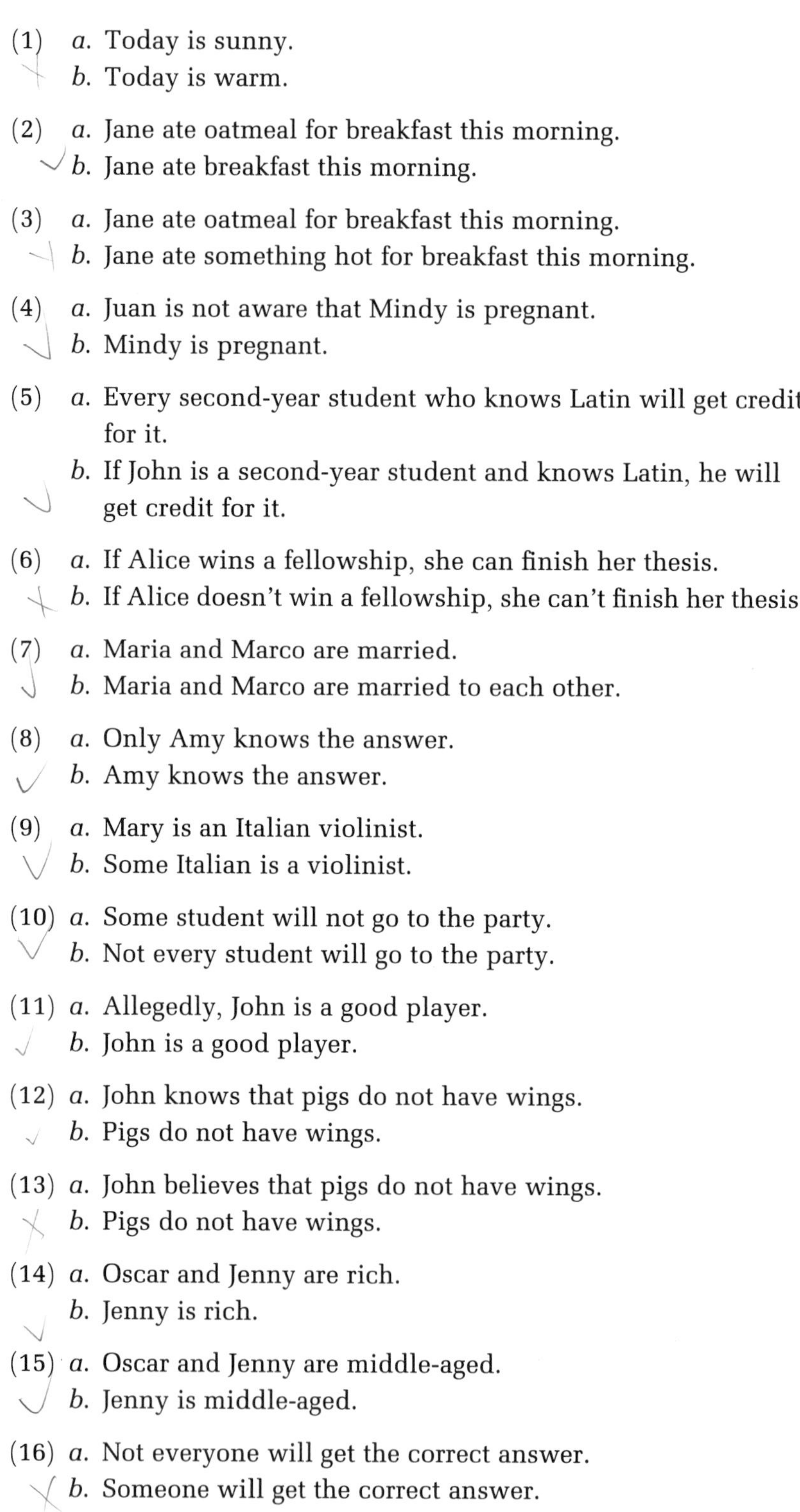

(1) *a.* Today is sunny.
b. Today is warm.

(2) *a.* Jane ate oatmeal for breakfast this morning.
b. Jane ate breakfast this morning.

(3) *a.* Jane ate oatmeal for breakfast this morning.
b. Jane ate something hot for breakfast this morning.

(4) *a.* Juan is not aware that Mindy is pregnant.
b. Mindy is pregnant.

(5) *a.* Every second-year student who knows Latin will get credit for it.
b. If John is a second-year student and knows Latin, he will get credit for it.

(6) *a.* If Alice wins a fellowship, she can finish her thesis.
b. If Alice doesn't win a fellowship, she can't finish her thesis.

(7) *a.* Maria and Marco are married.
b. Maria and Marco are married to each other.

(8) *a.* Only Amy knows the answer.
b. Amy knows the answer.

(9) *a.* Mary is an Italian violinist.
b. Some Italian is a violinist.

(10) *a.* Some student will not go to the party.
b. Not every student will go to the party.

(11) *a.* Allegedly, John is a good player.
b. John is a good player.

(12) *a.* John knows that pigs do not have wings.
b. Pigs do not have wings.

(13) *a.* John believes that pigs do not have wings.
b. Pigs do not have wings.

(14) *a.* Oscar and Jenny are rich.
b. Jenny is rich.

(15) *a.* Oscar and Jenny are middle-aged.
b. Jenny is middle-aged.

(16) *a.* Not everyone will get the correct answer.
b. Someone will get the correct answer.

3.2 Implicature

As we have set things up, it might look as if implicature is simply implication minus entailment. Implicature, however, is characterized more positively: we say that an utterance *A* implicates *B* only if we take *B* to be (part of what) the utterer of *A* meant by that utterance. An implicature must be something that the utterer might reasonably mean by making the utterance, something she expects to convey. And, critically, if *A* implicates *B*, there is a certain kind of explanatory account of that relation, one that invokes general principles of conversation, as well as (perhaps) certain specific assumptions about the particular context in which *A* happens to have been uttered. Grice says that implicatures must be *calculable*: there should be an argument that *A* implicates *B*, an argument that draws on the linguistic meaning of *A* and on expectations that speakers generally have of one another (e.g., that what is said will be "relevant" and "informative") and, in some cases, on particular features of the utterance context.

Suppose, e.g., that we have the dialogue in (28).

(28) *A*: Did you enjoy the dinner?
B: We had mushroom salad and mushroom sauce on the pasta.

What might speaker *B* be implicating? Given a question like that asked by *A*, what becomes immediately relevant is for *B* to choose one of the possibilities in (29).

(29) *a*. I (namely *B*) enjoyed the dinner.
b. I (namely *B*) didn't enjoy the dinner.

Thus, unless there's some reason to think that *B* is dodging the question, we will generally take *B*'s utterance to implicate either (29*a*) or (29*b*). But no general principles allow us to decide whether the implicature is positive or negative: to do that, we have to know more. Perhaps it is common knowledge that *B* hates mushrooms with a passion or, conversely, that *B* absolutely adores mushrooms in virtually any dish. In the first case, (29*b*) is implicated, whereas (29*a*) is implicated in the other case. If *A* knows nothing about *B*'s opinions of mushrooms, *A* will likely interpret *B*'s response as evasive. (An evasive answer might be in order if, e.g., *B* fears that *A* will report the evaluation to the person who hosted the dinner.) When the implicature to one of (29) works, then we are dealing with a *particularized* conversational implicature. Linguistic theories cannot really predict such implicatures (except insofar as they can shed light on such issues as how questions make certain next contributions relevant). Not surprisingly, no one is likely to think that the relation between (28*B*) and either of the sentences in (29) is entailment, that it is the semantic content of the sentence in (28*B*) that licenses the inference to either (29*a*) or (29*b*).

What linguists have studied most systematically are what Grice called *generalized* conversational implicatures. These are the cases that often seem close to entailments. Take example (23) from the preceding section, repeated here.

(23) *a.* Mary used to swim a mile daily.
b. Mary no longer swims a mile daily.

We argued that the relation between these sentences was not entailment, because we could follow an utterance of (23*a*) with an utterance of (25), also repeated here.

(25) I wonder whether she still does.

What (25) does is *defeat* the inference from (23*a*) to (23*b*): an empirical hallmark of conversational implicatures is that they are, in Grice's words, *defeasible*. An implication that can be defeated just by saying something that warns the hearer not to infer what might ordinarily be implied is not an entailment but something different. Notice that if we try to "defeat" entailments, we end up with something contradictory:

(30) #Lee kissed Kim passionately, but Lee didn't kiss Kim.

But even though the implication from (23*a*) to (23*b*) is defeasible, that implication is a very general one that holds unless it is specifically defeated. In contrast to the implication from (28*B*) to one of the sentences in (29), the implication from (23*a*) to (23*b*) does not depend on any special features of the contexts in which sentences like (23*a*) might be uttered. What, then, is the general argument, the calculation, that takes us from (23*a*) to (23*b*)?

Roughly, the argument goes like this. Hearers expect speakers to be adequately informative on the topic being discussed, and speakers know that hearers have this expectation. Sentence (23*a*) reports a past habit, in contrast to (31), which reports a present habit.

(31) Mary swims a mile daily.

Present habits, however, began earlier, and thus (31) might well be true of the same situation as (32*a*), which cancels implicature (23*b*).

(32) *a.* Mary used to swim a mile daily, and she still does.
b. Mary used to swim a mile daily, but she no longer does.

Unless there is some special reason that the conversationalists are interested only in Mary's past habits, if the speaker is in a position to inform the hearer by uttering (31) rather than (23*a*), then she should do so (and, furthermore, she knows that the hearer expects her to do so). Thus to utter (23*a*) suggests one is not in a position to make the stronger claim (31), and in many circumstances it suggests that the stronger claim is false, i.e., (23*a*) conveys that (23*b*) holds. Indeed, it is normal to make the move from (23*a*) to (23*b*)—and, more generally, from *used to* to *does no longer*—unless there are explicit indicators to the contrary as in (32*a*). The strength of the implication is one reason why it is so often confused with entailment. Sentence (32*b*) illustrates another empirical test that distinguishes implicatures from entailments: they are typically *reinforceable*, without any flavor of the redundancy that generally accompanies similar reinforcement of entailments. Although (32*b*) sounds fine, (33), where an entailment is reinforced, sounds quite strange.

(33) #Lee smokes and drinks, but/and she smokes.

Reinforceability is the flip side of defeasibility. Because generalized implicatures are not part of the linguistic meaning of expressions in the same sense that entailments are, they can readily be explicitly set aside or explicitly underscored. However, they are strongly recurrent patterns, most of them found in similar form crosslinguistically.

Here are some more examples where a generalized implicature seems to hold between the (*a*) and the (*b*) sentences.

(34) *a.* Joan likes some of her presents.
b. Joan doesn't like all of her presents.

(35) *a.* Mary doesn't believe that John will come.
b. Mary believes that John won't come.

(36) *a.* If you finish your vegetables, I'll give you dessert.
b. If you don't finish your vegetables, I won't give you dessert.

Exercise 2 Choose one of the pairs of sentences in (34) to (36) and show that the relation between (*a*) and (*b*) is both defeasible and reinforceable.

We return to the topic of conversational implicature in chapter 4, where we say more about Grice's account of the conversational principles that underlie these relations.

3.3 Presupposition

Many expressions seem to "trigger" certain presuppositions; i.e., they signal that the speaker is taking something for granted. Utterances of sentences containing such expressions typically have two kinds of implications: those that are asserted (or denied or questioned or otherwise actively entertained) and those that are presupposed. As we noted above, presupposition is more than a species of implication: it is a matter of the discourse status of what is implied. If *A* presupposes *B*, then *A* not only implies *B* but also implies that the truth of *B* is somehow taken for granted, treated as uncontroversial. If *A* entails *B*, then asserting that *A* is true commits us to the truth of *B*. If *A* presupposes *B*, then to assert *A*, deny *A*, wonder whether *A*, or suppose *A*—to express *any* of these attitudes toward *A* is generally to imply *B*, to suggest that *B* is true and, moreover, uncontroversially so. That is, considering *A* from almost any standpoint seems already to assume or presuppose the truth of *B*; *B* is part of the background against was we (typically) consider *A*.

Consider, for example, the sentences in (37). Any one of (*a–d*) seems to imply (*e*) as a background truth. These implications are triggered by the occurrence of the phrase *the present queen of France*, a definite description. It is generally true of definite descriptions that they license such implications.

(37) *a.* The present queen of France lives in Ithaca.
b. It is not the case that the present queen of France lives in Ithaca (or more colloquially, the present queen of France does not live in Ithaca).
c. Does the present queen of France live in Ithaca?
d. If the present queen of France lives in Ithaca, she has probably met Nelly.
e. There is a unique present queen of France.

Or consider (38). Again (using) any of (*a–d*) will generally imply (*e*). In this case, the implications are attributable to *regret*, which is a so-called factive verb. Factive verbs generally signal that their complements are presupposed. Other examples are *realize* and *know*.

(38) *a.* Joan regrets getting her Ph.D. in linguistics.
b. Joan doesn't regret getting her Ph.D. in linguistics.
c. Does Joan regret getting her Ph.D. in linguistics?
d. If Joan regrets getting her Ph.D. and linguistics, she should consider going back to graduate school in computer science.
e. Joan got her Ph.D. in linguistics.

Look next at (39). Once again, each of the quartet (*a–d*) implies (*e*). In this case it is the quantifying determine *all* that is responsible. A number of quantificational expressions serve to trigger presuppositions.

(39) *a.* All Mary's lovers are French.
b. It isn't the case that all Mary's lovers are French.
c. Are all Mary's lovers French?
d. If all Mary's lovers are French, she should study the language.
e. Mary has (three or more?) lovers.

Finally, look at (40), where we find the same pattern. In this case it is the cleft construction that is responsible.

(40) *a.* It was Lee who got a perfect score on the semantics quiz.
b. It wasn't Lee who got a perfect score on the semantics quiz.
c. Was it Lee who got a perfect score on the semantics quiz?
d. If it was Lee who got a perfect score on the semantics quiz, why does she look so depressed?
e. Someone got a perfect score on the semantics quiz.

A distinguishing empirical feature of presupposition, then, is that it involves not just a single implication but a family of implications. By this we mean that not only assertive uses of sentence *A* (the affirmative declarative) imply *B* but also other uses of *A* where something is, for example, denied, supposed, or questioned. That we are dealing with a family of implications derives from the fact that the presupposition is background. Each of (*a–d*), what we will call the *P* family, is said to presuppose (*e*) because uttering each (typically) implies (*e*) and also implies that (*e*) is being taken for granted. It is convenient for testing purposes to identify the *P* family in syntactic terms: an affirmative declarative, the negative of that declarative, the interrogative, and the conditional antecedent. In semantic/pragmatic terms, these represent a family of different sorts of attitudes expressed towards *A*. We can thus informally characterize when *A* presupposes *B* as follows:

(41) *A* presupposes *B* if and only if not only *A* but also other members of the *P* family imply (and assume as background) *B*.

Presuppositions come in families, even if sometimes certain members of the family may be stylistically odd.

Notice that we have said that *A* and other members of its *P* family *imply B* when *A* presupposes *B*. We do *not* require that these implications be entailments. As we have defined entailment, it is not even possible for all these relations to be entailments. However, it is possible that some member of the family entails *B*. Sentence (40*a*), for example, not only presupposes (40*e*); it also entails (40*e*). If (40*a*) is true, then (40*e*) must also be true. The negation, (40*b*), also presupposes (40*e*) but does not entail it. The implication to (40*e*) is *defeasible*; that is, there are contexts in which it can be defeated, contexts in which (40*b*) is asserted yet (40*e*) is not assumed to be true. We might take (42) as a discourse context that defeats the implication from (40*b*) to (40*e*).

(42) *Speaker 1*: I wonder whether it was Lee or someone else who got a perfect score on the semantics quiz.
Speaker 2: It wasn't Lee who got a perfect score [on the semantics quiz]. I happen to know that Lee scored only 70 percent. I wonder if anyone managed to get a perfect score.

Speaker 2 has taken issue with speaker 1's presupposing that someone got a perfect score by suggesting that (40*e*) may be false and asserting that (40*b*) is indeed true. Of course, speaker 2 chooses this way of conveying the information that Lee did not get a perfect score because speaker 1 has already implied that someone did do that.

We need only look at noncleft counterparts of the sentences in (40) to see that *A* may entail *B* yet not presuppose *B*.

(43) *a.* Lee got a perfect score on the semantics quiz.
b. Lee didn't get a perfect score on the semantics quiz.
c. Did Lee get a perfect score on the semantics quiz?
d. If Lee got a perfect score on the semantics quiz, why does she look so depressed?
e. Someone got a perfect score on the semantics quiz.

If focal stress is not placed on *Lee*, then none of (43*b*–*d*) typically imply (43*e*), even though (43*a*) entails (43*e*). Someone's getting a perfect score on the semantics quiz is not part of the usual background for talking about Lee's achieving the feat in question, as stated by (43*a*). Indeed, it seems reasonable to say that a major semantic difference between the subject-verb-object (S-V-O) sentence (43*a*) and its cleft correlate (40*a*), "It was Lee who got a perfect score on the semantics quiz," is that the latter but not the former carries a presupposition that someone got a perfect score. Whether this difference can ultimately be explained in terms of some other difference between the two is an issue we cannot answer here.

What the sentences in (43) show is that *A* can entail *B* without other members of the *P* family also implying *B*. Presupposition and entailment are thus quite distinct. *A* may entail *B* but not presuppose it, as in (34); conversely, *A* may presuppose *B* but not entail it, as in (40). And given the way we have defined entailment and presupposition, it is also possible for *A* both to entail and to presuppose *B*. (Some accounts of presupposition do not admit this possibility; we will discuss this and related issues in more detail in chapter 6.)

Presupposition requires a family of implications, not all of which can be licensed by an entailment. Interrogatives, for example, would never entail other sentences, since they are not ordinarily valued as true or false; use of an interrogative may, however, imply something. Thus, one important question presupposition raises is about the nature of implications that are not backed by entailment relations. Some presuppositions, it has been argued, derive from quite general conversational principles and thus might be held to be licensed in much the same way as the conversational implicatures we briefly discussed in the preceding section. And there may be other mechanisms at work.

A related issue is the speaker's responsibilities with respect to what the utterance presupposes. What is presupposed in a discourse is what is taken for granted. Thus, a speaker who says *A*, presupposing *B*, in a context where *B* is at issue has thereby spoken inappropriately in some sense. For example, suppose that Sandy is on trial for selling illicit drugs and the prosecuting attorney asks question (44).

(44) Sandy, have you stopped selling crack?

As we know, the question is unfairly loaded, since it presupposes (45), which is very much at issue.

(45) Sandy has sold crack.

If Sandy simply answers yes or no, the presupposition is unchallenged, and she appears to go along with the implication that (45) is true. A defensive answer must explicitly disavow that implication:

(46) Since I never did sell crack, I have not stopped selling crack.

In many contexts, however, it is perfectly appropriate for a speaker to say *A*, presupposing *B*, even though the speaker does not believe that *B* is taken for granted by other discourse participants. For example, (47) might be uttered by a passenger to the airline representative, who can hardly be thought to know anything about the passenger's personal habits. Although the last clause in (47) presupposes the clause that precedes it in square brackets, it would seem unduly verbose to express that presupposed information overtly.

(47) I don't want to be near the smoking section because [I used to smoke and] I've just stopped smoking.

An obvious difference between the airline passenger and the prosecuting attorney is that the latter knows full well that what the utterance presupposes is controversial, whereas the former can safely assume that the reservations clerk has no opinion about what is being presupposed (and no real interest in the matter). With no reason to suppose otherwise, the clerk can quite reasonably be expected to accept the passenger's presupposition as if it were already taken for granted and discourse should proceed unproblematically. What happens in such cases is called *accommodation*.

We have barely begun to explore the topic of presupposition, and we will consider some of these phenomena in more detail in chapter 6. But it is clear already that presupposition raises questions not just about individual sentences and their truth or falsity but also about the uses of sentences in connected discourse (including uses of interrogatives, which are generally not said to be either true or false).

Exercise 3 Consider the following:

(1) *a.* That John was assaulted scared Mary.
b. Mary is animate.
c. John was assaulted.
d. That John was assaulted caused fear in Mary.

(2) *a.* That John was assaulted didn't scare Mary.
b. Mary is animate.
c. John was assaulted.
d. That John was assaulted didn't cause fear in Mary.

(3) *a.* John didn't manage to get the job.
b. It was kind of hard for John to get the job.
c. John didn't get the job.

In each of these examples, the *a* sentences presuppose and/or entail the other sentences. Specify which is a presupposition and which a simple entailment and which is both an entailment and a presupposition. Explain what test convinced you of your answer.

What relationship holds between the sentences in the following examples? Explain why you think that that relation holds.

(4) *a.* It is false that everyone tried to kill Templeton.
b. Someone did not try to kill Templeton.

(5) *a.* That John left early didn't bother Mary.
b. John left early.

(6) *a.* Someone cheated on the exam.
b. John cheated on the exam.

(7) *a.* If John discovers that Mary is in New York, he will get angry.
b. Mary is in New York.

(8) *a.* Seeing is believing.
b. If John sees a riot, he will believe it.

---

4 More Semantic Relations and Properties

Implication relations are not the only kind of semantic relations speakers recognize. In this section we look at a number of other semantic relations and properties.

4.1 Referential connections and anaphoric relations

Consider the sentences in (48).

(48) *a.* *She* called me last night.
b. Did you know that *he* is a Nobel Prize winner?
c. I had a terrible fight with *that bastard* yesterday.

Each of the italicized expressions is used to *refer* to someone, to pick out an individual about whom something is being said, but a pointing gesture or a nod or some similar nonlinguistic means may be needed to indicate who this is. These same expressions, however, can be used in contexts where such pointing is unnecessary because they are linked to other *antecedent* expressions. In (49) speakers judge that the bracketed italicized expressions can be understood as *coreferential* with, having the same reference as, the bracketed unitalicized expressions that serve as their antecedents, and furthermore, they can be understood as dependent for their reference on the reference assigned to their antecedents. Intuitive judgments are quite clear-cut in these cases: the italic expressions are *referentially dependent* on the unitalicized expressions.

(49) *a.* If [*she*] calls, please tell [Teresa] I've gone to the pool.
b. [The computer repairman] insists that [*he*] found nothing wrong.
c. I talked to [Kim] for an hour, but [*that bastard*] never once mentioned the gift I sent him from Peru.

Expressions are said to be interpreted *anaphorically* when their reference is derived from that of antecedent expressions. The italicized expressions in (49) illustrate this. There are some expressions that can only be interpreted anaphorically and not through anything like pointing. The reflexive pronoun *herself* falls in this category; compare (50*a*), where *she* can serve as antecedent, with (50*b*), where there is no antecedent for *herself*.

(50) *a.* [She] is proud of [*herself*].
b. *Be proud of herself.

In the syntactic literature, coindexing, as in (51), is the commonest device for indicating coreference.

(51) *a.* If $[\textit{she}]_i$ calls, please tell $[\text{Teresa}]_i$ I've gone to the pool.
b. $[\text{The computer repairman}]_j$ insists that $[\textit{he}]_j$ found nothing wrong.
c. I talked to $[\text{Kim}]_k$ for an hour but $[\textit{that bastard}]_k$ never once mentioned the gift I sent $[\textit{him}]_k$ from Peru.
d. $[\text{She}]_l$ is proud of $[\textit{herself}]_l$.

Chomsky (1981) discusses indexing as a formal process in some detail, but its informal use for this purpose far predates contemporary government-binding (GB) theory (see, for example, Postal (1971)).

What are called judgments of coreference in the literature typically involve judging not sameness of reference as such but dependence of reference of one expression upon that assigned to another.[6] Directed linking is another device sometimes used to show nonsymmetric dependence relations;[7] (52) shows a notation for linking.

(52) *a.* If [*she*] calls, please tell [Teresa] I've gone to the pool.

b. [The computer repairman] insists that [*he*] found nothing wrong.

c. I talked to [Kim] for an hour, but [*that bastard*] never once mentioned the gift I sent [*him*] from Peru.

d. [She] is proud of [*herself*].

Referential connections may be somewhat more complex. Much of chapter 3 is devoted to making precise the nature of the dependencies speakers recognize as possible in (53), where the dependencies are indicated by coindexing, just as in the simpler cases above. In (53) the anaphorically interpreted NPs (*she*, *her*, *himself*, *his*, and *themselves*) are said to be *bound* by their antecedent NPs.

(53) *a.* [Every woman]$_i$ thinks that [*she*]$_i$ will do a better job of child rearing than [*her*]$_i$ mother did.

b. [No man]$_i$ should blame [*himself*]$_i$ for [*his*]$_i$ children's mistakes.

c. [Which candidates]$_i$ will vote for [*themselves*]$_i$?

In (53) repetition of an index does not indicate straightforward sameness of reference, as it did in (51). Expressions like *every woman*, *no man*, and *which candidates* do not refer in the intuitive sense, though their relations to anaphors are often called "coreference." Although *she* in (53*a*) is not used to refer to any individual, the interpretation of (53*a*) can be understood in terms of sentences in which NPs in the analogous positions both refer to the same individual. Roughly, (53*a*) says that if we point to any particular woman and say (54), where each of the indexed NPs refers to that woman, then what is said will be true, no matter which woman we pick.

(54) [She]$_i$ thinks that [*she*]$_i$ will do a better job of child rearing than [*her*]$_i$ mother did.

Linguistic questions about the nature of anaphoric relations provided a major impetus for exploration of how classical logical theories might shed light on natural language semantics. In exploring how syntactic structures affect the possibilities of interpreting expressions, linguists and philosophers have discovered other cases of so-called coreference where referential dependency may be somewhat different both from simple sameness of reference and from the standard binding relations elucidated by quantification theory.

(55) *a.* Kath caught [some fish]$_i$, and Mark cooked [*them*]$_i$.
b. If [a farmer]$_j$ owns [a donkey]$_i$, [*he*]$_j$ beats [*it*]$_i$.
c. [Gina]$_i$ told [Maria]$_j$ that [*they*]$_{i+j}$ had been assigned clean-up duty.

In (55*c*) the plural pronoun *they* has what have been called *split antecedents*; the index $i+j$ indicates referential dependence on both the distinct indexes i and j. The notation i, j is often used for indicating split antecedents, but we want to reserve this notation for cases where an expression may be linked either to something with index i or to something with index j. In the rest of this section we ignore split antecedents.

These and many other examples have been widely discussed in the recent syntactic and semantic literature. Though there continues to be debate on the appropriate analysis of particular anaphoric relations, there is no question that speakers do recognize the possibility of some kind of interpretive dependencies in all these and indefinitely many other cases. Judgments of coreference possibilities (broadly understood) are fundamentally important semantic data.

There are also indefinitely many cases where the intuitive judgments are that such dependencies are not possible. These are usually called judgments of *disjoint reference*, a kind of independence of reference assignment. The terminology was introduced in Lasnik (1976), but as with "coreference," it must be understood somewhat loosely. The asterisks in (56) mean that the indicated referential dependencies are judged impermissible. The NPs in question are, according to speakers' judgments, necessarily interpretively independent of one another and are not anaphorically relatable.

(56) *a.* *Behind [Teresa]$_i$, [*she*]$_i$ heard Mario.
b. *[*He*]$_i$ insists that [the computer repairman]$_i$ found nothing wrong.
c. *If [*that bastard*]$_i$ calls, tell [Kim]$_i$ I've gone to Peru.
d. *[*Herself*]$_i$ is proud of [her]$_i$.

Sentences (56*a–c*) are bad with the indicated coindexing; they can be used only if the italicized expressions are interpreted non-anaphorically (through pointing or something similar). Sentence (56*d*) is unusable because *herself* happens to be an expression that requires anaphoric interpretation.

Much interesting recent linguistic research in semantics has tried to elucidate and systematize judgments about referential relations, and such data have figured prominently in developing theories of the map between syntactic structures and their interpretation.

Exercise 4 Each of the following sentences contains some nonpronominal NPs and a pronoun (in some cases, a possessive pronoun). Assign a distinct index to each nonpronominal NP. Copy all such indices on the pronoun in the sentence, and star those indices copied from NPs that cannot be antecedents for the pronoun. For example,

(1) *a.* John believes that few women think that they can be successful.
b. John$_1$ believes that [few women]$_2$ think that they$_{2,*1}$ can be successful.

(2) *a.* They know few women.
b. They$_{*1}$ know [few women]$_1$.

(3) She thinks that Barbara is sick.

(4) If she is sick, Barbara will stay home.

(5) When he is unhappy, no man works efficiently.

(6) Neither of Ann's parents thinks he is adequately paid.

(7) That jerk told Dick what Mary thinks of him.

(8) If she wants to, any girl in the class can jump farther than Mary.

(9) Her mother is proud of every woman.

(10) Her mother is proud of Lisa.

(11) My friends think that Joan's parents met each other in college.

(12) John promised Bill to help him.

(13) John persuaded Bill to help him.

(14) Every girl on the block jumps rope, but she knows few rhymes.

(15) The man who likes him will meet Bill tomorrow.

(16) John needs to talk to Bill about himself.

(17) John needs to talk to Bill about him.

(18) She does not realize that every girl is talented.

4.2 Ambiguity

Ambiguity arises when a single word or string of words is associated in the language system with more than one meaning. Each of the sentences in (57) illustrates a different way in which a single expression may be assigned multiple interpretations.

(57) *a.* You should have seen the bull we got from the pope.
b. Competent women and men hold all the good jobs in the firm.
c. Mary claims that John saw her duck.
d. Someone loves everyone.

Sentence (57*a*) illustrates what is called lexical ambiguity: the form *bull* can be assigned at least three quite different interpretations (roughly, a papal communication, a male cow, or nonsense). The sentence is ambiguous because *bull* is ambiguous. To understand sentences containing that form, to identify their entailments, we need to know which of its three interpretations is being used. Lexical disambiguation is exactly like knowing which word has been used, like knowing, for example, that someone has uttered *cow* rather than *sow.* That is, an ambiguous lexical item can be thought of as several different lexical items that happen to be written and pronounced in the same way.

Sentence (57*b*) shows a simple kind of structural, or syntactic, ambiguity. We need not interpret any individual word as ambiguous but can attribute the ambiguity to distinct syntactic structures that give rise to distinct interpretations. Is *competent* modifying the conjunction *women and men*, or is the NP *competent women* conjoined with the single-word NP *men*? One interpretation entails that the men holding the good jobs are competent, whereas the other does not. The English sentences in (58) unambiguously convey the two possible interpretations and thus allow us informally to disambiguate the original sentence.

(58) *a.* Women who are competent and men hold all the good jobs in the firm.
b. Women who are competent and men who are competent hold all the good jobs in the firm.

Example (57*c*) illustrates both syntactic and lexical ambiguity. Is Mary claiming that John saw the bird she possesses or that he saw her lowering herself? These two interpretations are associated with radically different syntactic structures (*her duck* is in one case like *me jump* and in the other case like *my dog*) and also with distinct lexical meanings (the noun and the verb *duck* have the same spelling and pronunciation but quite distinct interpretations).

Sentence (57*d*) illustrates scope ambiguity. We can interpret the sentence as simply assigning some lover to each person (there is always the person's mother!) or as saying that someone is a universal lover (perhaps a divinity). The ambiguity here arises from the relation between *someone* and *everyone*: a scope ambiguity is not lexical but structural. But (57*d*) differs from (57*b*) and (57*c*) in having only a single surface syntactic structure. There have been arguments offered that sentences like (57*d*) do have multiple syntactic structures at some nonsurface level; we adopt such an approach in chapter 3. It is controversial, however, whether all scope ambiguities reflect syntactic ambiguities. If there are sentences whose ambiguity is nonlexical and that do not involve distinct syntactic structures, then structures or constructional principles that play no syntactic role are needed for semantic interpretation. We leave it as an open question whether there are any nonlexical, nonsyntactic ambiguities of this kind.

For linguistic purposes, ambiguity (multiplicity of interpretations assigned by the language system) is distinguished both from vagueness and from deixis or indexicality.

Vagueness is a matter of the relative looseness or of the nonspecificity of interpretation. For example, *many linguists* is noncommittal as to the precise number of linguists involved. It seems to be part of what we know about *many* that it is imprecise in this sense. We discuss semantic imprecision in chapter 8. Virtually all expressions are general: *kiss* does not specify whether the kiss lands on the lips or cheek, etc., of the one kissed. But neither *many linguists* nor *kiss* would count as having multiple meanings on these grounds (that is, as synonymous with, for example, *350 linguists*, *400 linguists*, *379 linguists*, or again with *kiss on the lips*, *kiss on the cheek*).

Deixis, or *indexicality*, is involved when the significance of an expression is systematically related to features of the contexts in which the expression is used. For example, the first-person pronoun *I* is an indexical expression, but it is hardly ambiguous simply because it is sometimes interpreted as referring to Gennaro, sometimes to Sally, sometimes to you.

It is not always as easy to distinguish ambiguity from vagueness and indexicality as our examples might suggest, and we will return to these topics in later chapters. One test of ambiguity is the existence of distinct paraphrases for the expression in question, each of which conveys only one of the interpretations in question. An expression is a paraphrase of a declarative sentence for these purposes if it expresses exactly the same information as the original does on one way of understanding it; paraphrases will share all entailments with the given interpretation. Distinct paraphrases will usually have distinct entailments. The distinct interpretations must not be explicable in pragmatic terms; for example, "I'd like a glass of water" probably does not count as ambiguous, because how it is understood depends on pragmatic factors: on what an utterance of it is intended to accomplish. In general, expressions that are ambiguous can be used only with one of their meanings in any given situation. Exceptions are cases of punning and are clearly very special. There are many clear cases of lexical, structural, and scope ambiguities, and there are also some instances where intuitions do not settle the question of how different interpretations should be analyzed. For now, however, we simply want to emphasize that ambiguity is an important semantic phenomenon and that it is distinct from both vagueness and indexicality.

Exercise 5 For each of the following sentences, state whether you judge it to be ambiguous, and for ambiguous sentences, disambiguate them by providing unambiguous distinct paraphrases of their possible interpretations.

(1) Everyone didn't like the movie.

(2) Someone came.

(3) Joan should be in New York.

(4) The missionaries are too hot to eat.

(5) The students are revolting.

(6) A lot of people came to Chomsky's lecture.

(7) Andrea is feared.

(8) Mindy likes Cynthia better than Jonathan.

(9) Visiting relatives can be tedious.

(10) Elizabeth didn't finish her thesis to please Jim.

(11) She was upset.

(12) John hit a boy with a book.

(13) John left early and Bill left early or Sue left early.

(14) Zelda ran the Boston marathon.

(15) Every faculty member was met by two student guides.

(16) Every student thinks that she is a genius.

4.3 Synonymy

In discussing ambiguity, we mentioned the notion of one expression's being a paraphrase of another, or synonymous with it. Judgments of *synonymy*, or semantic equivalence—that distinct expressions have the same meaning—turn out to be somewhat complex: they are relative to certain purposes or restricted to certain domains. If explicit content, that is, informational significance, is all that is at stake, then the sentences in (59) count as synonymous with one another: they share all their entailments, which is what we required of a disambiguating paraphrase.

(59) *a.* Those women at the corner table look ready to order.
b. Those ladies at the corner table look ready to order.
c. Those dames at the corner table look ready to order.

Suppose that one of these sentences is uttered by the head waiter to his underling. She doesn't quite catch what was said and asks another one of the servers, who, to report what was said, might perfectly well reply,

(60) He said that . . .

and choose any one of the sentences in (59) to complete (60). It is irrelevant to the server's immediate purposes how the other server identifies the customers that the head waiter says are ready to place an order, so long as she does so accurately. Even if the report is not the same sentence that the head waiter actually uttered, the reporter has not misrepresented the content of what he said. She has made a judgment of synonymy, or semantic equivalence, that fits with judgments of other native speakers.

The notion of synonymy involved here we call *content synonymy*, and we can define it in terms of mutual entailment.

(61) *A* is (*content*) *synonymous* with $B =_{df}$ *A* entails *B* and *B* entails *A*.

We could equally well have required that *A* and *B* share all their entailments, that is, that for any *C*, if *A* entails *C*, then *B* entails *C*, and vice versa. Two sentences will satisfy definition (61) if and only if they have all the same entailments. What content synonymy requires is just that *A* and *B* are true in exactly the same set of circumstances.

There is another sense in which speakers judge that the sentences in (59) have different meanings and thus are not (fully) synonymous. In choosing to utter one rather than another of these sentences to describe a situation, speakers can convey something important about their attitudes toward that situation and those involved in it. The differences involved are traditionally said to be connotations or a matter of tone; they may ultimately be a matter of presuppositions. In any case, they can be quite consequential. Suppose, for example, that the head waiter must later defend himself in a sex-discrimination suit filed by the server who was told what he had said. In this case how he said it does indeed matter.

Let us turn to some different examples. Speakers judge that the sentences in (62) share the same informational significance; they are content synonymous.

(62) *a.* The police searched Sarah.
b. Sarah was searched by the police.

Again, this judgment seems to be grounded in the fact that (62*a*) entails (62*b*) and vice versa, that they share all their entailments. Yet doubt has been raised about the claim that passives are always content synonymous with the corresponding actives. Why? Precisely because in some cases it is not obvious that corresponding actives and passives do share all their entailments. For example, (63*a*), first discussed in Chomsky (1957), certainly does not entail (63*b*); (63*a*) is true, and (63*b*) false, if the circumstances are as described in (63*c*).

(63) *a*. Everyone in this room speaks two languages.
  b. There are two particular languages such that all the people in the room speak those languages.
  c. There are four people in the room, one of whom speaks only Italian and English, another only Finnish and Swedish, another only Hebrew and Russian, another only Yoruba and French.

The question is whether (64), the passive counterpart of (63*a*), is also true in the situation described by (63*c*) or in any other situation where (63*b*) fails to be true.

(64) Two languages are spoken by everyone in this room.

Here judgments are much less clear. What is clear is that the syntactic difference in (63*a*) and (64) leads to a difference in what an interpreter is likely to infer. From an utterance of (64) we are inclined to infer that the situation is not that described in (63*c*) but rather one where there are two particular languages that all speak, perhaps English and Japanese. Is this inclination a matter of entailment, or is it some less strong kind of implication? Here judgments are divided. The important point for our present purposes is not whether (63*a*) and (64) are content-synonymous, whether they express the same literal content. What matters for this discussion is the strong link between negative judgments on equivalence of content and negative judgments on identity of entailments.

No one is likely to deny, of course, that the difference between the active and passive can be important in interpretation. As we have just noted, (64) certainly suggests something that (63*a*) does not. And even where an active and passive clearly entail one another, as in (62) and many other pairs, substitution of one string for the other in certain contexts may fail to preserve mutual entailments. The sentences in (65), for instance, clearly do not entail one another.

(65) *a.* Unwillingly the police searched Sarah. [The mayor forced them.]
b. Unwillingly Sarah was searched by the police. [They had to tie her down.]

In other words, how a sentence structures the content it expresses can apparently matter to the contribution that sentence makes to the content of sentences in which it is embedded. Even if *A* and *B* have exactly the same entailments, it seems that two sentences *C*(*A*) and *C*(*B*) that differ from one another only in that *C*(*B*) contains *B* where *C*(*A*) contains *A* may differ in their entailments.

There are other ways in which sentences that express the same content can, in some sense, differ in meaning. For example, consider the different utterances in (66), the first of which places focus on *Mary*, the second of which places focus on *cake* (italics indicate focal stress). The sentences in (67), while structurally different, are identical in focal structure (and arguably also in entailments) to those in (66).

(66) *a.* *Mary* baked the cake.
b. Mary baked the *cake*.

(67) *a.* It was Mary who baked the cake.
b. It was the cake that Mary baked.

Sentences (66*a*) and (67*a*), which focus on *Mary*, might both be used, for example, to answer someone who uttered (68*a*), whereas (66*b*) and (67*b*), which focus on *cake*, strike us as badly suited for that job but just what is needed to answer someone who asks (68*b*).

(68) *a.* Who baked the cake?
b. What did Mary bake?

It is sometimes claimed that perfect synonymy does not exist. What is usually meant by this is that formally distinct expressions are nearly always used in somewhat different ways, are appropriate in somewhat different contexts. This can involve their syntactic structure, their tone, what they suggest, the metaphoric possibilities they evoke, even matters of phonological and phonetic structure. If synonymy of distinct expressions means that we judge them appropriate in exactly the same range of contexts, effective for precisely the same purposes, then it is no surprise that plausible candidates are hard to find.

On the other hand, mutual entailment can be quite reliably judged, as can certain other properties relevant to semantic equivalence (for example, identity of focal structure). Mutual entailment, however, is basic; it generally provides the minimal basis for judgments of synonymy relied on in assessing accuracy of translations from one language to another and of second-party reports of what someone has said. Sometimes more is needed for an adequate translation or report, but mutual entailment is the necessary starting point.

4.4 Contradiction

Contradiction is intimately linked to entailment. When we said that (14), "Lee kissed Kim passionately," entails (15*d*), "Lee touched Kim with her lips," for example, we were guided by the judgment that (69), the conjunction of (14) with the negation of (15*d*), is contradictory.

(69) Lee kissed Kim passionately, but she [Lee] didn't touch him [Kim] with her lips.

What is meant by saying that (69) is contradictory? We can informally define contradiction in either of the following ways:

(70) *A* is *contradictory* $=_{\text{df}}$
- *A* can never be true
- there is no possible situation describable by *A*

That is, in judging (69) to be contradictory, we deem that it is false no matter what the facts might be, that it describes no possible situation. Contradiction can also be thought of as a relation between sentences; the informal definitions in (71) can get us started.

(71) *A* and *B* are *contradictory* $=_{\text{df}}$
- *A* and *B* cannot both be true; whenever *A* is true, *B* is false, and whenever *B* is true, *A* is false.
- a situation describable by *A* cannot also be a situation describable by *B*

When we speak of one *person* *x* contradicting another *person* *y*, we mean that what *x* has asserted contradicts what *y* has asserted. Lois's response of no to her mother's assertion *A* is tantamount to an assertion by Lois of "not *A*," which contradicts her mother. *A* and *B* are said to be contradictories if each contradicts the other; *A* and *not A* are contradictories par excellence. If a sentence is contradictory, it will have entailments that are contradictories. More specifically, among its entailments will be a pair of sentences one of which is the negative of the other.

As with intuitions about entailments, initial judgments about contradictoriness can be subjected to further tests. We can defeat a claim that *A* and *B* are contradictory by showing a situation to which they both apply.

Sometimes sentences that overtly express contradictions are used for other purposes. For example, (72*a*) might receive as an answer (72*b*), which looks like a contradiction but is interpreted along the (noncontradictory) lines suggested in (72*c*). We do not simply interpret the speaker who utters (72*b*) as committed to an impossibility.

(72) *a.* Is Andrea smart?
b. She [Andrea] is [smart], and she [Andrea] isn't [smart].
c. Andrea is smart in some respects but not smart in other respects.

We consider similar examples in more detail in chapter 8, section 5.

4.5 Anomaly

Contradictions are clearly incoherent; we might well say that (69) doesn't make sense because it entails contradictories. Few would be tempted to say that (69) is ungrammatical, however, or that it is completely meaningless. The problem seems to be that its meaning includes, in some sense, obviously incompatible parts, the two clauses that are conjoined. Each of the constituent clauses is, however, perfectly fine on its own; incoherence arises from combining them.

Incoherent sentences that are not surface conjunctions of contradictory sentences do not so blatantly generate contradictory entailments. Indeed, their incoherence is often such that we are hard pressed to see that they have any entailments at all. Linguists have spoken of *anomaly* in cases like those illustrated in (73).

(73) *a.* The square root of Milly's desk drinks humanity.
b. Colorless green ideas sleep furiously.

c. To laugh is very humid.
d. The fact that cheese is green skipped inadvertently.
e. Being a theorem frightens consternation.
f. My toothbrush is blonde and buxom.
g. That rock thinks it's too good to hold the door open.

Chomsky (1965) introduced the notion of selectional restrictions to mark such sentences as ungrammatical. A verb like *drink*, he noticed, carries the information that its object designates something drinkable—a liquid or semiliquid substance perhaps, but at the very least something concrete rather than abstract—and that its subject designates something that might be a drinker, minimally, an animate being, we might suppose. The idea, then, was to provide a mechanism to ensure that *drink* selects only arguments satisfying such restrictions. From information given in its lexical entry, *drink* would be marked by something like the following "selectional feature":

(74) [+[+animate] ____ [−abstract]]

This is a contextual feature indicating that *drink* must only be inserted where there is a preceding animate subject and a following nonabstract object. Subject and object NPs, it was assumed, would receive feature specifications from their head nouns; *humanity*, for example, would be marked [+abstract] and *square root* [−animate]. Violations of selectional restrictions would arise from mismatches between features and would be ungrammatical.[8]

Sentences like those in (73) do seem very strange, and their strangeness seems different from that of a simple contradiction like (69), "Lee kissed Kim passionately, but she didn't touch him with her lips." The constituent clauses in (69), "Lee kissed Kim passionately" and "she [Lee] didn't touch him [Kim] with her lips," are each semantically unproblematic; each describes a possible situation. The oddness of (69) is that passionate kissing and not touching with the lips are brought together in a single event. The anomalous sentences in (73) are not strange in precisely the same ways or to the same degree. Some of them even seem more susceptible to being put to good use than does (69). We can imagine ways of interpreting sentences like (73*f*) and (73*g*), for example (someone might, for instance, have a toothbrush that looks like a woman, or someone might pretend or even believe that rocks are thinking beings). Yet (73*a*) and (73*e*) seem virtually impossible to make any sense of (the very notion of square root would seem to preclude a desk's having one or it's being something that might drink, and similarly, consternation seems incomparable to the kinds of things that can be frightened: people and other sentient beings).

It has often been pointed out that poetic uses of language are sometimes anomalous if interpreted in the usual and most obvious ways. Personification, for example, is a familiar poetic device, and (73*f*) and (73*g*) might easily be interpreted from that perspective. But the very fact that interpretation of these sentences typically suggests that their utterers are presenting toothbrushes and rocks as personlike calls for some explanation. Sentence (73*b*), famous from Chomsky's use of it in *Syntactic Structures* to illustrate the possibility of divergence between grammatical and semantic well-formedness, is the final line of a poem by John Hollander, where it seems vaguely evocative.[9] Again, the question of how its appropriateness there is achieved needs to be addressed.

The point is not that the sentences in (73) are semantically acceptable (although some of them may be) but rather that they are semantically distinct from one another, and a theory that simply marks them all as meaningless does not reveal this. As in the case of straightforward contradictions, the individual words and the syntactic constructions are semantically unproblematic; what is odd are the combinations, and some are much odder than others.

In some cases the oddness seems linked more to the structure of the world than to facts about linguistic meaning: rocks just aren't the kind of thing that thinks, as it happens, but this seems less a matter of what *rock* and *think* mean than a matter of what rocks and thinking are like. People are inclined to say that someone might wonder or claim or wish that rocks think. The study of artificial intelligence has raised the possibility of machines' thinking, a possibility that might well have been deemed as strange a century or so ago as that of rocks' thinking. On the other hand, (73*e*) seems far more peculiar; because it is an abstract entity, consternation is completely outside the realm of things than might be frightened. We cannot begin to understand someone's wondering whether consternation has been frightened. Someone who utters (73*e*) with apparent seriousness will be thought to have made a slip of the tongue or some other linguistic mistake (perhaps not knowing the meanings of some of the words used), to be suffering from some form of aphasia, to be mentally disturbed in some way. It would be quite strange for another to report the event by saying,

(75) Lindsey wonders whether being a theorem frightens consternation.

Sentence (75) seems hardly easier to interpret than sentence (73*e*). Similarly, sentence (73*a*) seems to resist any kind of interpretation: a desk is not a number and therefore in some fundamental way not the sort of thing that could have a square root, and numbers are not the sort of things that drink.

The correct conclusion may be that judgments of anomaly pick out a somewhat heterogeneous set of expressions, some of which are simply contradictions (with the incompatible entailments perhaps less immediate than in the cases that are obvious contradictions), others of which describe situations that are bizarre because of how the world works, and others of which involve a kind of semantic incompatibility other than that of contradiction (perhaps a semantic analogue of the notion of a violation of selectional restrictions).

What might this special kind of semantic incompatibility be like? It might somehow be part of the meaning of *drink*, for example, that it is only predicable of a certain range or *sort* of object, a sort that does not (at least in normal or literal uses) include square roots. Though it might be difficult to decide for a particular sentence whether it is *sortally deviant* (what is often called a *category mistake* in the philosophical literature) or anomalous in some other way, semantic anomaly, as illustrated in (73), is quite pervasive, is apparently distinct from the other phenomena we have considered, and seems clearly to call for some kind of semantic account.

One proposal is that some kinds of anomaly involve incompatible presuppositions. This would make anomaly analogous to contradiction, which involves incompatible entailments. The problem of distinguishing (certain cases of) anomaly from contradiction would then reduce to the problem of distinguishing presupposition from entailment, a matter we have touched on already and will later take up in more detail.

4.6 Appropriateness

One characteristic of anomalous expressions is that they are inappropriate for use in most contexts. People seem able to judge that particular expressions are or are not *appropriate* for uttering in particular contexts, and some have tried to incorporate an account of appropriateness conditions into a theory of linguistic semantics.

As we noted above in section 3.2, sentences are often judged inappropriate for contexts where their presuppositions are at issue or somehow controversial. Appropriateness is sometimes held to be a more general and useful notion for semantic theory than that of truth, or descriptive applicability, which was central to our discussion of entailments and contradictions. Only declaratives are sensibly said to describe a situation, or to be true of certain circumstances; interrogatives and imperatives are susceptible to the defect of inappropriateness rather than that of falsity. It is sometimes thought that a theory of appropriateness might replace a semantic theory based on truth. Appropriateness is often appealed to in explaining how speech acts are performed, how we manage to "do things with words": assert, inquire, promise, entreat, and the like. Some examples will illustrate. It is inappropriate for us to promise you to do something that we do not believe ourselves capable of doing (teach you all there is to know about meaning) or to do something we have no intention of doing (resign our positions if you don't like our book). It is inappropriate to assert something that we do not ourselves believe or that we do not want to give you reason to believe. It is generally inappropriate to inquire whether pigs have wings if we know whether pigs have wings (though, of course, examiners in pig biology may put the question to their students, knowing full well its answer). In chapter 4, we discuss speech acts in some detail. To perform a certain speech act is, in part, to adopt a certain attitude toward the content of what one says and perhaps also sometimes to urge a certain attitude on the part of the hearer ("Is that a promise or a threat?").

A related but slightly different area where appropriateness is appealed to is in judgments of whether a particular expression fits in a particular discourse slot, whether the discourse itself is sensible, coherent. If you have just uttered (76*a*) to the instructor, then (76*b*) seems highly inappropriate as her response.

(76) *a.* Can I have a copy of the answer sheet?
b. Yes, and Joan is similar.

There are clearly many more factors involved in assessing discourse appropriateness than what linguistic expressions mean. For example, relevance is a factor in assessing discourse appropriateness, and knowing what is relevant may involve all kinds of nonlinguistic knowledge. It seems quite unlikely that we could explicitly specify for all sentences of the discourse all the contexts in which they might be appropriate, though for some expressions we might be able to characterize at least partially the class of inappropriate contexts (see the discussion of presupposition in chapter 6).

Appropriateness is also invoked in dealing with matters of stylistic register: certain forms are reserved for church services, others are appropriate for the locker room, others for family dinners. It is generally inappropriate to mix registers, to use them in the wrong contexts, just as it is inappropriate to wear tennis shoes with a ball gown or to wear a ball gown to your linguistics class. Appropriateness here seems linked to cognitive significance: choosing a certain style signals a certain attitude toward the speech situation.

The notion of appropriateness is thus something of a mixed bag. Appropriateness does not seem to be structured like truth. There is no generally recognized relation of one expression's being dependent on another for its appropriateness parallel to the entailment relation, where one sentence must be true if another is. Nor does appropriateness seem to be readily amenable to a compositional treatment; certainly, no one has offered any general account of how to project appropriateness of (indefinitely many) complex expressions from appropriateness-related properties of their constituents. In other words, it does not seem that appropriateness will replace truth as a fundamental notion for semantic theory.

Nonetheless, recent work on such topics as presupposition has suggested that certain aspects of appropriateness may be characterizable in a much more rigorous way than was once thought possible. As we pointed out, the sentences "Lee got a perfect score on the semantics quiz" and "It was Lee who got a perfect score on the semantics quiz" entail one another; truth-based considerations do not distinguish them. The latter sentence, however, presupposes that someone got a perfect score, whereas the former does not. As we shall see in chapter 6, the presupposition of the cleft restricts the range of contexts in which its utterance is appropriate. It would be inappropriate to utter it in response to the question "Did anyone get a perfect score on the semantics quiz?" for example. Considerable progress is being made in developing empirically sound and theoretically sophisticated discourse theories that elucidate what is involved in such judgments for these and certain other kinds of cases. We will also see that something systematic can be said about how presuppositions of complex sentences relate to the presuppositions of constituent sentences.

5 Summary

We have given the reader an indication of the main aspects of language that a theory of meaning must deal with. Meanings form a productive system in which new meanings can always be expressed. There are aspects of meaning that may be constant across all human languages. Furthermore, meaning encodes information about the world and plays a role in giving a shape to our mental states. A theory of meaning must shed light on all these issues. We have also discussed the different types of semantic judgments in which what we know about meaning manifests itself, and we have provided a preliminary classification of such judgments. We are capable of assessing certain semantic properties of expressions and how two expressions are semantically related. These properties and relationships and the capacity that underlies our recognition of them constitute the empirical base of semantics.

In presenting a theory of semantics that tries to shed light on all these aspects of meaning, we are guided throughout by what Jackendoff (1983, 13) dubs the "grammatical constraint": "prefer a semantic theory that explains otherwise arbitrary generalizations about the syntax and the lexicon." The adherence to this constraint is what perhaps most sharply distinguishes our approach from that of philosophical logicians.

2 Denotation, Truth, and Meaning

1 Introduction

We have outlined what we think the empirical coverage of a theory of meaning should be. This will help us in directly addressing the question, What is meaning? Answers should be evaluated on the basis of how well they account for the phenomena singled out in chapter 1.

The question of what meaning is, is important to any discipline concerned, directly or indirectly, with cognition, that is, with how humans process information. To indicate where we stand with respect to some of the traditional views of meaning, it is convenient to classify approaches to meaning in three groups.

The first family of theories can be labeled "referential" or "denotational." This kind of theory is outward looking; its main emphasis is on the informational significance of language, its aboutness. Meaningfulness lies, according to this view, in the relations of symbols and configurations thereof to objects of various kinds. The study of meaning is the study of such relations. This tradition is the basis of the semantic techniques that have been developed within mathematical and philosophical logic.

It seems reasonable to maintain that the study of the relation of symbols to what they stand for must indeed be part of an account of meaning. For otherwise, how could we understand the fundamental fact that configurations of symbols carry information about all the diverse aspects of our experience?

A second family of theories of meaning might be labeled "psychologistic" or "mentalistic." Theories of this sort are inward looking and focus on the cognitive significance of language. The meaning of a configuration of symbols, according to this view, lies in what we grasp when we manipulate them; that is, it lies in the internalized representation of their retrievable content. The study of meaning is the study of how contents are mentally represented, the study of semantic representations. This tradition is the basis of much semantic work in psychology and artificial intelligence.

It seems reasonable to maintain that a given configuration of symbols has meaning for us only if we are able to grasp its content, which involves mentally representing it. If such representations are crucial in mediating between symbols and their content, we must not exclude them from semantics.

A third family of theories might be labeled "social" or "pragmatic." Its emphasis is on communication as a social activity. According to this view, meaningfulness lies essentially in the way agents use symbols in the course of their interactions with each other.

Again, it seems indubitable that we actually *do* things with words (saying "I promise to behave" constitutes, under the right circumstances, making a promise) and that key semantic notions like referring or making sense of some set of symbols involve activities. The way we actually use symbols, what we do with words, must play a central role in semantic considerations.

We believe that these three perspectives are by no means incompatible. On the contrary, meaning has all three aspects (namely, the denotational, representational, and pragmatic aspects). Any theory that ignores any of them will deprive itself of a source of insight and is ultimately likely to prove unsatisfactory.

Suppose that we adopted an approach of the second kind, an approach that studied meaning by relating symbols to mental representations or mental procedures of some sort, and stopped there. That would amount to limiting the domain of semantics to the relations between a language, which is a form of representation, and another representation. In other words, one would be relating two representations, translating one into the other (for example, translating our public language into an internal mental code, our "language of thought," say[1]). But how can mapping a representation onto another representation explain what a representation *means*, that is, what its information content is? Representations, routines, and procedures that manipulate symbols are precisely the kinds of things that have meaning. Mapping a representation *A* onto a representation *B* will not in itself tell us what representation *A* means. It will simply transform the problem of what *A* means into the problem of what *B* means. Only if we know what *B* means, what information *B* carries, will mapping *A* onto *B* help. In other words, even if our interaction with the world is always mediated by representation systems, understanding such systems will eventually involve considering what the systems are about, what they are representations of.[2]

Thus, what is needed is some way of talking about what a representation represents, that is, a theory of the information content of a system of symbols. We have to understand how information flows when we interact in certain ways. Only that, we think, can give to a theory of semantic representation its actual semantic bite.

The denotational perspective (the first one of those outlined above) seems to be promising in connection with the problem of explaining the link between symbols and their information content, in connection with the aboutness of language. In a nutshell, from a denotational point of view, symbols stand for objects. Consequently, configurations of symbols can be used to encode how objects are arranged and related to one another. We believe that this simple idea can be further articulated and developed into a full-fledged theory of what we are calling "information content." We will try to argue that such a theory leads to valuable insights about the structure and role of semantic representations and also meshes well with a view of language as a social activity. We hope, however, that even the reader who is not fully convinced by these arguments will find in what follows a battery of puzzles, techniques, and ideas crucially relevant to semantic analysis.

2 Denotation

It is often said that a name, *Pavarotti*, say, refers to or denotes its bearer (the popular singer). We shall use *denotation*, *denotatum*, *reference*, and *semantic value* for what a name (or some other expression) denotes.

The significance of a name does appear to consist largely of its being related to a given semantic value, a certain individual, say. Conceivably, the same paradigm might be extended to kinds of expressions other than proper names; perhaps it might be extended to expressions of any kind whatsoever. If that turned out to be the case, the denotation relation might constitute the most fundamental semantic relation.

2.1 Denotation and the foundations of semantics

Other noun phrases (NPs) besides proper names seem to derive their significance or semantic power from their reference. For example,

(1) *a.* It is a pencil.
b. This is yellow.
c. The tallest man in the world lives in Los Angeles.

For an utterance of (1*a*) to be felicitous, there must be some salient object in the context that is taken as the semantic value of the pronoun *it*. Similar considerations apply to (1*b*), where the reference of the demonstrative *this* might be individuated in our perceptual space by means of an act or demonstration. Sentence (1*c*) is an example that contains a definite description. The reference of the subject NP in (1*c*) is determined by whoever satisfies or fits the descriptive content expressed by the nominal *tallest man in the world*. Typical properties of definite descriptions are that they sound odd if nothing or more than one thing satisfies their descriptive content, as illustrated by the following examples:

(2) *a*. The present queen of France is smart.
b. The book that Agatha Christie wrote is about Hercule Poirot.

What is strange about utterances of these sentences is that there is no present queen of France and that Agatha Christie has written more than one book about Hercule Poirot. A theory of definite descriptions would have to account for these oddities.

Let us go back to referential NPs in general. To convince oneself that the notion of reference is central for the NPs in (1), it is sufficient to ask the following simple question: Could we say that we understand the meaning of the NPs in (1) if we didn't know what they referred to? Hardly, it would seem. The NPs in (1*a*) and (1*b*) clearly convey no information by themselves. The NP in (1*c*) does, yet its semantic role is to create an appropriate referential connection with some entity, and there is something distinctly odd (as we have seen in connection with (2)) if such a referential connection cannot be established. Thus, the notion of reference appears to be a fundamental component of what the NPs in question mean.

Of course, to grant this is not enough. Even if we believed that what makes the NPs in (1) meaningful is their relation to a denotation, one would still need an account of, for example, the much more direct role that the context plays in, say, fixing the reference of (1*a*, *b*) as compared to (1*c*). Even remaining within the limits of referential NPs, there is a wide variety of issues that a theory of reference faces.

NPs can refer not just to individuals but also to pluralities or collections of individuals:

(3) *a*. The students in my class are American.
b. The students in my class outnumber those in yours.

In (3*a*) the subject NP refers to a plurality of students in a distributive way. That is, the property of being American is attributed individually to each student in the relevant class. In contrast, in (3*b*) the subject NP refers to a plurality in a collective way. No individual student in the relevant class outnumbers anything; only the students as a group do. NPs can also refer to substances, actions, and abstract entities:

(4) *a.* Gold is expensive.
   b. Running is healthy.
   c. Justice should be prized.

They can refer to fictional characters:

(5) Bond is my hero.

What these examples suggest is that saying that the meaning of NPs such as those we have been considering consists of their relation to some denotatum is not saying much. Even at this preliminary level one can see that this view needs to be supplemented by theories of pluralities, abstract entities, fictional characters, etc.

In fact, there is a general point that is appropriate to make in this connection. To say that an NP like those we have been considering refers to an individual does not commit us to any preconceived view of what individuals are, nor does it presuppose that the notion of an individual is unproblematic. This comes up in an obvious way when we deal with, say, abstract nouns, as in (4*c*), but it is true of ordinary physical objects as well. Physical objects form causal patterns whose individuation across time or whose location in our perceptual space raise very interesting puzzles. To use a classical example, all the material parts of a table can be gradually changed in subsequent repairs and yet the table might be regarded as the same object before and after such repairs. Thus what we must mean by *the table* cannot be simply identified with the sum of portions of matter that make it up at a given time. Questions of this sort actually turn out to have direct semantic relevance.[3]

In spite of all the problems that there are, it is hard to see how in semantics one could dispense with the notion of an individual or with the notion of reference. Among other things, such notions seem to support a compositional theory of semantic relations (such as entailment or presupposition), even if all they do is link semantics to theories of how objects of various sorts are conceptualized. We hope that this idea will become clearer as we go along.

The following considerations add a further dimension to the problem of reference. Take the example in (6).

(6) A/some/every/no student in my class is blond.

In all these cases we have a nominal (*student in my class*) that is combined with what is generally called a determiner (*a*, *some*, *every*, *no*, etc.). What could the resulting NPs in (6) denote? It is far from clear. One is tempted to say, Nothing at all. In fact, these NPs are often called nonreferential.

There just is no obvious simple way to find a reference for NPs like *every student*. One might try to argue that *every student* denotes the class of students. Then the sentence "Every student outnumbers the professors" should have a sensible meaning that is roughly paraphrasable as "The class of students outnumbers the professors." But it doesn't. Furthermore, one would expect that a sentence like "Every Italian doesn't like Pavarotti" should be unambiguous and mean roughly "The class of Italians does not like Pavarotti." But such a sentence has (at least) two readings: "Not every Italian likes Pavarotti" and "Every Italian dislikes Pavarotti." Arguments in a similar vein can be constructed against other similar attempts to find a straightforward and intuitively simple denotation for the other NPs in (6).

Exercise 1 Assume that *a woman* denotes an arbitrarily chosen woman. What problems does this assumption run into? (Hint: consider what sentences like "In my class, a woman is blond and a woman is red-haired and ..." and "Every man loves a woman" would be expected to mean under the assumption in question.) Assume that *no woman* denotes a class that contains no women. Argue for or against such an hypothesis.

So, if we wish to pursue the idea that meaning can be accounted for in terms of a relation between expressions and their denotata, then the problem of nonreferential NPs constitutes a formidable challenge.

Now as pointed out in the introduction to this chapter, part of the appeal of the idea that semantics is essentially denotational lies in the fact that it would enable one to explain the aboutness of language, how it is that expressions have content. As a very rough first approximation one might say, for instance, that "Pavarotti is cute" conveys information about Pavarotti, because the name occurring in that sentence refers to that singer. Thus, what we say using the name *Pavarotti* will be understood as being about that particular entity. However, we have argued in chapter 1 that there are other empirical phenomena that a theory of meaning should account for, such as what we have called the productivity of meaning and judgments of semantic relatedness. How can we extend the denotational approach that we are considering so as to account for these other phenomena?

To account for productivity, it seems that we need two things: first, a way to determine what expressions of syntactic categories other than that of NPs denote, second, a procedure to determine how the reference of complex expressions depends on the reference of their components.

Let us see what the problems involved are by looking at a simple example.

(7) Pavarotti is an Italian singer.

Sentence (7) is generated by combining the NP *Pavarotti* with the verb phrase (VP) *is an Italian singer*. We might say that the VP *is an Italian singer* has a property as its semantic value. Properties can be predicated of individuals. The result of predicating a property of an individual is something like a state of affairs or situation. So sentence (7) might be regarded as having a situation (or a state of affairs) as its semantic value, intuitively, one in which *Pavarotti* has the property of being an Italian singer.

It might be possible to extend this strategy to more complex constructions. Forming an hypothesis concerning the denotation of other categories besides NPs, and in particular concerning the denotation of sentences, might help us in this task. To see this, let us take a first stab at the hard problem of such nonreferential NPs as *every woman* or *no woman*. We might try to analyze such NPs along the following lines. Let us say that these NPs indeed lack a denotation. This does not mean that they do not play any semantic role. The semantic role of, say, *no woman* would be that of combining with a property (such as, say, the one associated with the VP *smokes*) to yield a situation or state of affairs in which no woman smokes. The idea is to specify the semantic role of nonreferential NPs indirectly via the contribution that they make to the specification or description of the state of affairs associated with the sentences in which they occur. The same strategy might be applied to other nonreferential expressions (such as *and*, *because*, etc.).

Of course, to pursue this line of analysis we would have to overcome many more problems (for example, nonreferential NPs combine with expressions of many different syntactic categories, prepositions, for example, as in "I walked with every student, " etc.). But the above considerations do lend some preliminary support to the idea that our overall strategy of providing a referential analysis for various kinds of expressions may be viable. If so, we could have an arguably elegant account for the productivity of meaning in terms of a primitive denotation relation.

Here is how we proceed. We can classify objects in various semantic categories (say, individuals, properties, situations, etc.), and we can individuate various ways of combining those objects (for example, predication combines individuals with properties to give states of affairs). Expressions of different syntactic categories would be associated with objects of different semantic categories (or types); syntactic modes of putting expressions together would correspond to ways of combining the objects that those expressions denote. In this way one could always compositionally figure out the object that any given expression denotes in terms of objects that its component expressions denote and the way in which they are put together. This also explains more precisely how configurations of symbols carry information about arbitrarily complex states of affairs.

This program is thus of potential interest, for there are grounds to believe that it might account for both the aboutness of language and the productivity of meaning, two important desiderata for a semantic theory. There are, however, some further problems that call for attention. We can bring them into focus by considering in more detail the kinds of entities that we need to assume as semantic values for expressions of categories other than NP. Let us consider in particular sentence denotations, what we have intuitively called "situations" or "states of affairs."

First notice that the notion of a situation or state of affairs that we need to support the notion of a sentence denotation is itself quite problematic. To see this consider the following examples:

(8) *a.* Pavarotti is French.
b. If Pavarotti sings "O che gelide manine," I want to be there.

What states of affairs can (8*a*, *b*) denote? There is no actual state of affairs or situation that corresponds to (8*a*). Perhaps we might say that (8*a*) denotes a "hypothetical" or "possible" situation. Similarly, what sort of a state of affairs or situation can (8*b*) denote? It must be some kind of "conditional" state of affairs.

But notations like "possible state of affairs" or "conditional situations" are quite abstract and not immediately clear; in particular, they do not appear to be any clearer than the notion of a sentence denotation, which is what we want to explain. And objections of this kind are not confined to sentence denotations. They also apply, for example, to the notion of "property," that is, what we have indicated as a possible candidate for the role of VP denotations.

What about intuitions of semantic relatedness? Here lies the heart of the problem for the kind of semantic approach we have been considering. To see this, take the following example:

(9) Someone is an Italian singer.

Clearly, (7) is related to (9). The information that (9) conveys is somehow implicit in (7), and this knowledge is part of what we know about the meanings of (7) and (9). So, for example, it is impossible to assert (7) and deny (9). The relation between (7) and (9) is that of entailment, discussed in chapter 1.

We know that any sentence can enter a potential infinity of such relationships. That is, any sentence entails and is entailed by a potential infinity of other sentences, and when confronted with a pair of sentences, we are in general able to judge what entails what. Appealing to properties, predication, situations, and the like will not suffice, unless these notions are able to support a theory of semantic relatedness, among other things, a theory of entailment. In particular, to enable us to characterize entailment, the structure of properties or situations must be rich enough to support a logic. Appealing to properties or situations without specifying their logic is, in Donald Davidson's words, labeling a problem rather than solving it.

Again, it should be intuitively clear that the above argument applies not just to properties or situations but also to sorts of things that we might want to assign to expressions as semantic values. Appealing to any kind of thing whatsoever will be of little help if the logical structure of such a kind is not specified, that is, if no theory of entailment comes with it.

Now it is appropriate to ask the following question: what would it mean for, say, a theory of situations (or states of affairs) to be able to support a characterization of entailment? Let's go back to examples (7) and (9). A plausible first guess would be to say that the situation or state of affairs that (9) refers to is somehow contained in the situation that (7) is associated with. Equivalently, we might say that whenever the situation described by (7) occurs, the one described by (9) must occur. This, in turn, is equivalent to saying that whenever (7) is true, (9) must also be: saying that the situation denoted by a sentence occurs is tantamount to saying that the sentence in question is true. These preliminary considerations suggest that the logic of notions of potential semantic interest is linked in some crucial way to the notion of truth. In section 3 we will begin to explore this line of thought.

But before addressing directly the relation of denotation to truth, we would like to point out another interesting puzzle that specifically concerns the notion of sentence reference. The solution to this puzzle, advocated by the mathematician and philosopher Gottlob Frege, appeals to the notion of sense. First, we turn to the puzzle.

2.2 Reference and sense

We have assumed so far that a sentence denotes something like a state of affairs, or a situation. We shall now argue that this assumption, along with two rather plausible principles, leads to highly counterintuitive results.[4] The principles in question are the following:

(10) *a.* Two expressions that entail each other (that are content-synonymous) have the same reference.
b. If we have an expression *A* containing an expression *B* and we replace *B* in *A* with an expression *C* that has the same reference as *B*, the reference of *A* does not change.

We claim that these principles constitute valid generalizations about referential NPs. Let us convince ourselves that (10*a*, *b*) are true of referential NPs. Consider

(11) *a.* the sister of John
b. the daughter of John's parents

Content synonymy has been defined so far only for sentences. However, it is possible to generalize it to expressions of other categories. In particular, we can say that a referential NP *A entails* another NP *B* whenever the sentence "*x* is *A*" entails "*x* is *B*." Clearly, "*x* is John's sister" and "*x* is the daughter of John's parents" entail each other. Thus, by the definition just given, the NPs (11*a*) and (11*b*) entail each other. And our semantic competence tells us clearly that they also *must refer* to the same individual (whoever that may be). Thus principle (10*a*) appears to be true as applied to referential NPs.

Consider now principle (10*b*). It is easy to see that this too is true of referential NPs. Relevant examples are of the following kind:

(12) *a.* the sister of John
b. the sister of Mary's husband

Suppose that John is Mary's husband; that is, suppose that *John* and *Mary's husband* have the same reference. Expression (12*b*) is the result of substituting "Mary's husband" for "John" in (12*a*). Using the schema given in (10*b*), (12*a*) is our *A*, *John* is our *B* and *Mary's husband* our *C*. Again, our intuitions are pretty sharp on this score: if John is Mary's husband, the reference of (12*a*) and (12*b*) *must* be the same, just as (10*b*) would predict.

So, the principles in (10) appear to characterize correctly two properties of the denotation (or reference) relation, as exhibited by referential NPs. We are trying to build our semantics on (some version of) such a relation by generalizing it from NPs to other categories of expressions. Thus, we ought to expect such principles to hold also with respect to the denotation of expressions different from NPs. There is no reason to expect these principles to be limited just to the denotation of NPs if denotation is a unitary semantic relation. In particular, these principles should apply to the reference of sentences. Let us see what happens.

Take two arbitrary sentences (say, "It snows" and "Pavarotti is cute") and suppose that the only thing that they have in common is that they happen to be both true or both false. Let us introduce some handy terminology. If a sentence is true, we say that its truth value is true (abbreviated as T). If a sentence is false, we say that its truth value is false (abbreviated as F). Consider now the following:

(13) *a.* Pavarotti is cute.
b. The truth value of "Pavarotti is cute" = T.
c. The truth value of "It snows" = T.
d. It snows.

We are going to show that by principles (10*a*, *b*), (13*a*) and (13*d*) must refer to the same thing. First, notice that (13*a*) and (13*b*) entail each other. For suppose that (13*a*) is true. Then the truth value of "Pavarotti is cute" is T, and (13*b*) would be saying that the truth value of "Pavarotti is cute" (namely T) equals T, which, of course, is indeed the case. Suppose, on the other hand, that (13*a*) is false. Then (13*b*) will be false too, since the truth value of "Pavarotti is cute" would be F, and (13*b*) would be saying that F equals T, which is clearly false. Since (13*a*) and (13*b*) entail each other, they must have the same reference, by principle (10*a*).

Now (13*b*) and (13*c*) must also have the same reference, this time in virtue of (10*b*), since by hypothesis (13*a*) and (13*d*) have the same truth value and (13*c*) is obtained from (13*b*) by replacing in it the definite description *the truth value of "Pavarotti is cute"* with the coreferential definite description *the truth value of "It snows."* Finally, (13*c*) and (13*d*) must have the same reference, because they too entail each other (the reasoning here is fully parallel to that used to show the content synonymy of (13*a*) and (13*b*)).

Thus, if (10*a*, *b*) are true generalizations about reference, as they appear to be in the case of NP reference, then two *arbitrary* sentences with the same truth value must have the same reference, or denotatum.

But now look: in the cases where the truth value of sentences can be determined, there are going to be only two truth values (true and false). We have chosen in (13) two sentences that, aside from truth values, have nothing in common semantically. At the same time we have shown that they must have the same denotatum. But then what can this denotatum be? Clearly, the denotatum must be something that those sentences have in common, namely, their truth value. That is, if the principles in (10) are valid, then the denotation of a sentence must be its truth value. To put this in different terms, if we want to maintain the principles in (10*a*, *b*), and also the idea that sentences refer to states of affairs, we are forced to conclude that there can be at most two such things: the true state of affairs and the false one. But this seems counterintuitive at best.

What way out do we have? Perhaps there is something wrong with the principles in (10) as applied to semantic values of sentences. But it seems hard to tell what and why if the logical structure of the notion of a sentence denotation isn't spelled out more clearly. Or perhaps we can say that the denotation of sentences is indeed their truth value. In other words, our strategy of developing a semantic theory in which referential NPs are the model for reference generally has as one of its consequences that sentences must be taken to refer to truth values. We do not in fact have an obvious pretheoretical understanding of a notion of sentence reference; our everyday talk is of sentences' *describing* situations, not referring to them. Still, many find it odder to think of sentences as referring to or denoting truth values than to think of them as referring to or denoting situations. However, such a result need not necessarily be regarded as a negative one if our theory delivers what it should (a theory of entailment, presupposition, etc.).

Nonetheless, if sentences denote their truth values, then there must be something more to sentence meaning than denotation, for we don't want to say that any two sentences with the same truth value have the same meaning. This is what led Frege to posit the notion of *sense*. Let us explore it briefly.

Frege proposes that sentences (and indeed, expressions of any category) have not only a reference (a standard translation of the German word *Bedeutung*) but also a sense (Frege's term was *Sinn*). The reference of an expression is what it stands for on a given occasion of its use. Its sense, Frege says, is the way in which the reference is presented. To illustrate the distinction, Frege uses an example along the following lines. Suppose we are looking at the moon by means of a telescope. The moon corresponds to the reference. The sense corresponds to the moon's image as projected on the telescope's lens. The image on the retina corresponds not to the sense but to its mental representation. The sense (like the image projected on the telescope's lens) is "objective." The retinal image is subjective and may vary from perceiver to perceiver.

More specifically, table 2.1 shows how Frege classified the sense and reference of expressions of the categories we have been considering. The reference of an expression depends on its sense and on what the circumstances are. For example, we can determine the reference of *the morning star* by finding out what fits that description, given what we understand of it and what the facts are. According to this view, meaning is to be analyzed along two complementary dimensions. The meaning of an expression *A* lies in the relation that *A* has with its sense and its reference.

Similar ideas have several historical antecedents and have also been elaborated by other researchers independently of Frege. For example, Ferdinand de Saussure (1916) has a distinction between

Table 2.1 Frege's classification of sense and reference

	EXPRESSION	REFERENCE	SENSE
Category	Referential NPs	Individuals	Individual concepts
Example	*the morning star*	Venus	The concept of the star that disappears last in the morning
Category	VPs	Classes of individuals	Concepts
Example	*is Italian*	The Italians	The concept of being Italian
Category	Ss	True or false	Thoughts
Example	"Pavarotti is Italian."	True	The thought that Pavarotti is Italian

signification and *signifié* that appears to be conceptually similar to Frege's distinction between reference and sense.

It is worth reiterating that for Frege senses are not to be thought of as mental or psychological entities. In particular, the sense of a sentence, say, "Pavarotti is Italian," is not what we grasp in hearing it, for the latter is intrinsically a subjective matter, and varies to a degree from individual to individual. Senses are what enable us to communicate with each other, and as such they must be intersubjective (or objective). So the notion of a thought for Frege should be construed as something like the information content that we grasp in understanding a sentence. Henceforth we will follow the common practice of using the term *proposition* for this purpose. A proposition is the sense of a sentence.

Of course, it is conceivable to adopt Frege's distinction without being radical Fregean objectivists about what sense are. For example, one could hold the view that senses are a characterization of the common structure that our semantic representations must share (given that communication is successful). But the question of the nature of senses has no easy answer. Luckily, as we will see, it is possible to do semantics even in the absence of a complete understanding of this.

In later formal work stemming from the tradition originated by Frege (see especially Carnap 1947), the sense/reference contrast is understood in terms of *intension* versus *extension*. Carnap's notion of the intension of an expression is intended as a more precise rendering of what Frege called its sense; the extension is what Frege called its reference (or denotation). Sometimes we use Carnap's terminology, sometimes Frege's.

Frege put forth other arguments that point to the need for an appeal to sense (or intension) in semantic considerations. Here are two. The first is concerned with identity statements. Consider

(14) *a.* The morning star is the evening star.
  b. The morning star is the morning star.

Both definite descriptions *the morning star* and *the evening star* happen to pick out the same entity, namely, Venus. So (14*b*) is derived from (14*a*) by replacing coreferential expressions. If reference is all there is to meaning, then (14*a*) and (14*b*) should have the same information content. But they clearly do not. Sentence (14*b*) is utterly uninformative: we know it a priori. Sentence (14*a*) is informative: in fact, it was an astronomical discovery. Using the notion of sense, we can account for this contrast. Sentence (14*b*) is uninformative because the two expressions being equated are identical, and thus both have the same sense and the same reference. The two expressions in (14*a*), on the other hand, have different senses, and it is an empirical fact that they happen to pick out the same reference, whence the informativeness of (14*a*).

The second argument has to do with what Frege called "indirect" and Quine "opaque" contexts:

(15) Sophia Loren believes that Pavarotti is French.

Sentence (15) attributes a certain belief to Loren. What Loren believes is somehow described by the sentence "Pavarotti is French." Consequently, it must be systematically recoverable from the meaning of the latter. But clearly the actual truth value of "Pavarotti is French" does not determine what Loren may believe. Thus, the notion of sense is needed to account for contexts such as these. Sentence (15) can be interpreted as saying that Loren bears the *believe* relation to the thought (or proposition) expressed by "Pavarotti is French." Examples such as these could be multiplied and elaborated upon in many ways.

At this point we should ask the following questions. Does appealing to the notion of sense really help us? Does it provide a base from which we can study meaning in natural language? Recall that what we want is a compositional theory of meaning that accounts for the properties discussed in chapter 1. In particular, such a theory should account for our intuitions concerning semantic relations. If meaning is to be studied along two dimensions (the intensional and the extensional), we need a way to determine compositionally both the intension and the extension of an expression in terms of the intension and extension of its parts. We also need to know precisely how intensions and extensions are related. Moreover, they should provide an account of the various semantic relations, such as entailment and presupposition. In the absence of all this, appealing to intensions will not help us much. To say that "Pavarotti is French" has the thought (or proposition) that Pavarotti is French as its sense links the notion to be explained (namely, that of meaning) to the notion of a thought (or proposition), and this latter notion is equally in need of an account. Furthermore, this move in itself buys us nothing in terms of explaining the various semantic relations. This is precisely the criticism that we have leveled against accounting for sentence meaning in terms of the notion of a situation or state of affairs. It seems, therefore, that we have reached an impasse.

We started out by exploring the notion of reference or denotation and giving some general reasons why such a notion could play a central role in semantics. However, we have met some difficulties in extending such a notion beyond referential NPs; in particular, we have had trouble with the notion of sentence reference. We first saw some of the difficulties that arise from adopting the view that sentences denote situations or states of affairs. In essence, we argued that this claim is nearly vacuous if its connection to a theory of semantic relations (such as entailment and presupposition) is not made clear. We have also argued that generalizations that seem to be true of the notion of NP denotation lead to counterintuitive results if we try to maintain that the semantic content of sentences be analyzed in terms of situations or states of affairs. We then considered Frege's way out of these difficulties, which appeals to the notion of a sense (or intension). Such a notion, however, also appears to be nearly vacuous if its connection to a theory of semantic relations is not made clear.

We don't think, however, that these difficulties constitute an insurmountable obstacle to constructing a semantics in which the notion of denotation plays a central role. Nor do we believe that they conclusively show that Frege's notion of sense has no use in semantics. In fact, in chapter 5 we argue that it does. But we do seem to need a different starting point.

3 Truth

3.1 Nur im Zusammenhange eines Satzes bedeuten die Wörter etwas

One of the recurrent problems that we observed in section 2 has to do with how to characterize sentence meaning. In particular, we have tried to focus on the reasonably clear name-bearer relation and adopt it as paradigmatic for all key semantic notions. But what sentences denote and how one gets to such a denotation remain outstanding problems. Perhaps before trying exactly to identify the denotation of words (or morphemes), we should try to make some progress toward a viable characterization of the semantic content of sentences.

In fact, it is not even clear that the notion of denotation can be understood independently of sentence meaning. This is arguably true even of the best understood referring expressions, like proper names. Consider how we could go about explaining the "meaning" of the name *Pavarotti* to someone who doesn't know it. Two obvious possibilities would be pointing at the famous singer and giving a description of him. We can of course combine these two possibilities in various ways as the circumstances require. But even if we use a simple ostension, or deixis (pointing), what our act expresses is something like a complete utterance with roughly the same meaning as "This person is Pavarotti." So it would seem that we are dealing with a propositional kind of knowledge. Moreover, for the pointing to make sense, we must already be able to distinguish and classify people from other objects. In other words, as Quine (1960) argued, the perceptual stimuli from which deixis can be drawn are insufficient to characterize the objects that constitute the frame of reference for our language. We can refer to something and individuate it within a given background only by using a conceptual system. It follows that in grasping the meaning of a word, any word, for the first time, we cannot get at it directly (whatever that may involve). We never deal with labels and objects in isolation. We are typically confronted with complex states of affairs in which objects stand in relations to other objects. Indeed, one can say that we arrive at objects via a process of abstraction that enables us to identify them as, say, causal structures, regularities across states of affairs.

What this suggests is that to get started, we should pursue units more complex than names (or words). Language, as an information code, provides an association between two systems: what signifies and what is signified. Sentences, as opposed to whole texts, appear to be the smallest autonomous information units in a language (with some qualification having to do with context dependency—see below). Sentences comprise a category of well-formed structures capable of expressing thoughts that can stand on their own, of describing whole situations. Thus, perhaps getting at sentence meaning might be easier than getting at the meaning of other units. What we might try to do is to define "S means *p*" precisely, where S is a sentence. We might then be able to identify further crucial semantic notions in terms of sentence meaning. This, in fact, is one way of capitalizing on the famous (and controversial) dictum by Frege that we use as title for this section: "Only in the context of a sentence do words have meaning."

Before seeing how such a program might be pursued, we should clear up some obvious problems. First, what are sentences? How do we define them? For the time being, we will consider only ordinary declarative sentences. We hope to be able to convince the reader that the approach developed in connection with this kind of sentence does extend to the other kinds. Second, it is a commonplace observation that the content of (declarative) sentences can depend on the situation, or context, in which they are uttered. Consider, for example,

(16) I am tired.

What (16) can convey is going to depend partly on who the speaker is and when the sentence is uttered. And there are, of course, many other more complex ways in which what a sentence means depends on the context (ways having to do with intersentential anaphora, focus, presuppositions, etc.). Trying to address fully the issue of context dependency at this stage would complicate our task considerably. Therefore, we adopt a simplification known as the "fixed-context assumption." We assume that the context of use (who the speaker is, what the time of the utterance is, etc.) is a known quantity. Consequently, so-called indexicals such as *I* in (16) come to have a definite reference and behave just like other referential expressions (such as proper names). This assumption will then be abandoned when we specifically address the issue of indexicality.

Within these restrictions a conspicuous property of declarative sentences is that they can be true or false in a given situation or circumstance. Consider, for example, (17), and assume that its context of utterance is known, say, September 10, 1986, in a classroom on the Cornell campus in Ithaca (as per the fixed-context assumption).

(17) The pope talked to Reagan between 3:00 and 4:00 P.M. on September 9.

When is (17) true? Of course, even if the context is fixed, truth depends on more: what the facts are. Sentence (17) is going to be true if, in fact, the two relevant people were talking at the specified time. We may never know whether such an event actually took place. Perhaps neither of the protagonists has been seen at the designated time. Perhaps they have been struck by amnesia concerning the event described in (17). However, even though we may lack actual knowledge of facts, we know, for example, that a transatlantic phone call could suffice for (17) to be true, but (17) would not be true if John Paul spent all the relevant time talking to Pavarotti. The important thing to notice here is that though we might not know what the facts are, we do know what they ought to be in order to make the sentence true. This knowledge, we claim, is semantic (and hence grammatical) in nature: it is constitutive of our knowledge of what (17) means.

Conversely, someone who did not know what (17) means (for example, a monolingual speaker of Russian) could not make use of a specification of the facts to evaluate it. To judge whether (17) is true, one needs not only knowledge of the facts; one also needs to know what (17) means, to know something about the grammar of the language. If we didn't know what (17) means, we would have no clue as to what circumstances would make (17) true.

Notice that we are not trying to provide effective criteria for checking the truth of sentences. We don't think that semantics could or should aim so high. What we want to do is simpler. Are there criteria to determine when it is appropriate to say that a sentence is true? We think that there are. The examples illustrate them. A declarative sentence like (17) describes a corner of reality, claims that a certain condition (John Paul's talking to Reagan) obtains. Saying "S is true" amounts just to saying that the conditions that S claims to obtain do obtain. Thus we have at least a criterion of adequacy for the predicate *is true*. It may seem a trivial one, but consider that we don't have even that much for "S means *p*." The notion of truth, whatever problems it may have, is a little bit clearer than the notion of meaning.

Tarski (1935, 1944) has shown that we can draw further consequences from having a clear criterion of application for the truth predicate. To give a characterization of this predicate for a whole language, we need to have a theory that, for any *S* in *L* and any *v*, gives us the following:

(18) *S* is true in *v* if and only if (iff) *p*.

Here S is a structural description of a sentence of a language *L*, *v* is a situation or a specification of the relevant facts, and *p* describes the conditions that have to obtain for S to be true in *v* (that is, the truth conditions for S). The reader may be worried by the fact that we are still relying in (18) on the notion of a situation (or circumstance), which gives rise to problems. We will show later, however, that the way we use this notion in giving a truth definition is quite unproblematic.

Sentences of the form (18) are called T-sentences. Now, if the language contains only a finite number of sentences, then one could simply list all the relevant T-sentences, and we could directly pair up all members of the syntactic category of sentences with their truth conditions. But if the language contains an infinite number of sentences, then a theory of truth must incorporate a mechanism for generating all of the correspondingly infinite number of T-sentences. Presumably, such a mechanism will have to be based on the generative device that characterizes the syntax of the language. In other words, a characterization of the truth predicate for an infinite language must be compositional. As we shall see, to obtain a compositional definition of truth for a sufficiently rich language is not exactly trivial.

We should perhaps point out that we are not claiming that meaning is completely exhausted by truth conditions. What we are claiming is that if we ignore the conditions under which S is true, we cannot claim to know the meaning of S. Thus, knowing the truth conditions for S is at least necessary for knowing the meaning of S. We cannot have the latter without the former. Suppose we did not know whether sentence (19*a*) is true or false in the situation represented in (19*b*).

(19) *a*. The door is closed.
b.

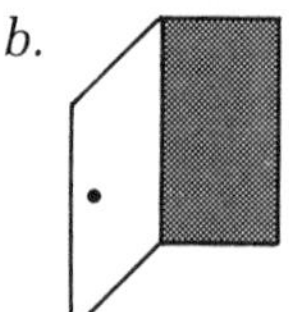

Could we be said to know what (19*a*) means? We think not. But then truth conditions must surely be a necessary component of sentence meaning: there is no meaning without truth conditions.

In fact, various philosophers have gone beyond this and argued that knowing the meaning of S is just knowing its truth conditions.[5] If that is so, one could propose the following definition:

(20) S *means* $p =_{\text{df}}$ S is true in *v* if and only if (iff) *p*.

What we have on the left hand side is quite obscure: an intensional relation involving an entity whose nature is unknown (*p*, viewed as the meaning of S). What we have on the right hand side is a lot clearer: a biconditional between two sentences of our semantic metalanguage, "S is true in *v*" and *p* (viewed as a sentence describing when this holds). From the perspective of definition (20), a theory of sentence meaning (for a language *L*) is just a formal device that compositionally generates all the T-sentences for *L*.

Perhaps before discussing this claim any further, we should see what such a formal device would actually look like. We do so by providing a phrase-structure grammar for an elementary fragment of English and developing a Tarski-style truth definition for it.

3.2 The fragment F_1

The syntax of F_1 is specified in terms of a very simple set of phrase-structure rules and hardly requires any comment. The semantics of F_1 corresponds essentially to the semantics of the propositional calculus. Its design, however, differs from what can be found in most introductory logic textbooks, as the emphasis here is on the actual linguistic applications of propositional logic. The simplest sentences in F_1 are made up of noun-verb (N-V) or N-V-N sequences. We shall call such sentences *atomic*. Complex sentences are obtained by conjoining, disjoining, and negating other sentences. Even though the grammar of F_1 is so simple, it generates an infinite number of sentences.

3.2.1 Syntax of F_1 In specifying the syntax of F_1, we use more or less traditional grammatical categories (S for sentences, VP for verb phrases, V_t for transitive verbs, V_i for intransitive verbs, etc.). These categories are adopted purely for pedagogical purposes. Discussing syntactic categories and phrase structures goes beyond the limits of the present work. As far as we can tell, any of the major current theories of syntactic categories (such as X′ theory, or extended categorical grammars) can be adopted with the semantics that we are going to develop.

The rules in (21) generate sentences like those in (22) and associate with them structures like those in (23) for (22*a*).

(21) *a.* S → N VP[6]
b. S → S conj S
c. S → neg S
d. VP → V_tN
e. VP → V_i
f. N → Pavarotti, Sophia Loren, James Bond
g. V_i → is boring, is hungry, is cute
h. V_t → likes
i. conj → and, or
j. neg → it is not the case that

(22) *a.* Pavarotti is hungry, and it is not the case that James Bond likes Pavarotti.
b. It is not the case that Pavarotti is hungry or Sophia Loren is boring.

(Henceforth we simplify and freely use *Loren* and *Bond* for *Sophia Loren* and *James Bond*, respectively).

(23) *a.*

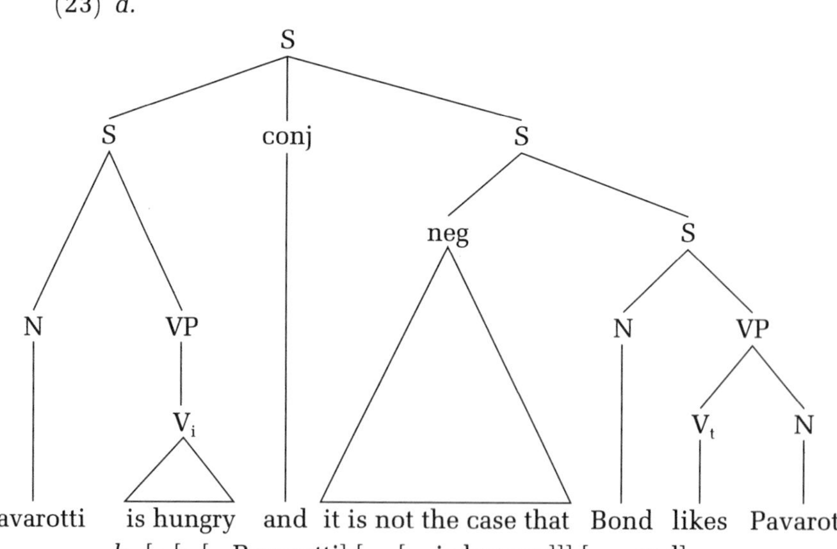

b. [S [S [N Pavarotti] [VP [V_i is hungry]]] [conj and] [S [neg it is not the case that] [S [N Bond] [VP [V_t likes] [N Pavarotti]]]]]

In (23*a*) the syntactic analysis of (22*a*) is displayed in the form of a tree diagram (its phrase-structure marker, or P-marker for short).

In (23*b*) the same information is represented in the form of a labeled bracketing. These two representations are known to be equivalent. Roughly put, each (nonterminal) tree node in (23*a*) corresponds to a subscripted label in (23*b*), and the brackets to which the label is subscripted represent the branches stemming from the corresponding node. We switch between these two notations as convenience requires. To enhance readability, we also follow the common practice of occasionally representing syntactic structures incompletely, that is, showing only that part directly relevant to the point we are trying to make.

3.2.2 Semantics for F_1 As F_1 generates an infinite number of sentences, we can specify the truth condition associated with each sentence only compositionally, by looking at the way it is built up in terms of smaller units. We have to look at the semantic value of such smaller units and provide an algorithm for combining them. If β is a well-formed expression of F_1, we shall write $[\![\beta]\!]^v$ for its semantic value in circumstance v. For example, we will write $[\![\text{Pavarotti}]\!]^v$ for the semantic value of the expression *Pavarotti* in circumstance v. What should $[\![\text{Pavarotti}]\!]^v$ be? In F_1, just as in English, we will let the semantic value of *Pavarotti* in any circumstance v be the celebrated tenor in flesh and blood.

Our goal is to provide a fully explicit, that is, fully formalized, specification of truth conditions for sentences in F_1. We will have done this if we assign semantic values in each circumstance to all lexical entries and give combinatorial rules that together with those lexical values permit us to assign to each sentence S the truth value of S in circumstance v. Thus, $[\![\text{S}]\!]^v$ will be the truth value of S in v. We do not have to worry about what truth values are, so long as we provide for distinguishing two of them. It is handy to use 1 for what true sentences denote and 0 for what false sentences denote, but these choices have no special significance. Thus $[\![\text{S}]\!]^v = 1$ is just shorthand for "S is true in v" or less naturally but equivalently "*S* denotes 1 in v." Although it may look somewhat unfamiliar and frightening at first, the mathematical notation is ultimately an enormous convenience. To achieve formal explicitness without using it would require much lengthier specifications and quite tortured prose, which would prove harder to understand in the long run. The combinatorial semantic rules and the semantic values for lexical expressions will have to be chosen so that for any sentence S and circumstance v, whether $[\![\text{S}]\!]^v$ is 1 or 0 depends only on the values in v of the lexical expressions occurring in S and the semantic rules applied in interpreting S. What we present is just one of several equivalent ways of carrying out this program.

A further preliminary point that should be noted is that some terminal strings generated by the syntax of F_1 are ambiguous. For example, (22*b*) is associated with two distinct trees (or labeled bracketings), namely,

(24) *a.* $[_S$ neg $[_S$ Pavarotti is hungry or Loren is boring$]]$
b. $[_S [_S$ neg $[_S$ Pavarotti is hungry$]]$ or Loren is boring$]$

These syntactic ambiguities correspond to semantic ones. (24*a*) negates a certain disjunction, namely, that Pavarotti is hungry or Loren is boring. Thus, (24*a*) is a way of saying that Pavarotti is not hungry and Loren is not boring. But (24*b*) says that either Pavarotti isn't hungry or Loren is boring. It follows, therefore, that if we want to assign a unique semantic value to each sentence in any given situation, we should interpret not terminal strings but trees (or labeled bracketings). Thus, for any well-formed tree or labeled bracketing Δ, $[\![\Delta]\!]^v$ will be its semantic value in v. How can such a semantic value be determined in general? Well, we first have to assign a lexical value to every terminal node. Terminal nodes (or lexical entries) are finite and can thus be listed. Then we look at the syntactic rules of F_1. Each rewrite rule, say of the form $A \rightarrow BC$, admits as well-formed a tree of the form

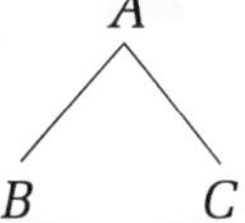

(or equivalently a labeled bracketing of the form $[_A\ B\ C]$). We have to specify the value of the tree whose root is A in terms of the values of the subtrees rooted in B and C. This means that the semantic value for the terminal string dominated by A is determined in terms of the values of the substrings dominated by B and C and the way these substrings are put together. If we do this for every syntactic rule in the grammar, we can interpret any tree admitted by it. A definition of this kind (with a finite number of base clauses and a finite number of clauses that build on the base clauses) is called *recursive*.

We start off by assigning values to each basic lexical entry. Our Ns are all proper names, and we let them denote individuals. It is less obvious what V_is, intransitive verbs, and V_ts, transitive verbs, should denote. Intransitive verbs, or one-place predicates, can be used to say something about an individual. It is plausible, therefore, to associate an intransitive verb with a set of individuals in a circumstance; intuitively, this set includes those individuals of whom the verb can be truly predicated in the given circumstance. For example, $[\![\text{is boring}]\!]^v$ will be the set of individuals that are boring in *v*. Transitive verbs can be used to say that one individual stands in some relation to a second individual. We can associate these expressions (two-place predicates) in a circumstance with a set whose members are ordered pairs of individuals. Intuitively, an ordered pair is in this set in given circumstances iff the first member of the pair stands in the relation designated by the verb to the second member in those circumstances. For example, the *love* relation can be thought of as the set of pairs $\langle x, y \rangle$ such that *x* loves *y*. We first specify the values for the members of N, V_i, and V_t. We assume familiarity with the concepts and notation of elementary set theory; symbols and brief explanations appear in the appendix, but readers who want a fuller discussion should consult an elementary book on set theory (for example, Halmos (1960) or Stoll (1963)).

(25) For any situation (or circumstance) *v*,
$[\![\text{Pavarotti}]\!]^v = \text{Pavarotti}$
$[\![\text{Loren}]\!]^v = \text{Loren}$
$[\![\text{Bond}]\!]^v = \text{Bond}$
$[\![\text{is boring}]\!]^v =$ the set of those individuals that are boring in *v* (in symbols, $\{x : x \text{ is boring in } v\}$)
$[\![\text{is hungry}]\!]^v = \{x : x \text{ is hungry in } v\}$
$[\![\text{is cute}]\!]^v = \{x : x \text{ is cute in } v\}$
$[\![\text{likes}]\!]^v =$ the set of ordered pairs of individuals such that the first likes the second in *v* (in symbols, $\{\langle x, y \rangle : x \text{ likes } y \text{ in } v\}$)

As the semantics for F_1 must be given in a (meta)language, we choose English, enriched with some mathematics (set theory). Within this metalanguage we first stipulate that proper names are associated with the respective individuals named by them. This association does not depend on circumstances in the way in which the extension of a predicate like *is hungry* does. Thus, we assume for now that the reference of proper names is fixed once and for all in a given language. The reader should not be misled by the fact that in ordinary natural languages there are many proper name forms that denote more than one individual; for example, the form *Jim Smith* names many different men. This is a kind of lexical ambiguity where the language contains a number of distinct proper names that happen to have the same form; the distinct proper names are pronounced and spelled the same. To keep matters simple, proper names in our fragment are not ambiguous; each form denotes only one individual. The extension of a predicate, on the other hand, can vary across circumstances. Such an extension in different situations is determined by the predicate itself. The theory thus exploits our competence as English speakers. There is nothing circular about this, as throughout (25) on the left hand side of "=" we mention or quote the relevant words, and on the right hand side we use them. The appearance of circularity would vanish if we used English to give the semantics for a different object language, say Italian.

Let us now turn to a consideration of the logical words *and*, *or*, and *it is not the case that.* To understand how negation works, we have to look at the truth conditions of sentences that contain negations. Intuitively, a sentence like "It is not the case that S" will be true exactly when S is false. We can represent this by means of the following table:

(26) $[\![S]\!]^v$	$[\![\text{neg S}]\!]^v$
1	0
0	1

A conjunction of the form "S and S′" is true just in case both S and S′ are true:

(27) $[\![S]\!]^v$	$[\![S']\!]^v$	$[\![\text{S and S}']\!]^v$
1	1	1
1	0	0
0	1	0
0	0	0

In ordinary English discourse, conjunctions sometimes imply more than the truth of both conjuncts; for example, "Bond jumped into the waiting car, and he [Bond] chased the gangsters" suggests that Bond's chasing the gangsters followed his jumping into the car. But a speaker could go on and say "but not in that order" without contradiction and thus such a suggestion is not part of what *and* itself contributes to truth conditions. We discuss pragmatic explanations of such further implications in chapter 4.

For disjunction we seem to have an option. In natural language, *or* sometimes seems to be interpreted *exclusively* (as in "Gianni was born in Rome, or he was born in Florence," where both disjuncts cannot be true) or *inclusively* (as in "Maria is very smart, or she is very hardworking," which will be true even if Maria is both very smart and very hardworking). We might hypothesize that *or* is ambiguous between an exclusive and an inclusive interpretation. Note, however, that the inclusive *or* is more general than the exclusive one. For any situation *v*, if either one of *p* and *q* is true, "p or_{exc} q" and "p or_{inc} q" will both be true in *v*. If, however, *p* and *q* are both true, then "p or_{exc} q" will be false, while "p or_{inc} q" will be true. The state of affairs that we have can be illustrated by the following diagram of situations:

(28)

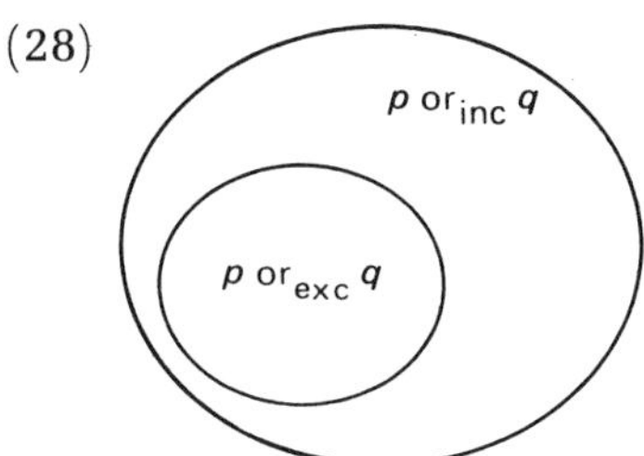

Whenever such a circumstance arises, we can try the strategy of assigning the more general interpretation to the relevant construction as its semantic value. The narrower interpretation would not thereby be excluded and could then arise as the intended one by extrasemantic (pragmatic) means. For the time being, we will follow this strategy without further justification but will try to justify it more when we specifically discuss various pragmatic theories. We therefore adopt the following semantics for *or*:

(29)

$[\![S]\!]^v$	$[\![S']\!]^v$	$[\![S \text{ or } S']\!]^v$
1	1	1
1	0	1
0	1	1
0	0	0

Some of our readers will recognize (26), (27), and (29) as the truth tables familiar from elementary logic. We could use these truth tables directly to provide the truth conditions for complex sentences without assigning a semantic value for *and*, *or*, etc. However, it is quite easy to construct an abstract semantic value for each connective that will achieve exactly the same results as the truth tables in specifying truth values for sentences in which the connectives occur. We can view the connectives as functions that map truth values (or ordered pairs of truth values in the case of conjunction and disjunction) onto truth values.

A function is simply a systematic connection between specified inputs and outputs such that for any given input there is a unique corresponding output (see appendix for further discussion). We can represent a function by indicating what output is associated with each input. This is what we have done in (30) using the arrow notation.

(30) For any situation v,

$$[\![\text{it is not the case that}]\!]^v = \begin{bmatrix} 1 \to 0 \\ 0 \to 1 \end{bmatrix}$$

$$[\![\text{and}]\!]^v = \begin{bmatrix} \langle 1,1\rangle \to 1 \\ \langle 1,0\rangle \to 0 \\ \langle 0,1\rangle \to 0 \\ \langle 0,0\rangle \to 0 \end{bmatrix}$$

$$[\![\text{or}]\!]^v = \begin{bmatrix} \langle 1,1\rangle \to 1 \\ \langle 1,0\rangle \to 1 \\ \langle 0,1\rangle \to 1 \\ \langle 0,0\rangle \to 0 \end{bmatrix}$$

We have chosen to regard the truth tables from elementary logic as (truth) functions. We have then assigned these abstract objects as the semantic values of logical words. This enables us to talk about the meaning of conjunction: a function that maps truth values into truth values. Notice that the value of logical words is in an interesting way language-independent. Of course, the conjunction operation expressed by English *and* will be expressed by other forms in other languages. Nonetheless, languages generally appear to provide constructions whose meanings correspond to the functions we have associated with *and*, *or*, and *it is not the case that*. Such meanings are thus strong candidates for semantic universals.

We have assigned a semantic value to the basic entries. At this point we need to provide an interpretive rule corresponding to each syntactic rule. This will guarantee the interpretability of any tree that is admitted by such rules (and consequently of any terminal string generated by the language).

In what follows, we use category symbols for the trees they dominate. Thus, for example, we use A to indicate the tree dominated by A. And we use $[_A\ B\ C]$ to indicate a tree dominated by A, whose immediate constituents are B and C. Thus, $[\![[_A\ B\ C]]\!]^v$ stands for the value of a tree whose root is A such that B and C are A's daughters. Furthermore, if g is a function and u a possible argument for g, $g(u)$ will indicate the result of applying g to u. The symbol $\in$ indicates set membership and is to be read "is an element of" or "belongs to." We follow standard practice in abbreviating *if and only if* as *iff*. The letters of the formulas in (31) indicate the correspondence with the syntactic rules in (21).

(31) *a.* $[\![[_S \text{ N VP}]]\!]^v = 1$ iff $[\![\text{N}]\!]^v \in [\![\text{VP}]\!]^v$ and 0 otherwise
b. $[\![[_S \text{ S}_1 \text{ conj S}_2]]\!]^v = [\![\text{conj}]\!]^v(\langle [\![\text{S}_1]\!]^v, [\![\text{S}_2]\!]^v \rangle)$
c. $[\![[_S \text{ neg S}]]\!]^v = [\![\text{neg}]\!]^v([\![\text{S}]\!]^v)$
d. $[\![[_{VP} \text{ V}_t \text{ N}]]\!]^v = \{x : \langle x, [\![\text{N}]\!]^v \rangle \in [\![\text{V}_t]\!]^v\}$
e–j. If A is a category and a is a lexical entry or a lexical category and $\Delta = [_A\ a]$, then $[\![\Delta]\!]^v = [\![a]\!]^v$

3.2.3 Some illustrations To see how this works, let us interpret the sentence given in (22*a*). To facilitate this task, let us index every node in the relevant tree:

(32)

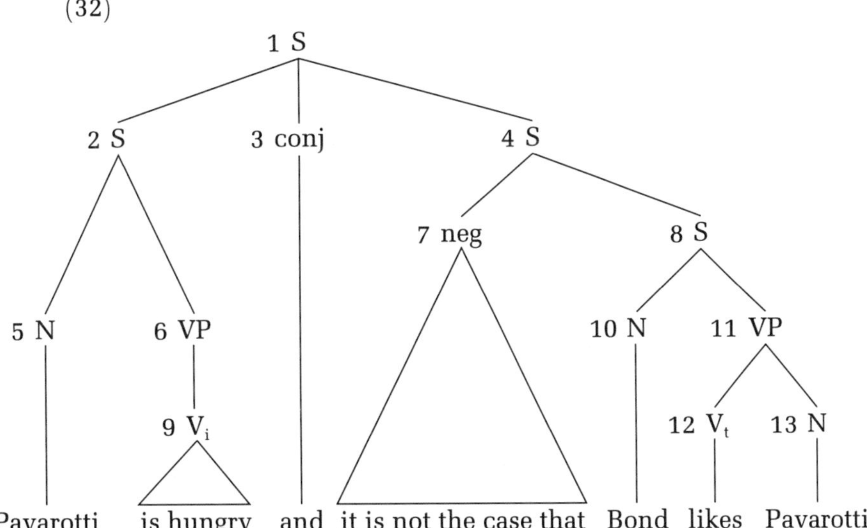

Our interpretive procedure works bottom up. Here is a step by step derivation of the truth conditions associated with (22*a*):

(33) $[\![5]\!]^v =$ Pavarotti, by (31*e*)
$[\![9]\!]^v = \{x : x \text{ is hungry in } v\}$, by (31*e*)
$[\![6]\!]^v = \{x : x \text{ is hungry in } v\}$, by (31*e*)
$[\![2]\!]^v = 1$ iff Pavarotti $\in \{x : x \text{ is hungry in } v\}$, by (31*a*)
$[\![13]\!]^v =$ Pavarotti, by (31*e*)
$[\![12]\!]^v = \{\langle x, y \rangle : x \text{ likes } y \text{ in } v\}$, by (31*e*)

$$
\begin{aligned}
[\![11]\!]^{v} &= \{x : \langle x, [\![13]\!]^{v}\rangle \in [\![12]\!]^{v}\} \\
&= \{x : \langle x, \text{ Pavarotti}\rangle \in \{\langle x, y\rangle : x \text{ likes } y \text{ in } v\} \\
&= \{x : x \text{ likes Pavarotti in } v\}, \text{ by } (31d) \\
[\![10]\!]^{v} &= \text{Bond, by } (16e) \\
[\![8]\!]^{v} &= 1 \text{ iff Bond} \in \{x : x \text{ likes Pavarotti in } v\}, \text{ by } (31a) \\
[\![7]\!]^{v} &= \begin{bmatrix} 1 \rightarrow 0 \\ 0 \rightarrow 1 \end{bmatrix}, \text{ by } (31e) \text{ and } (30) \\
[\![4]\!]^{v} &= \begin{bmatrix} 1 \rightarrow 0 \\ 0 \rightarrow 1 \end{bmatrix} ([\![8]\!]^{v}), \text{ by } (31c) \\
[\![3]\!]^{v} &= \begin{bmatrix} \langle 1,1\rangle \rightarrow 1 \\ \langle 1,0\rangle \rightarrow 0 \\ \langle 0,1\rangle \rightarrow 0 \\ \langle 0,0\rangle \rightarrow 0 \end{bmatrix}, \text{ by } (31e) \text{ and } (30) \\
[\![1]\!]^{v} &= \begin{bmatrix} \langle 1,1\rangle \rightarrow 1 \\ \langle 1,0\rangle \rightarrow 0 \\ \langle 0,1\rangle \rightarrow 0 \\ \langle 0,0\rangle \rightarrow 0 \end{bmatrix} (\langle [\![2]\!]^{v}, [\![4]\!]^{v}\rangle), \text{ by } (31b)
\end{aligned}
$$

Now suppose we are in a situation where Pavarotti is indeed hungry and Bond does not like him. Call such a situation v'. We thus have that Bond $\notin \{x : x$ likes Pavarotti in $v'\}$. Therefore, $[\![8]\!]^{v'} = 0$, by (31*a*). So $[\![4]\!]^{v'} = 1$, by (31*c*). Furthermore, Pavarotti $\in \{x : x$ is hungry in $v'\}$. Therefore, $[\![2]\!]^{v'} = 1$, by (31*a*). Thus, $[\![1]\!]^{v'} = 1$, since $[\![\text{and}]\!]^{v'}(\langle 1, 1\rangle) = 1$, by (30).

Suppose instead that we have a different situation, call it v'', where Pavarotti is hungry and Bond does like him. Then it is easy to see that by performing the relevant computations, we get that $[\![4]\!]^{v''} = 0$ and thus that $[\![1]\!]^{v''} = 0$.

This simple example shows how a Tarski-style truth definition provides a procedure that can associate the right truth conditions with the infinitely many sentences of F_1 with only a finite machinery. The truth conditions for a sentence S determine how, given particular facts, one can determine whether S is true or false as a function of the simpler expressions occurring in it. This is just what the procedure exemplified above does. For example, we have seen how sentence (22*a*) comes out with different truth values in the two different situations we have described. To illustrate further, consider (22*b*) on the analysis given in (24*a*) and let v''' be a situation where Pavarotti is not hungry and Loren is boring. That is, let us assume that we have $[\![\text{Pavarotti is hungry}]\!]^{v'''} = 0$ and $[\![\text{Loren is boring}]\!]^{v'''} = 1$. Then, $[\![[_S \text{ Pavarotti is hungry or Loren is boring}]]\!]^{v'''} = 1$, since $[\![\text{or}]\!]^{v'''}(\langle 0, 1\rangle) = 1$, by (30). And consequently, $[\![(24a)]\!]^{v'''} = 0$, since $[\![\text{not}]\!]^{v'''}(1) = 0$. Thus, sentence (22*b*) on the analysis in (24*a*) is false in v''' according to our procedure.

Exercise 2 Compute the truth value of sentence (22*b*) on the analyses in (24*a*) and (24*b*), repeated below, in the following three situations.

(22) *b.* It is not the case that Pavarotti is hungry or Loren is boring.

(24) *a.* [$_S$ neg [$_S$ Pavarotti is hungry or Loren is boring]]
b. [$_S$[$_S$ neg [$_S$ Pavarotti is hungry]] or Loren is boring]

Situation 1. Pavarotti is hungry; Loren is boring.
Situation 2. Pavarotti is not hungry; Loren is not boring.
Situation 3. Pavarotti is hungry; Loren is not boring.

One of our basic semantic capacities is that of matching sentences with situations. For example, we can intuitively see, perhaps after a bit of reflection, that sentence (22*b*) on analysis (24*a*) is indeed false in a situation where Pavarotti is hungry, which corresponds to the results of our interpretive procedure. This shows how our procedure can be regarded as an abstract representation of our capacity of pairing sentences with the situations that they describe and also how the theory makes empirically testable claims (since the pairing of sentences with the truth conditions generated by the theory can clash or agree with our intuitions).

In fact, one way of understanding the notion of sentence content that we are characterizing is the following. Sentence content can be regarded as a relation between sentences and situations, or circumstances. Our notation $[\![\text{S}]\!]^{v} = 1$ (or 0) can be interpreted as saying that S correctly characterizes or describes (or does not correctly describe) situation v. The meaning of sentences of a language L is adequately characterized by such a relation if the speakers of L behave as if they knew the value of $[\![\text{S}]\!]^{v}$ as a function of the values assigned in v to the lexical items in S for any situation or set of circumstances v and any sentence S. To borrow a metaphor from cognitive psychology, imported into the semantic literature by Barwise and Perry (1983), speakers of L are "attuned" to a certain relation between sentences and circumstances. This is one way of understanding what our theory is doing.

There is a further crucial thing that our theory can do: it can provide us with a formal definition of entailment. Here it is:

(34) S *entails* S′ (relative to analyses Δ_S and $\Delta_{S'}$, respectively) iff for every situation v, if $[\![\Delta_S]\!]^v = 1$, then $[\![\Delta_{S'}]\!]^v = 1$.

This is just a first approximation. Ultimately, we will want to regard entailment as a relation between utterances (that is, sentences in context), where the context crucially fills in certain aspects of meaning. Here the only feature of context that we are considering is that it must specify a syntactic analysis for ambiguous terminal strings (by means of prosodic clues, for example). In what follows, we sometimes talk of entailment as a relation between sentences, even if phrase markers (and ultimately utterances) are meant.

It should be clear that (34) is simply a way of saying that S entails S′ iff whenever S is true, S′ also is; that is, it is a way of formally spelling out our intuitive notion of entailment. This definition enables us to actually prove whether a certain sentence entails another one. Let us illustrate. Let us prove that sentence (22*b*) on analysis (24*a*) entails

(35) [$_S$[$_S$ it is not the case that Pavarotti is hungry] and [$_S$ it is not the case that Loren is boring]]

To show this, we assume that (22*b*) is true on analysis (24*a*) and show, using our semantic rules, that (35) must also be true. The outermost connective in (24*a*) is negation. The semantics for negation, (31*c*), tells us that for any v if $[\![(24a)]\!]^v = 1$, as by our hypothesis, then $[\![$Pavarotti is hungry or Loren is boring$]\!]^v = 0$. But the semantics for *or*, (30), together with (31*b*), tells us that a disjunctive sentence is false iff each disjunct is false. Thus we have that $[\![$Pavarotti is hungry$]\!]^v = 0$ and $[\![$Loren is boring$]\!]^v = 0$. Now if this is so, again by the semantics of negation we have that $[\![$it is not the case that Pavarotti is hungry$]\!]^v = 1$ and $[\![$it is not the case that Loren is boring$]\!]^v = 1$. But (35) is just the conjunction of the latter two sentences, and the semantics for conjunction thus yields $[\![(35)]\!]^v = 1$.

Let us show that (36*a*) does not entail (36*b*).

(36) *a.* [[it is not the case that Pavarotti is hungry] or [Loren is boring]]

b. [[Pavarotti is hungry] or [it is not the case that Loren is boring]]

To show this we construct a situation, call it v', such that (36*a*) is true in v' while (36*b*) is false in it. Now, since we want it to be the case that $[\![(36b)]\!]^{v'} = 0$, by the semantics for disjunction we must have $[\![\text{Pavarotti is hungry}]\!]^{v'} = 0$ and $[\![\text{it is not the case that Loren is boring}]\!]^{v'} = 0$. By the semantics for negation this means that $[\![\text{Loren is boring}]\!]^{v'} = 1$. Thus, v' is a situation where "Pavarotti is hungry" is false and "Loren is boring" is true. It is easy to see that in such a situation (36*a*) will be true. This follows immediately from the semantics for disjunction and the fact that "Loren is boring" (one of the disjuncts) is true in v'. We have thus constructed a situation where (36*a*) is true and (36*b*) is false, and hence the former does not entail the latter.

Exercise 3 A. Prove that "Pavarotti is hungry and Loren is boring" entails "Loren is boring."

B. Prove that (35) entails (24*a*).

C. Prove that (36*b*) does not entail (36*a*).

We can also define a number of other semantic notions closely related to entailment, such as logical equivalence (what we also called "content synonymy"), contradiction, and logical truth (validity).

(37) S is *logically equivalent* to S′ (relative to analyses Δ_S and $\Delta_{S'}$) iff S entails S′ (relative to Δ_S and $\Delta_{S'}$) and S′ entails S (relative to Δ_S and $\Delta_{S'}$).

(38) S is *contradictory* (relative to analysis Δ_S) iff there is no situation v, such that $[\![\Delta_S]\!]^v = 1$.

(39) S is *logically true* (or *valid*) relative to analysis Δ_S iff there is no situation where $[\![\Delta_S]\!]^v = 0$.

To illustrate, let us show that the following is contradictory:

(40) Pavarotti is boring, and it is not the case that Pavarotti is boring.

Assume that there exists a v such that $[\![(40)]\!]^v = 1$. By the semantics for conjunction we have $[\![\text{Pavarotti is boring}]\!]^v = 1$ and $[\![\text{it is not the case that Pavarotti is boring}]\!]^v = 1$. But the semantics for negation yields the result that the same sentence is assigned two distinct truth values, which is a contradiction.

The preceding proof can be straightforwardly modified so as to show that the negation of (40) ("It is not the case that [Pavarotti is boring and Pavarotti isn't boring]") is valid.

All these notions can be extended to relations involving not simply sentences but *sets* of sentences:

(41) A set of sentences $\Omega = \{S_1, \ldots, S_n\}$ *entails* a sentence S (relative to analyses $\Delta_{S_1}, \ldots, \Delta_{S_n}$ and Δ_S, respectively) iff whenever in any situation v we have for all $S' \in \Omega$, $[\![\Delta_{S'}]\!]^v = 1$, we also have that $[\![\Delta_S]\!]^v = 1$. (That is, any situation v that makes all of the sentences in Ω true also has to make S true.)

(42) A set of sentences Ω is *contradictory* (relative to analyses $\Delta_{S_1}, \ldots, \Delta_{S_n}$) iff there is no situation v such that for all $S \in \Omega$, $[\![\Delta_S]\!]^v = 1$.

Exercise 4 A. Show that sentences (1) and (2) jointly entail (3).

(1) [[it is not the case that Pavarotti is hungry] or Loren is boring]

(2) Loren is not boring.

(3) Pavarotti is not hungry.

B. Show that (4) and (5) are contradictory.

(4) [[it is not the case that Bond is cute] and Pavarotti is boring]

(5) Bond is cute.

C. Let "$\vee$" be the standard inclusive *or* and "+" the exclusive one. (*And* is expressed with "$\wedge$.") If *or* in natural language is ambiguous, a sentence like (6*a*), expressed more idiomatically in (6*b*), would be ambiguous four ways; it would have the four readings given in (7).

(6) *a.* John smokes or drinks, or John smokes and drinks.
b. John smokes or drinks or both.

(7) *a.* $[\text{smoke}(j) \vee \text{drink}(j)] \vee [\text{smoke}(j) \wedge \text{drink}(j)]$
b. $[\text{smoke}(j) + \text{drink}(j)] \vee [\text{smoke}(j) \wedge \text{drink}(j)]$
c. $[\text{smoke}(j) + \text{drink}(j)] + [\text{smoke}(j) \wedge \text{drink}(j)]$
d. $[\text{smoke}(j) \vee \text{drink}(j)] + [\text{smoke}(j) \wedge \text{drink}(j)]$

Consider now (8*a*) and (8*b*).

(8) *a.* $[\text{smoke}(j) \vee \text{drink}(j)]$
b. $[\text{smoke}(j) + \text{drink}(j)]$

Prove that (7*a*–*c*) are all equivalent to (8*a*) and that (7*d*)is equivalent to (8*b*). What does this result show about the hypothesis that *or* is ambiguous between an inclusive and an exclusive reading?

(From A. C. Browne, "Univocal 'Or'—Again," *Linguistic Inquiry* 17 (1986): 751–754.)

We have shown that a theory of truth conditions enables us to come up with a precise characterization of several key semantic notions. Furthermore, such a theory enables us to derive as theorems claims about semantic relationships (claims about what entails what, for example). To the extent that what the theory predicts (or yields as theorems) actually matches our intuitions, we have confirming evidence for it. If, for example, it turned out that our theory didn't allow us to show that "Pavarotti is hungry and Loren is boring" entails "Pavarotti is hungry," the theory would be inadequate, as our intuitions clearly tell us that the former sentence does entail the latter. Thus, a truth-conditional theory appears to be a promising candidate as an approximation to a full-fledged theory of meaning.

3.2.4 An alternative method for interpreting F_1 What we have done in specifying the semantics for F_1 is to provide, for each syntactic rule listed in (21), a corresponding semantic rule listed in (31). The semantics is defined recursively off the syntax. This is the standard approach in treatments of formal languages and is the one adopted by Montague (1973) in his ground-breaking formal semantic treatment of (a fragment of) English. This *rule-to-rule* method of semantic interpretation offers interpretive procedures that are specific to particular constructions.

However, if we look at our semantic rules, we see that there is a lot of redundancy. The principle of interpretation for terminal nodes or lexical entries, the "base" for the recursion, is the same for all basic expressions: the value they get is that assigned directly in situation *v*. And for phrasal nodes that do not branch, the interpretation of the daughter is just passed up to the mother. Thus in a structure like (43), the value of *run* is passed up all the way to the VP.

(43) 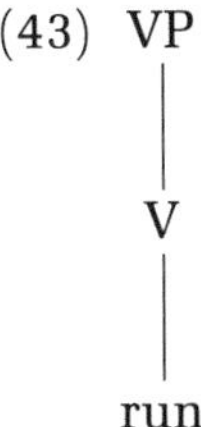

Things look a bit more complicated when we turn to the interpretations associated with nodes that branch. For example, subject-predicate configurations are interpreted as designating 1 or 0 on the basis of whether or not the individual designated by the subject belongs to the set designated by the VP. A VP that consists of a verb and object will designate a set of individuals; the transitive verb itself designates a binary relation, a set of ordered pairs of individuals, and the VP denotation consists of just those individuals that stand in that relation to the individual designated by the object NP. We haven't introduced ditransitive verbs yet. They would, however, be interpreted as three-place relations (i.e., sets of ordered triples). The interpretation assigned to a VP like "give *War and Peace* to Mary" would be a set of individuals (those who give *War and Peace* to Mary) and thus would combine semantically with a subject in exactly the same way as the interpretation assigned to a VP with a transitive verb, e.g., "like Mary." (In Exercise 8 at the end of this chapter the reader is asked to provide a rule for interpreting VPs containing ditransitive verbs that is parallel to (31d), the rule for interpreting VPs containing transitive verbs.) Finally, conjunctions and negations are both interpreted by means of functions, but in the case of conjunction the function has two arguments, whereas in the case of negation it has only one.

Klein and Sag (1985) pointed out that rule-to-rule interpretive procedures in principle do not place any constraints on possible semantic rules, which suggests that whenever a new syntactic configuration is encountered, the language learner must simply learn the appropriate semantic procedure for its interpretation. But as a matter of fact, we see that the semantic rules actually found appear to be of a highly restricted sort. So, they argued, it may be possible to set up a semantic theory with only a very limited set of interpretive procedures that need minimal syntactic information to work. If this program turns out to be feasible, we would have in semantics a situation parallel to that of syntax, where a wide range of constructions across different languages can be analyzed in terms of a small set of rules and principles. This is made all the more plausible by the observation that when the semantic values of sentences and lexical entries are set, then how one gets from the latter to the former is also virtually determined (modulo a few variants). Thus, as Klein and Sag pointed out, combinatorial processes can be constrained to depend only on the *types* of values assigned to the combining nodes if those types—the kinds of

Table 2.2 Initial type assignments for F_1

SYNTACTIC CATEGORY	SEMANTIC TYPE
S	Truth values (0, 1)
N	Individuals
V_i, VP	Sets of individuals
V_t	Sets of ordered pairs of individuals
conj	Function from two truth values to one truth value
neg	Function from one truth value to one truth value

semantic values assigned to various sorts of nodes—are chosen carefully. Semantic interpretation will then be, as they put it, *type-driven*, rather than construction-specific.

Table 2.2 lists the semantic types we have currently specified for the various categories in F_1. The semantic type for a category is the kind of thing that the interpretation function $[\![\ ]\!]^V$ assigns to expressions in that category. The two basic types we have identified are individuals and truth values. Each of them in some sense stands on its own: they have no internal structure. The other types we list above are various set-theoretic constructions out of elements of one or both of these two basic types. In particular, we have sets of individuals, sets of ordered pairs, and functions (from truth values and pairs thereof into truth values).

Now functions in general take input arguments from some specified domain and yield an output value. In the case of a function f with a single argument x, applying f to x yields the value of the function for that argument, namely $f(x)$. This mode of combining two values is called *functional application*, and we have already made use of it to interpret negated sentences. The principle itself does not depend on having any particular kind of function or argument: it could work to interpret any syntactic structure with two branches (which is what most of ours have) if one branch is interpreted as a function and the other branch is interpreted as a possible argument of the function. It turns out that we can indeed revise our interpretive principles so that functional application is the only combinatory semantic principle we need for F_1.

Let's start by seeing how we can think of the interpretation of an intransitive verb as a function. The best way to see it is via an example. Consider a particular situation v in which the meaning of *is boring* is as follows:

(44) $[\![\text{is boring}]\!]^v = \{x : x \text{ is boring in } v\} = \{\text{Bond, Pavarotti}\}$

Suppose now that the domain of discourse U, i.e., the individuals we talk about in v, is restricted to Bond, Pavarotti, and Loren. In such a situation, the meaning of *is boring* can be construed as a function f that applied to an individual u yields *true* just in case u is boring and otherwise yields *false*:

(45) $[\![\text{is boring}]\!]^v =$ the function f from individual entities to truth values such that $f(x) = 1$ if $x \in \{x : x \text{ is boring in } v\}$ and $= 0$ otherwise.

If Bond and Loren are the members of this set in v, then

$$\begin{aligned} \text{Bond} &\rightarrow 1 \\ \text{Pavarotti} &\rightarrow 0 \\ \text{Loren} &\rightarrow 1 \end{aligned}$$

Notice that we started from our original set of individuals and used it to define this function. We could have done exactly the same thing had we started with any other set of individuals. Any function that assigns one of two distinct values to the members of a domain is called a *characteristic function*, and given the output values (for convenience we use 0 and 1), each subset of the domain defines such a function uniquely and any such function corresponds to a unique subset of the domain. (See the appendix, p. 538.) Thus we can move back and forth between sets and the characteristic functions of those sets. In particular, we can model the meaning of intransitive verbs as characteristic functions over the domain of individuals; where we assigned a set of individuals as the denotation of a particular verb before, we will now assign the characteristic function of that set. Clearly, the functional perspective on intransitive verb denotations is simply a different way of looking at the same facts we considered before. But now we can interpret the combination of an intransitive verb and its subject by functional application and get exactly the same results we got before.

It is useful to have a way to represent the general type of functions from individual entities to truth values. Let e (for "entity") be the type of individuals and t the type of truth values; then $\langle e, t\rangle$ will represent the type of functions from individuals (things of type e) into truth values (things of type t).

Exercise 5 Provide the appropriate functional values for *is hungry* and *is cute.*

The next challenge we turn to is how to interpret transitive verbs so that a VP consisting of a verb and its object will also designate a function of type $\langle e, t\rangle$. In our initial formulation of denotations of transitive verbs, we have, for example, the following:

(46) $[\![\text{likes}]\!]^v = \{\langle x, y\rangle : x \text{ likes } y \text{ in } v\}$.

If we imagine that in *v*, Bond and Pavarotti like Loren (and nobody else likes anybody else), we get this:

(47) $[\![\text{likes}]\!]^v = \{\langle \text{Bond, Loren}\rangle, \langle \text{Pavarotti, Loren}\rangle\}$

For our functional-application program to work, we need two things: (1) transitive verbs need to be able to combine with their objects by functional application—that is, they need to be functions that take individual entities as arguments—and (2) VP interpretations produced by combining transitive verbs with their objects need themselves to be able to combine by functional application with subjects—that is, the output value of combining a transitive verb with its object should itself be a function of type $\langle e, t\rangle$, the type we just used for interpreting VPs consisting solely of an intransitive verb.

Intuitively, if we combine *likes* and *Pavarotti* to get the VP *likes Pavarotti*, we want the result to be the characteristic function of the set of people who like Pavarotti, and similarly for all other individuals in the domain of discourse that might be values of the object. Transitive verbs can thus be viewed as functions whose output value is itself a function. The function-valued function corresponding to (47) would be the following:

(48)
$$\begin{bmatrix} \text{Pavarotti} & \rightarrow & \begin{bmatrix} \text{Pavarotti} & \rightarrow & 0 \\ \text{Bond} & \rightarrow & 0 \\ \text{Loren} & \rightarrow & 0 \end{bmatrix} \\ \text{Bond} & \rightarrow & \begin{bmatrix} \text{Pavarotti} & \rightarrow & 0 \\ \text{Bond} & \rightarrow & 0 \\ \text{Loren} & \rightarrow & 0 \end{bmatrix} \\ \text{Loren} & \rightarrow & \begin{bmatrix} \text{Pavarotti} & \rightarrow & 1 \\ \text{Bond} & \rightarrow & 1 \\ \text{Loren} & \rightarrow & 0 \end{bmatrix} \end{bmatrix}$$

So what we want to do is to assign to *likes* a function that takes the value assigned to the object, the "likee," as its argument. Functional application then yields as output a new function, which will be the value of the VP. This VP function yields value 1 when applied to an individual who likes the individual designated by the object.

As in the case of intransitive verbs, it is useful to have a way to represent functions of the type we are using to interpret transitive verbs. With intransitive verbs, we used an ordered-pair notation. The type of their arguments, i.e., e, was the first member of the pair, and the type of their values i.e., *t*, was the second. That is, we used $\langle e, t \rangle$ to represent functions from type *e* to type *t*. Following this same principle, since transitive verbs designate functions whose arguments are individuals and whose values are functions of type $\langle e, t \rangle$, we will assign them to type $\langle e, \langle e, t \rangle \rangle$, i.e., functions from things of type *e* to things of type $\langle e, t \rangle$.

In discussing the interpretation of *likes*, we started with a two-place relation, whose characteristic function can be thought of as having two arguments, and ended up with a single argument function whose value is another function. What we did is follow a standard way of reducing any function with multiple arguments (or its corresponding multiple-place relation) to a one-place function. This technique is due to M. Schönfinkel (1924) and was further developed by Curry (1930). (See the appendix for further discussion of how to "curry" a function.) Let R be any two-place relation between individual entities; the corresponding function f of type $\langle e, \langle e, t \rangle \rangle$ will be the function whose value for any y is the function g_y such that $g_y(x) = 1$ iff $\langle x, y \rangle \in R$. It follows from this definition that $f(y)(x) = 1$ iff $\langle x, y \rangle \in R$. So now we can provide an appropriate denotation for transitive verbs.

(49) $[\![\text{likes}]\!]^v$ = the function f in $\langle e, \langle e, t \rangle \rangle$ such that $f(y) = g_y$, the characteristic function of $\{x : x \text{ likes } y \text{ in } v\}$.

To say that transitive-verb denotations are in type $\langle e, \langle e, t \rangle \rangle$ is just to say that they are functions whose domain is things in *e*, the type of individual entities, and whose output values are things in $\langle e, t \rangle$, the functional type we have associated with intransitive verbs (that is, functions from individual entities to truth values, the functional equivalent of sets of individuals).

Exercise 6 A. Assume that in situation v' we have that

$$[\![\text{likes}]\!]^{v'} = \{\langle\text{Bond}, \text{Bond}\rangle, \langle\text{Pavarotti}, \text{Pavarotti}\rangle, \langle\text{Loren}, \text{Loren}\rangle, \langle\text{Loren}, \text{Bond}\rangle\}$$

Recouch $[\![\text{likes}]\!]^{v'}$ as a function-valued function. Having done that, give the values of $[\![\text{likes Bond}]\!]^{v'}$ and $[\![\text{likes Loren}]\!]^{v'}$.

B. Consider the following function of type $\langle e, \langle e, t\rangle\rangle$:

$$\begin{bmatrix} \text{Pavarotti} & \rightarrow & \begin{bmatrix} \text{Pavarotti} & \rightarrow & 0 \\ \text{Bond} & \rightarrow & 1 \\ \text{Loren} & \rightarrow & 0 \end{bmatrix} \\ \text{Bond} & \rightarrow & \begin{bmatrix} \text{Pavarotti} & \rightarrow & 1 \\ \text{Bond} & \rightarrow & 1 \\ \text{Loren} & \rightarrow & 0 \end{bmatrix} \\ \text{Loren} & \rightarrow & \begin{bmatrix} \text{Pavarotti} & \rightarrow & 0 \\ \text{Bond} & \rightarrow & 1 \\ \text{Loren} & \rightarrow & 1 \end{bmatrix} \end{bmatrix}$$

Give the corresponding set of ordered pairs.

In general, given the type e of individuals and the type t of truth values as our basic types, we can construct functions of arbitrary complexity, using the following recursive schema:

(50) *a.* If a and b are types, so is $\langle a, b\rangle$.
b. Things of type $\langle a, b\rangle$ are functions from things of type a to things of type b.

Clearly, $\langle e, t\rangle$, and $\langle e, \langle e, t\rangle\rangle$ are instances of this general schema. So is $\langle e, \langle e, \langle e, t\rangle\rangle\rangle$ (which would correspond to the type of three-place relations), $\langle\langle e, t\rangle, t\rangle$, $\langle t, t\rangle$, and so on. The schema in (50) defines in simple terms the space of all possible functions one might want to define. When functional types become complex, these angle-bracket expressions can seem quite forbidding. But the basic principle is very simple and straightforward. Natural languages use just a small subset of these possible types.

Let's now see how this new approach might work for calculating the truth conditions of simple sentences. All we have done so far is to replace the set-theoretic values for transitive and intransitive verbs given in (25) with appropriate functional alternatives. And we have two rules in our recursive definition of the interpretation function. The first, which we'll call "pass-up," is essentially the same as (31*e*–*j*); pass-up says that nonbranching nodes inherit the interpretation of what they directly dominate. The second is functional application, which tells us how to interpret a node with two branches, one of which denotes a function and the other of which denotes something in the domain of that function. The interpretation of the branching node is obtained simply by applying the function to the argument. Here, then, is the new recursive definition for the interpretation function.

(51) *a.* *Pass-up* If Δ is a nonbranching node that dominates a, then $[\![\Delta]\!]^v = [\![a]\!]^v$.
b. *Functional application* If Δ is a branching node with daughters a and b and $[\![a]\!]^v$ is a function whose domain contains $[\![b]\!]^v$, then $[\![\Delta]\!]^v = [\![a]\!]^v([\![b]\!]^v)$.

Note that these rules make no reference to particular syntactic configurations beyond the distinction between branching and nonbranching nodes.

Let's see how interpretation works for (52).

(52)

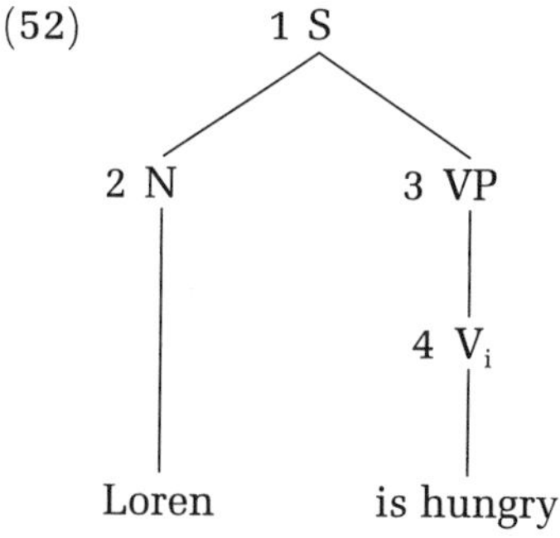

In (53) we give a derivation of the truth conditions of (52).

(53) *a.* $[\![2]\!]^v =$ Loren, by pass-up and (25)
b. $[\![4]\!]^v =$ the function f in $\langle e, t\rangle$ such that $f(x) = 1$ if $x \in \{x : x \text{ is hungry in } v\}$ and $= 0$ otherwise, by pass-up and the value assigned in exercise 5
c. $[\![3]\!]^v =$ the function f in $\langle e, t\rangle$ such that $f(x) = 1$ if $x \in \{x : x \text{ is hungry in } v\}$ and $= 0$ otherwise, by pass-up and the preceding calculation of $[\![4]\!]^v$
d. $[\![1]\!]^v = [\![3]\!]^v([\![2]\!]^v)$, by functional application

e. $[\![3]\!]^v([\![2]\!]^v) = 1$ if Loren $\in \{x : x$ is hungry in $v\}$ iff Loren is hungry in v and $= 0$ otherwise

The truth conditions we have calculated are exactly the same as we would have gotten following our earlier procedures. Now let's look at (54), whose truth conditions we calculate in (55).

(54)

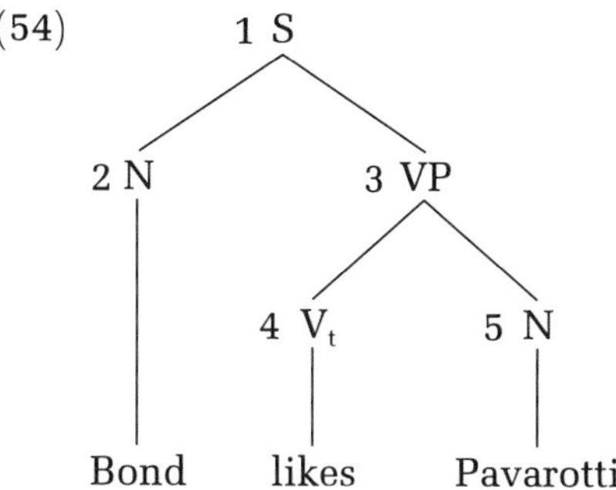

(55) a. $[\![2]\!]^v =$ Bond, by pass-up and (25)

b. $[\![4]\!]^v =$ the function f in $\langle e, \langle e, t \rangle \rangle$ such that $f(y) = g_y$, the characteristic function of $\{x : x$ likes y in $v\}$, by pass-up and exercise 6

c. $[\![5]\!]^v =$ Pavarotti, by pass-up and (25)

d. $[\![3]\!]^v = [\![4]\!]^v([\![5]\!]^v)$, by functional application

e. $[\![4]\!]^v([\![5]\!]^v) =$ the characteristic function of $\{x : x$ likes Pavarotti in $v\}$

f. $[\![1]\!]^v = [\![3]\!]^v([\![2]\!]^v)$, by functional application

g. $[\![3]\!]^v([\![2]\!]^v) = 1$ if Bond $\in \{x : x$ likes Pavarotti in $v\}$ iff Bond likes Pavarotti in v and $= 0$ otherwise

Again, we come up with exactly the same truth conditions that our original formulation provided.

Besides reducing the stock of interpretive rules we need, there are other benefits of this way of doing things. We can let the semantics carry the burden of distinguishing verb subcategorization and thus do not need distinct syntactic rules for constructing VPs with transitive verbs and VPs with intransitive verbs (and ultimately VPs with ditransitive and other verbs as well). Instead of (21*d*–*e*) and (21*g*–*h*), we have (56*a*, *b*), respectively.

(56) a. VP $\rightarrow$ V(N)

b. V $\rightarrow$ is boring, is hungry, is cute, likes

The syntax then will generate not only well-formed sentences such as we had before but also sentences where an intransitive verb is followed by an object, (57*a*), or a transitive verb appears without its object, (57*b*).

(57) *a.* Loren is cute Pavarotti.

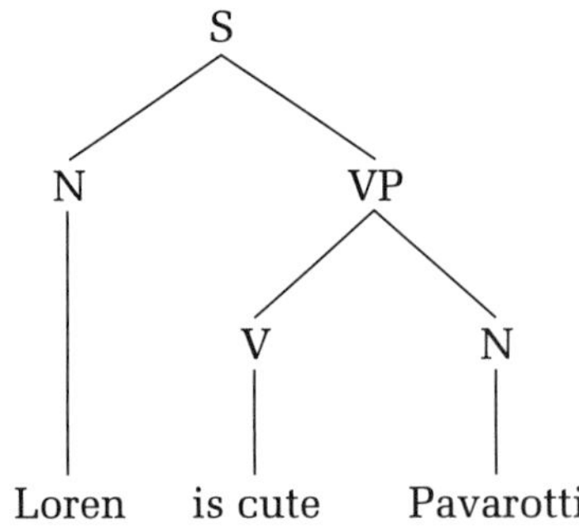

b. Bond likes.

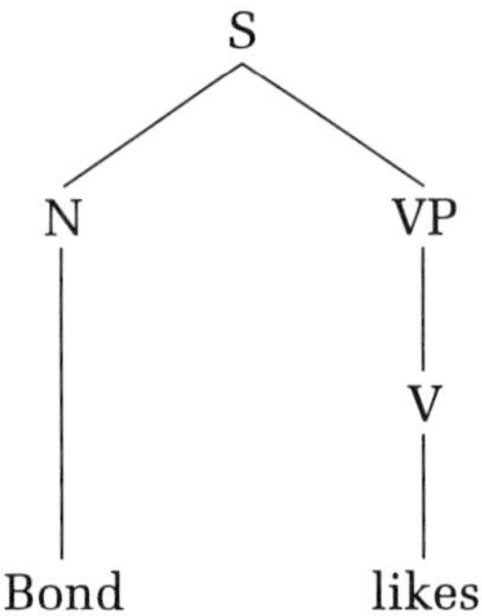

As we saw above, *is cute* will denote a function in $\langle e, t \rangle$. The V node dominating it can take Pavarotti as an argument but will then yield a VP value of 1 if Pavarotti is cute in v and 0 otherwise. This truth value, however, cannot combine with the subject N, and thus we cannot assign any semantic value at all to the S node in (57*a*). In the case of (57*b*), the value of *likes* will pass up to V and then to VP, to yield the characteristic function of $\{x : x \text{ likes } y \text{ in } v\}$. When we combine this with Bond, the value passed up to the subject NP, we get 1 if Bond likes y in v and 0 otherwise. But these truth conditions are not fully specified and cannot yield a truth value in v. Thus in both cases the constructions are not properly interpretable. On this approach, whether or not a verb takes an object is a matter of its semantics and not its syntactic categorization. In the rule-to-rule approach, the argument structure associated with a verb is a matter of its syntactic and semantic properties.

We still have said nothing about the logical connectives on this new approach. Readers may remember that in (30) *it is not the case that* is already interpreted as a function from truth values to truth values, i.e., a function in type $\langle t, t\rangle$. A neg node gets this function as its interpretation by pass-up, and then rule (31*c*) is no more than an instance of function application. The lexical entries in the category conj are also interpreted as functions, but these functions have two arguments, and our syntactic rules have the conjoined structure dominated by a node with three branches rather than two. Functional application is applicable, however, only to binary branching nodes where one daughter is a function whose domain includes the other daughter. Thus we need to change the syntax of F_1 slightly by replacing (21b) by the following two rules:

(58) *a.* S → S conjP
b. conjP → conj S

In other words, the conjunction and the second conjunct themselves form a phrase, which we've called conjP, and this phrase then combines with the first conjunct. This is just a device to guarantee that our branching nodes are all binary, so that functional application can apply. If natural languages in fact syntactically require nonbinary branching nodes, we will need something different from our present principle of functional application. But for present purposes we can assume binary structures and readily provide lexical entries for *and* and *or* that will do the job. What the lexical entries have to do is to provide a function whose argument is a truth value and whose output is a function that maps a truth value into a truth value; that is, *and* and *or* should be of type $\langle t, \langle t, t\rangle\rangle$. That is exactly what we get when we play the same trick with *and* and *or* that we played with *likes*: to reduce a two-argument to a one-argument function. So instead of the value for $[\![\text{and}]\!]^V$ that we gave in (30), we could use

$$(59)\ [\![\text{and}]\!]^V = \begin{bmatrix} 1 & \rightarrow & \begin{bmatrix} 1 & \rightarrow & 1 \\ 0 & \rightarrow & 0 \end{bmatrix} \\ 0 & \rightarrow & \begin{bmatrix} 1 & \rightarrow & 0 \\ 0 & \rightarrow & 0 \end{bmatrix} \end{bmatrix}$$

Exercise 7 Redo the function given in (30) for $[\![\text{or}]\!]^V$ so that it is of type $\langle t, \langle t, t\rangle\rangle$ and thus can be used to interpret conjP and structures containing it.

Table 2.3 Functional type assignments for F_1

SYNTACTIC CATEGORY	SEMANTIC TYPE
S	t
N	e
V_i, VP	$\langle e, t\rangle$
V_t	$\langle e, \langle e, t\rangle\rangle$
conj	$\langle t, \langle t, t\rangle\rangle$
neg	$\langle t, t\rangle$

A type-driven approach to semantic interpretation does seem to have some advantages over the rule-to-rule approach. The inventory of semantic rules gets reduced; for F_1, we need only "pass-up" and "apply." And once the types corresponding to key syntactic categories (like S and N) are set, the types corresponding to the remaining categories can readily be obtained in a uniform functional format. There is also the possibility of simplifying the syntax by letting semantic uninterpretability filter out certain unacceptable strings, as illustrated in the discussion of (57) above. As that discussion shows us, limiting semantic procedures allows us to have lexical items with different semantic types in the same syntactic category, e.g., a single category V rather than the distinct categories V_i and V_t. Type-driven approaches make the project of arriving at a simple universal semantic procedure look viable. Table 2.3 shows the type assignments we have used in showing how to develop a type-driven alternative for interpreting F_1.

At the same time, we often can more readily see what is going on in particular cases if we are not worrying about letting semantic types do all the interpretive work. Sets of ordered pairs, for example, seem easier to grasp than functions that map individual entities into functions that then map from individual entities into truth values (i.e., elements of $\langle e, \langle e, t\rangle\rangle$). What we have done in this section is to illustrate the possibility of replacing rule-to-rule truth-conditional interpretive procedures by ones that are type-driven. Although we will not show it in any detail, the further techniques we develop and the analyses we illustrate in the rest of the book do have type-theoretic analogues.

4 Problems

There are several questions that the approach we have introduced leaves unanswered. We will try to address them at various points in the course of this book. A preliminary discussion of some of them, however, might be useful already at this point. This section is devoted to such preliminary discussion, and it can be skipped without in any way undermining the comprehension of subsequent material.

4.1 Situations, circumstances, states of affairs

Our definition of truth depends on a given specification of what the facts are, one could say, on a data base. It is relativized to what we have loosely called situations, circumstances, or states of affairs. The formal counterpart of the notion of situation or state of affairs that we have adopted in our formal definition of truth is so far very rudimentary. We model situations or states of affairs as alternative assignments of truth values to atomic sentences. Each assignment tells us which of the atomic sentences are true and which are false and thus in a sense offers a characterization or description of a situation. Alternatively, we could think of situations as assignments of extensions to predicates: this would amount to a specification of which individuals satisfy which predicates and thus again could be viewed as a characterization of a state of affairs. Admittedly, this way of modeling situations or states of affairs does not do justice to their intuitive content. But for our present purposes it suffices. In the grammar of F_1 we do not deal yet with sentence embedding, and thus we can get by with a very rough hypothesis as to the denotation of sentences. This enables us to avoid the problems discussed in section 2.1 and 2.2.

Of course, at some point the question of sentence embedding will have to be addressed, and a more articulated way of modeling states of affairs will perhaps be needed. In fact, it is possible that the analysis of more complex constructions will lead us not only to the introduction of more refined notions of states of affairs or situations but also to the introduction of other semantic concepts such as, say, events, actions, properties, and the like. The point worth emphasizing in this connection is that introducing such concepts will certainly not exempt us from seeking a match of sentences with their truth conditions, for truth conditions are our link to logic. As we have seen, part of our semantic competence enables us to make judgments of entailment. And a theory of entailment has to resort, directly or indirectly, to the notion of truth, we think.[7]

Our strategy can, thus, be summarized as follows. As a result of the work of Tarski we know how truth can be formally characterized. Our aim is to get a Tarski-style definition of truth for ever larger fragments of natural languages. At the outset it seems reasonable to base our definition on fairly elementary concepts so that we can be reasonably sure that we are not sneaking in obscure notions in our attempt to characterize meaning. For example, to interpret F_1, we have simply used the following notions: individual, set, circumstances (regarded as ways of evaluating atomic sentences). In carrying out this program, we may find constructions whose truth conditions seem to require making an appeal to further semantic notions (say, events, actions, etc.). These notions will then be construed as components of a recursive definition of truth and come to have the status that theoretical concepts have in any other empirical inquiry. Their justification will be a matter of overall theory evaluation, which, complicated as it may be, is ultimately an empirical question. A strategy of this kind should be appealing also to those who, like us, are convinced that there is more than truth conditions to sentence meaning.

4.2 The variability of speech acts

Another difficulty that one might think besets any kind of truth-conditional semantics is that it appears to be limited to a small and artificial fraction of language. Even granting that our approach works for ordinary uses of simple declarative sentences, how is it ever going to generalize to the indefinite variety of uses that language can be put to? And if it does not generalize, why should it be interesting as a theory of natural language meaning? The problems that this question raises are serious. To see what our line is in dealing with them, let us consider some specific examples.

For one thing, we lie. That is, we use declarative sentences with some systematicity, knowing them to be false. This might be taken to suggest that in large parts of real-life situations we couldn't care less for truth. We, however, think that this pessimistic conclusion is misguided. To be able to lie, we must know that something is true and pretend that it isn't. So if we didn't know under what conditions sentences are true, how could we lie? How could we even define what a lie is? Moreover, even professional liars are bound to aim at truth most of the time. What would happen if they lied in trying to purchase food, getting medical assistance, etc.? Donald Davidson (1977, 295) has made this point very clearly: "We work on one or another assumption about the general pattern of agreement. We suppose that much of what we take to be common is true, but we cannot of course assume we know where the truth lies." In fact, it is hard to see how our species could have survived without being endowed with this disposition to utter truths. Such a disposition must be based on a capacity to tell whether a sentence is true or false in a given situation where the relevant facts are available, a capacity that a theory of truth is designed to represent. A truth-conditional semantics seems to be a necessary ingredient in the attempt to explain an extremely widespread pattern of behavior: our tendency to utter true sentences.

Still, there is no denying that truth seems plainly irrelevant to much of our use of language. This applies, for example, to all nondeclarative sentences. Consider, for example,

(60) *a.* Open the door.
b. What was open?

To ask whether the sentences in (60) have a truth value seems to be inappropriate. Yet from this it does not follow that truth conditions are irrelevant to a characterization of the meaning of (60*a*) and (60*b*). To see this, think of what it takes to understand, say, the imperative sentence (60*a*) as an order. To understand an order, we must know what it is to carry it out, that is, what situation must be brought about. In the case of (60*a*) we are asked to bring about a situation where a certain door is open. In other words, orders have a content: what it is that has to be brought about. It is this content that a truth-conditional theory enables us to characterize. For example, we can imagine a characterization of a notion of satisfaction of an order along the following lines:

(61) Order δ is satisfied iff p is carried out.

Here δ is an order, and p a description of the conditions to be carried out. We see no difficulty, in principle, in providing a recursive characterization of such a notion. In fact, it could be directly modeled on a Tarski-style definition of truth.[8]

Consider next a question, such as, say, (60*b*). What does someone who asks it want to know? Well, take the set of all the objects x, such that "*x* is open" counts as an accurate, true answer to (60*b*), that is, the set {*x* : "*x* is open" is a true answer to (60*b*)}. Someone who asks (60*b*) is in fact wondering what the membership of this set is, what objects belong to it. So perhaps constituent questions might be semantically associated with sets of this kind, which would also be recursively definable in terms of true answers. Looking at true answers can thus constitute a good starting point in the investigation of the semantics of questions.[9]

These suggestions are very sketchy. Many different approaches are possible in the case of nondeclaratives. Some of them will be discussed at more length when we deal with speech-act theories in chapter 4. The general point is that any description of nondeclaratives must characterize what their content is. It seems very hard to even start talking sensibly about questions or comands without somehow isolating what is being asked or commanded. We think that truth-conditional semantics is well designed to characterize the relevant notion of content. The above suggestions are simply meant to give some intuitive plausibility to this general strategy.

Considerations of a similar kind apply to the multitude of acts that we can perform by speaking and that go well beyond the simple exchange of truthful information, acts such as threatening, imploring, denying, investigating, etc. To perceive a linguistic act as an act of a certain type, we have to be able to isolate what is literally said, that is, the actual content of the speech act. A truth-conditional theory of meaning can do that rather well, and that is why we believe a theory of speech acts needs such a theory (just as much as the latter needs the former).

A related issue concerns the emphasis that we are putting on the notion of entailment with respect to other semantic notions. Such an emphasis might appear to be unjustified, since from the point of view of language users, entailments are simply one of the many kinds of intuitions that we have about sentences. There are, however, two points to consider in this connection. The first is that our capacity for evaluating entailments does appear to be grounded in what we know about meaning, that is, in our semantic competence. Thus a theory of entailments is a necessary component of a characterization of such competence. Furthermore, we think that there are grounds to believe that such a theory can be applied in interesting ways to deal with presuppositions and perhaps semantic anomaly, as we shall see in subsequent chapters. For these reasons we feel entailments should play a central role in any approach to meaning.

Finally, it should be understood that exchange of information presupposes linking sentences to their content (in our terms, to their truth conditions). Such a link appears to be based on the intention to communicate and must be sustained by a pattern of conventions and beliefs among the members of the community of speakers. Thus, meaning is a particular kind of action (one that involves bringing about a link between form and content) and can be properly understood only in the general context of our behavior as socially and historically conditioned rational agents. The specifics of this idea will be discussed at some length in chapter 4. But more generally, this entire work is an attempt to show that truth-conditional semantics is an interesting theory of this form of action (and of the competence that underlies it).

4.3 Vagueness

Another phenomenon that might be thought to undermine our approach is vagueness. Consider the following sentence:

(62) This is a chair.

Suppose we utter (62) by pointing at some object that is something in between a chair and a stool. It is not hard to come across such objects. We might have a very hard time deciding whether (62) is true or false of it. Perhaps the criteria that we use to decide whether something is a chair are just not sharp enough to let us settle the question. What then of truth conditions? Doesn't this situation show that even a simple sentence like (62) can easily fail to have truth conditions? Words in natural language are intrinsically vague, and our semantics seems to be poorly equipped for dealing with vagueness.

We will try to get by for now by pointing out that there are many cases that the criteria for the application of the predicate *chair* does settle: certain things are definitely chairs and others are definitely not chairs. Those cases are the ones we are talking about in developing our semantics. There is a gray area in between that we are disregarding at this point. Or rather, we are relativizing our semantics to some way of resolving vagueness. Our assignment of truth conditions to sentences of English is exactly as vague as the meaning of the basic expressions in those sentences. This is not a trivial achievement, however. It gives us a way of projecting the vagueness of words (as well as the precision) into the infinite number of sentences in which they occur, in a systematic fashion. In chapter 8 we will try to show that there are interesting formal ways of dealing with vagueness that build on the general approach to meaning that we are adopting.

4.4 Truth versus reference

In section 1 of this chapter we criticized the claim that meaning is some kind of (internal) representation, as it merely shifts the problem of what sentences mean to the one of what their associated representations mean. Now, a similar criticism could be leveled against the present approach. What a Tarski-style definition of truth does is to associate sentences with a description of the conditions under which they are true *in a certain metalanguage*. It thereby seems to shift the issue of meaning from the object language to the metalanguage without really telling us what meaning is. However, the point to note in this connection is that specifying truth conditions (*a*) forces one to specify what exactly words and phrases contribute to sentence content and (*b*) enables us to define entailment and a variety of other semantic notions and to prove claims about them. These, we think, are the specific merits of a truth-conditional approach, and they enable us to make some progress toward characterizing the notion of semantic content.

But there is more to this issue. The careful reader will have noticed a further problem in our presentation. We started out in section 3 arguing that instead of taking reference as basic, we needed a characterization of sentence meaning in order to define other semantic concepts. We then argued that sentence meaning can be characterized by means of a Tarski-style truth definition. But what does such a definition actually do? It reduces the truth conditions of sentences to identification of the extension of terms (nouns) and predicates in various situations. Thus it seems that our grasp of the latter must be prior to our understanding of truth conditions. In other words, a Tarski-style truth definition can do its job only if we know how to get at the reference of words first. *If* the meaning of the lexical entries is understood, *then* truth conditions of arbitrary sentences can be computed. So maybe for our approach to really work, we must, after all, assume as our basic notion the notion of reference (across different circumstances) rather than the notion of truth conditions as such. Is this a sound strategy in view of our overall approach?

4.4.1 The causal theory of reference To answer the latter question, we should ask again what it is for a word to refer to something in a given circumstance. What is it, for example, to claim that *Pavarotti* denotes Pavarotti? Many different answers have been given to this question. One kind of answer might be that Pavarotti can be uniquely identified by means of descriptions like *the greatest Italian tenor who ever lived* or *the tenor that performed in the Arena di Verona on July 7, 1986*. A proper name like *Pavarotti* might be thought to be associated with a cluster of such descriptions, Pavarotti being the individual that uniquely falls under them. Together such descriptions could be regarded as a criterion that uniquely picks out Pavarotti from what there is. As such they seem to form a plausible candidate for being the meaning of *Pavarotti*. The same point seems to apply to general terms (or predicates) like *water* or *tiger*. They can be thought of as being associated with a set of criteria or descriptions that determine what falls under such concepts. Such criteria are reasonable candidates for being the meaning of common nouns.

Kripke (1972), Putnam (1975), and others have pointed out several problems with this view and have proposed an alternative. They have noted, among other things, that the view just sketched has the following curious consequence. Suppose that the criteria associated with a term happen to go wrong. Suppose, for example, that Pavarotti turns out not to be the tenor who performed in the Arena di Verona on July 7, 1986. Suppose that the tenor who performed in the Arena di Verona on July 7, 1986, turns out to be a man whose name is *Cipputi* (who sang disguised as the better known Pavarotti). Indeed, suppose that all the descriptions used as semantic criteria for applying the name *Pavarotti* actually describe Cipputi instead. The view sketched above of proper names as having descriptive criteria is then committed to a striking claim: the name *Pavarotti* actually refers to Cipputi. This is so because on this view proper names are not directly linked to their bearers.

But the example given above suggests that this is just false. To reiterate this point with one of Kripke's examples, suppose that the only description we associate with the name *K. Gödel* is *the one who proved the incompleteness of arithmetic*. Suppose that we then find out that a certain Herr Schmidt rather than Gödel proved the famous theorem. The description theory predicts that the name *Gödel* should then refer to Schmidt. In other words, "Gödel proved the incompleteness of arithmetic" is true by definition, since *Gödel* simply means *prover of the incompleteness theorem.* But surely this is wrong. Examples of this kind can be constructed, it seems, for any description or feature cluster we can conceive.

The view that reference is mediated by a cluster of descriptions seems initially even more appealing for common nouns than for proper names. We may be willing to admit that proper names are linked directly to their bearers and lack descriptive content to mediate that link, yet we are accustomed to thinking of the meaning of words like *water*, *tiger*, and *woman*—words that refer to what Kripke calls "natural kinds"—as more directly involving definitional criteria. The Kripke-Putnam arguments for abandoning this view of the meaning of such common nouns are more complex (and have won fewer converts) than those dealing with proper names. Yet notice that when our identificational criteria for applying such a noun go wrong, our mistakes do not change what it is we are talking about or referring to when we use the word. People used to think that whales were fish and not mammals, but it seems intuitively plausible that we, who are biologically more sophisticated than they and have different criteria, are nonetheless talking about the same creatures our ancestors were when we use the word *whale.* Suppose that *whale* used to "mean" a kind of fish. Then when these earlier speakers spoke about whales, they were not speaking about Moby Dick and his kin. But this seems wrong. They believed that the very same creatures we think are mammals were fish. It is not the meaning of *whale* that has changed but beliefs about the creatures included in its reference.

The above considerations suggest that the semantics of proper names and perhaps also some basic general terms like *tiger* can be articulated in three components. First, there is the issue of what determines the reference of *Pavarotti* or *tiger*, that is, what determines the association of a particular word with a particular object or class of objects. The Kripke and Putnam view proposes a direct "causal" link between words like *Pavarotti* and *tigers* and objects like Pavarotti and tigers, respectively. For example, at one point Pavarotti was registered in the city hall of his birth place as "Luciano Pavarotti," and that act, in virtue of the conventions associated with it, created a direct causal link between *Pavarotti* and Pavarotti. The man himself figured in the chain of events leading to his naming. His parents spread the name, and others acquired it and with it a direct link to him, whether or not they ever encounter him in the flesh. As members of the same language community, we rely on that link when we use the name. We talk about the man who was so registered, no matter what beliefs we might have about him. With words like *tiger* the story is considerably more complicated but nonetheless plausibly similar. In general, a crucial class of words appears to get directly attached to referents in a variety of ways, of which an original dubbing ceremony may be one.

Second, there is the issue of what makes something a tiger and Pavarotti Pavarotti. This is the problem of what determines membership in a certain class or the identity of a certain individual. On such matters the language community often relies on experts. For instance, in the case of applying *tiger* and other kind-denoting terms, we tend to rely on genetic templates as biology currently characterizes them. The best theory available on the matter is what we use to settle disputes. For *Pavarotti* his parents may be our best experts where identification is problematic.

Third, there is the issue of what kind of information the competent speaker of English normally relies on in trying to use words like *tiger* or *Pavarotti*. We certainly must cognitively represent concepts of tigers and of Pavarotti and somehow use these representations in processing the words *tiger* and *Pavarotti*. But it is unclear whether these concepts play any semantic role. On the causal theory of reference, such cognitive representations do not enter into determining truth conditions. What is crucial for truth is the referential link itself, and that is a matter of the causal history of the world (which baby it was whose parents named it *Luciano Pavarotti*, for example) rather than of conceptual structure (the concept a speaker has of Pavarotti). What emerges from the Kripke and Putnam line is that words of an important class have to be somehow directly linked to their possible extensions. There is in their meaning an inescapable demonstrative component. For them we can't do much better than saying things like "Pavarotti is this man" or "Tigers are animals like these," pointing at the right things. This does not mean that all words work like this, however. Many words have, for example, semantic relations to other words or semantically relevant internal structure. We will discuss this issue further in chapter 8.

From the perspective of our semantics there are certain general consequences that it might be tempting to draw from Kripke's and

Putnam's work. Maybe what Tarski-style truth definitions accomplish is the reduction of the notion of meaning to the notion of reference (via the notion of truth). This reduction succeeds where other previous attempts have failed because it can provide a compositional account of sentence meaning, a characterization of notions like entailment, and a plausible account of the meaning of function words, among other things. Reference is then to be understood along the lines that Kripke and Putnam have independently argued for, namely, as a direct causal link of words to objects and classes of objects that propagates through the language community by means of various conventions. Of course, much more work is needed to spell out what counts as a "direct causal link" between words and their referents and exactly how a community maintains such connections through the language-using practices that prevail among its members. But we do seem to have a useable preliminary picture of how the meaning of basic expressions might ultimately be rooted in (and hence depend on) ways of referring.

4.4.2 Atomism versus holism in semantics One might think that the picture we have just sketched yields a form of "semantic atomism."[10] It reduces the problem of determining the meaning of a complex expression to the problem of determining the reference of its parts. In a Tarski-style definition the truth conditions of "Hobbes is a lion" depend on what *Hobbes* and *lion* refer to. This might be taken to presuppose that each part can be linked in isolation to its reference, where reference is understood as a direct link between an expression and its denotation causally brought about and transmitted through the community of speakers. The references of basic expressions are the atoms out of which truth conditions are built.

But this view is questionable. How can reference be established without a conceptual frame that allows us to identify and classify individuals? How can a causal link between the expressions of a language and any aspect of reality be brought about and transmitted without a network of intentions, conventions, and beliefs about that language shared by its speakers? Try to imagine the situation where a link between *Pavarotti* and Pavarotti, or *tiger* and tigers is brought about. Saying "This is a tiger" and pointing at a tiger will not suffice. How do we know that one intends to refer to tigers rather than to, say, striped animals in general? This type of problem is at the root of Quine's (1960) worries about the "radical indeterminacy of translation." From our point of view, the issue is the following. A compositional semantics for a language like English seems to require causal links between lexical items and their references. But such causal links seem to presuppose a set of collective intentions, beliefs, etc., about a language like English. Truth seems to depend on reference. And reference on truth. Aren't we running in a circle?

Not necessarily. To show this, let us sketch a highly idealized picture of how a semantic system like the one we have sketched might come about. One might start with a language much simpler than English, perhaps one that only contains a finite number of sentences. The truth conditions for the sentences of this language might be agreed upon globally. In other words, sentences may be linked to aspects of states of affairs holistically (all at once and without analyzing them into components and establishing references for such components). If the language is small enough, this will be possible, for it involves only agreeing upon a list pairing each sentence with the conditions that must hold for its truth. Once such a language is in place, reference of some sentence components may be determined by a process of abstraction. Suppose, for example, that the language in question contains sentences like "Hobbes is a tiger," "Hobbes is not a lion," and "Hobbes is striped," and suppose furthermore that we have somehow agreed on the truth conditions associated with them. By looking at the role of the word *tiger* in channeling the truth conditions of the sentences in which it occurs, we may then be able to agree on the fact that *tiger* refers to tigers. That is, we may be able to articulate a component of a sentence, identify a regularity in our experience, and establish a causal or conventional link between the two.

At this point, having established a common, if limited, frame of reference, we may expand our language by adding new sentences and establishing their truth conditions, using our original language and our newly acquired frame of reference. So the process starts again, going through stages where new sets of sentences are holistically mapped onto aspects of the world and stages where new frames of reference are established by abstraction. A language like English can be viewed as a point where this process stabilizes (to a degree, for languages change constantly). A Tarski-style semantics can be viewed as characterizing a language that has reached its point of equilibrium.

The very same ideas can be developed as a picture of language acquisition. Consider how the child might acquire a semantic system like the one that underlies English. Conceivably, the child might start off by figuring out the truth conditions of a small set of English sentences, those that are somehow more salient in her experience. Our language learner will globally link sentences to situations without necessarily analyzing the contributions of their components. The child can then figure out the reference of words from the role they play in channeling the truth conditions of sentences. This process of abstraction leads the child to acquire aspects of the frame of reference and of the system of causal links prevailing in her community. Familiarity with the reference frames associated with certain word families will prompt the acquisition of truth conditions for new sentences, and the process enters a second cycle. And so on. Throughout this process the child is presumably guided by an innate apparatus, say, general capacities for concept formation that our species may be endowed with, perhaps along with some machinery specific to language. On this view, a compositional semantic system arises only as a culmination or point of equilibrium of a complex process of abstractive reflection that goes through stages. Reference as such is not there initially but comes into play only through the contribution that it makes to the truth conditions of sentences.

These considerations, as much armchair theorizing on cognition and language acquisition, should not be taken as realistic descriptions of how a semantic system like that of English gets established or is acquired by the child. Their purpose is to demonstrate that our theory of meaning and the causal theory of reference are not *logically* committed to a kind of semantic atomism. Nor do truth and reference depend on one another in a circular way.

There is no way that we could do justice here to the richness of the positions that emerge from the philosophical debate associated with truth-conditional semantics. But pedagogical considerations required us not to bypass completely discussion of some of the claims most often associated with it.

Exercise 8 Add the following to F_1.

$VP \rightarrow V_{dt}$ N to N

$V_{dt} \rightarrow$ introduces

What is $[\![[_{VP} V_{dt} \text{ N to N}']]\!]^{v}$ equal to?

Consider next the following situations:

(v_1) $[\![\text{Pavarotti is cute}]\!]^{v_1} = 1$
$[\![\text{S}]\!]^{v_1} = 0$ for every atomic S different from "Pavarotti is cute."

(Recall that S is atomic iff it does not contain any sentential connective, like *and*, *or*, or negation.)

(v_2) $[\![\text{Pavarotti is boring}]\!]^{v_2} = 1$
$[\![\text{Loren is boring}]\!]^{v_2} = 1$
$[\![\text{Bond is cute}]\!]^{v_2} = 1$
$[\![\text{Bond likes Bond}]\!]^{v_2} = 1$
$[\![\text{Bond likes Pavarotti}]\!]^{v_2} = 1$
$[\![\text{Loren introduces Pavarotti to Bond}]\!]^{v_2} = 1$
$[\![\text{Bond introduces Pavarotti to Bond}]\!]^{v_2} = 1$
$[\![\text{S}]\!]^{v_2} = 0$ for any atomic S different from the ones listed above.

(v_3) $[\![\text{is cute}]\!]^{v_3} = \{\text{L}\}$
$[\![\text{is hungry}]\!]^{v_3} = \varnothing$
$[\![\text{is boring}]\!]^{v_3} = \{\text{P, B, L}\}$
$[\![\text{likes}]\!]^{v_3} = \{\langle \text{B}, \text{B}\rangle, \langle \text{B}, \text{P}\rangle, \langle \text{B}, \text{L}\rangle\}$
$[\![\text{introduces}]\!]^{v_3} = \varnothing$

Here P = Pavarotti, B = Bond, and L = Loren. Give the values of the following in each of the above situations.

(1) is cute

(2) introduces Pavarotti to Bond

(3) Pavarotti is boring or [Loren is boring and it is not the case that Bond likes Loren]

(4) [Pavarotti is boring or Loren is boring] and it is not the case that Bond likes Loren

(5) [Pavarotti is boring or Loren is boring] or [Pavarotti is boring and Loren is boring]

(6) it is not the case that it is not the case that [Bond introduces Pavarotti to Loren or Loren introduces Pavarotti to Bond]

(7) Pavarotti likes Loren and [Bond likes Pavarotti or Bond likes Bond]

Show whether the following pairs of sentences are logically equivalent.

(8) *a.* [Pavarotti is boring and Loren is boring] and Bond is boring
b. Pavarotti is boring and [Loren is boring and Bond is boring]

(9) *a.* Pavarotti is boring and [Loren is boring or Bond is boring]
b. [Pavarotti is boring or Loren is boring] and [Pavarotti is boring or Bond is boring]

(10) *a.* Pavarotti is boring and [Loren is boring or Bond is boring]
b. Pavarotti is boring or Bond is boring

---

3 Quantification and Logical Form

1 Introduction

We introduced truth-conditional (or logical) semantics by considering a simple language, F_1, in which we could attribute certain properties (being boring, being hungry, liking James Bond, etc.) to certain individuals (Bond, Loren, and Pavarotti). The language F_1, however, provides no way to move beyond talk of particular individuals to the expression of generalizations, such as those in (1).

(1) *a.* Everyone likes Loren.
b. No one is boring.
c. Someone is hungry.

One might suggest that we can express the content of the sentences in (1) by using sentences like those in (2).

(2) *a.* Loren likes Loren, and James Bond likes Loren, and Pavarotti likes Loren.
b. It is not the case that [Loren is boring or Bond is boring or Pavarotti is boring].
b′. Loren is not boring, and Bond is not boring, and Pavarotti is not boring.
c. Loren is hungry, or Bond is hungry, or Pavarotti is hungry.

This is almost right *if* our domain of discourse includes only Bond, Loren, and Pavarotti. In such contexts the sentences in (2) will be truth-conditionally equivalent to those in (1). But suppose that there are some additional individuals under consideration. The sentences in (1) would automatically take account of those individuals in addition to our familiar three, whereas the sentences in (2) must be amended. Moreover, it does not seem necessary for us to be able to name the additional individuals to include them in our generalizations, since expressions like *everyone, no one*, and *someone* automatically include them.

Such expressions are quantificational, as are many others: *most, many, two, all*. Quantificational expressions introduce the power to express generalizations into language, that is, the power to move beyond talk about properties of particular individuals to saying what *quantity* of the individuals in a given domain have a given property. The quantificational apparatus of a language is a central plank of its expressive capacity.

Quantification in natural language is an extremely complex phenomenon, one that we will not address directly at first. Instead, we will first present the syntax and semantics of an artificial language that contains constructions capable of representing some very common quantificational tools of natural languages. This is the language of what is known as (first-order) predicate calculus with identity. The semantic techniques for interpreting languages of this kind form the core of standard quantification theory and can be extended to apply directly to English and other natural languages. Before presenting the formal language, however, we will introduce its distinctive semantic idea informally.

As the sentences in (2) suggest, there is indeed a systematic connection between the truth conditions of sentences with quantified expressions as subjects and the truth conditions of sentences with such ordinary referring expressions as personal pronouns or proper names as subjects. It is this connection that quantification theory exploits. Our approach to evaluating sentences like those in (2) seems to have something to do with our evaluations of sentences like those in (3).

(3) *a.* She/he likes Loren.
a′. Bond/Pavarotti/Loren likes Loren.
b. She/he is boring.
b′. Bond/Pavarotti/Loren is boring.
c. She/he is hungry.
c′. Bond/Pavarotti/Loren is hungry.

The basic semantic insights of quantification theory can be implemented so as to emphasize the connection to sentences with proper names in place of quantificational expressions, sentences like those in (3*a′*–*c′*), *Substitutional* approaches to quantification work in this way and have strategies for dealing with some of the problems we pointed to in discussing the sentences in (2) as possible paraphrases of those in (1). For example, languages can be "extended" so that all objects about which we want to generalize are provided with names. Then we would say, for example, that (1a) is true if and only if substitution of names for every individual yields truth. But we will not pursue the substitutional approach. Instead, we will present an *objectual* approach, developing the connection with sentences with pronouns, like those in (3*a*–*c*).

Both approaches share the fundamental idea that the interpretation of sentences with quantificational expressions is systematically related to the interpretation of nonquantificational sentences about individuals.

We can think of the truth-conditional import of the sentences in (1) by imagining the sentences in (3*a*–*c*) uttered again and again, each time accompanied by a pointing at a different individual until each individual in the domain has been pointed at. With each pointing, the sentences are understood as saying of the particular individual in the domain pointed at that she or he likes Loren, is boring, or is hungry. Relative to that pointing, each of these sentences can be assigned a truth value of either true or false, as we elaborated in the preceding chapter. But what about the sentences in (1)? They say something about the pattern of these successive valuations, something that holds regardless of the order in which we choose to point, provided that we eventually point at all the individuals. Sentence (1*a*) says that (3*a*) is true relative to every pointing, sentence (1*b*) says that (3*b*) is true with respect to no pointing (that it is false relative to every pointing), and sentence (1*c*) says that (3*c*) is true relative to some pointing or other.

The basic idea can be applied to other quantified expressions.

(4) *a.* Three cats have whiskers.
    b. Most cats have whiskers.
    c. Many cats have whiskers.
    d. One cat has whiskers.

Each of these sentences can be thought of as having two components. One is a simple subject-predicate sentence with something like a pronoun as its subject, something like (5), which can be evaluated as true or false only with respect to some individual contextually taken as a value for the pronoun (demonstrated by pointing, for example) and which by itself expresses no generalization.

(5) It has whiskers.

The other component, the quantified expression, tells us something about how many different values of the pronoun we have to consider (in this case the quantified expression can also be thought of as instructing us to limit the domain of individuals being considered to cats). The quantified expression is the generalizing component. Sentence (4*a*) is true just in case there are at least three different cats to point to of whom (5) is true; (4*b*) requires that most (more than half) of our pointings at cats pick out cats of which (5) is true; (4*c*) is true just in case "many" of our pointings pick out cats of which (5) is true (and how many this requires depends on various contextual factors); finally, (4*d*) requires only one pointing at a cat of whom (5) is true. In other words, we seem to have analyzed the sentences in (4) roughly along the lines indicated in (6):

(6) *a.* (three cats)(it has whiskers)
b. (most cats)(it has whiskers)
c. (many cats)(it has whiskers)
d. (one cat)(it has whiskers)

This may seem unnatural, since the sentences in (4) do not contain any overt pronouns. But now consider a sentence like (7).

(7) Every cat is proud of its whiskers.

Whereas (5) is incomplete without some contextual demonstration to supply a referent for the pronoun, (7) does not seem to need such a demonstration, even though (7) also contains an occurrence of the pronoun *it*. The pronoun in (7), however, does not refer to some particular cat or set of cats. This might seem mysterious, but it is very natural if we analyze (7) as having two components, just as we did with our earlier sentences.

(8) (every cat)(it is proud of its whiskers)

The pronoun *it*(*s*) in (8), our abstract representation of (7), serves as a placeholder for successive pointings: each successive pointing must assign to both occurrences of the pronoun *it*(*s*) the same object. The semantic value of both occurrences must covary. The analysis in (8) makes this explicit by having the placeholder occur twice, though, of course, it is only the second occurrence that actually surfaces as a pronoun in natural English. The pronoun that surfaces in (7) seems to do exactly what the (abstract) subject pronouns we hypothesized in (5) and (6) do.

It was Frege who first had the idea of analyzing quantified statements such as those we have considered as having two components: one a singular sentence with a placeholder element like a pronoun and the other a component that says how many of the possible values for that placeholder are such that the singular sentence is true relative to that value for the placeholder. Truth conditions for these quantified statements are defined in two stages: first, truth conditions are defined for the singular sentence relative to some value for the placeholder(s), and then truth conditions are defined in terms of generalizations about values assigned to the singular sentence.

Though it may seem simple now, this two-stage approach was an enormous breakthrough. It provided us with the first fully general treatment of multiply quantified sentences (sentences with interdependent occurrences of several quantified expressions, like "Every student meets two professors every week"). In the following section we are going to see how multiple quantification can be made more explicit by incorporating it into the syntax of a formal language (the predicate calculus).

1.1 The standard theory of quantification

1.1.1 The syntax of the predicate calculus The syntax of the predicate calculus (PC) can be given in terms of a simple set of phrase-structure rules such as those in (9). In stating these rules, we abbreviate a set of rules of the form $A \rightarrow C_1, \ldots, C_n$.

Form is the category of formulas; Pred_n is the category of n-placed predicates; t is the category of terms; const is the category of (individual) constants; var is the category of (individual) variables; conn is the category of connectives; neg is the category of negation. To keep the presentation simple, we have included only one-place (monadic), two-place (dyadic), and three-place (triadic) predicates, but (9*b*) could easily be expanded to include predicates with more argument places, since rule (9*a*) is written in a general form. The

(9) *a.* Form $\rightarrow \text{Pred}_n(\text{t}_1, \ldots, \text{t}_n)$
b. i. $\text{Pred}_1 \rightarrow P, Q$
ii. $\text{Pred}_2 \rightarrow K$
iii. $\text{Pred}_3 \rightarrow G$
c. t $\rightarrow$ const, var
d. i. const $\rightarrow j, m$
ii. var $\rightarrow x_1, x_2, x_3, \ldots, x_n, \ldots$
e. Form $\rightarrow$ Form Conn Form
f. Conn $\rightarrow$ $\wedge$ (to be read "and"), $\vee$ (to be read "or"), $\rightarrow$ (to be read "if ... then ..."), $\leftrightarrow$ (to be read "if and only if")
g. Form $\rightarrow$ Neg Form
h. Neg $\rightarrow$ $\neg$ (to be read "it is not the case that")
j. Form $\rightarrow \forall x_n$ Form, $\exists x_n$ Form. $\forall x_n$ should be read "for every x_n"; $\exists x_n$ should be read "for some x_n" or "there is (at least) a x_n such that"
k. Form $\rightarrow$ t = t

number of places associated with a predicate is sometimes called its *adicity*. We also simplified by including only two expressions as one-place predicates (P and Q), two expressions as constants (j and m), one two-place predicate (K), and one three-place predicate (G). Adding more expressions in any of these categories is perfectly straightforward. We have adopted symbols for connectives and quantifiers that are frequently used. But in the logic and semantic literature there is a fair amount of variation, unfortunately, when it comes to notation.

In (10*a*, *b*) we give as illustrations two phrase-structure trees admitted by (9) together with the corresponding labeled bracketings. In giving the labeled bracketings, we omit representing lexical categories, for simplicity. Note that parentheses and commas belong to no category; they are simply introduced by rule (9*a*).

(10) *a.*

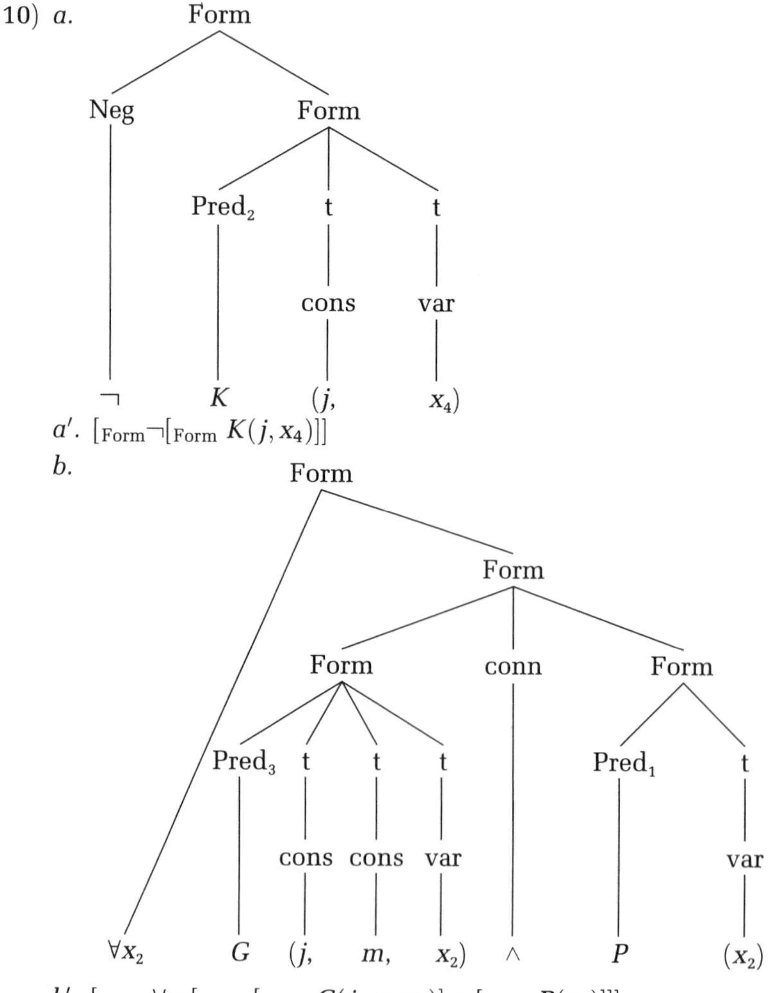

a′. $[_{\text{Form}} \neg [_{\text{Form}}\ K(j, x_4)]]$

b.

b′. $[_{\text{Form}}\ \forall x_2 [_{\text{Form}}\ [_{\text{Form}}\ G(j, m, x_2)] \wedge [_{\text{Form}}\ P(x_2)]]]$

In representing syntactic structures it is generally useful to leave out some details to keep things simple. Thus, for example, in representing labeled bracketings, we can go further than we did in (10*a*′, *b*′) and omit category labels and brackets whenever no ambiguity in syntactic structure results. Under this convention, we can rewrite (10*a*′, b′) as (11*a*, *b*), respectively. Formulas (11*c*–*f*) give further examples of well-formed structures associated with formulas generated by (9).

(11) *a.* $\neg K(j, x_4)$
b. $\forall x_2[G(j, m, x_2) \wedge P(x_2)]$
c. $\forall x_1 \exists x_2[K(x_1, x_2)]$
d. $\forall x_7 \neg[Q(x_7) \rightarrow K(x_7, j)]$
e. $\exists x_3[P(x_3) \vee Q(j)]$
f. $[[\exists x_3 Q(x_3)] \vee P(x_3)]$

Formula (11*b*) can be read "For every x_2, the G relation holds between j, m, and x_2, and x_2 has the property P."

Quantificational sentences are built out of sentences containing variables. This is a way of representing the idea informally presented in the introduction that quantification has two components: a sentence containing ordinary (unquantified) attributions of properties to referents and an instruction as to how many such referents should have the properties. Variables are going to play the semantic role that pronouns were playing in that earlier informal discussion. In a formula like $\exists x_3 Q(x_3)$, the variable x_3 is said to be bound. As we will see when we turn to the semantics of PC, the contribution of a bound variable is completely determined by the quantifier with which it is coindexed: this particular formula says that something is Q. In a formula like $Q(x_3)$, the variable x_3 is free, and the formula says that x_3, which must somehow get assigned a particular value, is Q. The syntax of PC distinguishes bound and free variables.

Let us spell this out. We can say that an occurrence of a variable x_n is *syntactically bound* iff it is c-commanded by a quantifier coindexed with it (that is, it is of the form $\forall x_n$ or $\exists x_n$); otherwise we say that x_n is free. *C-command* (which abbreviates *constituent command*) is defined as follows:

(12) *A c-commands B* iff the first branching node that dominates *A* also dominates *B*.

Accordingly, the first occurrence of x_3 in (11*f*) is bound, the second one is free. Perhaps this can be best appreciated by switching from the labeled bracketing notation to the corresponding phrase marker:

(13)

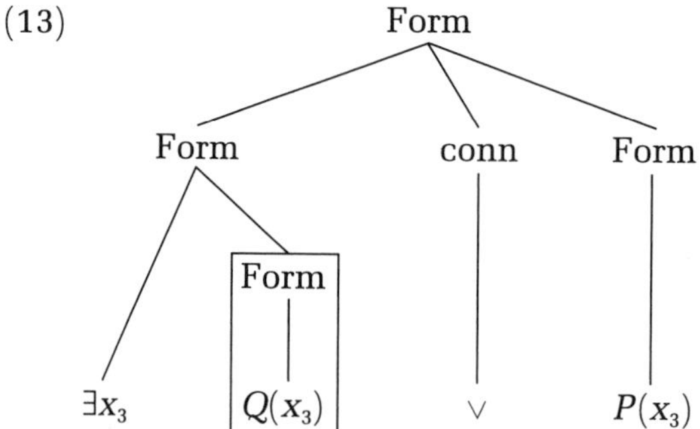

We also say that the *syntactic scope* of a quantifier is what it c-commands (or, equivalently, its c-command domain). Thus, the scope of $\exists x_3$ in (13) is the boxed occurrence of $Q(x_3)$. The notion of scope can be generalized to any connective or operator. That is to say, we can talk of the scope of negation, disjunction, and so on in exactly the same sense in which we talk of the scope of quantifiers.

Finally, we say that an occurrence of x_n is *syntactically bound by* a quantifier Q_n iff Q_n is the *lowest* quantifier c-commanding x_n. Thus, in (14*a*), $\forall x_3$ binds only the second occurrence of x_3, while $\exists x_3$ binds the first one. In fact, as we will shortly see, the formula in (14*a*) will turn out to be equivalent to the one in (14*b*), where quantificational dependencies are expressed in a graphically clearer way.

(14) *a.*

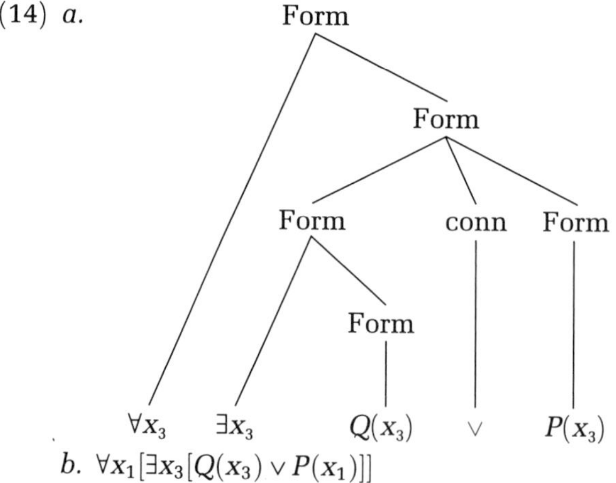

b. $\forall x_1[\exists x_3[Q(x_3) \vee P(x_1)]]$

The two formulas in (14) are said to be *alphabetic variants* of one another and will turn out to be equivalent on our semantics; for clarity, we will generally have distinct variables bound by distinct quantifier occurrences.[1] The syntactic notions of bondage and freedom have a semantic basis that will become clear as we work through the interpretation of PC. Essentially, if an occurrence of variable x is syntactically bound by a quantifier Q in a formula ϕ, what x contributes to the truth conditions of ϕ is determined by Q: a bound occurrence of x does not have any independent fixed value.

Customarily, the syntax of PC is specified by means of a recursive definition, rather than by means of phrase-structure grammars. In (15) we give a recursive characterization of the syntax of PC, which is equivalent to (9). It is easy to verify that the structures in (11) are also admitted by the clauses in (15).

Exercise 1 Prove the last claim for the first two examples in (11) by generating them using the rules in (15).

There are two rather trivial differences between the syntax in (9) and the one in (15). The first concerns the fact that (9) generates terminal strings of the category Form that are ambiguous, as they can be associated with different phrase markers or bracketings. Thus, as in the case of F_1, in order to do semantics we have to refer to sentences under an analysis. On the other hand, (15) is designed to encode directly a certain amount of syntactic structure in the string of symbols that are admitted as members of the category of formulas. In particular, (15) encodes structural information into terminal strings in the form of (*un*labeled) bracketings. As a consequence, (15) generates unambiguous formulas, and semantics can be done directly in terms of the members of category Form, rather than in terms of the members of category Form under a certain analysis. The second difference concerns the fact that the connectives $\wedge$, $\vee$, and $\neg$ are assigned to the categories conn and neg by the

(15) *a.* For any integer n, x_n is an (individual) variable.
b. j, m are (individual) constants.
c. Variables and constants are terms.
d. P, Q are in Pred_1 (one-place predicates), K is in Pred_2, G is in Pred_3.
e. If A is an n-place predicate and $t_1, \ldots, t_n$ are n terms, then $A(t_1, \ldots, t_n)$ is a Form (formula).[2]
f. If A and B are formulas, then so are $\neg A$, $[A \wedge B]$, $[A \vee B]$, $[A \rightarrow B]$, $[A \leftrightarrow B]$, $\forall x_n A$, $\exists x_n A$.
g. If t_1, t_2 are terms, then $t_1 = t_2$ is a formula.

grammar in (9). In the grammar in (15), they are assigned to no category at all. In the latter case, we say that they are treated *syncategorematically*. It wouldn't be hard to modify (15) so as to introduce in it the categories conn and neg.

Exercise 2 A. How would you define bound and free variables, given the syntax in (15)?
B. Consider the formula $[\neg(P(x) \wedge Q(x)]$. What is the scope of negation according to (15)? And what is the scope of the quantifier in $[\forall x Q(x) \rightarrow P(x)]$?

1.1.2 The semantics for PC In what follows we provide a semantics for PC based on the syntax in (15). For F_1 we defined truth conditions recursively on the basis of syntactic recursion. We follow the same sort of procedure in treating the semantics of PC, but now we must consider variables and quantifiers, which are quite different from the names, predicates, and connectives we encountered in F_1.

We have already suggested that variables in PC play some of the roles associated with pronouns in natural languages. It is part of their semantics that they can refer to any individual at all in a given set and can be used with quantifiers to say something general about such a set.

In understanding variables, we must consider the possibility of assigning them different values. For present purposes we can think of these as something like the pointings we imagined for contextually specifying the values of antecedentless pronouns. The main difference is that we can use different ostensions or pointings to fix references of different occurrences of a single pronoun in a sentence, but different occurrences of a single variable in a formula are to be understood as having the same reference. Let us illustrate what we mean. Consider (16).

(16) *a.* She thinks that she is smart.
b. $K(x_1, x_1)$
c. $K(x_1, x_3)$

Interpret $K(x, y)$ as x thinks that y is smart. (This is just a convenience for illustrating our point about variable interpretation; we will not actually deal with formal representations of English sentences like (16*a*) until chapter 5.) When using (16*a*), we can point at one person as we utter the first *she* and to another when the second *she* is pronounced. In contrast, in (16*b*) we are required to assign the same value to x_1 in each of its occurrences: thus (16*b*) must be read as saying that the individual assigned to x_1 stands in the *K* relation to itself (in this case, she thinks that she herself is smart), whereas (16*c*) says that the individual assigned to x_1 stands in the *K* relation to the individual assigned to x_3 (which says nothing about whether the individuals involved are one and the same individual and certainly does not require that they are). We can think of variables as abstract pronouns, with the proviso that in a given context we can point to only one individual for each distinct variable.

In interpreting variables, the critical thing is that we will need to consider alternative assignments of values, just as we need to consider alternative values for a pronoun whose antecedent is a quantified expression, as in (8). We already noted in connection with F_1 that predicates have an extension in a given set of circumstances that depends on what the circumstances are like, what the facts are. For variables, it is crucial that we allow for alternative assignments even where the facts are fixed.

One way of achieving such a goal in interpreting PC is to use two independent value-assigning functions. We will have a function *V* that assigns a value to individual constants and to predicative expressions and a different function *g* that assigns a single value to each distinct variable. It can be helpful to think of *g* as fixing the value of each variable much as an act of ostension can fix the value of an antecedentless third-person pronoun.[3] The semantics for quantifiers will then be given as an instruction as to how to process value assignments to variables.

Perhaps the best way to understand the semantics for PC is by looking at a concrete example. In what follows, we will present first a specific interpretation for PC; later on we will discuss the general form that any interpretation of PC must have.

Interpreting PC involves choosing a set of entities we want to talk about (let's say the set that contains our old friends Bond, Pavarotti, and Loren) and assigning a specific extension to the constants. We can, for example, decide that *m* stands for Loren, and *j* for Pavarotti. Moreover, we can think of *Q* as having as its extension those who are hungry (on a certain occasion), *P* as standing for being boring, *K* as the relation of liking and the three-place relation *G* as standing for introducing (i.e., $G(x, y, z)$ might be read as "*x* introduces *y* to *z*"). Formally, the model we have in mind is specified as follows.

(17) *a.* Let M_1 be a pair $\langle U_1, V_1 \rangle$, where U_1 is a set of individuals (which we will call the *domain* or *universe of discourse*) and V_1 assigns an extension in U_1 to each individual constant of PC and an extension of n-tuples built from U_1 to each predicate. In particular,

$U_1 = \{\text{Bond, Pavarotti, Loren}\}$
$V_1(j) = \text{Bond}$
$V_1(m) = \text{Loren}$
$V_1(P) = \{\text{Loren, Pavarotti}\}$
$V_1(Q) = \{\text{Loren, Bond}\}$
$V_1(K) = \{\langle\text{Bond, Bond}\rangle, \langle\text{Bond, Loren}\rangle, \langle\text{Loren, Pavarotti}\rangle, \langle\text{Pavarotti, Loren}\rangle\}$
$V_1(G) = \{\langle\text{Bond, Loren, Pavarotti}\rangle, \langle\text{Loren, Loren, Bond}\rangle, \langle\text{Loren, Bond, Pavarotti}\rangle, \langle\text{Pavarotti, Pavarotti, Loren}\rangle\}$.

b. Let g_1 be a function that assigns to any variable a value drawn from U_1. In particular, let $g_1(x_1) = \text{Bond}$, let $g_1(x_2) = \text{Loren}$, and for all $n \geq 3$, let $g_1(x_n) = \text{Pavarotti}$. The function g_1 can also be represented as a list of the following kind:

$$g_1 = \begin{bmatrix} x_1 \rightarrow \text{Bond} \\ x_2 \rightarrow \text{Loren} \\ x_n \rightarrow \text{Pavarotti} \end{bmatrix} \quad \text{where } n \geq 3$$

M_1 is called a model for PC. In general, models are abstract structures that we use as auxiliary devices in providing interpretations. Model theory is a branch of modern logic that deals with the semantics of formal systems. Our ultimate goal is applying model theory to natural-language semantics.

So, selecting M_1 means that we are going to talk about Bond, Loren, and Pavarotti. Furthermore, by assigning an extension to predicates, we describe, in a sense, a situation or state of affairs. For example, M_1 as we have set it out represents a situation where Loren and Pavorotti are hungry but Bond is not and where Loren has introduced herself to Bond but Bond has not been introduced to her. Particular models such as M_1 can be thought of, then, as ways of representing situations, collections of facts, or data. Furthermore, in (17*b*), we single out a function g_1 to assign values to variables. When we give the semantics for $\forall$ and $\exists$ along the lines described in section 1, this will enable us to keep the facts fixed while considering different assignments to variables.

We now proceed to give a semantics for PC relative to the situation encoded in M_1 and the value assignment to variables g_1. We have to relativize interpretation to both the model and the assignment because complex expressions can contain both constants and variables. Our interpretation will be recursive. Consequently, the first thing we have to do is to provide the base for the recursion. In (18) we provide the base for the recursive definition of the interpretation of PC, relative to the situation encoded in M_1 and the assignment of g_1.

(18) If A is either a predicate or an individual constant, then $[\![A]\!]^{M_1,g_1} = V_1(A)$. If A is a variable, $[\![A]\!]^{M_1,g_1} = g_1(A)$.

What (18) does is ground our interpretive function $[\![\;]\!]$ (now relativized to a model and an assignment) in the previously defined V and g functions so that constants are interpreted with respect to what the facts are and variables with respect to an assignment function. We now provide the recursive clauses that concern the quantifier-free portion of PC.

(19) For any formulas A, B, any Pred$_n$ R, and any terms $t_1, \ldots, t_n$,
  a. $[\![R(t_1, \ldots, t_n)]\!]^{M_1,g_1} = 1$ iff $\langle [\![t_1]\!]^{M_1,g_1}, \ldots, [\![t_n]\!]^{M_1,g_1} \rangle \in [\![R]\!]^{M_1,g_1}$
  b. $[\![A \wedge B]\!]^{M_1,g_1} = 1$ iff $[\![A]\!]^{M_1,g_1} = 1$ and $[\![B]\!]^{M_1,g_1} = 1$
  c. $[\![A \vee B]\!]^{M_1,g_1} = 1$ iff $[\![A]\!]^{M_1,g_1} = 1$ or $[\![B]\!]^{M_1,g_1} = 1$
  d. $[\![A \rightarrow B]\!]^{M_1,g_1} = 1$ iff $[\![A]\!]^{M_1,g_1} = 0$ or $[\![B]\!]^{M_1,g_1} = 1$
  e. $[\![A \leftrightarrow B]\!]^{M_1,g_1} = 1$ iff $[\![A]\!]^{M_1,g_1} = [\![B]\!]^{M_1,g_1}$
  f. $[\![\neg A]\!]^{M_1,g_1} = 1$ iff $[\![A]\!]^{M_1,g_1} = 0$
  g. $[\![t_i = t_j]\!]^{M_1,g_1} = 1$ iff $[\![t_i]\!]^{M_1,g_1}$ is the same as $[\![t_j]\!]^{M_1,g_1}$

Before moving to the semantics of quantifiers, perhaps we can look at how (19) enables one to interpret quantifier-free formulas of PC. On the next page we compute the value of (20) in M_1 with respect to g_1. After of each step of the computation, we give its justification.

(20) $P(m) \wedge Q(x_3)$

In (h) of the computation for (20) we have what can be thought of as the truth *conditions* of formula (20), relative to M_1; (k) gives the truth *value* of (20), given what the facts of M_1 are.

Exercise 3 State the most efficient way to compute the truth values of the following formulas:

(1) $[R(x, y) \wedge P(x)] \rightarrow Q(x)$

(2) $[[P(y) \wedge R(x, y)] \rightarrow P(x)] \vee [P(x) \vee P(y)]$

(3) $[P(x) \rightarrow Q(y)] \wedge [R(y, y) \leftrightarrow [Q(x) \vee P(y)]]$

Compute the value in M_1 with respect to g_1 of the following formulas:

(4) $G(x_3, j, x_3)$

(5) $\neg P(x_1) \leftrightarrow K(x_2, j)$

(6) $\neg[G(x_1, x_1, x_1) \rightarrow j = m] \wedge [\neg Q(j) \wedge K(j, m)]$

(7) $\neg x_1 = j \rightarrow \neg G(x_1, x_1, x_1)$

(8) $\neg[[Q(x_3)/P(j)] \leftrightarrow K(m, m)] \rightarrow x_1 = m$

Let us now turn to the interpretation of formulas with quantifiers, which is where the real novelty of the present semantics lies. The basic idea is that we look at the formula to which a quantifier is attached and consider its values relative to alternative assignments to the variable with which the quantifier is coindexed. After we present our formal definition and explain it informally, we will work through some illustrative examples.

(21) *a.* $[\![\forall x_n A]\!]^{M_1, g_1} = 1$ iff for all $u \in U$, $[\![A]\!]^{M_1, g_1[u/x_n]} = 1$, where $g_1[u/x_n] = g_1$, except that $g_1[u/x_n](x_n) = u$
b. $[\![\exists x_n A]\!]^{M_1, g_1} = 1$ iff for some $u \in U$, $[\![A]\!]^{M_1, g_1[u/x_n]} = 1$

Let us go through (21*a*) slowly. What (21*a*) says is that a formula of the form $\forall x_n A$ will be true (relative to an assignment function g_1 and a model M_1) if and only if the following conditions hold. For each individual u in the domain of M_1 we evaluate A by assigning u

Computation of (20)

(*a*) $[\![P(m) \wedge Q(x_3)]\!]^{M_1, g_1} = 1$ iff $[\![P(m)]\!]^{M_1, g_1} = 1$ and $[\![Q(x_3)]\!]^{M_1, g_1} = 1$ By (19*b*)
(*b*) $[\![P(m)]\!]^{M_1, g_1} = 1$ iff $[\![m]\!]^{M_1, g_1} \in [\![P]\!]^{M_1, g_1}$ By (19*a*)
(*c*) $[\![m]\!]^{M_1, g_1} \in [\![P]\!]^{M_1, g_1}$ iff $V_1(m) \in V_1(P)$ By (18)
(*d*) $V_1(m) \in V_1(P)$ iff Loren $\in$ {Loren, Pavarotti} By (17*a*)
(*e*) $[\![Q(x_3)]\!]^{M_1, g_1} = 1$ iff $[\![x_3]\!]^{M_1, g_1} \in [\![Q]\!]^{M_1, g_1}$ By (19*a*)
(*f*) $[\![x_3]\!]^{M_1, g_1} \in [\![Q]\!]^{M_1, g_1}$ iff $g_1(x_3) \in V_1(Q)$ By (18)
(*g*) $g_1(x_3) \in V_1(Q)$ iff Pavarotti $\in$ {Bond, Loren} By (17*a*, *b*)
(*h*) $[\![P(m) \wedge Q(x_3)]\!]^{M_1, g_1} = 1$ iff Loren $\in$ {Loren, Pavarotti} and Pavarotti $\in$ {Bond, Loren} By (*a*), (*d*), and (*g*)
(*i*) $[\![P(m)]\!]^{M_1, g_1} = 1$ By (*b*), (*c*), (*d*), and definition of set membership
(*j*) $[\![Q(x_3)]\!]^{M_1, g_1} = 0$ By (*e*), (*f*), (*g*), and definition of set membership
(*k*) $[\![P(m) \wedge Q(x_3)]\!]^{M_1, g_1} = 0$ By (*i*), (*j*), and (19*b*)

to every occurrence of x_n in A and leaving the value assigned to all other variables by g_1 the same; that is, we evaluate A relative to $g_1[u/x_n]$, a function that assigns u to x_n and is otherwise identical to g_1 (we will say more about these modified assignment functions below). If for some u, A is false relative to $g_1[u/x_n]$, then we can stop and conclude that $\forall x_n A$ is false relative to g_1 and M_1. If, however, A comes out true relative to $g_1[u/x_n]$ for all u, then we can conclude that $\forall x_n A$ is true relative to assignment function g_1 and M_1.

For (21*b*), which interprets the existential quantifier, the idea is pretty much the same. The difference is that for $\exists x_n A$ to be true, it suffices to find some u or other in the domain such that the result of interpreting A by assigning u to x_n gives us the truth value 1. In evaluating universals we can stop if any u gives us falsehood; in evaluating existentials we can stop if any u give us truth. Using modified assignment functions is the formal analogue of our informal conception of alternative pointings for evaluating sentences like those in (3*a*–*c*) as a way to evaluate quantified sentences like those in (1).

The basic trick of our semantics for each quantifier is thus to start with an assignment function and then modify that function with respect to the value it assigns to the variable coindexed with that quantifier. In (17*b*) we have specified an assignment g_1 as follows:

$$g_1 = \begin{bmatrix} x_1 \rightarrow \text{Bond} \\ x_2 \rightarrow \text{Loren} \\ x_n \rightarrow \text{Pavarotti} \end{bmatrix} \quad \text{where } n \geq 3$$

Out of g_1 we can construct any assignment of a particular variable to any individual as demanded by the occurrences of quantifiers we encounter. For example, we can construct an assignment $g_1[\text{Bond}/x_3]$, which assigns Bond as the value of x_3 and is just like g_1 in what it assigns to all the other variables. This is the x_3-modification of g_1 with respect to Bond:

$$g_1[\text{Bond}/x_3] = \begin{bmatrix} x_1 \rightarrow \text{Bond} \\ x_2 \rightarrow \text{Loren} \\ x_3 \rightarrow \text{Bond} \\ x_n \rightarrow \text{Pavarotti} \end{bmatrix} \quad \text{where } n \geq 4$$

Some modifications of assignment functions might be vacuous. Note for example that $g_1[\text{Bond}/x_1] = g_1$, since g_1 already assigns Bond as the value of x_1. We also may have to consider (as will be the case with nested quantifiers) modifications of already modified assignments. For example, we might want to take $g_1[\text{Bond}/x_3]$ and modify it by assigning Loren to x_1. We represent this new function as $g_1[[\text{Bond}/x_3]\text{Loren}/x_1]$:

$$g_1[[\text{Bond}/x_3]\text{Loren}/x_1] = \begin{bmatrix} x_1 \rightarrow \text{Bond} \\ x_2 \rightarrow \text{Loren} \\ x_3 \rightarrow \text{Bond} \\ x_n \rightarrow \text{Pavarotti} \end{bmatrix} \quad \text{where } n \geq 4$$

What we do is this. First we modify g_1 by assigning Bond to x_3 and then, keeping that constant, we assign Loren to x_1. Although the notation can become intimidating, the basic idea is a very simple one.

In fact, in doing computations we do not need to bother with keeping track of all details of the modified functions. What we need to know about modified assignment functions in the course of our computing is either told to us by the notation itself or by the specification of the initial assignment function. The notation tells us, e.g., that $g_1[\text{Pavarotti}/x_1](x_1) = \text{Pavarotti}$ and that $g_1[[\text{Pavarotti}/x_2]\text{Loren}/x_3](x_3) = \text{Loren}$ (and also, of course, that $g_1[[\text{Pavarotti}/x_2]\text{Loren}/x_3](x_1) = \text{Pavarotti}$). What about variables whose assignment has not been directly modified, the variables not indicated in the notation? For such variables, we rely on our original assignment function; that is, we know immediately that $g_1[[\text{Pavarotti}/x_2]\text{Loren}/x_3](x_8) = g_1(x_8) = \text{Pavarotti}$.

Let us look now at a few examples where we will work with modified assignments. Let us consider first a sentence with only one quantifier.

(22) $\exists x_1 P(x_1)$

What (22) basically says is that something in the domain satisfies the predicate P. Given the interpretation specified in (17), it says specifically that something in U_1 is hungry. Such a statement is true in M_1, as the set of those individuals satisfying P, those who are hungry, is not empty in M_1. Thus the result of evaluating (22) in M_1 should yield the truth value 1. The computation is in the box on the next page.

We did the computation in a dumb way by taking Bond as our first individual to assign to the coindexed variable. That meant we had to do a second evaluation with respect to another member of our domain. The point is that we do not need to know in advance which individual or individuals might satisfy our predicate. We took Loren as our target individual for the second evaluation, but

Computation of (22) relative to M_1 and g_1

(*a*) $[\![\exists x_1 P(x_1)]\!]^{M_1,g_1} = 1$ iff for some $u \in U_1$, $[\![P(x_1)]\!]^{M_1,g_1[u/x_1]} = 1$ By (21*b*)
(*b*) Assign Bond to x_1; i.e., consider $g_1[\text{Bond}/x_1]$
(*c*) $[\![P(x_1)]\!]^{M_1,g_1[u/x_1]} = 1$ iff $[\![x_1]\!]^{M_1,g_1[u/x_1]} \in [\![P]\!]^{M_1,g_1[u/x_1]}$ By (19*a*)
(*d*) $[\![x_1]\!]^{M_1,g_1[u/x_1]} \in [\![P]\!]^{M_1,g_1[u/x_1]}$ iff $g_1[\text{Bond}/x_1](x_1) \in V_1(P)$
$= \{\text{Loren, Pavarotti}\}$ By (18)
(*e*) $g_1[\text{Bond}/x_1](x_1) = \text{Bond}$ By definition (21*a*)
(*f*) $[\![P(x_1)]\!]^{M_1,g_1[u/x_1]} = 1$ iff Bond $\in$ {Loren, Pavarotti} By (*c*), (*d*), (*e*)
(*g*) $[\![P(x_1)]\!]^{M_1,g_1[u/x_1]} = 0$ By (*f*) and definition of set membership
(*h*) Assign Loren to x_1; i.e., consider $g_1[\text{Loren}/x_1]$
(*i*) $[\![P(x_1)]\!]^{M_1,g_1[\text{Loren}/x_1]} = 1$ iff $[\![x_1]\!]^{M_1,g_1[\text{Loren}/x_1]} \in [\![P]\!]^{M_1,g_1[\text{Loren}/x_1]}$ By (19*a*)
(*j*) $[\![x_1]\!]^{M_1,g_1[\text{Loren}/x_1]} \in [\![P]\!]^{M_1,g_1[\text{Loren}/x_1]}$ iff $g_1[\text{Loren}/x_1](x_1) \in V_1(P)$
$= \{\text{Loren, Pavarotti}\}$ By (18)
(*k*) $g_1[\text{Loren}/x_1](x_1) = \text{Loren}$ By definition (21*a*)
(*l*) $[\![P(x_1)]\!]^{M_1,g_1[\text{Loren}/x_1]} = 1$ iff Loren $\in$ {Loren, Pavarotti} By (*i*), (*j*), (*k*)
(*m*) $[\![P(x_1)]\!]^{M_1,g_1[\text{Loren}/x_1]} = 1$ By (*l*) and definition of set membership
(*n*) $[\![\exists x_1 P(x_1)]\!]^{M_1,g_1} = 1$ By (*m*) and (21*b*)

as it happens, we could have taken Pavarotti and gotten the same result. Relative to either of those individuals, $P(x_1)$ gets the value 1 in our model and thus the existentially quantified formula in (22) gets the value 1, as we predicted.

The real power of using assignment functions comes when we consider formulas with multiple quantifiers. Look at (23*a*). Again, before evaluating it formally, we will consider it intuitively. The syntactic structure of (23*a*) can be displayed as in (23*b*).

(23) *a.* $\forall x_1 \exists x_2 K(x_1, x_2)$
b.

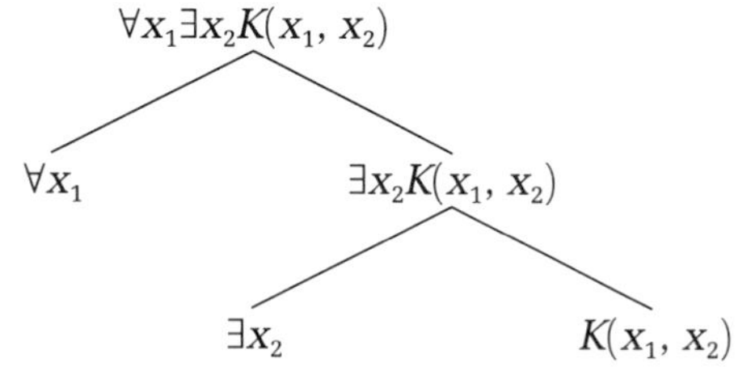

```
              ∀x1∃x2K(x1, x2)
             /               \
          ∀x1            ∃x2K(x1, x2)
                          /          \
                       ∃x2          K(x1, x2)
```

When quantifier Q_n includes Q_j in its scope or, as we also say, has scope over Q_j, then Q_n is said to have *wide scope* relative to Q_j, and Q_j is said to have *narrow scope* relative to Q_n. In (23), $\forall x_1$ has scope over $\exists x_3$; in (24) below, we examine the semantic effects of the opposite scope relations. Formula (23*a*) says that everything in the domain has something that it bears the relation K to, something that it likes. In M_1 we see that this is true. Take Bond; he likes himself. Turning to Loren, we see that she does not like Bond but she does like Pavarotti. And finally, Pavarotti likes Loren. Our formal procedure mimics this informal way of evaluating (23*a*). We work our way from the outermost layers of syntactic structure inward, applying the corresponding semantic rules as we parse the formula. Because our superscripts get hard to read as matters get more complex, we will omit them and instead write out "$[\![\beta]\!]$ relative to M and g," where M and g are the model and assignment functions relevant at a given stage. This is lengthier but a bit easier to process. In the first subbox we focus on Bond and try to find someone he likes. We try Bond himself, and indeed that works. In the second subbox we focus on Loren. First we try Bond but find she does not like him. Next, however, we try Pavarotti and are successful. Finally, we focus on the third member of our domain, Pavarotti. Our first try for someone he might like is Loren, and because he does, the computation is successful. In the final step we put together the results of these three subcomputations and conclude that everyone in our domain does indeed have someone whom they like.

The process of evaluation just illustrated is, of course, tedious. Luckily, semanticists do not spend their time doing such computations. In fact (*d*) in the main box gives us the truth *conditions* of interest (relative to M_1); it is only in calcuating actual truth *values* that we need to consider particular assignments explicitly. Semanticists do need, however, to know that there is a formal semantics for quantification that can treat cases of any complexity whatsoever. And what we have outlined can indeed do that. Complicated though the computations in the preceding box may seem, they really are just explicit versions of the rather simple process that we went through informally before beginning the formal computations.

Quantifiers are construed as instructions to check assignments to the variables that they bind: how many assignments must yield a value of 1 is what each quantifier specifies. How many we need actually consider may depend on where we happen to start. In the worst-case scenario the number of assignments that must be considered is the number of elements in the universe raised to the power n, where n is the number of distinct variables bound by the quantifiers. In the relatively simple example above, this was $3^2 = 9$. We actually considered only four. The first was with Bond assigned to both x_1 and x_2, that is, $g_1[[\text{Bond}/x_1]\text{Bond}/x_2]$, which is what we

Computation of (23) relative to M_1 and g_1

(*a*) $[\![(23a)]\!] = 1$ relative to M_1 and g_1 iff $[\![\exists x_2 K(x_1, x_2)]\!] = 1$ relative to M_1 and $g_1[u/x_1]$ for all u in U_1 By (21*a*)
(*b*) $[\![\exists x_2 K(x_1, x_2)]\!] = 1$ relative to M_1 and $g_1[u/x_1]$ iff for some u' in U_1 $[\![K(x_1, x_2)]\!] = 1$ relative to M_1 and $g_1[[u/x_1]u'/x_2]$ By (21*b*)
(*c*) $[\![K(x_1, x_2)]\!] = 1$ relative to M_1 and $g_1[[u/x_1]u'/x_2]$ iff $\langle g_1[[u/x_1]u'/x_2](x_1), g_1[[u/x_1]u'/x_2](x_2)\rangle \in V_1(K)$ By (19*a*)
(*d*) $[\![K(x_1, x_2)]\!] = 1$ relative to M_1 and $g_1[[u/x_1]u'/x_2]$ iff $\langle u, u'\rangle \in V_1(K) = \{\langle$Bond, Bond$\rangle$, $\langle$Bond, Loren$\rangle$, $\langle$Loren, Pavarotti$\rangle$, $\langle$Pavarotti, Loren$\rangle\}$ By definition of modified assignments, (*c*), and (17*a*)

Go to subbox 1 and assign Bond to x_1; i.e., consider $g_1[\text{Bond}/x_1]$.

1 (*a*) $[\![\exists x_2 K(x_1, x_2)]\!] = 1$ relative to M_1 and $g_1[\text{Bond}/x_1]$ iff there is some u in U such that $[\![K(x_1, x_2)]\!] = 1$ relative to M_1 and $g_1[[\text{Bond}/x_1]u/x_2]$ By (21*b*)

Assign Bond himself also to x_2; i.e., consider $g_1[[\text{Bond}/x_1]\text{Bond}/x_2]$.

(*b*) $[\![K(x_1, x_2)]\!] = 1$ relative to M_1 and $g_1[[\text{Bond}/x_1]\text{Bond}/x_2]$ iff $\langle g_1[[\text{Bond}/x_1]\text{Bond}/x_2](x_1), g_1[[\text{Bond}/x_1]\text{Bond}/x_2](x_2)\rangle \in V_1(K)$ By (18) and (19*a*)
(*c*) $\langle g_1[[\text{Bond}/x_1]\text{Bond}/x_2](x_1), g_1[[\text{Bond}/x_1]\text{Bond}/x_2](x_2)\rangle \in V_1(K)$ iff $\langle$Bond, Bond$\rangle \in V_1(K)$ By definition of $g_1[[\text{Bond}/x_1]\text{Bond}/x_2]$
(*d*) $\langle$Bond, Bond$\rangle \in V_1(K)$ iff $\langle$Bond, Bond$\rangle \in \{\langle$Bond, Bond$\rangle$, $\langle$Bond, Loren$\rangle$, $\langle$Loren, Pavarotti$\rangle$, $\langle$Pavarotti, Loren$\rangle\}$ By (17*a*)
(*e*) $[\![\exists x_2 K(x_1, x_2)]\!] = 1$ relative to M_1 and $g_1[\text{Bond}/x_1]$ By (*a*) through (*d*) and definition set membership

Go to subbox 2 and assign Loren to x_1; i.e., consider $g_1[\text{Loren}/x_1]$.

2 (*a*) $[\![\exists x_2 K(x_1, x_2)]\!] = 1$ relative to M_1 and $g_1[\text{Loren}/x_1]$ iff there is some u in U such that $[\![K(x_1, x_2)]\!] = 1$ relative to M_1 and $g_1[[\text{Loren}/x_1]u/x_2]$ By (21*b*)

Assign Bond to x_2; i.e., consider $g_1[[\text{Loren}/x_1]\text{Bond}/x_2]]$.

(*b*) $[\![K(x_1, x_2)]\!] = 1$ relative to M_1 and $g_1[[\text{Loren}/x_1]\text{Bond}/x_2]$ iff $\langle g_1[[\text{Loren}/x_1]\text{Bond}/x_2](x_1), g_1[[\text{Loren}/x_1]\text{Bond}/x_2](x_1)\rangle \in V_1(K)$ By (18) and (19*a*)
(*c*) $\langle g_1[[\text{Loren}/x_1]\text{Bond}/x_2](x_1), g_1[[\text{Loren}/x_1]\text{Bond}/x_2](x_1)\rangle \in V_1(K)$ iff $\langle$Loren, Bond$\rangle \in \{\langle$Bond, Bond$\rangle$, $\langle$Bond, Loren$\rangle$, $\langle$Loren, Pavarotti$\rangle$, $\langle$Pavarotti, Loren$\rangle\}$
(*d*) $[\![K(x_1, x_2)]\!] = 0$ relative to M_1 and $g_1[[\text{Loren}/x_1]\text{Bond}/x_2]$ By (*b*), (*c*), and definition of set membership

Assign Pavarotti to x_2; i.e., consider $g_1[[\text{Loren}/x_1]\text{Pavarotti}/x_2]$.

(*e*) $[\![K(x_1, x_2)]\!] = 1$ relative to M_1 and $g_1[[\text{Loren}/x_1]\text{Pavarotti}/x_2]$ iff $\langle g_1[[\text{Loren}/x_1]\text{Pavarotti}/x_2](x_1)$, $g_1[[\text{Loren}/x_1]\text{Pavarotti}/x_2](x_1)\rangle \in V_1(K)$ By (18) and (19*a*)

(*f*) $\langle g_1[[\text{Loren}/x_1]\text{Pavarotti}/x_2](x_1)$, $g_1[[\text{Loren}/x_1]\text{Pavarotti}/x_2](x_1)\rangle \in V_1(K)$ iff ⟨Loren, Pavarotti⟩ ∈ {⟨Bond, Bond⟩, ⟨Bond, Loren⟩, ⟨Loren, Pavarotti⟩, ⟨Pavarotti, Loren⟩} By definition of $g_1[[\text{Loren}/x_1]\text{Pavarotti}/x_2]$ and (17*a*)

(*g*) $[\![\exists x_2 K(x_1, x_2)]\!] = 1$ relative to M_1 and $g_1[\text{Loren}/x_1]$ By (*e*) through (*f*) and definition of set membership

Go to subbox 3 and assign Pavarotti to x_1; i.e., consider $g_1[\text{Pavarotti}/x_1]$.

3 (*a*) $[\![\exists x_2 K(x_1, x_2)]\!] = 1$ relative to M_1 and $g_1[\text{Pavarotti}/x_1]$ iff there is some u in U such that $[\![K(x_1, x_2)]\!] = 1$ relative to M_1 and $g_1[[\text{Pavarotti}/x_1]u/x_2]$

Assign Loren to x_2; i.e., consider $g_1[[\text{Pavarotti}/x_1]\text{Loren}/x_2]$.

(*b*) $[\![K(x_1, x_2)]\!] = 1$ relative to M_1 and $g_1[[\text{Pavarotti}/x_1]\text{Loren}/x_2]$ iff $\langle g_1[[\text{Pavarotti}/x_1]\text{Loren}/x_2](x_1)$, $g_1[[\text{Pavarotti}/x_1]\text{Loren}/x_2](x_2)\rangle \in V_1(K)$ By (19*a*) and (18)

(*c*) $\langle g_1[[\text{Pavarotti}/x_1]\text{Loren}/x_2](x_1)$, $g_1[[\text{Pavarotti}/x_1]\text{Loren}/x_2](x_2)\rangle \in V_1(K)$ iff ⟨Pavarotti, Loren⟩ ∈ {⟨Bond, Bond⟩, ⟨Bond, Loren⟩, ⟨Loren, Pavarotti⟩, ⟨Pavarotti, Loren⟩} By definition of $g_1[[\text{Pavarotti}/x_1]\text{Loren}/x_2]$ and (17*a*)

(*d*) $[\![\exists x_2 K(x_1, x_2)]\!] = 1$ relative to M_1 and $g_1[\text{Pavarotti}/x_1]$ By (*a*) through (*c*) and definition of set membership

Conclusion: $[\![(23a)]\!] = 1$ relative to M_1 and g_1 By (*a*) through (*c*) and subboxes 1, 2, and 3

used in the subbox 1 computation. The second and third we used in subbox 1; both of these assigned Loren to x_1 but one assigned Bond to x_2—this was $g_1[[\text{Loren}/x_1]\text{Bond}/x_2]$—and the other assigned Pavarotti to x_2—this was $g_1[[\text{Loren}/x_1]\text{Pavarott}/x_2]$. In this subbox, the assignment $g_1[[\text{Loren}/x_1]\text{Bond}/x_2]$ yielded 0 for the unquantified formula $K(x_1, x_2)$ and thus did not help us determine whether $\exists x_2 K(x_1, x_2)$ was true relative to $g_1[\text{Loren}/x_1]$, which is what we were investigating at that point (whether there was someone Loren liked). That's why we had to look at the effects of assigning someone else—we chose Pavarotti—as the value of x_2. And finally in subbox 3 we assigned Pavarotti to x_1 and Loren to x_2—this was $g_1[[\text{Pavarotti}/x_1]\text{Loren}/x_2]$.

It is clear that matters could quickly get out of hand were we to consider longer nestings of quantifiers or larger domains of discourse. But it is also clear that this limitation is only due to the limited character of our psychophysical resources (memory, life span, etc.). The procedure we have specified will eventually yield a truth value for each formula if we abstract away from such limits, that is, if we imagine being able to extend our memory space, for example, indefinitely. Compare our semantics for quantifiers with the algorithm for computing addition. Two numbers can well be too big to be added by any human. Yet (for finite domains) the algorithm for addition will eventually yield a value if we let it run for a sufficiently long time. We do not intend to suggest that people actually use the computational procedures specified above but only that these procedures show the structure of their semantic competence.

Readers might want to familiarize themselves more with these techniques by evaluating a few more formulas. Consider, for example, (24):

(24) $\exists x_2 \forall x_1 K(x_1, x_2)$

Formula (24) is the result of permuting the quantifiers in formula (23*a*). For (24) to be true, we have got to find some $u \in U_1$ such that all u' in U_1 bear the *K*-relation to u. Given our particular model, there must be some individual who is universally liked. That is, we must find some u in U_1 such that $[\![\forall x_1 K(x_1, x_2)]\!] = 1$ relative to relative to M_1 and $g_1[u/x_2]$; to return to our superscript notation, we need a u such that $[\![\forall x_1 K(x_1, x_2)]\!]^{M_1, g_1[u/x_2]} = 1$. (To save space, we will return to using the superscript notation from now on to indicate the model and assignment function to which interpretation is relativized.) But there is no such u. To see this, consider that

$$[\![\forall x_1 K(x_1, x_2)]\!]^{M_1, g_1[\text{Bond}/x_2]} = 0,$$

since

$$[\![K(x_1, x_2)]\!]^{M_1, g_1[[\text{Bond}/x_2]\text{Loren}/x_1]} = 0.$$

Similarly,

$$[\![\forall x_1 K(x_1, x_2))]\!]^{M_1, g_1[\text{Loren}/x_2]} = 0,$$

since

$$[\![K(x_1, x_2)]\!]^{M1, g_1[[\text{Bond}/x_2]\text{Loren}/x_1]} = 0.$$

And finally,

$[\![\forall x_1 K(x_1, x_2)]\!]^{M_1, g_1[\text{Pavarotti}/x_2]} = 0,$

since

$[\![K(x_1, x_2)]\!]^{M_1, g_1[[\text{Pavarotti}/x_2]\text{Bond}/x_1]} = 0.$

Thus, (26) is false in M_1.

Exercise 4 Consider a model $M_2 = \langle U_2, V_2 \rangle$ such that the following hold:

$U_2 = \{0, 1, 2, 3, 4, 5, 6, 7, 8, 9\}$

$V_2(j) = 0$

$V_2(m) = 9$

$V_2(P) =$ the odd numbers in $U_2 = \{1, 3, 5, 7, 9\}$

$V_2(Q) =$ the numbers in U_2 whose representation in standard arabic notation Pavarotti could recognize by his third birthday $= \{0, 1, 2, 3, 4, 5, 7, 8\}$

$V_2(K) =$ the set of pairs $\langle x, y \rangle$ of elements of U_2 such that x is less than or equal to y

$V_2(G) =$ the set of ordered triples $\langle x, y, z \rangle$ of elements of U_2 such that $x + y = z$

Furthermore, let $g_2(x_1) = 1$, $g_2(x_2) = 5$, $g_2(x_3) = 6$, and for all $n \geq 4$, $g_2(x_n) = 2$. What do the following formulas say in English, and what is their truth value in M_2?

(1) $\forall x_1 \exists x_2 [K(x_1, x_2) \wedge \neg x_1 = x_2]$

(2) $\exists x_1 [Q(x_1) \wedge \neg P(x_1)] \wedge \exists x_1 [Q(x_1) \wedge P(x_1)]$

(3) $\forall x_1 [[P(x_1) \wedge \neg x_1 = m] \rightarrow Q(x_1)]$

(4) $\forall x_1 [Q(x_1) \rightarrow [P(x_1) \wedge \neg x_1 = m]]$

(5) $\forall x_1 [\neg Q(x_1) \rightarrow [x_1 = m \wedge \exists x_2 G(x_2, x_2, x_1)]]$

(6) $\exists x_1 [G(x_1, x_1, x_1) \wedge \forall x_2 [G(x_2, x_2, x_2) \leftrightarrow x_2 = x_1]]$

(7) $\forall x_1 \forall x_2 [G(x_2, x_1, x_1) \leftrightarrow x_2 = j]$

(8) $\exists x_1 \exists x_2 \exists x_3 \neg [G(x_1, x_2, x_3) \leftrightarrow G(x_2, x_1, x_3)]$

(9) $\neg \exists x_1 \neg K(x_1, x_1)$

(10) $\forall x_1 \forall x_2 \forall x_3 [G(x_1, x_2, x_3) \rightarrow [K(x_2, x_3) \wedge \neg x_2 = x_3]]$

Evaluate the following formulas in M_2, with respect to g_2, showing the crucial steps.

(11) $G(x_1, x_2, x_3)$

(12) $\forall x_1 G(x_1, j, x_1)$

(13) $\neg P(m) \leftrightarrow Q(m)$

(14) $\forall x_2 \exists x_3 [G(x_1, x_2, x_3) \vee x_2 = m]$

It is important to note that it will not matter at all which assignment we begin with in evaluating (24), (22), or (23*a*). Although g_1 was in the background, we never actually used it to assign variable values entering into our calculations. We used only the *modified* assignment functions. This contrasts sharply with what we did in evaluating (20), $P(m) \wedge Q(x_3)$, where x_3 is free. Its interpretation crucially depends on the assignment, in a way reminiscent of how the interpretation of sentences with pronouns depends on a contextually specified way of getting at the intended referent. Notice, in particular, that in (g) of the boxed computation following (20), we relied crucially on the fact that $g_1(x_3) = \text{Pavarotti}$. There is no quantifier in (20) that would permit us to modify variable assignments, whereas in (23*a*) each variable comes with an instruction, provided by the quantifier, to consider modified assignments (i.e., each variable is bound). This should make it clear how the syntactic notions of free and bound variables are linked directly to semantic dependencies. We will see shortly in exactly what sense.

The notion that we have defined for formulas is "true with respect to a model and an assignment." Tarski's original notion was that of "satisfaction of a formula by an assignment." If a formula does contain syntactically free variables, it can only be true or false with respect to an assignment. But when a formula contains no free variables, as noted above in connection with (23*a*), it will get a value independently of which particular assignment is chosen. It follows that if a formula without free variables is true with respect to an assignment, it will be true with respect to *all* assignments. And if it is false with respect to an assignment, it will be false with respect to all assignments. This is simply because which particular assignment we start with does not enter in any relevant way into the computation of the value of the formula. The semantic rule for interpreting quantifiers guarantees that we confine our attention to assignments that are modified with respect to the variables coindexed with the c-commanding quantifiers. We can exploit this fact to define truth formally.

(25) *a.* A formula A is true in a model M iff for any assignment g, $[\![A]\!]^{M,g} = 1$.
b. A formula A is false in M iff for any assignment g, $[\![A]\!]^{M,g} = 0$.

Thus, by this definition, $[\![(23a)]\!]^{M_1} = 1$; more simply, in M_1, (23*a*) is true. Any formula without free variables that is true with respect to a model M and an assignment g is simply true with respect to M; that is, assignments do not matter to the truth of a formula unless there are free variables in the formula.

We are now able to see the interest of the syntactic definitions of bondage and freedom given in section 1.1.1. The value of a formula ϕ in a model M may or may not depend on what an assignment g assigns to a variable x_i. If it does, in view of how the interpretation of PC is set up, it must be because x_i is syntactically free in ϕ; if it does not, it must be because x_i is syntactically bound.[4] We can exploit this fact in defining what it is to be semantically free (or bound):

(26) *a.* The occurrence of a variable x_i in a formula ϕ is semantically free iff for some M and some g the value of ϕ in M may vary depending on what g assigns to x_i.
b. The occurrence of a variable x_i in a formula ϕ is semantically bound iff the value of ϕ in a model M relative to an assignment g does not change no matter how we vary what g assigns to x_i.

So we wind up with two notions of bondage and freedom. One uses syntactic terms (*indices* and *c-command*); the other semantic ones (*values in a model relative to assignments*). Now, it can be shown (though we will not do that here) that there is a virtually perfect correspondence between the two; that is, (the occurrence of) a variable is syntactically bound iff it is semantically bound, and is syntactically free iff it is semantically free (but see note 4). This is due, of course, to how PC is set up, and it justifies talking of free or bound variables without further specification.

We are interested in applying the PC treatment of quantification to the study of English quantificational structures. It would be interesting if a similar correspondence between syntactic and semantic notions of binding could be established for natural language. Can one define a syntactic notion of binding for English that (under plausible syntactic assumptions and a simple interpretive procedure) turns out to have a natural semantic counterpart? And is this the best way of understanding how quantification works in natural language? These are the sort of questions that will be taken up in the next sections. Even though we will not be able to provide definite answers, we believe that one can learn a lot by pursuing them.

The semantics for PC is made up of three components: the assignment to variables, a characterization of the class of models, and the recursively specified semantic rules. The structure of the models of PC is quite simple. Any structure of the following form will qualify as a model for PC:

(27) $M = \langle U, V \rangle$, where U is a set of individuals, and V is a function such that if c is an individual constant, $V(c) \in U$, and if c is an n-place predicate, $V(c)$ is a set of ordered n-tuples of elements drawn from U. In symbols, $V(c) \subseteq U_1 \times \cdots \times U_n$, where $U_1 \times \cdots \times U_n$, the Cartesian product of U times itself n times, is the set of all ordered n-tuples built on U. (See the appendix for an explanation of Cartesian products.)

The content of the model (that is, the particular choice of a universe of discourse and the way it is carved up into suitable extensions for predicative and individual constants) may vary. The recursive part of the semantics then provides a way of computing the truth values of sentences of indefinite complexity relative to a model. This represents how the semantics for PC provides a way of determining the truth values of sentences across different circumstances (which are represented here by different particular models). A semantics for more complex constructions is generally specified in this same format.

We can now proceed to define entailment, logical equivalence, validity, and contradiction along the lines familiar from the preceding chapter.

(28) a. A set of formulas Ω *entails* a formula β iff for every model M such that $[\![S]\!]^M = 1$ for every $\delta \in \Omega$, $[\![\beta]\!]^M = 1$.
b. A formula β is *logically equivalent* to a formula δ iff β entails δ and vice versa (that is, iff they are true in exactly the same models).
c. A formula β is *valid* iff for every model M, $[\![\beta]\!]^M = 1$.
d. A formula β is *contradictory* iff for every model M, $[\![\beta]\!]^M = 0$.

Given our semantics for PC and the definitions in (19) and (28), a number of entailments will automatically be allowed. The entailments in the semantics for F_1 had to do with the relations among conjunction, disjunction, and negation, and PC has parallel entailments. The new entailments that fall out of the semantics for PC concern the relations among quantifiers and sentential connectives. Because we are generalizing over all models for PC, it is only the interpretation of these logical constants that remains fixed, and thus the only entailments we derive are those that depend solely on them. This is as it should be for PC, but when we turn to fragment F_2, we will generalize only over models that interpret our constants as they are interpreted in English.

Let us now look at some of the entailments involving quantifiers and sentential connectives in PC. First, let us show that (29) entails (30) and vice versa.

(29) $\forall x \neg P(x)$

(30) $\neg \exists x P(x)$

Thus starting with the assumption that (29), $\forall x \neg P(x)$, is true relative to some arbitrary M and g, we arrived at the conclusion that (30), $\neg \exists x P(x)$, is also true relative to the same arbitrary model M and assignment g. We never used the specific content of M or g. Therefore, we have shown that (29) entails (30). Let us go in the other direction. Again, our proof holds for arbitrary M and g, and thus we show in the next box that (30) entails (29). So we have shown on the basis of the two boxed proofs that (29) and (30) are logically equivalent. This equivalence is one that is often useful.

Proof that (29) entails (30)

(*a*) Let $M = \langle U, V \rangle$ be any model such that $[\![(29)]\!]^M = 1$ By assumption
(*b*) For every assignment g, $[\![(29)]\!]^{M,g} = 1$ From (*a*), by definition of truth in (25)
(*c*) For all $u \in U$, $[\![\neg P(x)]\!]^{M,g[u/x]} = 1$ From (*b*), by the semantics for $\forall$ in (21*a*)
(*d*) For all $u \in U$, $[\![P(x)]\!]^{M,g[u/x]} = 0$ From (*c*), by the semantics for $\neg$ in (19*f*)
(*e*) There is no $u \in U$ such that $[\![P(x)]\!]^{M,g[u/x]} = 1$ From (*d*)
(*f*) $[\![\exists x P(x)]\!]^{M,g} = 0$ From (e), by the semantics for $\exists$ in (21*b*)
(*g*) $[\![\neg \exists x P(x)]\!]^{M,g} = 1$ From (*f*), by the semantics for $\neg$ in (19*f*)

Proof that (30) entails (29)

(a) Let $M = \langle U, V \rangle$ be any model such that $[\![(30)]\!]^{M} = 1$ By assumption
(b) For every g, $[\![\exists x P(x)]\!]^{M,g} = 0$ From (a), by the definition of truth in (25) and the semantics of $\neg$ in (19f)
(c) There is no $u \in U$ such that $[\![P(x)]\!]^{M,g[u/x]} = 1$ From (b), by the definition of $g[u/x]$
(d) For all $u \in U$, $[\![P(x)]\!]^{M,g[u/x]} = 0$ From (c)
(e) For all $u \in U$, $[\![\neg P(x)]\!]^{M,g[u/x]} = 1$ From (d) and the semantics of $\neg$ in (19f)
(f) $[\![\forall x \neg P(x)]\!]^{M,g} = 1$ From (e), by the semantics of $\forall$ in (21a)

Proof that (31) entails (32)

(a) Let M be any model such that for all g, $[\![(31)]\!]^{M,g} = 1$ By assumption
(b) For all $u \in U$, $[\![P(x) \rightarrow Q(x)]\!]^{M,g[u/x]} = 1$ From (a), by the semantics for $\forall$ in (21a)
(c) For all $u \in U$, $[\![P(x)]\!]^{M,g[u/x]} = 0$ or $[\![Q(x)]\!]^{M,g[u/x]} = 1$ From (c), by the semantics for $\rightarrow$ in (17d)
(d) Either there is some $u \in U$ such that $[\![P(x)]\!]^{M,g[u/x]} = 0$ (we explore this possibility in (e)) or there is not (this possibility is explored in (f))
(e) i. Assume that there is some $u \in U$ such that $[\![P(x)]\!]^{M,g[u/x]} = 0$
ii. $[\![\forall x P(x)]\!]^{M,g} = 0$ From (e.i), by the semantics for $\forall$ in (21a)
iii. $[\![(32)]\!]^{M,g} = 1$ From (e.ii), by the semantics for $\rightarrow$ in (19d). (The formula in (e.ii) is the antecedent of the conditional in (32), and conditionals with false antecedents are automatically true.)
(f) i. Assume that there is no $u \in U$ such that $[\![P(x)]\!]^{M,g[u/x]} = 0$
ii. $[\![\forall x P(x)]\!]^{M,g} = 1$ From (f.i), by the semantics for $\forall$ in (21a)
iii. For all $u \in U$, $[\![Q(x)]\!]^{M,g[u/x]} = 1$ From (c) and (f.ii)
iv. $[\![\forall x Q(x)]\!]^{M,g} = 1$ From (f.iii), by the semantics for $\forall$ in (21a)
v. $[\![(32)]\!]^{M,g} = 1$ From (f.iv) and the semantics for $\rightarrow$ in (19d). (The formula in (f.ii) is the consequent of the conditional in (31), and conditionals with true consequents are automatically true.)
(g) $[\![(32)]\!]^{M,g} = 1$ From (a) through (f)

Model showing (32) does not entail (31)

(a) Let $M' = \langle U', V' \rangle$ such that $U' = \{a, b\}$, $V'(P) = \{a\}$, and $V'(Q) = \{b\}$, and let g by any assignment function.
(b) $[\![P(x)]\!]^{M', g[b/x]} = 0$ By (a), (19a), and the definition of $g[b/x]$ in (21a)
(c) $[\![\forall x P(x)]\!]^{M'} = 0$ From (b) and the semantics for $\forall$ in (21a)
(d) $[\![(32)]\!]^{M'} = 1$ From (c) and the semantics for $\rightarrow$ in (19d). ((c) is the antecedent of the conditional in (31).)
(e) $[\![P(x) \rightarrow Q(x)]\!]^{M', g[a/x]} = 0$ From (a) and the semantics for $\rightarrow$ in (19d). (Note that when (a) is assigned as the value of x, $P(x) = 1$ and $Q(x) = 0$.)
(f) $[\![\forall x[P(x) \rightarrow Q(x)]]\!]^{M'} = [\![(31)]\!]^{M'} = 0$ By (e) and the semantics for $\forall$ in (21a)
(g) M' is a model relative to which (32) is true and (31) false

Now let us show that (31) entails (32) but not vice versa.

(31) $\forall x[P(x) \rightarrow Q(x)]$

(32) $\forall x P(x) \rightarrow \forall x Q(x)$

What we did in the preceding box was to assume that (31) is true relative to some (arbitrary) model M and assignment g and then to show that (32) also had to be true relative to M and g and thus that (31) entails (32), by the definition of entailment in (27a). Next we want to show that (32) does not entail (31). To show nonentailment, we have to find a model where (32) is true but (31) is false, which we do in the next box. Finding one such model works because of our definition of entailment, which says that (32) entails (31) only if for *any* model relative to which (32) is true, then (31) is also true. The model M' given in the box below thus shows that (32) does not entail (31).

Exercise 5 A. Show that the following pairs are equivalent:

(1) $a.$ $\forall x P(x)$
$b.$ $\neg \exists x \neg P(x)$

(2) $a.$ $\exists x P(x)$
$b.$ $\neg \forall x \neg P(x)$

B. Show whether the following pairs are logically equivalent:

(3) $a.$ $\forall x[P(x) \wedge Q(x)]$
$b.$ $\forall x P(x) \wedge \forall x Q(x)$

(4) *a.* $\exists x[P(x) \wedge Q(x)]$
b. $\exists xP(x) \wedge \exists xQ(x)$

(5) *a.* $\forall x[P(x) \vee Q(x)]$
b. $\forall xP(x) \vee \forall xQ(x)$

(6) *a.* $\exists x[P(x) \vee Q(x)]$
b. $\exists xP(x) \vee \exists xQ(x)$

(7) *a.* $\forall x_1 \exists x_2 K(x_1, x_2)$
b. $\exists x_2 \forall x_1 K(x_1, x_2)$

C. What do you think would be the fastest way to compute the truth value of the formula below?

(8) $[\forall x \exists y L(x, y) \vee \exists z[L(z, z) \wedge z \neq j]] \wedge \exists y \forall x L(x, y)$

It should be noted that the syntax of PC allows for vacuous binding of variables. So, for example, (33*a*, *b*) are as well formed as (33*c*, *d*):

(33) *a.* $\exists xP(y)$
b. $\forall xP(j)$
c. $P(y)$
d. $P(j)$

But natural languages generally want their quantifiers to do some work; sentences like "Every cat is such that the grass is green" sound quite odd. It turns out, however, that the semantics that we have provided makes (33*a*, *b*) logically equivalent to (33*c*, *d*), respectively. The quantifiers in (33*a*, *b*) make no contribution to the content of the formula they operate on; they are semantically void. To see this, consider the model M and an assignment g such that $[\![(33a)]\!]^{M,g} = 1$. This can be so iff for some $u \in U$, $[\![P(y)]\!]^{M,g[u/x]} = 1$, which is the case iff $g[u/x](y) \in V(P)$. But $g[u/x](y) = g(y)$ because $g[u/x]$ is defined to be just like g in the value it assigns to all variables other than x and thus of course in the value it assigns to y. In other words, if $g(y) \in V(P)$, then for any $u \in U$, $g[u/x](y) \in V(P)$. That is, whether $P(y)$ holds is not going to depend on what one assigns to x. Parallel reasoning shows that if (33*c*) is true, so is (33*a*). Thus formulas containing vacuous quantifiers turn out to have the same truth conditions as the corresponding formulas without them. This is just a technical convenience and is not important for our purposes, given that English and other languages do not use vacuous quantification.

1.2 Quantification in PC versus quantification in English

Quantification in PC bears a connection with quantification in English, but the connection is not straightforward. For example, given our semantics for PC, how would you express some of the most normal quantificational locutions of English, such as those in (34)?

(34) *a.* Some odd number is less than 9.
b. Every odd number is less than 9.
c. (At least) two odd numbers are less than 9.
d. (Exactly) two odd numbers are less than 9.

For concreteness, let us adopt the model M_2 for PC described in exercise 4, and let us further adopt the following simplifying conventions:

(35) *a.* is an odd number $= P$
b. is less than $= <$ (where $\forall x \forall y[x < y \leftrightarrow [K(x, y) \wedge x \neq y])$

Standard practice is to render (34*a*–*d*) as (36*a*–*d*).

(36) *a.* $\exists x[P(x) \wedge x < m]$
b. $\forall x[P(x) \rightarrow x < m]$
c. $\exists x \exists y[x \neq y \wedge P(x) \wedge P(y) \wedge x < m \wedge y < m]$
d. $\exists x \exists y[[x \neq y \wedge P(x) \wedge P(y) \wedge x < m \wedge y < m]$
$\wedge \forall z[[P(z) \wedge x < m] \rightarrow x = z \vee y = z]]$

Sentence (36*a*) literally says that there is something that is an odd number and it is less than 9. It seems uncontroversial that if this is true, then some odd number is less than 9, and vice versa. Thus (36*a*) and (34*a*) appear to have the same truth conditions, which in some sense justifies using (36*a*) as a PC rendering of (34*a*). The same point can be made, perhaps less smoothly, with respect to (36*b*). This says that if anything is an odd number, it is also less than 9. This does seems to be synonymous in content with (34*b*); we cannot think of any situation where one of (34*b*) and (36*b*) would be false and the other true. The only controversial case is a situation where there aren't any odd numbers in the domain. In this case our semantics for PC predicts that (36*b*) is true. What truth value the English sentence (34*b*) receives, however, is not quite so clear-cut.

Let us consider some further English examples:

(37) *a.* Every student registered in Joan's seminar is a genius.
b. Every holder of a winning ticket receives a prize; the problem is that no one ever holds a winning ticket.

c. Mary read every book assigned last semester, if any were assigned.

If you tell us that no students are registered in Joan's seminar, we will not conclude that (37*a*) is thereby rendered false; no one would respond to an utterance of (37*a*) with "No, that's false because no students registered," although one might respond, "Yes, but only because there are no students registered." Certainly it seems odd to utter (37*a*) in a context in which it is apparent that there are no students registered. The degree of oddity associated with universal quantifiers whose domain is potentially empty seems to vary significantly; (37*b*) seems not so bad, and (37*c*) is fine, even though it explicitly allows for the possibility that the domain is empty. So when we say *every student*, we generally (though not always) take for granted or presuppose that there are some. That this piece of information should not be part of the truth-conditional meaning of sentences like (36*a–c*) is supported by its removeability. (See chapter 4, section 5, for discussion of similar cases.)

Consider next (36*c*). It says that there are at least two distinct things that are odd numbers and less than 9. The truth-conditional equivalence of (34*c*) and (36*c*) appears uncontroversial.

Finally, consider (36*d*). It says that there are two distinct things that are odd numbers and less than 9, and furthermore that anything that is an odd number and less than 9 must be identical to one of those two things. This makes (36*d*) false in every situation where there aren't exactly two odd numbers less than 9. The philosopher Bertrand Russell proposed that the definite article expresses the same sort of quantificational import: it says that there is one and only one thing that satisfies the nominal expression to which it is attached. In (38*b*) we give a Russellian rendering of (38*a*).

(38) *a*. The present queen of England is tall.
b. $\exists x[\mathrm{PQE}(x) \wedge \forall y[\mathrm{PQE}(y) \leftrightarrow y = x] \wedge \mathrm{tall}(x)]$

Take a situation where England has two queens: Elizabeth V and Mary III. In such a situation the second conjunct of (38*b*) would be false, for not every queen of England is identical with Mary, nor is every queen of England identical with Elizabeth.

Russell's analysis of the definite article has been widely discussed and is by no means universally endorsed. If someone were to utter (38*a*) at a time when there is no queen of England or when there are two queens of England, listeners might well think that the utterance simply did not come off rather than that it expressed something false. For this reason, use of the definite article is often said, as we mentioned in chapter 1, to *presuppose* that there is exactly one individual entity satisfying the nominal expression to which it is attached. (See chapter 6 for further discussion of presupposition.) Even this, however, seems to need some qualification. We clearly have to extend the analysis so that it can accommodate the use of the definite article with mass nouns (*the snow*) and plurals (*the cats*), neither of which are yet encompassed by our analysis, and we also need to show how to interpret sentences like (39), in which the subject noun phrase may seem to presuppose a unique cat but the prepositional-object noun phrase makes the non-uniqueness of that cat explicit.

(39) The cat hissed at the other cats she saw at the vet's.

There are other issues that we cannot explore here. There are also some ways to defend Russellian analyses in the face of facts like those mentioned above. For our purposes in this text, however, we will simply assume the Russellian account without further discussion.[5]

Notice that in writing formula (38*b*), we have added the one-place predicate *PQE* to the vocabulary of PC; obviously, we are interested in models where *PQE* is interpreted in the same way as the English expression *is presently queen of England*. From now on, we will freely add predicates to PC that correspond to English expressions when we want to use PC formulas to represent the truth conditions for English sentences.

Exercise 6 A. Assume M_2 as a model, and express the following sentences of English in PC.

(1) Everything is odd or not odd.

(2) For every n, the thing that yields n when added to n is 0.

(3) Everything is greater than or equal to itself.

(4) For every number n, the result of adding n to 9 is greater than or equal to 9.

(5) Everything has something greater than it.

B. Add *man*, *smoke*, and *get sick* to PC as one-place predicates (members of the category Pred_1), and assume models where these predicates are interpreted just as in English (that is, the extension of *man* is the set of those individuals in the domain who are men, the extension of *smoke* is those who smoke, and the extension of *get sick* is those who get sick). Give formulas of PC that have the same truth conditions as the following English sentences.

(6) More than two but fewer than five men smoke.

(7) Only men smoke.

(8) No man smokes.

(9) If someone smokes, she or he gets sick.

(10) No more than one man smokes.

In English and other natural languages, quantifying expressions like *every* and *some* are always accompanied by nominal expressions that seem intuitively to restrict the universe of discourse to individuals to which the nominal applies. We noted this in passing in our early informal discussion of sentences containing expressions like *every cat* or *some cat.* Even in maximally generic words like *everything* or *someone, every* and *some* are affixed to the nouns *thing or one*, respectively. In PC, however, we see that expressions like *cat* (or *thing*) have to be represented by a predicate. Sentences like (40*a*, *c*) will be represented as in (40*b*, *d*), respectively.

(40) *a.* Every cat prowls.
b. $\forall x[\text{cat}(x) \rightarrow \text{prowl}(x)]$
c. Some cat prowls.
d. $\exists x[\text{cat}(x) \wedge \text{prowl}(x)]$

Notice that representations of this kind do not make explicit our intuition that *cat* is playing quite a different role from *prowl.* Notice also that the formulas of PC change not only the quantifier but also the connective in the complex formula over which the quantifier has scope; in contrast, the English sentences differ only in the quantifying expression used. There is a way to make the dependence of the quantifier on the nominal explicit; its further advantage is that we need no longer use connectives in translating simple sentences like (40*a*, *c*). In (41*a*, *b*) we represent (40*a*, *c*) using what is called *restricted* quantification.

(41) *a.* $(\forall x\colon \text{cat}(x))\text{prowl}(x)$
b. $(\exists x\colon \text{cat}(x))\text{prowl}(x)$

In logics that use quantification of this type, the range of quantifiers is restricted to those individuals that satisfy the formula immediately following the quantifying expression, "cat(x)" in (41). The quantifiers are then interpreted as before: they require that (*a*) all or (*b*) some of the assignments of values to x that satisfy the restricting formula must also satisfy what follows, "prowl(x)" in (40). If we confine our attention to the quantifiers that we have considered so far, then we can say exactly the same thing whether we use restricted or unrestricted quantification. A difference seems to emerge, however, when we turn to examine expressions like *most.* It can be shown that a quantifier like *most* cannot be represented in PC. To see this, consider what one might try to substitute for the question mark in (42*b*) so that (42*b*) has the same truth conditions as (42*a*). It is easy to verify that neither $\rightarrow$ nor $\wedge$ will do. Yet (42*c*) does the job well if we interpret *most* as telling us that, say, more than half the assignments from the restricted domain of cats are also assignments for which "prowl(x)" is true.

(42) *a.* Most cats prowl.
b. most $x[\text{cat}(x)\ ?\ \text{prowl}(x)]$
c. (most $x\colon \text{cat}(x)$) $\text{prowl}(x)$

These observations have made some linguists conclude that using a notation with restricted quantifiers is more convenient for semantic purposes. While that might be right, it should also be noted that, as we will see, PC turns out to be in need of modifications on various other counts if it (or its semantics) is to be used for linguistic purposes. Such independently needed modifications of PC turn out to allow expression of *most* and similar quantifiers, and thus we see no compelling argument for (or against) the use of restricted quantification for PC itself.[6]

To sum up, PC seems capable of expressing many of the quantificational constructions that one finds in natural language. What we mean by this is that formulas of PC appear to have the same truth conditions (appear to describe the same situations) as sentences of English (relative to a suitable interpretation of the lexical items). This claim is simply based, however, on matching our intuitions about English sentences against the truth conditions explicitly associated with formulas of PC. The problem that we next face is how we match quantificational English sentences with their truth conditions in a more systematic or compositional way. The next section is devoted to this issue.

2 Quantification in English

We have been assuming that semantic interpretation is driven by syntactic structure. We now want to look at how quantificational expressions can be compositionally interpreted, which means that we have to look at what the syntax of English tells us about quantifier scope. Here we run into an interesting problem.

In discussing the syntax and semantics of PC, we said that an occurrence of a variable x_n is bound iff it is c-commanded by a quantifier of the form Qx_n; the syntactic definition we gave of binding was chosen to coincide with the semantic notion of a bound variable as independent of particular assignments. More generally, we defined the scope of a quantifier as what it c-commands, which, in our semantics, will include any variable it might bind and may also include other quantifiers and operators with which its interpretation interacts. The syntax of PC is designed to express scope relations unambiguously: if quantifier Q_1 is in the scope of Q_2, then the interpretation of Q_1 is in some sense embedded within or dependent on that of Q_2, as we saw in calculating truth conditions. Unfortunately, in English overt syntactic dominance does not provide a reliable guide to semantic dominance.

Exercise 7 In exercise 2 you provided a definition of bound and free variables applicable to the PC syntax specified in (15). How would you define the scope of a quantifier for that same syntax?

You may remember that in chapter 1 we briefly discussed some examples of scope ambiguity. For example, sentences like (43*a*) appear to be semantically ambiguous. The two readings that (43*a*) seems to have can be represented by the two formulas (43*b*, *c*):

(43) *a.* Everyone loves someone.
b. $\forall x \exists y[\text{love}(x, y)]$
c. $\exists y \forall x[\text{love}(x, y)]$

In (43*b*) the existential quantifier associated with the direct object in (43*a*) is in the scope of the universal quantifier associated with the subject. In this situation we say that the universal quantifier has *wide scope*, the existential quantifier *narrow scope*. Formula (43*b*) says that everyone loves some person or other. In (43*c*) the opposite is true; the existential quantifier has wide scope, the universal quantifier narrow scope. Formula (43*c*) says that there is (at least) one person that everybody loves.

In chapter 2, F_1 allowed distinct syntactic structures to correspond to a single surface string; by interpreting structures rather than strings, we could assign a single interpretation to each sentential structure and at the same time allow multiple interpretations for syntactically ambiguous strings. Many English strings of words can be shown to be associated with distinct structures on syntactic grounds alone; frequently the distinct syntactic structures are associated with distinct interpretations, as we mentioned in chapter 1. Various constituency tests can be used to justify the assumption that (44*a*), for example, has the two structures shown in (44*b*, *c*).

(44) *a.* John hit a boy with a pair of binoculars.
b. [John hit [$_{NP}$ a boy with a pair of binoculars]]
c. [John hit [$_{NP}$ a boy][$_{PP}$ with a pair of binoculars]]

In (44*b*) the prepositional phrase (PP) forms a constituent with and semantically modifies the NP *a boy*; in (44*c*) it does not form a constituent with the NP *a boy*; it modifies the V *hit*. (We leave it open as to whether the PP in (44*c*) is attached to the VP or the S.) These hypotheses can be confirmed in various ways. For example, under the assumption that only equal categories can conjoin, one would expect that [$_{NP}$ a boy with a pair of binoculars] in (44*b*) could conjoin with other NPs and that the result should be semantically unambiguous. This is indeed so.

(45) John hit a dog, a boy with a pair of binoculars, and a girl.

Sentence (45) can only mean that John hit a dog, a boy who was carrying a pair of binoculars, and a girl.

Furthermore, on the assumption that one cannot extract PPs out of NPs, only in (44*c*) should we be able to question the PP. Thus one would expect the result of questioning the PP to be unambiguously associated with the reading (44*c*). Again, this seems to be so:

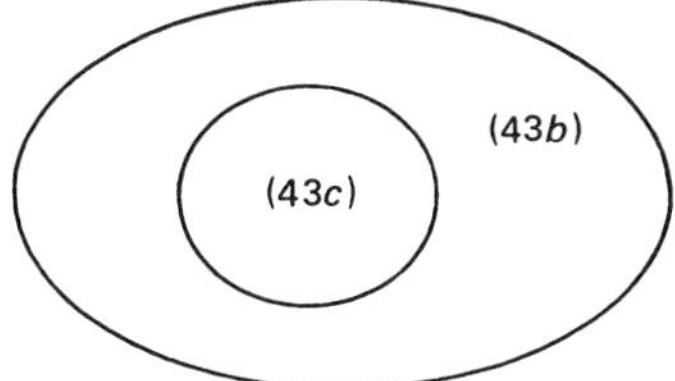

Figure 3.1

(46) With what did John hit a boy?

Introductory syntax textbooks provide abundant discussions of such cases.

It is far less clear, however, that the string in (43*a*) is associated with distinct syntactic structures corresponding to formulas (43*b*, *c*). The problem here is that independent syntactic evidence that there are distinct structures associated with (43*a*) is not so easy to come by. In particular, no simple-minded (surface) constituency test, like the ones illustrated in (45) and (46), appears to be able to detect ambiguities of any kind.

One might try to argue, as has been done in, for example, Reinhart (1979), that there is no ambiguity in (43*a*), on the grounds that the two readings are not logically independent: (43*c*) entails (43*b*) (but not vice versa). This means that the set of circumstances where (43*b*) obtains is a proper superset of the set of circumstances where (43*c*) obtains, as is shown in figure 3.1.

In chapter 2 a similar situation came up in connection with exclusive versus inclusive *or*, and we used it to argue *against* the ambiguity of *or*. By parallel reasoning we could argue that (43*a*) is semantically associated with the more general reading (43*b*). The more specific reading, where the loved one happens to be the same for everybody, is not thereby excluded and can be the intended one under suitable contextual conditions.

To implement this view, one must claim that some principle fixes the scope of quantifiers so that no scope ambiguity arises. For instance, on the basis of examples like (43*a*) one could claim that quantifiers are interpreted in their linear left-to-right order (in terms of c-commanding at the surface structure, the c-commanding quantifier has wide scope, as in Reinhart's proposal). The problem is, however, that any such principle should provide a procedure that always associates the most general reading with a certain sequence of quantifiers, in the way that the principles just mentioned do with respect to (43*a*). But this does not seem very likely, as the following examples suggest:

(47) *a.* There was a name tag near every plate.
b. A flag was hanging in front of every window.[7]
c. A student guide took every visitor to two museums.

In (47*a*, *b*) the preferred reading is not the one that one would expect in terms of the left-to-right (or c-command) condition. Such a principle would assign *a name tag* (or *a flag*) wide scope over *every plate* (*every window*), which yields the more restrictive of the two possible readings. Thus the reading where *every plate* (*every window*) has wide scope, the preferred one, cannot be derived by appealing to contextual or pragmatic factors. A mechanism for assigning wide scope to the rightmost NPs seems to be needed. Furthermore, in (47*c*), of all six possible quantifier construals, the most general one (the one entailed by all the others) is the one where the second quantifier has scope over the other two. It is difficult to see what principle could account for cases like those in both (43) and (47).

Perhaps one way to rescue the idea that sentences like (43) are unambiguous might be the following: in interpreting a sentence, always assign wide scope to *every* and narrow scope to *some, two*, etc. But this too appears to run into difficulties. Consider the following:

(48) *a.* Everyone loves someone I know.
a′. $\forall x \exists y[\text{know}(I, y) \wedge \text{love}(x, y)]$
b. It is not the case that everyone loves someone I know.
b′. $\neg \forall x \exists y[\text{know}(I, y) \wedge \text{love}(x, y)]$

According to the proposal just outlined, (48*a*) would have only the reading specified in (48*a′*). The other alleged reading (where there is just one person I know that everyone loves) would be a special case of (48*a′*), one where the person everyone loves happens to be the same one. It follows, then, that since (48*a*) on such a proposal would be unambiguous, the only possible reading for the negation of (48*a*), namely (48*b*), would be the one shown in (48*b′*). Imagine now the following scenario. I know many people, and everyone likes someone or other among them. However, there is no person I know that everyone loves: not everyone loves Sue, not everyone loves John, not everyone loves Mary, and so on. It seems to us that it would be perfectly appropriate to report such a situation by

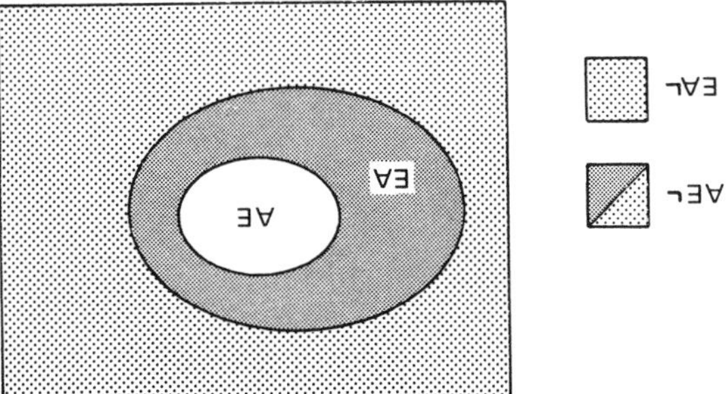

Figure 3.2

means of (48*b*). That is, (48*b*) could well be true in the scenario we just set up. (If you have trouble getting this interpretation for (48*b*), try uttering the sentence with focal stress on *not* and with the embedded sentence carrying no focal stresses.) However, notice that (48*b*′) would be false in such a scenario, for everyone does love one of my friends or another. So the proposal we have considered seems to predict that a certain reading is absent from (48*b*), contrary to what appear to be the facts.

One can see what goes wrong with such a proposal by examining its logic again, which goes as follows. The two alleged readings of a sentence like (49*a*) stand in the relation shown in (49*b*).

(49) *a*. Everyone loves someone.
b. $\exists\forall \rightarrow \forall\exists$
c. $\neg\forall\exists \rightarrow \neg\exists\forall$

So one can assign the more general $\forall\exists$ reading to (49*a*) and argue that the $\exists\forall$ reading arises as a special case. This is appealing, as it prevents us from positing an ambiguity for which we have no evidence other than these scope phenomena. The problem, however, is that negation reverses entailments such as the one in (49*b*). Under negation we get the pattern in (49*c*), where $\neg\exists\forall$ is the more general reading (the entailed one). This is illustrated in figure 3.2. In this figure the situations associated with (a certain reading of) a sentence are represented as a portion of a space, and entailment can be visualized as inclusion (*A* entails *B* if the space of possibilities corresponding to *A* is included in the space of possibilities corresponding to *B*). Negation takes us from the space associated with a sentence to the space excluded by it. The reader can easily check that if *A* is a subregion of *B*, then $\neg B$ must be a subregion of $\neg A$.

The interpretation assigned to a negative sentence ought to be just the negation of the interpretation assigned to its positive counterpart. But, as we have seen, the interpretation of $\neg\forall\exists$ is not general enough to cover all readings associated with negative sentences like (48*b*), and thus the strategy of assigning positive sentences like (48*a*) only the more general $\forall\exists$ reading is problematic. (In contrast, negated disjunctions *do* have the narrow range of interpretations predicted by assigning only the general inclusive reading to *or* [see chapter 4, p. 251].)

It has often been noted that intonational phenomena interact with scopal-interpretation possibilities. If (49a) is uttered with focal stress on *someone*, it is virtually obligatory to give it the more general interpretation, that is, to understand the unstressed subject NP as having wide scope. The speaker will be understood as making only the general claim and as refusing to endorse the more specific claim. But if focal stress is on *everyone* and *someone* is destressed, then the more narrow reading seems equally plausible (though the more general interpretation does not disappear). There has been considerable interesting work on focus in recent years (see, e.g., Rooth 1996), and a better understanding of just how focal stress and other focal constructions constrain the interpretation of scopal relations is becoming possible. Unless there are potential scopal ambiguities, however, it is hard to see how focus could help disambiguate scopal relations. Thus the intonational facts, complex as they are, seem to support our claim that scope ambiguities are encountered in English.

So we are led to conclude that, on our current understanding of quantificational dependencies, scope ambiguities are real. A sentence containing quantified NPs is, in general, semantically ambiguous as to how the scope relations of its NPs may be understood. Even if no single sentence may allow us to construe the scope of its NPs in any old order, nevertheless, any old order seems to occur in some sentence or other. It appears less ad hoc, then, to assume that any quantifier-scope construal is possible in principle as far as the basic semantics of quantification goes, and that other factors may rule certain construals out. In addition to pragmatic factors, which are always important in ambiguity resolution, we will almost certainly find that the semantics of focus plays some role, along with perhaps properties of certain particular lexical items. To avoid positing scopal ambiguities for quantified phrases looks ultimately more complicated than dealing with them, and examples like (47) suggest that it is also empirically inadequate.

If there are scope ambiguities, the problem is *where* to resolve them. Two major kinds of strategies come to mind as we try to develop compositional rules that can assign (43*a*) both the truth conditions associated with (43*b*) and those associated with (43*c*). The first treats the scope ambiguities of a sentence as basically semantic and complicates rules of semantic interpretation to allow them to assign distinct specifications of truth conditions to a single syntactic structure. The second hypothesizes a more abstract level of syntactic structure than the surface structure and provides distinct syntactic structures to associate with sentence (43*a*) and to serve as input to the recursive rules of semantic interpretations.

Cooper (1983) is the earliest explicit attempt to pursue the first strategy, and other researchers (e.g., Jacobson 1992) have developed some quite sophisticated and subtle semantic analyses of quantification and related phenomena that allow us to keep the approach to English syntax very simple. The semantic techniques involved, however, are significantly more complex than those afforded us by PC. And they are often easier to understand if one already has a grounding in the more standard semantic ideas of PC and similar languages. We will thus pursue the second kind of strategy here.

PC itself is, of course, an example of a strategy of the second kind in dealing with scope, as it provides a syntactic characterization of the scope of a quantifier. What we might hope to do is find evidence for a more abstract level of English syntax that somehow resembles more closely the syntax of PC.

Recent syntactic theories of all kinds have found it necessary to articulate and enrich syntactic structure with notions that go well beyond representing the immediate surface constituents on which we relied in testing the syntactic structure of (44). What we do below is adapt one such proposal that uses the notions of *movement* and *traces* developed in the Chomskyan Revised Extended Standard Theory and its successor, Government Binding Theory. There are other syntactic theories around, and Chomsky himself has recently developed the somewhat different minimalist framework. Our interest, however, is not in endorsing any particular syntactic proposals but in finding an intuitively accessible and relatively familiar framework that allows us to illustrate how a grammar might deal with some of the quantificational phenomena we have noted.

2.1 Syntactic preliminaries

In this section we summarize briefly the main syntactic notions that we are going to use in what follows. As we noted above, our interest is in illustrating how a grammar of English might represent some of the quantificational phenomena we have noted, and we are adopting a very simple syntax that allows us to do that relatively easily. Readers familiar with post-1965 transformational approaches may skip this section.

The development of transformational syntax after 1965 (the date of publication of *Aspects of the Theory of Syntax*) led to a model of grammar usually schematized as follows:

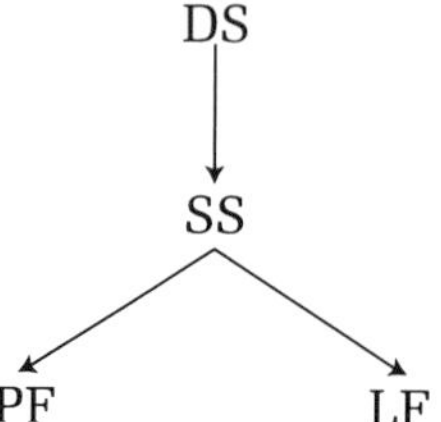

Each node in the diagram (namely, DS, SS, PF, and LF) stands for a distinct level of grammatical representation. DS stands for deep structure (also abbreviated as D-structure), SS stands for surface structure (also abbreviated as S-structure), PF stands for phonological form, and LF for logical form. These levels are derivationally linked as indicated by the arrows. In generating a sentence, the grammar first produces its D-structure. This is then mapped onto the corresponding S-structure. The S-structure is the input to two interpretive components. On the one hand, the S-structure of a sentence is mapped onto a phonological form. On the other hand, it is mapped onto one or more logical forms, which are then semantically interpreted. We will say more about LF shortly.

Each level is subject to certain conditions of well-formedness. For a sentence to be well formed, it must be well formed at each level. D-structure represents, in the form of phrase-structure markers, the structural properties of sentences that can be directly projected from their lexical makeup. D-structure is mapped onto S-structure by moving constituents out of their allowable D-structure positions by application of a very general rule: move any constituent α anywhere.[8] Various independent constraints prevent the "move α" rule from overgenerating. Sentences like (50*b*, *d*) can be seen as derived via the "move α" rule from the D-structures associated with (50*a*, *c*), respectively.

(50) *a.* John likes beans.
b. Beans, John likes.
c. John wonders Bill bought what.
d. John wonders what Bill bought.

In the case of (59*a*, *b*), both structures are well formed, whereas the "unmoved" structure in (50*c*) is ungrammatical (although syntactic arguments can be provided for positing something like it as the DS source of (50*d*)). One can describe the relation between (50*a*, *c*) and (50*b*, *d*) by saying that in (50*b*, *d*) a constituent has been dislocated to clause-initial position. Various properties of dislocated constituents, such as interrogative and relative pronouns or topicalized expressions, depend on their DS position. For example, case markings on dislocated constituents may depend on where they come from:

(51) *a.* *Whom did you say ____ came late?
b. Whom did you say John met ____?
c. To whom did Joan give the book ____?

As (51) illustrates, accusative case on interrogative pronouns in English is acceptable only if the question concerns what would be an accusative case complement of a verb or preposition. This shows that the position of the dislocated constituent in (51*b*, *c*) and the position of the gap—a position with which accusative case marking is associated—must be somehow related. Movement is one plausible way of capturing such relatedness.

More specifically, it is assumed that moved constituents leave behind either a silent copy, as in (52*a*), where it is marked in italics, or an empty node coindexed with the moved constituent, as in (52*b*):

(52) *a.* [$_{S'}$ whom [$_S$ did you say [$_S$ John met [$_{NP}$ *whom*]]]]
b. [$_{S'}$ whom$_i$ [$_S$ did you say [$_S$ John met [$_{NP}$ e_i]]]]

The constituent left behind by a moved element is called a *trace*. We will adopt the notation in (52*b*), though nothing we say hinges on this assumption. These phonologically unrealized or empty elements are argued to produce audible effects in certain contexts. In English, for instance, there is a contraction process that turns *want* + *to* sequences into *wanna*. *Wanna* contraction appears to be blocked by traces intervening between *want* and *to*, as illustrated in (53).

(53) *a.* Who do you wanna invite?
b. $[_{S'}$ who$_i$ $[_S$ do you want to invite $e_i]]$
c. *Who do you wanna come?
d. $[_{S'}$ who$_i$ $[_S$ do you want e_i to come$]]$

If syntactic structure encodes information about positions that are not pronounced (via movement as we have just described or by some other method, e.g., copying a trace into the appropriate position), then facts such as those in (53) can be plausibly explained as the blocking of a phonological process triggered by structural elements (traces). Data such as those in (53) are arguably more difficult to explain in terms of theories of syntax that eschew abstract empty nodes.

The view of movement just sketched can be useful in dealing with quantifier scope as well. One can imagine representing the scope of quantified NPs by adjoining them to the site over which they are supposed to have scope. Thus, for example, the two NPs in (54*a*) could be fronted (by the "move α" rule) in either order, which yields the two structures in (54*b*, *c*).

(54) *a.* Everyone loves someone.
b. $[_S$ everyone$_i$ $[_S$ someone$_j$ $[_S$ e_i loves $e_j]]]$
c. $[_S$ someone$_j$ $[_S$ everyone$_i$ $[_S$ e_i loves $e_j]]]$
d. $\forall x \exists y[\text{loves}(x, y)]$
e. $\exists y \forall x[\text{loves}(x, y)]$

The two structures in (54*b*, *c*) could then be unambiguously mapped onto the truth conditions associated with (54*d*, *e*) respectively. Note that we actually do have overt though somewhat stilted structures in English that make the scopal relations explicit. Sentence (55*a*) has the truth conditions of (54*d*), whereas the truth conditions of (55*b*) are those of (54*e*).

(55) *a.* Everyone is such that someone loves them.
b. Someone is such that everyone loves them.[9]

Thus one can imagine having both overt movement that actually dislocates constituents in surface structure (as in the examples in (50)) and covert movement whose role is purely interpretive, perhaps with properties similar to those of overt movement (and perhaps obeying similar constraints). Covert movement yields disambiguated structures that constitute the input to semantic interpretation. Movement used to represent quantificational scope is generally called *quantifier raising* (QR), and the level of syntactic structure that QR gives rise to is called *Logical Form* (LF).

Although the notion of LF in linguistics bears some relation to the characterizations of logical form one finds in the logico-philosophical literature (which we will discuss in section 3), it is not to be identified with it. LF is a level of syntactic representation where scope and possibly other relations relevant to semantic interpretation are overtly displayed.[10] LF mediates between surface syntactic structures and meaning (truth conditions). As such it is a technical notion of syntactic theory, and we restrict the use of the acronym *LF* accordingly.

In some recent developments of the Principles and Parameters framework, it has been argued that no principle of grammar actually makes reference to D-structure or S-structure. Words are taken from the lexicon, merged together, and moved according to general principles. At some point of the derivation (a point that may vary from language to language), a process spells out the structure at that stage; the derivation then goes on until the input to semantic interpretation, namely LF, is reached. As our interest here is how LF is interpreted, we can afford to stay neutral on syntactic issues such as these. We will keep referring to S-structure, which under the developments just mentioned could be reinterpreted as the level at which "spell out" applies. What is important to us is that there is a level of syntactic representation at which quantifier scope is structurally represented. We assume that this spelling out happens by whatever is responsible for overt syntactic movement. Other ways of dealing with scope have been proposed within the generative tradition. The semantic methods to be illustrated in the next section can be modified, as far as we can see, to apply to most ways of disambiguating surface syntactic structures with regard to the scope of quantified NPs, though not all (see, e.g. Jacobson's variable-free approach, illustrated in Jacobson 1992 and elsewhere).

This discussion gives only a very rough overview of some widely used syntactic terminology that we will adopt in setting up our sample grammar in the form of a fragment of English with quantified NPs. As before, our English fragment is offered for pedagogical purposes only: in particular, our interest is in the semantic techniques it lets us illustrate and not in the particular syntactic analyses of English it embodies.

2.2 The fragment F_2

To illustrate some of the problems involved in spelling out the truth conditions of sentences containing quantified NPs, we will now formally describe a fragment of English, F_2, that includes some elementary forms of quantification. F_2 is generated by a set of phrase-structure rules. The syntactic structures admitted by this set of rules undergo a quantifier-raising transformation. In light of what we discussed in 2.1, we shall call the phrase markers associated with sentences generated by the phrase-structure rules *S-structures* and the phrase markers generated by applying quantifier raising to S-structures *LF structures*. A compositional model-theoretic interpretation is provided for LF structures. Thus sentences are going to interpreted *relative to* (one of their) LF structures. As we are not dealing in this fragment with relative clauses, questions, or other constructions involving overt syntactic movement, we will not need distinct levels for D-structure and S-structure.

2.2.1 The syntax of F_2 With this in mind, let us consider the syntactic rules for F_2. As is usual, we will use $\rightarrow$ for phrase structure rules and $\Rightarrow$ for transformations.

(56) *a.* S $\rightarrow$ NP VP
b. S $\rightarrow$ S conj S
c. S $\rightarrow$ neg S
d. VP $\rightarrow$ V_t NP
e. VP $\rightarrow$ V_i
f. VP $\rightarrow$ V_{dt} NP PP[to]
g. NP $\rightarrow$ Det N_C
h. PP[to] $\rightarrow$ to NP
i. Det $\rightarrow$ the, a, every
j. N_p $\rightarrow$ Pavarotti, Loren, Bond
k. N_c $\rightarrow$ book, fish, man, woman
l. V_i $\rightarrow$ is boring, is hungry
m. V_t $\rightarrow$ likes, hates
n. V_{dt} $\rightarrow$ gives, shows
o. conj $\rightarrow$ and, or
p. neg $\rightarrow$ it is not the case that
q. NP $\rightarrow$ N_p

The rule for quantifier raising is (57), where NP is [Det N_C].

(57) $[_S \text{ X NP Y}] \Rightarrow [_S \text{ NP}_i [_S \text{ X } e_i \text{ Y}]]$

Notice that QR, the rule given in (57), coindexes the moved NP with the trace that it enters in the original position of the NP.

Here is an example of a sentence generated by F_2, along with its (six!) possible LF structures. One of these structures is presented in full, the others in abbreviated form.

(58) *a.* Every man gave a book to the woman.

b.

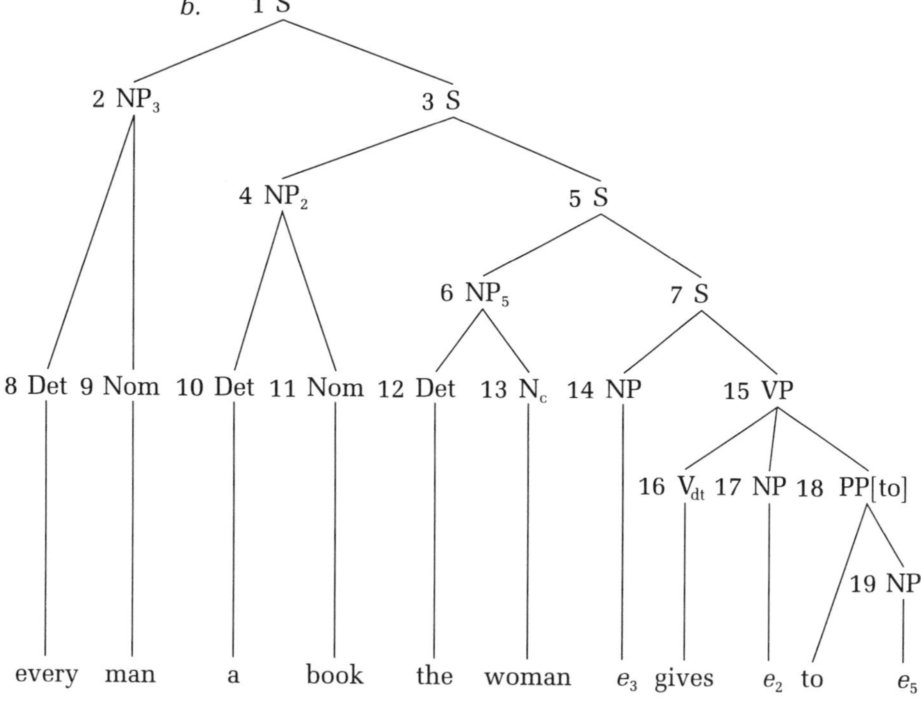

c. [[every man]$_3$ [[the woman]$_5$ [[a book]$_2$ [e_3 gives e_2 to e_5]]]]

d. [[a book]$_2$ [[every man]$_3$ [[the woman]$_5$ [e_3 gives e_2 to e_5]]]]

e. [[a book]$_2$ [[the woman]$_5$ [[every man]$_3$ [e_3 gives e_2 to e_5]]]]

f. [[the woman]$_5$ [[every man]$_3$ [[a book]$_2$ [e_3 gives e_2 to e_5]]]]

g. [[the woman]$_5$ [[a book]$_2$ [[every man]$_3$ [e_3 gives e_2 to e_5]]]]

2.2.2 The semantics of F_2 We begin by first providing an example of a particular model for F_2. Let $M_3 = \langle U_3, V_3 \rangle$, where U_3 and V_3 are defined as follows:

(59) *a.* U_3 = {Bond, Pavarotti, Loren, *War and Peace, Aspects*}

b. V_3(likes) = {⟨Bond, Loren⟩, ⟨Pavarotti, Loren⟩, ⟨Loren, *Aspects*⟩, ⟨Bond, *War and Peace*⟩, ⟨Pavarotti, Pavarotti⟩}

V_3(hates) = {⟨Bond, Pavarotti⟩}

$V_3(\text{gives}) = \{\langle \text{Bond, } \textit{Aspects}\text{, Loren}\rangle,$
$\quad\langle \text{Pavarotti, } \textit{War and Peace}\text{, Loren}\rangle\}$
$V_3(\text{is hungry}) = \{\text{Pavarotti, Bond}\}$
$V_3(\text{is boring}) = \varnothing$
$V_3(\text{Pavarotti}) = \text{Pavarotti}$
$V_3(\text{Bond}) = \text{Bond}$
$V_3(\text{Loren}) = \text{Loren}$
$V_3(\text{book}) = \{\textit{War and Peace}, \textit{Aspects}\}$
$V_3(\text{man}) = \{\text{Bond, Pavarotti}\}$
$V_3(\text{woman}) = \{\text{Loren}\}$
$V_3(\text{fish}) = \varnothing$

$$V_3(\text{and}) = \begin{bmatrix} \langle 1,1\rangle \to 1 \\ \langle 1,0\rangle \to 0 \\ \langle 0,1\rangle \to 0 \\ \langle 0,0\rangle \to 0 \end{bmatrix}$$

Similarly for *or* and *it is not the case that.*

The model itself says nothing about the interpretation of traces. Along with model M_3, we will also define a particular assignment function, g_3, to assign a value to traces. In particular, let us assume that for any $n, g_3(e_n) =$ Pavarotti.

What we have done above is provide a *particular* model and assignment function for evaluating sentences relative to particular LFs in the English fragment F_2. Particular models can be thought of as part of what speakers in some sense access on particular occasions of language use. The domain, what is being talked about, can vary, and of course the facts will vary, that is, the extension of particular lexical constants can vary. But certain aspects of lexical interpretation are fixed. Speakers may not know the full details of the model, e.g., they may not know who is hungry (that is not part of semantic knowledge), but they do know that *is hungry* is picking out the set of those with a certain property, being hungry.

All models for F_2 have certain general properties, e.g., they assign sets of individuals as the value of intransitive verbs. These and the recursive semantic rules, which we give below, constitute part of speakers' semantic competence. But as we have noted, speakers also have more specific knowledge about the allowable interpretation of lexical constants in F_2 models they might access. Let us define an *admissible model for F_2* as one in which the general interpretation of lexical constants is constrained by the semantic knowledge of English speakers. Because F_2 is intended as a fragment of English, we will also speak of F_2 models for English. An admissible F_2 model for English is any model $M = \langle U, V \rangle$ such that

$$V(\text{gives}) = \{\langle x, y, z \rangle : x, y, \text{ and } z \text{ are in } U \text{ and } x \text{ gives } y \text{ to } z\},$$

$$V(\text{is hungry}) = \{x : x \text{ is in } U \text{ and } x \text{ is hungry}\},$$

and so on. Similarly, if Bond is a member of U, then $V(\text{Bond}) =$ Bond.

There may be some variability allowed in interpretation of lexical constants on different occasions of use—e.g., in this book we ask you to interpret some ordinary English words in special technical ways—and thus admissible models may not completely fix the concepts associated with particular words. But there seem to be substantial constraints on lexical interpretation that are part of speakers' semantic competence, and these constraints limit the class of admissible F_2 models for English. From now on, when we speak of models for the English fragment F_2, we will only be interested in F_2 models for English.

We provide next the recursive part of the semantic rules. As before, we want to associate each syntactic rule with a semantic one. After each semantic rule, we indicate the corresponding syntactic rule. As this part of the semantics is independent of any particular choice of model, we will relativize it to an arbitrary model for English M and an assignment g.

(60) *a.* If A is a lexical category and β a trace term,
$[\![[_A \beta]]\!]^{M,g} = g(\beta)$;
otherwise, $[\![[_A \beta]]\!]^{M,g} = V(\beta)$ (56*j–o*)
b. $[\![[_A B]]\!]^{M,g} = [\![B]\!]^{M,g}$ for A, B of any category (56*e, q*)
c. $[\![[_{PP} \text{ to NP}]]\!]^{M,g} = [\![\text{NP}]\!]^{M,g}$ (56*h*)
d. $[\![[\text{NP VP}]]\!]^{M,g} = 1$ iff $[\![\text{NP}]\!]^{M,g} \in [\![\text{VP}]\!]^{M,g}$ (56*a*)
e. $[\![[\text{S}_1 \text{ conj S}_2]]\!]^{M,g} = [\![\text{conj}]\!]^{M,g}(\langle [\![\text{S}_1]\!]^{M,g}, [\![\text{S}_2]\!]^{M,g} \rangle)$ (56*b*)
f. $[\![[\text{neg S}]]\!]^{M,g} = [\![\text{neg}]\!]^{M,g}([\![\text{S}]\!]^{M,g})$ (56*c*)
g. $[\![[\text{V NP}]]\!]^{M,g} = \{x : \langle x, [\![\text{NP}]\!]^{M,g} \rangle \in [\![\text{V}]\!]^{M,g}\}$ (56*d*)
h. $[\![[\text{V NP PP}]]\!]^{M,g} = \{x : \langle x, [\![\text{NP}]\!]^{M,g}, [\![\text{PP}]\!]^{M,g} \rangle \in [\![\text{V}]\!]^{M,g}\}$ (56*f*)
i. $[\![[[\text{every } \beta]_i \text{ S}]]\!]^{M,g} = 1$ iff for all $u \in U$, if $u \in [\![\beta]\!]^{M,g}$,
then $[\![\text{S}]\!]^{M,g[u/e_i]} = 1$ (QR)
j. $[\![[[\text{a } \beta]_i \text{ S}]]\!]^{M,g} = 1$ iff for some $u \in U$, $u \in [\![\beta]\!]^{M,g}$
and $[\![\text{S}]\!]^{M,g[u/e_i]} = 1$ (QR)
k. $[\![[[\text{the } \beta]_i \text{ S}]]\!]^{M,g} = 1$ iff for some $u \in U$, $[\![\beta]\!]^{M,g} = \{u\}$
and $[\![\text{S}]\!]^{M,g[u/e_i]} = 1$ (QR)

Except for relativizing our interpretation to a model and assignment function rather than simply to a situation, semantic rules

(60*a*–*h*) look just like the rules in chapter 2 for F_1 (expanded by exercise 8 at the end of the chapter). And the clauses that interpret the semantic contribution of raised quantificational NPs work very much like our semantics for the logical quantifiers in PC. The indefinite article, *a*, works just like the existential quantifier except that we do not have access to the entire domain of individuals but just those satisfying the nominal to which the article is attached; with *every*, we have similarly restricted universal quantification. The semantic contribution made by NPs with the definite article, *the*, is what the Russellian analysis specifies (see pp. 143–144 above). In all three rules interpreting the contribution of quantificational NPs, we make use of modified assignment functions, as we did for PC. Traces are the expressions in F_2 that work semantically like the variables of PC.

Let us illustrate the working of the present semantics with an example. We will first compute the truth conditions of (58*a*), relative to the LF in (58*b*), in an arbitrary F_2 model for English and then go on to compute its truth value in the particular model M_3. Of course, we also need a particular assignment function to assign a value to traces, and we will use g_3, defined above as $g_3(e_n) =$ Pavarotti for all *n*. We repeat (58*a*–*b*) here.

(58) *a.* Every man gave a book to the woman.

b.

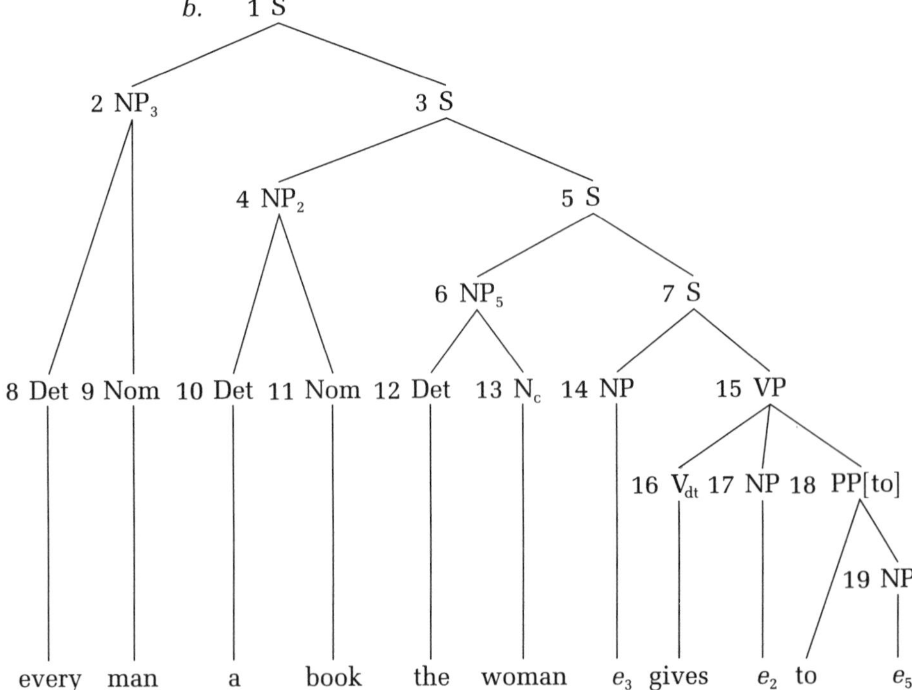

Our strategy is essentially the same as that we used for calculating the semantic values of expressions in PC. We start with the outermost quantifying expression and work our way in. We will calculate the truth conditions for an arbitrary F_2 model for English M and assignment function g in tedious detail. In calculating the truth conditions for the particular model M_3 and assignment function g_3, we will be less thorough. (Numbers refer to nodes in (58*b*).) Notice that we made critical use of our assumption that M was an F_2 model for English in the last step. If we had not made that assumption, we would have had to stop with (*j*). In that case, our truth conditions would have made reference just to membership in V(man), V(book), V(woman), and V(gives), and we would not have been guaranteed anything about men giving books to women. Now let's calculate the truth value of our LF structure relative to M_3 and g_3 (see the box on p. 164). The computation is in some respects just like that above, but our interest in M_3 will be the particular facts it

Calculation of the truth conditions of (58*a*) relative to LF (58*b*)

(*a*) $[\![(55b)]\!]^{M,g} = 1$ iff for all $u \in U$, if $u \in V(\text{man})$, then $[\![3]\!]^{M,g[u/e_3]} = 1$ By (60*i*)

(*b*) $[\![3]\!]^{M,g[u/e_3]} = 1$ iff for some $u' \in U, u' \in V(\text{book})$, $[\![5]\!]^{M,g[[u/e_3]u'/e_2]} = 1$ By (60*j*)

(*c*) $[\![5]\!]^{M,g[[u/e_3]u'/e_2]} = 1$ iff for some $u'' \in U$, $V(\text{woman}) = \{u''\}$ and $[\![7]\!]^{M,g[[[u/e_3]u'/e_2]u''/e_5]} = 1$ By (60*k*)

(*d*) $g[[[u/e_3]u'/e_2]u''/e_5](e_3) = u$
$g[[[u/e_3]u'/e_2]u''/e_5](e_2) = u'$
$g[[[u/e_3]u'/e_2]u''/e_5](e_5) = u''$
By definition of modified assignment functions

(*e*) $[\![7]\!]^{M,g[[[u/e_3]u'/e_2]u''/e_5]} = 1$
iff $[\![14]\!]^{M,g[[[u/e_3]u'/e_2]u''/e_5]} \in [\![15]\!]^{M,g[[[u/e_3]u'/e_2]u''/e_5]}$ By (60*d*)

(*f*) $[\![14]\!]^{M,g[[[u/e_3]u'/e_2]u''/e_5]} = u$ By (*d*) and (60*a*)

(*g*) $[\![16]\!]^{M,g[[[u/e_3]u'/e_2]u''/e_5]} = V(\text{gives})$ By (60*a*)
$[\![17]\!]^{M,g[[[u/e_3]u'/e_2]u''/e_5]} = u'$ By (60*a*), (*d*)
$[\![18]\!]^{M,g[[[u/e_3]u'/e_2]u''/e_5]} = u''$ By (60*a*), (60*c*), (*d*)

(*h*) $[\![15]\!]^{M,g[[[u/e_3]u'/e_2]u''/e_5]} = \{x : \langle x, u', u''\rangle \in V(\text{gives})\}$ By (*g*) and (60*h*)

(*i*) $[\![17]\!]^{M,g[[[u/e_3]u'/e_2]u''/e_5]} = 1$ iff $\langle u, u', u''\rangle \in V(\text{gives})$ By (*h*) and definition of set membership

(*j*) $[\![(55b)]\!]^{M,g} = 1$ iff for all $u \in U$, if $u \in V(\text{man})$, there is some $u' \in U$, $u' \in V(\text{book})$, and some $u'' \in U$, such that $V(\text{woman}) = \{u''\}$ and $\langle u, u', u''\rangle \in V(\text{gives})$ By (*a*) through (*i*)

(*k*) $[\![(55b)]\!]^{M,g} = 1$ iff for all $u \in U$ such that u is a man, there is some $u' \in U$, u' a book, and some $u'' \in U$, u'' the only woman in U, such that u gives u' to u'' By (*j*) and the assumption that M is an F_2 model for English

Computation of the truth value of (58*b*) relative to M_3 and g_3

(a) $[\![(58b)]\!]^{M_3, g_3} = 1$ iff for all $u \in U$, if $u \in V_3(\text{man})$, then $[\![3]\!]^{[M_3, g_3[u/e_3]} = 1$ By (60*i*)

(b) $V_3(\text{man}) = \{\text{Pa}, \text{Bo}\}$ By (59*b*)

Go to subbox 1, and assign Pa to e_3; i.e., consider $g_3[\text{Pa}/e_3]$.

1 (a) $[\![3]\!]^{M_3, g_3[\text{Pa}/e_3]} = 1$ iff for some $u' \in U, u' \in V(\text{book}) = \{W\&P, Asp\}$, $[\![5]\!]^{M, g[[\text{Pa}/e_3]u'/e_2]} = 1$ By (59*b*) and (60*j*)

(b) Assign $W\&P$ to e_2; i.e., consider $g_3[[\text{Pa}/e_3]W\&P/e_2]$

(c) $[\![5]\!]^{M_3, g_3[[\text{Pa}/e_3]W\&P/e_2]} = 1$ iff for some $u'' \in U$, $V(\text{woman}) = \{u''\}$ and $[\![7]\!]^{M_3, g_3[[[\text{Pa}/e_3]W\&P/e_2]u''/e_5]} = 1$ By (60*k*)

(d) $V(\text{woman}) = \{\text{Lo}\}$ By (59*b*)

(e) $[\![5]\!]^{M_3, g_3[[\text{Pa}/e_3]W\&P/e_2]} = 1$ iff $[\![7]\!]^{M_3, g_3[[[\text{Pa}/e_3]W\&P/e_2]\text{Lo}/e_5]} = 1$ By (c), (d)

(f) $[\![7]\!]^{M_3, g_3[[[\text{Pa}/e_3]W\&P/e_2]\text{Lo}/e_5]} = 1$ iff $\langle \text{Pa}, W\&P, \text{Lo} \rangle \in V(\text{gives})$ For details, see (e) to (i) in the calculation of the truth conditions for (58*a*)

(g) $[\![3]\!]^{M_3, g_3[\text{Pa}/e_3]} = 1$ By (a) through (f) and (59*b*)

Go to subbox 2 and assign Bo to e_3; i.e., consider $g_3[\text{Bo}/e_3]$.

2 (a) $[\![3]\!]^{M_3, g_3[\text{Bo}/e_3]} = 1$ iff for some $u' \in U$, $u' \in V(\text{book}) = \{W\&P, Asp\}$, $[\![5]\!]^{M, g[[\text{Bo}/e_3]u'/e_2]} = 1$ By (59*b*) and (60*j*)

(b) Assign Asp to e_2; i.e., consider $g_3[[\text{Bo}/e_3]Asp/e_2]$

(c) $[\![5]\!]^{M_3, g_3[[\text{Bo}/e_3]Asp/e_2]} = 1$ iff for some $u'' \in U$, $V(\text{woman}) = \{u''\}$ and $[\![7]\!]^{M_3, g_3[[[\text{Bo}/e_3]Asp/e_2]u''/e_5]} = 1$ By (60*k*)

(d) $V(\text{woman}) = \{\text{Lo}\}$ By (59*b*)

(e) $[\![5]\!]^{M_3, g_3[[\text{Bo}/e_3]Asp/e_2]} = 1$ iff $[\![7]\!]^{M_3, g_3[[[\text{Bo}/e_3]Asp/e_2]\text{Lo}/e_5]} = 1$ By (c), (d)

(f) $[\![7]\!]^{M_3, g_3[[[\text{Pa}/e_3]W\&P/e_2]\text{Lo}/e_5]} = 1$ iff $\langle \text{Pa}, W\&P, \text{Lo} \rangle \in V(\text{gives})$ For details, see (e) to (i) in the calculation of the truth conditions for (58*a*)

(g) $[\![3]\!]^{M_3, g_3[\text{Pa}/e_3]} = 1$ By (a) through (f) and (59*b*)

(c) $[\![(58b)]\!]^{M_3, g_3} = 1$ By (a), (b), and the two subbox results encodes. To keep our notation shorter, we'll designate Bond by Bo, Pavarotti by Pa, Loren by Lo, *War and Peace* by *W&P*, *Aspects* by *Asp*. We kept things relatively brief by not going down any blind alleys. In the first subbox we might have tried, for example, *Asp* rather than *W&P* to see whether Pavarotti gave it to Loren. Had we done so, that particular calculation would have yielded a 0, and then we would have had to try *W&P* before being able to close the first subbox. But the basic idea is simple and not very different from what we did in PC.

On the basis of the semantics for F_2, we can provide the usual definitions of truth, entailment, and related notions.

(61) *a.* A sentence S of F_2 is *true* in a model M relative to one of its LF structures β iff for all assignments g, $[\![\beta]\!]^{M,g} = 1$. S is false in M relative to β iff for all g, $[\![\beta]\!]^{M,g} = 0$.

b. A set of sentences $\Omega = \{S_1, \ldots, S_n\}$ of F_2, each S_i taken relative to one of its LF structures β_i, *entails* a sentence S' of F_2 relative to one of its LF structures β', iff for all M, M an F_2 model for English, in which each S_i is true in M relative to β_i, S' also is true in M relative to β'.

Restricting our attention to admissible F_2 models for English in defining entailment means that we will potentially have more entailments than just those due to the quantifiers and connectives. For example, in all models for English the intersection of V(hates) and V(likes) is arguably empty; that is, although there may be a middle ground, hating and liking are incompatible. On this assumption, then, (62*a*), relative to LF (62*a*′), entails (62*b*).

(62) *a.* Loren likes a man.

a′.

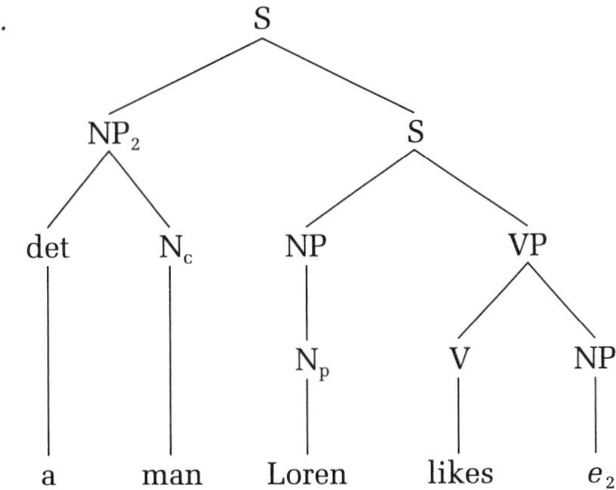

b. It is not the case that Loren hates every man.

b′.

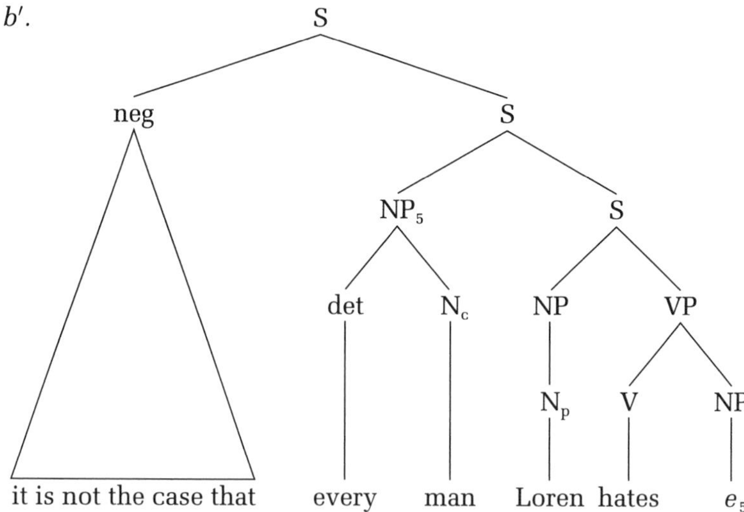

We will just sketch how a proof of this entailment would go. Assume that (62*a′*) is true in model *M*. By (60*j*), this implies that for some *u* in *V*(man), if *u* is assigned to e_2, then $[\![$Loren likes $e_2]\!] = 1$ relative to that assignment of a value to e_2. This, however, is true iff Loren is in $\{x : \langle x, u\rangle \in V(\text{likes})\}$ iff $\langle \text{Loren}, u\rangle \in V(\text{likes})$. But $V(\text{likes}) \cap V(\text{hates}) = \varnothing$ (by the assumption that *M* is an admissible F_2 model for English). Therefore, $\langle \text{Loren}, u\rangle \notin V(\text{hates})$ for some *u* in *V*(man), and thus $[\![$Loren hates $e_5]\!] = 0$ if *u* is assigned as the value of e_5. But by (60*i*), this means that $[\![$[every man]$_5$ [Loren hates e_5]$]\!] = 0$ in *M*, and thus, by (60*f*), (62*b′*) is true in *M*. This entailment depends on grammatical structure, the properties of the "logical" words (the quantifying determiners and the negative), and also the lexical relation of the content words *hates* and *likes.*

Readers may have noticed that so far we have always raised quantifier NPs and then interpreted the resulting LFs. If QR is optional, what happens with sentences with quantified NPs left *in situ* (that is, not raised by means of QR)? Such sentences are uninterpretable and thus, for that reason, ultimately ungrammatical. All sentences are interpreted relative to an LF, but for sentences without quantified NPs their only LF is identical with their surface structure. Sentences that do have one or more LFs distinct from their S-structure, i.e., sentences containing a quantified NP, have to be interpreted relative to one of their LFs.

Now we could make QR obligatory and thus rule out sentences with quantified NPs *in situ* as syntactically deviant. Given the semantics of F_2, however, it turns out to be easy to filter out sentences with unraised quantified NPs. Such NPs lack a denotation, and thus rules like (57*d*), which interpret subject-predicate constructions, will not work if the NP is a quantified one. Quantified NPs receive an interpretation only in fronted position, and then only indirectly by means of the contribution they make to the truth conditions of the sentences they occur in. There is no value assigned to a quantified NP as such.

Of course, the fact that quantified NPs lack an independently definable value is a major drawback of the present approach. It forces us to deal with each determiner within an NP in terms of a separate semantic rule, as (60*i*–*k*) illustrate. Not only is this inelegant; it will not be viable in the long run. Notice that there are an indefinite number of determiners that can occur within NPs (complex NPs like *every man and some woman, every man and some woman and three boys, a chicken in every pot, two candidates from every city, some but not all men, not every but some man, most or all men*, etc.). If each type of quantified NP is simply associated with a separate semantic rule, our capacity to interpret such an indefinite variety of NP types would be a mystery. Clearly, the semantic value of NPs, just like that of other nonlexical phrases, has to be compositionally derived from the semantic values of their parts. But then NPs have to have a semantic value and cannot be treated indirectly just by looking at their semantic role in the structures in which they occur.

These considerations show that our semantics for F_2 is compositional only in a weak sense: sentences are compositionally interpreted in terms of the meanings of their parts, but other phrases, such as NPs, are not. As we have seen, this has undesirable consequences. However, there is no way to find an object that can play the role of quantified NP meanings within the limits of the semantics for PC. More powerful semantic techniques are called for. We will come back to these and related issues in chapter 9, where we introduce the theory of generalized quantifiers. Even this more powerful theory, however, makes use of semantic variables and techniques like modifying assignment functions, concepts that may be easiest to introduce in this simpler framework. In the meantime, PC and the fragment F_2 also let us explore many basic scopal phenomena.

Although we will eventually make some modifications, we want to stress that we take the recursive semantic rules in (60) and the constraints on admissible F_2 models of English informally described on pp. 160–161 to constitute a partial characterization of the semantic competence of English speakers, which includes their basic linguistic knowledge and what they know about how their language links to the world. Using these rules and conditions, we are able to calculate truth conditions, as shown on p. 163 and, relative to knowledge of particular facts, truth values, as shown on p. 164. We are also able to demonstrate entailment relations, as shown on p. 166. In other words, the semantic rules and conditions on admissible models for F_2 do go a long way toward specifying the semantic knowledge of English speakers (with respect to this fragment): the results we got in deriving truth conditions and judging entailments match speakers' intuitive judgments quite well. In using English in particular contexts, speakers make use of something like the F_2 rules and particular admissible models, we think. (We discuss questions of language use in chapter 4 and pay particular attention to the contribution of contextual factors to interpretation in chapter 6.) We have specified our recursive rules and the constraints on admissible models by using a mixture of mathematical terminology and English. We have said nothing about what speakers might know about particular English words like *woman*, what the real significance is of claiming that speakers only entertain models in which $V(\text{woman}) = \{x : x \text{ is a woman}\}$. How much of what is involved in this constraint on the models that speakers use is linguistic knowledge? How much is socially based linguistic practice? How much is a matter of extralinguistic beliefs about the world? There are many deep and difficult questions involved here, some of which we will address (though by no means fully answer) in chapter 8. In the meantime, our approach seems very promising: we have an explicit theory that yields results that agree with the semantic judgments of native speakers. Not surprisingly, the current fragment does not do all we want, and thus we will continue to expand and modify our approach. But the general program is off to a satisfactory beginning.

Exercise 8 For each of the LFs associated with (58*a*), determine which of the other LFs it entails.

2.3 Pronouns as bound variables and some scope restrictions in English

As pointed out in Cooper (1983, sec. 3.2.1), any mechanism, like QR, that allows assignment of wide scope to syntactically embedded quantified NPs can be used to account for three things:

a. Ambiguities due to the presence of several quantified NI clause ("Every man loves a woman")
b. Ambiguities that quantified NPs generate in interaction with intensional contexts (to be discussed in chapter 5)
c. Bound uses of pronouns ("Every cat loves its whiskers")

We just saw how (a) is accommodated in F_2. We will see what phenomena (b) refers to and how to accommodate them when we discuss intensionality. For you to see (c), we have to introduce pronouns into F_2, which we now do. This again will illustrate some of the problems involved.

Personal pronouns in English are inflected with respect to gender, number, and case, and the actual distribution of pronominal forms is far more complex than is often acknowledged. Here we cannot deal properly with the issues that arise in connection with the status of these notions. Instead, we simply add he_n, she_n, and it_n, along with him_n and her_n, as new lexical entries of category $\mathrm{N_p}$; n is just an unpronounced arbitrary numerical index. Pronouns are distinguished from other members of category $\mathrm{N_p}$ by the fact that they have an inherent index.

(63) $\mathrm{N_p} \rightarrow he_n, she_n, it_n, him_n, her_n$, for arbitrary n

Of course, in most of their uses the feminine she_n/her_n and the masculine he_n/him_n respectively presuppose female or male sex in the values they might be assigned for plausible interpretations; unlike it_n, they also presuppose animacy in those potential value assignments. For present purposes, however, we can simply assume that sentences with coindexings with a gender clash are somehow filtered out. That is to say, NPs with the same index must agree in gender features. Syntactic position determines the different distribution of nominative case he_n/she_n and their accusative counterparts, him_n/her_n, but here too we will simply assume that case forms in inappropriate locations are somehow excluded without worrying about the precise mechanism that accomplishes this.

With these modifications F_2 can generate sentences like (64*a*) below. Before looking at it, however, we need also to modify slightly the semantics of F_2 so that our newly introduced pronouns can be interpreted. The idea is to interpret them just as we interpreted variables in PC and as we have interpreted traces in F_2; that is, their initial values will be determined by the assignment function g, with possible modification if they happen to be bound by a quantifying expression. We will require that pronouns with the same index are mapped onto the same individuals, regardless of case (so that, e.g., $g(he_n) = g(him_n)$). We will also assume that assignments of values to pronouns respect their genders. For example, let us assume that g_3 is specified as follows: $g_3(he_1) =$ Pavarotti, $g_3(he_2) =$ Bond, $g_3(she_3) =$ Loren, $g(it_4) =$ *War and Peace*, and for any $n > 4$, $g_3(he_n) =$ Pavarotti. (Gender, as noted above, contributes semantic information, presumably as a presupposition, but we will not try here to spell out formally how this happens.) We present next the amended version of (60), italicizing the parts that have been modified. We omit (*b*) to (*h*), which are unchanged.

(64) *a.* If A is a lexical category and β a trace *or pronoun*, $[\![[_A\beta]]\!]^{M,g} = g(\beta)$; otherwise, $[\![[_A\beta]]\!]^{M,g} = V(\beta)$

i. $[\![[[\text{every } \beta]_i \text{ S}]]\!]^{M,g} = 1$ iff for all $u \in U$, if $u \in [\![\beta]\!]^{M,g}$, then $[\![\text{S}]\!]^{M,g[u/t_i]} = 1$, *where t_i is a trace or a pronoun; that is, $g[u/t_i] = g$ except that $g[u/t_i](e_i) = u$ and $g[u/t_t](he_i) = g[u/t_t](she_i) = g[u/t_t](it_i) = g[u/t_t](him_i) = g[u/t_t](her_i) = u$*

j. $[\![[[\text{a } \beta]_i \text{ S}]]\!]^{M,g} = 1$ iff for some $u \in U$, $u \in [\![\beta]\!]^{M,g}$ and $[\![\text{S}]\!]^{M,g[u/t_i]} = 1$, *where t_i is a trace or a pronoun*

k. $[\![[[\text{the } \beta]_i \text{ S}]]\!]^{M,g} = 1$ iff for some $u \in U$, $[\![\beta]\!]^{M,g} = \{u\}$ and $[\![\text{S}]\!]^{M,g[u/t_i]} = 1$, *where t_i is a trace or a pronoun*

F_2 so amended serves as a preliminary illustration of how our formal semantics for quantification can be applied to a natural language. We think that such an approach helps bring into focus some interesting empirical properties of grammars. In what follows, we briefly discuss a sample of such properties.

Let us first familiarize ourselves with how F_2 with pronouns works. In (65*b*) we illustrate the surface structure of (65*a*), and then we compute the value of (65*b*) in M_3 relative to g_3.

(65) *a.* Pavarotti likes her.

b.

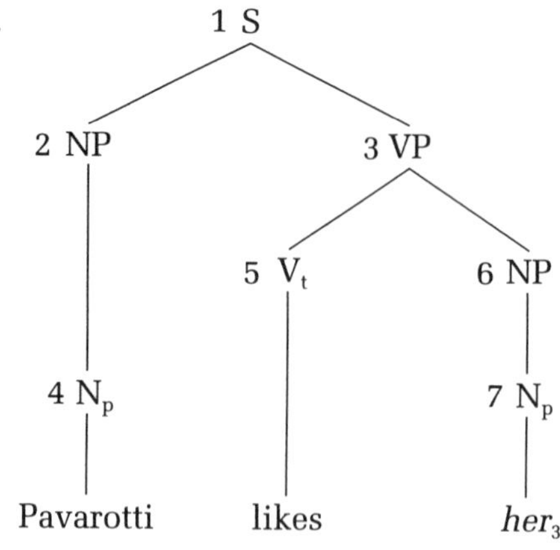

Calculation of the truth conditions and value of (65*b*)

(*a*) $[\![(65b)]\!]^{M_3, g_3} = 1$ iff $[\![2]\!]^{M_3, g_3} = [\![3]\!]^{M_3, g_3}$ By (60*d*)
(*b*) $[\![2]\!]^{M_3, g_3} = \text{Pavarotti}$ By (59*b*)
(*c*) $[\![3]\!]^{M_3, g_3} = \{x : \langle x, g_3(her_3)\rangle \in V_3(\text{likes})\}$ By (60*a*, *g*) and (64*a*)
(*d*) $g_3(her_3) = \text{Loren}$ By expanded definition of g_3 above
(*e*) $V_3(\text{likes}) = \{\langle \text{Bond}, \text{Loren}\rangle, \langle \text{Pavarotti}, \text{Loren}\rangle, \langle \text{Loren}, Asp\rangle, \langle \text{Bond}, W\&P\rangle, \langle \text{Pavarotti}, \text{Pavarotti}\rangle\}$ By (59*b*)
(*f*) $\text{Pavarotti} \in \{x : \langle x, \text{Loren}\rangle \in V_3(\text{likes})\} = \{\text{Bond}, \text{Pavarotti}\}$ By (*d*), (*e*), and the definition of set membership
(*g*) $[\![(64b)]\!]^{M_3, g_3} = 1$ By (*a*) through (*f*)

If we assume that $V_3(\text{likes}) = \{\langle x, y\rangle : x \text{ likes } y\}$ in M_3, then our result is that (65*a*) is true in M_3 relative to g_3 just in case Pavarotti likes Loren. Notice that we had to use the value assigned by g_3 to her_3 to get this result. The pronoun her_3 in (65a) is what is called a deictic pronoun: it gets its interpretation from a pointing or some other contextual way of identifying a particular referent. English pronouns used deictically are treated just like free variables in PC: they get their value directly from an assignment function.

Just as some English pronouns are interpreted like free variables, some are interpreted like bound variables. Typical examples of bound-variable uses of pronouns are the following:

(66) a. *Every teenager* likes *her* mother.
  b. *Every professor* thinks that *she* is busy.

At present we are unable to accommodate such uses because we haven't dealt with the semantics of possessives or with embedding. If we had a semantics for such constructions, the treatment of bound pronouns in F_2 would apply to them (as we will see when we deal with embedding). To show binding in F_2, we will just add reflexive pronouns with -$self_n$ to our stock. In the next section, we will discuss the distribution and interpretive constraints on reflexives. We can, however, simply add them to our fragment now in anticipation and actually work through a straightforward example of the binding of a pronoun by a quantified NP. So let us further increase the stock of lexical items in category N_p by adding the following:

(67) $N_p \rightarrow$ $itself_n$, $himself_n$, $herself_n$, for arbitrary n

For now, these reflexive pronouns will be given their initial value by the assignment function, just like our other pronouns, and be subject to binding by quantified NPs. We will require that for all n, $g(itself_n) = g(it_n)$, $g(himself_n) = g(he_n) = g(him_n)$, and $g(herself_n) = g(she_n) = g(her_n)$. Sentence (68*a*) and its LF (68*b*) are generated by our expanded fragment, and we can calculate the truth conditions and value of (68*b*) in M_3 relative to g_3. The process is familiar.

(68) *a.* Every man likes himself.

b.

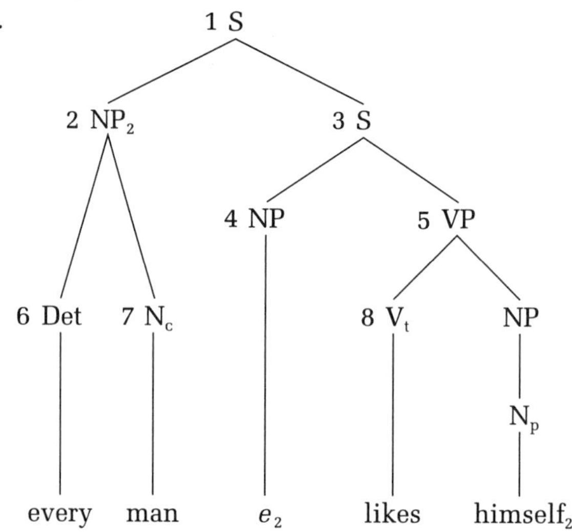

Notice that the values of g_3 themselves do not enter into the calculation and thus the sentence is false in M_3. This is because the pronoun and the trace are bound by the raised quantificational NP. Notice also that we had to raise the quantifier *every man* in order to

Calculation of the truth conditions and value of (68*b*)

(*a*) $[\![(68b)]\!]^{M_3,g_3} = 1$ iff for all u in U if $u \in [\![7]\!]^{M_3,g_3} = V_3(\text{man})$, then $[\![3]\!]^{M_3,g_3[u/t_2]} = 1$ By (64*i*)

(*b*) $[\![3]\!]^{M_3,g_3[u/t_2]} = 1$ iff $[\![4]\!]^{M_3,g_3[u/t_2]} \in [\![5]\!]^{M_3,g_3[u/t_2]}$ By (60*d*)

(*c*) $[\![4]\!]^{M_3,g_3[u/t_2]} = u$ By (64*a*) and the definition of $g_3[u/t_2]$

(*d*) $[\![5]\!]^{M_3,g_3[u/t_2]} = \{x : \langle x, g_3[u/t_2](himself_2)\rangle \in V_3(\text{likes})\}$ By (64*a*) and (60*g*)

(*e*) $g_3[u/t_2](himself_2) = u$ By (64*a*) and the definition of $g_3[u/t_2]$

(*f*) $[\![3]\!]^{M_3,g_3[u/t_2]} = 1$ iff $u \in \{x : \langle x, u\rangle \in V_3(\text{likes})\}$ iff $\langle u, u\rangle \in V_3(\text{likes})$ By (*b*) through (*e*) and the definition of set membership

(*g*) $[\![(68b)]\!]^{M_3,g_3} = 1$ iff for all u in U, if $u \in V_3(\text{man}) = \{\text{Bond}, \text{Pavarotti}\}$, $\langle u, u\rangle \in V_3(\text{likes})$ By (*a*) through (*f*) and (59*b*)

(*h*) $\langle \text{Bond}, \text{Bond}\rangle \notin V_3(\text{likes}) = \{\langle \text{Bond}, \text{Loren}\rangle, \langle \text{Pavarotti}, \text{Loren}\rangle, \langle \text{Loren}, Asp\rangle, \langle \text{Bond}, W\&P\rangle, \langle \text{Pavarotti}, \text{Pavarotti}\rangle\}$ By (59*b*) and the definition of set membership

(*i*) $[\![(68b)]\!]^{M_3,g_3} = 0$ By (*g*) and (*h*)

interpret the sentence: quantificational NPs need an index to be interpreted, and they get their index only when moved. Expanding the fragment to include reflexives has given us an example of pronoun binding.

Even without reflexives, F_2 does display what look like bound-variable uses of nonreflexive pronouns, but these raise some interesting problems. Here are some examples.

(69) *a.* The man is hungry, and he is boring.
b. $[_S$ [the man]$_3$ [e_3 is hungry and $[_{NP}$ he_3] is boring]]
c. $\exists y[\text{man}(y) \wedge \forall x[\text{man}(x) \leftrightarrow x = y] \wedge \text{hungry}(y) \wedge \text{boring}(y)]$

(70) *a.* A man is hungry, and he is boring.
b. $[_S$ [a man]$_2$ [e_2 is hungry and $[_{NP}$ he_2] is boring]]
c. $\exists y[\text{man}(y) \wedge \text{hungry}(y) \wedge \text{boring}(y)]$

In these two examples (*b*) is the LF of (*a*), and (*c*) is a PC formula whose truth conditions are the same as those that the semantics in (64) associates with these constructions. In these sentences we see an NP assigned scope over both conjuncts in a conjunction. As the sentences in question are indeed grammatical (if one is willing to tolerate a certain stylistic awkwardness), the fact that these constructions can be accommodated in F_2 and can be interpreted as shown in (69*c*) and (70*c*) appears prima facie to be a positive result. Examples of the same kind can be constructed for disjunction:[11]

(71) [A package]$_4$ (that I was waiting for) either got delayed, or it$_4$ was sent to the wrong address.

Notice also that the sentences in (72*a*) below are interpreted conjunctively and the existential quantifier associated with *a man* binds the pronoun *he*, which is schematically illustrated by the PC rendering in (72*b*).

(72) *a.* *A maniac* has damaged this painting. *He* evidently used a knife.
b. $\exists x[\text{maniac}(x) \wedge \text{damaged-this-painting}(x) \wedge \text{used-a-knife}(x)]$

These examples show that definite and indefinite NPs can have scope over coordinated structures and even across stretches of discourse, a fact that can perhaps be accommodated within the grammar of F_2.

However, it must also be observed that universally quantified NPs behave differently in this respect from existentially quantified ones, as is shown by the following examples (where the asterisk is used to indicate ungrammaticality in the intended interpretation).

(73) *a.* *[Every man]$_4$ is hungry, and he$_4$ is boring.
b. $\forall x[\text{man}(x) \rightarrow [\text{hungry}(x) \wedge \text{boring}(x)]]$

(74) *a.* *[Every man]$_4$ walked in. He$_4$ was wearing a hat.
b. $\forall x[\text{man}(x) \rightarrow [\text{walked-in}(x) \wedge \text{wearing-a-hat}]]$

The (*a*) sentences in these examples show that in English a universal quantifier contained within a conjunct cannot in general bind pronouns contained in other conjuncts (unlike the existential quantifier associated with the indefinite article).[12] This behavior of universal quantifiers is reminiscent of the coordinate-structure constraint, familiar to linguists since the work of Ross (1966). This constraint describes a crucial property of movement dependencies, namely, the impossibility of extracting a constituent out of just one of two conjuncts, as illustrated by the following examples:

(75) *a.* *Which boy did John see ____ and Mary likes Bill.
b. *Beans John likes ____ and Mary hates potatoes.

It is hard to avoid the conclusion that quantifiers like *every* are governed by the same constraint (whatever a correct account of it might be). However, if we follow this line, then (69*a*) and (70*a*) become a problem. We have to explain why NPs whose determiner is a definite or indefinite article (as in (69*a*) and (70*a*) respectively) do not appear to be subject to such a constraint. We will come back to this problem shortly. The interesting thing to note here is that if it is correct that *every* is subject to the coordinate-structure constraint, an interpretive phenomenon (the scope properties of a quantifier) would be subject to a restriction governing syntactically overt movement. This in turn would suggest that a unified treatment of overt movement and scope phenomena (which the theory we are adopting provides) is empirically supported. If *wh* dependencies and quantifier scope were dealt with in terms of totally different mechanisms, there should be no reason to expect them to obey similar restrictions.

In fact, parallelisms in the behavior of *wh* dependencies and quantifier scope are not limited to coordinate structures. They show up in other grammatical structures, especially what Ross called "island" environments, which seem to prevent movement "off island." For example, it is impossible to question a constituent contained inside an NP of the form [$_{\text{NP}}$ NP S] (a relative or an appositive clause, for example). Consider, e.g., the ungrammaticality of the following sentences:

(76) *a.* *[Which class]$_j$ did you correct the homework that$_i$ the teacher assigned ____$_i$ to ____$_j$?
b. *[Which assignment]$_i$ did you hear the claim that a student copied ____$_i$?

Here the indices represent the dependency between dislocated constituents and gaps. The particular constraint illustrated in (76) is known as the complex NP constraint; it appears to hold also of quantifier scope. Rodman (1976) points out the following minimal pair:

(77) *a.* Guinevere has a bone in every corner of the house.
a′. $\forall x[\text{corner-of-the-house}(x) \rightarrow \exists y[\text{bone}(y) \wedge \text{has}(g, y) \wedge \text{in}(y, x)]]$
b. Guinevere has a bone which is in every corner of the house.

The preferred reading of (77*a*) is the one represented in (77*a′*), where the universal quantifier has widest scope. On the other hand, such a reading is unavailable for (77*b*), where to obtain it we would have to move the universally quantified NP out of a complex NP. Again, there must be a good reason why these parallelisms hold. Although there may be alternative explanations, such parallelisms seem unsurprising if overt *wh* dependencies and quantifier scope do indeed have a common structure. Our present approach does not really explain these generalizations. It does, however, provide a framework within which such an explanation might be found.

In light of these examples the hypothesis that quantifier scope is subject to constraints similar to those on *wh* movement gains further plausibility, which makes the behavior of the NPs illustrated in (69) to (72) especially puzzling. What is it that allows them to extend their scope beyond what is possible for *every*?

The mystery that surrounds NPs whose determiner is a definite or indefinite article is not confined to their behavior with respect to coordinated structures. Consider the contrast in (78).

(78) *a.* *Every farmer who owns [every donkey]$_1$ beats it$_1$.
b. Every farmer who owns [a donkey]$_1$ beats it$_1$.

Sentence (78*a*) on the intended reading is ungrammatical. This is to be expected if *every* is subject to something like the complex NP constraint: *every donkey* can bind the pronoun *it* only if we extract the former out of the relative clause in which it is embedded (a complex NP). On the other hand, (78*b*) is perfectly grammatical. This appears to be a further instance of the capacity of NPs with articles to extend their scope beyond that possible for universally quantified NPs.

But there is something about (78*b*) that is even more puzzling. So far we have assumed that NPs with indefinite articles are semantically associated with existential quantifiers, a hypothesis that seems to work remarkably well for many cases. However, this hypothesis does not help us with (78*b*). If *a donkey* is existentially quantified, we have essentially two options in assigning truth conditions to sentences like (78*b*):

(79) *a.* $\forall x[[\text{farmer}(x) \wedge \exists y[\text{donkey}(y) \wedge \text{own}(x, y)]] \rightarrow \text{beat}(x, y)]$
b. $\forall x \exists y[[\text{farmer}(x) \wedge [\text{donkey}(y) \wedge \text{own}(x, y)]] \rightarrow \text{beat}(x, y)]$

In (79*a*) the existential quantifier is assigned narrow scope with respect to the conditional. However, in such a case the second occurrence of *y*, the one that represents the pronoun in (78*b*), is not bound by $\exists$, and thus its value is referentially independent of the NP *a donkey*, which does not give us the reading we want. In (79*b*) the existential quantifier is assigned wide scope over the conditional, and so the second occurrence of *y* is bound. But this still gives us the wrong truth conditions. Sentence (79*b*) is true whenever there is anything that makes the antecedent false. The existence of something that is not a donkey is sufficient to make (79*b*) true, independently of what every farmer does to donkeys. Thus, for example, in a situation in which there is a cat and no farmer beats his donkey, (79*b*) would be true, for the cat would suffice to make the antecedent of the conditional false and hence the whole conditional true. But this is clearly not a reading that (78*b*) allows. Thus, (79*b*) does not adequately represent the truth conditions of (78*b*).

A better approximation to what (78*b*) means is given by the truth conditions of (80).

(80) $\forall x \forall y[[\text{farmer}(x) \wedge \text{donkey}(y) \wedge \text{own}(x, y)] \rightarrow \text{beat}(x, y)]$

Formula (80) seems to represent fairly well the truth conditions associated with (78*b*), though perhaps only under the further presupposition that each farmer owns just one donkey. However, in

(80) we are interpreting the indefinite NP *a donkey* in terms of a universal quantifier rather than an existential quantifier. Why and how does this come about?

This phenomenon is perfectly general. In fact, it also shows up in other types of constructions, notably conditionals, as the following illustrates:

(81) *a.* *If Kim owns [every donkey]$_1$, she beats it$_1$.
b. If Kim [owns a donkey]$_1$, she beats it$_1$.
c. $\exists y[\text{donkey}(y) \wedge \text{own}(k, y)] \rightarrow \text{beat}(k, y)$
d. $\exists y[[\text{donkey}(y) \wedge \text{own}(k, y)] \rightarrow \text{beat}(k, y)]$
e. $\forall y[[\text{donkey}(y) \wedge \text{own}(k, y)]\ \text{beat}(k, y)]$

Again, the scope of an NP with an indefinite article seems able to span beyond the scope of a universally quantified NP (see (81*a*, *b*)). And again, the usual existential interpretation of the indefinite article gives wrong results (consider (81*c*, *d*)). The phenomenon under discussion has been known at least since the ancient Stoics. In recent debates it goes under the name of *donkey anaphora*, because of the examples used to illustrate it by Geach (1962), which have become standard in the literature.

To summarize, we have found good evidence that universally quantified NPs are subject to constraints similar to those to which question formation is subject (like the coordinate-structure constraint and other island constraints). NPs with indefinite (or definite) articles do not appear, prima facie, to obey restrictions of this sort. Furthermore, indefinite articles appear to undergo what might look like a change in meaning when they occur in the restrictive portion of a universal quantifier or in the antecedent of a conditional. It may be that some pronouns whose interpretation seems to depend on an antecedent—i.e., they are not deictic—may not be "bound" in quite the sense our semantics for quantification elucidates. Much recent work has been devoted to the solution of these mysteries, and this work suggests that the phenomena illustrated in (66) to (69) and those illustrated in (75) to (78) are indeed related.[13] Such work focuses on how the truth conditions of sentences can affect, as well as be affected by, the dynamics of discourse. It calls for techniques that go well beyond the limits of this book, however. At any rate, we hope to have aroused the curiosity of the reader about these matters.

2.4 Coreference and noncoreference

In chapter 1, sec. 3.3, we informally introduced some observations about the possible referential dependence of pronouns on other NPs, traditionally called their antecedents. Referential dependence of the pronoun might mean reference to the same entity as the antecedent, or it might mean, as we have come to see in this chapter, being quantificationally bound by the antecedent. In the linguistic literature, referential dependence is often called *coreference* and is indicated by coindexing, although the precise semantic significance of coindexing is typically not spelled out (nor did we spell it out in our informal discussion). Even though the term "referential dependence" is better than "coreference" (which is potentially misleading), we will not try to reform this aspect of linguistic practise here. As we also pointed out, there are cases where a pronoun cannot depend referentially on a particular NP. This phenomenon has been dubbed *disjoint reference* or *noncoreference* and is indicated by having distinct indices on the pronoun and the NPs that cannot serve as its antecedent. There is a significant linguistic literature on the subject of coreference and noncoreference, which began to attract attention in the 1970s.[14] In this section we explore these phenomena in more detail and show how the syntax and semantics we have developed for F_2 can help articulate a semantically more precise account of the possible and impossible coreference relations discovered in syntactic theory.

A quite pervasive generalization about natural languages is that pronouns cannot corefer if they are somehow too close. Thus, for example, (82*a*) cannot in general have the same truth conditions as the F_2 LF in (82*b*), which is equivalent to the PC formula (82*c*):

(82) *a.* He loves him.
b. He_1 loves him_1.
c. $\text{love}(x_1, x_1)$

The two occurrences of pronouns in (82*a*) are not expected to refer to the same entity, whereas the two pronouns in (82*b*) (or the two variables in (82*c*)) are required to refer to the same entity.

If we introduce reflexives, however, matters look very different. Sentence (83*a*) not only can but must have the truth conditions associated with (82*b*, *c*). We also find that a sentence like (83*b*), in which the different gender presuppositions rule out coreference, is not acceptable.

(83) *a.* He loves himself.
b. *She loves himself.

Reflexives seem to need coreference or semantic dependence on something "close," whereas ordinary pronouns reject such "local" coreference. What counts as "close" or "local" must, of course, be spelled out, but as a starting point one might say that two constituents are "close" if they are in the same clause. To a significant degree the domains over which pronouns must be disjoint in reference coincide in languages like English with the domains within which reflexives must find an antecedent. Much work has been done on the individuation of the syntactic domains (and on the exact conditions) with respect to which such a generalization holds. There are some interesting crosslinguistic variations, but the basic ideas seem to apply universally. For convenience, we will confine ourselves to generalizations that hold of English. The question, then, is how to elucidate these generalizations in a semantic theory of the kind we have been developing.

A possible first guess is to try to constrain the way in which the indices are associated with pronouns, so that, for example, the two pronouns in (84*a*) are never coindexed, whereas the two in (84*b*) always are. The pronouns in (84*c*, *d*), on the other hand, may or may not be coindexed.

(84) *a.* John spoke with *him* about *him*.
b. John spoke with *her* about *herself*.
c. *He* thinks that *he* is smart.
d. *She* loves *her* mother.

In other words, coindexing might be constrained to yield the following pattern of grammaticality:

(85) *a.* John spoke with him_1 about him_2.
a′. *John spoke with him_2 about him_2.
b. John spoke with her_3 about herself_3.
b′. *John spoke with her_3 about herself_2.
c. He_1 thinks that he_1 is smart.
c′. He_1 thinks that he_3 is smart.
d. She_1 loves her_1 mother.
d′. She_2 loves her_3 mother.

The rationale behind this move is the following. Our semantics treats pronouns like variables in a logical calculus, as the notion of a variable appears to be our current best formal tool for dealing with the way pronouns behave. The data in (84) and (85) suggest that we should keep the variables that interpret two (or more) nonreflexive pronouns in the same local domain distinct from each other and that we should make sure that the variables that interpret reflexive pronouns have a suitable antecedent with which they might be coindexed. What our account offers in addition to that in the syntactic literature is a clear account of the semantic significance of coindexing or disjoint indexing.

Interestingly, effects of a closely related sort are detectable elsewhere. Specifically, disjoint-reference constraints seem to apply to relations between pronouns and other kinds of NPs, as illustrated in (86).

(86) *a.* Pavarotti likes him.
b. Every student likes her.
c. Every student thinks that she is smart.

In (86*a*) *him* is not expected to refer to Pavarotti. In (86*b*) *her* cannot be bound by (and thus referentially dependent on) *every student*, while in (86*c*) *she* can. It seems reasonable to assume that these facts can be accounted for by the same general principles that account for the facts in (84).

In our sample grammar F_2, each pronoun carries an arbitrary inherent index, and all raised quantifier NPs are also given an arbitrary index (the traces left behind are, of course, automatically coindexed with the moved NP). Thus the grammar already generates all sorts of combinations of indexing. Suppose that we retain this feature of the fragment's grammar (and also retain it when we expand the fragment later to include embedded sentences and other more complex constructions) but then filter out the unwanted types of coindexing it will generate and also filter out sentences that lack desired coindexing relations. The following principles, based on the syntactic literature, are a first start.

(87) *a.* A reflexive pronoun must be coindexed with a c-commanding argument within the minimal NP or S that contains it.
b. A nonreflexive pronoun must not be coindexed with a c-commanding NP within the minimal NP or S that contains it.
c. A nonpronominal NP must not be coindexed with a c-commanding NP.

The principles in (87) constitute a rudimentary version of what is called syntactic binding theory. Let us briefly see how they work to constrain the interpretation of some English sentences. For illustrative purposes, we will include some sentences not in the current fragment, simply assuming that the F_2 treatment of pronouns and their relations to antecedents is to be retained when our fragment grows to include them. Principle (87*a*) yields the following pattern:

(88) *a.* *Himself$_1$ likes him$_1$.
b. *He$_1$ likes herself$_1$.
c. *He$_1$ thinks that Mary likes himself$_1$.

Sentence (88*a*) is ruled out because of the c-command condition on coindexing. Sentence (88*b*) is ruled out because the coindexed pronouns do not carry the same gender specifications. Although sentence (88*c*) is not yet in our fragment, it would be ruled out in an expanded fragment because the antecedent of the reflexive is not in the same local domain (in this case, the embedded S) as the reflexive. Principle (87*b*) yields the following pattern, (89*a*, *b*) being the English sentences and (89*a*′, *b*′) being their potential LFs generated by the fragment, some of which are filtered out by the principles in (87):

(89) *a.* Every student likes her.
a′. *[Every student]$_1$ [e_1 likes her$_1$]
b. Every student thinks that she is smart.
b′. [Every student]$_1$ [e_1 thinks that she$_{1,2}$ is smart]

Finally, principle (87*c*) rules out (90*a*′) as a possible LF for (90*a*) and (90*b*′) as a possible LF for (90*b*):

(90) *a.* He thinks that every student is tired.
a′. *He$_1$ thinks that [[every student]$_1$ [e_1 is tired]]
a″. *[every student]$_1$ [he$_1$ thinks that [e_1 is tired] (From (90*a*) via long QR)
b. Every student likes every student.
b′. *[Every student]$_1$ [[every student]$_1$ [e_1 likes e_1]]

To understand the full significance of these patterns, we have to determine their actual semantic import. Indexing in F_2 already plays an explicit role in semantic interpretation. This allows us to make quite precise what truth conditions are being allowed or disallowed by the binding theory in particular cases. We are then able to ask whether the predicted possible truth conditions match our intuitions concerning the possible meanings of the constructions we are examining.

Given the binding theory and the general semantics that we are assuming, the English sentence (91*a*) must be assigned an LF like (91*b*), and it gets the truth conditions spelled out in (91*c*), which are exactly the same as those assigned to the PC formula (91*d*). (Which index is used does not matter; readers can confirm that the truth conditions are the same, relative to suitable assignment functions.) What is crucial is that the LF in (91*e*), whose truth conditions are equivalent to those of the PC formula (91*f*), is filtered out by the binding theory and thus cannot be used in interpreting (91*a*).

(91) *a.* He likes himself.
b. He_1 likes himself_1.
c. $\langle g(\text{he}_1), g(\text{he}_1)\rangle \in V(\text{likes}) = \{\langle x, y\rangle : x \text{ likes } y\}$
d. $\text{like}(x_1, x_1)$
e. *He_1 likes himself_2.
f. $\text{like}(x_1, x_2)$

Notice that both pronouns in (91*b*) and both variables in (91*d*) are free: their interpretation depends on a particular assignment function rather than being controlled by a c-commanding quantifier. The second pronoun, however, gets exactly the same value assigned as the first, and in this sense its interpretation depends on that of the first. In such cases syntacticians say that the first pronoun *binds* the second; as this example shows, what syntacticians mean by binding does not always coincide with what is meant in the logical-semantic tradition (although sometimes it does). The context in which you encounter such terminology will generally make clear which meaning is intended.

Now consider sentence (92*a*).

(92) *a.* Every professor likes herself.
b. $[\text{Every professor}]_1\ [e_1 \text{ likes herself}_1]$
c. $\forall x_1[\text{professor}(x_1) \rightarrow \text{like}\ (x_1, x_1)]$
d. *$[\text{Every professor}]_1\ [e_1 \text{ likes herself}_2]$
e. $\forall x_1[\text{professor}(x_1) \rightarrow \text{like}(x_1, x_2)]$

The binding theory in (87) allows us to interpret (92*a*) as having LF (92*b*), which has the same truth conditions as the PC formula in (92*c*). The binding theory, however, filters out LF (92*d*), the truth conditions of which are equivalent to those of PC formula (92*e*). (We often give PC formulas to represent the truth conditions of LFs in our fragment rather than spelling out the truth conditions directly. This is just for convenience and it is always possible to calculate the truth conditions directly for the F_2 fragment and forget about the PC equivalents; readers new to logic may sometimes find the LFs generated by the F_2 English fragment easier to process semantically than PC formulas.) We appear to get the right truth conditions. Thus our rudimentary binding theory provides a good first approximation to the meaning of reflexives.

A further consequence of the binding theory is that sentences like (93*a*) can never be assigned the LF in (93*b*), whose truth conditions are equivalent to those of formula (93*c*).

(93) *a.* Every professor likes her.
b. [Every professor]$_1$ [e_1 likes her$_1$]
c. $\forall x_1[\text{professor}(x_1) \rightarrow \text{like}(x_1, x_1)]$

To obtain the reading in (93*b*), the trace left by the raised quantified NP *every professor* would have to be coindexed with *her*. But this is ruled out by principle (87*b*). Notice that the grammar of F_2 would indeed generate (93*b*) as a possible reading of (93*a*) if something like principle (87*b*) were not adopted. This shows that a set of binding principles along the lines we are considering is necessary on truth-conditional grounds, for otherwise we would be predicting that (93*b*) is a possible meaning of (93*a*).

The truth-conditional relevance of binding theory can be further confirmed by considering what would happen if, contrary to binding theory, a sentence like (90*b*) could be assigned LF (90*b*′), repeated here as (94*a*). The truth conditions for (94*a*) turn out to be equivalent to those of the PC formula (94*b*), which in turn is equivalent to (94*c*).

(94) *a.* [[every student]$_1$ [[every student]$_1$ [e_1 likes e_1]]]
b. $\forall x_1[\text{student}(x_1) \rightarrow \forall x_1[\text{student}(x_1) \rightarrow \text{like}(x_1, x_1)]]$
c. $\forall x_1[\text{student}(x_1) \rightarrow \text{like}(x_1, x_1)]$

But clearly the sentence "Every student likes every student" lacks the reading represented by (94*c*), which attributes liking oneself to every student (and is consistent with each student's liking none of the other students, a situation in which our original sentence would be false). Similar considerations apply to (90*a*). Thus the binding theory seems to yield a wide range of correct results.

But how can we generalize the above results to the case of proper names? Consider a sentence like (95).

(95) Pavarotti likes himself.

Currently we have no way to assign indices to proper names. If we add such a provision, we then have to spell out how proper names with indices on them are interpreted. There are several ways to go in this connection. Perhaps the simplest one within the present setting is to assimilate proper names to quantified NPs. That is, we could let proper names undergo QR, receiving an index in the process and leaving behind a coindexed trace. The semantic rule that interprets structures with raised proper names is very easy to state:

(96) If NP_i is a proper name, $[\![[\mathrm{NP}_i\ \mathrm{S}]]\!]^{M,g} = 1$ iff $[\![\mathrm{S}]\!]^{M,g'} = 1$, where $g'(t_i) = [\![\mathrm{NP}_i]\!]^{M,g}$ (here $t_i = x_i$ or $t_i = e_i$) and otherwise $g' = g$. (In our earlier notation, $g' = g[[\![\mathrm{NP}_i]\!]^{M,g}/t_i]$; putting this all in a superscript would impair readability.)

By extending QR to proper names, we now have LF (97*a*) to associate with sentence (95), which has the truth conditions in (97*b*) (for details, see some of our earlier computations). These truth conditions are exactly the same as those for the PC formula in (97*c*).

(97) *a.* [Pavarotti$_1$ [e_1 likes himself$_1$]]
b. $[\![[\text{Pavarotti}_1\ [e_1 \text{ likes himself}_1]]]\!]^{M,g} = 1$
iff $[\![[e_1 \text{ likes himself}_1]]\!]^{M,g[\text{Pavarotti}/t_1]} = 1$
iff $\langle\text{Pavarotti, Pavarotti}\rangle \in V(\text{likes}) = \{\langle x, y\rangle : x \text{ likes } y\}$
c. like(Pavarotti, Pavarotti)

We can maintain that QR of proper names is optional. However, the binding condition (87*a*) on reflexives can only be met in sentences like (95) if the proper name does undergo QR, for nonpronominal NPs do not carry inherent indices. This gets us the results we want. In general, all the above considerations concerning quantified NPs will extend to proper names if they are interpreted in raised position.

Careful consideration of our semantics will reveal an interesting puzzle. Consider (98*a*). Our grammar requires that the pronouns be assigned different indices, and this yields an LF like that represented in (98*b*); (98*c*) gives the equivalent PC formula.

(98) *a.* He likes him.
b. He_1 likes him_2
c. $\text{like}(x_1, x_2)$

But now nothing prevents he_1 and him_2 (or x_1 and x_2) from referring to the same individual. Similar considerations apply to (99*a*), with (99*b*) being the LF and (99*c*) the equivalent PC formula.

(99) *a.* John likes him.
b. [John_1 [e_1 likes him_2]]
c. like(John, x_2)

Nothing prevents him_2 in (99*b*) (or x_2 in (99*c*)) from accidentally referring to John. These possibilities might seem not to do justice to our intuitions about the meaning of these sentences.

We might try to get out of this problem by to requiring that distinctly indexed pronouns and traces be mapped into distinct individuals (or, for PC, that distinct variables get distinct values). That is, we could restrict ourselves to assignments that require that whenever $n \neq m$, $g(he_n) \neq g(he_m)$ and $g(he_n) \neq g(e_m)$ (and similarly for the feminine and neuter pronouns). However, this condition appears to be far too strong. As applied to PC, it would make formulas like (100*a*) always false, and if we extended our fragment to include identity statements in English, it would also seem to make sentences like (95b) always false:

(100) *a.* $x_1 = x_2$
b. She is Joan.

Even putting identity statements aside, there are cases where noncoreference seems to be suspended. The following examples adapted from Evans (1980) illustrate:

(101) *a.* I know what John and he [pointing at Bill] have in common.
John likes Bill, and he [pointing again at Bill] likes Bill also.
b. Look, fathead, if *everyone* likes him [pointing at Bill], then Bill must also like him.

Examples of this kind appear to be perfectly sensible and are fairly systematic. They call, therefore, for an account of some sort. The nature of the facts in question suggests that we might be dealing with a partly pragmatic strategy of some sort. An interesting proposal has been made in this connection by Reinhart (1983a, 1983b, 1997).[15] Though we cannot do justice to the extent of her discussion, her basic idea can be sketched in the following terms. Sentences like (102*a*) and (103*a*) are assigned LFs such as those in (102*b*) and (103*b*) respectively.

(102) *a.* He likes him.
b. He_1 likes him_2

(103) *a.* Pavarotti likes him.
b. [Pavarotti_1 [e_1 likes him_2]]

But the LFs in (102) and (103) are accompanied by a general interpretive strategy of the following sort:

(104) Do not interpret distinct free variables as coreferential where the option of having bound variables is available.

So, for example, in (102a) if we wanted to express referential dependence of the object on the subject, we should have used a reflexive pronoun. Not choosing such an option will induce the expectation that coreference is not intended. The interpretive strategy in (104) has a default character. There can be special reasons for using pronouns rather than reflexives (e.g., in identity statements and in Evans's example), in which case the expectation of noncoreference will be suspended.

In fact, this view meshes well with general pragmatic strategies, which we will discuss in more detail in chapter 4. The point is that the grammar provides us with a specific tool for expressing obligatory coreference: reflexives. If speakers have grounds for asserting the coreferential reading, they are misleading their audience by using nonreflexives. Note that such a strategy must still appeal to a theory of binding along the lines sketched above. Without it, there would be no way to show the truth-conditional effects we saw earlier with quantificational NPs and no source for a principle like (104).

The topics at hand are quite intricate. Our discussion is preliminary, and there are many related phenomena that we haven't even begun to discuss (such as, for instance, the interactions of binding theory with *wh* dependencies). Yet the above considerations illustrate that a theory of binding along the lines we have been considering appears to be necessary to get the right truth conditions for a substantial number of sentences and also has a wide-ranging set of semantic consequences that must be carefully weighed.

2.5 Summary

This section has focused on giving a precise account of the truth conditions of sentences containing quantified expressions and has also considered the semantics of pronouns. We provided a sample grammar, F_2, that associates a certain class of English sentences with a syntactic analysis similar to PC, and this allowed us to transfer the model-theoretic semantic tools we introduced for PC to the English fragment. Fragment F_2 associated with sentences structures much like those that GB syntactic studies hypothesize are assigned at the LF level. We have also considered some of the scope and binding phenomena that have come to constitute a standard set of problems for any theory of natural-language meaning. This enabled us to illustrate some of the issues that arise in trying to identify a principled interface between syntax and semantics.

3 Logical Form (*lf*)

A main strength of the approach to meaning that we have been developing is that it provides a theory of entailment and thereby characterizes one central aspect of our semantic competence. There are other ways of approaching this task that are relevant to our enterprise and that we should therefore discuss, however briefly.

Consider the sentences below:

(105) *a.* All mothers are women, and Loren is a mother.
  b. Loren is a woman.

It is clear that (105*a*) entails (105*b*). In fact, for any pair of sentences that bear to one another the same structural relationship as (100*a*) to (100*b*), we can tell that the first will entail the second.

(106) *a.* All *A*s are *B*s and *x* is an *A*.
  b. *x* is a *B*.

The thing to note here is that we have to know virtually nothing about what (106*a*) and (106*b*) mean in order to determine that (106*b*) follows from (106*a*). We are able to determine it just by looking at the syntactic structure of (106*a*) and (106*b*), in which we treat the noncontent expressions *all*, *and*, and *is a* as part of that structure. This suggests that we may be able to characterize something closely resembling entailment in purely syntactic terms just by looking at the form of argument patterns.

In fact, techniques of this sort have been widely and successfully studied within logic. The complexity and ambiguity of natural language, however, have made it very hard to characterize a sufficiently general notion of inference (proof or deduction) directly in terms of natural language syntax. This has led logicians to construct artificial languages that are on the one hand capable of expressing significant portions of what natural language expresses and at the same time are endowed with a simple syntax that supports a purely syntactic characterization of the notion of a valid inference. PC is one such language.

To get the flavor of what is involved in syntactically characterizing the notion of a valid inference, let us define some of the key concepts that this requires. A formal system consists of a language (a set of symbols and a set of formation rules that determine what strings of symbols are well formed) and a deductive apparatus. The deductive apparatus generally consists of a (possibly empty) set of axioms and a set of inference rules. The axioms are certain formulas of the language that are taken as valid without proof. Inference rules determine how formulas can be inferred or deduced from other formulas.

In the present chapter we have formulated the PC language. Such a language was used to introduce certain semantic techniques. But we have provided no deductive apparatus for PC. To see how such an apparatus may be specified, let us give one of the standard axiomatizations of the predicate calculus.

(107) *a.* $\psi \rightarrow (\phi \rightarrow \psi)$
b. $(\psi \rightarrow (\phi \rightarrow \theta)) \rightarrow ((\psi \rightarrow \phi) \rightarrow (\psi \rightarrow \theta))$
c. $(\neg\psi \rightarrow \neg\phi) \rightarrow ((\neg\psi \rightarrow \phi) \rightarrow \psi)$
d. $\forall x\psi \rightarrow \psi(t/x)$
e. $\forall x(\psi \rightarrow \phi) \rightarrow (\forall x\psi \rightarrow \forall x\phi)$

Here ψ and ϕ are arbitrary formulas of PC and $\psi(t/x)$ is the result of uniformly substituting t for x in ψ. The choice of the axioms is determined not by their intuitiveness but by considerations of formal simplicity. The standard rules of inference for PC are given in (108) (*modus ponens*) and (109) (generalization).

(108) From ψ and $\psi \rightarrow \phi$ you can infer ϕ.

(109) From ψ you can infer $\forall x\psi$.

The predicate calculus as a formal system is made up of PC plus the axioms in (107) and inference rules (108) and (109). In terms of this apparatus we can now explicitly define the notions of proof and theorem.

(110) A sequence of well-formed formulas $\langle \psi_1, \ldots, \psi_n \rangle$ is a *proof* iff for $1 \leq i \leq n$, ψ_i is either an axiom or is derived from $\psi_1, \ldots, \psi_{i-1}$ by one of the inference rules.

(111) A formula ϕ is a *theorem* iff there exists a proof $\langle \psi_1, \ldots, \psi_n \rangle$ such that $\psi_n = \phi$.

So informally, a proof is a sequence of formulas such that each member of the sequence is either an axiom or derivable from already proven formulas by means of inference rules. A theorem is the last line of a proof. For the benefit of the reader unfamiliar with these notions, let us give an example of a proof. In (112) we show that $p \rightarrow p$ (where p is any formula) can be derived from the axioms in (101) and hence is a theorem of PC.

(112) *a.* $\underset{\psi}{\underline{p}} \rightarrow ((\underset{\phi}{\underline{p \rightarrow p)}} \rightarrow \underset{\theta}{\underline{p}})) \rightarrow ((\underset{\psi}{\underline{p}} \rightarrow (\underset{\phi}{\underline{p \rightarrow p)}} \rightarrow (\underset{\psi}{\underline{p}} \rightarrow \underset{\theta}{\underline{p}}))$
Axiom (107*b*)

b. $\underset{\psi}{\underline{p}} \rightarrow ((\underset{\phi}{\underline{p \rightarrow p)}} \rightarrow \underset{\psi}{\underline{p}}))$ Axiom (107*a*)

c. $((p \rightarrow (p \rightarrow p)) \rightarrow (p \rightarrow p))$ From (*a*) and (*b*) by *modus ponens*

d. $\underset{\psi}{p} \rightarrow (\underset{\phi}{p} \rightarrow \underset{\psi}{p})$ Axiom (107*a*)

e. $p \rightarrow p$ From (*c*) and (*d*) by *modus ponens*

The Greek letters written under the formulas indicate what part of the axiom each subformula corresponds to. The sequence of formulas $\langle (112a), \ldots, (112e) \rangle$ comprises a proof and its last line, (112*e*), is a theorem of PC. Not all theorems of PC are so trivial, but they are all proved by means of the same machinery.

We can further define the notion that ψ is derivable from ϕ by saying that if we take ϕ as a premise (as an additional axiom, if you wish), ψ is provable in terms of the deductive machinery of PC. This gives us a notion closely related to the notion of entailment but defined in purely syntactic terms, that is, solely in terms of the structural properties of configurations of symbols and independently of their meaning.

A natural question to ask is, What exactly is the relation between the syntactic characterization "ψ is derivable in PC from ϕ" and the semantic characterization "ϕ entails ψ"? Both are relations between sentences of a certain language. They are defined totally independently of one another and yet they intuitively appear to be related. They can both be regarded as characterizing the conditions under which the information that ψ conveys is in some relevant sense included in the information that ϕ conveys.

The question of how the syntactic notion of provability relates to the semantic notion of entailment breaks down into two subparts. Let us examine them separately. The first subpart can be put in the following terms: if ψ is derivable from ϕ (in some formal system such as PC), does ϕ entail ψ (with respect to a given semantics for the language)? This question is equivalent to the following: if ψ is derivable from ϕ, is ψ true whenever ϕ is true? An affirmative answer to this question would tell us something very important concerning our formal system. It would tell us that the system does what it is supposed to do, namely, enable us to infer conclusions from premises without ever letting us infer *false* conclusions from *true* premises. If our formal system meets this requirement, it is consistent or *sound.*

We cannot rely on the self-evidence of the axioms or inference rules to conclude that a formal system is sound. Seemingly unproblematic assumptions have often turned out to be inconsistent. And an inconsistent calculus is pretty useless: it is unable to separate valid inferences from invalid ones.

How can we prove that a formal system (for example, PC) is sound? One way of doing it is by showing inductively that all its axioms are logically valid and that its inference rules are truth preserving. We illustrate the strategy by showing that (101*a*) is logically valid (or true in every model) and that *modus ponens* is truth preserving.

Assume that for some model M and assignment g, $[\![\psi \rightarrow (\phi \rightarrow \psi)]\!]^{M,g} = 0$. Then, by the semantics for $\rightarrow$ it must be the case that $[\![\psi]\!]^{M,g} = 1$ and $[\![(\phi \rightarrow \psi)]\!]^{M,g} = 0$. The latter is possible iff $[\![\phi]\!]^{M,g} = 1$ and $[\![\psi]\!]^{M,g} = 0$, again by the semantics for $\rightarrow$. But then we should have that $[\![\psi]\!]^{M,g} = 1$ and $[\![\psi]\!]^{M,g} = 0$, a contradiction. Therefore, for every model M and assignment g, we must have that $[\![\psi \rightarrow (\phi \rightarrow \psi)]\!]^{M,g} = 1$.

Let us next show that *modus ponens* is truth preserving. Assume that there is a model M and an assignment g such that $[\![\psi]\!]^{M,g} = 1$ and $[\![\psi \rightarrow \phi]\!]^{M,g} = 1$ but $[\![\phi]\!]^{M,g} = 0$. By the latter two assumptions and the semantics for $\rightarrow$, it follows that $[\![\psi]\!]^{M,g} = 0$. But this contradicts our first assumption. Thus for any model M and assignment

g, if $[\![\psi]\!]^{M,g} = 1$ and $[\![\psi \to \phi]\!]^{M,g} = 1$, it must also be the case that $[\![\phi]\!]^{M,g} = 1$.

To complete our soundness proof, we would have to show that all the axioms in (101) are logically valid and that the generalization rule preserves truth. It turns out that this is indeed the case: PC is a sound system.

The second question that we can ask about the relation between provability and entailment is the following: whenever ψ entails ϕ, is it also the case that ϕ is syntactically derivable from ψ? An answer to the latter question tells us whether our formal system is *complete*, whether it characterizes as provable all the arguments that our semantics independently characterizes as valid. If we can show that ψ entails ϕ but ϕ is not derivable from ψ, then the formal calculus would be incomplete (with respect to the given semantics). It can be proved that PC is complete in this sense. There are many interesting standard formal systems that turn out to be incomplete. Completeness, however, signals that the system is in an important sense nonarbitrary: provable inferences, syntactically characterized, coincide exactly with valid inferences, semantically characterized.

So formal systems (or calculi) can be studied from both a syntactic and a semantic point of view. The branch of logic that focuses on formal systems as provability devices is called proof theory, while the one that studies them from a semantic point of view is called model theory. The notion of truth is absolutely central to the latter. It is by playing the syntactic and semantic perspective against each other that we can learn the most about the properties of a given calculus.

These considerations enable us to address several questions concerning the notion of logical form. The term *logical form* tends to be used very differently by different people, which leads to considerable confusion.

Consider, for example, the notion of LF introduced in section 2.1. LF is defined as a level of syntactic structure that arises when certain rules (specifically, QR) are applied to S-structures. In particular, we are using LF as a level of structure at which quantifier scope and anaphoric dependencies are disambiguated. If we were to stop at that, there would be nothing specifically logical about LF. Logic, we think, has to do with valid inference patterns. LF as such doesn't characterize them. To do that, we need either to specify a proof theory for LF or a way of interpreting it that supports a definition of entailment.

This is not merely a quibble about the word *logical*. The point is rather that something is needed to give to LF (or some other relevant level of syntactic structure) its actual semantic bite. That something must incorporate at least a characterization of our intuitions about what entails what.

Conceivably, one might want to explore the following strategy for semantics. We might systematically (or compositionally) map the relevant level of syntactic structure into a formal calculus and use the deductive machinery of the calculus to characterize the relevant semantic notions. After all, we have just seen that in a significant class of cases (sound and complete systems) the definitions of "ψ is derivable from ϕ" and "ϕ entails ψ" pick out exactly the same pairs of formulas (that is, ψ is derivable from ϕ iff ϕ entails ψ). We could view such a map onto a formal calculus as providing us with logical forms (*lfs*) for English sentences. (Note that the *lfs* provided by formal calculi are different from LFs produced by quantifier raising.) Such logical forms can further be viewed as abstract characterizations of the mental representations that we associate with sentences. One basis for such a claim is the following. If the mind is a computational device, our recognizing semantic relatedness, and in particular our recognizing what entails what, would seem to be based on some mental calculus that specifies semantic relations among sentences on the basis of their formal properties. And our theory of logical form provides us with a formal calculus that characterizes how sentences are semantically related and makes empirically testable predictions. This does not mean, of course, that the mind actually goes through derivations such as the one in (112) to assess entailments. As Stanley Peters put it, our theory is a theory of *what* it is that the mind must compute, not of *how* it computes it (see Johnson-Laird (1983), p. 167).

A view such as this, or some more refined variant of it, however appealing, must, we think, be modified by two considerations. First, mapping English into an uninterpreted calculus cannot exhaust all there is to say about meaning. We use English to talk about reality, and we need some way of characterizing how this happens. As we have tried to show, the notions of truth and denotation give us a handle, an indispensable one, we think, on how this happens.

Second, a calculus must be sound, for otherwise it is useless. And unless it is complete, we have no guarantee that the correspondence between its theorems and valid arguments is nonarbitrary. How do we know that a calculus has these properties?

Again, as we have seen above, the notions of truth and denotation in a model have proved to be formidable tools on this score.

Thus this approach to the notions of logical form and semantic representation might well be viable. But we fail to see how this can be if these notions are not solidly grounded on a truth-conditional and denotational perspective to ensure that the truth-conditional interpretation of the calculus we use is a known quantity.

Exercise 9 Add to F_2 (display (56)) the following syntactic rules:

(56) *r.* NP → no N
s. NP → not every N

Give the semantics for (56*r*) and (56*s*). According to the semantics you have given, does (1*a*) entail (1*b*) and does (2*a*) entail (2*b*)? Does the result you get match your intuitive judgment?

(1) *a.* No man smokes.
b. Not every man smokes.

(2) *a.* Some man drinks, and no man smokes.
b. Not every man smokes.

4 Speaking, Meaning, and Doing

1 Introduction

How do people use language to convey what they mean? In this chapter we suggest how a model-theoretic semantics can help answer this question. The English fragment F_2 generates declarative sentences and includes an interpretation function $[\![\ ]\!]$ that recursively assigns truth conditions to them. This program helps us provide a precise account of entailment relations and other semantic notions. We have also used it to explore some of the complexities of possible structural constraints in English on anaphoric relations. But it is not immediately obvious just what role a formal account of the semantics of a language can play in helping us understand language production and its subsequent interpretation. We know that people use language to implement their various aims and intentions, to *do* things. What we want to explore is the connection between linguistic meaning and these activities.

We are not attempting to describe directly the uses of language. Those uses, however, are part of the empirical data to which our theoretical account of semantic competence must be responsive. Knowing "how to do things with words," as J. L. Austin (1962) so nicely put it, depends on our having the linguistic knowledge that a semantic theory attempts to model. And what people do with their language provides evidence about the nature of the grammar of that language, including its semantic rules.

F_2 is an abstract system, a formal language that is describable in terms that make no reference to how or why speakers might use such a system, to their intentions, goals, or attitudes. In F_2, for example, we can prove that sentences (1*a*) and (1*b*) together entail (1*c*).

(1) *a*. Pavarotti hates every woman.
b. Sophia Loren is a woman.
c. Pavarotti hates Loren.

This entailment relation is independent of what speakers believe or do; it is a matter of the relation that holds between $[\![(1a)]\!]$, $[\![(1b)]\!]$, and $[\![(1c)]\!]$ in all models for F_2. If, however, English speakers who utter strings like these are indeed using a system like F_2, we expect this entailment relation to place constraints on the kinds of utterances they can successfully use.

For example, we would be surprised indeed to find a speaker who utters (1*a*) and (1*b*) assertively while denying (1*c*) in the same discourse. Of course, (1*a*) could be offered as a supposition or somewhat tentative assertion and then considered together with (1*b*). In such a discourse the denial of (1*c*) would constitute good grounds for rejecting the earlier supposition (1*a*). In other words, what F_2 is like places certain limits on how its sentences will be used by rational linguistic agents.

There are not only constraints but also possibilities of use that F_2 helps us understand. For example, someone who takes you already to believe that (1*b*) is true can sensibly assert (1*a*) with the aim of conveying (1*c*) to you: (1*a*) might be offered, for instance, to challenge your assertion that no one hates Sophia Loren. Sentence (1*a*) will be a good tool for that job in the imagined context precisely because of the entailment relations that F_2 specifies (and the speaker's belief that you recognize those relations). In offering F_2 as a fragment of English, we make a claim that ordinary speakers of English can in fact use its sentences in certain ways in situated discourse and cannot use them in other ways. It is facts about English speakers that constitute our evidence that they know and use a system something like F_2. The grammar of F_2 does not itself, however, specify how speakers might use and hearers interpret its sentences. The relation between that grammar and facts like these about linguistic communication is necessarily indirect. To understand it better, we will draw on work in linguistic pragmatics and the philosophy of language.

2 Expression Meaning and Speaker's Meaning

Our focus so far has been on assigning meaning to linguistic expressions. The meaning of a declarative sentence, we have said, is associated with its truth conditions: a sentence α means that p just in case α is true in situation v iff p, where p is some sentence of our metalanguage that gives the truth conditions for α. So, for example, we say that the meaning of (2*a*) is a proposition that is true in model M just in case $[\![(2a)]\!]^M = 1$ in M; this proposition is expressed by the set-theoretic statement (2*b*).

(2) *a.* Pavarotti doesn't like Loren.
   b. $\langle [\![\text{Pavarotti}]\!]^M, [\![\text{Loren}]\!]^M \rangle \notin [\![\text{like}]\!]^M$

F_2 is a formal language, but we have claimed that it models a fragment of English and that our account of the truth conditions of its sentences is a partial account of the semantic knowledge of English speakers. We have also claimed that knowledge of this kind underlies the capacity of English speakers to use (2*a*) to convey the information that Pavarotti doesn't like Loren. If Joan believes that Pavarotti doesn't like Loren and wants to share this belief with Alan, Joan can utter (2*a*), and we say that in so uttering, Joan herself means that Pavarotti doesn't like Loren. If in uttering (2*a*) to Alan, Joan cannot mean that Pavarotti doesn't like Loren, then we are inclined to say that F_2 is not a fragment of the language Joan uses for communicating with Alan. That a sentence means that *p* in a language is somehow connected to its being reliably useable by speakers of that language to mean that *p* and to communicate that meaning to one another.

We already have some account of what it is for a sentence, a linguistic *expression*, to mean that *p*. In this section we want to say something about what it is for a *speaker* to mean that *p*, and we want to consider in somewhat more detail how these two distinct notions of meaning might be related to one another. (As is customary in linguistic discussions, the word *speaker* is not confined to those who are audibly uttering expressions but includes any utterer of a linguistic expression, no matter what medium the expression is uttered in.)

What is it for a *speaker A* to mean that *p* in uttering sentence α? When you read sentence (2*a*) above, you undoubtedly did not understand us, the authors of this book, to mean that Pavarotti doesn't like Loren even though you understand that the expression we produced means that. We have simply *mentioned* that sentence as an example without really *using* it. We are expressing no opinions at all about Pavarotti's attitude toward Loren when we cite this sentence to illustrate our general points about sentence meaning. In general, we don't intend you to draw any conclusions about what we think of Pavarotti or Loren on the basis of the many example sentences we provide. Although the sentences in our examples are associated with meanings in English and thus can be understood both by us and our readers, our uttering those sentences as examples does not involve our using them to mean something. In such cases the expressions mean something, but the speakers are not using them to mean something. For someone to mean something in uttering a sentence, more is required than just producing a written or phonetic realization of the sentence, knowing what the sentence itself means, and expecting one's addressee to share that knowledge.

What more is needed? Grice (1957; 1989, chap. 14) provided a ground-breaking discussion of this question that linked meaningful use of linguistic expressions with various other ways people might communicate and also with the more general notion of meaning as evidence ("Those clouds mean rain"). These ideas are developed further in Grice (1968; 1969; 1982; reprinted as 1989, chaps. 6, 5, and 18). Part of Grice's answer is implicit in our explanation of why our mentioning example sentences like (2*a*) does not involve our using them to mean anything. We do not mean that Pavarotti doesn't like Loren because we do not intend for you to take our utterance of sentence (2*a*) as evidence of anything at all about Pavarotti and Loren. This suggests that one who does utter (2*a*) to mean that Pavarotti doesn't like Loren is using the sentence in order to produce in others a certain opinion about Pavarotti's feelings toward Loren. A speaker who means that Pavarotti doesn't like Loren must intend addressess to take the utterance as evidence about Pavarotti's relation to Loren.

Intending one's utterance to count as evidence that some proposition p is true is not all that is required for one to mean that p. Suppose that Joan utters (2*a*) intending to impress others by giving them evidence of intimate acquaintance with certain famous people. We would not say that in uttering (2*a*), Joan means that she is intimately acquainted with Pavarotti and Loren. Although she intends her addressees to take the utterance as evidence of such an acquaintance, she does not intend to accomplish this effect through getting the addressees to recognize her intention to give them information about her relation to Pavarotti and Loren. To mean that p, says Grice, is to intend addressees to recognize one's intention that one's utterance is to count as evidence that p, and furthermore, to intend that the addressee's recognition of one's intention be instrumental in achieving the intended effect. In the case of Joan's name-dropping, her intention to impress could be achieved even if the hearer did not take her to have intended that effect (perhaps the hearer assumes she is modest but reasons that she must know these famous folk to be so well informed about their relationship). In fact, Joan's chances of success in impressing others are probably enhanced if her addressees do not recognize what she seeks to accomplish.

Grice considers a number of examples of utterances for which we might say that a speaker intended to convey that *p* but where we would nonetheless not be willing to say that the speaker meant that *p*. On the basis of such examples he arrives at something like the following definition:

(3) Speaker *A* means that *p* in uttering α to hearer *B* iff *A* intends the utterance of α to lead *B* to adopt a certain attitude toward *p*, and *A* also intends *B*'s recognition of *A*'s intention to be instrumental in producing in *B* the intended attitude toward *p*.

The phrase *a certain attitude* in definition (3) is neutral about exactly what sort of attitude might be involved. Different attitudes in the addressee will be aimed at if the speaker is doing something like directing or inquiring rather than stating. We set aside such complications for now but discuss some of them in subsequent sections.

Suppose a speaker utters (2*a*), "Pavarotti doesn't like Loren," and means exactly what it literally says, that is, what is expressed by the set-theoretic statement in (2*b*). Such a speaker, according to (3), is intending to produce in a potential audience something like the belief that Pavarotti is not linked by the *like* relation to Loren, or at least a recognition in that audience that the speaker so believes. We might say that in uttering (2*a*), the speaker intends to express the information that Pavarotti doesn't like Loren and to mean thereby that Pavarotti doesn't like Loren. The speaker presents that proposition as true in some situation, as a piece of information about that situation. The information is conveyed if the audience is led to believe on the basis of understanding the utterance (and taking the speaker to be a reliable informant) that Pavarotti doesn't like Loren in the situation being discussed.

When the speaker means that *p* in uttering α, *p* is said to be the *speaker's meaning* (or the *occasion meaning*) of that utterance of α. What α itself means is *expression meaning* or *timeless meaning* (Grice's expression) or *linguistic meaning* or the *semantic value* of α. If in uttering sentence (2*a*) Joan means that (2*b*) is true, then the speaker's meaning of that utterance of (2*a*), what Joan herself means, and the expression meaning, what the sentence she uttered means, completely coincide. Joan means just exactly what the sentence she has uttered means.

Grice proposes that speaker's meaning is fundamental. A sentence α has proposition p as its timeless meaning, he suggests, when there is some sort of convention in uttering α to mean that p. We can recast this suggestion as (4):

(4) Sentence α means that p in community C iff there is some convention established among the members of C that to utter α is to mean that p (or that the speaker's meaning of utterances of α is p).

More concretely, the English sentence "Pavarotti doesn't like Loren" has the truth conditions that it does in F_2 because English speakers have established certain conventions specifying that in uttering the sentence, they mean that Pavarotti doesn't like Loren. Actually working out the details of such a proposal requires elaboration of the notion of a convention; Lewis (1969) and Schiffer (1972) are examples of the many philosophical contributions to this endeavor that are relevant for thinking about how humans endow bursts of sound (or assemblages of marks) with conventional meaning. Grice himself (1982; 1989, chap. 18) moved to the view that it is communitywide social norms or canons of propriety governing speaker's meaning that underlie expression meaning rather than conventions as such. But the central idea is much the same: conventional linguistic meaning derives from socially regulated or conventionalized intentional actions.

Of course, norms that regulate what speakers mean in uttering sentences cannot be established sentence by sentence. Defining expression meaning as suggested in (4) cannot be the full story, since speakers must know how to calculate sentential meanings recursively. When we said that there is a convention for meaning that Pavarotti does not like Loren in uttering "Pavarotti doesn't like Loren," we were speaking somewhat loosely. Rather, there must be norms for using words and syntactic structures that yield the result that utterances of the sentence in question conventionally convey the informational content in question. What might such usage conventions be like?

Certain lower-level expressions can be linked in a fairly direct way to speaker's intentions in using them. For example, in using *Pavarotti*, speakers can intend to refer to Luciano Pavarotti. We can say that the *speaker's reference* of *Pavarotti* is Pavarotti if it is Pavarotti to whom the speaker intends to refer when uttering *Pavarotti*. Or in saying of someone that she is hungry, we can say that one intends to attribute to her the property of being hungry. Then we can speak of a convention to refer to Pavarotti when uttering *Pavarotti* or a convention to attribute hunger to the subject when uttering is *hungry*. But we need not link linguistic expressions so directly with the actions that the speaker conventionally performs in using them. Speaker's meaning for many expressions below the clausal level may be just a matter of what the speaker intends the expression to contribute to the overall speaker's meaning of the utterance in which it occurs; that is, it may be just a matter of the contribution the expression makes to what the speaker means in producing that utterance.

The fundamental idea, however it is elaborated, is that conventions of language exist to help language users with their projects of affecting one another by producing bursts of noise, stretches of written symbols, or manual displays (as in American Sign Language). Utterances are reliably informative because conventions regulate what speakers mean in producing them.

It might be objected that we cannot equate what sentences mean with norms for what speakers mean in uttering them because many natural language sentences are ambiguous or include context-dependent elements and thus are not assigned truth conditions directly but only relative to something else. Suppose we have an utterance of (5*a*); then the proposition that the sentence expresses is defined only relative to an *lf* (logical form), either an *lf* interpreted in the same way as the PC formula (5*b*) or one interpreted like (5*c*).

(5) *a.* Someone likes everyone.
b. $\exists x \forall y$ like (x, y)
c. $\forall y \exists x$ like (x, y)

In using such a sentence to mean something, the speaker must select one logical form rather than the other (and intend addressees to select that same logical form). What the speaker means coincides with what the expression she utters means if what she means is identical with either the proposition expressed by (5*b*) or that expressed by (5*c*). It is plausible to think of the speaker as selecting not just a string to utter, something like (5*a*), but a structured expression in which the relative scopes of the quantified NPs are indicated (for example, a structure in which QR is applied to the subject NP before it is applied to the object NP, a structure interpreted like (5*c*)). If we take the uttered expression to consist not just of a string of words but also of an *lf*, we can think of someone producing (5*a*) as also uttering (5*b*) or (5*c*) and thus able to mean exactly what the expression she uttered means. English often uses stress and intonation to help convey which *lf* is associated with the uttered string. Nonetheless, it is quite possible for the same surface phonetic form to be associated with different *lf*s. But to understand what is meant a hearer must know which expression, which *lf*, the speaker is uttering.

Other sorts of ambiguities can be thought of in much the same way. In the case of lexical ambiguities, for example, we make the plausible assumption that there are multiple lexical entries for the ambiguous form, several "words" at some abstract level, and we define an interpretation relative to a particular entry in the lexicon (associating, for example, *bull* with the entry equivalent to *male bovine* rather than with that equivalent to *nonsense*). Syntactic ambiguities in surface structure require that we interpret relative to a particular constituent structure (associating *competent women and men*, for example, with [[competent women] and [men]] rather than with [competent [women and men]]).

Similarly, to associate an utterance of (6*a*) with a unique proposition, say (6*b*), we need some contextual specification of a value for the pronoun, and in the preceding chapter we used the assignment function *g* for this job.

(6) *a.* He likes Loren.
 b. $\langle g(\text{he}_1), [\![\text{Loren}]\!]^M \rangle \in [\![\text{like}]\!]^M$

Again the speaker is responsible for the pointing needed to establish just what she has said. In this case too there is a sense in which we might say that a speaker means exactly what she has said if we include in what she has said the contextually established assignment of a value to the pronoun. What the speaker has said tells the hearer to look for a pointing. Actually figuring out who is so indicated may be a complex matter and certainly involves more than just linguistic knowledge. For example, the speaker may point at a group that the hearer judges to include only one man (on the basis of a cursory assessment of clothing, hairstyles, body types, etc.); the hearer will use perceptual information, beliefs about sex-based differences in appearance, and various other kinds of data. Nonetheless, someone who points at Pavarotti and utters (6*a*) to mean that Pavarotti likes Loren has said directly and literally what she means. It is just that what has been uttered is in some sense incomplete. A sentence with a free pronoun does not express a proposition by itself. A contextual parameter must be supplied for interpreting the pronoun in order to arrive at the propositional content expressed by such a sentence. Something like the assignment function must be included in any account of the semantic contribution of pronouns. As we will see in chapters 5 and 6, pronouns are not the only expressions whose semantic interpretation requires reference to such parameters set by speakers. For a sentence with context-sensitive elements, what a speaker conventionally means in uttering it is what that sentence means relative to some contextual parameter (often one that the speaker may help set by pointing or in some other way).

The speaker's intentions are relevant both to disambiguation—choosing a particular logical form or lexical item—and to completing meaning for expressions that require further contextual specification—establishing reference for pronouns, for example. But our descriptions of disambiguation and of such phenomena as reference fixing can be given without referring to a speaker's interest in producing certain kinds of effects, as we have seen in the preceding chapters.

Grice introduces the notion of the *applied timeless meaning* of the utterance of α to cover disambiguation and contextual specification. In his view the semantic rules of the language will tell us what propositions are potentially available as applied timeless meanings for a particular sentence α, what speakers might conventionally mean in uttering α. Where a string is ambiguous or incomplete, the rules tell us that an utterance of α expresses one of the propositions available as a disambiguation or completion. The linguistic rules themselves do not say which such proposition is expressed by uttering the string, just as the syntactic rules do not tell us what string will be uttered. A speaker selects one of the applied timeless meanings associated by "timeless" linguistic conventions with the string uttered.

Can we now stop? If Alice means that *p* in uttering α as an English sentence, must we conclude that the (applied timeless) meaning of α in English is that *p*? Not always. Alice's meaning may be different from the meaning of α because Alice made a mistake. She intended to utter a sentence with applied timeless meaning that *p*, but what she actually said does not have *p* as an applied timeless meaning. A slip of the tongue and the word *like* is subtituted for *hate*: Alice utters (7*a*), although she actually intended to utter (7*b*).

(7) *a*. Pavarotti likes Loren.
b. Pavarotti hates Loren.

Or perhaps Alice is new to English and mistakenly thinks that (7*a*) means in English what (7*b*) actually means. In both cases her mistake is linguistic; for some reason the expression actually uttered does not have in English the meaning that she intended her utterance to have.

There are also nonlinguistic mistakes that create a divergence between the speaker's meaning and the meaning of the sentence uttered. For example, Keith may see Pavarotti and Bond standing in the corner at a cocktail party; Pavarotti is drinking a colorless liquid with an olive floating in it from a martini glass, and Bond is drinking a colorless liquid with ice cubes in it from a tall tumbler. Believing that Pavarotti is drinking a martini and Bond water, Keith utters (8), thinking that what it expresses is the proposition that Pavarotti doesn't like Loren.

(8) The man drinking the martini doesn't like Loren.

Unbeknownst to Keith, however, Pavarotti's martini glass contains only water (and an olive), whereas Bond is drinking not water but a very large martini poured over ice in a tall glass. So what the sentence uttered actually expresses is the proposition that Bond doesn't like Loren, though what Keith intended to say was that Pavarotti doesn't like Loren. Suppose Keith is speaking to Sheila, who knows about the deceptive glasses. Sheila may understand perfectly well what he means because she correctly realizes that he intended simply to refer to a particular person—Pavarotti, the man who is actually drinking water from a martini glass. It intuitively seems that Sheila also knows that what Keith said was not what he meant. If she further knows that Pavarotti doesn't like Loren whereas Bond does, Sheila will probably be willing to take Keith as having expressed a truth, although she is aware that, literally interpreted, his words expressed a falsehood.

Donnellan (1966) speaks of *referential* uses of definite descriptions in cases like this where the speaker uses the content of the description only as a device for referring to some individual. Had Keith known that the individual was Pavarotti, he might have uttered our familiar (2*a*), "Pavarotti doesn't like Loren." Or if he had known about the glasses and their contents, he might have uttered (9).

(9) The man drinking water doesn't like Loren.

We are generally quite charitable in our interpretations in such cases. So long as the hearer is able to zero in on the same individual as the speaker, little significance is attached to whether the content of the description offered by the speaker to establish the individual as referent does or does not actually apply to that individual.

Donnellan contrasts such cases with *attributive* uses of definite descriptions, where the speaker wants to say something about whoever the description fits. Suppose Keith had uttered (10) in the circumstances above.

(10) The man drinking a martini will get drunk.

It is still possible that Keith simply wants to refer to Pavarotti and to say that he will get drunk. It seems more likely, however, that he means that whoever is drinking the martini will get drunk. Keith might only have been told that one man is drinking a martini and have no idea which one that is (being too far away to see their glasses) and want to say that the one who is will get drunk.

Kripke (1977) has argued persuasively that *the man drinking the martini* has the same *semantic reference* at the party (it happens to be Bond), whether Keith uses it referentially or attributively. Semantic reference is determined by timeless meaning and the circumstances. The *speaker's reference* of that NP, however, may vary, according to whether it is being used to refer to some individual independently identified by the speaker or to refer to whatever individual the chosen description actually applies to. In the case described above where Keith uttered (8) and was using the definite description to refer to Pavarotti (inaccurately, as it happens), what Keith means in uttering (8), the speaker's meaning of that utterance, is different from the applied timeless meaning of his utterance of (8), the linguistic meaning of what he said. We don't even need to suppose that Keith is mistaken about the facts. He might know of the deceptive glasses but take his hearer to be confused and thus use a description that he has reason to think will work for the hearer, even though he himself knows the description is inaccurate.

Of course, whether or not semantic and speaker reference coincide, a speaker who uses a description referentially often means something different from one who uses it attributively. The attributive speaker may intend to convey that there is some connection between an individual's satisfying the description and having the property ascribed to the referent of the description, whereas the referential speaker intends to attribute the property on the basis of what is believed about some individual independently of whether that individual satisfies the definite description used to refer to him (or her). But these further messages that might sometimes be conveyed do not support the view that there is a systematic semantic ambiguity underlying the distinction between referential and attributive uses of a definite description. Notice that sentence (10) could be used in circumstances where we might hesitate to say that its use was either purely attributive or purely referential. Keith might want to say of some particular man that he will get drunk, but he might be using as evidence for his saying so his belief that the man is drinking a martini. Keith might believe that if Bond is drinking a martini, he will not get drunk, but that Pavarotti is particularly susceptible to martinis. The difference between attributive and referential uses of definite descriptions thus seems to be a matter of the sort of evidence a speaker is depending on in stating that some property or other holds of the individual who satisfies the description.

Exercise 1 As evidence that a purely referential interpretation of a definite description like *the man drinking the martini* is assigned by semantic rules as a sense of that expression, some have pointed to Sheila's willingness to accept Keith's utterance of (8) as true just in case the intended referent of *the man drinking the martini* (Pavarotti) doesn't like Loren. That is, they claim that she is willing to understand the utterance on the referential interpretation and appraise its truth on that interpretation. Interpreted attributively, the sentence is false; the martini drinker (Bond) does like Loren.

Let us now suppose a different scenario in which Keith utters (1) below, intending thereby to say of the man holding the martini glass (Pavarotti, as it happens) that he doesn't like Loren.

(1) Bond doesn't like Loren.

Again, a hearer who realizes which man is Bond and which is Pavarotti may nonetheless also realize to which man Keith intended to refer and thus charitably treat him as having expressed a truth, while nonetheless recognizing that if *Bond* is interpreted as referring to Bond, then the sentence expresses a falsehood. Should we conclude that sentence (1) above is ambiguous? Discuss this example and its implications for this argument in support of the claim that the referential/attributive distinction reflects systematic ambiguity in definite descriptions.

Grice himself was especially interested in cases where no linguistic or other mistakes are involved and yet we are still inclined to say that what the speaker means is not the same as the applied timeless meaning of the utterance. One kind of example is illustrated by the sentences in (11).

(11) *a.* [Linda]$_i$ met the love of [her]$_i$ life, and [she]$_i$ got married.
b. [Linda]$_i$ got married, and [she]$_i$ met the love of [her]$_i$ life.

We typically interpret (11*a*) as part of a happy story, whereas (11*b*) suggests an impending tragedy, or at least a hard choice for Linda. Yet the semantic value we have assigned to *and* would lead us to assign the same applied timeless meaning to utterances of the two sentences (relative to some particular reference for *Linda*).

Consider (12), an example Carston (1988) attributes to Deirdre Wilson.

(12) It is better to meet the love of your life and get married than to get married and meet the love of your life.

Utterance of such a sentence would be pretty near incomprehensible if we supposed that the speaker meant the same thing by *to meet the love of your life and get married* and *to get married and meet the love of your life*. In actual discourse the proposition a speaker means to convey in uttering a particular expression often goes beyond what the expression itself means. A cooperative hearer will interpret the sentences in (11) as if the speaker had actually uttered the corresponding sentences in (13).

(13) *a.* [Linda]$_i$ met [the love of [her]$_i$ life]$_j$, and then [she]$_i$ got married to [him]$_j$.
b. [Linda]$_i$ got married to [someone]$_j$, and then [she]$_i$ met [the love of [her]$_i$ life]$_k$.

This filling in or expansion of what linguistic meaning provides is similar to looking for the referent of a free pronoun. But there is an important difference: the grammar directs the hearer to find a pronominal referent but not to provide a further specification of what the speaker means with the kind of sentence illustrated above. Nonetheless, there are principles that guide hearers in their interpretive tasks, whether disambiguating, fixing referents, or adding to what the speaker has actually encoded further aspects of the propositional content intended to be taken as if expressed. We need not spell out everything unambiguously and in full detail to one another. The reason is that interpretation can make use not only of linguistic knowledge but also of knowledge about the context in which we attempt communication and of expectations about one another as conventionally cooperative communicators.

There is a fable about the boy who cried "Wolf!" many times when no wolf was around and then was unable to issue the proper warning when a wolf finally did show up. The people who first heard the boy utter (14*a*) filled in his incomplete utterance. In doing this, they took him to mean that something like the proposition expressed by (14*b*) was true rather than something like what is expressed by (14*c*, *d* or *e*).

(14) *a.* Wolf!
b. I have just seen a wolf near here.
c. I have just been thinking about a wolf.
d. My father once saw a wolf in a field far from here.
e. A wolf can be dangerous.

Why? There is a general presumption that what the boy means in uttering (14*a*) will be a proposition that is immediately relevant to the addressees. It must also be a proposition addressees can be reasonably expected to identify just by recognizing the boy's intention to convey it. The boy crying "Wolf!" is responsible for somehow making the proposition he intends to convey manifest in his behavior (of which his utterance of the expression in question is one component) in the context in which he produces the utterance. Otherwise, he cannot intend to have it recognized without undue work on the part of his audience. Again it was Grice who first tried to explain in such terms how we are able to interpret beyond the letter of what is said. In section 5 we will say more about Grice's theory of conversation, a theory that has been developed in a variety of different ways (see, for example, Bach and Harnish 1979, Horn 1989, Levinson 1983, and Sperber and Wilson 1986). The central point is that the proposition in (14*b*) is a message of more critical importance or relevance to the audience than the others and is also easier to retrieve from the boy's utterance, on the assumption that the boy is doing his communicative job properly. The extreme brevity of the utterance might be a clue, since it is more appropriate for a warning, for which time is short, than for reports on one's own mental states, recountings of past history, or statements of general truths.

Let us recall what happened to the boy in this old tale. Because he uttered (14*a*) time after time in the absence of any wolf, the townspeople ceased to heed his cries. When the wolf finally did show up, the boy was unable to use "Wolf!" to convey that information to them. Lewis (1969) has argued that there are conventions of truthfulness for speakers and of trust for hearers that prevail in communities that successfully use some language for communicating with one another. The boy who cried "Wolf!" when none was there had failed to heed the truthfulness convention, eventually eroding the convention of trust on the part of his hearers and finally undermining completely his capacity to convey information to them.

The central point is that what an expression means is directly tied to conventions for what speakers can mean in uttering it. What a sentence means can be thought of as its truth conditions relative to disambiguation and contextual specification. But what an expression means is only part of the evidence available to the hearer for interpreting what the speaker means in uttering it. Speakers may succeed in meaning something different or more than the meaning of the expressions they have uttered because they and their audience share certain expectations about one another as communicators and certain beliefs about the situation in which they are placed. We may succeed in meaning propositions that have not been fully stated: recall sentence (14), "It is better to meet the love of your life and get married than to get married and meet the love of your life." Cooperative hearers use not only their linguistic knowledge but other information as well to figure out what speakers mean in their utterances, correcting linguistic and other mistakes and providing necessary specifications of propositional content that speakers have not overtly expressed.

So far we have considered only cases where speakers intend to speak directly and conventionally. Although the speaker may have made mistakes or not been fully explicit, the point of the utterance is not tied to any contrast between expression meaning and speaker meaning. Yet language can be used in more complex ways. A speaker can suggest some proposition and an attitude toward it but at the same time present this proposition and associated attitude as only suggested and not as directly part of what the utterance means. In such cases there is a clear sense in which there are different *levels* on which the speaker performs acts of meaning something.

For an example let's return to (2*a*), "Pavarotti doesn't like Loren." It is quite possible for Joan to utter this to Alan and to mean not only that Pavarotti doesn't like Loren but also the stronger proposition that Pavarotti hates Loren, the proposition that would be assigned as the timeless meaning of sentence (1*c*), "Pavarotti hates Loren." Joan may make this stronger proposition manifest to Alan in a number of ways. She can pronounce the utterance with intonation and stress that direct Alan to examine it critically. She can rely on his using their shared belief in Pavarotti's passionate nature (he is never neutral about his acquaintances: he either loves them or hates them). But her understatement is intended to be noticed as such: we cannot properly report her as simply having said that Pavarotti hates Loren, for such a report omits the effect achieved by her choice of the less direct mode of expression. She does not intend simply to get Alan to come to believe that Pavarotti hates Loren by recognizing that she so believes (and intends him to recognize that belief). If that had been her only purpose, the sensible strategy would have been to utter "Pavarotti hates Loren." Her circumlocution must be intended to get Alan to recognize something else, perhaps her own delicacy in putting the matter. Or Joan might utter (2*a*) ironically, intending to convey to Alan that Pavarotti does like Loren (perhaps very much indeed). Here too it will be important for Alan to take Joan not only as informing him that Pavarotti like Loren but also as doing so by uttering something that both she and he take to mean just the opposite.

In either case Joan is doing something more complicated than straightforward communication. There is an explicit level on which she means something, and there is an implicit level on which she means something else—something more in the case where she has understated the situation and something quite opposite in the case where she is speaking ironically. In each case, part of the effect she intends her utterance to have is produced by the contrast between these two different levels of her meaning.

Another kind of multilevel communication is illustrated by the example we used in chapter 1 to illustrate that interpreting utterances involves more than just semantic knowledge. We noted that Molly might utter "I'd like a glass of water" and thereby suggest that the hearer ought to do something to satisfy the desire she has expressed (such as bring her a glass of water). In such an utterance Molly's meaning is complex. On one level there is the proposition that she would like a glass of water presented as something to be believed by the hearer (on the basis of trusting her report). On another level there is the proposition that she will receive a glass of water, whose truth Molly intends to be ensured by an act of the hearer's. We will consider such cases of so-called *indirect speech acts* in more detail in section 4 below.

Fresh metaphors and many other figurative uses of language are also to be understood in terms of multiple levels of speaker's meaning. All such cases of multileveled communication go beyond simply conveying information and do other things as well: they amuse or give aesthetic pleasure or enhance social relationships. A speaker may utter an expression that is conventionally informative, yet conveying that information or any other propositional content may be quite secondary to the speaker's intentions, or perhaps not even a purpose at all. Nonetheless, analyzing straightforward communication will be an essential preliminary to developing illuminating accounts of these more complex uses of language, and so we will focus on the simpler cases.

Grice notes only that the speaker's meaning can diverge from what the uttered expression means; he does not comment on the fact that such divergence may sometimes itself also be part of what the speaker means. But the general spirit of Grice's proposal seems to us quite compatible with these added complexities. We can use Grice's ideas to help flesh out an account of the relation between linguistic meaning and what speakers mean in uttering linguistic expressions. The abstract semantic systems we are exploring in developing a partial account of the truth conditions for English sentences represent theories of conventions developed by communities of English speakers for what members of the community are to mean in uttering such sentences. These are conventions that regulate speakers' actions in presenting their beliefs (and other attitudes) to produce effects on the beliefs (and other attitudes) of their audience. Speakers need not always adhere to these conventions in order to achieve the effects they intend to achieve through their utterances: they sometimes make mistakes, and they often rely on hearers to fill in aspects of meaning they have not explicitly expressed. In other words, what a speaker means may be different from what the expression uttered means on the occasion of its utterance. In addition, there may be multiple levels of speaker's meaning: a single utterance may be the instrument for a complex communicative act that depends for its effect in part on contrast between explicit and implicit levels of speaker's meaning. Nonetheless, linguistic meaning—truth conditions for declarative sentences, for example—can be fruitfully thought of as in some sense created by conventions for performing certain kinds of actions intended to affect others in specific ways.

Thus the pragmatic notion of speaker's meaning complements our semantic account of linguistic meaning in two ways. First, it provides insight into what it is for a linguistic expression to be used meaningfully: it provides a way to connect abstract linguistic meaning with what people do by means of using language. We will further explore these connections in the following two sections on sentential force and speech acts. Second, it helps us understand how interpretations of actual utterances might sometimes fail to coincide with the linguistically assigned interpretations of the expressions uttered. In the final section on conversational implicatures we explore pragmatic principles of conversation that supplement semantic knowledge in successful communication.

3 Sentential Force and Discourse Dynamics

We might think of assigning truth conditions to a sentence as equivalent to representing the circumstances in which the sentence is true, the *content* of the sentence. As our discussion above of speaker's meaning makes clear, however, talk does not consist simply of presenting sequences of such representations of content in a way analogous to projecting a series of pictures on a screen. Consider the sentences in (15).

(15) *a.* Bond gives every fish to Loren.
b. Does Bond give every fish to Loren?
c. Give every fish to Loren, Bond.

In uttering (15*a*) and thereby meaning what that sentence expresses, a speaker must be thought of not only as producing a representation of certain circumstances (those in which Bond gives every fish to Loren) but also as doing something more in which the content of what is said will figure. A speaker might, for example, be affirming that the circumstances of which she is speaking can be accurately so represented and inviting the other conversationalists to join in such an affirmation. Among other things, in stating that (15*a*), a speaker expresses the view that Bond's giving every fish to Loren holds in, and in some sense describes, the circumstances that are being spoken of (which are often but not always those of the context in which the sentence is being uttered). And although (15*b*) and (15*c*) seem in some sense to involve the same circumstances as those described by (15*a*), we do not speak of either (15*b*) or (15*c*) as true or false relative to a circumstance.

Sentence (15*a*) is, of course, declarative, (15*b*) interrogative, and (15*c*) imperative. Only sentence (15*a*) is generated by the grammar in F_2, which also assigns it truth conditions of the appropriate kind. Relative to any circumstance in which (15*a*) is assigned a value of 1, (15*b*) is truly answerable by (15*a*) or more briefly with *yes*. And relative to such a circumstance, (15*c*) is complied with or satisfied; if Bond responds with acceptance to an utterance of (15*c*), then he undertakes to bring such a circumstance into existence. Our truth-conditional analysis of (15*a*) thus seems also to be relevant to an analysis of (15*b*) and (15*c*), but we will want to assign a different semantic value to each of the three sentences.

One thing that seems obvious is that sentences (15*a*–*c*) are designed to do different things when produced in a discourse. Thus whatever semantic value we assign to them should reflect and help explain this distinction in potential discourse functions. Suppose Pavarotti utters the sentences in (15). In English we can report each act by using the corresponding sentence in (16).

(16) *a.* Pavarotti stated that Bond gives every fish to Loren.
b. Pavarotti asked whether Bond gives every fish to Loren.
c. Pavarotti told Bond to give every fish to Loren.

Putting it so suggests why it seems so natural to distinguish two aspects of the meaning of a sentence: its content (what (15*a*–*c*) seem, more or less, to have in common) and *sentential force* (what the grammar assigns to the sentence to indicate how that content is conventionally presented). Sentential force in this sense would be the semantic correlate of sentence type (what differentiates the three sentences in (15) most sharply). Informally, declarative, interrogative, and imperative sentence forces can be identified with stating that, asking whether, and telling to, respectively, as suggested by the verbs and complementizers in (16) that introduce the common subordinate clause. (The subordinate clause in (16*c*) is tenseless in contrast to the tensed clauses in (16*a*, *b*); we will here ignore this difference.) Most of this section will be devoted to exploring the question of how an account of declarative force, stating that, might be incorporated in an expanded semantic theory.

The idea of treating the meaning of a sentence as consisting of two components, force and content, is an old one. For example, Frege distinguished the thought that a declarative sentence expresses from the assertion that what is expressed by the sentence is true. More generally, he took sentential force to be what distinguishes the meaning or semantic value of different sentence types:

An interrogative sentence and an assertoric [or declarative] one contain the same thought; but the assertoric sentence contains something else as well, namely, assertion. The interrogative sentence contains something more too.... Therefore, two things must be distinguished in an assertoric sentence: the content, which it has in common with the corresponding propositional question; and assertion.[1]

Frege introduced ⊢ to mark what he called "assertoric force" and what we have called "declarative force." Others have used symbols such as ? and ! to mark interrogative and imperative forces. Thus representations like those in (17) are sometimes proposed (see, for example, Lyons 1977).

(17) *a.* ⊢ [Bond give every fish to Loren]
b. ? [Bond give every fish to Loren]
c. ! [Bond give every fish to Loren]

Early transformational grammar had abstract syntactic markers Q and Imp that were supposed to be interpreted as interrogative and imperative force, respectively. But just writing such markers gives us no account of their value. In this section we will discuss some recent formal approaches to declarative force.

Linguistically assigned sentential forces need not be thought of as something mysterious and completely unlike the values available within a formal model-theoretic approach to semantic analysis. Considerable recent work in formal semantics and discourse theory is developing the view that sentential force can be modeled as a context-changing function: the change that uttering a particular sentence type produces in a discourse context. Extending the proposals made in Stalnaker (1974, 1978) and elsewhere, Heim (1983) suggests that we take our ⟦S⟧, the value assigned to a declarative sentence by the recursive rules of interpretation, to be not a truth value (in circumstance *v*) but a function that takes S together with the discourse context in which it is uttered and yields a new discourse context. Where S is a declarative sentence, this function will indirectly also specify the truth conditions of S. These ideas are developed with the help of some formal machinery that we present in chapters 5 and 6, and we will give a somewhat fuller (though still sketchy) picture of them in our discussion of presupposition in chapter 6. At this point we just want to outline a bit of the intuitive picture that underlies recent formal discourse theories and the dynamic semantics associated with them.

How can we formally characterize a conversation or a narrative or any other situation in which language is used? Adopting the simplifying idealization that each utterance is a sentence, we can start by thinking of a discourse as a sequence of sentences, $S_1, S_2, \ldots, S_n$. (Of course, in conversation many utterances are not complete sentences, but we can ignore this complication for our present purposes.) The effect of uttering sentence S_j generally depends not just on S_j itself but on what has been uttered before, on the preceding sentences $S_1, \ldots, S_{j-1}$. The sentences may all be produced by the same person (perhaps an author or a monologuist), or in the more interesting case of interactive discourse, different people may utter different sentences. The purpose of the discourse may be to amuse or inspire by speaking of some fictional beings and their affairs, to impress someone by assuming certain attitudes or access to information, to gossip about friends and colleagues, to make plans for dinner together next week, to work on revising the book one is writing, to pool information on a murder in an effort to crack the case, and so on. The abstract structure of discourse dynamics is essentially the same, however, no matter what particular aims and attitudes the participants happen to have.

As a discourse progresses, its participants jointly develop a slate of discourse commitments. Here we follow Stalnaker and Heim and call this slate the *common ground*. Other things can (and generally do) happen as discourse proceeds, but we want to focus on this component of the discourse context. The common ground is the participants' mutually developed public view of what they are talking about. It always includes the thoughts they have stated to one another insofar as such thoughts have not been challenged or withdrawn.

The common ground is of special importance in understanding Frege's assertive force. In conversations where we each express what we genuinely believe (and the others protest if someone expresses a belief from which they dissent), the common ground is mutually believed, although it may not include all that we believe, since we may keep some beliefs private. And, of course, we often engage in discourse in which no participant takes the thoughts expressed to be genuine beliefs (perhaps there is some pretense for the benefit of a third party). In all such cases, however, discourse participants are acting as if they mutually believe the common ground. As the philosopher G. E. Moore observed many years ago, there is something paradoxical in following an assertion of *p* with "but I don't believe *p*." Such a tag can only be construed as being on a different discourse level—an aside, perhaps, to signal that the common ground to which *p* is added is not one to be taken seriously. Although the proposition that the asserter of *p* does not believe *p* is perfectly consistent with *p*, the common ground cannot include at the same level as *p* the proposition that a discourse participant does not believe *p*. It is in this sense that the common ground represents what the conversationalists purport to mutually believe.

The discourse need not start with a clean slate. Most discourses take some commonplaces to be already in play (for example, that humans direct utterances toward one another intending thereby to achieve some kind of effect) or accessible if needed (for example, that water relieves thirst). Where the discourse starts depends on the previous shared history of the participants, the purposes of the discourse, and so on. Of course, one participant might take certain implicit assumptions as "in play," as part of the common ground, that the other participant was leaving out. For analytical purposes we can ignore this complication, since conversationalists who discover such differences usually make adjustments in order to ensure successful communication.

The common ground is not just a set of unconnected thoughts. As new propositions are added to it, participants consider what those added thoughts entail in light of their being joined to those previously entered. We "put two and two together" and draw conclusions. Where these conclusions seem blatantly obvious, participants often don't bother to state them explicitly but simply add them unspoken to the growing common ground. If a proposition is a candidate for joining the common ground but is recognized as inconsistent with what is already there, then either the new candidate is rejected or some earlier commitment is abandoned. In any case, conversationalists aim at consistency in developing the common ground. (We put aside for the moment the special kind of playing with paradox that Lewis Carroll has immortalized.) Whether we are constructing the common ground as fantasy or fact, the same general process goes on. Constructing the common ground as fact does have a kind of analytical priority, however. Even telling a story is a matter of speaking as if we were recounting real events.

Discourse participants look at the common ground as a coherent and connected set of thoughts because the discourse process is a collaborative delineation of a story or a view of circumstances—actual, possible, or perhaps desirable. As new thoughts are added, they serve to refine and further specify which circumstances participants are speaking of. An example will illustrate. Suppose someone utters (18*a*), and suppose the common ground already contains (18*b*).

(18) *a.* Pavarotti likes Loren.
b. Loren is a woman.

The common ground will now contain not only (18*a*) but also (19), which is entailed by the set consisting of (18*a*) and (18*b*).

(19) Pavarotti likes a woman.

In light of the inconsistency of liking and hating (which is not explicitly represented in fragment F_2), the common ground as now developed would be inconsistent with the proposition expressed by (20).

(20) Pavarotti hates every woman.

Thus in this discourse all circumstances in which (20) is true are eliminated from consideration after acceptance of (18*a*). If an utterance of (18*a*) is followed by an utterance of (20), the common ground must be revised, for (20) challenges (18*a*) and, where the domain includes women other than Loren, tries to add additional information. It may be that one or another conversationalist will win out; then either (18*a*) or (20) is added to the common ground. If (20) is added and (18*a*) abandoned but (18*b*) retained, then, of course, (21) is also added.

(21) Pavarotti hates Loren.

If there's an impasse, then neither (18*a*) nor (20) can remain in the common ground. (The exchange will still leave some mark: the common ground will include certain higher-level propositions to the effect that one speaker stated that Pavarotti likes Loren and that another speaker stated that Pavarotti hates every woman.) What we can't do is to act as if the circumstances we are speaking of are ones in which both (18*a*) and (20) express truths, because no such circumstances could exist in light of our assumptions about Loren and the incompatibility of liking and hating.

Of course, without (18*b*) in the common ground, (20) is not incompatible with (18*a*). Suppose the common ground so far does not include (18*b*); for all that has been said or tacitly assumed, Loren is a man or a fish or a book. In such a discourse (18*a*) can easily be joined by (20) and the common ground will then also be enriched to include (22).

(22) Loren is not a woman.

And so on. At each stage the common ground determines a set of circumstances that remain as live possibilities for the discourse. A *live possibility* at a given discourse stage is any circumstance *v* such that all the propositions in the common ground at that point of the discourse are true in *v*. The view being developed in the discourse does not encompass circumstances where some unchallenged uttered sentence gets a value of 0 or where some proposition that is recognized as a consequence of what has been said is false. Semantic theory cannot, of course, provide any insight into how conversationalists resolve conflicts that arise as they participate in the collaborative development of the common ground. Yet it does have quite a lot to say about the options open to them.

Although assertive utterances are generally intended to enrich the common ground and narrow the live possibilities, this isn't essential to stating that *p*. So, for example, at some later stage in a discourse where (18*a*) was added unchallenged to the common ground, someone might utter that same sentence again, perhaps as a way of reminding everyone that it is on the slate. Or after the first utterance of (18*a*) someone might utter (19), which is already conveyed by assertion (18*a*) plus assumption (18*b*); one might want to do this to make sure that the commitment to (19) receives explicit attention. The formal structure of the declarative is the same in both cases, however: the proposition expressed by the simple declarative sentence uttered is added to the common ground (though the addition may sometimes be redundant), and any possibilities inconsistent with it are excluded from the set of live possibilities.

Because *assert that* tends to suggest that what is asserted is supposed not to be already part of the common ground, the more neutral *state that* is a less misleading designation of the sentential force of declaratives uttered in a discourse. Authors frequently do, however, use *assert* in the very abstract sense we are associating with *state*. (See Grice 1989, 18, for a discussion of different uses of *assert*.) Indeed, even *state* is sometimes used to imply something about the speaker's beliefs and motives that goes beyond what we mean here, but this seems to be the best familiar term for our present purposes.

In chapter 6 we show how ideas of this kind can be incorporated in a formal account of the meaning of declaratives in discourse. Matters are considerably more complex than we have indicated here, of course. We address some of these complexities in chapter 6.

One complication that we do not consider in chapter 6 is the possibility of subordinated commitment slates or grounds: assumptions entertained simply to explore their consequences, for example. Someone might utter (23*a*), and someone else respond with (23*b*), which might lead the first speaker to state (23*c*).

(23) *a*. Suppose Bond hates every woman.
b. Then $[\text{Bond}]_i$ would hate $[\text{Loren}]_j$, but $[\text{he}]_i$ likes $[\text{her}]_j$.
c. So, Bond doesn't hate every woman.

We also, of course, need to elaborate our account of discourse structure and context-changing functions in order to deal with interrogative and imperative forces. In chapter 2 we discussed an approach to the semantics of an interrogative (originally due to Karttunen 1977) as a set of propositions; intuitively, these are the propositions that constitute true answers to the interrogative. Other more recent work has developed related ideas (see, for example, Groenendijk and Stokhof 1984 and Engdahl 1986). Dynamic or discourse-theoretic accounts of interrogative meaning might, for example, take the interrogative to indicate that the common ground is to include some family of propositions whose membership is to be identified. Imperative meaning has been far less extensively studied; an informal proposal in Sperber and Wilson (1986) is that an imperative presents some proposition as controllable by the addressee and as desirable for someone, typically the speaker (requests or commands) or the addressee (suggestions). Much more detailed work needs to be done to develop these and similar ideas explicitly enough to incorporate them into either a static truth-conditional semantics or the dynamic discourse semantics that we have begun to sketch here.[2]

The dynamic approach seems especially promising for developing an abstract semantic theory of sentential meaning that goes beyond truth conditions. The fundamental idea is that there is a formal discourse structure associated with contexts of utterance. We have informally discussed the common ground it includes and the associated live possibilities. The interpretation function $[\![\ ]\!]$ can be thought of as recursively specifying functions that map the set of live possibilities at one discourse stage into another set (or perhaps change discourse structure in some other way). As we have presented it, $[\![S]\!]$, the interpretation of a simple declarative sentence, maps the preexisting common ground onto a new common ground enriched by addition of the content expressed by that sentence (and concomitantly maps the live possibilities onto a set restricted by the elimination of prior possibilities inconsistent with that expressed content). We will give actual examples of rules assigning such functions in chapter 6. These rules can plausibly be thought of as encompassing both what Frege meant by sentential content and what he meant by sentential force. They give some substance to the notion that the meaning of a sentence involves both static truth-conditional content and dynamic force, which specifies something of how that content functions in discourse.

There are many unanswered questions about how best to implement a dynamic approach to sentential force. A more complex view than we have suggested could well emerge even for declarative sentences. It might be desirable, for example, to assign different dynamic semantic values to declaratives with the same truth-conditional content but distinct structures (for example, "Joan cried, or she laughed" and "If Joan didn't cry, she laughed"). We can proceed at this point, however, without addressing such issues as these.

4 Speech Acts

Our reconstruction of Fregean sentential force is, as we have noted, very abstract. What we called "stating that," for example, is much less concrete than claiming, guessing, reminding, warning, or threatening, the kinds of speech acts that many have thought must be the literal force associated with sentences by the language system. A sentence like (24) may be uttered with any one of these illocutionary forces.

(24) The bull is in the field.

Yet in all cases, we are proposing, an utterance of a declarative sentence S in which the speaker means anything at all is a statement: it places the proposition expressed by S in the common ground and discards any possibilities rendered no longer live because of their inconsistency with that (possibly new) information. Where does this abstract stating act fit in a larger theory of the actions we perform when speaking?

4.1 The kinds of things we do with words

It is useful at this point to draw from Austin's analysis of speech acts. Austin introduced a tripartite classification of acts performed when a person speaks. We have already mentioned two such classes: locutionary and illocutionary acts. The *locutionary act*, Austin said, "is roughly equivalent to uttering a certain sentence with a certain sense and reference, which again is roughly equivalent to 'meaning' in the traditional sense."[3] That is, a locutionary act is an act of producing a meaningful linguistic expression as such: the parrot producing a string of sounds that sound like "Polly wants a cracker" is not performing a locutionary act, because the bird does not have access to the linguistic structure and meaning that would underlie an English speaker's making the same noises. An *illocutionary act* is performed in saying something. In engaging in locutionary acts, we generally "also perform illocutionary acts such as informing, ordering, warning, undertaking, etc., i.e. utterances which have a certain (conventional) force." Here the speaker's motives go beyond simply saying something. An illocutionary act is part of the speaker's strategy in meaningfully using language; the speaker offers the utterance as a particular sort of interactional move. And we may, if lucky, also "perform *perlocutionary acts*: what we bring about or achieve by saying something, such as convincing, persuading, deterring" (italics added). Unlike locutionary and illocutionary acts, perlocutionary acts are performed only if the speaker's strategy actually succeeds in accomplishing its desired aims. Austin's interest lay primarily in elucidating the nature of illocutionary acts, for it is in them, his discussion makes clear, that full-blooded force resides, what an utterance is *meant as* by its utterer, how it figures in the utterer's general plan of action.

We will use Austin's notion of locutionary act to cover the very abstract notion of sentential force that we sketched for declaratives in section 3.1. The locutionary act performed in uttering sentence (24) can be thought of as the act of stating that the bull is in the field: the act of placing the proposition in question in the common ground (at some level) of some discourse or other. But which discourse, and what are the aims of that discourse? Does the common ground include propositions about bulls being dangerous, about whether the addressee is considering entering the field, about whether the speaker intends to attempt to place the addressee in the field along with the bull, about what the addressee might want (imagine uttering (24) to someone longing to display bull-handling capabilities)? What are the motives prompting performance of this particular locutionary act in this particular context? Just stating that the bull is in the field is not enough to make the speaker an illocutionary agent engaged in a goal-directed course of action: abstract sentential force alone, what we could call *locutionary force*, does not result in illocutionary force.

To use language is to perform some kind of illocutionary act: any actual performance of a locutionary act will figure in some way or other in a plan of action that gives it illocutionary significance. But it is by no means clear that the speaker needs to make particular elements of that plan manifest to the addressee to have successfully accomplished the illocutionary act that the utterance is meant as. Suppose the speaker means utterance (24) as a warning, yet the addressee does not so take it, perhaps having no thought of any potential peril from the bull's being in the field. Has the addressee failed to retrieve the message that the speaker intended to convey? Not necessarily, although the addressee would not be fully cognizant of why the speaker spoke as she or he did. Of course, if a speaker means the utterance of (24) to serve not only as a direct statement that the bull is in the field but also as an indirect directive to the addressee to shut the gate to the field, then the speaker means to convey to the hearer more than what the sentence itself expresses. But is that directive meant as a suggestion or an order? It is not clear that the speaker must intend to convey what kind of directive the utterance is meant as. In other words, intended illocutionary acts need not be a part of what the speaker means in the sense elucidated by Grice's notion of speaker's meaning.

What an utterance is meant as, what illocutionary act the speaker intends, depends on how the utterance fits into the speaker's purposes for the particular discourse and conceptions of what role this particular utterance might play in advancing those purposes. If the speaker is a sergeant and charged with responsibility for fish distribution and Bond is a private serving under the speaker's command, then an utterance of (15*c*), "Give every fish to Loren, Bond," is likely to be meant as an order. Suppose, however, that the speaker knows that Loren adores people who give her fish and utters (15*c*) in response to Bond's uttering (25).

(25) I'd do anything to get Sophia Loren to like me.

In this case, (15*c*) is almost certainly meant as a suggestion.

The same locutionary act seems to have been performed in both cases. The imperative sentence (15*c*) tells Bond to give every fish to Loren in each case. There is no inclination to say that in either case the speaker is somehow using language nonliterally or indirectly (as when one uses (24), "The bull is in the field," as a way to tell someone to close a gate). We need not suppose multiple levels of speaker meaning for either the order or the suggestion. There seems to be a clear sense in which the speaker means the same thing in both cases, even though the two utterances count as quite different interactional moves. On the face of it, the difference seems to lie in how the act fits with the rest of the discourse and with the larger contextual factors relevant to understanding what the speaker is doing (such as the rank relation between speaker and addressee and assumptions about the relative interests of speaker and addressee in the addressee's acting as the imperative says).

Of course, speakers can, and often do, make their specific illocutionary aims explicit. We have a vocabulary for distinguishing among kinds of illocutionary acts. The speaker might utter (15*c*) and follow that utterance by saying one of the sentences in (26).

(26) *a.* And that's an order.
b. That's the best suggestion I can come up with.

Interestingly, indirect illocutionary aims cannot be made explicit in this same way. Even where it is abundantly clear that the speaker intends an utterance of (24) to convey a directive to close the gate, the force of that implicit directive cannot be explicitly specified just by continuing with one of the tags in (26). Thus it seems plausible to say that (15*c*), "Give every fish to Loren, Bond," but not (24), "The bull is in the field," may be pragmatically specified as intended directly to convey an order or a suggestion and that this difference is linked to differences in the locutionary force associated with declaratives and imperatives. But the possibility of specifying imperatives as orders or suggestions or some other variety of directive does not mean, we think, that the imperative is ambiguous between ordering and suggesting and other kinds of directive. Indeed, not all meaningful uses of imperatives need be characterizable as any specific kind of illocutionary act of the directive variety. The imperative sentences in (27), for example, would rarely, if ever, be used to direct the addressee to do something, yet they need not be viewed as therefore nonliteral or indirect.

(27) *a.* Have a wonderful time. [A wish]
b. Swim at your own risk. [A warning]
c. Help yourself to whatever you want. [Permission or an offer]

In other words, whatever imperative meaning might amount to, it seems that it must be sufficiently abstract to accommodate a wide range of actions.

We offered no specific proposal for imperative force, for imperative meaning as a function that maps the discourse structure at one stage into a new structure. But we did make some suggestions about declarative force, and declaratives are used with an even wider range of apparently direct illocutionary force than imperatives.

(28) *a.* I'll be there right away. [A promise or an offer]
b. She must get better. [A wish]
c. You may watch "Sesame Street" tomorrow. [Permission]

How can promises, wishes, and permissions be literal acts of stating? We'll say something more about cases like those in (28) when we discuss modal semantics in chapter 5. Sentence (28*a*) in particular points to a class of utterances that Austin examined in some detail and that might prima facie seem to undermine our claim that what declaratives do by virtue of their meaning is state: add propositions to the common ground. We now turn to consider explicitly performative utterances of declarative sentences.

4.2 Performative utterances

A *performative* utterance of a declarative does not simply convey a message but performs some substantive action (or initiates a state), indeed, the very action (or state) that the content of the declarative in some sense describes. The sentences in (29) can all be uttered as performatives.

(29) *a.* We find the defendant guilty as charged. [To utter (*a*) is to find the defendant guilty as charged.]
b. I bid three clubs. [To utter (*b*) is to bid three clubs.]
c. I promise to split any lottery winnings with you. [To utter (*c*) is to promise to split any lottery winnings with the addressee.]
d. You're fired. [To utter (*d*) can be to fire the addressee.]
e. You may have dessert tonight. [To utter (*e*) can be to grant permission to the addressee to have dessert on the night of the utterance.]
f. Gentlemen are requested to wear jackets and ties to dinner. [To utter (*f*) can be to request gentlemen to wear jackets and ties to dinner.]

As with the declaratives in (28) used to promise, wish, or give permission, it seems pointless for anyone to appraise the truth of any of the sentences in (29) on the occasion of its performative utterance. What is special about these performative utterances is that the utterance itself is what makes the circumstances fit the words: the utterance of sentence S brings into existence the very (nonlinguistic) facts that S states obtain. As Searle noted recently, it is only because of beliefs we have about causal relations that we don't think that sentences like those in (30) can be uttered performatively by ordinary people.[4]

(30) *a.* You can now see. [Addressed to a blind person by a healer]
b. The engine is turning over. [Used as a way of starting one's car]

Someone's seeing or an engine's starting requires, most of us believe, more than a verbal trigger. Social actions, however, are different. Words have the power, for example, to terminate a person's employment.

On our account, the grammar itself specifies that utterances of declaratives with content *p* (literally) state that *p*. Such statements may be true or false as applied to particular circumstances, so one question is why appraisal of truth seems quite beside the point for performative utterances of declaratives. According to the view we sketched of sentential force, linguistic rules assign to (29*c*) the locutionary act of stating that the speaker promises to share any lottery winnings with the addressee. How, then, can we explain the intuitive judgment that uttering this sentence counts as making the promise that, according to our analysis, it states has been made? Promising is not a species of stating in the way that ordering is a species of telling someone to do something, yet there is nothing indirect, nonconventional, or multileveled about using (29*c*) to make a promise. Indeed, its potential as a tool for promising seems intimately tied to what it means. Yet we have claimed that illocutionary forces are not in general a part of sentential meaning.

What Austin did was force analysts to recognize and think about the vast number of apparent counterexamples to an account like the one we have offered of the sentential force of declaratives. Declarative sentences used performatively seem prima facie to be counterexamples to a unified account of declarative sentential force because what they principally do is so very different from stating. With ordinary statements, which Austin called *constatives*, it is appropriate to challenge or confirm them with a *no* or *yes*. The *no* or *yes* is an assessment of whether the statement fits the circumstances being described, whether the statement ought to remain in the common ground to which the speaker adds it. Whether the words fit the circumstances is a matter of their truth in those circumstances (of what we think of as truth *simpliciter*, where the circumstances being spoken of are conversationalists' actual surroundings). But it would generally be absurd to say "Yes" or "No" or "That's right" or "That's wrong" to a performative utterance of the kind illustrated in (29). Such utterances actually create the circumstances they speak of, so the question of whether they fit those circumstances seems quite irrelevant.

Sentences (29*a–c*) are explicit performatives; the matrix verb phrase labels the illocutionary act that an utterance of the sentence performs (finding guilty, bidding three clubs, promising, etc.). Sentences (29*d–f*) are interesting because they can be used either to report (a constative use) or to do (a performative use). Uttering (29*d*) is indeed to fire someone *if* the speaker has the appropriate position with respect to the addressee; if not, the sentence may be used to convey news of a firing to the affected party (for example, the receptionist might so inform an employee headed into the boss's office). And (29*e*) may either report on some third party's having given permission or actually confer that permission ((28*c*) can also be used either to report or to grant permission). Similarly, (29*f*) can be performatively issued by the hotel management or constatively uttered by a disgruntled man who has just learned the hotel's policy and is explaining to his companion why they ought to go buy themselves jackets and ties.

Performativity of an utterance is a matter of what the words mean and the powers accorded people by virtue of certain social institutions (the legal system with provision for trial by jury in the case of issuing a verdict, the rules of a game in the case of bidding, a particular form of labor organization in the case of firing). In some cases the relevant social institutions are very diffuse and little is needed beyond the words themselves for a speaker to succeed in performing the act in question (promising, for example).

This is not to say that performatives always work as they should any more than so-called constatives do. Just as constatives can be appraised as true or false in particular circumstances, performatives can be appraised as *felicitous* or *infelicitous* in various ways, Austin noted. We have, he claimed, certain conventions that in some sense regulate our use of performatives; he called these *felicity conditions*. If felicity conditions governing use of a certain form fail to be satisfied, then use of the form may *misfire*. If an utterance misfires, then the act in question does not come off (because the proper kinds of conventions are nonexistent, the persons and circumstances for such a performance are wrong, or the procedures are executed improperly or incompletely). The rules of bridge, for instance, don't permit (29*b*) to effect the indicated bid (three clubs) at a point in the game where another player has just bid three hearts or if the speaker is the partner of the person who just completed the preceding bid. In such contexts we sometimes say things like "No you don't" (perhaps more often, "No; you can't") to indicate that the attempted alteration of the circumstances to fit the words did not take place.

Failure to satisfy other conditions may yield what Austin calls an *abuse* rather than a misfire. For example, an act is *insincere* if participants don't have the thoughts and feelings they purport to have in performing it. If I utter (29*c*), "I promise to split any lottery winnings with you," yet have no intention of sharing any winnings with you, then my promise is insincere. We do, of course, abuse performatives in such ways. As insincere promise is nonetheless a promise: the promiser has made a commitment whether or not she or he intends to honor it.

Constatives too can suffer abuses or misfires, Austin notes. Lying would be an abuse in the constative case. A misfire might be an utterance of (31) in a context with no elephant in view.

(31) That elephant is huge. [Speaker points to empty space.]

What makes the explicit performatives like those in (29*a–c*) so interesting is that they seem to wear their illocutionary forces on their linguistic sleeves. It is tempting to say that an utterance of (29*c*), "I promise to split any lottery winnings with you," counts as a promise simply by virtue of what the sentence means, in almost the same way as a constative utterance of sentence (31) counts as the literal making of a statement. In the following section we discuss Searle's account of the felicity conditions that govern the act of promising, an act that does not require the explicit rules and institutional arrangements that govern bidding or issuing a legal finding or discharging an employee.

Several approaches have been suggested for explaining performative utterances of declaratives like those in (28) and (29) while at the same time continuing to maintain that such declaratives do indeed state in our abstract sense. We have observed that performative utterances are not sensibly assessed in terms of their correspondence to the facts because in a real sense they create, rather than simply report, that correspondence. (Here we except the reporting uses that (29*d–f*) allow.) Even so, a possible explanation of performative power may be found in a more thorough consideration of truth conditions. It seems plausible that certain words (*bid*, *promise*, *fire*) are such that their contribution to truth-conditional content ensures that their utterance in certain contexts is self-verifying. Because of the nature of bidding, to state that one is doing so is to do so and thus to state a truth. Indeed, it seems plausible, as Ginet (1979) proposed, that the statement that one is bidding three clubs serves as the instrument for doing so. Performatives, he argues, both state and do, and the doing is effected by means of the stating.

Our interest in an utterance of (29*b*) is in its effect on the nonlinguistic circumstances, on the bridge game, for example. At the same time, though, we take the utterance to expand the common ground like other assertive utterances: just after it is made, other players will act as if there is a general commitment to the utterer's having made the bid in question. The utterer issues a statement that the bid is being made, and the statement is instrumental in making the bid. That the utterer is viewed as having stated that she bids three clubs seems supported by the fact that considerations of consistency and of commitment to the consequences of propositions added to the common ground operate in exactly the same way that they do when a bid is reported after it is made. Thus either of the sentences in (32) could be used to report an utterance of (29*b*) (perhaps one of the other bridge players is getting deaf and did not hear what was said).

(32) *a.* She bid three clubs.
b. She said that she bid three clubs.

As soon as the utterance is interpreted, the proposition that the utterer bid three clubs is entered into the common ground. In other words, to utter (29*b*) is not only to bid three clubs but also to state that one is so doing, a statement that is true unless the act misfires. And, as Ginet observes, the statement is not just an incidental accompaniment to the bid but the very means of making the bid.

We discuss briefly in chapter 5 a truth-conditional analysis of *may* by Angelika Kratzer that suggests why and how, in certain contexts, its use can be thought of as granting permission rather than merely informing the addressee that permission has been granted. Roughly, the idea is that a sentence like (29*e*), "You may have dessert tonight," says that the proposition that the addressee have dessert on the night of the day of the utterance is compatible with some contextually supplied set of propositions. The propositions in this case delimit permissible actions of the addressee. The set may be given in various ways: linguistic rules do not specify how membership in the set is determined. If there is some third party with authority over the addressee, the speaker may simply be reporting on the proposition that the authority has placed in the set of permissible actions. Perhaps, however, the speaker is the addressee's mother, with authority over the dessert issue. In this case the speaker herself may place the proposition about eating dessert into the set of propositions describing permissible actions and may report that action at the same time she does it.

Exercise 2 We will say that a verb is a performative verb if it can be used as the highest verb in a sentence that can be uttered performatively. Which of the following verbs is a performative? For those that are, illustrate their performative potential in a sentence that can be uttered performatively. For those that are not, explain briefly why. Here are the verbs: concede, apologize, believe, say, thank, frighten, deny, forget, wish, hint, nominate, oppose, joke, congratulate, doubt.

Performatives offer a strong prima facie challenge to any theory that distinguishes sharply between locutionary force, which is associated with sentences as such and makes no reference to the goals or plans of speakers, and the action that gives illocutionary forces their potency, the action fueled by conversationalists' aims, attitudes, and beliefs. We do not think, however, that performatives constitute an insuperable problem for a program that places illocutionary force outside the realm of semantics proper. Work like Kratzer's makes us optimistic that continued detailed investigations of the truth-conditional content of a wide range of expressions will help explain many of the very interesting observations that have been made about language functions by focusing on the performative utterances. We turn to look next at Searle's account of the conventions that delineate the activity of promising, drawing from that account a rather different moral than Searle does.

4.3 Illocutionary acts as the subject of semantics

Searle (1969) took the Austinian program one step further, denying that there is any useful distinction between locutionary and illocutionary acts. If Searle is right, then there is no justification for treating the meaning of a sentence uttered in a discourse as distinct from the illocutionary force of that utterance. While we disagree sharply with Searle on this point, we do think that there is much to be learned from his thoughtful analyses of different kinds of illocutionary acts and the conventions governing them. Searle develops the idea that social conventions for selecting particular linguistic expressions to achieve particular aims in some sense constitute the linguistic meaning of the expressions used. Searle's idea is similar to Grice's view of linguistic meaning as deriving from social norms that regulate speaker's meaning (see section 2 above), but unlike Grice, Searle sees no place for a truth-conditional notion of linguistic meaning. Some of the proposed conventions are very general ones relevant for virtually all felicitous uses of language and can be compared with Gricean maxims for conducting conversations, which we discuss below in section 5. Those specific to particular kinds of illocutionary acts are more interesting for our present purposes of considering whether sentential meaning specifies illocutionary force, as Searle has urged.

Searle's account of promising can illustrate his general program of explaining how utterances accomplish the illocutionary aims agents intend them to serve. What does it take for an utterance to be a felicitous promise? Searle, in an important early paper (1965), discusses this question in some detail.[5] For an utterance to be a felicitous illocutionary act of any kind, Searle suggests, conditions of normal "input" (speaking) and "output" (understanding) are required. Presumed are knowledge of the language, non-impaired cognitive functioning, adequate peripheral processing, and so on. (Is a promise defective or infelicitous if the addressee cannot understand it? There is disagreement on such matters, but the controversy is not really over analysis of illocutionary acts but over the more general notion of speaker's meaning.) The utterance must not be simply offered for inspection but must be meant by its utterer. Searle proposes to exclude jokes, playacting, and similar nonserious uses, but as noted earlier, we presumably understand what is going on in such cases through reference to serious communications. The actor is a locutionary agent serving as a mouthpiece for a different illocutionary agent, the character in the play. A speaker who is joking in promising to give the addressee caviar for breakfast every morning achieves her effect through pretending to make such a promise. The joke lies in seeing that the speaker is assuming the guise of some fictive illocutionary agent. Searle's general input and output conditions are intended to focus attention on canonical cases of a fully competent speaker's straightforwardly meaning an utterance to convey some message to a fully competent addressee in a situation where external factors do not interfere with the exercise of linguistic competence.

As Frege did, Searle draws a distinction between propositional content and force, although for Searle propositional content is what a speaker (not a sentence) expresses and force is illocutionary force. The conventions that govern an illocutionary act of a certain kind (usually) include a basic *propositional content condition* (a convention that the speaker must express some proposition) and a more specific condition about the content of the expressed proposition that arises from the nature of the particular illocutionary act in question. In general, Searle suggests, there will be two components to an utterance: a component that expresses its propositional content and the *illocutionary force indicating device* (IFID). IFIDs include syntactic devices like inversion, intonational markers, and of course the various performative verbs: *warn*, *apologize*, and *promise*. Often the context "will make it clear what the illocutionary force of the utterance is, without its being necessary to invoke the appropriate function indicating device."[6] This caveat is ignored in Searle's later discussion, but we will return to it below.

In the case of a promise, Searle proposes, the propositional content must predicate a future act or acts of the speaker (and not of anyone else). Some utterances seem to be promises yet do not explicitly express propositions that predicate an act of the speaker ("I promise that our dog will not chase your cat again"). Searle views promises whose overt content concerns events that are not acts of the speaker as elliptical expressions of promises to take an action to ensure that the (explicitly) promised event will occur ("I promise to see to it that our dog will not . . ."). He could also, of course, take a similar line with other promises that do not explicitly predicate actions (such as "I promise not to smoke" or "I promise to be awake when you return"). The specific propositional content conditions that Searle elaborates for the illocutionary act of promising are not peculiar to promising but are shared by other illocutionary acts in the general class that Searle calls commissives, acts in which agents commit themselves to some course of action (including not only promises but also offers and threats). In the discussion of Searle's conditions on promising, we will use *A* to designate the act that a speaker makes a commitment to perform when she utters a commissive.

Certain *preparatory conditions* constrain the common ground that must be in place for the promise to occur. Intuitively, an illocutionary act must be thought to have some point; there must be some reason for the speaker to perform it. For a promise and other commissives, this amounts to the requirement that it is not already part of the common ground prior to the speaker's commissive act that she will perform *A*. The condition that distinguishes a promise from other commissives is that it is part of the common ground that the addressee would like the speaker to perform *A*. Of course, the speaker may think the addressee wants *A* but be wrong in that judgment; in cases where the common ground is differently appraised or where the common ground includes false propositions, the promise is arguably defective.

Besides preparatory conditions, illocutionary acts also generally have *sincerity conditions*. Basically, these require that agents actually have the aims and intentions that their acts present them as having, guaranteeing that the illocutionary force is a reliable indicator of the motives producing the utterance. A promise is only sincere if the speaker actually intends to do *A*. To allow for insincere promises, we might weaken this requirement and require only that the speaker intends to assume responsibility for doing *A*. An insincere promise is nonetheless a promise, just as a lie is nonetheless a claim about how things are.

The *essential condition* of a promise, Searle proposes, is that promisers intend their utterances to be understood as placing them under an obligation to do *A*. Exactly what this obligation amounts to is not spelled out. Note, however, that the speaker's assuming an obligation to do *A* entails that *A* is a future act of the speaker, so this essential condition entails the propositional content condition mentioned earlier. In general, what Searle identifies as essential conditions for particular illocutionary acts constrain propositional content conditions for the acts in question.

Finally, Searle formulates conditions intended to ensure both that the speaker means the promise to be understood as such by the addressee, and that the expression uttered is a conventional means of accomplishing that illocutionary aim. What concerns us here is Searle's formulation of this second condition, namely, that the semantic rules of the language used by speaker and addressee are such that the expression in question "is correctly and sincerely uttered if and only if [the preceding] conditions ... obtain" (Searle 1965, 236). Taken at face value, this might seem to imply that no other expression could also perform the same function, that there is only one way "correctly and sincerely" to make a given promise. Searle must intend that the expression in question is correctly and sincerely uttered only if conditions like the above hold and that if those conditions obtain, its utterance would be correct (and sincere) though there might also be other expressions that could be correctly and sincerely uttered.

Indeed, what Searle finally offers us is a formulation of the putative "semantical" rules governing use of an IFID *P* for promising (for example, a simple present tense *promise* whose subject is *I*). We simplify Searle's account slightly.

(33) *a.* *The propositional content rule. P* is to be uttered only in the context of a sentence (or larger stretch of discourse) predicating some future act *A* of the speaker.

b. *The preparatory rule. P* is to be uttered only if the addressee is positively oriented toward *A* and the speaker so believes (and only if it is not obvious to the addressee prior to this utterance that the speaker will do *A*).

c. *The sincerity rule.* *P* is to be uttered only if the speaker intends to do *A*.

d. *The essential rule.* Uttering *P* counts as undertaking an obligation to do *A*.

As Searle notes, the sincerity rule can be dropped, in which case the rules govern correct (and not correct and sincere) uses of the promising device; insincerity is always a possibility and nothing special needs to be said about it in the case of promises. The first half of the preparatory rule specifies what is taken for granted when an act is offered as a promise; the second half is designed to rule out pointless or unnecessary promises, although such promises can be made. The propositional content rule must be taken somewhat more loosely than stated: for example, the act(s) in question need not be explicitly stated but need only be somehow inferrable from the context. The essential rule guarantees that an utterance of a promise must somehow allow us to infer some act or class of acts that the speaker can undertake an obligation to do. The essential rule and the positive half of the preparatory rule constitute the core of what it is to perform the illocutionary act of promising.

As Searle also notes, explicit devices for indicating illocutionary force are not always needed. What is accomplished by uttering (34*a*) can in many contexts be done simply by uttering (34*b*), which explicitly states only the propositional content required by (33*a*).

(34) *a.* I promise to write you next week.
b. I'll write you next week.

In uttering (34*b*) a speaker can state that she will write the addressee in the week following the utterance and at the same time promise to do so (although she does not explicitly state that she promises). The promise is not indirect or nonliteral: it is simply not overtly indicated (compare our discussion in section 2 of uses of *and* that convey more than logical conjunction). The sentences in (35), though predicating future acts of their utterers, are less likely to be used to promise than (34*b*).

(35) *a.* I'm going to write you next week.
b. I'm writing you next week.
c. I write you next week.

Even the sentences in (35), however, can be followed by (36).

(36) That's a promise.

An explanation of such facts should be found in an account of the differences among alternative ways of talking about the future.

Interestingly, the rules in (33) seem relevant not only to specifying what is required for correct use of a device for indicating a promise such as that in (34*a*) but also to specifying what is required for a correct use of *promise* in a sentence like (37), where it contributes to propositional content and does not indicate illocutionary force.

(37) Joan promised to write Lee next week.

Like bidding three clubs, promising is an activity governed by certain rules. Both promising and bidding can be effected just by saying something. The rules of bridge that define bidding are explicit; the social conventions that define promising are implicit and closely tied to conventions for using language. To utter (34*a*) and mean what one says is to make a promise; an obligation henceforth exists. We have further suggested (contra Searle) that uttering (34*a*) is also to state that one is making such a commitment to the addressee, just as uttering (37) states that Joan has so committed herself to Lee. Sentence (34*a*), we propose, gives an on-the-spot report of what it does: it explicitly displays what we think of as its primary illocutionary force.

Thus, on the one hand, Searle characterizes what counts in general as an act of promising. As we have just seen, this cannot be viewed as something that could or should be part of the grammar, for (*a*) to the extent that language is involved, promising presupposes that the grammar is already in place (note the propositional content rule), and (*b*) form and illocutionary force are not directly linked.

On the other hand, the lexicon, a part of grammar, does reflect classifications of actions by the language-using community. Thus we can recast (33) as describing the conditions of correct use for the word *promise*, as delineating (at least partially) which actions are promises. We will say more in chapter 8 about ways to expand our semantic theory to incorporate analyses of the contribution made by lexical meaning to truth conditions for sentences.

In the heady days following the publication of Chomsky's *Aspects*, a number of linguists tried to combine Searle's view that illocutionary force was a matter of linguistic meaning with the standard logical conception of semantics as concerned with truth conditions for sentences. We turn now to examine this alternative approach to making the illocutionary force of a sentence a matter of linguistic semantics.

4.4 The performative hypothesis

The idea behind the *performative hypothesis* is that every sentence determines a literal illocutionary force and that explicit performative utterances overtly indicate this literal illocutionary force. Ross (1970) was the first to suggest that a sentence like (34*b*), "I'll write you next week," when uttered as a promise, might be essentially identical to the overt performative (34*a*), "I promise to write you next week," at some more abstract linguistic level than surface syntactic structure. Similar ideas were further developed in work by Sadock (1974) and others.

More generally, what was proposed was that in relatively deep structure every sentence has some performative verb as its highest verb with a first-person subject and a second-person object. This underlying performative verb determines how someone else can accurately characterize what the utterance was meant as. Thus (34*b*), "I'll write you next week," might look like (34*a*), "I promise to write you next week," on one interpretation and like one of the sentences in (38) on others.

(38) *a.* I claim that I will write you next week.
b. I predict that I will write you next week.

From saying that overt performative utterances do indeed bear truth values, it can seem only a short step to saying that utterances of interrogatives and imperatives are also assigned truth values. This move assumes that we derive sentences like (15*b*), "Does Bond give every fish to Loren?" and (15*c*), "Give every fish to Loren, Bond," from explicit performatives like those in (39).

(39) *a.* I ask you whether Bond gives every fish to Loren.
b. I tell you, Bond, to give every fish to Loren.

Lewis (1972) takes this tack. Although such an approach might be viable, it is important to note that it does not remove the necessity of providing semantic values for the embedded interrogatives (introduced by the complementizer *whether*) and for the tenseless infinitival complements that occur in such contexts.

As we noted, Ross's proposal went even further, associating with every sentence, including declaratives, a higher performative verb. For example, he would derive (40*b*) from the structure underlying (40*a*).

(40) *a.* I say to you that grass is purple.
b. Grass is purple.

But this kind of move is semantically untenable if (40*a*) is to provide the basis for assigning truth conditions to (40*b*). To utter (40*a*) is *ipso facto* to say something true; the same can certainly not be said for (40*b*). Saying that these two sentences are semantically identical just does not work. Many, probably most, sentences do not report the illocutionary force with which they are uttered, even at some abstract level.

4.5 Grammar and illocutionary force

The performative hypothesis and Searle's speech act theory both attempt to treat the illocutionary force of an utterance as a component of its (literal) linguistic meaning. As Levinson points out (1983, chap. 5), a single sentence can be used to perform a whole host of illocutionary acts, and the same illocutionary act can be performed by any number of different sentences (some of which may perform other acts as well). And this, he correctly observes, creates enormous difficulties for any theory that attempts to make the illocutionary force of an utterance a component of its linguistic meaning.

Take sentence (34*b*), "I'll write you next week," which can be uttered as a promise, a threat, or a report of a decision. If illocutionary force were a matter of linguistic meaning, then we would have to say that (34*b*) is ambiguous. The most likely source of such an ambiguity would be the auxiliary *will*. Yet whether the utterance counts as a promise, a threat, or just a report of a decision seems to be a matter not of which sense of *will* a speaker has selected but of assumptions about the addressee's attitudes toward the projected letter writing. The speaker may in fact make the sort of commitment that promises and threats share without having even considered whether the addressee is positively, negatively, or neutrally oriented toward the projected act. Even more problematic for an ambiguity account of illocutionary forces is the fact that a single utterance of (34*b*) might both report a decision and make a promise. Generally in a single utterance of an ambiguous expression, speakers convey only one of the linguistically assigned meanings (exceptions are puns, which are perceived as special). Rather few surface sentences are restricted to a single illocutionary force when uttered, and it is common for a single utterance to carry multiple illocutionary forces with there being no suggestion of punning.

There also seem to be many different ways to accomplish a given illocutionary aim. The two sentences in (34) can be used to perform the illocutionary act reported in (37), "Joan promised to write Lee next week," and so also can those in (41), given suitable circumstances surrounding their utterance.

(41) *a.* Count on a letter from me next week.
b. I promise to comply with your request next week.
c. I'll resume my daughterly duties again next week.
d. You'll get a letter from me next week.

We hardly want to say that these sentences are synonymous. Nor do we want to say that in uttering (41*a*), Joan would mean just what she would mean in uttering (41*b*), even if in both cases she meant her utterance as a promise to Lee to send a letter next week.

Linguistic meaning does constrain the illocutionary acts that utterance of a sentence can perform. Some illocutionary acts seem less directly accomplished than others. The sentences in (42) are far less direct than the sentences in (34) and (41) if uttered as the promise reported in (37); they contrast with those more direct promises in that their nonexplicit promissory value cannot be overtly signalled by continuing with (36), "That's a promise."

(42) *a.* How would you like a letter from me next week?
b. The orthopedist says I'll definitely be able to use the typewriter next week.

The explanation of how the sentences in (42) can serve as indirect promises to write the addressee next week will presumably draw on some of the more general theories of pragmatic inferencing inspired by Grice's work on conversational implicature, which we discuss in the next section. Although the sentences in (41) can directly promise, we are not entitled to conclude that their being potential promises depends on some linguistic properties other than their truth conditions and abstract locutionary force.

Exercise 3 For each of the following illocutionary acts, give five nonsynonymous sentences that could be used to perform them.

(1) Reminding someone to pick up the cleaning

(2) Offering to help someone wash the dishes

(3) Asking someone to hurry in the shower

For each of the following sentences, name at least two illocutionary acts their utterance could simultaneously perform. Where special contextual factors must be present, specify them.

(4) Assignments will be collected next week.

(5) I'm cold.

(6) Is Linda there?

(7) Our dinner reservations are at seven o'clock.

(8) You may want to review chapter 3 before Friday's test.

---

5 Conversational Implicature

Speakers mean more than the sentences they utter mean, as we have already observed at a number of points in this chapter. What is amazing is how good language users are at going beyond what is overtly said to whatever is contextually or pragmatically implied. We suggested in section 2 that we sometimes even take what is pragmatically implied to be part of what the speaker straightforwardly means. How is this possible? As we noted in chapter one, Grice was the first to attempt an explanation of how we can so successfully convey more than what our words overtly say, the first to attempt a systematic account of the principles underlying pragmatic implication.[7]

Subsequent research has led to major revisions in Grice's original proposals, and there are currently several competing pragmatic theories, for example, "relevance" theory as presented in Sperber and Wilson (1986) and the neo-Gricean approaches of Horn (1989) and Levinson (1983, forthcoming). We will not try to lay out and compare these alternatives. Instead, we will just sketch Grice's original program, which has been the major reference point for virtually all current work in linguistic pragmatics, and then use it to help explain some of the divergences between interpretations assigned by F_2 and those that English speakers assign to occurrences of expressions in actual utterances. We will then briefly consider pragmatic approaches to such rhetorical devices as irony.

In chapter 1 we said that (an utterance of) sentence S implies proposition *p* (or has *p* as an implication) just in case in uttering S the speaker invites or licenses the addressee to infer that the speaker is making a commitment to *p*. To Grice we owe not only the distinction between entailments and implications licensed in some other way but also the technical terminology now standardly used in drawing the distinction. As Grice puts it, S (or its utterance or utterer) may *implicate* a proposition, which is its *implicatum* (plural, *implicata*). In such a case the relation between an utterance of S and what it implies is one of *implicature*; the implicata of an utterance are also called implicatures.

As we noted in note 5 to chapter 1, Grice divides implicatures into two classes: *conversational implicatures*, which are derived on the basis of conversational principles and assumptions, and *conventional implicatures*, which are assigned on the basis of the conventional meanings of the words occurring in a sentence. We briefly introduced conversational implicatures in chapter 1, and they will be our focus in the rest of this chapter. Before further discussing them and the theory of conversation Grice offers to explain them, however, we will say just a few words about conventional implicatures.

What Grice calls *conventional implicatures* are implications that are triggered by linguistic meaning but seem different from (ordinary) entailments in two ways: (*a*) the exact content of what is implied is not readily made explicit, and (*b*) the content of the implication does not seem at issue in the way that truth-conditional content standardly is. Let us illustrate with an example adapted from Grice.

(43) *a.* [John]$_i$ is an Englishman, but [he]$_i$ is cowardly.
b. [John]$_i$ is an Englishman, and [he]$_i$ is cowardly.
c. [John's]$_i$ being cowardly is somehow unexpected or surprising in light of [his]$_i$ being English.

Sentence (43*a*), but not (43*b*), implies (43*c*). We might say that uttering (43*a*) adds the same propositional content to the common ground as uttering (43*b*), but that (43*a*) differs from (43*b*) in presupposing something along the lines of (43*c*).

Grice denies that (43*c*) is entailed by, or part of, the truth-conditional content of (43*a*), claiming that (43*c*) might be false yet (43*a*) nonetheless true. There is general agreement that something like (43*c*) is part of what (43*a*) implies by virtue of its meaning and that at the same time this implication has some kind of special status. The question of what status (43*a*) has if (43*c*) is false is not settled, however. We will postpone further discussion of conventional implicatures until chapter 6, where we consider in some detail the phenomenon of presupposition. Conventional implicatures, Karttunen, Peters, and others have suggested, are conventionally presupposed. Certainly, every case that Grice presented as a matter of conventional implicature is also a case where what is implicated is presupposed.

In the remainder of this chapter we will focus on nonconventional or conversational implicature, sometimes speaking simply of implicature. Part of what we mean by the conversational implicata of S is that the propositions in question are not entailed by S, or more generally, that the implication relies on more than the linguistic meaning of S. What more is involved?

What Grice proposed was that conversation is regulated by an overarching *principle of cooperation* between speaker and hearer to achieve the purposes at stake in their talk:

(44) Make your conversational contribution such as is required, at the stage at which it occurs, by the accepted purpose or direction of the talk in which you are engaged.

The purposes of central importance in elaborating a general theory of meaning and comprehension are those at stake in successfully and efficiently conveying information. Given these purposes, rational speakers, Grice proposes, choose what to say in light of something like the following *maxims*:

(45) *a.* *Relation*. Be relevant.
b. *Quantity*. Be only as informative as required for current conversational purposes.
c. *Quality*. Say only what you believe true and adequately supported.
d. *Manner*. Be perspicuous: be brief and orderly and avoid obscurity and ambiguity.

In other words, Grice is suggesting that something like these maxims articulate a conversational strategy for cooperatively conveying information. We can see that some of them might be connected to the earlier discussed convention of truthfulness and to the need to make what one means readily accessible to one's audience. In figuring out implicatures, hearers rely on the assumption that these maxims are being observed or there is a good reason why some particular maxim has been "flouted." Sometimes conversational implicatures are part of what the speaker straightforwardly means; sometimes they introduce additional levels of speaker meaning. Let us now turn to concrete examples.

Many different kinds of implicatures have been discussed in the literature; we will illustrated a few here. To say something like (46*a*) is in most contexts to implicate (but not entail) the proposition expressed by (46*b*), whereas what (46*c*) expresses is entailed by (46*a*).

(46) *a.* Joan has a husband.
b. Joan has only one husband.
c. Joan has one or more husbands.

How do we know that (46*a*) does not entail (46*b*) and does entail (46*c*)? Well, if we discover that Joan is a biandrist, (46*b*) is false, but this discovery does not show that (46*a*) is false. One could sensibly respond to (46*a*) with (47*a*) but not with (47*b*), which contradicts (46*a*). (The symbol # indicates that the following sentence is infelicitous or pragmatically inappropriate in the discourse context described.)

(47) *a.* Yeah, in fact she has two.
b. #Yeah, in fact she has none.

A speaker who utters (46*a*) knowing that Joan is a biandrist (and issues no qualifiers along with that utterance) has been deceptive, since the speaker must know that the hearer will infer that Joan is a monandrist. In our culture there is a strong background assumption that people do not have more than one spouse. It would be disingenuous to claim not to have meant that Joan had only one husband, since the hearer will commonly draw such an inference. If the speaker is caught, the attempted defense is usually something like "I didn't *say* she had only one."

The American legal system has ruled on occasion that people (advertisers, for instance) can be held responsible not just for what is explicitly said but also for implicatures that most rational hearers would take them to have meant. Similarly, a hearer can deliberately "misunderstand" what has been meant by refusing to draw an obvious implicature: "But you didn't say that you thought she would not come, only that you didn't think she would come." Of course, there can also be genuine misunderstandings due to hearers' failing to draw the inferences that speakers take themselves to have meant and genuine differences of opinion on what hearers should infer in a given context.

Grice proposes that conversational implicatures are calculable from (1) the linguistic meaning of what is said (what the speaker conventionally or normatively is taken to mean), (2) the assumption that the speaker is observing the conversational maxims, and (3) contextual assumptions of various kinds (for example, that one spouse per woman is generally the upper limit). It is not simply that we intuitively grasp what is implied, he says, but that "the intuition is replaceable by an argument" involving general principles of conversation (Grice 1975, 50).

Although Grice is not completely explicit on this point, he seems to think of these arguments as deductive. Speakers rely on hearers' being able to calculate implicatures. Why? Because the speaker needs to intend the hearer to understand simply by recognizing that the speaker so intends, and just retrieving linguistic meaning will not suffice. Of course, calculation may go awry because the hearer and speaker don't assess contextual factors in the same way, because they give different weights to conflicting conversational principles, or because the hearer does not (perhaps cannot) make the effort to work things out. What is remarkable is how highly successful we seem to be in conveying to one another what we implicate.

That implicatures are calculable does not mean that speakers and hearers actually calculate them; the cognitive processes at work need not involve deduction. Perrault (1987), Levinson (forthcoming), and others have recently proposed nondeductive default logics as models of language users' knowledge of (at least some) implicatures; such a model is also suggested by the theory presented in Gazdar (1979).[8] Speakers need not supply the premises that would allow an implicature to be worked out; hearers simply apply default inference rules, such as one permitting the inference from "*x* has a husband" to "*x* has exactly one husband." Such logics are "nonmonotonic" in that additional premises—for example, that Joan comes from a culture in which biandry is the norm—can defeat the default inference. Such nondeductive systems, though consistent with, do not in themselves provide any account of, Grice's observation that the inferences in question are motivated by conversational principles. Nonetheless, there probably are default kinds of inferences that are made in the absence of counter-evidence; certainly generalized conversational implicatures are both very robust and to some extent conventionalized. For our present purposes, however, we will simply assume deduction from tacit premises, what are sometimes called enthymemes (arguments that require certain unexpressed premises). Such inferences are defeated if some of the implicit premises on which they depend have to be abandoned.

As we noted in chapter 1, a fundamental characteristic of conversational implicatures is that they are cancelable or defeasible, as well as calculable. This property follows immediately if the calculability is a matter of deducibility from contextually supplied or tacit premises, some of which may have to be abandoned in the face of their inconsistency with other contextual premises. It is easy to provide illustrations of cancellation or suspension of implicatures, as in (48), for example.

(48) *a.* Joan has a husband, perhaps even two.
b. Nicky got a job at Harvard and moved to Cambridge but not in that order.

In contrast, we can't in the same way cancel or suspend implications licensed simply by linguistic meaning (entailments or conventional implicatures).

(49) *a.* #Joan has a husband, yet perhaps she's unmarried.
b. #Nicky got a job at Harvard and therefore moved to Cambridge, but her move was quite unconnected to her job.

There is a close link between the extrasemantic calculability of implicature, its dependence on implicit pragmatic premises, and its defeasibility. We return to this issue in chapter 6, section 3.3.

Grice has also suggested that expressions with the same linguistic meaning should generate the same implicatures relative to a fixed context; he calls this the nondetachability of implicature. The nondetachability assumption may be problematic and is certainly difficult to examine without some independently supported account of what linguistic meaning amounts to. It has been pointed out that (50*a*) will almost always implicate (50*c*), whereas (50*b*), which might seem to be synonymous (and is certainly assigned the same literal linguistic content), does not seem to share this implicature.

(50) *a.* Can you pass the salt?
b. Are you able to pass the salt?
c. Please pass the salt.

There are, however, uses of sentences like (50*b*) to implicate requests like (50*c*); (51) provides an example.

(51) *a.* Are you able to lend me $15 until Friday?
b. Please lend me $15 until Friday.

The fact that literal synonymy does not guarantee identical implicatures in all contexts shows that factors other than literal or conventional linguistic content are relevant for calculating implicatures. Although the literal content of an utterance always enters into calculating conversational implicatures, which may be what Grice had in mind when formulating his nondetachability principle, it is clear that the form in which that content is expressed is also often a significant factor (a fact of which Grice was well aware, as we will see). Compare the sentences in (52), which generate rather different implicata though strictly expressing the same truth-conditional content.

(52) *a.* It is possible that Jesse Jackson will be president some day.
b. It is not impossible that Jesse Jackson will be president some day.

Belief that the speaker is indeed adhering to the general cooperative principle will generate implicatures. So-called *scalar implicatures*, first discussed in detail in Horn (1972), are said to exploit the maxims of quantity and quality. Thus in many contexts a speaker will implicate (53*b*) by uttering (53*a*).

(53) *a.* Some students did very well on the exam.
b. Some students did not do very well on the exam.

The argument through which the implicature can be calculated goes something like the following: The proposition that every student did well on the exam is informative in the context. If it is thought to be true on the basis of adequate evidence, then it should be stated. Since the speaker did not so state, one can infer either that the speaker does not believe it or has inadequate evidence. Since the speaker is presumed to have good evidence about how all the students did, the speaker does not believe that every student did very well and, on the assumption about the speaker's access to evidence, the speaker knows that not all students did well and intends to convey this.

In other words, the implicature in this case relies for its calculability on the maxims of quantity and quality. It would be defeated or weakened to something like (54) in contexts where the speaker is believed to have only partial information about performance on the exam.

(54) It is possible, on the basis of what the speaker knows, that some students did not do very well on the exam.

Horn has proposed a number of different linguistic scales that seem much like that relating *some* and *all* or *every* (for example, *warm* and *hot*, *good* and *excellent*, *possible* and *necessary*). There are many questions raised by positing such scales. But there is now much work (especially by Horn) that supports the view that implications like that in (53) are implicatures and do not require that we abandon standard logical accounts of the truth-conditional contribution of words like *some* and *all*. (The further link in the reasoning from (53*a*) to (53*b*) is the entailment from the proposition that not all did well to the proposition that some did not do well.) Fragment F_2, which lacks plurals, has scaled determiners *a* and *every*, which for these purposes might be expected to work like *some* and *all*.

Scalar implications like that in (53) are ubiquitous, and they often seem completely direct in the sense of being part of what speakers mean where there is only one level of speaker meaning. At the same time such implications are in general defeasible: stronger elements on a scale are consistent with weaker ones. In (55) the scaled expressions are italicized, with the weaker occurring first.

(55) *a.* *Some* of the students did very well on the exam, perhaps *all*.

b. The novel will certainly be *good*, and it may well be *excellent*.

c. It is *possible*, perhaps even *necessary*, to treat these inferences as implicatures.

Data such as these are prima facie evidence against the view that the implications like that in (53) are entailments.

Nonetheless, as Horn (1989) explains in some detail, there is a venerable tradition that tries to treat the weaker scaled items—*some*, *good*, *possible*—as ambiguous between a "two-sided" sense, in which they are inconsistent with the stronger member of the scale (this two-sided sense would make (53) an entailment), and a "one-sided" sense in which they are consistent with the stronger item (the one-sided sense appears in (55)). The problems with the ambiguity approach are manifold. One anomaly is that these so-called ambiguities are paralleled in language after language; to the best of our knowledge, no language has different morphemes translating one-sided and two-sided *some*. Another is that distribution of the putatively different senses of *some* is linked to exactly the kinds of factors that play a role in the pragmatic implication arguments (a fact that is unexplained on the ambiguity account). For example, we don't seem able to interpret (55*a*) as involving the two-sided *some*, an interpretation that would make the sentence inconsistent. Still another is that which item in a scaled pair is "ambiguous" is predictable on the basis of relative strengths on the scale: "ambiguity" is consistently imputed to the weaker member of the scale. There are others as well. Yet the ambiguity approach continues to be attractive to many, presumably because the two-sided understanding involved in interpreting (53*a*) as implying (53*b*) is apparently assigned so directly and does not involve multiple levels of speaker meaning. We certainly do not consciously go through a calculation like that given for (53) even if the possibility of such an argument is what ultimately supports the inference in (53).

One kind of data sometimes offered in support of the ambiguity analysis involves what Horn (1985) calls "metalinguistic" or "pragmatic" negation. We do find people uttering sentences like those in (56), where italics indicate intonational prominence.

(56) *a.* That novel isn't *good*; it's absolutely superb.
b. She didn't get *some* of the questions right; she answered every single one correctly.

What Horn argues is that the negative here does not serve to negate propositional content; that is, we do not interpret these sentences as denying the truth of the two-sided reading of the weak scalar item. Rather, he suggests, the emphasized weak-scalar item is being mentioned here and not used.

To use an expression is to be responsible for an illocutionary act in which the locution figures directly. To mention an expression is to disavow illocutionary agency in performing the locutionary act. We did not put it quite this way in section 2, not then having available the distinction between locutionary acts and illocutionary acts. One reason to mention an expression can be to comment on the possible illocutionary act of someone who might utter it. This is what seems to be happening in (56); the speaker is dissociating herself from one who would (simply) say that the novel is good or that some of the questions were answered correctly, in order to emphasize that what such a way of speaking implicates is false. What is negated seems to echo some other utterance and to criticize the speaker who chose the locution in question. What negatives do in the sentences in (56) seems very similar to what they do in the sentences in (57); in (57) the negatives criticize pronunciation, choice of register, or other unwanted implications, and the criticized locution is followed by the one endorsed.

(57) *a.* I don't like to/mah/toes but to/mey/toes.
b. You didn't go *pee-pee*: you *urinated.*
c. No, I didn't have lunch with the *girls*: we *women* ate together.

What seems to clinch the case for treating some uses of negatives as involving something very different from negation of propositional content is that the material with which the negative is associated need not be linguistic at all. This point is beautifully made in person by Larry Horn performing on his kazoo, the brackets indicating the points at which he demonstrates two musical performances, the first to be avoided and the second to be imitated.

(58) It's not $[\quad]_1$ but $[\quad]_2$.

It seems clear in (57) that in uttering the initial apparently negative clause, the speaker means only that some other speaker has failed to choose the most appropriate or effective locution to do the job; she then demonstrates what a better locution might be. A similar account of the import of the negatives in (56) seems quite plausible, in which case such utterances provide no evidence at all in favor of scalar ambiguities.

What are sometimes called *clausal implicatures* have also been much discussed. Uttering a sentence that contains an embedded clausal complement may generate an implicature about the epistemic status of that clause: for example, that the speaker is taking the proposition expressed by the subordinate clause as still an open question. Gazdar (1979) is the first extensive discussion of clausal implicatures as a class, and he proposes that they are governed by (59).

(59) If a sentence does not entail either the proposition expressed by the subordinate clause or its negation, then uttering the sentence implicates the (epistemic) possibility of both those propositions.

But (59) does not always work. Sentences (60*a*) and (60*b*) are alike in entailing neither the subordinate clause (60*c*) nor its negation (60*d*).

(60) *a.* I guess Joan is smart.
b. I am certain that Joan is smart.
c. Joan is smart.
d. Joan is not smart.

Thus Gazdar's principle (59) predicts that both (60*a*) and (60*b*) should implicate (61).

(61) For all I know, Joan is smart, and for all I know, Joan is not smart.

Now (60*b*) certainly does not implicate (61); indeed, it tends to implicate (62).

(62) I know that Joan is smart.

It might seem somewhat more plausible that (60*a*) implicates (61). But even this somewhat more plausible prediction is dubious. Sentences like (60*a*) are typically used as hedged assertions of their complement clauses, thus implicating those complements; in many contexts, uttering (60*a*) would implicate (60*c*).

Nonetheless, Gazdar is quite right in observing that certain complex sentential forms imply (though they do not entail) propositions about the speaker's epistemic position with respect to the propositions expressed by constituent clauses. So for example, (63*a*) and (63*b*) each implies all the remaining sentences in (63), though these implications are defeasible.

(63) *a.* Either [Joan]$_i$ bought steak, or [she]$_i$ bought swordfish.
b. If [Joan]$_i$ did not buy steak, [she]$_i$ bought swordfish.
c. For all the speaker knows, Joan did not buy steak.
d. For all the speaker knows, Joan did buy steak.
e. For all the speaker knows, Joan did not buy swordfish.
f. For all the speaker knows, Joan did buy swordfish.

We do not need principle (59), however, but can calculate these implicatures by appeal to the assumption that the speaker is cooperative in the purposes of the exchange and has adhered to maxims of quality and quantity. Let's see how the argument works.

In chapter 2 we semantically analyzed *or* as inclusive (as requiring only that at least one disjunct be true). Now we can say more about how the exclusive interpretation arises. A sentence like (63*a*), which is entailed on our account by (64*a*), is often taken to implicate (64*b*).

(64) *a.* Joan bought both steak and swordfish.
b. Joan didn't buy both steak and swordfish.

The implicature is easily calculated from the observation that (63*a*) is entailed by, but does not entail, (64*a*). Thus (63*a*) is weaker. As is generally the case with such relations of relative strength, someone who states only that (63*a*) is true suggests she is not in a position to claim (64*a*) and thus (in many circumstances) implies that (64*b*), the negation of (64*a*), is true. In this way we can use the maxim of quantity to arrive at the pertinent implication; we do not need to posit a special exclusive sense of *or*. The exclusive interpretation can be explained pragmatically rather than semantically.

Nonetheless, as with other scalar items, many have taken the ambiguity path. As evidence it is alleged that Latin *autem* actually expressed a disjunction true only in case exactly one of the disjuncts it joins is true, but the facts are not so simple. (Horn 1989 includes some discussion of this question.) It seems that *autem* may simply have been used in contexts where exclusiveness of the disjunction was presupposed.

Some negative sentences seem at first glance to offer evidence in support of the claim that the truth of exactly one disjunct is entailed.

(65) Joan didn't buy *either* steak or swordfish: she came home with *both*.

Both stress and discourse constraints on the use of such sentences, however, strongly argue for their being cases of metalinguistic rather than propositional negation. In other words, the negative in (65) attacks the use of the word *either* as an ill-advised choice rather than negating the proposition expressed by (63*a*). Without focal stress as indicated or a preceding assertion of (63*a*), (65) seems interpretable only as a contradiction. Thus sentence (65) does not show the existence of a sense of *or* relative to which (60*a*) entails (61*b*); once again, apparent evidence of ambiguity evaporates once we see that *not* can indicate metalinguistic negation.

What is interesting is that *neither* ... *nor* is only interpretable as negating an inclusive *either* ... *or*. Note that the conjunction of sentence (66*a*) with (66*b*) is blatantly contradictory.

(66) *a.* Joan bought neither steak nor swordfish.
b. Joan bought both steak and swordfish.

As we have observed in earlier chapters, ambiguities in a sentence are matched by ambiguities in the negation of that sentence. In general, *neither* ... *nor* constructions express the negations of their *either* ... *or* counterparts. Thus if *either* ... *or* is ambiguous, we should expect a parallel ambiguity in *neither* ... *nor*. If (66*a*) were interpreted as the negation of the exclusive sense posited for *either* ... *or*, then on that interpretation (66*a*) would be true in the situation in which both (and not simply one) of its disjuncts is true. The fact that there is no available interpretation for (66*a*) compatible with (66*b*) strongly argues against the existence of an exclusive sense of *or*. Indeed, even (67) is incompatible with (66*b*), unless (67) is interpreted as metalinguistic negation (with tell-tale stress and discourse restrictions).

(67) It is not the case that Joan bought either steak or swordfish.

There are further considerations that can be offered against the ambiguity analysis, but these will serve for now. As Grice observes, the principle of Occam's razor—do not multiply entities beyond necessity—is generally relevant. Why multiply senses if one suffices? In this case it seems clear that one sense not only can but must suffice.

Both scalar and clausal implications are instances of what Grice calls *generalized conversational implicatures* (GCIs). GCIs hold in a wide range of conversational contexts: a hearer could calculate them with access only to some very basic beliefs about communication and perhaps some other widely available assumptions about social norms and the subject matter being discussed. They are also typically direct in the sense we discussed in section 2; that is, the speaker does not mean to draw attention to the contrast between what is literally said and what is conversationally implicated. A GCI is like a second sense in being immediately available. It is not surprising then that GCIs are so often thought to be entailments, their defeasibility then being attributed to some putative ambiguity rather than to the failure of a conversational premise.

In contrast, *particularized conversational implicatures* (PCIs) depend crucially on contextual features specific to a given utterance and not just on a standard background. Sperber and Wilson (1986) discuss many examples of such contextually specific implications. For example, someone uttering (68*b*) in response to (68*a*) would implicate (68*c*) and (68*d*).

(68) *a.* Have you read E. O. Wilson's *Sociobiology*?
b. I don't read science fiction.
c. I have not read *Sociobiology*.
d. I view *Sociobiology* as (like) science fiction (and thus as bad science).

One might think initially that particularized implicatures are limited to face-to-face communication, since it is only there that producer and interpreter are in (essentially) the same context. But there can be particularized implicatures that draw on the particular background generated by preceding text. That is, preceding text produces a partial but nonetheless particular context. A sentence in the middle of a book might be interpreted quite differently from the same sentence placed near the beginning. And sometimes an author assumes familiarity on the part of the reading audience with other texts she has produced. The contrast between generalized and particularized implicatures may not always be sharply defined. Indeed, most implicatures (even quite generalized ones) probably rely on premises that some community members cannot supply (the relatively young, newcomers, and some unusually ill-informed people). Not surprisingly, however, most attention has been paid to systematizing the account of clear cases of GCIs, although Sperber and Wilson's work does not draw a real distinction (and offers analyses of many implicatures that Grice and those who have followed him more closely would treat as PCIs).

In the arguments supporting calculability that we gave above, there was tension between maxims but they were not abandoned. Sometimes, though, maxims are apparently flouted, and yet, Grice suggests, we still assume that the cooperative principle is in play, and we try to infer what the speaker intends to convey on this basis. In such cases we are reading between the lines: drawing inferences on the basis of beliefs of the sort embodied in the maxims about strategies and speaker's purposes.

For example, a letter of recommendation for someone applying for a faculty position in a linguistics department that consists only of (69*a*) would implicate (69*b*).

(69) *a.* Lee has a nice smile and draws beautiful phrase-structure trees.
b. Lee is no good as a linguist.

The letter writer has obviously failed to give a full enough picture of Lee's qualifications for the post. How then do we actually infer (69*b*) rather than assuming that the letter writer has said no more because this is all she knows (or believes with adequate evidence) about Lee? Presumably, we have to appeal to principles beyond the maxims themselves in order to generate this inference, because if the letter writer does indeed believe with evidence something along the lines of (69*b*), quantity would seem to require that this be said. But it was not said. So quantity is blatantly flouted. And in this extreme case what is communicated about smiling and drawing trees is irrelevant to the communicative task at hand. But we need additional assumptions to conclude that the writer is implicating (69*b*) in writing (69*a*). We may assume that people typically refrain from saying overtly negative things in job recommendations, even where such negative evaluations are highly relevant, whereas they do not refrain from saying positive things that are relevant. Along with this assumption there must also be the overarching assumption that the letter writer is attempting to cooperate in spite of appearances to the contrary.

Such indirect communication can be risky. One hears arguments about what a recommender intended to implicate.

(70) *A*: She said nothing about his teaching, so she must be implying that it is terrible.
B: Oh no, I think she assumes that his teaching is fine unless otherwise stated.

As we noted earlier, there can be reasons for choosing such indirect ways of conveying what one means. One way of being polite is to "pretend" that one means one thing—what one directly says—while actually conveying something rather different: consider (71*a*) as a way of conveying (71*b*), purporting to offer the addressee a choice of seats while at the genuinely operative level issuing a directive as to where to sit.

(71) *a.* Would you like to sit here?
b. Sit here, please.

Alert children frequently refuse to play this game: their answer to (72*a*) is (72*b*).

(72) *a.* Would you like to set the table?
b. No, but I will.

After all, to act as if setting the table is what one wants to do is to lose moral credit for having agreed to do it (and to let the requester avoid the debt for having asked to have it done). Brown and Levinson (1978) discuss "linguistic universals of politeness," drawing on a general Gricean pragmatic theory.

Exercise 4 In each of the pairs below sentence (*a*) conversationally implicates sentence (*b*). For each pair, provide a reason for thinking that the implication is not an entailment, and calculate the implicature as best you can, indicating where contextually specific premises need to be supplied.

(1) *a.* Joan swung at the ball.
b. Joan missed the ball.

(2) *a.* I don't think your solution works.
b. I think your solution doesn't work.

(3) *a.* Mary brought a man from New York as her guest.
b. The man was not Mary's husband.

(4) *a.* I wonder what time it is.
b. The speaker wants to be told what time it is by the addressee.

(5) *a.* Jim's research is respected.
b. Many people respect Jim's research.

(6) *a.* Jill and Greg went to the movies.
b. Jill and Greg went to the movies together.

Many rhetorical strategies and figures of speech depend on what we called in section 2 multiple levels of speaker meaning. Sperber and Wilson (1986) discuss a number of cases. Their analysis of verbal irony, for example, makes it echoic in much the same sense as Larry Horn's pragmatic negation. The point of ironic utterances, they suggest, is to caricature an echoed utterance by performing essentially the same locutionary act in a manner designed to suggest that what such a locution explicitly expresses is inappropriate and thus to present those who might utter it as stupid, insensitive, or unsophisticated by mockingly imitating them. (There need not actually have been a previous utterance of the type so caricatured.) Thus two lovers might be happily walking in pouring rain, and one might say the following in a tone of mock surprise to the other:

(73) Why, it seems to be raining.

What might be meant? Here are some possibilities: that these two are above ordinary mortals, who notice such mundane details as whether it is raining, that they are so elevated because of the grandeur of their passion, that they cannot concern themselves with the possible disapproval of more conventional and prosaic souls, and so on. The particular inferences to be drawn about the speaker's attitudes cannot be identified simply on the basis of what one knows about the language system and about the appropriateness of the utterance in the given context. These are cases where what is conveyed is relatively open-ended: the main aim seems to be simply to evoke a general atmosphere or a family of attitudes.

A thorough exploration of indirect and nonliteral uses of language lies outside the scope of this book. We are inclined to be optimistic, however, that explicit accounts of what expressions literally mean and of the systematic processes of directly implicating will help us understand these more complex uses of language. Indirectness and figurativeness are in some ways parasitic on canonical situations, where language use is direct and conventional (though perhaps less than fully explicit) and where the aims of communication are the cooperative exchange of information.

Although the details are still far from clear, there continues to be considerable interest in the general Gricean idea that to attribute to others communicative intentions is to have certain expectations that can be exploited to enhance communicative ability. This idea has been especially important in trying to show how the logician's analysis of the semantic value of certain words and constructions can be maintained in the face of evidence that speakers often mean more than the logical analysis itself would seem to warrant. It is also crucial in extending analyses beyond canonical communicative situations of cooperatively sharing information. Some such theory is an essential complement to the kind of truth-conditional semantic analyses we propose as an analysis of the meaning of disambiguated and contextually specified English sentences.

5 Intensionality

1 Introduction

In this chapter we will explore ways in which intensional phenomena can be approached from the point of view of truth-conditional semantics. We will begin by discussing contexts that appear to resist an analysis in purely extensional terms.

1.1 Intensional contexts

To specify the truth conditions for the sentences in F_2, we had to consider only the referential value of their components in a given situation. Thus, for example, the truth conditions of (1*a*) are specified in (1*b*):

(1) *a*. Pavarotti is boring.
b. (1*a*) is true in *v* iff Pavarotti is in the set of things that are boring in *v*.

To determine the value of (1*a*) in *v*, we just have to check whether Pavarotti is in the set that constitutes the extension in *v* of the predicate *is boring*. Individuals and sets, whatever mysteries may surround them, are paradigmatic extensional notions.

We know, however, plenty of constructions that are more complex. Consider, for example, the sentences in (2).

(2) *a*. Pavarotti is hungry.
b. Pavarotti was hungry.

To know whether (2*b*) is true in a situation *v*, it is not sufficient to know the extension of *is hungry* in *v*. The latter knowledge suffices only to assess the truth value of (2*a*). To evaluate (2*b*) in *v*, we must know the extension of *is hungry* in circumstances that occurred prior to *v*. Thus if we want to say something about the semantics of tense, we need more than the extension of expressions in a given situation.

Consider (3) next:

(3) It is possible for John to travel to Russia.

To evaluate (3) in a situation *v*, knowing the extension in *v* of *to travel to Russia* will not suffice. Nor will it suffice to know what has happened before *v* and what will happen after *v*. It might be that John has never traveled to Russia and never will. Yet traveling to Russia is quite possible for him, while for others perhaps it isn't. Thus the notion of possibility also calls for more than extensions, and it does so in a way that appears to be different from tense, for knowing what has been the case or what will be the case does not suffice to assess the truth value of (3).

Another example is provided by counterfactual conditionals, such as the ones in (4).

(4) *a.* If Proust had taken a cruise on the *Titanic*, the *Titanic* would not have sunk.
b. If Proust had taken a cruise on the *Titanic, Remembrance of Things Past* would not have been completed, and literature would have suffered a great loss.

We are inclined to judge (4*a*) as false and (4*b*) as true. Now we know that in fact Proust never was on the *Titanic*. Yet the sentences in (4) invite us to consider a situation where he was and make a claim as to what follows from that. Clearly, the truth values of (4*a*) and (4*b*) do not depend on the truth values of the antecedents (or of the consequents), for in both cases the antecedents (and the consequents) are both actually false (Proust never cruised on the *Titanic, Remembrance of Things Past* was completed, and the *Titanic* sank).

Another striking case is provided by sentences like

(5) John believes that Mary is hungry.

Clearly whether (5) is true or not does not depend in any way on the truth value of the embedded clause. John might believe that Mary is hungry, whether she is in fact or not. But we as yet have no way to assign a more plausible semantic value to the embedded clause in (5). We have argued that the meaning of sentences is related to their truth conditions. On this basis we would expect that John's belief has something to do with the truth conditions of the embedded clause, that it is somehow related to the conditions under which "Mary is hungry" is true. But we are so far unable to use this idea in providing a compositional semantics for sentences like (5).

All these constructions are said to be *intensional*; their analysis will require sharpening our view of such intensional notions as those of *proposition* and *property*, which we discussed informally in chapter 2 in connection with Frege's notion of sense. Now something that the sentences in (2*b*) to (5) all seem to have in common is that they call for a consideration of the extension that expressions have in circumstances other than the one in which we are evaluating them. In the case of (2*b*) this claim hardly requires further comment. It should also be clear with respect to (3). To claim that for John to travel is possible we must consider what options John might have. Such options must include some in which John's traveling takes place. Envisioning a possibility is simply considering an alternative way in which the world might have been, that is, a nonactual circumstance. A similar point can be made in connection with (4). Conditionals in general invite us to imagine that certain hypotheses hold (whether they in fact do or not) and to consider their consequences.

And something in very much the same vein can also be said about (5). Consider the ways in which the world could be, the alternative states of affairs that might obtain. We can regard them as forming a logical space: the space that delimits all the possible alternatives to the state of affairs in which we in fact are. Belief can be thought of as a way of locating oneself in this logical space. Accordingly, (5) says that John believes himself to inhabit a region of the logical space where Mary is hungry. He is disposed to act as if the actual world were in that region. For example, he may offer her something to eat or start cooking a meal for her, etc. His expectations, desires, and so on depend on what it would be like if Mary were hungry.

In fact, all predicates that can take *that* clauses as complements are amenable to an analysis similar to that just sketched for *believe*. To fear, to hope, and to wish that Mary is hungry can all be thought of as attitudes in favor of or against those (possibly nonactual) circumstances where Mary is hungry. In chapter 3 we said that different models might reflect different circumstances or states of affairs, but the semantic machinery presented there did not allow us to consider more than one such state of affairs in interpreting a sentence. Yet a semantic analysis of (2*b*) to (5) and related constructions seems to call for consideration in a given circumstance of alternative sets of circumstances, states of affairs, or more picturesquely, *possible worlds*.

Roughly speaking, a possible but nonactual state of affairs is what would be the case if some (many, most, or even all) events had different outcomes from those that they in fact have. For example, one can imagine a possible state of affairs exactly like the one we are in except that this text is printed in red rather than in black. David Lewis (1973, 84) offers a vivid characterization of possible worlds in the following often quoted paragraph:

It is uncontroversially true that things might have been otherwise than they are. I believe, and so do you, that things could have been different in countless ways. But what does this mean? Ordinary language permits the paraphrase: there are many ways things could have been besides the way they actually are. On the face of it, this sentence is an existential quantification. It says that there exist many entities of a certain description, to wit, "ways things could have been." I believe permissible paraphrases of what I believe; taking the paraphrase at its face value, I therefore believe in the existence of entities which might be called "ways things could have been." I prefer to call them "possible worlds."

The formal apparatus of possible worlds, a number of whose applications to semantic questions we discuss later in this chapter, was introduced in Kripke (1959) as a tool for investigating the semantic properties of certain formal systems. There has since been, and continues to be, much controversy in the philosophical literature over what assumptions that apparatus requires. In accepting Lewis's point we do not deny that possible worlds might raise deep metaphysical issues, but we think that the formal apparatus can be adopted without resolving these issues, just as we can successfully use the notion of an individual in set theory and logic without resolving all the thorny problems it raises, for example, the mysteries of criteria for identifying individuals. Such skeptics about possible worlds as Quine or, more recently, Barwise and Perry have not abandoned set-theoretic methods just because they lack adequate criteria for identifying individuals (and thus ultimately sets). Nor should they.

Our position is the following. We find possible worlds an extremely useful tool in understanding meaning. Evaluating the notion is a matter of evaluating the role it plays in the various enterprises of which it is part, and we should not be misled by the science fiction flavor of the terminology. This is, we think, in the same spirit as Stalnaker (1984). Stalnaker argues very strongly that possible worlds should be regarded as "not concrete objects or situations, but abstract objects whose existence is inferred or abstracted from the activities of rational agents. It is thus not implausible to suppose that their existence is in some sense dependent on, and that their natures must be explained in terms of, those activities" (p. 50). Kripke makes a similar comment: "'Possible worlds' are *stipulated*, not *discovered* by powerful telescopes" (1972, 267).

The human activities on which the existence of possible worlds depends (through which they are stipulated) include using language and interpreting expressions. Semantics, as we understand it, seeks to develop a model (or part of a model) of such activities. In fact, using the formal apparatus of possible worlds in semantics has produced some very interesting and nontrivial accounts of various intensional phenomena, and many quite enlightening semantic studies have been generated. It certainly seems to us a fruitful hypothesis that our semantic competence can be elucidated in this framework. We now turn to introducing the main ideas underlying possible world semantics.

1.2 Possible worlds

A sentence S is semantically associated with a way of dividing circumstances (or, as we can now say, possible worlds) into two groups: those adequately characterized by S (those in which S is true) and those that are not. This much was implicit in our discussion in chapter 2 of the meaning of a sentence as (at least partly) constituted by its truth conditions (not, you will remember, by its truth value as such). To understand the content of a sentence "is to have the capacity to divide the relevant alternatives in the right way" (Stalnaker 1984, 4). This way of putting it suggests that we might identify the content of a sentence, the proposition it expresses, with the set of circumstances or possible worlds in which it is true, at least as a first approximation. Equivalently, we can think of a proposition as a function that associates with each relevant world or circumstance a truth value: true with the worlds in which it is true, false with the others. This is illustrated in figure 5.1. The box in figure 5.1 includes all the worlds that we are capable of discriminating from one another (with the conceptual resources available to us). The circle within the box includes all the worlds associated with some proposition p. Figure 5.1 illustrates how one can also view p as a function from worlds to truth values rather than as a set. It is easy to see that these two ways of characterizing p are equivalent: given the two sets of worlds, we can

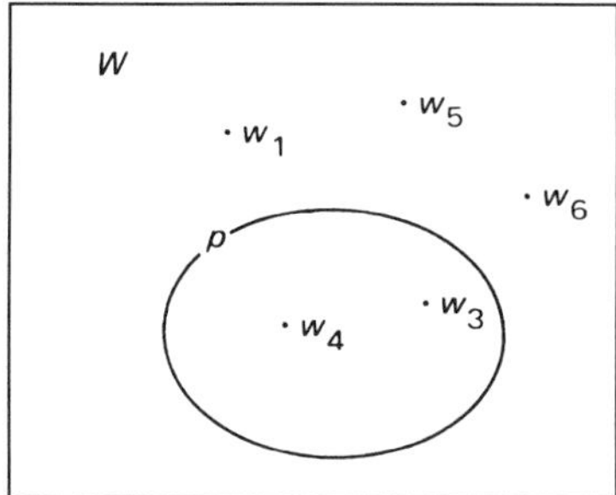

$$p = \begin{bmatrix} w_1 \to 0 \\ w_5 \to 0 \\ w_6 \to 0 \\ \vdots \\ w_3 \to 1 \\ w_4 \to 1 \\ \vdots \end{bmatrix}$$

Figure 5.1

construct the function from worlds to truth values and vice versa (see the appendix for the notion of the characteristic function of a set). Thus we will feel free to switch from one characterization to the other.

To accommodate temporal discourse, we will want to consider not just possible worlds, but possible worlds at different times. Thus our logical space can be represented as having (at least) two coordinates, as illustrated below:

(6)

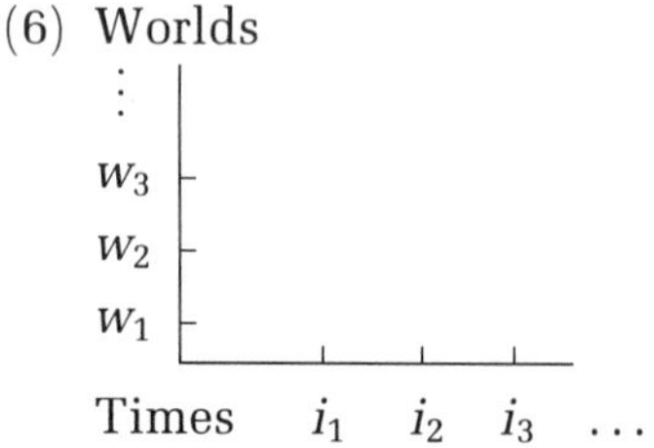

Propositions are to be construed as (possibly noncontinuous) regions of this logical space, as sets of world-time pairs. From now on, we will use *circumstance* to indicate a world-time pair, and we will accordingly talk of propositions as sets of circumstances or as functions from circumstances to truth values. We will nevertheless still refer to the semantics we are describing here as possible world semantics.

On this view, propositions do not appear to be very sentencelike. For example, they don't have a subject-predicate structure or constituents of any kind. As Stalnaker puts it (1984, 23), internal structure is taken to be part not of the content of sentences but of the way in which such content is represented. This seems to go against the intuitive picture of propositions that many have. According to Frege, for example, propositions (the senses of sentences) are the thoughts that sentences express. And it is tempting to take those thoughts as something like sentences in an internalized language, what Lewis (1970) dubs "mentalese." Indeed, there are certain sentencelike attributes that we definitely want propositions to have. For example, we want to be able to say that a proposition entails another proposition, for the content of a sentence may certainly commit us to the content of another sentence, independently of how such contents may be described. We may also want to conjoin propositions, for the content of two sentences can be conjoined. And so on. A notion of proposition that did not allow us to make such ideas precise would be pretty useless for doing semantics. Fortunately, even though the notion of possible circumstances is nowhere close to having the rich structure of sentences, it does allow us to define the structural properties that propositions should definitely have in terms of elementary set-theoretic operations, as sketched in (7). (See the appendix for an explanation of set-theoretic concepts and notation.) Let p and q be subsets of W (where W is the set of all possible circumstances).

(7) *a.* p entails $q =_{\mathrm{df}} p \subseteq q$

b. p is equivalent to $q =_{\mathrm{df}} p = q$ (that is, $p \subseteq q$ and $q \subseteq p$)

c. p and q are contradictory $=_{\mathrm{df}} p \cap q = \varnothing$ (there is no circumstance in which p and q are both true)

d. $\neg p =_{\mathrm{df}} \{w \in W : w \notin p\}$ (the worlds in which p is not true)

e. $p \wedge q =_{\mathrm{df}} p \cap q = \{w \in W : w \in p \text{ and } w \in q\}$

f. $p \vee q =_{\mathrm{df}} p \cup q = \{w \in W : w \in p \text{ or } w \in q\}$

g. p is possible $=_{\mathrm{df}} p \neq \varnothing$ (p is nonempty; there is at least one circumstance in which it is true)

h. p is necessary $=_{\mathrm{df}} p = W$ (there is no circumstance in which p is false)

All the notions in (7) were previously defined on sentences. Now we have a language-independent characterization of sentence content with respect to which they can be defined, a characterization that, even if very simple, will enable us to attempt a semantic analysis of sentences like (2*b*) to (5). So the present view does justice to the intuition that propositions should have a certain amount of structure. In fact, if we could give a satisfactory account of sentences like (2*b*) through (5), that would constitute evidence that the structure that the present theory assigns to propositions is exactly what is called for.

In other ways as well the notion of a proposition that we are considering is not as far from Frege's notion of sense as it might at first appear to be. In general, senses, according to Frege, are the way in which reference is given. Yet he didn't characterize much further the notion of sense (and more specifically the notion of proposition or thought). However, given that the reference of a sentence for him is its truth value, its sense (the thought associated with it) must be the way in which the truth value is given. Functions are mathematical constructs that can be thought of as representing ways of giving things as they depend on something else. Hence, to represent senses as functions would seem appropriate. The question is, then, What is the input of sense functions? What do senses depend on? In particular, what do the senses of sentences depend on? Well, if their reference is a truth value, it must depend on what might be the case, the circumstance that one is envisioning. But then Frege's notion of thought becomes just what we have: a function from circumstances into truth values. The notion of a proposition that we are considering can be seen as at least a partial formal rendering of Frege's notion of a thought (though Frege may well have had more in mind).

Similar considerations can be applied to other kinds of Fregean senses. For example, the reference or extension of a predicate like *is hungry* is a set; the corresponding sense, the way in which the extension is presented, is what Frege thought of as a property. In our terms, properties can be thought of as functions from possible circumstances to sets: the property of being hungry is a function that in any circumstance $\langle w, i \rangle$ tells us what is the set of things that have the property of being hungry in w. Frege also thought that singular terms like *the president* have individuals as their extension (or reference) and what he called individual concepts as their intensions. Again, we can reconstruct individual concepts as functions from possible circumstances to individuals: the individual concept associated with *the president* would yield at a circumstance $\langle w, i \rangle$, the individual that falls under that concept in $\langle w, i \rangle$. All this can be summed up as shown in table 5.1.

Table 5.1 Fregean semantics and possible world semantics

SYNTACTIC CATEGORY	EXAMPLE	INTENSION OR SENSE	EXTENSION OR REFERENCE
Fregean semantics			
VP	is hungry	Property	Set of individuals
S	It rains.	Thought	Truth value
NP	the president	Individual concept	Individual
Possible world semantics			
VP	is hungry	Function from possible circumstances to sets	Set of individuals
S	It rains.	Function from possible circumstances to truth values	Truth value
NP	the president	Function from possible circumstances to individuals	Individual

This constitutes a precise and simple characterization of the kind of objects that Frege and others thought are necessary for doing semantics. A few comments are perhaps in order. We are not claiming that sets of worlds are what propositions *really* are. We claim only that sets of worlds have got the right structure to do what we think propositions do: mediate between sentences and their truth conditions. A crucial component of our semantic competence, what we understand when we understand the content of a sentence, is our capacity to match sentences and situations. Functions from worlds to truth values can be regarded as an abstract way of characterizing such a capacity.

From a slightly different perspective, we can regard meaning in a Saussurean way as a relation between sentence types and the type of circumstances that they describe, along the lines already discussed in chapter 3. We represent the former as phrase markers of some kind and the latter as sets of points in a bidimensional space. Speakers of the language are attuned to such a relation; their interactions with the environment can be accounted for on the basis of it. There is, of course, no denying that part of what speakers do (part of their being attuned to the right meaning) is to form a representation of what is spoken about. The present approach doesn't specify the exact form of this representation. It specifies the structure that any such representation must have in order to be a representation of what we talk about: ways in which the world can be.

To specify *how* we mentally represent what we grasp in understanding a sentence seems feasible only if there is a specification of *what* we grasp. Moreover, if our characterization of what we grasp works (that is, gets the truth conditions of natural language sentences right), this cannot fail to constrain dramatically what our mental representation of such content can be. A good (nonmisleading) representation will reflect faithfully the structure of what it represents, and in the absence of evidence to the contrary, we have no reason to suppose that our internalized representations are bad ones. Differently put, the structure of a good representation will be isomorphic to the structure of its content.

This metaphor could be and has been made more precise in much work on formal semantics (for example, Montague (1973) and subsequent work inspired by this article). But rather than following this line, it is handier to try to explain ourselves further by means of an example. We have just seen that propositions as defined above have a certain structure: they can be conjoined, disjoined, and negated, where conjunction, disjunction, and negation are related in a certain way. Technically, they form what is known as a Boolean algebra (see the appendix). A faithful representation of propositions will contain operators that impose on the representation itself the same structure that propositions have (that is, it too will form a Boolean algebra). This leads to the claim that a system of semantic representations forms a Boolean algebra at some level, a nontrivial claim: not all systems have this structure.

It is now time to make these ideas more concrete by putting them to work. We first develop an artificial language (an extension of PC) that accommodates modal and temporal contexts, and then provide a (fairly standard) possible world semantics for it. We then go on and apply the techniques so developed to a semantic analysis of English.

2 IPC: An Elementary Intensional Logic

There are many ways of designing an intensional predicate calculus (IPC). Our choices are motivated, as throughout this work, mostly by pedagogical considerations. In reading what follows, the reader should bear in mind that other options are available. As suggested by the discussion above, we will include both possible worlds and times in the semantics for IPC.

The syntactic rules for IPC are the same as those of PC (see the recursive formulation in (15), chap. 3, pp. 96–97), with the following addition:

(8) If ψ is a formula, then so are $\Box\psi$ (to be read "it is necessarily the case that ψ"), $\Diamond\psi$ (to be read "it is possibly the case that ψ"), $\mathbf{P}\psi$ ("it *was* the case that ψ") and $\mathbf{F}\psi$ ("it *will* be the case that ψ").

These new operators—$\Box$, $\Diamond$, **P**, and **F**—can be used to model some of the intensional contexts discussed in section 1 (in particular those having to do with tenses and with VPs like *is possible* or *is necessary*). In virtue of (8), in addition to containing all the well-formed formulas of PC, IPC will also contain formulas like those in (9).

(9) *a.* $\Box\exists x[P(x)]$
b. $\exists x[\Box P(x)]$
c. $\forall x[P(x) \to \mathbf{F}P(x)]$
d. $\mathbf{P}\forall x[P(x)]$
e. $[\mathbf{P}P(x) \vee P(x) \vee \mathbf{F}P(x)]$
f. $\Diamond\Box\forall x[P(x)]$
g. $\neg\mathbf{P}[P(j)]$
h. $\mathbf{P}\neg[P(j)]$

A model for IPC is going to include a set of individuals U and an interpretation function for the constants V (just like a model for PC). But since we are in an intensional setting, a model for IPC will also include a set of worlds W and a set of times I, ordered by an earlier than relation $<$, and the interpretation function V will assign intensions to constants. For any constant a, $V(a)$ is a function from circumstances into extensions of the appropriate kind. So for any circumstance $\langle w, i\rangle$, $V(a)$ applied to $\langle w, i\rangle$, i.e., $V(a)(\langle w, i\rangle)$, is a's extension. More explicitly:

(10) $\langle W, I, <, U, V\rangle$, where the following constraints hold:
a. W is a set of worlds.
b. I is a set of instants ordered by the relation $<$. (For i, i' in I, $i < i'$ is to be read "i precedes i'," or colloquially, "i is earlier than i'.")
c. U is a domain of individuals.

d. V is a function that assigns an intension to the constants of IPC. In particular, if β is an individual constant of IPC, $V(\beta)$ is a function from $W \times I$ $(= \{\langle w, i\rangle : w \in W \text{ and } i \in I\})$ to U, so for any $w \in W$ and $i \in I$, $V(\beta)(\langle w, i\rangle) \in U$. If β is a one-place predicate of IPC, $V(\beta)$ is a function from $W \times I$ to sets of elements of U; that is, for any $w \in W$ and $i \in I$, $V(\beta)(\langle w, i\rangle) \subseteq U$ (or equivalently, $V(\beta)(\langle w, i\rangle) \in \mathcal{P}(U)$). If β is a two-place predicate, then $V(\beta)$ is a function from $W \times I$ to sets of ordered pairs of elements of U; that is, for any $w \in W$ and $i \in I$, $V(\beta)(\langle w, i\rangle) \subseteq U \times U$ (or equivalently, $V(\beta)(\langle w, i\rangle) \in \mathcal{P}(U \times U)$). In general, if β is an n-place predicate of IPC, $V(\beta)$ is a function from $W \times I$ to $\mathcal{P}(U^n)$, where $U^n = U \times \cdots \times U$, n times.

A value assignment to variables will be a function g from variables to individuals, as before. There are some intensional logics where assignment functions are also relativized to worlds, but this leads to technical complications that we want to avoid at this point.

We now recursively define the notion of an interpretation of an expression of IPC. The interpretation function $[\![\ ]\!]$ will be relativized not only to a model M of the form described in (10) and an assignment to variables g but also to a world w and a time i. To interpret modal and temporal operators, we have to consider the intensions of expressions involved, or what under the present analysis amounts to the same thing, we have to consider how the extension of expressions varies across different circumstances. Thus our interpretation function $[\![\ ]\!]$ must enable us to represent such a variation directly, hence its relativization to circumstances (world-time pairs).

(11) *a*. If β is a constant, $[\![\beta]\!]^{M,w,i,g} = V(\beta)(\langle w, i\rangle)$.

b. If β is a variable, $[\![\beta]\!]^{M,w,i,g} = g(\beta)$.

c. If $\beta = \delta(t_1, \ldots, t_n)$, then $[\![\beta]\!]^{M,w,i,g} = 1$ iff $\langle [\![t_1]\!]^{M,w,i,g}, \ldots, [\![t_n]\!]^{M,w,i,g}\rangle \in [\![\delta]\!]^{M,w,i,g}$.

d. If $\psi = \neg\phi$, then $[\![\psi]\!]^{M,w,i,g} = 1$ iff $[\![\phi]\!]^{M,w,i,g} = 0$. Similarly for the other connectives ($\vee$, $\wedge$, $\rightarrow$, $\leftrightarrow$).

e. If $\psi = \forall x\phi$, then $[\![\psi]\!]^{M,w,i,g} = 1$ iff for all $u \in U$, $[\![\phi]\!]^{M,w,i,g[u/x]} = 1$. Similarly for the existential quantifier.

f. If $\psi = \Box\phi$, then $[\![\psi]\!]^{M,w,i,g} = 1$ iff for all $w' \in W$ and all $i' \in I$, $[\![\phi]\!]^{M,w',i',g} = 1$.

g. If $\psi = \Diamond\phi$, then $[\![\psi]\!]^{M,w,i,g} = 1$ iff there exists at least one $w' \in W$ and one $i' \in I$ such that $[\![\phi]\!]^{M,w',i',g} = 1$.

h. If $\psi = \mathbf{P}\phi$, then $[\![\psi]\!]^{M,w,i,g} = 1$ iff there exists an $i' \in I$ such that $i' < i$ and $[\![\phi]\!]^{M,w,i',g} = 1$.

i. If $\psi = \mathbf{F}\phi$, then $[\![\psi]\!]^{M,w,i,g} = 1$ iff there exists an $i' \in I$ such that $i < i'$ and $[\![\phi]\!]^{M,w,i',g} = 1$.

Apart from the explicit relativization to worlds and times, the interpretation function is essentially the same as the one familiar from PC. Strictly, in IPC (as in PC) we have only up to three-place predicates, and thus clause (*c*) is too general. However, such excess generality might be desirable, for at some point we might want to introduce in IPC relations that take more arguments, without having to revise the interpretive procedure each time. The real novelty with respect to the comparison with PC comes from clauses (*f*) through (*i*), which assign an interpretation to the modal and temporal operators of IPC. Clause (*f*) can be regarded as a formalization of the Leibnizian idea that a sentence is necessarily true in a given circumstance iff it is true in every possible circumstance. According to (*g*), a sentence is possibly true iff there exists at least one possible circumstance in which it is true. So necessity is interpreted as universal quantification over circumstances (or world-time pairs), and possibility as existential quantification over circumstances. The interpretation of the temporal operators should also be fairly transparent, and it's due, in the form we have adopted, to A. Prior (1967). According to (*h*), a sentence of the form "It was the case that β" is true iff there is a moment that precedes the time of evaluation at which β is true. For the present purposes we can assume that the time at which we evaluate a sentence is the time of utterance, although in the long run this assumption will have to be revised (see, for example, Kamp 1971). So sentences are generally evaluated with respect to the actual world at the time of utterance (relative to a model). This approach tries to model (in a still very approximate way) the way tense seems to function in natural language. When we say, "Bond kissed Loren," we do not seem to refer explicitly to a particular time. As participants in a speech act, we have access to what the time of utterance is, and the past morpheme in *kissed* signals that the event in question occurred before the time of utterance. Similarly, in IPC the past temporal operator does not explicitly refer to a particular past time but directs us to evaluate the sentence for times before the time of utterance. The future tense operator works the same way, but for times that follow the time of utterance.

The definitions of truth, validity, entailment, and equivalence are straightforward extensions of the familiar ones:

(12) *a.* A formula ψ is *true* in a model M with respect to a world w and a time i iff for any assignment g, $[\![\psi]\!]^{M,w,i,g} = 1$.

b. A formula ψ is *valid* iff for any model M, any world w, and any time i, ψ is true in M with respect to w and i.

c. A formula ψ *entails* a formula ϕ iff for any model M, any world w, any time i, and any assignment g, if $[\![\psi]\!]^{M,w,i,g} = 1$ then $[\![\phi]\!]^{M,w,i,g} = 1$.

d. A set of formulas $\Omega = \{\psi_1, \ldots, \psi_n\}$ *entails* a formula ϕ iff for any model M, any world w, any time i, and any assignment g, if $[\![\psi_i]\!]^{M,w,i,g} = 1$ for all ψ_i in Ω, then $[\![\phi]\!]^{M,w,i,g} = 1$.

e. Two formulas ψ and ϕ are *equivalent* iff they entail each other.

We might familiarize ourselves more with an intensional semantics of this kind by providing a specific model and evaluating a few formulas in it. Even if we try to keep things as concise as possible, it rapidly becomes very long and tedious to specify completely a model for IPC. So we will compromise and explicitly assign an interpretation to just one one-place predicate P, and two individual constants m and j of IPC. This will suffice for the purpose of illustration. The model M_4, a variant of a model in Dowty, Wall, and Peters (1981, 113), contains two worlds, w' and w'', and three instants i', i'', and i''' (ordered $i' < i'' < i'''$). The intensions of P and m are given in the form of matrices and should be self-explanatory.

(13) $M_4 = \langle W_4, I_4, <_4, U_4, V_4 \rangle$, where

a. $W_4 = \{w', w''\}$, $I_4 = \{i', i'', i'''\}$,
$<_4 = \{\langle i', i'' \rangle, \langle i'', i''' \rangle, \langle i', i''' \rangle\}$, $U_4 = \{a, b, c\}$

b. $V_4(j)$ is a constant function such that for any $w \in W_4$ and $i \in I_4$, $V_4(j)(\langle w, i \rangle) = a$. Furthermore,

$V_4(m) =$	i'	i''	i'''
w''	b	b	a
w'	a	a	c

$V_4(P) =$	i'	i''	i'''
w''	$\{b, c\}$	$\{a, b\}$	$\{a\}$
w'	$\{a, b, c\}$	$\{a, b\}$	$\{c\}$

We also need to select an assignment to variables. Let us take the following:

$$g_4 = \begin{bmatrix} x \rightarrow a \\ y \rightarrow b \\ z \rightarrow b \\ \vdots \end{bmatrix}$$

Now we will consider a few examples. We will consider three simple formulas that contain the necessity operator. As there are six circumstances in M_4, in order to compute the truth values of our formulas we will typically have to compute it six times (one for each world-time pair). As usual, we set apart computation of truth conditions from computation of truth values. The first formula contains no quantifier, the other two do and illustrate the interaction between the modal operator and the existential quantifier. The truth conditions of the third formula will require us to look for something that is in the extension of P in every world. We try all the individuals in the domain and we see that none of them is in P in all the worlds. Hence we conclude that the formula is false.

The truth conditions of $\square P(m)$ relative to M_4 in w'', at i', relative to g_4

(a) $[\![\square P(m)]\!]^{M_4, w'', i', g_4} = 1$ iff for all $w \in W_4$ and $i \in I_4$, $[\![P(m)]\!]^{M_4, w, i, g_4} = 1$ By ($11f$)

(b) For all $w \in W_4$ and $i \in I_4$, $[\![P(m)]\!]^{M_4, w, i, g_4} = 1$ iff $V(m)(\langle w, i\rangle) \in V(P)(\langle w, i\rangle)$ By ($11c$) and ($11a$)

(c) $[\![\square P(m)]\!]^{M_4, w'', i', g_4} = 1$ iff for all $w \in W_4$ and $i \in I_4$, $V(m)(\langle w, i\rangle) \in V(P)(\langle w, i\rangle)$ By (a), (b)

The truth value of $\square P(m)$ relative to M_4 in w'', at i', relative to g_4

(i) $[\![P(m)]\!]^{M_4, w', i', g_4} = 1$ iff $a \in \{a, b, c\}$, which is the case
(ii) $[\![P(m)]\!]^{M_4, w', i'', g_4} = 1$ iff $a \in \{a, b\}$, which is the case
(iii) $[\![P(m)]\!]^{M_4, w', i''', g_4} = 1$ iff $c \in \{c\}$, which is the case
(iv) $[\![P(m)]\!]^{M_4, w'', i', g_4} = 1$ iff $b \in \{b, c\}$, which is the case
(v) $[\![P(m)]\!]^{M_4, w'', i'', g_4} = 1$ iff $b \in \{a, b\}$, which is the case
(vi) $[\![P(m)]\!]^{M_4, w'', i''', g_4} = 1$ iff $a \in \{a\}$, which is the case

(d) $[\![\square P(m)]\!]^{M_4, w'', i', g_4} = 1$ By (c) and (i) through (vi)

The truth conditions of $\exists x\Box P(x)$ relative to M_4 in w'', at i''', relative to g_4

(a) $[\![\Box\exists xP(x)]\!]^{M_4, w'', i''', g_4} = 1$ iff for all $w \in W_4$ and $i \in I_4$, $[\![\exists xP(x)]\!]^{M_4, w, i, g_4} = 1$ By ($11f$)

(b) For all $w \in W_4$ and $i \in I_4$, $[\![\exists xP(x)]\!]^{M_4, w, i, g_4} = 1$ iff for some $u \in U_4$, $[\![P(x)]\!]^{M_4, w, i, g_4[u/x]} = 1$ By ($11e$)

(c) For all $w \in W_4$ and $i \in I_4$ and for some $u \in U_4$, $[\![P(x)]\!]^{M_4, w, i, g_4[u/x]} = 1$ iff $[\![u]\!]^{M_4, w, i, g_4[u/x]} \in [\![P]\!]^{M_4, w, i, g_4[u/x]}$ By ($11c$)

(d) For all $w \in W_4$ and $i \in I_4$ and for some $u \in U_4$, $[\![u]\!]^{M_4, w, i, g_4[u/x]} \in [\![P]\!]^{M_4, w, i, g_4[u/x]}$ iff $g_4[u/x](x) \in V(P)(\langle w, i\rangle)$ By ($11a$)

(e) For all $w \in W_4$ and $i \in I_4$ and for some $u \in U_4$, $g_4[u/x](x) \in V(P)(\langle w, i\rangle)$ iff for all $w \in W_4$ and $i \in I_4$ and for some $u \in U_4$, $u \in V(P)(\langle w, i\rangle)$ By def. of $g_4[u/x]$

(f) $[\![\Box\exists xP(x)]\!]^{M_4, w'', i''', g_4} = 1$ iff for all $w \in W_4$ and $i \in I_4$ and for some $u \in U_4$, $u \in V(P)(\langle w, i\rangle)$ From (a) and (e)

This ends the computation of the truth conditions. As for the truth value of $\Box\exists xP(x)$ relative to M_4 in w'', at i''', relative to g_4, we note that (f) requires that the extension of P be nonempty in any of the circumstances of the model; by inspection we immediately see that this is so.

The truth conditions of $\exists x\Box P(x)$ relative to M_4, in w'', at i''', relative to g_4

(a) $[\![\exists x\Box P(x)]\!]^{M_4, w'', i''', g_4} = 1$ iff for some $u \in U_4$, $[\![\Box P(x)]\!]^{M_4, w'', i''', g_4[u/x]} = 1$ By ($11e$)

(b) For some $u \in U_4$, $[\![\Box P(x)]\!]^{M_4, w'', i''', g_4[u/x]} = 1$ iff for all $w \in W_4$ and $i \in I_4$, $[\![P(x)]\!]^{M_4, w, i, g_4[u/x]} = 1$ By ($11f$)

(c) For some $u \in U_4$, for all $w \in W_4$ and $i \in I_4$, $[\![P(x)]\!]^{M_4, w, i, g_4[u/x]} = 1$ iff $u \in V(P)(\langle w, i\rangle)$ By ($11a$–c) and def. of $g_4[u/x]$

(d) $[\![\exists x\Box P(x)]\!]^{M_4, w'', i''', g_4} = 1$ iff for some $u \in U_4$, for all $w \in W_4$ and $i \in I_4$, $u \in V(P)(\langle w, i\rangle)$ From (a) and (c)

This completes computation of the truth conditions.

For the truth value, we try out the three different individuals in our domain.

(i) $[\![\Box P(x)]\!]^{M_4, w''', i'', g_4[a/x]} = 0$, since $a \notin V(P)(w'', i')$

(ii) $[\![\Box P(x)]\!]^{M_4, w''', i'', g_4[b/x]} = 0$, since $b \notin V(P)(w', i''')$

(iii) $[\![\Box P(x)]\!]^{M_4, w''', i'', g_4[c/x]} = 0$, since $c \notin V(P)(w', i'')$

(e) $[\![\exists x\Box P(x)]\!]^{M_4, w'', i''', g_4} = 0$ From (d) and (i) to (iii)

Exercise 1 Evaluate the following sentences in M_4 in the worlds and at the times indicated:

(1)	(9*c*)	$\langle w', i' \rangle$, $\langle w'', i' \rangle$, $\langle w'', i'' \rangle$
(2)	(9*d*)	$\langle w'', i' \rangle$, $\langle w', i''' \rangle$, $\langle w'', i'' \rangle$
(3)	(9*e*)	$\langle w'', i' \rangle$, $\langle w', i'' \rangle$
(4)	(9*f*)	$\langle w'', i''' \rangle$, $\langle w', i' \rangle$
(5)	$\mathbf{FP}\neg P(j)$	$\langle w'', i' \rangle$, $\langle w'', i'' \rangle$, $\langle w'', i''' \rangle$
(6)	$\neg\mathbf{F}\neg P(j)$	$\langle w', i' \rangle$, $\langle w'', i' \rangle$, $\langle w', i''' \rangle$
(7)	$\neg\mathbf{P}\neg P(j)$	$\langle w', i''' \rangle$, $\langle w'', i''' \rangle$, $\langle w'', i' \rangle$
(8)	$\Diamond\mathbf{F}P(j)$	$\langle w'', i''' \rangle$
(9)	$\Box\Diamond\mathbf{F}P(j)$	$\langle w'', i''' \rangle$
(10)	$\forall x \Diamond P(x)$	$\langle w'', i''' \rangle$
(11)	$\forall x[P(x) \rightarrow \mathbf{F}P(x)]$	$\langle w', i''' \rangle$, $\langle w'', i''' \rangle$
(12)	$\Box\Box\mathbf{P}(m)$	$\langle w', i'' \rangle$
(13)	$\forall x[P(x) \rightarrow \Box[P(x) \vee \mathbf{P}P(x)]]$	$\langle w', i''' \rangle$, $\langle w'', i''' \rangle$
(14)	$\Diamond\Box\Diamond\ \forall x[P(x) \rightarrow x = j]$	$\langle w'', i' \rangle$
(15)	$\exists x \Box[x = j]$	$\langle w'', i' \rangle$
(16)	$\exists x \Box[x = m]$	$\langle w'', i' \rangle$
(17)	$\neg\Diamond\neg\forall x[P(x) \rightarrow \mathbf{P}P(x)]$	$\langle w'', i' \rangle$, $\langle w', i'' \rangle$

The semantics associated with IPC allows us to study the structural relationships that hold among various operators (thereby bringing into sharper focus the notions that such operators are designed to express).

The necessity and the possibility operators are related as in (14):

(14) *a.* $\Box\psi \leftrightarrow \neg\Diamond\neg\psi$ (cf. $\forall x P(x) \leftrightarrow \neg\exists x \neg P(x)$)
b. $\Diamond\psi \leftrightarrow \neg\Box\neg\psi$ (cf. $\exists x P(x) \leftrightarrow \neg\forall x \neg P(x)$)

It is easy to see that our semantics makes (14*a*, *b*) valid no matter how ψ is instantiated. If ψ is true in every world, then it is not the case that there exists a world where ψ is false, and vice versa.[1] Thus, the relation between $\Box$ and $\Diamond$ is directly parallel to the one between $\forall$ and $\exists$, as indicated by the formulas in parentheses in (14*a*, *b*). In technical terms, one is the *dual* of the other. It isn't hard to see where this parallelism comes from: necessity and possibility are semantically interpreted in terms of universal and existential quantifications, respectively, over circumstances. Bringing out a nonobvious parallelism between quantifiers and modal notions (whether they are construed as adverbs, as in "Necessarily, John will be fired," as auxiliarlike verbs, as in "John must leave," or as sentential predicates, as in "For John to leave is impossible") is one of the interesting features of the present semantics, a feature that has several consequences. In particular, $\Box$ will behave just like $\forall$, and $\Diamond$ like $\exists$, with respect to $\rightarrow$, $\wedge$, and $\vee$. For example, we know that $\forall x[P(x) \rightarrow Q(x)]$ entails $[\forall xP(x) \rightarrow \forall xQ(x)]$ but not vice versa. By the same token, $\Box[\psi \rightarrow \phi]$ entails $[\Box\psi \rightarrow \Box\phi]$ but not vice versa.

Exercise 2 Convince yourself of the last claim. Show, furthermore, that (1*a*) entails (1*b*) and vice versa, and that (2*b*) entails (2*a*) but not vice versa.

(1) *a*. $\Box[\psi \wedge \phi]$
    b. $\Box\psi \wedge \Box\phi$

(2) *a*. $\Box[\psi \vee \phi]$
    b. $\Box\psi \vee \Box\phi$

What are the entailment relations that hold between the pairs in (3) through (5)?

(3) *a*. $\Diamond[\psi \rightarrow \phi]$
    b. $\Diamond\psi \rightarrow \Diamond\phi$

(4) *a*. $\Diamond[\psi \wedge \phi]$
    b. $\Diamond\psi \wedge \Diamond\phi$

(5) *a*. $\Diamond[\psi \vee \phi]$
    b. $\Diamond\psi \vee \Diamond\phi$

Further interactions between modal operators and quantifiers can be observed by looking at the following formulas.

(15) *a*. $\exists x\Box P(x)$
     b. $\Box\exists xP(x)$

(16) *a.* $\exists x \Diamond P(x)$
b. $\Diamond \exists x P(x)$

(17) *a.* $\forall x \Box P(x)$
b. $\Box \forall x P(x)$

(18) *a.* $\forall x \Diamond P(x)$
b. $\Diamond \forall x P(x)$

According to the semantics that we have given, (15*a*) entails (15*b*). For if something, say *u*, has property *P* in every world, then $\exists x P(x)$ will be true in every world (since assigning *u* to *x* will make $P(x)$ true in every world). On the other hand, (15*b*) does not entail (15*a*). In fact, M_4 is a model that makes (15*b*) true and (15*a*) false. This corresponds to the fact that formulas of the form $\forall x \exists y \psi$ are entailed by, but do not entail, $\exists y \forall x \psi$. It should not be hard to see that (16*a*) and (16*b*) entail one another (compare the validity of $\exists x \exists y \psi \leftrightarrow \exists y \exists x \psi$). Our semantics also makes (17*a*) and (17*b*) equivalent. This is perhaps less intuitively obvious. The key to understanding why (17*a*, *b*) come out equivalent is to notice that we quantify over the whole domain in every world, or what amounts to the same thing, that the things over which we quantify are drawn from the same set in every world. Thus if every $u \in U$ necessarily has property *P*, then in every world, every $u \in U$ will have property *P*. This corresponds to the validity of $\forall x \forall y \psi \leftrightarrow \forall y \forall x \psi$. The formula $\Box \forall x P(x) \leftrightarrow \forall x \Box P(x)$, known in the literature as the Carnap-Barcan formula, can be invalidated by a semantics that assigns different domains of quantification to different worlds. Such a semantics would have to be more complex than the one we have got. Finally, it is easy to see that (18*b*) entails (18*a*) but not vice versa, for if there exists one world where every $u \in U$ is *P*, then every $u \in U$ is such that there exists a world where it is *P*, but not the other way around.

Another aspect of the semantics of IPC is that it does not validate inferring (19*b*) from (19*a*):

(19) *a.* $\Box P(m)$
b. $\exists x \Box P(x)$

If *m* is necessarily *P*, it does not follow that some *u* in *U* has property *P* in every world, since the individual that *m* picks out can be different in every world. In fact, M_4 (given in (13)) is a model where (19*a*) is true but (19*b*) false. The failure of the inference from (19*a*) to (19*b*) is symptomatic of intensional (or, as they are also called, opaque or oblique) contexts. Only if some constant c refers to the same entity in every world will we be able to draw the inference in question. This can be expressed as follows:

(20) $[\exists x\Box[x = c] \rightarrow [\Box P(c) \rightarrow \exists x\Box P(x)]]$

where c is a metavariable ranging over individual constants of IPC. Kripke (1972) called expressions that satisfy condition (20) *rigid designators* and argued that proper names in natural language rigidly refer, which might explain our feeling of uneasiness with the claim that saying something like (19*a*) should not commit one to (19*b*). In model M_4 for IPC, j is a rigid designator, but m is not. An expression like *Miss America* is clearly not a rigid designator, and in fact while "In every world and at every time, Miss America is Miss America" is certainly true "Some person u is such that she is Miss America in every world and at every time" is certainly false.

Another feature of our semantics is that it makes (21*a*) and (21*b*) equivalent.

(21) *a.* $\Box\Diamond\psi$
b. $\Diamond\psi$

The inference from (21*a*) to (21*b*) is an instance of the general schema according to which if ψ is possible in all possible worlds, ψ must be possible in the particular world where it is evaluated. The other direction can be thought of as saying that if something can be seen as possible from the vantage point of the world where it is evaluated, or true in one of the worlds being considered, then it can be seen as possible from any world at all. Since our models for IPC offer only an unstructured set of possible worlds, any member of that set is seen as possible from any other. Every world is accessible from every other, and both directions of inference are valid. This is fine if we are talking about logical necessity and possibility, but certain other kinds of necessity and possibility (practical necessity and possibility, for example) seem to work somewhat differently. Kripke (1963) developed the idea that different semantic conceptions of necessity and possibility (different kinds of modality) can be elucidated by examining different constraints on the accessibility relation between worlds. The inference from (21*b*) to (21*a*) might fail, for example, if some possibility is accessible from one world (say, the world in which ψ is evaluated) but not from another.

A number of different modal logics have this feature. The inference from (21*a*) to (21*b*) remains valid in normal modal systems where the accessibility relation is reflexive (each world is accessible from itself).

There are other ways to impose structure on the set of worlds in order to explore varieties of necessity and related notions. Analysis of conditionals such as those in (22) offers an example.

(22) *a.* If you drop that glass, it will break.
b. If John had played, our team would have won.
c. If the Americans destroyed their nuclear arsenal, the Russians would destroy theirs.

Clearly, the connection between antecedent and consequent in (22*a*–*c*) is much stronger than what the ordinary truth function $\rightarrow$ can capture. The consequent is somehow a necessary consequence of the antecedent under a certain set of implicit assumptions generally associated with conditionals. For example, in uttering something like (22*a*), we assume that the glass is not being dropped on soft material (that it is not dropped into a net); we further assume that no one is going to catch it before it reaches the floor, etc. Similar "everything else being equal" conditions appear to be associated with (22*b*) and (22*c*). This notion of normal background assumptions can be fleshed out using the idea that possible worlds may resemble one another in various respects. We can try to formulate more adequate truth conditions for something like (22*a*) by saying that it would be true in a world w iff all the worlds where the antecedent is true and *that most closely resemble* w are such that the consequent is also true. Thus the notion of relevant background is analyzed in terms of a notion of similarity among worlds. This is one illustration of how the set of worlds might be structured more finely than what we have been assuming here. They can be more or less similar to one another. While there is no uniquely defined notion of similarity, there is a family of plausible conditions that such a notion should meet. This enables one to provide fairly articulate semantic analyses of conditionals that can be tested against the entailment patterns they give rise to (see, for example, Stalnaker 1968 or Lewis 1973). Whatever its ultimate outcome, this approach has proven to be extremely fruitful.

Many of the above considerations can be easily applied to temporal operators. For example, it is fairly easy to check the equivalence of (23*a*) and (23*b*), which is parallel to the equivalence of (16*a*) and (16*b*).

(23) *a.* $\exists x\mathbf{F}P(x)$
  b. $\mathbf{F}\exists xP(x)$

Furthermore, we can define duals of **F** and **P** as shown in (24):

(24) *a.* $\mathbf{G}\psi =_{\mathrm{df}} \neg\mathbf{F}\neg\psi$
  b. $\mathbf{H}\psi =_{\mathrm{df}} \neg\mathbf{P}\neg\psi$

On the basis of the semantics for the future tense operator, the newly defined operator **G** will mean something like *it will always be the case that* or *always in the future*, while **H** will mean something like *it has always been the case that.* The behavior of **G** and **H** is essentially parallel to that of □, as they amount to universal quantifiers restricted to future and past instants respectively.

The structure that we have assigned to time is extremely rudimentary. Many different questions can be raised in this connection. For example, is time adequately modeled as potentially discrete, which we have not ruled out here, or must it be treated as dense? That is, in doing semantics must we assume that given any two instants, we can always find an intermediate one? Again, is it semantically adequate to think of each world as having only one fully determinate future, or is it better to allow for several possible futures? And so on. By imposing further structure on the times in our model, we can explore which patterns of entailment will be validated for temporal notions. Conversely, finding one set of entailments rather than another will impose various constraints on the structure of time in our model. Many interesting and difficult semantic puzzles are raised by the interaction of tense and aspect expressions that we can observe in English and other natural languages. For example, the past progressive and the simple past in English have a complex relation to one another. Sentence (25*a*) entails (25*b*), but (26*a*) does not entail (26*b*).

(25) *a.* Joan was pushing a cart.
  b. Joan pushed a cart.

(26) *a.* Mary was crossing the street.
  b. Mary crossed the street.

To see that we do not have an entailment relation in (26), consider that a truck might hit Mary while she's in the middle of the street.

How are such facts to be explained? There exists a substantial and constantly growing body of work in the area of temporal semantics, which we cannot report on here.[2]

The variety of intensional logics that have been and are currently being studied is vast, and applications proposed for such logics are both numerous and diverse. Within the limits of the present work it is impossible to discuss even just those that have been claimed to have linguistic applications. The application of an intensional semantics to English that we develop in what follows, though still extremely rudimentary, will illustrate what some of the issues involved are.

3 Some Intensional Constructions in English

This section is devoted to a discussion of three major intensional constructions in English: tense, modals, and sentence-embedding verbs.

3.1 Tense

Sentences in natural languages typically contain temporal information. Often such information is expressed either through bound morphemes, as with the past tense in English (see (27*a*)), or through modals, as with the future in English (see (27*b*)).

(27) *a.* John arrived.
b. John will arrive.

Information about time can be also be carried by adverbial modifiers of various sorts:

(28) John arrived yesterday/at two o'clock/on February 4.

Here we will focus on the temporal information coded in the main verb of a (finite) clause. If we try to apply the semantics for tense developed in section 2 to English, we run into an immediate problem. Tense in IPC is a sentential operator. Its semantics instructs us to evaluate *whole sentences* at past or future times. Yet in natural languages we tend to find temporal information attached to the verb. Now think about trying to formulate some systematic interpretive procedure for interpreting English tense. As we have seen, it must have the form of a recursive definition of some sort, with syntactic structures as inputs. Suppose that we state the procedure bottom-up, starting from the leaves of syntactic trees, the way we did for F_2. If we have tensed verbs, we are going to hit the tense morpheme as soon as we hit the verb, as illustrated in the following example.

(29)

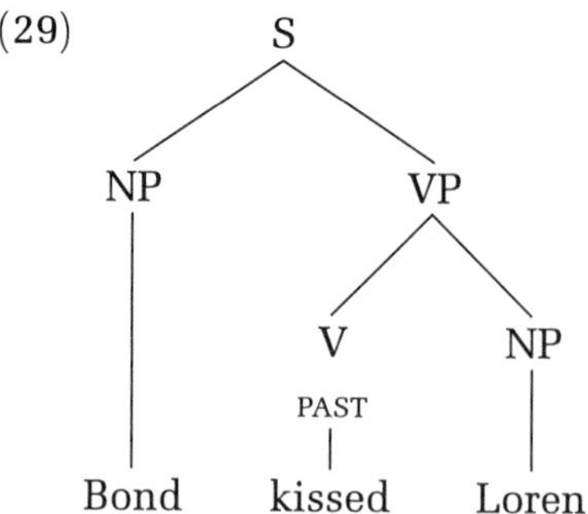

But we will not be able to use the corresponding semantic information at that point, for that information concerns the whole sentence. So we somehow have to store the information conveyed by tense while we interpret the rest of the sentence, pretend that we are dealing with a tenseless verb, and retrieve the information once we have interpreted the whole sentence. It should be clear that defining our interpretive procedure top-down (that is, starting with the root of the tree) will not help: we simply run into the mirror image of the same problem. We want to employ temporal information at the S level, yet that information is just not there. We seem to have a mismatch between syntax and semantics.

There are many different approaches that are being explored in this connection. Tense interacts in complicated ways with the auxiliary system, inflectional morphemes, and negation, and its treatment involves addressing questions that are central to the overall organization of the grammar. The fragment that we are going to present should be taken just for what it is: a pedagogical tool to illustrate some of the issues associated with the semantics of tense in natural languages.

3.1.1 Tense as a functional category In the spirit of much recent work, let us assume that there are three main tenses—PRES, FUT, and PAST—and that they are introduced as heads of a functional category T. Accordingly, the structure of a clause would look roughly as follows:

(30)

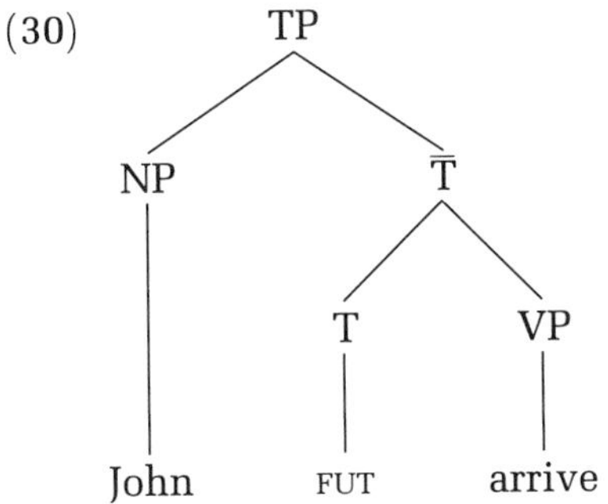

The categorial label TP stands for "Tense Phrase" and replaces the more traditional label S, although in discussing issues not related to tense we will often revert to using S instead of TP. Following current practise (see, e.g., Haegeman 1990 or any other current syntax textbook), we will call TP the maximal projection of T. $\bar{T}$ is an intermediate projection of T. The subject in (30) is adjoined to $\bar{T}$ (in what is often referred to as the *specifier* position of the clause). Things like FUT or PAST are to be thought of as proxy for modals or bound temporal morphemes. In English, FUT is spelled out as the modal *will.* PAST is spelled out as *-ed.* Since PAST (unlike *will*) is a bound morpheme, it will eventually have to attach to the verbal head (via, e.g., a process of incorporation of V into T), and its ultimate realization will be morphologically conditioned. For example, the sequence PAST-*arrive* is spelled out as *arrived*, whereas PAST-*give* is spelled out as *given*. The details of these processes do not seem to be semantically relevant and thus do not concern us here (but see, e.g., Pollock 1989 or Belletti 1990 for discussion of some of the morphosyntactic issues). Languages may vary as to just how tense is expressed in finite clauses. Some languages may lack some tenses. In fact, there are languages (e.g., Chinese) that are described as completely lacking tense as discussed here; in such languages temporal information is carried by adverblike modifiers and by what are called *aspectual* morphemes.[3] Although developed explicitly for dealing with tense morphemes, some of the techniques discussed below will be relevant to the analysis of temporal semantics in such languages as well.

Now while some story along the present lines may be adequate to characterize the syntax and morphology of English tense, the compositional interpretation of structures like (30) is problematic for the reasons discussed above in considering (29). If tense operates semantically on formulas (i.e., things that are true or false), we must assume that in English it operates on clauses. This means that a structure like (30) cannot be interpreted as is (unless we devise an interpretive procedure fancier than the one pursued so far). How could this structure be modified to yield something more readily interpretable? One possibility is to assume that the temporal head moves up, yielding a structure like (31*a*).

(31) *a.* *b.*

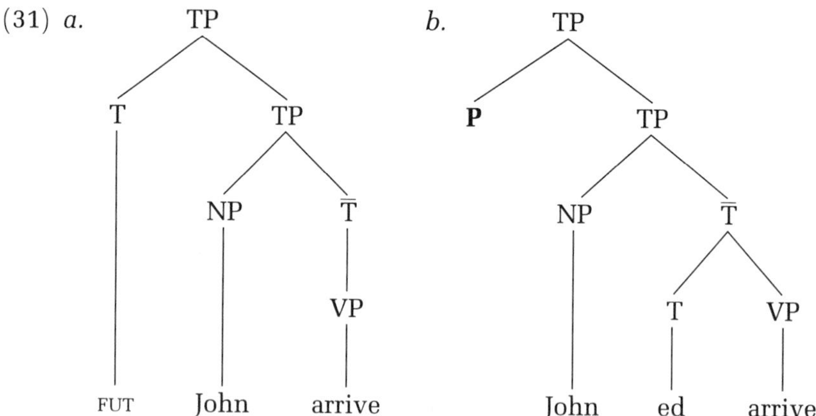

Structure (31*a*) is derived from (30) by adjoining T to its own projection TP; (31*a*) can be regarded as the LF of sentence (30). To simplify things, we are assuming that movement of the temporal head leaves no traces, as such traces would be interpretively inert. But nothing hinges on this. A variant of our T-raising approach is to think that the temporal morpheme as such has no meaning, but requires the presence of a matching (phonologically null) tense operator adjoined to its projection, as illustrated in (31*b*). Yet another strategy is to adopt the so called VP-internal-subject hypothesis, i.e., the idea that the subject originates within the VP and is then moved up to the specifier position of TP. At LF, the subject would be "reconstructed" in its base position for interpretive purposes. Whichever route one chooses, the end result doesn't change. At the point where semantic interpretation takes place, we wind up with structures that for our purposes are just like those in (31). In these structures, tense operates on a clause and works essentially like a Priorian operator, familiar from section 2. For illustrative purposes, we will adopt the LF in (31*a*).

If one wants to be a bit more explicit, to get the structures in (30) and (31*a*) one can resort to the following set of rules:

(32) *a.* TP → NP T̄
b. T̄ → T VP
c. Tense raising: $[_{\text{TP}}$ NP T VP$]$ ⇒ $[$T $[_{\text{TP}}$ NP VP$]]$[4]

Given Logical Forms for temporal expressions like (31), the job of semantics becomes quite easy. The interpretation of every expression will be relativized to worlds and times (besides, of course, models and assignments). For example, $[\![\text{arrive}]\!]^{M,w,i,g}$ will be the set of people that arrive in w at time i. Strictly speaking, we need only instants and their ordering to interpret tenses and could manage without possible worlds. However, no harm is going to result from introducing worlds now, and we will do so to make it easier to provide various extensions to modalities in subsequent sections. The interpretation of the inner TP in (31a) is the obvious one, namely (33):

(33) 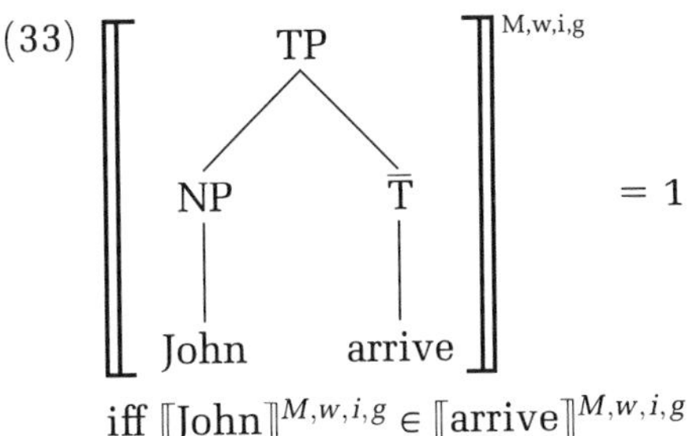

iff $[\![\text{John}]\!]^{M,w,i,g} \in [\![\text{arrive}]\!]^{M,w,i,g}$

We are going to assume that there is no semantic rule corresponding to the syntactic rule in (32b). This means that phrases of the form $[_{\bar{T}}\ \text{T VP}]$ are not interpretable as such, much as, under our current assumptions, quantified NPs cannot be interpreted *in situ*. In the latter case this forces QR. In the present case it forces raising of tense, via (32c). The interpretation of tense operators then becomes straightforward:

(34) $[\![\text{FUT TP}]\!]^{M,w,i,g} = 1$ iff for some i' such that $i < i'$,
$[\![\text{TP}]\!]^{M,w,i',g} = 1$

Applied to LF (31a), this assigns to sentence (30) the intuitively correct truth conditions that "John will arrive" is true at time i just in case there is a time i' after i at which John arrives. The interpretation of the past tense is analogous, except that the time of the arrival has to precede the evaluation time. The present tense leaves the evaluation time unchanged.

3.1.2 The fragment F_3 We can now practise the ideas discussed in the previous section by working out a fragment of English with some elementary tenses. The fragment F_3 is an extension of F_2.

(35) Syntax of F_3

a. i. TP $\rightarrow$ NP $\bar{\text{T}}$

ii. $\bar{\text{T}}$ $\rightarrow$ T VP

b. i. TP $\rightarrow$ TP conj TP

ii. TP $\rightarrow$ neg TP

c. VP $\rightarrow$ V_t NP

d. VP $\rightarrow$ V_i

e. VP $\rightarrow$ V_{dt} NP $PP_{[to]}$

f. T $\rightarrow$ PAST, PRES, FUT

g. NP $\rightarrow$ Det N_c

h. $PP_{[to]}$ $\rightarrow$ to NP

i. Det $\rightarrow$ the, a, every

j. N_p $\rightarrow$ Pavarotti, Loren, Bond, ..., he_n, ...

k. N_c $\rightarrow$ book, fish, man, woman, ...

l. V_i $\rightarrow$ be boring, be hungry, walk, talk, ...

m. V_t $\rightarrow$ like, hate, kiss, ...

n. V_{dt} $\rightarrow$ give, show, ...

o. conj $\rightarrow$ and, or

p. NEG $\rightarrow$ it is not the case that

q. NP $\rightarrow$ N_p

r. Quantifier Raising (QR)

$[_{\text{TP}}\ X\ \text{NP}\ Y] \Rightarrow [_{\text{TP}}\ \text{NP}_i\ [_{\text{TP}}\ X\ e_i\ Y]]$

s. Tense Raising (TR)

$[_{\text{TP}}\ \text{NP T VP}] \Rightarrow [_{\text{TP}}\ \text{T}\ [_{\text{TP}}\ \text{NP VP}]]$

As is easy to see, different applications of QR and TR assign to a sentence like (37*a*) two distinct LFs, namely (37*b*) and (37*c*):

(36) *a.* Every man arrived.

b.

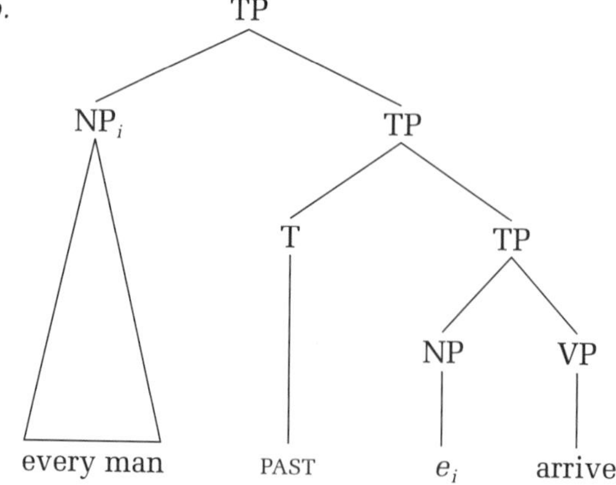

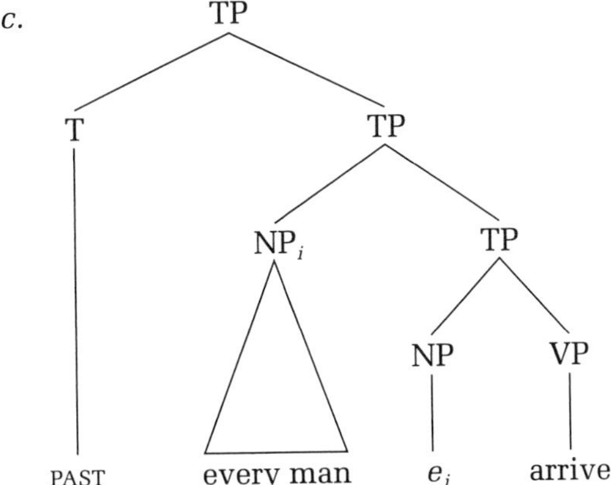

For simplicity, we omit representing in (36) the nonbranching node $\bar{T}$. In LF (36*b*), the quantified NP *every man* has scope over tense. The semantics for the fragment will assign to this structure an interpretation according to which for every man there is some time or other in the past at which he arrives (i.e., the arrivals need not happen simultaneously). In LF (36*c*), the past-tense operator has scope over the NP *every man*. On this interpretation, sentence (36*a*) winds up saying that there is a time in the past at which every man arrived; i.e., the arrivals must be simultaneous. These appear indeed to be the admissible interpretations of (36*a*). Thus the present approach seems to capture correctly the scope interaction between quantified NPs and the tense operator. But to see this more concretely, we must spell out the semantics for F_3.

(37) An F_3 model for English M is an ordered tuple of the form $\langle W, I, <, U, V\rangle$ where the following conditions hold.

a. W is a set of worlds.

b. I is a set of instants ordered by $<$.

c. U is the domain of quantification.

d. V is a function that assigns intensions to the constants of F_3. In particular, if b is a proper name, then $V(b)$ is a constant function from $W \times I$ into U denoting the bearer of the proper name in the relevant community. Moreover:

$V(horse)\langle w, i\rangle = \{x : x \text{ is a horse in } w \text{ at time } i\}$,

$V(love)\langle w, i\rangle = \{\langle x, y\rangle : x \text{ loves } y \text{ in } w \text{ at time } i\}$,

$V(give)\langle w, i\rangle = \{\langle x, y, z\rangle : x \text{ gives } y \text{ to } z \text{ in } w \text{ at time } i\}$.

And similarly for other members of Nom or V.

$$V(\text{it is not the case that}) = \begin{bmatrix} 1 \rightarrow 0 \\ 0 \rightarrow 1 \end{bmatrix}$$

$$V(\text{and}) = \begin{bmatrix} \langle 1,1\rangle \rightarrow 1 \\ \langle 1,0\rangle \rightarrow 0 \\ \langle 0,1\rangle \rightarrow 0 \\ \langle 0,0\rangle \rightarrow 0 \end{bmatrix}$$

By the same token, V(or) is the truth function associated with *or.*

The models for F_3 are trivial variants of those for IPC and consequently require little comment. One difference is that in (37) we interpret connectives (*and, or,* and *it is not the case that*) in terms of truth functions rather than syncategorematically. As usual, we assume that the English constants have the same interpretation in every model. Furthermore, we follow Kripke (1972) in assuming that proper names are rigid designators, and we accordingly require that proper names have constant functions as their intensions (functions that pick the same individual in every circumstance).

We now provide the recursive part of the semantics for F_3 relative to an F_3 model for English M, a world w, an instant i, and an assignment g to traces and pronouns. As in IPC, instants are ordered by the relation $<$.

(38) *a.* If A is lexical and β is a trace or a pronoun, $[\![[_A\ \beta]]\!]^{M,w,i,g} = g(\beta)$;
otherwise, $[\![[_A\ \beta]]\!]^{M,w,i,g} = V(\beta)(\langle w,i\rangle)$

b. If A and B are any categories, $[\![[_A\ B]]\!]^{M,w,i,g} = [\![B]\!]^{M,w,i,g}$,
and $[\![[_A \text{ to } B]]\!]^{M,w,i,g} = [\![B]\!]^{M,w,i,g}$

c. $[\![[\text{NP } \bar{\text{T}}]]\!]^{M,w,i,g} = 1$ iff $[\![\text{NP}]\!]^{M,w,i,g} \in [\![\bar{\text{T}}]\!]^{M,w,i,g}$

d. i. $[\![[\text{TP}_1 \text{ conj } \text{TP}_2]]\!]^{M,w,i,g}$
$= V(\text{conj})(\langle [\![\text{TP}_1]\!]^{M,w,i,g}, [\![\text{TP}_2]\!]^{M,w,i,g}\rangle)$

ii. $[\![\text{NEG TP}]\!]^{M,w,i,g} = V(\text{NEG})\ ([\![\text{TP}]\!]^{M,w,i,g})$

e. $[\![[\text{V NP}]]\!]^{M,w,i,g} = \{x : \langle x, [\![\text{NP}]\!]^{M,w,i,g}\rangle \in [\![\text{V}]\!]^{M,w,i,g}\}$

f. $[\![[\text{V NP PP}]]\!]^{M,w,i,g}$
$= \{x : \langle x, [\![\text{NP}]\!]^{M,w,i,g}, [\![\text{PP}]\!]^{M,w,i,g}\rangle \in [\![\text{V}]\!]^{M,w,i,g}\}$

g. Structures of the form $[\text{NP}_i\ \text{TP}]$
$[\![\text{a } \beta_i \text{ TP}]\!]^{M,w,i,g} = 1$ iff for some $u \in U$, $u \in [\![\beta_i]\!]^{M,w,i,g}$ and $[\![\text{TP}]\!]^{M,w,i,g[u/t_i]} = 1$, where $t_i = e_i$ or $t_i = he_i$
$[\![\text{every } \beta_i \text{ TP}]\!]^{M,w,i,g} = 1$ iff for all $u \in U$, if $u \in [\![\beta_i]\!]^{M,w,i,g}$, then $[\![\text{TP}]\!]^{M,w,i,g[u/t_i]} = 1$, where $t_i = e_i$ or $t_i = he_i$

$[\![\text{the } \beta_i \text{ TP}]\!]^{M,w,i,g} = 1$ iff for some $u \in U$, $[\![\beta_i]\!]^{M,w,i,g} = \{u\}$ and $[\![\text{TP}]\!]^{M,w,i,g[u/t_i]} = 1$, where $t_i = e_i$ or $t_i = he_i$

h. Structures of the form $[_{\text{TP}}$ T TP$]$

$[\![\text{PRES TP}]\!]^{M,w,i,g} = [\![\text{TP}]\!]^{M,w,i,g}$

$[\![\text{PAST TP}]\!]^{M,w,i,g} = 1$ iff for some $i' \in I$ such that $i' < i$, $[\![\text{TP}]\!]^{M,w,i',g} = 1$

$[\![\text{FUT TP}]\!]^{M,w,i,g} = 1$ iff for some $i' \in I$ such that $i' > i$, $[\![\text{TP}]\!]^{M,w,i',g} = 1$

The definitions of truth, validity, and entailment are straightforward.

If we look at (38), we see that clauses (38*a–g*) are virtually identical to those we have for F_2 ((60) in chap. 3) except that now the interpretation function is relativized to worlds and times as well. The real novelty is (38*h*), which introduces the semantics for the (raised) tense morphemes. Such a semantics is modeled on the semantics for IPC.

(39) *a*. A sentence S is *true* in an F_3 model for English *M*, in a world *w*, and at a time *i* relative to one of its LFs β iff for every assignment *g*, $[\![\beta]\!]^{M,w,i,g} = 1$. It is *false* iff for every *g*, $[\![\beta]\!]^{M,w,i,g} = 0$.

b. A sentence S is *valid* relative to one of its LFs β iff for every F_3 model for English *M*, every world *w*, and every time *i*, S is true in *M*, in *w*, and at *i* relative to β.

c. A set of sentences $\Omega = \{S_1, \ldots, S_n\}$ relative to LFs $\beta_1, \ldots, \beta_n$ respectively *entails* a sentence S′ relative to LF δ iff for every F_3 model for English *M*, world *w*, and time *i*, whenever every S_j in Ω is true relative to its LF β_j in *M*, in *w*, and at *i*, then S′ is also true in *M*, *w*, and *i* relative to δ.

To illustrate the workings of the present semantics, we provide next a concrete example by partially specifying a model M_5 as follows:

(40) Let $M_5 = \langle\{w', w''\}, \{i', i'', i'''\}, \{\langle i', i''\rangle, \langle i'', i'''\rangle, \langle i', i'''\rangle\}, \{a, b, c\}, V_5\rangle$, where for every $w \in W_5$ and $i \in I_5$, $V_5(\text{Pavarotti})(\langle w, i\rangle) = a$, $V_5(\text{Bond})(\langle w, i\rangle) = b$, and $V_5(\text{Loren})(\langle w, i\rangle) = c$. Furthermore, let

$V_5(\text{walk}) =$		i'	i''	i'''
	w''	$\{a, c\}$	$\{a, b, c\}$	$\{b\}$
	w'	$\{a\}$	$\{c\}$	$\varnothing$

We also assume that *man* and *woman* are interpreted in the natural way (that is, for every world-time pair $\langle w, i \rangle$, $V_5(\text{man})(\langle w, i \rangle) = \{a, b\}$ and $V_5(\text{woman})(\langle w, i \rangle) = \{c\}$). Finally, let g be an assignment that maps every pronoun and trace t_i to c.

Let us now evaluate example (36*a*) in M_5, w', i''' relative to LF (36*b*), repeated here for convenience.

(36) *b.*

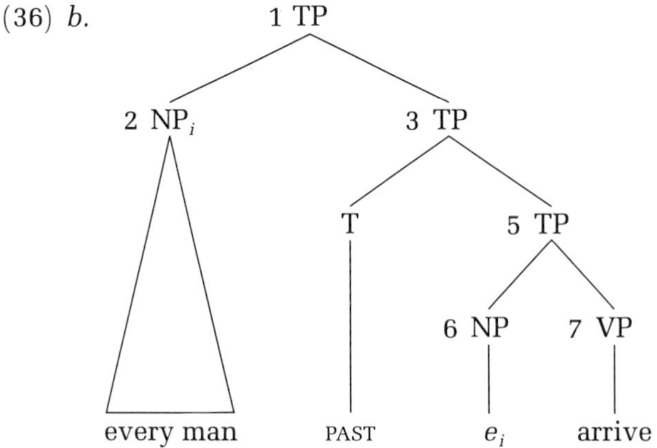

Intuitively, (36*b*) says that for every man, there is an instant in the past at which he arrived. In the model M_5, there are two men, Bond (*b*) and Pavarotti (*a*). By looking in world w' at time t''', we see that there is a time preceding t''' (namely t') at which Pavarotti arrives and a different time preceding t''' (namely t'') at which Bond arrives. So in w' at t''' it is true that every man arrived on the reading represented by (36*b*). However, in this world there is no moment at which every man simultaneously arrives. Hence sentence (36*a*) on the reading represented by (36*c*) would be false all times of w' (while it would be true in w'' at t'''). In the following example we show the main steps of the computation of the value of (36*b*) relative to M_5 in w' at t'''.

Exercise 3 A. Evaluate "Every man arrived" with respect to LF (36*b*) in $\langle w', i' \rangle$ and $\langle w'', i''' \rangle$. Evaluate (36*a*) relative to LF (36*c*) in $\langle w', i''' \rangle$, $\langle w'', i''' \rangle$, and $\langle w'', i''' \rangle$.

B. Show that (36*c*) entails (36*b*).

As should be clear by now, the present analysis assigns to sentences like "Every man arrived" two distinct LFs, (36*a*) and (36*b*),

Evaluation of (36b) in M_5, w', i''' relative to g

(*a*) $[\![1]\!]^{M_5, w', i''', g} = 1$ iff for every $u \in [\![\text{man}]\!]^{M_5, w', i''', g}$, $[\![3]\!]^{M_5, w', i''', g[u/e_i]} = 1$
By (38*g*)

Since, by (38*a*), $[\![\text{man}]\!]^{M_5, w', i''', g} = \{a, b\}$, where a is Pavarotti and b is Bond, we have to evaluate $[\![3]\!]^{M_5, w', i''', g[a/e_i]}$ and $[\![3]\!]^{M_5, w', i''', g[b/e_i]}$ and see how they come out. Let us try the former (namely Pavarotti).

(*b*) $[\![3]\!]^{M_5, w', i''', g[a/e_i]} = 1$ iff for some $i \in I_5$ such that $i < i'''$, $[\![5]\!]^{M_5, w', i, g[a/e_i]} = 1$ By (38*h*)

Now we have to check what happens at different times in the past relative to i'''. Let us try i'.

(*c*) $[\![5]\!]^{M_5, w', i', g[a/e_i]} = 1$ iff $[\![6]\!]^{M_5, w', i', g[a/e_i]} \in [\![7]\!]^{M_5, w', i', g[a/e_i]}$ By (38*c*)

Since by (38*a*), $[\![6]\!]^{M_5, w', i', g[a/e_i]} = g[a/e_i](e_i) = a$ and by (38*b*) and (38*a*), $[\![7]\!]^{M_5, w', i', g[a/e_i]} = V_5(\text{arrive})(\langle w', i' \rangle) = \{a\}$, we conclude that $[\![3]\!]^{M_5, w', i''', g[a/e_i]} = 1$.

Now we have to compute $[\![3]\!]^{M_5, w', i''', g[b/e_i]}$. That is, we go through essentially the same computations focusing on Bond.

(*d*) $[\![3]\!]^{M_5, w', i''', g[b/e_i]} = 1$ iff for some $i \in I_5$ such that $i < i'''$, $[\![5]\!]^{M_5, w', i, g[b/e_i]} = 1$ By (38*h*)

Let us see what Bond does at i'':

(*e*) $[\![5]\!]^{M_5, w', i'', g[b/e_i]} = 1$ iff $[\![6]\!]^{M_5, w', i'', g[b/e_i]} \in [\![7]\!]^{M_5, w', i'', g[a/e_i]}$ By (38*c*)

We see that by (38*a*), $[\![5]\!]^{M_5, w', i'', g[b/e_i]} = g[b/e_i](e_i) = b$, and by (38*b*) and (38*a*), $[\![7]\!]^{M_5, w', i'', g[b/e_i]} = V_5(\text{arrive})\ (\langle w', i'' \rangle) = \{b\}$. Since the former is indeed a member of the latter, we have shown that $[\![3]\!]^{M_5, w', i''', g[b/e_i]} = 1$. Since in world w', for every man (Pavarotti and Bond) there is a moment in the past with respect to i''' where that man arrives, we conclude that $[\![1]\!]^{M_5, w', i''', g} = 1$.

which generate two nonequivalent readings. The different readings arise by differently fixing the relative scope of tense and quantified NPs.

3.1.3 Further issues There are many problems that our approach leaves open. Here we will discuss, in a necessarily preliminary way, some of the most important ones having to do with negation and its interaction with tense.

So far we have discussed only sentence-embedding negation (*it is not the case that*). However the most common way of expressing negation is by placing a negative morpheme (in English, *not* or its contracted form *'nt*) within the clause. Languages vary as to where clause-internal negation gets placed. Consider, for instance, the English sentence in (41*a*) and its Italian counterpart in (41*b*).

(41) *a.* Lee hasn't arrived.
b. Lee non e′ arrivato.
Lee not au-PAST arrived

English places negation relatively "low" in the tree, after the auxiliary element that carries temporal information. Italian places it higher up, before the auxiliary. One can capture this by saying that in English negation is adjoined somewhere in the VP (i.e., lower than TP), while in Italian it is adjoined higher up (somewhere within TP):

(42)
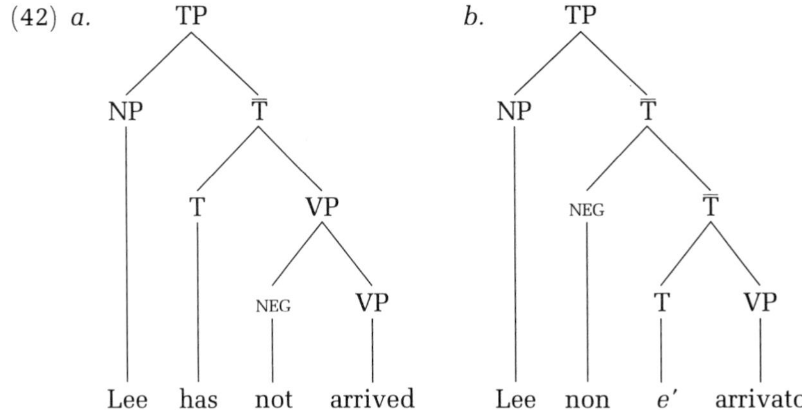

It has also been argued that negation heads a special functional projection (NEG Phrase) having to do with the polarity of a sentence (see, e.g., Laka 1990), but since what we have to say is not affected by this hypothesis, we will stick to the representations in (42). In both (42*a*) and (42*b*), under the present assumptions, sentence-internal negation cannot be interpreted where it occurs. Semantically, negation operates on formulas (i.e., truth values). But syntactically, it appears as a sister to smaller, subclausal units that do not denote truth values. Evidently, we face a problem analogous to that which we encountered in interpreting tense. Some scope-shifting operation must take place if we want to interpret negation as a truth function. Ideally, the same mechanisms we use for tense might work in the case of negation, as the interpretive problems that these cases pose appear to be closely related. For tenses, we suggested several ways to go and ended up adopting, for illustrative purposes, the operation of tense raising. Similarly, we might say that at LF negation gets adjoined to TP, where it is a sister to something that can be naturally interpreted as a truth value. This move has as its immediate consequence that a sentence like (43*a*)

will get two readings, depending on how the respective scope of negation and the subject is fixed.

(43) *a.* Every American doesn't smoke.
b. [$_{TP}$ every American$_i$ [$_{TP}$ not [$_{TP}$ e_i smoke]]
c. [$_{TP}$ not [$_{TP}$ every American$_i$ [$_{TP}$ e_i smoke]]

LF (43*b*) is interpreted as saying that every American is such that he or she doesn't smoke, LF (43*c*) says that it is not the case that every American smokes. This is a welcome result, as sentence (43*a*) does intuitively appear to be ambiguous. Modulo certain quite interesting complications (which we cannot get into here), this generalizes to NPs other than universally quantified ones and positions other than the subject position. In other words, negation interacts with quantified NPs and gives rise to scope ambiguities. The approach just sketched is a simple way of capturing them.

When it comes to tenses, however, we find an unexpected restriction. Consider sentence (44*a*):

(44) *a.* Lee didn't kill Kim.
b. NEG [PAST [Lee kill Kim]]
c. PAST [NEG [Lee kill Kim]]

Sentence (44*a*) is predicted to have two readings, corresponding to the two Logical Forms in (44*b*) and (44c). According to the first, sentence (44*a*) says that there is no time that precedes the evaluation time at which Lee kills Kim. This is indeed how (44*a*) is interpreted. However, this sentence is also predicted to have the reading in (44*c*). The latter LF says that there is a time in the past at which Lee did not kill Kim. This is not a sensible reading. It's too weak. For any activity, there are always going to be infinitely many instants at which one is not engaged in it. Hence any sentence with a logical form parallel to (44*c*) expresses a trivial truth. This runs against our intuitions on sentences like (44*a*), which do not appear to have such an interpretation.

What seems to be going on is that if tenses are understood as Priorian operators, which existentially quantify over times, then negation must have scope over tense. At present, insofar as we know, this has to be stipulated. It does not seem to follow from independent properties of how negation (or tense) is coded in natural languages.

While readings like that expressed by (44*b*) appear to be a good approximation to the interpretation of sentences like (44*a*), it must be pointed out that the interpretations predicted are also not fully adequate in all cases. Consider, for example, our treatment of the simple past in connection with (45), an example due to Partee (1973):

(45) John didn't turn off the stove.

According to our semantics, (45) would be true at $\langle w, i \rangle$ iff it is not the case that there is a previous instant i' such that "John turns off the stove" is true at $\langle w, i' \rangle$. But now imagine (45) being uttered by Mary as she drives to a friend's house. Clearly, Mary is not saying that John has never turned off the stove; (45) seems to be about a specific point in the past (which Mary has in mind) at which he failed to turn it off. She is right even if he has sometimes turned it off but failed to do so this time: John can't defend himself by pointing out that he turned it off last year. Suppose that she calls home and finds out she was happily mistaken and utters (46).

(46) John turned off the stove [after all].

She is saying not simply that John turned off the stove at any old time in the past, as F_3 would predict, but that he did so at the specific point she has in mind. For both negative and affirmative sentences the F_3 account must apparently be modified.

Various solutions have been proposed in this connection. One kind of approach resorts to something like a reference time, a notion proposed originally by Hans Reichenbach (1947). In a Priorian semantics for tense, sentences are interpreted relatively to a time (the evaluation time) and tenses shift the evaluation time to the past or future. Reichenbach argues for a substantial enrichment (and modification) of this picture whereby the evaluation of a sentence requires keeping track also of the utterance time and a reference time (the time from which the action is viewed). Tenses are construed not as existential quantifiers over times, but as conditions on how the evaluation time, the reference time, and the utterance time are related with respect to each other. One of the main motivations for the reference time lies in the analysis of compound tenses (which we haven't discussed and which are not easy to analyze in a Priorian framework). Consider (47):

(47) *a.* Joan arrived.
b. Joan has arrived.
c. Joan had arrived.
d. Joan had arrived by 5 P.M., Sunday.

According to Reichenbach, the evaluation time (i.e., the time of the action) and the reference time coincide in the case of (47*a*) and are both located in the past with respect to the utterance time. In contrast, in (47*b*) the reference time coincides with the utterance time and the action is in the past with respect to both. And in (47*c*) the action is considered as preceding some past moment that acts as the reference time, which, in (47*d*), is explicitly characterized through suitable time adverbials. The schema in (48) illustrates the general picture.

(48) Reichenbachian tenses

a. Schema for the simple past

```
----------------|-----------|———→ [time line]
               E,R          U
```

b. Schema for the present perfect

```
----------------|-----------|———→ [time line]
                E          U,R
```

c. Schema for the past perfect

```
--------|--------|----------|———→ [time line]
        E        R          U
```

U = time of the utterance

E = time of the event

R = reference time

For interpreting (47*d*), R will be identified with 5 P.M., Sunday. (The Sunday in question is typically the one immediately preceding the utterance, but not always; we cannot explore the full complexities of reference-time specification here.) The future perfect is slightly more complicated. Notice that (48*a*) can be uttered at noon and be true even if Joan's arrival was at 11 A.M.; indeed, (48*a*) might be followed by (48*b*) without contradiction.

(49) *a.* Joan will have arrived by 1 P.M.

b. Joan may have already arrived.

The reader might want to specify what the future perfect seems to say about the relation of utterance, event, and reference times. (Hint: A single time line will not work.)

The Reichenbachian notion of reference time might also be helpful in connection with the problem posited by sentences like (45) above, and more generally in addressing the question of the scope of tense with respect to negation. It seems intuitively plausible to say that "John didn't turn off the stove" is true at a time *i* relative to a reference time R iff R precedes *i* and "John does not turn off the stove" is true at R. This kind of approach turns out to be helpful also in compositionally specifying how tense combines with other temporal expressions, such as *yesterday* or *last year*, which constitutes another difficult and open topic. Bennett and Partee (1978) and Dowty (1979) are classical references on this issue; Dowty (1982) adopts a reference-time approach especially to deal with the compositional puzzles he noted in the Priorian treatment in his earlier work. Many semantic investigations of tense and its interaction with other temporal expressions have abandoned Priorian time-shifting operators in favor of approaches that posit some kind of discourse-established reference time, but the debate is still open.[6]

This is a just a small sample of the host of intriguing issues that come up in providing a semantics for tense. Some topics central to current investigations we haven't even been able to mention—like the issue of tense in NPs (see, e.g., Enç 1981) or the phenomenon of tense sequences (see, e.g., Abusch 1997 and references therein). Temporal phenomena are very complex. They constitute an exciting area of research, and the body of semantic literature on them is constantly growing.

3.2 Modals

The modal concepts of necessity and possibility are expressed in a variety of natural-language forms.[8] The following are some of the most commonly observed forms in English and are typical of many languages.

Modal auxiliaries (*can, must, may, shall, should, will, would, might, could*) appear to be the most straightforward way of expressing various forms of necessity and possibility in English.

Some tenses (like the simple present in English) have a generic interpretation. One of the main functions of generic sentences appears to be that of expressing capability or possibility, as illustrated by the fact that the sentences in (50*a*–*b*) can be paraphrased as in the corresponding primed versions:

(50) *a*. John runs 50 miles without ever stopping.
  a′. John can run 50 miles without ever stopping.
  b. This program parses complicated sentences.
  b′. This program can parse complicated sentences.

We also use dispositional affixes on adjectives: *approachable, solvable, soluble, conceivable, washable, fragile, forgetful, mortal,* etc. Moreover, we also use sentential adverbs (*possibly, necessar-*

ily, *probably*, etc.) and adjective phrases (*be possible*, *be necessary*, *be able*, etc.).

In what follows, we would like to show how the semantics developed so far can be applied to the study of modalities in English by developing a first-approximation treatment of *can*, *might*, and *must*. This should suffice for the purposes of illustration, as it seems warranted to assume that other ways of expressing modal notions give rise to fundamentally similar semantic questions.

The syntax of modals is complex. There is disagreement as to whether they are main verbs or auxiliaries. Standard arguments in favor of treating modals as auxiliaries are the fact that, like auxiliaries, they undergo inversion in yes-no questions (*Joan can leave* ⇒ *Can Joan leave?*) and the fact that their paradigm is in various ways unlike that of full fledged verbs (they don't inflect for person, they often lack past-tense morphology, etc.). In view of these facts, we will treat them as auxiliaries, even though nothing in our semantic analysis of modals hinges on this choice. We cannot provide here a full fledged analysis of the English auxiliary system. The simplest thing for us to do is to treat modals as a particular manifestation of tense. Thus we will assume that the S-structure of a sentence like (51*a*) is roughly (51*b*), since modals will undergo tense raising; the logical form of (51*a*) will be (51*c*):

(51) *a.* Pavarotti can/must sing

b.

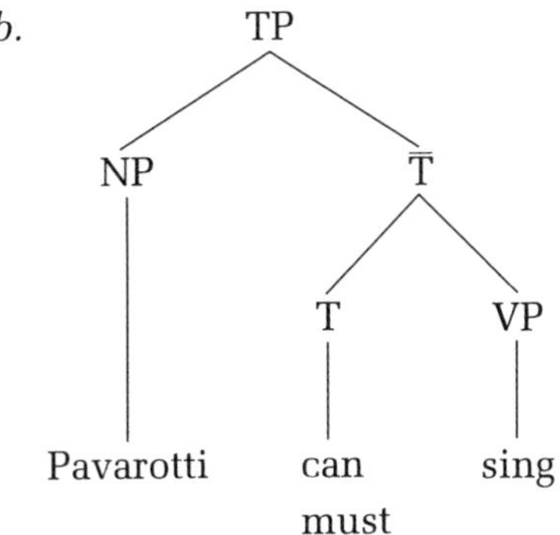

c. [can/must [$_{TP}$ Pavarotti sing]]

This will enable us to treat modals as propositional operators, which is what their semantics, as we know it from IPC, requires. And modals can interact with negation; sentence (52*a*) will have roughly the LF given in (52*b*):

(52) *a.* Pavarotti can't sing.

b. [NEG can [$_{TP}$ Pavarotti sing]]

When it comes to giving a semantics for *can* and *must*, however, an immediate application of the semantics for $\Diamond$ and $\Box$ will not do. For it would take (52*a*) as saying that there is no logically possible world where Pavarotti sings. But for any living individual *u*, conceiving of a circumstance where *u* sings is not logically impossible; there will in general be a logically possible world where *u* sings. Sentence (52*a*) makes a different claim. The semantics for logical possibility does not get us the right truth conditions for (52*a*).

What claim can one be making by uttering (52*a*)? We might be denying that Pavarotti has a certain capability. In his mental endowment there is no program that produces the kind of behavior classifiable as singing. Singing is not consistent with the actual state of his mental endowment. Or perhaps it is his physical endowment—his throat musculature and the shape of his vocal tract—that is problematic. In the actual world (52*a*) taken in either of these senses is clearly false. (And we can use this blatant falsehood to conversationally implicate a variety of things.)

Another possibility is that Pavarotti has a sore throat. He is capable of singing, but in general sore throats affect the performance of vocal cords. While this condition persists, Pavarotti cannot sing.

Many other scenarios are conceivable. What emerges from such possible scenarios is that the proper evaluation of sentences like (52*a*) requires a background of some kind. In the case at hand, a natural background is constituted by a set of relevant facts (such as evidence as to the existence of a certain mental program or Pavarotti's state of health). How can we characterize the relevant set of facts? In general by means of propositions that describe them. Under the current view, propositions are sets of worlds. Consequently, we can represent a set of facts as a set of sets of worlds.

So modals are context dependent. They require, in Kratzer's phrase, a conversational background: some assumptions in view of which the sentence is considered. Formally, a conversational background can be viewed as a set whose members are sets of worlds (that is, propositions).

The kind of background that seems to go well with the example in (52*a*) is constituted by certain relevant facts or actual circumstances. This use of modals is often called a "root" or "circumstantial" use and contrasts with "epistemic" uses, to be discussed shortly. Certain modal expressions (adjectives like *fragile* or *soluble*) are compatible just with circumstantial backgrounds; that is, they can only express root modalities. *Can*, *might*, and *must* are instead compatible with a wide variety of conversational backgrounds.

Consider, for example,

(53) Pavarotti might be the author of this letter.

Mary received an anonymous letter, some kind of practical joke. Pavarotti is a friend of hers. He knows her address and the relevant circumstances of her life. His being the author of the letter is consistent with all she knows. This is what she means by uttering (53).

In uttering (53) under the circumstances just described, Mary was relying on what she knows and is interested in what can turn out to be the case, given what she knows. The relevant conversational background can be called an epistemic one. Suppose that one gathers further evidence about the deed in question. For example, we discover that the characters in the letter display an idiosyncrasy that, around here, is to be found only on a typewriter that Pavarotti has sole access to. We could then truthfully utter

(54) Pavarotti must be the author of this letter.

It follows from what we know that he is the author. All the circumstances compatible with our knowledge have Pavarotti as the author of the letter. What is known can, of course, also be thought of as a set of propositions, the set of propositions that are known in the relevant situation. A set of propositions characterizes a set of worlds: those where all the propositions in the set are true. Sentence (54) can be understood as saying that in all such worlds Pavarotti is the author of the letter.

Further kinds of conversational backgrounds are possible.

(55) I must give my seat to that senior citizen.

It is generally held that senior citizens have priority for seats in public places. This is for us a standard of politeness and a stereotype of kindness. In view of this ideal (that is, in all the worlds where it is realized), I stand up. Necessity or possibility involving such backgrounds is sometimes called "deontic." Even (52*a*) can be so interpreted if, for example, Pavarotti's mother has forbidden him to sing and we hold to an ideal of obeying one's mother. His singing would be inconsistent with that ideal and is thus not possible if he is to adhere to the standards set.

Let us consider a further example of deontic uses of modals. If Pavarotti's mother decides to grant him permission to sing, she must make his singing consistent with the ideal. She can do that simply by saying that the ideal is now one with which his singing is consistent: "Luciano, you can sing." Because a deontic conversational background can be changed by a person with appropriate authority (Pavarotti's mother), deontic modals can be used performatively, as we noted in chapter 4. Pavarotti's mother makes it true that he can sing (on a deontic interpretation) just by saying that he can and thereby changing the relevant conversational background.

Thus, the interpretation of modals depends on the contextual specification of certain kinds of background information: what the relevant facts are, what is known, what is polite, what the authorities permit, what someone's goals are, etc. Each of these backgrounds can be represented as a set of propositions, which in turn determines a set of worlds, those in which all of the propositions are true. It is this set of worlds and not the set of all logically possible ones that we take as our *modal base*, as the logical space with respect to which the modal is evaluated. The semantics of modal expressions will thus specify (i) what kinds of backgrounds a modal admits (*can*, *might*, and *must* are pretty unrestricted in this regard) and (ii) what modal relation is associated with it. The modal relation associated with *can* and *might* is possibility; they express consistency with the given modal base. The modal relation associated with *must* is necessity; *must* says that something is a logical consequence of a given model base.

This will become clearer if we provide a more concrete example by implementing these ideas in F_3. To do so, we must find a way of expressing the context dependency of modalities. Our treatment of context so far is extremely rudimentary. The only kind of context-dependent items that we have in F_3 are pronouns (whose complex behavior is far from receiving a full treatment). We represent their dependency on context by assigning to them a value in terms of an assignment function g. In the same spirit we need to relativize our interpretation to an assignment of conversational backgrounds. For this purpose we can use g itself. We can extend the function g so that it not only maps pronouns to individuals but also maps circumstances $\langle w, i \rangle$ to sets of propositions: the conversational background relevant to that circumstance. So, for example, suppose that the propositions in the common ground at $\langle w, i \rangle$ are $p_1, \ldots, p_n$. We express this by saying that $g(\langle w, i \rangle) = \{p_1, \ldots, p_n\}$. The set of propositions $\{p_1, \ldots, p_n\}$ determines the set of circumstances $\{\langle w', i' \rangle$: for every $p \in \{p_1, \ldots, p_n\}$, $\langle w', i' \rangle \in p\}$. This set is the modal base at $\langle w, i \rangle$, and we will use $\bigcap\{p_1, \ldots, p_n\}$ (or $\bigcap g(\langle w, i \rangle)$) to refer to it. In general, if A is a set of sets, $\bigcap A$ will be the set of objects that belong to all the sets in A (that is, $\{u : \forall X[X \in A \rightarrow u \in X]\}$). In the example just given, the set of propositions in the common ground was assumed to be finite. But there might well be common grounds that contain an infinite number of propositions.

In terms of these notions we can now provide an explicit semantics for the modals we are considering. We will treat *can* and *might* alike, even though this is certainly not right. But at present we don't have the tools to attempt a more refined analysis of their differences.

(56) *a.* $[\![\text{must TP}]\!]^{M,w,i,g} = 1$ iff
$\bigcap g(\langle w, i\rangle) \subseteq \{\langle w', i'\rangle : [\![\text{TP}]\!]^{M,w',i',g} = 1\}$
b. $[\![\text{can TP}]\!]^{M,w,i,g} = [\![\text{might TP}]\!]^{M,w,i,g} = 1$ iff
$\bigcap g(\langle w, i\rangle) \cap \{\langle w', i'\rangle : [\![\text{TP}]\!]^{M,w',i',g} = 1\} \neq \emptyset$

Intuitively, a sentence whose LF is of the form [must TP] is true at $\langle w, i\rangle$ relative to a background $g(\langle w, i\rangle)$ iff the proposition that TP expresses follows from (or is entailed by) the propositions in $g(\langle w, i\rangle)$. In the possible worlds analysis of entailment this means that we have to intersect all the propositions in $g(\langle w, i\rangle)$ with one another and check whether the set of worlds so obtained is a subset of the set of worlds in which TP is true. Similarly, a sentence whose LF is of the form [can TP] is true in $\langle w, i\rangle$ relative to background $g(\langle w, i\rangle)$ iff the proposition that TP expresses is consistent with the propositions in the background taken jointly. This means that if we intersect all the propositions in the background and intersect what we obtain with the set of worlds at which TP is true, the result must be nonempty: there must be one or more worlds at which TP and the propositions in the background are jointly true.

Now consider example (53) again. Before gathering evidence concerning Pavarotti's typewriter, it was consistent with what we knew then that Pavarotti is the author of the anonymous letter Mary got. That is, in some of the circumstances compatible with what we knew, Pavarotti is the author of the letter; in others he isn't. Later we find out new facts concerning the typewriter with which the letter was written: it was a typewriter that only Pavarotti had access to. At this point the relevant conversational background shifts to a new one, and in all the worlds compatible with it Pavarotti is the one who writes the letter: no one else could have done it. This makes (54) true. This is how the analysis proceeds.

It is worth noting that the logical modalities associated with $\square$ and $\Diamond$ can be seen as just a special case where the conversational background is empty (and thus the modal base includes all possible worlds). And we do find our modal auxiliaries expressing these modalities.

(57) No number can be divided by zero.
If Joan smokes and drinks, then she must smoke.

There are many ways in which the present line of analysis should and could be extended and improved. Perhaps it is worth discussing, at least informally, what some of the problems and directions of inquiry are. Let us go back to the example of the anonymous letter. Suppose that instead of finding conclusive evidence against Pavarotti, we find merely strong reasons for suspecting him. For example, he is one of the few people acquainted with the relevant circumstances of Mary's life. And with regard to those few, the kind of practical joke played on Mary fits perfectly with only his kind of humor. In such a situation one might truthfully say

(58) It is probable that Pavarotti wrote this letter.

If, on the other hand, the evidence points strongly to another suspect without excluding Pavarotti, one might say

(59) There is a slight chance that Pavarotti wrote the letter.

The apparatus developed so far is insufficient to analyze the kind of modal locutions in (58) and (59). What (58) and (59) seem to call for is a way of ranking the relevant possibilities. Some of them are more likely to occur than others. The criteria that we use to rank the relevant situations can vary from context to context. In the case at hand we have a modal base determined by what we know about the circumstances in which the letter was written. But beyond that, we also have ideas about what normally is the case. What normally is the case can also be regarded as a conversational background, a stereotypical one. It describes worlds where only what is normal happens: a total bore, as Kratzer puts it. A stereotypical conversational background will also be a set of propositions. So we have a first conversational background that determines the relevant set of worlds and a second conversational background that provides us with standards that we can use to rank or impose an ordering on the relevant set of worlds. Intuitively, we can say that a world w in the modal base will be closer to our standards of normality than a world w' iff w makes true more propositions in the stereotypical background than w'.

Having defined how the relevant worlds are ranked, we are now able to state explicit truth conditions for (58) and (59) along the following lines:

(60) *a.* Sentence (58) is true in $\langle w, i \rangle$ iff Pavarotti is the author of the letter in all the relevant situations (those compatible with what we know) that come closest to our standards of normality.
b. Sentence (59) is true at $\langle w, i \rangle$ iff Pavarotti is the author of the letter in a situation that is relevant (or compatible with what we know) but not close enough to the standards of normality.

The analysis in (60) constitutes just an informal approximation to an analysis of the locutions in (58) and (59). Using the machinery of possible world semantics, one can give a fully explicit content to (60), but we will not try to do this here.

We should point out that the idea illustrated in (60) can be used to analyze many other modal locutions. For example, we can give for (61*a*) the truth conditions in (61*b*).

(61) *a.* It could well be that β.
b. Sentence (61*a*) is true in $\langle w, i \rangle$ iff it is not the case that $\neg\beta$ is probable.

Statement (61*b*) analyzes *could well be* as the dual of *is probable* (just like $\Diamond$ is the dual of $\Box$). This makes certain predictions as to what entailment patterns one should expect. For example, it predicts that (62*a*) and (62*b*) should be compatible (by analogy with the compatibility of $\Diamond\beta$ and $\Diamond\neg\beta$). That is, there should be at least one circumstance in which both (62*a*) and (62*b*) are true.

(62) *a.* It could well be that β.
b. It could well be that not β.

It further predicts that (62*a*) should follow from (63) and that (62*b*) and (63) should be incompatible, which also seems to be the case.

(63) It is probable that β.

To sum up, we can say that in general the analysis sketched here claims that modal locutions are understood relative to two contextually specified conversational backgrounds. One determines a modal base: the range of possibilities to be considered. The other acts as an ordering source: it ranks the modal base according to certain standards. Possible world semantics allows one to make this analysis fairly precise and to incorporate it in a compositional semantics for a wide variety of modal locutions (which we have just begun to do here). When tested against the entailment patterns that those locutions enter into, this analysis appears to be fairly successful.

We think that an analysis along these lines is at least a good start. But beyond its specific results we are interested in the general point that it illustrates. Our understanding of the modal system of English crucially involves the ability to engage in various forms of modal reasoning. The theory that we have presented provides us with an empirically testable model of what the relevant cognitive capacities are based on.

Exercise 4 Consider the following sentence:

(1) Every person can read.

Sentence (1) is assigned two logical forms by the grammar of modalities developed above. Specify them. In prose form, give a clear paraphrase of what truth conditions these logical forms are associated with, in a way that makes it clear whether they are equivalent or not.

Consider the following sentences:

(2) *a.* The president must vote.
b. Reagan is the president. (That is,
$\exists x[\text{president}(x) \wedge \forall y[\text{president}(y) \leftrightarrow x = y] \wedge x = \text{Reagan}]$)
c. Reagan must vote.

Assume that (2*b*) is interpreted as indicated and that (2*a*–*c*) are uttered in the same context. For (2*a*) and (2*b*) jointly to entail (2*c*) what LF must be assigned to (2*a*)? Why?

Next consider the following sentences:

(3) *a.* Reagan must vote.
b. Reagan can vote.

In the context-dependent theory of modalities developed above, under what conditions would (3*a*) entail (3*b*)?

3.3 Complementation

3.3.1 Sentence embedding The possible-world analysis of intensional notions that we have been exploring here is sufficiently articulated and rich to permit a compositional treatment of various forms of embedding. Embedded clausal constructions (for example, *that* clauses) are naturally analyzed as propositions. On this view, verbs taking *that* clauses turn out to express properties of (or relations of individuals to) sets of worlds. Perhaps the best way to grasp what this amounts to is to introduce *that* clauses in fragment F_3.

Let us assume, in line with much recent work, that the syntactic category of embedded clauses is CP (for "Complementizer Phrase") and that the structure of a sentence embedding is as illustrated in (64):

(64) *a.* Loren believes that Pavarotti is hungry.
b.

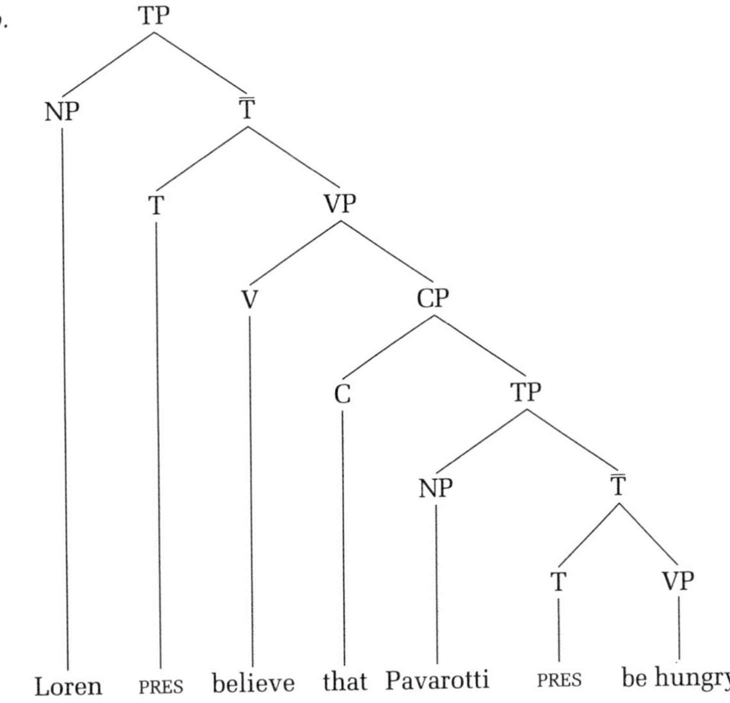

Structures such as (64*b*) can be readily obtained by adding the following syntactic rules to those already given for F_3.

(65) *a.* CP → C TP
b. VP → V CP

c. V $\rightarrow$ believe, know, regret, ...
d. C $\rightarrow$ that, ...

The question now is, How are sentence-embedding verbs interpreted? A prototypical example of such verbs is *believe*, which we used in example (64). What is it to believe that Pavarotti is hungry? Roughly, it is to believe oneself to be in a world where that is the case. To put it slightly differently, our beliefs identify a set of worlds, namely those where we think we might be. In trying to realize our desires or guard against our fears, for example, we act as if we were in one of those worlds. Thus, for example, if we believe that Pavarotti is hungry and we want him to be happy, we may give him some food. Here is one way to spell this intuition out in giving the semantics of *believe* and related verbs:

(66) For any $\langle w, i\rangle$, $V(\text{believe})(\langle w, i\rangle) = \{\langle u, p\rangle$: u is an individual and p is a proposition, and p is true in all those w', i', compatible with what u believes in w at $i\}$

What (66) says is that the intension of *believe* is a function from worlds and times into a two-place relation; for similar verbs—e.g., *know*, *wish*, *fear*, etc.—we will assign the same sort of relation-valued function. The first member of any such relation will be an individual, the second member will be a proposition. What is it for an individual to stand in the *believe* relation to a proposition? Each individual u is associated with a set of worlds that represents u's beliefs (the set of worlds compatible with u's beliefs, or, as they are also called, the set of doxastic alternatives for u). For instance, if u believes that the earth is flat, that ocean water is salty, that u's brother is a Democrat, and so on, the set of u's belief worlds will be those in which all such propositions are true. If u isn't sure whether Bond is a spy, in some of u's belief worlds Bond is a spy and in some others he is not. Now, for u to believe p is simply for p to be true in all of u's belief worlds. Different sentence-embedding verbs correspond to different sets of worlds: u's desires correspond to the worlds where all u's wishes comes about, u's fears to all the worlds u would not want to be actualized, and so on.

With this analysis of sentence-embedding verbs, let us now turn to *that* clauses, which, as noted above, are naturally analyzable as proposition-denoting. Propositions can be modeled either as functions from worlds into truth values, or, equivalently, as sets of worlds. Here we will adopt the first alternative (but the reader should be ready to switch to the second); we are going to assume, moreover, that the complementizer is what turns sentence denotations into propositions—a plausible enough move. For any sentence S, *that* S is going denote a function p such that for any world w' and time i', p is going to map $\langle w', i' \rangle$ into *true* just in case S is true in w' at time i':

(67) *a.* $[\![[_{CP} \text{ that TP}]]\!]^{M,w,i,g} = p$, where for any world w' and any time i', $p(\langle w', i' \rangle) = 1$ iff $[\![\text{TP}]\!]^{M,w',i',g} = 1$
b. $[\![[_{VP} \text{ believe CP}]]\!]^{M,w,i,g} = \{u : \langle u, [\![\text{CP}]\!]^{M,w,i,g} \rangle \in [\![\text{believe}]\!]^{M,w,i,g}\}$

Clause (67*b*) is simply a routine extension of our VP semantic rule to clausal complements. It says that the denotation of a VP like *believe that Pavarotti is hungry*, for example, is the set of those individuals that stand in the *belief* relation to the proposition that Pavarotti is hungry. To put it all together, a sentence like (64) is analyzed as being true in a world w at a time t iff in all of Loren's belief worlds, Pavarotti is hungry. The following box displays how these truth conditions for sentence (64) are formally derived (we ignore, for simplicity, the contribution of tense).

So far we have analyzed *that* clauses and sentence-embedding verbs with a possible-world account of intensionality. Now we are going to show how this analysis interacts with our treatment of quantifier scope in an interesting way. Consider the following example.

(68) *a.* Bond believes that a student in that class is a spy.
b. [[a student in that class]$_i$ [Bond believes that [$_{TP}$ e_i is a spy]]]
c. [Bond believes that [$_{TP}$ [a student in that class]$_i$ [e_i is a spy]]]

(*a*) $[\![(64)]\!]^{M,w,i,g} = 1$ iff $[\![[_{NP} \text{ Loren}]]\!]^{M,w,i,g} \in [\![[_{VP} \text{ believes that Pavarotti is hungry}]]\!]^{M,w,i,g}$ By (39*c*)
(*b*) $[\![[_{NP} \text{ Loren}]]\!]^{M,w,i,g} \in [\![[_{VP} \text{ believes that Pavarotti is hungry}]]\!]^{M,w,i,g}$ iff $[\![[_{NP} \text{ Loren}]]\!]^{M,w,i,g} \in \{u : \langle u, [\![[_{CP} \text{ that Pavarotti is hungry}]]\!]^{M,w,i,g} \rangle \in [\![\text{believe}]\!]^{M,w,i,g}\}$ By (67*b*)
(*c*) $[\![[_{NP} \text{ Loren}]]\!]^{M,w,i,g} \in \{u : \langle u, [\![[_{CP} \text{ that Pavarotti is hungry}]]\!]^{M,w,i,g} \rangle \in [\![\text{believe}]\!]^{M,w,i,g}\}$ iff $\langle [\![[_{NP} \text{ Loren}]]\!]^{M,w,i,g}, [\![[_{CP} \text{ that Pavarotti is hungry}]]\!]^{M,w,i,g} \rangle \in [\![\text{believe}]\!]^{M,w,i,g}$ By definition of $\in$
(*d*) $\langle [\![[_{NP} \text{ Loren}]]\!]^{M,w,i,g}, [\![[_{TP} \text{ that Pavarotti is hungry}]]\!]^{M,w,i,g} \rangle \in [\![\text{believe}]\!]^{M,w,i,g}$ iff $\langle \text{Loren}, p \rangle \in V(\text{believe})(\langle w, i \rangle)$, where for any w', i', $p(\langle w', i' \rangle) = [\![[_{TP} \text{ Pavarotti is hungry}]]\!]^{M,w',i',g}$ By (67*a*)
(*e*) $\langle \text{Loren}, p \rangle \in V(\text{believe})(\langle w, i \rangle)$ iff in all of Loren's belief worlds, Pavarotti is hungry By (66)

Sentence (68*a*) contains two possible sites to which the indefinite NP *a student in that class* can be raised. This yields the two LFs schematically given in (68*b*) and (68*c*). The truth conditions associated with (68*b*) and (68*c*) by the semantics for F_3 are clearly distinct. Perhaps the easiest way to see this is to see how (68*b*) and (68*c*) can be represented in IPC. To this end let us introduce in IPC an operator that plays a role similar to *that* in English. We will follow Montague (1973) and use ^ for such an operator. This is done as follows:

(69) *a.* If ψ is a well-formed formula, $^\wedge\psi$ is a propositional term.
b. $[\![{}^\wedge\psi]\!]^{M,w,i,g} = p$, where for any w', i', $p(\langle w', i'\rangle) = [\![\psi]\!]^{M,w',i',g}$

We also assume that a relational expression BELIEVE with the same meaning as *believe* in (66) is introduced in IPC. With the help of these additions, the LF in (68*b*) will turn out to be equivalent to IPC formula (70*a*) and that in (68*c*) to (70*b*), where S stands for *student in my class* and B for *Bond*. For convenience, we will henceforth use IPC formulas to represent the interpretations associated with the distinct LFs of the English sentences we are examining.

(70) *a.* $\exists x[S(x) \wedge \text{BELIEVE}(B, {}^\wedge\text{spy}(x))]$
b. $\text{BELIEVE}(B, {}^\wedge\exists x[S(x) \wedge \text{spy}(x)])$

If (70*a*) is the case, then there exists a particular student, say Bill, whom Bond believes to be a spy. If, on the other hand, (70*b*) is the case, then the set of worlds that Bond believes himself to be in is one where some student or other is a spy. Bond may have no belief as to *which* student is a spy. The proposition that Bond believes in the first case is one directly related to (or about) Bill. The proposition that Bond believes in the second case is not about any particular individual. In traditional terms, (70*a*) expresses a *de re* belief about a particular individual, and (70*b*) a *de dicto* belief (a belief about what is said, the propositional content of a sentence). A little care is required in using this terminology. Both (70*a*) and (70*b*) are relations of Bond to propositions. However, (70*a*) expresses Bond's belief of a proposition about a particular individual (what Russell would have called a "singular" proposition), while (70*b*) does not.

Sentences like (68*a*) do seem intuitively to be ambiguous between the two readings represented by (70*a*) and (70*b*). Moreover, we are led to expect a similar ambiguity to arise in connection with any other quantified NP. This too appears to be borne out. Thus, for example, F_3 associates the two LFs (71*b*, *c*) with (71*a*).

(71) *a.* Bond believes that the author of this letter is a spy.
b. [[the author of this letter]$_i$ [Bond believes that [e_i is a spy]]
c. [Bond believes that [[the author of this letter]$_i$ [e_i is a spy]]]

According to (71*b*), there exists a particular individual, say Bill, and Bond believes of Bill that he is a spy. Bond need not know or believe that Bill wrote this letter. That is simply a way for the utterer of the report in (71*a*) to identify Bill for her audience. On the other hand, according to the reading represented by (71*c*), Bond believes that the actual world is in a set of worlds where someone wrote this letter, and he further believes that that someone is a spy. His belief is a belief about whoever turns out to have written the letter in question.

The same point can be made in connection with the universal quantifier:

(72) Bond believes that every student in that class is a spy.

On the *de dicto* construal, Bond's belief concerns all the students in that class, whoever they turn out to be. On the *de re* construal, (72) is about the specific individuals that are in fact students in that class. Suppose that they are Bill, Sue, and John. Then (72) would be construed as saying that Bond believes of Bill, Sue, and John that they are spies.

Exercise 5 Assume that the following sentences were uttered in the associated contexts. Decide whether in that context they have a *de re* or a *de dicto* reading, and write the appropriate formula.

(1) Mary believes that a professor was caught shoplifting.
Context Mary is in the main office. The secretaries are all talking together, and she overhears the sentence "The police have caught a professor who was walking out of Tops with five tomatoes and no receipt."

(2) John suspects that one of the Swiss athletes took steroids.
Context John is a janitor at the 1988 Olympic Games. He goes into a changing room to clean it. On the floor he finds a vial. It says "steroids" on it and has instructions written in German, French, and Italian; it is manufactured in Geneva.

(3) Susan thinks that a Republican will be elected.
Context Susan lives in Southeast Asia. She doesn't know much about American politics. In particular, she doesn't know

that there are two main parties: the Republican and the Democratic. She is, however, interested in the presidential election and has read that the candidate who is leading is George Bush; she thinks he will win.

(4) John believes that the manager of Tops is a millionaire.
Context Bill is the manager of Tops, and he lives next door to John. He owns several expensive cars, his wife has many fur coats, the children go to expensive boarding schools, etc. John has no idea what Bill does for a living, but he thinks that Bill is a millionaire.

This treatment makes further claims as to how quantification and embedding interact in yielding valid reasoning patterns. Consider the following:

(73) *a.* Bond believes that the author of this letter is a spy.
b. Bill is the author of this letter.
c. Bond believes that Bill is a spy.

The semantics for F_3 predicts that we can infer (73*c*) from(73*a*, *b*) only under the *de re* construal of the definite description in (73*a*).

These considerations are not, of course, restricted to *believe.* They apply in general to all CP-taking verbs, as the reader can easily check. The interesting aspect of the present approach is that what might seem to be an ambiguity in the interpretation of NPs in embedded sentences is analyzed instead as a scopal ambiguity, a difference in the relative order of interpretation. In traditional linguistic terms, it was the NPs that were said to be ambiguous, with specificity said to distinguish the two understandings. On the present approach, the ambiguity is not in the NP as such but falls out of an independently needed mechanism, namely, the one that assigns scope to NPs. The notion of scope comes with an explicit semantics and is thus better understood than such notions as specificity. In addition, a scopal analysis allows for the possibility of more than two distinct interpretations when there are multiple sentence embeddings, and there have been a number of discussions arguing that this possibility does arise (Fodor 1970 is an early example in the linguistics literature).

The analysis we have sketched, though interesting and influential, leaves several problems unanswered. Here we will briefly discuss two. The first, in its classical form, is due to Quine (see, e.g.,

Quine 1960), and it is sometimes referred to as the "double vision" problem (Klein 1978). The second has to do with the scopal treatment of *de dicto/de re* ambiguities. Let us consider them in turn.

To see the double-vision problem, suppose that a guy, Ralph, sees a man in a brown hat, named Ortcutt, and from his behavior forms the opinion that he is a spy. He thus believes *de re* of Ortcutt that he is a spy. Later, Ralph meets Ortcutt again on the beach (this time Ortcutt is hatless) and forms the belief that the man he sees on the beach (without recognizing him as the man in the brown hat) is not a spy. He does so while not giving up his previous belief that the man he met before in the brown hat is a spy. Thus Ralph now also believes *de re* of Ortcutt that he is not a spy. Situations of this sort are surely common. Notice that Ralph is not being irrational. He simply is not recognizing somebody he has already met. Yet what our theory predicts is that Ralph *is* being irrational. Of one and the same individual, namely Ortcutt, Ralph simultaneously believes that he is and is not a spy. Evidently, there is something missing from our approach to *de re* belief. Representing *de re* beliefs as in (70*a*) leads us straight into this problem. Several philosophers (e.g., Kaplan 1969) have argued that the solution to it lies in how we enter in cognitive contact with the entities about which we form beliefs, expectations, etc. Whenever we enter into a cognitive relation to something, it always happens from a certain point of view or under a certain guise. For example, whenever we perceive something (a prototypical way of forming *de re* beliefs), we always perceive that entity from a certain partial perspective. Evidently, the perspective or guise under which we perceive an object is an essential component of the beliefs we come to have about it. Thus, in particular, we may believe that the man we saw in the brown hat is a spy while the man we saw on the beach is not, even if in the actual world these descriptions pick out the same man. What is missing from something like (70*a*), therefore, is a way of bringing out the implicit relativization of *de re* belief to guises or perspectives. Several attempts to spell this relativization out (and to assess its consequences for natural-language semantics) are being explored (see, e.g., Cresswell and von Stechow 1982), but we cannot pursue such lines of inquiry further within the limits of the present work.

We suggested above that the scopal treatment of the *de dicto/de re* contrast has the advantage of allowing for more than two interpretations. But multiplicities of scopal possibilities are a mixed blessing. We should point out that NP scope assignment out of embedded clauses is not as free as our discussion above might suggest. Contrast, for example, (74*a*) with (74*b*), both of which are from May (1977):

(74) *a.* Some politician will address every rally in John's district.
b. Some politician thinks that he will address every rally in John's district.

In (74*a*) the universally quantified NP *every rally* can be assigned either wide or narrow scope with respect to the existentially quantified NP *some politician*. So both (75*a*) and (75*b*) are possible readings for (74*a*), if we disregard irrelevant details.

(75) *a.* $\exists x[\text{politician}(x) \wedge \forall y[\text{rally}(y) \rightarrow \text{address}(x, y)]]$
b. $\forall y[\text{rally}(y) \rightarrow \exists x[\text{politician}(x) \wedge \text{address}(x, y)]]$

Things are more complicated for (74*b*). It seems intuitively impossible to assign widest scope to the universally quantified NP in (74*b*). That is, (74*b*) seems to lack the truth conditions associated with (76).

(76) $\forall y[\text{rally}(y) \rightarrow \exists x[\text{politician}(x) \wedge \text{think}(x, {}^\wedge\text{address}(x, y))]]$

However, in interpreting the contribution of *every rally in John's district*, there does seem to be something like a *de dicto/de re* contrast. In our terms, this means that both (77*a*) and (77*b*) are possible readings for (74*b*).

(77) *a.* $\exists x[\text{politician}(x) \wedge \forall y[\text{rally}(y) \rightarrow \text{think}(x, {}^\wedge\text{address}(x, y))]]$
b. $\exists x[\text{politician}(x) \wedge \text{think}(x, {}^\wedge\forall y[\text{rally}(y) \rightarrow \text{address}(x, y)])]$

By uttering (74*b*) under the *de dicto* interpretation, namely (77*b*), one is claiming that a politician thinks that he will talk at every rally, however the rallies turn out. Such a politician's thoughts are not claimed to be about any specific rally event. By uttering (74*b*) with the *de re* interpretation, the one represented by (77*a*), there have to be specific rally events (say *a*, *b*, and *c*, each with a specific spatiotemporal location) such that a politician believes that he will speak at all of them (*a*, *b*, and *c*). The politician need not believe that these specific rallies are all the rallies. These two types of situations are clearly different, and both can be easily described by using (74*b*). Thus if the scope treatment of *de dicto/de re* contrasts is adequate, then (74*b*) must indeed have both readings in (77).

The pattern of readings in (75) through (77) is rather puzzling. Why is the reading in (76) impossible? One could impose a restriction on QR that rules the relevant LF structure out. Such a restriction is likely to be complicated, however, for it has to disallow (76) while allowing for (77*a*). Moreover, rather than stating a brute-force constraint, one would like to find some good reason for why precisely this configuration of facts arises. This puzzle is interesting because the pattern of data in question is rather general. It appears to be quite hard to find sentences with embeddings where a universal quantifier in a lower sentence can have scope over an existential quantifier c-commanding it (at S-structure) from a higher clause. Several ideas relevant to finding a general solution to this puzzle are being currently debated (see, in particular, Reinhart 1997, Kratzer 1998).

Exercise 6 We have argued that sentence (1) below has two readings.

(1) John believes that a Russian student cheated.

Give the two logical forms, say (*a*) and (*b*), associated with (1) and describe informally but precisely two states of affairs, say (*A*) and (*B*), such that (*a*) is true in (*A*) and (*b*) false in it, and (*b*) is true in (*B*) and (*a*) false in it.

Give the logical forms associated with sentence (2) below and describe informally but precisely their respective truth conditions.

(2) John thought that Mary claimed that someone stole her purse.

To sum up, these considerations purport to illustrate how the possible-world analysis of propositions supports an elegant compositional semantics for sentence embedding. Such an analysis interacts with other components of truth-conditional semantics (such as the treatment of quantification) to yield an interesting but not problem-free account of various ways in which the contribution of NPs to embedded Ss can be understood.

The present approach to the semantics of embedded Ss also faces the most serious outstanding problem that besets the whole possible-world approach: the problem of logical omniscience. But before turning to it, let us discuss briefly other forms of embedding.

3.3.2 Infinitives and gerunds Another very widespread form of embedding is represented by infinitives and gerunds (IGs), illustrated in (78).

(78) *a.* John tried *playing tennis.*
b. John tried *to play tennis.*
c. John signaled to the man standing at the corner *to cross the road fast.*
d. John recommended *crossing the road fast* to the man standing at the corner.

These constructions have been the focus of much research within the generative tradition, at least since Rosenbaum (1967). In what follows, we would like to present briefly some questions raised by their semantics.

On the surface, IGs lack an overt subject but are undoubtedly understood as if they had one. In (78*a*, *b*) it is John's playing tennis that we are talking about. In (78*c*, *d*) John is concerned with the man at the corner crossing the road (and not with himself crossing the road). The problem of the interpretation of the missing subject is known as the problem of control (which NP in the matrix S controls the IG).

The standard approach to the problem of control within the generative tradition is as follows. IGs are taken to be embedded clauses with a phonologically null pronominal subject, usually represented as PRO. In our current notation, their structure would be as exemplified in (79).

(79) *a.* $[_{CP}\ \varnothing\ [_{TP}\ \text{PRO}_n$ to play tennis$]]$
b. $[_{CP}\ \varnothing\ [_{TP}\ \text{PRO}_n$ playing tennis$]]$

Here $\varnothing$ is the null complementizer and n is an arbitrary index standardly associated with pronouns (see chap. 3., sec. 2.3). The problem of control becomes one of determining what the antecedent of PRO_n is going to be (i.e., which NP is going to bind PRO_n). Even though these assumptions are controversial, in what follows we will adopt them without discussion, as our main interest here is the semantics of IGs.

Let us now turn to a discussion of the latter. Prima facie, the semantics of IGs, given the syntax in (79), appears to be straightforward. PRO_n is interpreted as a variable (just like other pronouns); IGs are interpreted as propositions, presumably formed by the null complementizer, just like other embedded clauses. Thus, for example, the meaning of (79) can be represented by (80) (in IPC):

(80) $^\wedge$play-tennis(x_n)

Here x_n could be bound by some NP, or perhaps it gets its reference from the context (depending on the kind ef embedding verb). Verbs like *try* would then have a semantics analogous to that of verbs likes *believe*. More specifically, one might say that, for example, John stands in the *try* relation to the proposition that John plays tennis iff in all the worlds where John's attempts succeed, John brings it about that he plays tennis. This can represented in IPC as follows:

(81) try(j, $^\wedge$play-tennis(j))

Exercise 7 Give the syntax, LF, and IPC representation of the semantics of "Every man tries to play tennis" according to the semantics for IGs just sketched.

There is, however, another possibility. One might say that verbs such as *try* express relations between individuals and properties. To try to play tennis is to try to have the property of playing tennis, to want to leave is to want to have the property of leaving, and so on. In a sense, *try to play tennis* can be thought of as forming a complex predicate, where the subject of *try* is understood as simultaneously filling in also the subject role of *to play tennis*. This too appears to be an a priori plausible way of accounting for the fact that we understand IGs as undergoing a kind of indirect predication. A way of implementing this view is as follows. We might assume that the contribution of PRO$_n$ is analogous to that of set abstraction. Accordingly, the interpretation of the IGs in (79) could be informally represented as follows:

(82) $\{x_n : x_n$ plays tennis (in w at t)$\}$

These structures are then operated on by the (null) complementizer. The complementizer, in general, creates an intensional entity. Intensions can be thought of as functions from worlds and times into extensions of the appropriate type (see table 5.1). In the case of ordinary *that* clauses, the complementizer creates functions from individuals into truth values (namely propositions). In the case of IGs, whose denotation, per our hypothesis, is a set, it will create functions from worlds into sets; functions of this sort are (our formal reconstruction of) properties.

According to the view just sketched, the semantics of something like (83*a*) could be represented in IPC as in (83*b*):

(83) *a.* John tries [PRO$_n$ to play tennis]
b. try(j, $^\wedge\{x : \text{play-tennis}(x)\}$)

Formula (83*b*) would require introducing in IPC set abstraction or something equivalent, which we will do, for independent reasons, in chapter 7. For the time being, readers can rely on their intuitive understanding of set abstraction. Informally, $^\wedge\{x : \text{play-tennis}(x)\}$ denotes a function that, applied to any world w and at time i, gives us the set of people who play tennis in w at i. The semantics for *try* that goes with this is the following:

(84) For any world w and time i, $V(\text{try})$ $(\langle w, i\rangle) = \{\langle x, P\rangle : u$ is an individual and P a property and in all worlds where u's attempts succeed, u brings it about that u has $P\}$

On the basis of this semantics, sentences like (83*a*) get the right truth conditions: (82*a*) comes out as true in w at i iff John tries to have the property of playing tennis in w, at i (i.e. iff in all the worlds where John's attempts succeed, John brings it about that he has the property of playing tennis).

Exercise 8 Consider the following sentence:

(*a*) John tries to wash himself.

Assume that its syntactic structure (in conformity with the binding theory) is (*b*).

(*b*) John tries [PRO$_j$ to wash himself$_j$]

Compute the truth conditions of (*b*). Do they get the right interpretation of the reflexive?

Summing up, we have sketched two views of the semantics of IGs and the predicates that embed them. According to the first view, IGs denote propositions. According to the second, they denote properties. Let us call the first the "propositional" approach and the second the "predicative" one. The truth conditions we seem to get as the end result on both approaches appear to be the same. Moreover, neither of the two compositional strategies necessary to obtain the semantics of these structures is formally more cumbersome than the other. The predicative view uses abstraction in order to form properties, the propositional one doesn't. One might say that this is a reason for regarding the propositional approach as simpler. But if set abstraction is an independently needed tool in the stock of our semantic operations (and as we shall see in chapters 7 and 9, it indeed is), arguments of this sort carry little weight. Thus it looks like this issue is difficult to settle. Perhaps it is even void of empirical consequences. Perhaps there is no fact that can be brought to bear in deciding it, and the choice between these two theories has to be relegated to the realm of the "overall conceptual elegance" of the final product and the like. In what follows, we would like to show that this isn't so; on the contrary, there are empirical facts that do seem to be directly relevant to choosing between the two theories we have presented.

Consider the argument in (85).

(85) *a.* Pavarotti liked Rome.
b. Loren liked the thing that Pavarotti liked.
c. Loren liked Rome.

It is clear that (85*c*) follows from (85*a*, *b*). It should also be fairly uncontroversial that, on some fairly plausible assumptions, the semantics that we have developed so far accounts for the validity of (85). The nominal phrase *thing that Pavarotti liked* is going to have as its extension the set of those things that Pavarotti liked. In fact, in *thing that Pavarotti liked* we have a head, namely *thing*, modified by a relative clause. When we look at the semantics for relative clauses in chapter 7, we will see how such a semantics would assign, in a compositional way, precisely this extension to the nominal in question. As a consequence of this and in view of our analysis of the determiner *the*, we must take (85*b*) to say that in the context at hand there is a unique thing that Pavarotti liked and Loren liked that same thing. Thus the truth-conditional import of (85*a*–*c*) can be represented, disregarding tense, as in (86*a*–*c*), respectively.

(86) *a.* $\text{like}(P, R)$
b. $\exists x[\text{thing-that-Pavarotti-likes}(x) \wedge \forall y[\text{thing-that-Pavarotti-likes}(y) \leftrightarrow y = x] \wedge \text{like}(L, x)]$
c. $\text{like}(L, R)$

It is straightforward to check that (86*a*, *b*) jointly entail (86*c*).

Consider now the argument in (87).

(87) *a.* Pavarotti tried playing tennis.
b. Loren tried the thing that Pavarotti tried.
c. Loren tried playing tennis.

Uncontroversially, (87*c*) follows from (87*a*, *b*). This is exactly what the predicative view of gerunds predicts (under the plausible assumption that the extension of *thing* can include properties). Just as we did in the case of (85*b*), we assume that the extension of *thing that Pavarotti tried* is the set of things that Pavarotti tries. This is exactly what the treatment of relative clauses needed for (85*b*) will compositionally associate with the nominal in question. The argument in (87) can be represented in IPC as follows (where Q and Z are variables ranging over properties):[9]

(88) *a.* $\text{try}(P, {}^\wedge\{x : \text{play-tennis}(x)\})$
b. $\exists Q[\text{thing-that-Pavarotti-tries}(Q) \wedge \forall Z[\text{thing-that-Pavarotti-tries}(Z) \leftrightarrow Z = Q] \wedge \text{try}(L, Q)]$
c. $\text{try}(L, {}^\wedge\{x : \text{play-tennis}(x)\})$

It is easy to see that (88*a*, *b*) entail (88*c*).

What is interesting to observe in this connection is that a propositional analysis of the semantics of IGs would *not* make the same prediction. According to that view, something like (87*a*) would be analyzed as a relation between Pavarotti and a proposition (or state of affairs). Such a proposition would have to be about Pavarotti: what (87*a*) says on such an analysis is that Pavarotti tries to bring about a situation where he plays tennis. This means that, everything else being equal, the truth conditions of the sentences in (87) will be as in (89), where *q* and *r* are variables over propositions.

(89) *a.* $\text{try}(P, {}^\wedge\text{play-tennis}(P))$
b. $\exists q[\text{thing-that-Pavarotti-tries}(q) \wedge \forall r[\text{thing-that-Pavarotti-tries}(r) \leftrightarrow r = q] \wedge \text{try}(L, q)]$
c. $\text{try}(L, {}^\wedge\text{play-tennis}(P))$

Clearly, (89*a*, *b*) entail (89*c*). Thus a propositional view of IGs predicts that it follows from (87*a*, *b*) that Loren tries to bring about a situation where Pavarotti plays tennis. But this clashes head-on with our intuitions. So, not only is the propositional theory not obviously capable of explaining our judgments about (87); on the face of it, it also seems to predict an unattested pattern of validity judgments.

It is not immediately obvious how one could rescue the propositional view. Perhaps one could try to argue that *thing that Pavarotti tries* is interpreted differently from ordinary relative clauses (like *thing that Pavarotti ate*). This amounts to the claim that relativization of the complements of verbs like *try* is somehow special. It is, of course, difficult to assess the consequences of this move in the absence of a general treatment of relative clauses (including their semantics). But it can be remarked that all other circumstances being equal, a uniform treatment of relative clauses is to be preferred to one that treats different cases of relativization differently. The predicative view of IGs allows for such a uniform treatment; it is not clear whether the propositional view also does.

It should perhaps be noted that the preceding argument can be constructed in a wide variety of forms. For example, one can also construct it by using the universal quantifier or free relatives (relative clauses that lack a head noun). This is illustrated in (90) and (91) respectively.

(90) *a.* John tried playing tennis.
b. Mary tried everything that John tried.
c. Mary tried playing tennis.

(91) *a.* John promised Mary to marry her.
b. Bill promised Mary whatever John promised her.
c. Bill promised Mary to marry her.

The predicative view predicts the validity of (90) and (91) in a way that is fully parallel to the account it provides for (87). And (90) and (91) create problems for the propositional view closely related to the problems that (87) poses for it.[10]

We are not so much interested here in defending the predicative view of IGs over the propositional one (even though we do feel that the above argument favors the former). Rather, we are interested in showing how very sharp judgments of semantic relatedness can be brought to bear in arguing for or against semantic hypotheses. Some questions that one raises in semantics appear prima facie to be closer to metaphysics than to linguistics. They are questions like these: What individuals should we put in our domain? Should a property be regarded as a particular sort of individual? Should we interpret IGs as properties or as propositions? What our discussion shows is that this appearance might be misleading; such questions can turn out to have an unexpectedly rich empirical content. The kind of answer to them that one chooses can have widespread effects on other aspects of grammar (in the case at hand, for example, on the treatment of relative clauses).

4 Problems with Belief Sentences

The analysis of propositions that we have presented is problematic in more than one way. In this section we will review one of the main problems and point out strategies that are being explored to solve it.

Imagine the following situation. Mary is at a party where several kinds of dishes and drinks are being served. She notices, however, that everyone at the party either doesn't eat (they only drink) or eats only chicken. She thus forms a certain belief, which might be reported in a number of ways. For example, one might report Mary's belief as follows.

(92) Mary believes that not everyone at the party ate and those who did ate only chicken.

(93) Mary believes that no one at the party ate anything other than chicken and some ate nothing.

The reason we can choose these two different ways of describing Mary's belief is that the embedded sentences in (92) and (93) have the same truth conditions; they are true in the same worlds. There are still other ways in which we might characterize Mary's attitude. For example, we might say that she believes that some people at the party didn't eat and those who did ate only chicken. And so on. In fact, it seems that while some sentences might turn out to be more felicitous than others, just about any sentence with the same truth conditions as the embedded clauses in (92) and (93) will do.

This state of affairs fits nicely with the possible world characterization of belief. According to such a characterization, to have a belief is to be related in a certain way to a set of worlds. Consequently, if a believes that ψ, and ϕ is true in the same worlds as ψ (ψ and ϕ entail each other), then a also believes that ϕ. This means that we are free to describe the relevant set of worlds by means of the sentence that we think most appropriate to the communicative purposes at hand. For cases like those illustrated in (93), this consequence seems to be a welcome one.

In fact, the possible-world analysis of belief has further interesting consequences. We have said that for an individual u to believe a proposition p is for p to be true in all of u's belief worlds. That is, if R_u are u's belief worlds, then u believes p iff $R_u \subseteq p$. Suppose now that p entails q. Then every p world is a q world: $p \subseteq q$. By putting these two facts together, we get that $R_u \subseteq p \subseteq q$. Hence q will be true in all of u's belief worlds as well, which is tantamount to saying that u believes q. Thus we seem to be committed to saying that if u believes p and p entails q, then u believes q. In other words, if someone believes something, they must believe all of its logical consequences. In many cases this seems to be right. We do want to say, for example, that if Mary has the specific belief we reported in (93), then she also has many other beliefs entailed by that belief, like those reported in (94).

(94) *a.* Mary believes that not everyone at the party ate.
b. Mary believes that only chicken was eaten at the party.

But there are more problematic cases. Consider (95).

(95) *a.* Only chicken was eaten at the party.
b. No tofu or veal was eaten at the party.
c. Only chicken and no tofu or veal was eaten at the party.

Sentence (95*a*) entails (95*b*) and, furthermore, is equivalent to (95*c*). The relation between (95*a*) and (95*b*) is diagrammed in figure 5.2. Conjunction corresponds semantically to set intersection, so the worlds in which (95*c*) is true will be $A \cap B$, but since $A \subseteq B$, $A \cap B = A$.

But in coming to believe (95*a*) (as reported in (94*b*)), Mary might have entirely failed to consider the possibility that the stuff she saw some partygoers putting in their mouths that looked like chicken might in fact be tofu or veal. So although she does not believe that anyone at the party ate tofu or veal, it is not clear that she has the belief expressed by (95*b*). Even worse, it is not clear that Mary has the belief expressed by (95*c*), yet we have seen that (95*c*) is logically equivalent to (95*a*): (95*a*) and (95*c*) pick out the same set of worlds, and an agent who believes one should believe the other if belief is indeed simply a relation to a set of worlds.

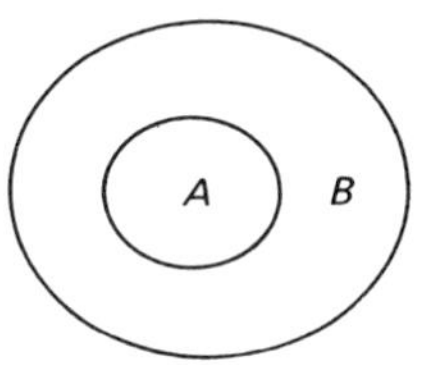

A: the worlds where only chicken was eaten at the party.
B: the worlds where no tofu or veal was eaten at the party.

Figure 5.2

The problems multiply when we turn to attitudes toward mathematical statements. Any true mathematical statement is necessarily true, that is, true in every possible world; every false mathematical statement is necessarily false, true in no world. There is just one necessarily true proposition (the set of all possible worlds) and one necessarily false proposition (the null set). Thus on the possible world account of propositions all true mathematical statements express the same proposition, so to believe (or know or consider) any one of the statements in (96) should be to believe (or know or consider) them all, a highly counterintuitive result.

(96) *a.* Two plus two equals four.
b. $19 \times 241 = 4579$.
c. There are infinitely many prime numbers.

The basic difficulty is that the possible world account of propositions cannot discriminate among logically equivalent or content-synonymous propositions. Yet we often fail to notice that two statements are logically equivalent, or we are quite ignorant of their equivalence. Possible world semantics, however, seems to imply a logical omniscience that humans notably lack.

The problem of logical omniscience arises in connection with any $\bar{S}$-taking verb. There is no definite solution to it at present. There are, however, many interesting proposals that often raise far-reaching foundational issues for semantics and cognitive science. The intricacy of the question is such that we certainly cannot do justice to it here. But we want to give the reader some idea of the various strategies being pursued.

In the following discussion one should keep in mind what our perspective is. We are concerned with the semantic characterization of *that* clauses. Such a characterization has to support a semantics of $\bar{S}$-taking verbs. The problem of logical omniscience seems to center around the fact that the notion of the semantic content of an S that the possible world approach characterizes is not fine-grained enough. We saw that propositions (on the possible world analysis) do share some of the structural properties of sentences. In particular, propositions and sentences share a Boolean structure (propositions can be negated, conjoined, disjoined, etc., just like sentences). But perhaps this is not enough: more of the structural properties of sentences might be relevant in characterizing the notion of sentence content. Most of the strategies being explored grant this point in some form or other.

4.1 Representationalist strategies

One strategy involves maintaining that belief and other attitudes involve in some crucial way representations of some sort. A radical way of pursuing this possibility is by bringing in sentence structure in a rather direct fashion. One might try to claim that belief and other attitudes involve dispositions to assent, dissent, or otherwise use sentences in deliberating and planning.[11] So belief becomes a relation of agents to public linguistic structures.

To see what this involves, it might be useful to sketch some simpleminded version of such an idea. Suppose we say that "*x* believes that S" should be analyzed as "*x* is disposed to assent to 'S'," where S stands for a sentence (or perhaps its P marker). A problem that immediately arises, then, is the problem of translation. Consider the following:

(97) *a.* John believes that it is raining.
b. John crede che sta piovendo.

Sentence (97*b*) is the Italian translation of (97*a*). Since the translation is accurate, it follows that (97*a*) is true iff (97*b*) is true. Yet, on the simpleminded quotational approach we have outlined, this is not predicted to happen, for (97*a*) is analyzed as John is disposed to assent to "It is raining," and (97*b*) as John is disposed to assent to "Sta piovendo." But "It is raining" and "Sta piovendo" are different sentences, and consequently one might be disposed to assent to the former but not to the latter. So the present view has as a consequence that (97*a*) might not have the same truth conditions as (97*b*), which is wrong.

One way out of this problem involves relativizing our characterization of belief to the notion of accurate translation. A first approximation might go as follows:

(98) The sentence "*x* believes that S" is true in a language *L* iff there exist a language *L*′ and a sentence S′ of *L*′ such that S is an accurate translation of S′ and *x* is disposed to assent to S′.

While this would solve the problem connected with (97), it does so by introducing the ill-understood notion of accurate translation. In particular, it seems very hard to characterize such a notion in a way that does not resort to what S and S′ mean. But if we had an adequate characterization of what S and S′ mean, then the nature of the problematic attitudes could probably be understood directly in terms of such a notion.

A second way out might be to say that belief is a relation involving syntactic objects but not sentences of some public language. Rather, the belief relation could be analyzed as a relation involving representations in some mental code, a "language of thought."[12] If such a mental code is universal, then the version of the translation problem outlined above would not arise. The universality of such a code could be taken to be directly related to a putatively universal level of linguistic structure such as LF. For example, believing might be a disposition to manipulate the LFs associated with sentences in deliberating, storing and retrieving information in memory, etc.

There are several further issues that this kind of approach raises, however. One thing to note is that the structure of a linguistically motivated level of representation might turn out to be unsuited for an analysis of belief sentences. For example, LFs might be limited in some ways. In particular, LF as currently conceived does not provide us with a characterization of the content of lexical items. The LF of "Pavarotti is bald" would be something very close to its surface form, except that the actual lexical entries "Pavarotti" and "bald" would be replaced by their LF translation/representation. Clearly, one would want such translation/representation to relate the English predicate "bald" to baldness (the property shared by people who have little or no hair on their head). It is far from clear how this is to be accomplished. Thus, linguistically motivated levels of representation as we understand them at this point seem to lack the characteristics that such a language of thought should have.

Two additional issues have been pointed out as problematic for attempts to analyze belief (and other attitudes) as relations involving crucially and solely syntactic structures or representations for some kind.[13]

The first has to do with the fact that our beliefs very often appear to be about things independently of how they are represented (mentally or otherwise). Take, for example, (99).

(99) *a.* John believes that this person is a genius.
b. There is someone that John believes is a genius.

An illocutionary agent who utters (99*a*) imputes to John a belief that involves someone regardless of how such a person is represented. This is shown, for example, by the fact that such an illocutionary agent will be committed also to the truth (99*b*). If belief were just a relation of individuals to representations, it is unclear how this aboutness of belief (and other attitudes) as manifested in such inference patterns as those in (99) would be accommodated.

An example from Partee (1979) that illustrates a similar point is the following:

(100) Smith believes that *that* door is locked, but she doesn't believe that *that* door is locked.

If the two demonstratives in (100) are interpreted as referring to different doors, then (100) attributes to Smith a noncontradictory belief. Yet there is only one sentence that we use to characterize what Smith might be related to, namely, "That door is locked." And it is not clear how to manufacture two different representations out of it without directly resorting to the contextually specified objects that form the demonstrata.

The second issue has to do with the fact that creatures that have limited capacities for representation might nevertheless have beliefs. My canary might believe that it rains or that someone will feed him. It is not so straightforward to conceive of canaries as standing in interesting relations to mental representations. For example, it is difficult to imagine my canary's dispositions to use mental representations in deliberating. It is even harder to imagine representations of the semantic contents of *that* clauses that could support a plausible analysis for sentences like "My canary believes that it will be fed."

The above problems all appear to be linked to the fact that while representations may well be a fundamental determinant of beliefs and other attitudes, a characterization of the meaning of *that* clauses that supports a plausible semantics for attitude reports appears to be hard to obtain without bringing into the picture in some systematic form the content of such representations. One way of doing this is along the following lines adapted from the discussion in Stalnaker (1984, 27 ff.).

(101) "x believes that S" is true iff x believes* $\rho(S)$ and $\rho(S)$ means that p.

Here $\rho(S)$ is some specified representation of S (perhaps something like its LF), *believe** is a relation to representations (perhaps retrieving and using them in specified ways determined by the type of attitude), and *means* is to be analyzed in terms of one's theory of meaning. In our case, "$\rho(S)$ means p" would be analyzed in terms of the truth conditions (or set of circumstances) associated with $\rho(S)$.

On the analysis just sketched, the problems that we have been discussing will not automatically disappear. But we are tackling them with better hope of success. In particular, an approach along these lines is clearly well equipped for dealing with logical omniscience. Two sentences can have the same truth conditions and yet be mapped onto very different representations. Our dispositions toward truth-conditionally equivalent representations might well vary. At the same time the relation of representations to their content enters in a crucial way in the characterization of attitudes and anchors such attitudes into the world. Puzzles surrounding *de re* beliefs can thus be dealt with in terms of the standard quantificational machinery of logic. Interesting proposals along these lines have been developed.[14]

However, one problem still remains. Consider the following pair of sentences:

(102) *a.* John believes that Kim is a genius.
 b. John does not believe that no one is a genius.

The truth of (102*b*) seems to follow from the truth of (102*a*). No matter how little developed John's logical skills may be, there is no way in which he can believe of someone that he or she is a genius and at the same time believe that no one is. Yet on the family of approaches we are considering, this does not automatically follow. The representations associated with the embedded clauses of (102*a*, *b*) will be different from each other. And hence, unless we say something more, standing in the belief relation to the one does not imply standing in the belief relation to the other. It looks as if in the attempt to get around the problem of logical omniscience, the family of approaches we are considering tend to go too far. They simply block every kind of inference involving embedded clauses. And it is not obvious how to bring back, in a general and non ad hoc way, those inferences that seem to be warranted.

4.2 Fine-grained meanings

Another important family of approaches tackles the problem of logical omniscience by seeking a more finely structured characterization of the notion of sentence content. One can try to introduce such notions as those of propositions, events, or situations as primitives and provide axioms (or algebraic conditions) to characterize their logical behavior where needed. There are many proposals that fall within the family, broadly construed. Let us consider briefly one that goes back to Carnap (1947).[15]

Take a sentence like the following:

(103) John runs.

Let *j* be John and *R* be the property of running, where the latter is construed as a function from individuals to sets of worlds (that is, for any individual *u*, *R*(*u*) is the set of worlds where *u* runs). We could associate with (103) the following structure:

(104)

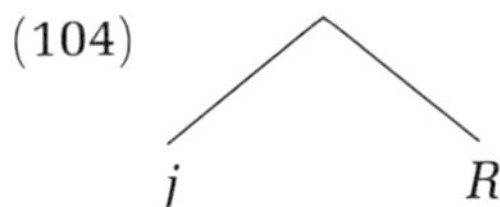

Now let – be set-theoretic complementation restricted to the set *W* of possible worlds.

We can then associate with sentence (105*a*) the structure (105*b*):

(105) *a.* John doesn't run.
b.

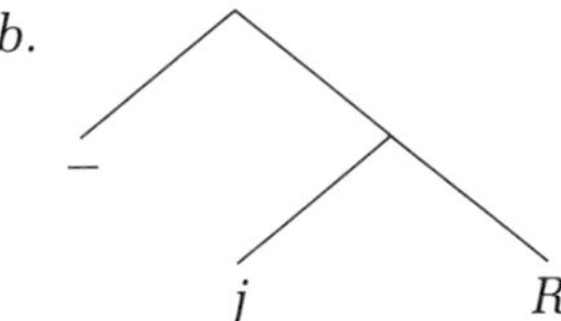

We can play the same game for other connectives and quantifiers. For example, where ∩ is set-theoretic intersection (restricted to *W*), we can associate with (106*a*) the structure in (106*b*):

(106) *a.* John runs, and Mary doesn't run.
b.

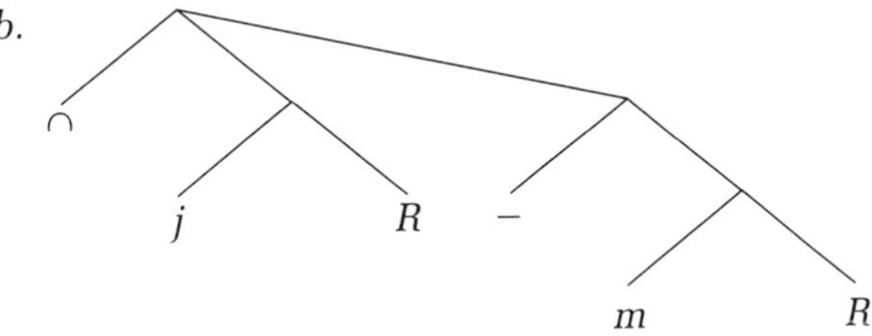

The objects that we are associating with sentences can be thought of as trees isomorphic to syntactic trees but whose terminals are objects rather than words. So we have "structured meanings," as Cresswell (1985) puts it. The structure comes from some relevant level of syntax, but the entities being structured are the meanings themselves (in the case at hand, the properties and individuals).

These structured objects are arguably candidates for a characterization of the notion of sentence content. For one thing, they can be compositionally specified. Moreover, the truth conditions of a proposition can systematically be recovered from them. For example, we can say that (105) is true in world w iff $w \in -R(j)$ (that is, w is in the complement of the set of worlds $R(j)$). Since structured meanings are so systematically linked to truth conditions, characterizing their logical behavior (and hence the logical behavior of the sentences they are associated with) can be done following known paths.

In addition, structured meanings are extremely fine-grained, and thus, treating S-taking verbs as relations to structured meanings will not get us into the problem of logical omniscience. For example, (107*a*) is a different structure from (107*b*), even if in classical logic the double negation of a formula ψ is equivalent to ψ itself.

(107) *a.* *b.*

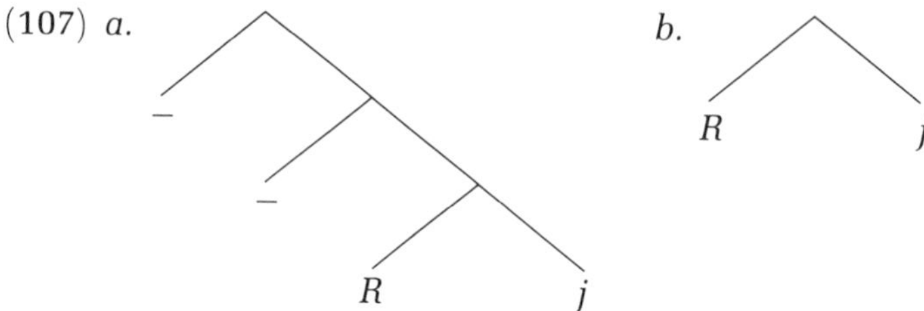

Thus we can stand in the belief relation with one of these objects, say (107*a*), without standing in the belief relations with, say, (107*b*).

Finally, if belief and other attitudes are relations to structured meanings, then they obviously are relations involving not just representations but actual objects. Thus the *de re* character of attitudes (and the pattern of entailments in which it is manifested) can be accommodated in a principled way.

The structured-meaning approach we have just sketched has quite a bit in common with the representationalist approach considered at the end of section 4.1. Both bring in an abstract kind of logical structure linked in systematic ways to the syntactic structure of sentences. Both have the actual denotation of phrases play an important role in characterizing the objects of belief (and the meaning of embedded clauses). And just like the representationalist approach, the structured-meaning one runs the risk of ruling out too much. If nothing is added, nothing follows from the fact that an agent stands in the belief relation to a given structured meaning.

Our rudimentary and unsophisticated discussion of these difficult topics doesn't show very much. Our main purpose is to give the reader some indication of the reasons why we are moderately optimistic on the outcome of research in this area. The problems involved in developing an account along the lines we have sketched are difficult. Nonetheless, serious attempts to spell out interesting characterizations of the notion of sentence content have been made.

Before concluding, we should point out what we think is an important aspect of the problems surrounding mental attitudes and the semantics of attitude reports, an aspect emphasized especially in Stalnaker (1984). There seems to be a notion of belief that the possible world approach, in spite of its limitations, captures in an arguably optimal way. This is the notion of belief as a disposition to act (as opposed to belief as a disposition to represent reality in a certain way). When we engage in action, we are confronted with ranges of possible outcomes. Our actions are guided by our attitudes for or against some such outcomes. Such actions are causally conditioned by the range of possibilities we can discriminate for certain purposes. From this perspective what appears to be crucial is that we discriminate between alternative states of affairs, not between alternative representations. Example (93) made this point. A further illustration can be constructed along the following lines. Consider the following:

(108) *a.* Pavarotti/my cat believes that some humans are friendly to him.
b. Pavarotti/my cat believes that not every human is unfriendly to him.

One plausible way of interpreting (108*a*) is as saying that Pavarotti (or my cat) is disposed to bring about his desires as if a certain condition obtained. The way we characterize such a condition (whether, for example, we characterize it as in (108*a*) or as in (108*b*)) is immaterial. The important thing is Pavarotti's capacity to distinguish between friendly humans and unfriendly humans. Any logically equivalent way of characterizing this distinction will serve the purpose. In this specific sense, his belief is closed under logical equivalence. From the point of view of how beliefs (and other attitudes) play a role in action, the form one uses for characterizing a set of possible outcomes is not crucial. Two agents may have the same attitude toward a given set of possible circumstances even if they individuate such a set by totally different means, up to logical equivalence.

This sense of what it is to have an attitude toward something and the notion of sentence content that goes with it appear to be adequately characterized by possible world semantics. It would seem on the face of things that any attempt to solve the problems that such an approach leaves open (such as the logical omniscience problem) should maintain in some form such a notion of sentence content.

In conclusion, there are some positive features as well as some serious problems in our current characterization of sentence meaning and in the way sentence meaning interacts with the semantics of attitude reports. Many exciting avenues of research are being pursued in this connection, and we have been barely able to give the reader a taste of some of the issues involved.

Exercise 9 Consider the following sentence:

(1) Every glass wasn't made in Italy.

Take "made in Italy" as an unanalyzed predicate. Adopt the Priorian analysis of tense and the constraint that negation must have scope over tense. On these assumptions, (1) is ambiguous. Give the two logical forms associated with (1) and their IPC representations. What is the relation between these two readings (i.e., are they, under our current assumptions, logically independent of each other)?

---

6 Contexts: Indexicality, Discourse, and Presupposition

1 Introduction

In the preceding chapter we generalized our model-theoretic semantics to deal with certain intensional notions. Truth definitions were given relative not only to a model and an assignment function but also to circumstances, world-time pairs. We have identified propositions with functions from circumstances to truth values (or sets of circumstances) and have defined an elementary intensional predicate calculus (IPC) with modal and temporal operators. The truth value of a sentence in IPC is assigned in two stages: (1) the sentence is associated with some proposition, and (2) that proposition is evaluated as true or false relative to a particular world and time. And we have used the techniques introduced in IPC in an account of tense, modal auxiliaries, modal adverbs, and complement-taking verbs like *believe* and *try*.

In this chapter we are going to look in more detail at the interaction of contextual factors with semantics. First we investigate the semantics of some indexical expressions like *I* and *here*. The basic idea is to increase the number of parameters relative to which truth conditions are defined. The most immediately obvious way to do this is to add such contextual coordinates as those specifying speakers and their locations to the worlds and times already needed for the analysis of intensionality; we call this the *multiple coordinate approach*. Multiple coordinates by themselves, however, do not support completely adequate notions of entailment and validity for sentences that include indexical expressions. We then turn to examine a view of context and circumstances as potentially independent of one another and propose a two-stage approach to the assignment of intensions.

The analysis of context we develop for the interpretation of indexicals can be used to talk about the dynamics of discourse. We illustrate this by further articulating some of our earlier informal suggestions about illocutionary forces as context-changing operations, developing the analysis of assertion as a function from one context into another. We make explicit the idea that what assertions do is to add the asserted propositional content to the set of propositions that conversationalists take for granted at later stages, the common ground. The conception of a context as including a set of background propositions and of discourse as involving ongoing changes in context helps provide the basis for a discussion of the contrast between presupposition and assertion by conversationalists and for an account of what it is for sentences to carry presuppositions. This approach suggests at least a partial solution to the projection problem for presuppositions, the question of the conditions under which embedded sentences project their presuppositions to the complex sentences containing them.

2 Indexicals

There are two ways in which the facts can enter into determining whether a sentence is true. Consider (1).

(1) I am hungry.

Were Bond to utter (1), it would express the same proposition as that expressed by (2*a*); were Pavarotti to utter it, it would express the same proposition as that expressed by (2*b*).

(2) *a*. Bond is hungry.
b. Pavarotti is hungry.

Whether (1) is true in *circumstances* $\langle w, i \rangle$ depends not just on which individuals are hungry in world w at time i but also on the *context* in which (1) is produced and that thereby determines whose hunger is relevant, who has uttered the sentence, and thus who the first-person pronoun *I* denotes. We follow the practice of Kaplan (1977) and use *context* when we mean something like the situation of utterance (the way things are that helps determine what is actually expressed by an utterance) and *circumstances* when we mean the state of affairs we are speaking about or describing (the way things are or might be that determines the truth value of what is expressed by the sentence uttered). Often we speak of the here and now in which the utterance occurs, and in such cases the context and the circumstances both involve aspects of the same concrete situation or state of affairs (where neither *situation* nor *state of affairs* is used in any special technical sense).

There are many different kinds of expressions that are similar to *I* in this sensitivity to variations in the context in which they are uttered. For example, whether (3) is true depends not only on what the circumstances are like with respect to who is boring; it also depends on the identify of the addressee, on the denotation of *you* in a particular context of using sentence (3).

(3) You are boring.

Imagine a context in which an utterance of (3) is addressed to Pavarotti, and the relevant circumstances are ones in which Pavarotti is boring but Bond is not boring. What has been said by uttering (3) in this context is thus true. Suppose further that Pavarotti mistakenly believes himself fascinating whereas Bond is fully aware of who is boring and who is not. If Pavarotti knows himself to be the addressee whereas Bond mistakenly takes himself to be addressed, then both Pavarotti and Bond will wrongly judge (3) to have been falsely uttered. Their reasons, however, are quite different. Pavarotti is wrong about what the relevant circumstances are, about who is boring, but he is quite right about what was said in the given context. Bond, in contrast, is in error over what was said but is quite right about who is boring. We are inclined to describe Bond as having simply misunderstood what was said, whereas Pavarotti's mistake we take to be one of substance.[1]

Another example is illustrated by the sentences in (4).

(4) *a.* Loren is behind the tree.
b. Loren is in front of the tree.

The facts about Loren and the tree—their particular locations in world w at time i—do not suffice to determine the truth of these sentences. Rather, whether (4*a*) is true and (4*b*) false or vice versa depends also on the location of the speaker; it is this location that determines what spatial relation of Loren to the tree counts as *behind* or *in front of*. Loren and the tree may be fixed in their locations and (4*a*) will be true relative to one speaker (located on the opposite side of the tree as Loren) but false relative to another (located on the same side of the tree as Loren). What the sentences say about Loren and her location with respect to the tree, their content, depends on features of the context relative to which they are uttered.[2]

In chapter 1 we used a similar contrast between *come* and *go* to illustrate how the way a particular circumstance is described can say something about the perspective from which the description is issued.

(5) *a.* The bear came into the tent.
b. The bear went into the tent.

As Barwise and Perry (1983) observe in discussing this example, each of the sentences in (5) may be used to correctly describe a single situation. Yet a hearer will learn something about the speaker's *perspective* on the situation from which verb is selected, and as a consequence he may infer something more about the speaker's attitudes toward the proposition she has expressed.[3]

Examples can be multiplied where what a sentence says, and thus whether it is true of circumstances $\langle w, i \rangle$, depends not just on those circumstances but on certain aspects of the context of its use. Tense and temporal adverbials (like *yesterday*), locative expressions (like *here*), and demonstratives (like *this*) all have a significance that depends on the context of their use. Someone who knows of a world w what, if anything, Sophia Loren gave to whom and where she was at all times may still fail to know whether (6) is true, for what (6) claims about Loren's givings, its content, depends on who utters it, when and where it is uttered, and what is demonstrated as it is uttered.

(6) Loren gave this to me here yesterday.

As an aside, we should note that demonstrative expressions sometimes act like anaphoric pronouns or bound variables to be interpreted in terms of their connection to an antecedent linguistic expression. Sentence (7*a*) might be a pure demonstrative occurrence of *that*, whereas (7*b*) is anaphoric.

(7) *a.* That is Melissa's favorite piece of clothing.
b. Every girl brought her favorite piece of clothing to school and wore that [her favorite piece of clothing] to the party rather than her uniform.

Ultimately, we might hope for an account that unifies these different uses, but for the present we will focus on occurrences of demonstratives that lack antecedents and that must be interpreted with reference to some contextual demonstration.

The philosopher Y. Bar-Hillel borrowed the term *indexical* from C. S. Peirce to apply specifically to expressions like first- and second-person pronouns, tense, and demonstratives, demonstratives having been discussed in Peirce (1902) under his much more general notion of an indexical sign. Like the more traditional linguistic term *deixis*, the word *indexical* is etymologically linked to a Greek word meaning indicating or pointing.

Indexical expressions are terms whose contribution to propositional content depends on the context in which they are used, and their meaning consists in specifying the aspect of context that determines what contribution to content they will make. Bar-Hillel (1954) seems to have been the first to propose that such expressions could and should be incorporated in formal systems and studied by logical methods.

It was Richard Montague and various students of his who really developed Bar-Hillel's proposal in a general way about a decade later. Significant work on tense logics had been undertaken much earlier. What was novel in Montague's program was the generalization of techniques already developed in model-theoretic semantics for dealing with indexical elements of all kinds.[4]

2.1 Multiple coordinates

The first step was suggested by analogies between tense and modal operators, which we discussed briefly in the preceding chapter. It is a very natural idea to treat times or histories as simply other factors relative to which truth conditions can be given and so to add a set of instants (or intervals) to the model along with a set of possible worlds. Just as modal expressions like *must* and *necessarily* can be understood as quantifying over possible worlds or circumstances, so temporal expressions like *always* and *will* can be understood as quantifying over times. In IPC we introduced simple tense operators. We then applied the same semantic techniques to interpreting the English tense morphemes in T; we assumed that present tense is interpreted as coincident with the time of the context in which the sentence is produced (much like *now*) and that future and past tenses quantify over times later or earlier than that denoted by *now*.

On the face of it, an indexical phenomenon like tense seems easy to deal with by extending the set of parameters to which interpretation is relativized, by adding *i*, an instant of time, to *w*, a world. It looks promising to generalize this strategy with respect to other contextual factors as well. The various types of information that the context supplies can be viewed as different coordinates to which an interpretation must be sensitive. This idea can be formalized in two simple steps where we (1) enrich the notion of a model by adding different relevant contextual parameters and (2) relativize the interpretation function ⟦ ⟧ to such further parameters.

We could add locations to our models, for example. Sentence (8*a*) will not be evaluated with respect to anything as global as what we have called a possible circumstance (a world-time pair) but will be understood as localized to a region centered on the place in which the sentence is produced. That is, (8*a*) is generally interpreted as synonymous with (8*b*), which contains an overt occurrence of the indexical *here.*

(8) *a.* It is raining.
 b. It is raining here.

In fact, we seem able to discriminate among indefinitely many locations within what can be viewed as the same context. The two distinct occurrences of *there* in (9) are associated with pointings to different places, which we have represented by giving them distinct (unpronounced) subscripts.

(9) Joan found a penny there_1 and there_2.

There is no difficulty in principle to continuing in the same way indefinitely: "and there_3 and ... and there_n." Of course, there are interesting issues in perceptual psychology about our capacity visually to identify and distinguish places. Practical limits on these perceptual capacities might put an end to the litany, although the speaker might also enlarge on the possibilities by walking around during the course of speaking, identifying a sequence of locations associated with occurrences of *there* with pointings from a sequence of distinct locations.

What is crucial for our present purposes is that visual demonstrations of places do provide essential information for the semantic interpretation of indexical expressions like *here* and *there.* The implication is that semantic interpretation has access to perceptually provided information, which might be taken to suggest some unified level of mental representation where perceptual and semantic information are both available. Jackendoff (1983) has made this point and further argues that there is no need for purely semantic or purely perceptual levels. Whatever the eventual answer to such questions about the nature of cognition and mental representation, indexicals demonstrate unequivocally that understanding involves not just linguistic processing but depends as well on such other cognitive faculties as perception.

Times and locations are, of course, not the only components of context relevant to interpretation of linguistic expressions. Some central instances of indexicals involve components of speech events as such. For example the speaker or illocutionary agent is referred to by *I* and the addressee by *you*. Why not simply add additional coordinates for speakers and for addresses?

There is no barrier in principle to continuing to add coordinates. In the happy phrase of Lewis (1979), coordinates "keep score in the language game." We can think of a scoreboard with slots reserved for contextually relevant factors. As the game of discourse proceeds, the values in the slots may change. At any stage where words like *I* and *here* are used, their value can be determined by checking the appropriate scoreboard slots, in this case the speaker slot and the discourse location slot.

We can illustrate these general ideas either by expanding IPC or by considering a larger fragment of English. Let us do the latter by expanding F_3 to include *I* as a new constant of category N. We now need a richer notion of models for F_3:

(10) A model M for F_3 is a sextuple of the form $\langle W, I, <, S, U, V \rangle$, where

a. $W, I, <, U$ are as before.

b. $S \subseteq U$ is a set of speakers.

c. V is a function that assigns to each constant α an intension of the right type, where intensions are now functions from $W \times I \times S$; in particular, for any $w \in W, i \in I$, and $s \in S$, $V(I)(\langle w, i, s \rangle) = s$.

The interpretation function $[\![\ ]\!]$ remains as before except that it too is now relativized to speakers. This means that we will recursively define $[\![\ ]\!]^{M,w,i,s,g}$ rather than $[\![\ ]\!]^{M,w,i,g}$. Let us illustrate by giving some of the key clauses in the definition of $[\![\ ]\!]^{M,w,i,s,g}$.

(11) *a.* If α is a basic constant, then $[\![\alpha]\!]^{M,w,i,s,g} = V(\alpha)(\langle w, i, s \rangle)$

b. If α is a trace or a pronoun, then $[\![\alpha]\!]^{M,w,i,s,g} = g(\alpha)$

c. $[\![[_S \text{ NP Pred}]]\!]^{M,w,i,s,g} = 1$ iff $[\![\text{NP}]\!]^{M,w,i,s,g} \in [\![\text{Pred}]\!]^{M,w,i,s,g}$.

This approach involves a different and more general notion of proposition than the one we used in the preceding chapter. All intensions are now functions from worlds, times, and speakers to extensions of the appropriate kind; thus a proposition is now a function from worlds, times, and speakers to truth values. Equivalently, a proposition can here be viewed as a set of relevant coordinates; the present generalization makes each such coordinate an ordered triple of a world, time, and speaker. Formally,

(12) $[\![\text{that S}]\!]^{M,w,i,s,g} = \{\langle w', i', s'\rangle : [\![\text{S}]\!]^{M,w',i',s',g} = 1\}$

Exercise 1 Assume that we have extended F_3 as in (10). Consider a model M_6 for this expanded F_3, where M_6 is just like M_5 in chapter 5, (40), except that (1) it includes the set of speakers $\{a, b\}$ in the fourth place and V_6 in the sixth place of the sextuple that constitutes the model, and (2) V_6 is different from V_5 only as much as is necessary to take account of the added relativization to agents. What are V_6(I), V_6(walk), V_6(Pavarotti), V_6(Bond), and V_6(Loren)? In lieu of a three-dimensional display, simply list values for V_6 at each of the 12 indices serving as its arguments.

This seems a quite straightforward extension of the techniques we have already become familiar with. Moreover, it is quite easy to see how we could go on in this way to deal with other aspects of context on which interpretation depends. For example, we could add to the model (and to the interpretation function) a set H of hearers or addresses to deal with *you*. For *here* and *there* we might add sets L_1 and L_2 of locations (more precisely, sequences of locations, since there is the possibility of changing locations or pointing at indefinitely many places within one context). And so on. While such an approach does not deal with all aspects of the context-dependency of language, it does provide a reasonable formal strategy for dealing with the contribution of context to the interpretation of indexicals. On the face of it, the multiple coordinate approach that simply adds coordinates seems to do what is needed. Its main immediately apparent problem is merely logistic: there seems to be no principled limitation to the stock of contextual coordinates that might prove relevant for interpretation of some linguistic expression or another.

A somewhat different approach to indexicality for which Stalnaker (1974) and Kaplan (1977) have argued is one that provides an additional stage of interpretation, another level of semantic value in addition to extensions and intensions. As a lead into their proposal, it is useful to consider how the speaker coordinate we have introduced in illustrating the multiple coordinate analysis of indexicals plays a different overall role from the world and time coordinates. Even at this early stage we can discern several such differences. Although we illustrate these differences by discussing the speaker coordinate s, exactly the same kinds of comments could be made about other purely contextual coordinates that might be introduced, like those for an addressee, a demonstrated location or locations, and so on. First, coordinates w and i play two different kinds of role in evaluating expressions, only the first of which seems to be paralleled by s and other purely contextual coordinates. On the one hand, w and i are explicitly relevant in the interpretation of the modal and temporal expressions: modal and temporal operators depend on the actual w and i. On the other hand, expressions in general have extensions that depend on worlds and times. An expression like *hungry*, for example, can have different extensions in a given world w at different instants i_1 and i_2 or in different worlds w_1 and w_2 at a given instant i. Perhaps Pavarotti and Loren are hungry in w at i_1, but no one is hungry in w at i_2. In contrast, the s coordinate seems to enter only into assigning values to the single form *I* (which includes, of course, the objective form *me* and the possessive *my*), whereas the extension of *hungry* and of other expressions is not tied to the s coordinate. This is what (13) says.

(13) If α is an expression that does not contain *I*, then for all s and s' in S, $[\![\alpha]\!]^{M,w,i,s,g} = [\![\alpha]\!]^{M,w,i,s',g}$

The second observation is that for a given s in S alternative values of w and i do not affect the value assigned as the interpretation of *I*; s is the only coordinate relevant for establishing the referent of *I*. It may seem odd to say that, relative to the speaker, *I* designates the same individual in all circumstances. Yet we can think of this as analogous to saying that the variable x_i designates the same individual in all circumstances relative to an assignment function g. The speaker coordinate is comparable to the assignment function in being independent of the differences in the world-time pairs that determine evaluation in the circumstances we speak of. Just like a variable expression, however, *I* has alternative values, namely, those assigned relative to alternative values of the speaker coordinate.

Third, notice that in the course of evaluating sentences, we often shift from one circumstances to another. For example, (14*a*) is true at $\langle w, i \rangle$ iff there is some i' prior to i such that (14*b*) is true at $\langle w, i' \rangle$.

(14) *a*. Pavarotti walked.
b. Pavarotti walks.

Furthermore, we generalize over circumstances by means of adverbs like *always* and *sometimes*. As far as contextual coordinates are concerned, we shift them in discourse (as, for example, speakers change) but we do not generalize over them: there is no *every I* or *some here* parallel to *always* or *sometimes*.

Differences such as these suggest that we might want to distinguish more sharply in our analysis between the context, which determines what is said, and the circumstances, which are the alternatives to be considered in determining whether whatever is said is true. The context gives information on who is speaking, what is being pointed at, and all the other factors relevant to interpretation of indexical expressions. Misinformation about the context can result in confusion about what is said; recall Bond's error in thinking that (3), "You are boring," was addressed to him, when in fact it was addressed to Pavarotti. But the substance of our talk is discriminating among circumstances. Unlike Bond, Pavarotti was correctly informed about the relevant context but differed from the speaker in what he took the circumstances to be.

Differentiating between context and circumstances allows us to say, for example, that, relative to a speaker, *I* designates the same individual (that speaker) in all circumstances. This is no different in principle from saying, as we do, that a variable x relative to an assignment g designates the same individual (namely $g(x)$) in all circumstances. For *I* this means that in evaluating a sentence like "I must be hungry" as uttered by Pavarotti, we really consider the proposition that Pavarotti is hungry in all the relevant circumstances (i.e., all the world-time pairs included in the modal base). We do not consider at all the values that "I must be hungry" has with respect to other possible speakers. Whether Bond, for example, is hungry is quite irrelevant to the value assigned to "I must be hungry" as uttered by Pavarotti. The fact that it might be Bond, rather than Pavarotti, who is speaking in some situation we consider is also not relevant to assigning a semantic value to "I must be hungry" in view of our initial focus on a context in which Pavarotti is taken as the speaker. Similar comments apply to "I was hungry" as uttered by Pavarotti; Bond's hunger at earlier times will not be relevant to evaluating this sentence. In other words, we want to hold the effects of the context on the assignment of interpretations to indexicals constant while considering alternative circumstances (in evaluating a modal or past tense, for example). This holds not just for *I* but also for *here, you, this*, and so on. The circumstances of evaluation—the sets of worlds that belong to the modal base in the case of a sentence with a modal auxiliary or the past times relevant for evaluating a past tense sentence—seem to play no role in the interpretation of context-dependent indexical expressions. There are minor exceptions with a joking or slightly paradoxical quality to them: "Tomorrow is always a day away."

Essentially the same point can be made in a slightly different way (also due to Kaplan and Stalnaker). The most natural way to interpret a complex index $\langle w, i, s\rangle$ is that s is speaking in world w at time i. This would have the result that for any M, w, i, s and g,

(15) $[\![\text{I}]\!]^{M,w,i,s,g} = [\![\text{the speaker}]\!]^{M,w,i,s,g}$

But then how could we explain the fact that the sentences in (16) are not synonymous? Sentence (16*a*) is perfectly coherent and contingent, but (16*b*) has a contradictory antecedent.

(16) *a.* If I were not the speaker, Joan would be talking.
b. If the speaker were not the speaker, Joan would be talking.

To make the same point more dramatically, treating *I* as synonymous with *the* (*present*) *speaker* would lead one to say that (17) is necessarily true.

(17) If the present speaker were now silent, there would be no present speaker, and thus I would not exist.

As Kaplan (1977, 44), puts it, "Beliefs such as [that expressed in (17)] could make one a compulsive talker."

The multiple coordinate approach must in fact give up the natural interpretation of complex indices and not require that s be speaking in w at i for $\langle w, i, s\rangle$ to be a well-formed index, so as to allow someone to speak about circumstances in which she is not speaking (or perhaps is absent altogether). The crucial point here is that in evaluating sentences, we sometimes need to consider circumstances that differ from the context that has provided the interpretation of the indexical expressions, and at the same time we need to hold constant the contextually determined interpretation of those indexical expressions. A possible world may lack speakers altogether, for example. Yet to interpret a sentence ϕ relative to some speaker s is to take s as a speaker producing ϕ, and this connection between s and ϕ is not captured by the multiple coordinate account of indexicality.

Such difficulties can be resolved if we treat the contextual elements as intrinsically connected to one another, as coherent in being aspects of some single situation or state of affairs but as potentially independent of the elements comprising the circumstances (which so far consist of just worlds and times but also potentially include elements like spatial locations that situate content more locally). In other words, contexts and circumstances can be treated as distinct components relative to which we define truth conditions, each of them further articulated into interrelated elements. Circumstantial coordinates can shift independently of one another, whereas contextual components are tied together by the utterance situation to which they belong.

One way of implementing this idea is to view semantic interpretation as proceeding in two stages. First we relativize interpretation to contexts, assigning each expression a function that determines for a given context an intensional value of the kind we discussed in the preceding chapter. Then, just as before, intensions will assign an extensional value of the appropriate type relative to each circumstance. For sentences we follow Stalnaker (1978) in calling the function from contexts to propositions a *propositional concept.* More generally, we also adopt the terminology of Kaplan (1977) and refer to the *character* of an expression as what is assigned at the first stage of interpretation, the relativization of intensions to contexts.

Frege saw that meaning involved both sense and reference. We can think of the Kaplan-Stalnaker approach as proposing that sense itself is further articulated and involves not only intension but also a propositional concept or more generally the character of an expression. An expression's character is what specifies the systematic contribution of a context of utterance to the interpretation of that expression. A similar idea based on Kaplan's work is being developed in situation semantics, where a sentence interacts with an utterance situation, roughly what we are calling a context, to determine an expressed proposition that represents a described situation. We turn now to a more detailed account of character and the notion of pragmatic validity that it permits us to define.

2.2 Expression character: mapping contexts to intensions

We define intensions as functions from circumstances, world-time pairs, to extensions, thus generalizing the referential notion of extension. Similarly, we can define expression characters as functions from contexts to intensions, thus generalizing the context-independent notion of intensions.

One way to accomplish this generalization is simply to treat contextual and circumstantial coordinates as two independent but essentially similar indices or dimensions, one representing possible worlds in their role as contexts and the other representing possible worlds in their role as circumstances. For our present purposes we can accomplish what is needed by including one further contextual coordinate c (for *context*) in our models; this added contextual coordinate in turn is articulated into distinct aspects as needed. The various aspects of contexts can be thought of as functions mapping each context c onto an appropriate range. Speakers are individual entities, and thus a speaker function sp maps each context c onto $\mathrm{sp}(c) \in U$, the speaker in c. An addressee function adr will map c onto $\mathrm{adr}(c) \in U$, the addressee in c. Similarly, a loc_n function (to interpret *here*) can map c onto $\mathrm{loc}_n(c)$, the nth location of c, and demloc_n function (to interpret *there*) can map c onto $\mathrm{demloc}_n(c)$, the nth demonstrated location of c, and so on. In chapter 5 we discussed modals and argued, following Kratzer, that they involved a contextually specified modal base and an ordering source. There we let the assignment function g determine modal bases and ordering sources. In our view of contexts a more adequate treatment is to regard them as contextual function mdb and ordsrc that map each context c onto the relevant sets of propositions: $\mathrm{mdb}(c)$ and $\mathrm{ordsrc}(c)$. In fact, since pronouns have deictic uses, the assignment function g should perhaps be recast as a component of the context, but we will refrain from doing so here. These ideas are very similar to the way context is treated in Cresswell (1973) and Bennett (1978).

To illustrate how this approach works let us replace (10) above by something like the following:

(18) A model M for F_3 is a sextuple of the form $\langle W, I, <, C, U, V \rangle$, where the following conditions hold.

a. W is a set of worlds.

b. I is a set of instants ordered by $<$.

c. U is the domain of quantification.

d. C is a set of contexts.

e. V is a function that assigns to the constants of F_3 an appropriate character. That is, for any constant α, $V(\alpha)$ is a function from C to a function from $W \times I$ to an extension of the appropriate kind. So $V(\alpha)(c)$ is the intension that α has in the context c, and $V(\alpha)(c)(\langle w, i\rangle)$ is the extension that α has relative to c in $\langle w, i\rangle$.

Thus according to (18), if α is a proper name, $V(\alpha)$ is a function such that for any c, $V(\alpha)(c)$ is the intention of α relative to c. Since α is a proper name, its intension will be a constant function from $W \times I$ (circumstances) to a member of U. Similarly, if α is a V_i or a Nom, then $V(\alpha)(c)$ is a function from $W \times I$ to sets of individuals ($\mathcal{P}(U)$), and if α is a V_t, then $V(\alpha)(c)$ is a function from $W \times I$ to sets of ordered pairs of individuals, and so on.

Exercise 2 Give the values of V(and) and V(not).

When we add *I*, *you*, *here*, and *there* to F_3, we will want to specify their characters along the following lines (ignoring for the present the fact that we do not have an appropriate syntactic category in F_3 for the locative adverbials *here$_n$* and *there$_n$*):

(19) For any c,

a. $V(I)(c)$ is a function such that for any w and any i, $V(I)(c)(\langle w, i\rangle) = \mathrm{sp}(c)$,

b. $V(\mathrm{you})(c)$ is a function such that for any w and any i, $V(\mathrm{you})(c)(\langle w, i\rangle) = \mathrm{adr}(c)$,

c. $V(\mathrm{here}_n)(c)$ is a function such that for any w and any i, $V(\mathrm{here}_n)(c)(\langle w, i\rangle) = \mathrm{loc}_n(c)$,

d. $V(\mathrm{there}_n)(c)$ is a function such that for any w and any i, $V(\mathrm{there}_n)(c)(\langle w, i\rangle) = \mathrm{demloc}_n(c)$.

Now we can proceed to define the interpretation function $[\![\ ]\!]^{M,w,i,c,g}$, which assigns an extension to each expression. We give only some of the key clauses of the recursion.

(20) a. If α is a constant, $[\![\alpha]\!]^{M,w,i,c,g} = V(\alpha)(c)(\langle w, i\rangle)$.

b. If α is a trace or pronoun, $[\![\alpha]\!]^{M,w,i,c,g} = g(\alpha)$.

c. If $\Delta = [\mathrm{NP\ Pred}]$, then $[\![\Delta]\!]^{M,w,i,c,g} = 1$ iff $[\![\mathrm{NP}]\!]^{M,w,i,c,g} \in [\![\mathrm{Pred}]\!]^{M,w,i,c,g}$.

d. If $\Delta = [\mathrm{S}_1 \text{ conj } \mathrm{S}_2]$, then $[\![\Delta]\!]^{M,w,i,c,g} = V(\mathrm{conj})(c)(\langle w, i\rangle)(\langle [\![\mathrm{S}_1]\!]^{M,w,i,c,g}, [\![\mathrm{S}_2]\!]^{M,w,i,c,g}\rangle)$.

e. If $\Delta = [\text{that S}]$, then $[\![\Delta]\!]^{M,w,i,c,g} = \{\langle w', i' \rangle : [\![\text{S}]\!]^{M,w',i',c,g}\}$.
f. If $\Delta = [\text{must S}]$, then $[\![\Delta]\!]^{M,w,i,c,g} = 1$ iff *for all* $\langle w', i' \rangle$ in $\text{mdb}(c)$, $[\![\text{S}]\!]^{M,w',i',c,g} = 1$.

Note that we once again maintain that propositions are sets of world-time pairs, just as in the preceding chapter.

Exercise 3 Assume that we have extended F_3 as in (20). Consider a model, M_7, like M_6 of exercise 1 in this chapter except that it includes a set of contexts $C = \{c', c''\}$ such that $\text{sp}(c') = a$ and $\text{sp}(c'') = b$ in its fourth place. Assume that V_7 and V_6 are different only as much as is necessary to take account of the changes in (18) to (20). Give the values of $V_7(\text{walk})$, $[\![\text{that Pavarotti walks}]\!]^{M_7,w',i',c',g}$, $[\![\text{that Pavarotti walks}]\!]^{M_7,w',i',c'',g}$, $[\![\text{that I walk}]\!]^{M_7,w',i',c',g}$, and $[\![\text{that I walk}]\!]^{M_7,w',i',c'',g}$.

On the basis of (20), three semantic levels can be individuated. First, interpretation (at least of sentences containing indexicals) is sensitive to context. Without contextual information as to its utterer, we cannot fully interpret a sentence like "I am hungry," sentence (1). Having fixed the utterer, we can then determine the intension of the sentence. For example, if (1) is uttered by Pavarotti, the contextually assigned intension of the sentence will be the set of worlds and times where Pavarotti is hungry. This is what (20*e*) gives us. Finally, on the basis of the intension, which represents the content or subject matter of the sentence, the truth value of the sentence is determined from a specification of the world(s) and time(s) being talked about.

So defining truth in terms of the recursion in (20), we must relativize our definition of truth for a sentence to a context (as well as to an LF that disambiguates it).

(21) *a.* A sentence S is *true* in a model M and a circumstance w, i relative to one of its LFs α and to a context c iff for every assignment g, $[\![\alpha]\!]^{M,w,i,c,g} = 1$. It is false iff for every g, $[\![\alpha]\!]^{M,w,i,c,g} = 0$.
b. A sentence S is *valid* relative to one of its LFs α iff for every model $M = \langle W, I, <, C, U, V \rangle$, $c \in C$, $w \in W$, and $i \in I$, S is true in M, w, i relative to α and c.
c. A sentence S relative to LF α *entails* a sentence S′ relative to LF β iff for every model $M = \langle W, I, <, C, U, V \rangle$, $c \in C$,

$w \in W$, and $i \in I$, if S is true in M, w, i relative to α and c, then S′ is true in M, w, i relative to β and c.

This approach helps us solve some of the problems we have pointed out above in connection with the multiple coordinate analysis. Consider, for example, the following inference from Bennett (1978):

(22) *a.* Loren believes that Pavarotti is hungry.
b. I am Pavarotti.
c. Loren believes that I am hungry.

Only if Pavarotti is the speaker can (22*b*) be true, and our semantics should reflect that (22*c*) is a valid inference from (22*a*, *b*) only with Pavarotti as speaker. This result will not follow from the approach we discussed in section 2.1. According to (10) through (12), $[\![\text{that Pavarotti is hungry}]\!]^{M,w,i,\text{Pavarotti},g} = \{\langle w', i', s'\rangle : \text{Pavarotti} \in [\![\text{hungry}]\!]^{M,w',i',s',g}\}$ and $[\![\text{that I am hungry}]\!]^{M,w,i,\text{Pavarotti},g} = \{\langle w', i', s'\rangle : s' \in [\![\text{hungry}]\!]^{M',w',i',s',g}\}$. But clearly these are in general different sets, and thus Loren might believe that proposition characterized by one of them without believing the other.

Exercise 4 Describe a model M where for some w, i, s and g, $[\![\text{that Pavarotti is hungry}]\!]^{M,w,i,s,g} \neq [\![\text{that I am hungry}]\!]^{M,w,i,s,g}$.

On the other hand, definition (20*e*) and the revised notions of truth and validity in (21) give a different result. Any c' such that (22*b*) is true is one in which $\text{sp}(c') = \text{Pavarotti}$. For all w and i, $[\![\text{that I am hungry}]\!]^{M,w,i,c',g} = [\![\text{that Pavarotti is hungry}]\!]^{M,w,i,c',g}$, and thus relative to c', if Loren believes one proposition, she also believes the other. Hence our revised semantics does capture the fact that (22) is valid relative to contexts where Pavarotti is the speaker.

What we have said so far about the context and character levels of semantic interpretation is not really enough, however, to resolve all the puzzles raised for the multiple coordinate approach. We have not yet made explicit the relation between sp(c) and any linguistic expression spoken by sp(c) in c. Nor have we specified the relationship between the various aspects of context. In (23) we suggest some more that might be said about well-formed contexts and admissible interpretations. Just to keep things simple, we will forget that speakers can change locations during an utterance and assume that we simply have loc(c) to provide a value for *here.* We also will take sentential expressions as paradigmatic utterances. We present in (23) a few more contextual functions and samples of the kind of constraints that a semantic-pragmatic theory might place on them.

(23) *a.* The function expr assigns expr(c) to each context c, where expr(c) can be thought of as the sentence uttered in c.
b. The functions tm and wrld assign tm(c) and wrld(c) to each context c, where tm(c) $\in I$ and wrld(c) $\in W$ are the time and world of context c.
c. For all $c \in C$, sp(c) is at loc(c) and is the illocutionary agent responsible for directing an utterance of expr(c) to adr(c) at tm(c) in wrld(c).

With an account of contexts along the lines sketched in (23), we are able to say something about sentences like those in (24).

(24) *a.* I am here.
b. I am speaking to you.

Such sentences have sometimes been said to be pragmatically valid because they are true whenever uttered (we need a few caveats about the possibility of using *here* accompanied by a pointing toward a map, and other such complications). Consider (24*a*), for example. Given (23*b*, *c*), we can conclude that for all c in C, $[\![\text{I am here}]\!]^{M,\text{wrld}(c),\text{tm}(c),c,g} = 1$. We can exploit this observation to define a new notion of pragmatic validity.

(25) S is *pragmatically valid* relative to LF α iff for all models M and contexts c, S is true in M at wrld(c) and tm(c) relative to α and c.

From this definition and our definition of necessity (20*f*) it follows that (24*a*), while being pragmatically valid, is not a necessary truth. Pragmatic validity looks at every possible context. Necessary truth keeps the context fixed and looks at every possible world. We can thus predict, for example, that (26) is satisfiable.

(26) I am here now, but I might be somewhere else.

Unlike the multiple coordinate approach to indexicals, our current account of the context dependence of interpretation permits us to say precisely what is special about pragmatically valid sentences without forcing us to treat them as necessarily true with the absur-

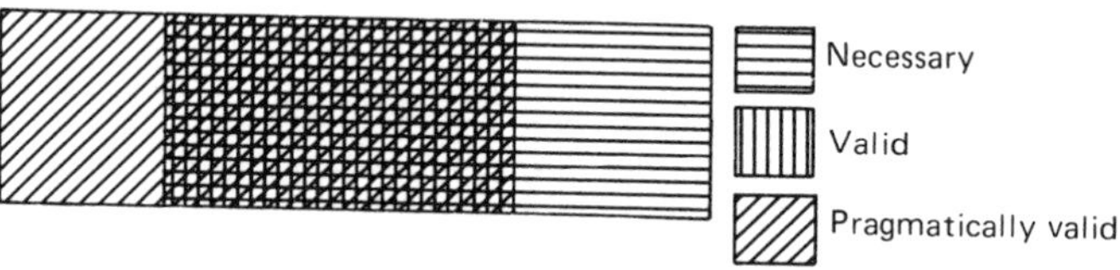

Figure 6.1

dities that would entail. (Recall our discussion of (16) and (17), where we wanted to consider circumstances in which the current speaker was silent.) Thus, on the basis of definitions (20*f*), (21*b*), and (25), we obtain the following classification of sentences:

- If a sentence S is valid, then it is necessarily true.
- A sentence can be necessarily true in a model *M* relative to a context *c* without being valid. (Such a sentence would be true relative to *M* and *c* in all the worlds of *M* but not true relative to some other model M' and context c'.)
- If a sentence is valid with respect to LF α, it is also pragmatically valid.
- Some sentences are pragmatically valid without being valid (or necessary) relative to some *c*.

The sentences in (24) are an example of the latter case. This is summarized in figure 6.1.

In the remainder of this section we discuss further aspects of the notion of a context as characterized by the semantics just given. More specifically, we point to semantic problems that can be explained in terms of the notion of character, a function from contexts to intensions.

How is indexicality to be distinguished from ambiguity such as that created by the association of multiple LFs with a single S? The borderline between the two phenomena may not always seen clear. The propositions associated with, for example, "I am hungry" and "Every man loves a woman" vary across different occasions of utterance. It seems reasonable to maintain, however, that "I am hungry" is unambiguous, that it has the same meaning on all occasions of use even though it may express different propositions on those different occasions. On the approach to context developed here, we can pinpoint its semantic constancy in the fact that its character is fixed by *V* and the rules of semantic composition, in the fact that its character is completely determined by the grammar of F_3 as expanded. In contrast, the rules of the language system do not specify which of its LFs a sentence like "Every woman loves some man" is associated with in a given utterance context. No linguistic rules settle this issue. The utterance situation does enter in assigning a proposition to both "I am hungry" and "Every man loves a woman." In the first case, semantic value is assigned relative to a linguistically specified contextual parameter: context in the technical sense supplies what is needed semantically. In the second case, two quite distinct characters are assigned to the sentence, one for each LF. The choice between them is often said to be presemantic, and it has nothing to do with context in our special sense, though, of course, it is tied to features of the world in which the utterance occurred, e.g., the speaker's intentions.

The notion of character also helps in understanding an important factor of cognitive significance that a sentence like (1), "I am hungry," retains throughout its different uses (a factor pointed out by Kaplan and Stalnaker).[5] We can put the like this: although Bond and Pavarotti express different propositions in uttering (1), the fact that those propositions are expressible by the same linguistic means reflects something similar in Bond's and Pavarotti's relation to the distinct propositions they have expressed. This is supported by the following example.

(27) *Bond*: I am hungry.
Pavarotti: I just said the same thing.

There is clearly a sense in which Pavarotti speaks truly if what he uttered is something like "I am hungry" or "I feel the need for some food" or even, using his native Italian, "Ho fame." In the case at hand, Bond and Pavarotti have not expressed the same proposition. Yet there is a sense in which they have said the same thing. For saying the same thing, identity of linguistic form is neither necessary or sufficient. Nor is identity of propositional content. What seems to be required is identity of character.

Contrast dialogue (27) with dialogue (28). Here what matters is propositional content rather than character.

(28) *Bond*: I am hungry.
Pavarotti: I thought so.

In this discourse Pavarotti speaks truly if what he thought was that Bond was hungry. He does *not* speak truly if his thoughts had nothing to do with Bond's hungry but only with his own hunger. (To express the proposition that he had been thinking of his own hunger, Pavarotti might respond "I was just thinking the same thing.")

Both character (which reflects the contextual perspective from which a thought is expressed) and the thought or propositional content are taken into account in what speakers are taken to be implying by their utterances. A further illustration of this is the following. It has been noted that there are few if any actually occurring contexts in which sentences like (29*a*, *b*) will be used.

(29) *a.* You feel a sinking sensation in the pit of your stomach.
b. Do I feel a sinking sensation and the pit of my stomach?
c. Joan feels a sinking sensation in the pit of her stomach.
d. Does Joan feel a sinking sensation in the pit of her stomach?

If usage were simply a matter of propositional content and did not also involve character, it would be difficult to see why sentences (29*c*, *d*) differ from sentences (29*a*, *b*) as to their utility.

In sum, there is considerable evidence to support the view that there is a level of meaning, character, that specifies the linguistically determined contribution of context to interpretation. The basic idea is that semantic competence includes knowledge of contextual functions, of how to use the context to assign interpretations. Presumably, part of what speakers learn about *this* is what aspects of context determine its reference: what *this* refers to in a context depends on a demonstration in that context (though precisely what is needed for an object to have been demonstrated raises difficult issues), and speakers know that they must search the context for such an event if they are to determine exactly what proposition has been expressed. Interpretation is incomplete if no such demonstration can be found.

We have hardly scratched the surface of the dependence of what is said on context. The major point we want to make here is that it is possible to use exactly the same kinds of mechanisms for accommodating indexicality that we used for introducing intensional notions. Just as we relativized extensional values of expressions to possible circumstances, so we can relativize intensions of expressions to appropriate contexts by introducing the more abstract notion of character.

A model of the kind introduced in (18) formally represents the two different ways in which a situation or state of affairs can contribute to determining the truth of a sentence uttered in it. (1) Aspects of the situation may fix interpretation of certain expressions to determine the thought or proposition the sentence expresses. The contextual coordinate c plays this interpretation-fixing role. (2) Whether the proposition expressed is true in the utterance situation depends on how things are, on the facts of that situation. The circumstantial coordinates $\langle w, i \rangle$ play this truth-evaluating role.

Contexts not only determine what is said. As we suggested informally in chapter 4, they also play an important role in elucidating the locutionary force associated with sentential meaning. With the more elaborate notion of context now available to us, we can begin to develop more precisely the discourse-theoretic or dynamic view of sentential semantics. This dynamic approach proves very useful in analyzing presupposition, to which we now turn.

3 Presuppositions and Contexts

What is presupposition? In our earlier informal discussion of presupposition we said that (an utterance of) a sentence S presupposes a proposition p if (the utterance of) S implies p and further implies that p is somehow already part of the background against which S is considered, that considering S at all involves taking p for granted. For example, (30*a*) presupposes (30*b*); (30*a*) implies that (30*b*) is taken for granted.

(30) *a.* Joan has stopped drinking wine for breakfast.
b. Joan used to drink wine for breakfast.

We are now able to make more precise this intuitive notion of presupposition. The rough idea is that the presuppositions of a sentence S constrain or limit the class of contexts C relative to which S can be felicitously uttered. Presuppositions of S must be satisfied by a context c in order for S to be *assertible*, for an utterance of S to be *felicitous.* Before elaborating these ideas, however, we want to make a few preliminary comments to set the stage.

3.1 Empirical tests and typologies

In the present section we want mainly to do two things: characterize presuppositions more sharply with respect to other forms of implications and identify the sort of facts a theory of presuppositions should account for.

For our present purposes the main empirical characteristics of presuppositions can be taken to be the following two: being backgrounded and being taken for granted. Let us consider them in turn.

In our previous discussion we took a sentence S to presuppose *p* just in case *p* was implied by S in the following family of sentences:

(31) *a.* S.
b. It is not the case that S.
c. Is it the case that S?
d. If S, then S′.

Thus, for example, for sentence (30*a*) the relevant P family is given in (32); each of these sentences does seem to imply (30*b*).

(32) *a.* Joan has stopped drinking wine for breakfast.
b. It is not the case that Joan has stopped drinking wine for breakfast.
c. Joan hasn't stopped drinking wine for breakfast.
d. Is it the case that Joan has stopped drinking wine for breakfast?
e. Has Joan stopped drinking wine for breakfast?
f. If Joan has stopped drinking wine for breakfast, she has probably begun to drink more at lunch.

What the P family test essentially tests for is backgroundedness of implications: it marks out implications that are attached to S not only when it is asserted but also when it is denied, questioned, or offered as a hypothetical assumption. Typically, if S implies that *p* is in the background, then someone who responds to an assertion of S with "I don't think so" or "Well, I wonder" or "Perhaps" does not thereby weaken or threaten the implication that *p*.

In contrast, nonbackgrounded implications of a sentence vanish unless the sentence is asserted and thus do not pass the P family test. For example, note the implication from (33*a*) to (33*b*) and that from (34*a*) to (34*b*).

(33) *a.* Lee kissed Jenny.
b. Lee touched Jenny.

(34) *a.* Mary has a child.
b. Mary has exactly one child.

The (*b*) implication is an entailment in (33) and a conversational implicature in (34). In each case the implication vanishes in members of the P family other than the affirmative or if the assertion of S is directly challenged by "I don't think so" or met with other reservations. The implied (*b*) propositions are neither backgrounded nor taken for granted by utterances of the implying (*a*) sentences.

Backgroundedness does not suffice, however, to identify presuppositions. Some implications seem to pass the tests for being backgrounded—they survive as implications throughout the P family—but are not presupposed. A case in point is that of nonrestrictive relative clauses (sometimes called appositive or parenthetical relative clauses). Consider, for example, (35*a*) and its implication family (35*b–d*). Each of (35*a–d*) implies (35*e*), the content of the relative clause. Yet (35*e*) is not presupposed.

(35) *a.* Jill, who lost something on the flight from Ithaca to New York, likes to travel by train.
b. Jill, who lost something on the flight from Ithaca to New York, doesn't like to travel by train.
c. Does Jill, who lost something on the flight from Ithaca to New York, like to travel by train?
d. If Jill, who lost something on the flight from Ithaca to New York, likes to travel by train, she probably flies infrequently.
e. Jill lost something on the flight from Ithaca to New York.

The proposition that Jill lost something on the flight from Ithaca to New York, expressed in (35*e*), is a backgrounded component of what is being asserted, not of what is being presupposed. In other words, in the sentences in (35) we articulate our assertions in two major parts: a main assertion in the foreground and a secondary one in the background. To see this more vividly, compare (35*a*) with (36), where the same proposition is presupposed.

(36) What Jill lost on the flight from Ithaca to New York was her new flute.

What sort of discourse might be required for uttering (35*a*) rather than (36)? Suppose someone starts a conversation with (37).

(37) Let me tell you about Jill Jensen, a woman I met while flying from Ithaca to New York last week.

Clearly such a beginning does not suppose any already existing information about Jill and, more specifically, does not establish that Jill lost something on the flight from Ithaca to New York. In such a context (35*a*), which contains the information that Jill lost something in a nonrestrictive relative clause, seems a perfectly fine thing to say next, whereas (36), a pseudo-cleft that presupposes that information, is quite bizarre. If (37) were followed by (38), which explicitly states that Jill lost something, then the pseudo-cleft (36) could easily come next.

(38) She lost something on the trip.

The difference seems to be that uttering (36) is infelicitous when the backgrounded proposition is not already established, whereas no such constraints are placed on uttering (35*a*).

What emerges from this discussion is the following. The hallmark of a presupposition is that it is taken for granted in the sense that its assumed truth is a precondition for felicitous utterance of the sentence and places a kind of constraint on discourse contexts that admit the sentence for interpretation. The P family provides a good way to test the presuppositional status of implications because a proposition cannot be presented as already assumed and simultaneously be presented as denied or hypothesized or queried. Failing the P family test is excellent evidence that an implied proposition is not presupposed but asserted. The P family test does not definitively identify presuppositions, because background status of an implied proposition is compatible with its being presented as not already assumed. If there is no suggestion of infelicity in using S in a discourse where *p* is clearly not taken to be part of the common ground, then S does not presuppose *p* even if *p* is backgrounded by S (as in the case of nonrestrictive relative clauses).

What a sentence conveys or implies can be classified not only in terms of its role in discourse (as we just did) but also in terms of how that implication comes about or how it is licensed. From the latter point of view we can distinguish between what depends strictly on truth conditions (entailments) and what depends on the interaction of truth conditions with something else. The latter kind of implications are Gricean implicatures.

As the reader will recall, Grice distinguished between conventional and conversational implicatures. Conventional implicatures have to do with aspects of meaning that do not seem to be strictly truth-conditional in nature. Consider, for example, the sentences in (39).

(39) *a.* Jim went to the store and bought nothing.
b. Jim went to the store but bought nothing.

It would appear that (39*a*) and (39*b*) are true in exactly the same situations. However, (39*b*) suggests something that (39*a*) does not.

It suggests that the speaker perceives a contrast between going to the store and buying nothing. Intuitively, this suggested contrast is conventionally conveyed by *but.* Considerations of this sort led Grice to regard the contrastive character of *but* as a "conventional implicature," an implication that is conventional in nature but not determinable by truth-conditional content as such. (In the final section of this chapter we suggest that perhaps conventional implications do make a contribution to truth conditions of a special context-dependent kind that reflects only the speaker's attitudes in a way analogous to certain uses of modals.)

The contrastive character of *but* does affect the felicity of an utterance containing it. Thus, for example, on standard assumptions about why people go to stores, (39*b*) would be taken to be perfectly felicitous and probably a more likely report, because more informative, than the neutral (39*a*). On these standard assumptions, replacing *nothing* with *something* in (39*b*) yields a sentence infelicitous in most contexts. However, if Jim has a compulsion to go to the store without ever buying anything (he prides himself on not buying anything) we might have contexts in which uttering (39*b*) is infelicitous and yet its twin with *something* replacing *nothing* could be uttered felicitously. Although the implication of a contrast is conventional, what is contrasted may vary from context to context.[6]

Furthermore, the contrastive nature of *but* appears to be backgrounded in general. For example, the sentence "If Jim went to the store but bought nothing, we are in trouble" seems to require for its felicitous utterance the same type of contrast as "Jim went to the store but bought nothing." Furthermore, the suggested contrast seems to be taken for granted. These considerations suggest that the conventional implicature associated with *but* is a presupposition. In fact, all Grice's examples of conventional implicatures seem to be presupposed, as Karttunen and Peters (1979) pointed out.

Conversational implicatures, on the other hand, depend on conversational dynamics. Thus, for example, implicatures such as the one in (34), repeated here, seem to follow naturally from the Gricean maxim of quantity.

(34) *a.* Mary has a child.
b. Mary has exactly one child.

A hearer will tend to infer (34*b*) upon hearing (34*a*) on the assumption that the speaker is being cooperative in conveying all the relevant information she has. As discussed above, (34*b*) is not presupposed. Some conversational implicatures, however, are presupposed. In other words, some presuppositions appear to be triggered by principles that guide conversational exchanges. This has been argued, for example, in connection with the presuppositions associated with factive verbs, like *discover*.[7] Thus, the P family tests and intuitive judgments of being taken for granted show that (40*a*) presupposes (40*b*). However, the contrast between (40*c*) and (40*d*) suggests that the presupposition is due not so much to an intrinsic property of *discover* (beyond its contribution to truth conditions) but to principles of conversation.

(40) *a.* Jim discovered that Bill is in New York.
b. Bill is in New York.
c. If Jim discovers that Bill is in New York, there will be trouble.
d. If I discover that Bill is in New York, there will be trouble.

The point is that (40*c*) can be taken to implicate or presuppose (40*b*), but (40*d*) cannot. If the implication to (40*b*) arises from the conventional meaning of *discover* in the case of (40*c*), it is hard to see why that implication should be absent in the case of (40*d*). On the other hand, if we assume that the implication to (40*b*) is conversationally triggered, an account for this could go roughly as follows. *Discover* is a factive, which is to say that if x discovers p, p must be the case. A speaker who has reason to doubt that Bill is in New York typically has no reason to conjecture what would happen if someone discovered it. Hence, asserting (40*c*) will lead the hearer to infer (40*b*), on the assumption that the speaker is being cooperative. But by the same token, if the speaker knew Bill's whereabouts, she would have discovered whether Bill is in New York or not and hence would have no reason to utter (40*d*), which implies that it is an open question whether she will discover that Bill is in New York. So again on the assumption that the speaker is being cooperative, (40*d*) does not license inferring (40*b*). And indeed, the implicature from (40*c*) to (40*b*) is defeasible. Suppose that the conversationalists know that Jim is investigating Bill's whereabouts but do not know what the outcome is. In such a context it would be perfectly appropriate to utter (40*c*) and speculate on the results of a particular outcome of Jim's inquiry, yet there would be no implication that (40*b*) is true. We will return to this sort of example below.

To summarize, we have classified what a sentence conveys along two dimensions. The first is the role in discourse of its different components, the basis of the distinction between what is presupposed and what is asserted. The second is how the different components of what is conveyed are licensed. On this dimension, we have distinguished entailments (licensed by truth conditions alone) from implicatures (licensed by the interplay of truth conditions with additional conventions or conversational principles). This leads us to the following classification:

(41) *a.* *A* entails *B* (if *A* is true, *B* is true).
b. *A* presupposes *B* (*B* is backgrounded and taken for granted by *A*).
c. *A* conventionally or conversationally implicates *B* (*B* follows from the interaction of the truth conditions of *A* together with either linguistic conventions on the proper use of *A* or general principles of conversational exchange).

This, in turn, gives us the following possibilities.

3.1.1 Entailment versus presupposition A sentence can entail another sentence without presupposing it. Example (33), repeated here, provides us with an illustration.

(33) *a.* Lee kissed Jenny.
b. Lee touched Jenny.

The implication of (33*b*) does not survive in the P family contexts and hence is neither backgrounded nor taken for granted by (33*a*).

A sentence can both entail and presuppose another sentence, as the former notion is based on how an implication is licensed, while the latter is based on its discourse status. Thus (42*a*) both entails and presupposes (42*b*).

(42) *a.* Joan realizes that syntax deals with sentence structure.
b. Syntax deals with sentence structure.

If (42*a*) is true, then (42*b*) is true; at the same time (42*b*) is backgrounded and taken for granted by (42*a*) (note the survival of the implication in P family contexts).

On the definition of entailment that we have so far, a sentence can presuppose another sentence without entailing it. For example, sentence (43*a*) presupposes but does not entail (43*b*).

(43) *a.* If Bill discovers that syntax is easy, he will be delighted.
b. Syntax is easy.

Sentence (43*a*) seems generally to need (43*b*) for felicity. Hence (43*a*) presupposes (43*b*). But in special circumstances this presupposition can be canceled (for instance, if the context makes it clear that the speaker doesn't know whether syntax is easy; see the discussion of (40)). So on the definition of entailment we have so far, (43*a*) does not entail (43*b*), for there are circumstances where (43*a*) is true but (43*b*) needn't be.

In sections 3.2 and 4 we will develop and modify this position. Our strategy involves viewing the presuppositions of a sentence as entailed contextually whenever the sentence is assertible. We could then revise the notion of entailment in such a way that a sentence does indeed entail its presuppositions in this special sense.

3.1.2 Presupposition versus implicature Sentence *A* may presuppose sentence *B* by means of a convention associated with the meaning of *A* or by means of conversational dynamics. In the former case it will be a conventional implicature; in the latter a conversational one. An example of a presupposition that is a conventional implicature is the one associated with *but* (see the discussion of (39)). Some other words and constructions with presuppositions that appear to be conventional in nature are *even, manage*, cleft constructions, and pseudo-cleft constructions. An example of a presupposition that is also a conversational implicature is the one associated with *discover* (see the discussion of (40)).

A sentence can conversationally implicate another sentence without presupposing it. Example are provided by implicatures like the one in (34), repeated here:

(34) *a.* Mary has a child.
b. Mary has exactly one child.

Sentence (34*b*) follows from (34*a*) by conversational principles, but the latter is not backgrounded; (34*b*) is not a felicity condition for uttering (34*a*). On the other hand, perhaps all conventional implicatures are also presupposed.

There are many more interesting and important issues related to various forms of implication that we are unable to address here. The literature on the topic includes a wide range of typologies and terminological uses, and we had to make some choices as to which to follow. We have tried to come up with some criteria that are as far as possible sharp and suitable to our present purposes, which are those of isolating presuppositions from other implications and discussing some of their properties. We do not claim, however, to have provided a completely problem-free classification of types of implications.

We now turn to a consideration of what sort of empirical tasks a formal theory of presupposition faces. A theory that gives formal structure to the notion of being taken for granted should help us address two main questions: how is a presupposition *triggered* (introduced) and how is it *projected* (associated with larger structures embedding the smallest clause containing its trigger)?

To ask about triggers is to ask about how presuppositions are introduced into sentences (or utterances thereof). As we just saw, presuppositions can be triggered in one of two ways: conventionally or by conversational maxims. What is interesting for our present purposes is that whether a presupposition is triggered conversationally or conventionally, the same questions arise about *projection* of the presupposition to larger sentences containing the clause with the trigger. Let us turn briefly now to the projection problem for presuppositions, first discussed in Morgan (1969) and Langendoen and Savin (1971).

To ask about projection is to ask about the conditions under which presuppositions, no matter how initially triggered, are projected from the clauses in which they are initially introduced to higher-level sentences in which these clauses are embedded. We have already seen that presuppositions associated with a simple affirmative declarative are often inherited by more complex sentences in which the simple sentence is embedded. Our P family test illustrates that presuppositions are typically maintained in negatives, interrogatives, and conditional antecedents. An hypothesis that comes to mind in this connection is that higher sentences always simply inherit the presuppositions of embedded clauses. This cumulative hypothesis was advanced by Langendoen and Savin in the 1969 talk on which their (1971) was based, but Morgan pointed out some difficulties for it. For example, the conditional in (44*a*) inherits the presupposition (44*c*) associated with its consequent clause but (44*b*) does not.

(44) *a.* If John were here, what Linda lost could be recovered.
b. If $[\text{Linda}]_i$ lost something, what $[\text{she}]_i$ lost was not valuable.
c. Linda lost something.

The presupposition of the consequent clause in (44*b*) is, as it were, filtered out. For this reason, environments of this kind were dubbed *filters* by Karttunen (1973), where they were contrasted with *holes*, which do essentially work cumulatively and let all presuppositions through (examples are the environments used in our P family: negatives interrogatives, and antecedents of conditionals), and with *plugs*, environments that always block inheritance of presuppositions. It has been claimed that the verb *say* is a presuppositional plug. Thus (45*a*) does not presuppose (45*b*) even though its complement clause does carry that presupposition.

(45) *a.* [Melissa]$_i$ said that [she]$_i$ knows that Elvis lives.
b. Elvis lives.

Whether there are any true plugs is not clear, since verbs like *say* do sometimes apparently allow presuppositions to ascend from an embedded clause and in such cases look like filters; Karttunen says that plugs all "leak." For example, (46*a*) seems to acquire presupposition (46*b*), which is triggered by the pseudo-cleft construction in the embedded clause.

(46) *a.* Anthony said that what Joan lost on the flight was her flute.
b. Joan lost something on the flight.

The projection problem for presuppositions is the problem of how to account systematically for the presuppositions of container sentences. Filters like conditionals are especially interesting, for they require some principled means for distinguishing the conditions under which presuppositions are inherited from those in which they are not. Intuitively, it seems that some principled explanation ought to be available. Sentence (44*b*), for example, is a conditional whose antecedent clause expresses the proposition that Joan lost something, which is the proposition that the consequent clause presupposes. Similarly, the conjunction in (47*a*) does not presuppose (47*b*), in spite of the fact that the second conjunct in isolation does presuppose (47*b*). This filtering effect seems to depend on the fact that the first conjunct of (47*a*) entails (47*b*).

(47) *a.* Keith has three children, and all Keith's children are asleep.
b. Keith has some children.

That sentence (47*a*) does not have (47*b*) as a presupposition can be seen from the fact that (47*a*) is a perfectly fine answer to the question in (48).

(48) Does Keith have any children?

Semantic relations between the proposition expressed by one contained clause and that presupposed by a second contained clause seem to affect filtering of presuppositions to a third higher clause. We not only want to describe precisely how this works; if possible, we also want to show why the inheritance of presuppositions in compound and complex sentences works as it does.

The valuable and vast literature on presuppositions can be mined for insights into how presuppositions are to be understood, how they are triggered, and how they are projected. Much of the discussion predates formal theories of discourse, however, and its import may not always be immediately apparent. In this chapter we will use the analytical tools already introduced to present what seems to us a useful approach to presuppositional phenomena, offering only highly selective references to the heated debates of the 1960s and 1970s on the status of presuppositions. We are well aware, of course, that the present perspective owes much to that earlier work as well as to more recent theoretical work.[8]

3.2 Defining presupposition

We can now make more precise the intuitive idea of a proposition's being presupposed. Presuppositions are based on a set of assumptions that impose felicity conditions on utterances, what we called the common ground in chapter 4. The presuppositional common ground can thus be identified with a set of propositions. We will represent presuppositional common grounds by another contextual function, comgrd; comgrd(c) will designate the common ground at context c, the set of propositions that conversationalists take for granted in c. We make the following assumptions about comgrd(c):

(49) For any proposition $p \in$ comgrd(c),
a. that sp(c) believes $p \in$ comgrd(c),
b. that adr(c) believes $p \in$ comgrd(c).

Condition (49*a*) says that the proposition that the speaker believes p is in the common ground if p is; (49*b*) does the same for the addressee. These conditions mean not that each conversationalist actually believes that *p* but simply that they each purport to believe that *p* for the purpose of that conversational exchange. Presuppositions in comgrd(c) are thus being treated as if they were mutually believed (at some discourse level), a fact that reflects their pragmatic character.[9]

The analogy of the present view of presuppositions with the analysis of modality and modal reasoning discussed in chapter 5 is obvious. In chapter 5 we argued, following Kratzer (1981), that modals can be analyzed in terms of a modal base and an ordering source, both of which were viewed as contextually supplied sets of propositions. While presuppositional common grounds, modal bases, and ordering sources are clearly related from an intuitive point of view, they cannot be altogether identified, at least not without further elaboration. This is shown by examples like the following:

(50) Loren didn't sing. But she might have.

The first sentence in (50) clearly excludes the proposition that Loren sang from what the conversationalists take for granted. Yet the second sentence states that her singing might have taken place (and thus is compatible with the relevant modal base). It follows that the modal base and the common ground must be viewed as distinct conversational backgrounds, for otherwise there would be no context with respect to which (50) could be true. Thus the picture that emerges from this is that the context supplies (in the form of distinct contextual functions) distinct conversational backgrounds: a presuppositional common ground (comgrd), a modal base (mdb), and ordering source (ordsrc) and probably more. Conversational backgrounds interact in complex ways that should eventually be integrated in a unified theory of conversational assumptions. But to pursue this would take us well beyond the limits of the present work. In the remainder of this chapter we will focus on the presuppositional common ground (comgrd) without considering its interaction with other conversational backgrounds.

The propositions in comgrd(c) uniquely determine a set of circumstances, given by the intersection of the propositions in the common ground, $\bigcap$comgrd(c). These circumstances are just those in which all the propositions in comgrd(c) are true—the circumstances belonging to all those propositions—and can be thought of as the live possibilities left open by the common ground being presupposed. We adopt the terminology of Stalnaker (1978) and call this the *context set*. (Heim (1983) calls it the context, since she is not concerned in her analysis with other contextual functions.) Because we will often need to refer to the context set, we will use c^* to designate it ($c^* = \bigcap \text{comgrd}(c)$). Note that as the common ground grows to include more propositions, the context set shrinks to exclude any worlds where some proposition in the common ground is false. In (51) we state the requirement that c^* never be empty.

(51) $c^* \neq \varnothing$

Condition (51) requires that there be some worlds in which all the propositions in c are true, which amounts to requiring that the propositions in the common ground be consistent. This seems to be the ideal norm to which speakers tend to conform: conversationalists tend to discard inconsistencies as they are detected in order to allow some world or worlds countenanced by the discourse. It might well turn out that the requirement in (51) is too strong, and there are various ways in which it could be weakened. Our discussion would be unnecessarily complicated, however, if we were to allow for inconsistent common grounds, so for the purposes of this discussion we stick to condition (51).

We can now use the notion of common ground, what the discourse or conversationalists presuppose, to explicate the notion of what (the utterance of) a sentence presupposes. To keep our exposition simple, we are going to restrict ourselves to sentences that do not contain indexical expressions like *I* or *you*, even though this assumption can (and must) eventually be modified.

(52) A sentence S presupposes a proposition p iff in any context c where S has a semantic value relative to c (is true or false relative to c), p follows from the common ground of c (that is, any world in c^* is a p world, a world in which p is true; in set-theoretic terms, $c^* \subseteq p$).

As it stands, (52) does not allow for presuppositions that are conversationally rather than conventionally triggered, but the basic framework can be developed before we provide for this possibility. The basic idea behind definition (52) is that in a given context the presuppositions of a sentence must be assumed in order for that sentence to be true or false. In other words, sentences fail to have a truth value (fail to be interpretable) if their presuppositions are not assumed to be true (or taken for granted). Like so much else in semantics, this can be traced back to ideas articulated by Frege: presuppositions place constraints on the assignment of semantic values to sentences. Consider the case of a declarative in a context with a presupposition that fails. Consider, for example, an utterance of (30*a*), "Joan has stopped drinking wine for breakfast," which presupposes (30*b*), "Joan used to drink wine for breakfast." Suppose a context where it is known that Joan never drank wine for breakfast. In such a context, c^* does not entail the proposition that Joan used to drink wine for breakfast (since c^* entails that Joan has never drunk wine for breakfast, which is inconsistent with the presupposition). What (52) says is that in this context sentence (30*a*) could not be judged as either true or false. Frege noted that we are indeed reluctant to say in such cases that the sentence is either true or false.

A number of further observations are called for in connection with (52). The first is that (52) does not actually require that a presupposition be a member of the common ground, which might have seemed the most natural reconstruction of the intuitive notion of being taken for granted. This definition requires only that a presupposition be entailed by the propositions in that common ground. In this respect it is analogous to our earlier definition of the truth conditions for *must,* which involve entailment of a proposition by the modal base but not membership in it. A consequence of this is that the necessarily true proposition T, which is identified with the set of all possible worlds, is presupposed by any sentence whatsoever. This reflects the fact that necessary truths place no constraint at all on common grounds. Notice, however, that on our definition of common ground, this does not mean that the conversationalists actually acknowledge that some particular sentence expressing T ("two plus two is four," for example) is true in all possible worlds. Although it does go beyond our ordinary terminology to say that "John walks" presupposes that two plus two is four, no dramatically bad consequences seem to follow. The main reason for dealing with c^* and its entailments rather than with the membership of comgrd(c) is formal simplicity. It will allow us to develop our account of projection properties more easily and does not seem to introduce undesirable consequences.

A second observation is that various nonstandard logics have been proposed for dealing with the truth-value gaps that failure of presupposition seems to bring. In particular, two general kinds of nonstandard logics have been applied to the study of presuppositions, three-valued and supervaluational logics (which have also been applied to analyses of certain kinds of vagueness or imprecision, discussed in chapter 8). However, pursuing treatments of presuppositions by means of three-valued logics or super-valuations and their relation to the approach considered here would take us too far afield, and we will therefore abstain from doing so.[10]

To put definition (52) in the right perspective, it is useful to recall Lewis's scoreboard metaphor. Slots on the contextual scoreboard show values for the various contextual functions. Just as the sections on the scoreboard in Candlestick Park change as the game progresses, contextual functions assume different values as discourse progresses. Immediately before an utterance is produced, no one is registered as speaker in the sp box: if what is said is "I am hungry," it is evaluated relative to the context as altered by the production of the sentence (with, for example, Alice as value of sp(c) if Alice uttered the sentence). Similarly, a demonstration that secures a reference for *that* will only get registered on the contextual scoreboard after the utterance is underway. Utterance of a sentence containing *that* will be infelicitous if the relevant slot remains empty after the utterance is complete.

The common ground too is affected by the utterance. Thus the common ground relative to which S is judged for admissibility and interpreted will include not only everything in the common ground before S was uttered but also propositions manifested to discourse participants during the utterance event, for instance, that sp(c) has indeed uttered S at tm(c) in wrld(c). Linguistic theory cannot say anything about which propositions these will be; it can start raining during our talk, and we may or may not register that fact in the common ground. It will depend on our attentiveness to our surroundings, including one another, and on what kind of discourse we take ourselves to be engaging in (suppose we're telling ghost stories).

What is especially interesting for our present purposes is that propositions that did not belong to the common ground prior to the utterance of S may enter the common ground in order to *accommodate* the presuppositions signaled by uttering S.

Sentence (53*a*), when uttered, presupposes the proposition that (53*b*) would express had it been uttered instead.

(53) *a.* I just stopped smoking.
b. I used to smoke.

It is not at all unusual, however, for someone to utter (53*a*) in contexts where the propositions in the common ground entail nothing about that person's smoking habits; in particular, we do not treat utterances of (53*a*) as infelicitous when (53*b*) is missing from the entailments of the common ground prior to the utterance of (53*a*). As mentioned in chapter 1, (53*a*) could be offered to an airline clerk by a passenger explaining a request for a nonsmoking seat. What seems to happen in such cases is that the proposition that sp(*c*) used to smoke is simply added to the common ground at *c* as if it had been there all along.

Lewis (1979) dubbed this phenomenon *accommodation,* suggesting that "if at time *t* something is said that requires presupposition *p* to be acceptable, and if *p* is not presupposed just before *t* then—ceteris paribus—presupposition *p* comes into existence" (p. 172). Of course, other things are not always equal, and accommodation is not automatic. If, for example, the presupposition required is inconsistent with what is already in the common ground, the utterance is infelicitous, because its presupposition cannot be accommodated by simple addition to the existing common ground. And there are various other constraints on accommodation (for limitations on possibilities for interpretation of definite NPs see Heim (1982), and see also Soames's (1979) suggestion that what is accommodated must be uncontroversial). Still, there seems to be a general tendency to accommodate by extending the common ground to include the needed presupposition *p* unless $\neg p$ is already in the common ground.

Note that accommodation can occur in a conversation even where the admitted presupposition is thought to be false by one of the conversationalists. For example, question (54*a*) may bring response (54*b*) even though (54*c*), which (54*a*) presupposes, is false.

(54) *a.* Would you like some more sherry?
b. No thanks.
c. The addressee of (54*a*) has had some sherry.

In this case, the addressee toward whom (54*a*) is directed allows (54*c*) to remain in the common ground, presumably because there is no reason to think that it will play any further role in developing that common ground, since it is peripheral to the general discourse purposes.

So if S presupposes *p*, what matters is not whether *p* is registered in the comgrd scoreboard slot immediately prior to the utterance of

S (what we might call the preutterance context) but whether it is so registered at the stage of assigning and evaluating propositional content (what we can call the context of utterance or the context relative to which S may potentially accomplish a shift to a new postutterance context). The common ground of the context of utterance typically includes information on the identity of the speaker and such propositions as that sp(c) has uttered S or that it has just begun raining in loc(c); it may also differ from the preutterance common ground in including (or at least entailing) an accommodated presupposition required to make the utterance of S felicitous, along with various propositions inferred from this enriched common ground. But as always, we do not add to the common ground a proposition p that is inconsistent with some other proposition q already there, at least not without discarding q.

4 Projecting Presuppositions Recursively

What we will do in this section is show how (52) can be made explicit in terms of the semantic apparatus we have developed and how presupposition projection can be dealt with.

4.1 Some empirical properties of filters

In section 3.1 we introduced some of the problems associated with presupposition projection. As pointed out there, the most interesting case is constituted by so-called filters like *and*, *or*, and *if . . . then*. Let us try to illustrate more explicitly what the problem is by trying to state informally the relevant empirical generalizations about the filtering properties of these items.

Consider *and* first. As a first shot, the projection properties of *and* seem to be that the presuppositions of a sentence of the form "p and q" are the presuppositions of both p and q, unless p entails the presuppositions of q. In the latter case the presuppositions of q are filtered out, and only the presuppositions of p are passed up. Let us illustrate. Consider the following:

(55) *a.* John doesn't know that syntax is easy, and Mary hasn't discovered that syntax is beautiful.
b. Syntax is easy.
c. Syntax is beautiful.

The first conjunct of (55*a*) presupposes (55*b*). The second conjunct presupposes (55*c*). The conjunction as a whole presupposes both (55*b*) and (55*c*). Consider next example (47) of section 3.1, repeated here:

(47) *a.* Keith has three children, and all Keith's children are asleep.
b. Keith has some children.

Here the second conjunct presupposes (47*b*). However, the first conjunct entails (47*b*), and thus the presupposition is filtered out and the second conjunct as such doesn't put any restriction on admitting contexts for the sentence. Notice that switching the conjuncts around in (47) makes a difference:

(56) All of Keith's children are asleep, and Keith has three children.

It would be odd to utter (56) in a context where (47*b*) is not presupposed. Thus, the presuppositional properties of a conjunction are not symmetric (the presuppositions of "*p* and *q*" are not the same as the presuppositions of "*q* and *p*"), while the truth-conditional content of a conjunction arguably is.

Indeed, even if *p* does not by itself entail the presuppositions of *q*, those presuppositions are filtered out in a context *c* where the addition of *p* to the common ground in *c* yields a set of propositions that jointly entail the presuppositions of *q*. Suppose, for example, that the common ground includes (57*a*). In such a context, asserting (57*b*) filters out the presupposition of the second conjunct, the proposition expressed by (47*b*).

(57) *a.* If Keith is married to Linda, then he has children.
b. Keith is married to Linda, and all his children are asleep.

So the correct generalization seems to be that "*p* and *q*" uttered in a context inherits all the presuppositions of both *p* and *q* except for any presuppositions of *q* that are contextually entailed by *p* (that is, entailed by *p* together with the propositions already in the common ground).

Essentially the same generalization seems to apply to conditionals. The presuppositions of "if *p* then *q*" are the presuppositions of both *p* and *q*, unless *p* contextually entails the presuppositions of *q*, in which case only the presuppositions of *p* are inherited by the conditional. Let us illustrate.

(58) *a.* If it was Linda who solved the projection problem, it was Bill who solved the problem of weak crossover.
b. Someone solved the projection problem.
c. Someone solved the problem of weak crossover.

The antecedent of (58*a*) presupposes (58*b*). The consequent presupposes (58*c*). The conditional as a whole presupposes both (58*b*) and (58*c*). Contrast this with the following:

(59) If someone solved the projection problem, it was Linda.

Here the antecedent entails the presuppositions of the consequent, which are accordingly filtered out. And as with conjunction, what matters is whether the antecedent together with other propositions already in the common ground entails the presuppositions of the consequent. Suppose again that the common ground includes the proposition expressed by (57*a*). In such a context, uttering (60) filters out the presupposition of its consequent clause, the proposition expressed by (47*b*), "Keith has some children."

(60) If Keith is married to Linda, all of his children are asleep.

Consider finally disjunction. Its presuppositional properties appear to be the following. A sentence of the form "*p* or *q*" generally inherits the presuppositions of both *p* and *q*, unless one of the disjuncts is contextually incompatible with the presuppositions of the other. In this case the incompatible presuppositions are filtered out. Consider (61).

(61) *a.* Either John doesn't know that syntax is easy, or Mary hasn't discovered that syntax is beautiful (I don't remember which).
b. Syntax is easy.
c. Syntax is beautiful.

Here the first clause presupposes (61*b*); the second (61*c*). The disjunction as a whole presupposes both (61*b*) and (61*c*). Consider now the following:

(62) *a.* Either no one has solved the projection problem, or it was Linda who did.
b. Someone solved the projection problem.

Here the second conjunction of (62*a*) presupposes (62*b*). But the first conjunct is incompatible with (62*b*); it entails the negation of (62*b*). Thus the presupposition of the second conjunct is filtered out. Notice that the order of the disjuncts here makes no difference:

(63) Either it was Linda who solved the projection problem, or no one did.

Sentence (63) does not presuppose (62*b*), although the first clause of (63) taken in isolation does. This seems to show that the presuppositional properties of disjunction (like its truth-conditional content) are symmetric (the presuppositions of "*p* or *q*" are identical with the presuppositions of "*q* or *p*").

Again we note that contextual incompatibility filters presuppositions of disjunctions. If the common ground at *c* includes (64*a*), then the disjunction (64*b*) does not presuppose (64*c*), even though the first disjunct of (64*b*) by itself would presuppose (64*c*) in that context.

(64) *a.* All lawyers are rich.
b. Either Mary discovered that John is poor, or she discovered that he is a lawyer.
c. John is poor.

If the common ground does not include (64*a*) or something similar that would make Mary's discovering that John is a lawyer incompatible with his being poor, then indeed uttering sentence (64*b*) would presuppose (64*c*).

Karttunen and Peters (1979) articulated essentially these filtering principles except that their account does not allow for the possibility that contextually available propositions can affect presupposition projection and thus fails to deal satisfactorily with cases like those in (57), (60), and (64). The discourse-theoretic approach we present below does not suffer from this limitation and is in this respect empirically more adequate.

Exercise 5 Consider a sentence of the form "If not *q* then (*p* and *r*)" and propositions *h*, *f*, and *g* such that *q* presupposes *h*, *p* presupposes *f*, and *r* presupposes *g*. Assume that *p* does not entail *g* and that not *f* entails *q*.

According to the generalizations discussed above, what do we expect the presuppositions of "If not *q* then (*p* and *r*)" to be in a null context (where the common ground is empty)?

Construct a concrete example of a sentence of the form "If not *q* then (*p* and *r*)" where the relations described at the beginning of this exercise obtain, and see whether its presuppositions in a null context are the expected one.

In simplified terms these appear to be the filtering properties of *and, if . . . then,* and *or.* Negation, as we saw, is instead a hole. Two questions now arise in this connection. First, how are these properties of the logical connectives to be formally captured? Second, why are these properties the way they are?

Answering the second question implies addressing such issues as the following: Can there be a language that associates with conjunction the projection properties that in English are associated with disjunction? Can there be a language where conditionals are presuppositionally like disjunction rather than conjunction?

A priori, positive answers to the above questions seem highly implausible. Why? Well, intuitively the projection properties described above seem strong candidates for being linguistic universals. This makes sense if the projection properties of the connectives considered above follow from their meanings (which also are strong candidates for universals) plus perhaps general principles concerning how discourse unfolds. In other words, we want a way of formally characterizing how presuppositions are projected that is not only empirically adequate but also sheds light on the relevant empirical generalizations by deriving them from general principles (and, of course, the truth-conditional semantics of the relevant connectives).

We think that recent work on this topic gives us reason for being optimistic about the possibility of attaining this goal. We will next try to show this by presenting a highly simplified version of the theory of presupposition projection developed in Heim (1983).

4.2 Dynamic sentential semantics and presupposition

So far we have been characterizing the truth-conditional content of sentences in static terms: a sentence has a truth value relative to a context, a value assignment to variables, and a world-time pair. However, we noted at several points in our previous discussion that sentences interact in a dynamic way with the context in which they are uttered. The result of uttering a sentence S in a context c leads to a new context c'. We can try to represent this by saying that sentences are associated with functions from contexts to contexts. We might call such functions context-change potentials. As Stalnaker (1978) proposes, the context-change potential of a sentence in simple cases can be viewed as narrowing down the set of live alternatives by excluding those incompatible with the sentence. Let p be the static semantic value of a sentence, the proposition it expresses according to the semantics we have developed so far. Its dynamic value can be represented as a function mapping a context set c^* to $c^* \cap p$. This amounts to excluding from the original c^* all the situations in which p is false; this is the effort of adding the proposition p to the set of propositions in comgrd(c), taking comgrd(c') = comgrd(c) $\cup \{p\}$.

Heim suggests that by developing Stalnaker's idea we can get some insight as to why presuppositions project the way they do. To see this, we will have to develop more explicitly the notion of context-change potential. Here is one way of doing it.

The interpretation function $[\![\ ]\!]^{M,g,w,i,c}$ as we have defined it is a fully defined (or total) function. It always assigns a value to sentences. This function is designed to deal with the static value of a sentence, the truth conditions it has if we abstract away from the impact sentences have on the context in which they are uttered. To deal with presuppositions, however, we need a more general characterization of the truth-conditional import of a sentence, one that takes into account its dynamic interaction with the context and consequently leaves open the possibility that some contexts may be unsuited for interpreting a given sentence, as our semi-formal characterization of presupposition in (52) assumes. To this end let us now redub the static truth conditions of a sentence S as characterized by $[\![\ ]\!]^{M,g,w,i,c}$ its *proto-truth-conditions*. Using the notion of proto-truth-conditions, we will be able to define recursively the context-change potential of a sentence as a function from context sets to context sets. Such a notion will then naturally lead to a more general characterization of the truth-conditional import of a sentence (which we will call its truth conditions proper).

Let $c + \mathrm{S}$ designate the context produced by uttering S in c. Formally, a context-change potential will be a *partial* function $|\mathrm{S}|^{g,c}$ (for an assignment to variables g and a context c) that maps the context set of its utterance c^* onto a new context set $|\mathrm{S}|^{g,c}(c^*)$. Let $c^* + \mathrm{S}$ designate $|\mathrm{S}|^{g,c}(c^*)$, the context set that results from the felicitous assertion of S (or the realization of whatever locutionary force is associated with S); $c^* + \mathrm{S}$ is the context set associated with $c + \mathrm{S}$. Clauses (65–67) below show how we might recursively define $|\mathrm{S}|^{g,c}$.

We will explicitly deal only with negation and conjunction. The same method can be generalized to conditionals, disjunctions, and quantifiers, but we will not do so here. The treatment of negation and conjunction should suffice to give the reader a fair idea of the main features of the present approach.

(65) Let S be an atomic sentence not containing connectives or modals. Let $\mathrm{Int}_{g,c}(\mathrm{S})$ (the intension of S relative to c and g) be $\{\langle w', i' \rangle : [\![\mathrm{S}]\!]^{M,g,w',i',c} = 1\}$. We then stipulate that $|\mathrm{S}|^{g,c}(c^*)$ $= c^* \cap \mathrm{Int}_{g,c}(\mathrm{S})$ if $c^* \subseteq p$ for any p that S presupposes. If for some p that S presupposes, $c \nsubseteq p$, $|\mathrm{S}|^{g,c}(c^*)$ is undefined.

Clause (65) is just what Stalnaker proposed in general for assertion of a simple declarative sentence S: when the proposition that S is added to the common ground, that proposition is intersected with the existing context set. To simplify the notation, we will omit reference to g and c in $|\ |^{g,c}$ and will write S^{i} for $\mathrm{Int}_{g,c}(\mathrm{S})$. In this unofficial notation (65) becomes either of the following equivalent formulas with the same provisos as in (65):

(65′) *a.* $|\mathrm{S}|(c^*) = c^* \cap \mathrm{S}^{\mathrm{i}}$
b. $c^* + \mathrm{S} = c^* \cap \mathrm{S}^{\mathrm{i}}$

Recall that we can think of propositions as regions of logical space, the sets of world-time pairs in which the proposition is true. A context set is itself a proposition (the conjunction of all the propositions in the set) and is thus a region of logical space. We further assume that the presuppositions associated with atomic sentences can be listed or otherwise finitely specified. Thus, for example, the atomic sentence "John managed to get the MIT job" presupposes that getting the MIT job was an achievement for John. In a context c where such a presupposition is not satisfied (or entailed by the context set c^*) |John managed to get the MIT job| would be undefined, reflecting the fact that such a context cannot be incremented by the information associated with "John managed to get the MIT job" (unless the relevant presupposition is accommodated in the context). Similarly, a sentence like "John regrets that he lost his job" presupposes that he did lose his job. In a context where it is assumed that he in fact did not, |John regrets that he lost his job| would be undefined.

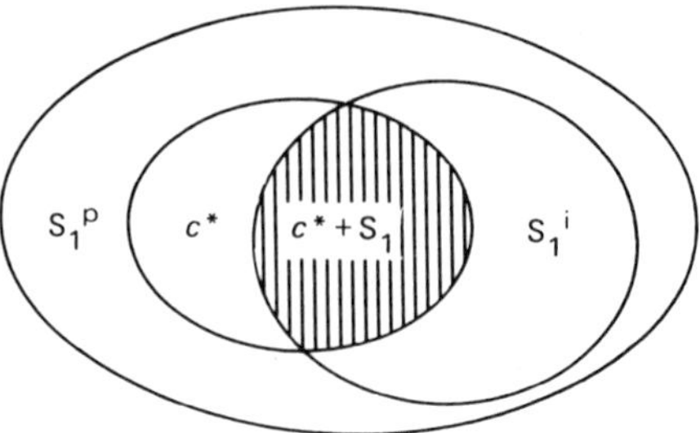

Figure 6.2

The presuppositions associated with specific grammatical constructions can be treated in the same way. For example, cleft sentences of the form "It was NP that S" presuppose that someone or something satisfies sentence S. We can illustrate what happens in calculating context incrementation involving simple cleft sentences (clefts where S in "It was NP that S" is atomic) by means of the example illustrated in figure 6.2. Let c^* be the proposition that Kermit was killed by either Ms. Piggy or by the butler. Let S_1 be "It was the butler who killed Kermit." And let S_1^p be the proposition that Kermit was killed by someone. S_1^i is the proposition expressed by S_1. Figure 6.2 shows a situation where c^* is taken as a context set of a context c that admits S_1. S_1^i is the proposition that the butler killed Kermit. S_1 presupposes that Kermit was killed by someone (S_1^p in figure 6.2). In general, we let S^p stand for the presupposition(s) associated with S. In the given context, S_1^p is satisfied (it is entailed by c^*). We show this graphically by including the region associated with the context set c^* in the region associated with S_1^p (the presupposition associated with S_1). The shaded area, which is the intersection of c^* and S_1^i, is $c^* + S_1$ (or $|S_1|(c^*)$); this is the context set of $c + S_1$.

Let us next consider in $c + S_1$ a new sentence S_2 (say "The butler regrets that he killed Kermit"), with presupposition S_2^p (the proposition that the butler killed Kermit). Figure 6.3 shows what happens. Let c^* be the proposition that Kermit was killed by either Ms. Piggy or by the butler. Let S_1 be "It was the butler who killed Kermit." Let S_1^p be the proposition that Kermit was killed by someone. Let S_2 be "The butler regrets that he killed Kermit." And let S_2^p be the proposition that the butler killed Kermit. S_1^i and S_2^i are the propositions expressed by S_1 and S_2 respectively. Note that $c^* + S_1$ is included in S_2^p, but the original c^* is not. In other words, S_2 is admitted in $c + S_1$ but is not admitted in the original c. This shows

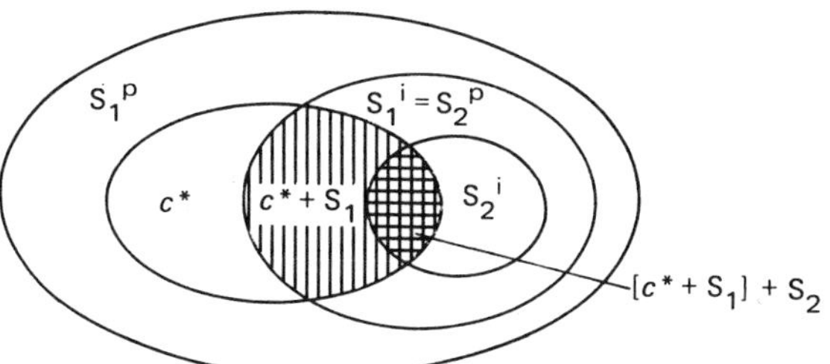

Figure 6.3

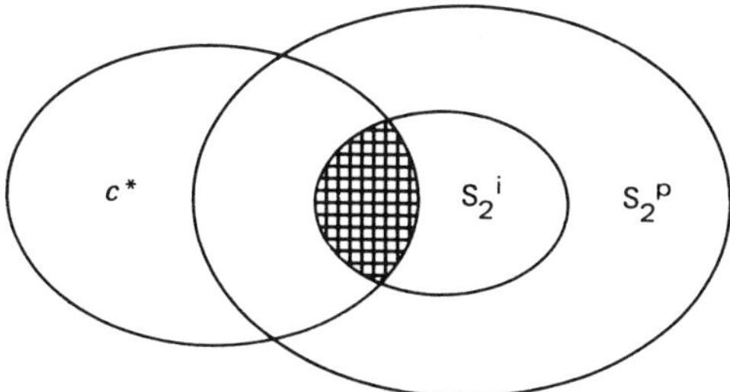

Figure 6.4

how an assertion, by altering the context set, can help satisfy presuppositions of subsequent utterances. Since $c^* + S_1$ entails S_2^p, the context set after S_2 is uttered is successfully restricted to $(c^* + S_1) + S_2$, which is indicated by the crosshatched area.

Figure 6.4 shows the original context set c^* with S_2^p, which it does not entail. In this case we cannot move to $c^* + S_2$ (indicated by the cross-hatched area). On our assumptions about the context c and its context set c^*, $|S_2|(c^*)$ is undefined, which captures the fact that S_2 is not felicitously assertible in c; context c cannot be incremented by S_2. In other words, to utter "The butler regrets that he killed Kermit" would be infelicitous in a context where, for all we know, he might not be the killer. We must add to the original context the information that it was indeed the butler who killed Kermit, either by an assertion or possibly by a process of accommodation.

Actually, the context set associated with $c + S_1$ can also be affected by the beliefs that the utterance of S_1 triggers for the conversationalists. However, for simplicity we will ignore the addition of these further implicit propositions in our discussion. Strictly speaking, a sentence S is uttered in a context c and is felicitous (or infelicitous) in c. However, it is the context set c^* that determines the felicity of S in the context c, so we will sometimes speak of S as uttered and felicitous in c^*. This is to be understood as shorthand for saying that S is uttered and felicitous in context c with context set c^*. We will also sometimes say that c or c^* admits S; this is shorthand for saying that the utterance of S in context c with context set c^* is felicitous (that c^* entails the presuppositions of S).

Let us now turn to negation. We want to define the context change potential of "not S" in terms of that of S. We can do so with either of the following equivalent formulas.

(66) *a.* $|\text{not S}|(c^*) = c^* - |\text{S}|(c^*)$
b. $c^* + [\text{not S}] = c^* - [c^* + \text{S}]$

The net effect of clause (66) is simply to subtract from c^* the worlds in which S is true. This happens in the following way. First we compute $|\text{S}|(c^*)$ (as if S were asserted in context c). Then we take the complement of the result with respect to the original context set.

The definition in (66) has an interesting consequence. Suppose that $|\text{S}|(c^*)$ is undefined. Then $|\text{not S}|(c^*)$ will also be undefined, as the latter is defined in terms of the former. Now $|\text{S}|(c^*)$ will be undefined if c^* does not satisfy (or entail) the presuppositions associated with S. It follows, then, that a context c for "not S" must satisfy the same presuppositions as a context for S, since $|\text{S}|(c^*)$ must be defined for $|\text{not S}|(c^*)$ to be defined. In other words, we derive the observation that negation is a hole as a simple consequence of the fact that the way "not S" affects the context is defined in terms of the way in which S does. Let us illustrate this further by means of an example. Let c^* be the proposition that the conversationalists know that Kermit was killed by either the butler or Ms. Piggy, that they don't know which of the two is the murderer, and that they do not believe that either Ms. Piggy or the butler has killed anybody else. Let S_1 be "It wasn't Kermit that Ms. Piggy killed." Let S_0 be "It was Kermit that Ms. Piggy killed." And let S_0^{p} be the proposition that Ms. Piggy killed someone. As noted above, S_1^{i} and S_0^{i} are the propositions expressed by S_1 and S_0 respectively. Intuitively, uttering S_1 in c^* (as described in figure 6.5) is infelicitous. In figure 6.5, S_1^{i} is represented by the horizontal lines. The infelicity of uttering S_1 in a context c with context set c^* follows, since to compute $c^* + \text{S}_1$, we first have to compute $c^* + \text{S}_0$. But $c^* + \text{S}_0$ is undefined, since the presupposition of S_0 (namely S_0^{p}) is not satisfied in c^* (that is, $c^* \not\subseteq \text{S}_0^{\text{p}}$).

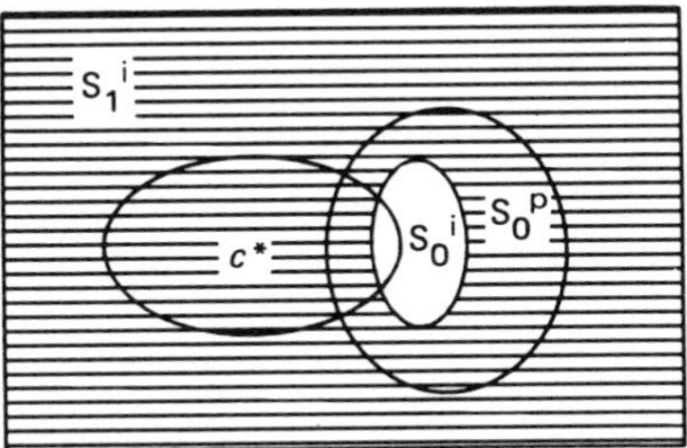

Figure 6.5

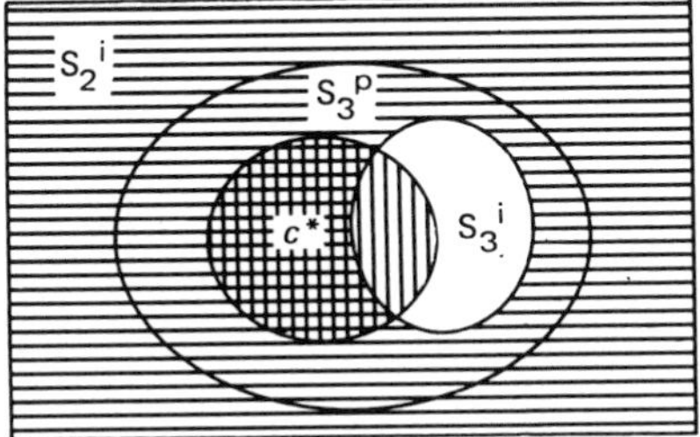

Figure 6.6

By way of contrast, consider uttering in c^* the sentence "It wasn't Ms. Piggy who killed Kermit." The results are illustrated in figure 6.6. Let c^* be as in figure 6.5. Let S_2 be "It wasn't Ms. Piggy who killed Kermit." Let S_3 be "It was Ms. Piggy who killed Kermit." And let S_3^p be the proposition that Kermit was killed by someone. S_2^i and S_3^i are the propositions expressed by S_2 and S_3 respectively. The result is felicitous. According to our rule, we proceed by computing first $c^* + S_3$. Since the presuppositions S_3^p are satisified in c (that is, $c^* \subseteq S_3^p$), this gets us to the worlds of c^* in which Ms. Piggy killed Kermit (indicated by vertical lines). We then take the complement of the resulting set (indicated by the crosshutching), and this will be the resulting context set, namely, $c^* - (c^* + S_2)$. We have now ruled out as live possibilities those where Ms. Piggy kills Kermit, which were admitted by the original c with context set c^*. This shows how the results of our algorithm match our intuitions with respect to how presuppositions are projected in negative contexts. The presuppositions of a sentence are passed up across negation. By assigning to negation the context-change potential in (66), we can derive this fact, since computing c^* + not S involves as a first step computing c^* + S, which will be undefined if c^* does not entail the presuppositions of S. We consider later how the status of

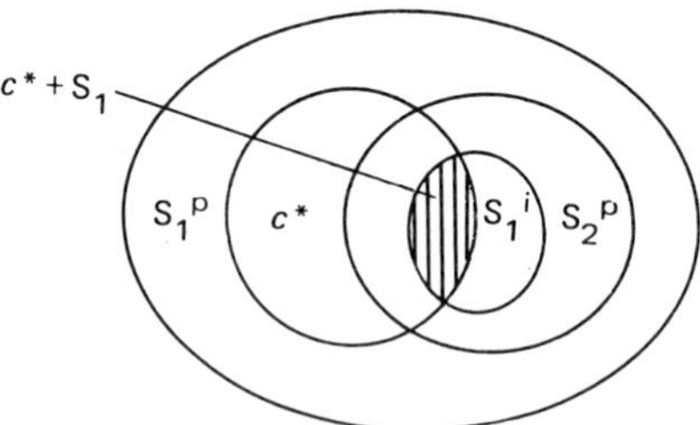

Figure 6.7

the negative as a hole is compatible with our earlier observation that some presuppositions appear to be defeasible in certain negative contexts.

Let us now consider conjunction. Here too we have the following equivalent formulas:

(67) *a.* $|\mathrm{S}_1 \text{ and } \mathrm{S}_2|(c^*) = |\mathrm{S}_2|(|\mathrm{S}_1|(c^*))$
b. $c^* + [\mathrm{S}_1 \text{ and } \mathrm{S}_2] = [[c^* + \mathrm{S}_1] + \mathrm{S}_2]$

The basic idea here is that conjunctions are processed linearly. To assert "S_1 and S_2" amounts to the same thing as asserting first S_1 and then following that assertion by an assertion of S_2 (in the same discourse). This gives to the conjuncts an asymmetric status in the spirit of Stalnaker's observation that when a conjunction is asserted, the relevant context set for the second conjunct has already been restricted by prior assertion of the first conjunct. An immediate consequence of this is that for c to admit "S_1 and S_2," it is *not* required that c admit both S_1 and S_2; rather, all that is required is that c admit S_1 and that the incremented context $c + \mathrm{S}_1$ admit S_2. That is, what is necessary is that c^* entails $\mathrm{S}_1^{\mathrm{p}}$ and $c^* + \mathrm{S}_1$ entails $\mathrm{S}_2^{\mathrm{p}}$. Recall our observation that any presuppositions triggered by S_2 that are contextually entailed by S_1 are filtered out. Let us see how our definition guarantees this result.

What our definition of conjunction requires is that the presuppositions of S_2 are entailed by $c^* + \mathrm{S}_1$. But this is just what it means to say that S_1 contextually entails $\mathrm{S}_2^{\mathrm{p}}$. In set-theoretic terms, what is required is that $c^* + \mathrm{S}_1 \subseteq S_2^{\mathrm{p}}$. Yet as figures 6.7 and 6.8 illustrate, this is possible even where $c^* \not\subseteq S_2^{\mathrm{p}}$. Figure 6.7 illustrates the case where S_1 actually entails $\mathrm{S}_2^{\mathrm{p}}$ (set-theoretically, $\mathrm{S}_1^{\mathrm{i}} \subseteq \mathrm{S}_2^{\mathrm{p}}$). In this case, it follows from set-theoretic principles that $c^* + \mathrm{S}_1 = c^* \cap \mathrm{S}_1^{\mathrm{i}} \subseteq \mathrm{S}_2^{\mathrm{p}}$. For figure 6.7 let c^* be the proposition that Keith has three children but it is not known whether any of them are asleep.

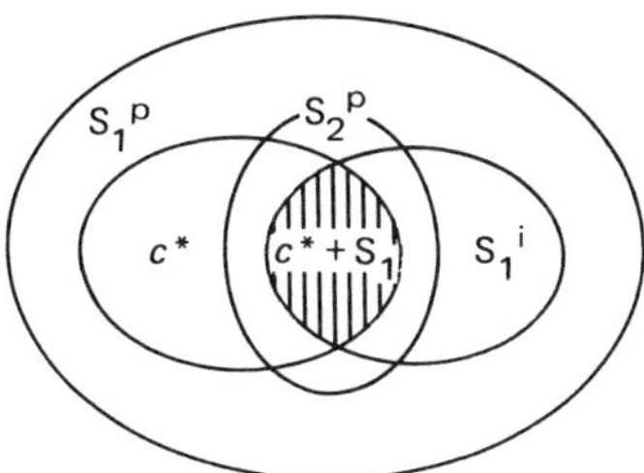

Figure 6.8

Let S_0 be "All of Keith's children are asleep, and Joan regrets it." Let S_1 be "All of Keith's children are asleep." Let S_1^p be the proposition that Keith has children. Let S_2 be "Joan regrets that all of Keith's children are asleep." And let S_2^p be the proposition that all of Keith's children are asleep. S_1^i and S_2^i are the propositions expressed by S_1 and S_2 respectively. We can see that although c^* does admit S_1 ($c^* \subseteq S_1^p$), it does not admit S_2 ($c^* \not\subseteq S_2^p$). But $c^* + S_1$ does admit S_2 ($c^* + S_1 \subseteq S_2^p$). Thus it is felicitous to utter S_0 ("S_1 and S_2") in c^*, although it would be infelicitous to utter just S_2 in c^*. The presuppositions of the second conjunct are filtered out because they are entailed by the first conjunct (set-theoretically, $S_1^i \subseteq S_2^p$). In this case the first conjunct automatically sets up the context for the felicitous utterance of the second conjunct.

Next let us consider figure 6.8. Let c^* be the proposition that it would be difficult for Joan to land a job on Wall Street, but if she does land a job on Wall Street, she'll be rich and furthermore that she may not land such a job and may remain poor. Let S_0 be "Joan managed to land a job on Wall Street, and she doesn't regret that she'll be rich." Let S_1 be "Joan managed to land a job on Wall Street." Let S_1^p be the proposition that it was difficult for Joan to land a job on Wall Street. Let S_2 be "Joan doesn't regret that she'll be rich." And let S_2^p be the proposition that Joan will be rich. S_1^i and S_2^i are the propositions expressed by S_1 and S_2 respectively. Again we see that it is felicitous to utter S_0 in context c with context set c^* because c^* itself entails the presuppositions of S_1 and although c^* doesn't entail the presuppositions of S_2 (it would not be felicitous just to utter S_2 in c), $c^* + S_1$ does entail those presuppositions. This case is different from that of figure 6.7, however, in that S_1 alone does not entail S_2^p ($S_1^i \not\subseteq S_2^p$); we have to add the assumptions in c that restrict c^* to get the required entailment. The first conjunct does not automatically set up a context for felicitous

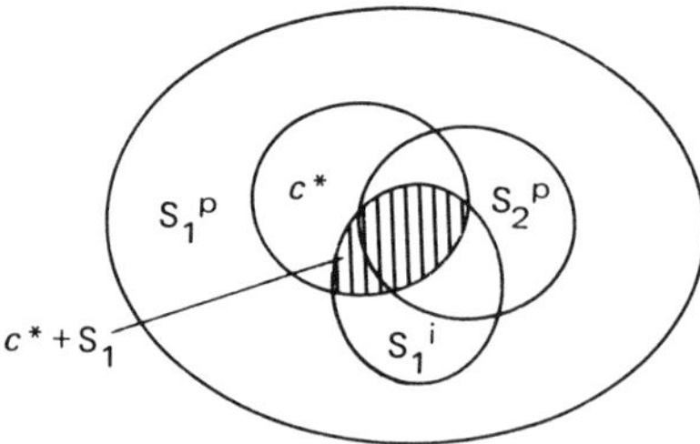

Figure 6.9

utterance of the second conjunct, but with the supporting propositions in the assumed context, uttering S_1 in the first context and moving to $c^* + S_1$ does indeed yield a context felicitous for utterance of S_2.

Finally, figure 6.9 illustrates a case where the first conjunct does not even contextually entail the second and where, although the context admits the first conjunct, it does not admit the second. In such a case the presuppositions of the second conjunct are not filtered out, and thus it is infelicitous to utter the conjunction in such a context. Let c^* be the proposition that Joan got lost but nothing is known about her health. Let S_0 be "Paul regrets that Joan got lost, and Bill that she got sick." Let S_1 be "Paul regrets that Joan got lost." Let S_1^p be the proposition that Joan got lost. Let S_2 be "Bill regrets that Joan got sick." And let S_2^p be "Joan got sick." S_1^i and S_2^i are the propositions expressed by S_1 and S_2 respectively. As we can see, $c^* + S_1 \not\subseteq S_2^p$, and thus the presuppositions of the second conjunct have not been satisfied. To summarize, our definitions guarantee that a conjunction can be uttered felicitously only in a context that satisfies the presuppositions of the first conjunct and satisfies all the presuppositions of the second conjunct that are not contextually entailed by the first conjunct. These filtering properties of conjunction, which we observed earlier, are a natural consequence of its dynamic properties and thus need not be separately stipulated.

Exercise 6 Consider (47*a*), repeated here as (1*c*).

(1) *a.* Keith has three children.
b. Keith has some children.
c. Keith has three children, and all Keith's children are asleep.

The second conjunct of (1*c*) presupposes (1*b*). However, (1*c*) does not, the reason being that its first conjunct, (1*a*), entails (1*b*). Diagram a context set c^* that does not entail the presuppositions of the second conjunct of (1*c*). Then diagram (1*a*) and (1*b*). Using the resulting diagram, show that the addition to c^* of the first conjunct sets up a new context set that entails the presuppositions of the second conjunct of (1*c*).

Definitions (65′), (66), and (67) illustrate how sentences can be assigned a dynamic semantic value that reflects the way in which they affect (and are affected by) the context in which they are uttered. We assume that definitions along these lines can also be provided for other constructions (such as quantifiers, modals, etc.). Then using our notion of context-change potential ($|\mathrm{S}|$), one can assign truth conditions to sentences in a way that directly reflects their presuppositional properties, that is, we can make explicit our semiformal definition (52). Such truth conditions can be represented in terms of a partial function $\| \ \|^{M,g,w,i,c}$ that assigns to a sentence S its truth value relative to model *M*, assignment *g*, and context *c* and in world *w* at time *i*. We will be interested only in contexts that are proper in a certain sense. For any interpretation function $\| \ \|^{M,g,w,i,c}$ we say that a context is *proper* iff $\langle w, i\rangle \in c^*$, that is, iff the world at which a sentence is evaluated is a member of the context set. This means that $\langle w, i\rangle$ is considered as a live alternative by the conversationalists. Accordingly, $\| \ \|^{M,g,w,i,c}$ is defined as follows:

(68) For every *M*, *g*, *w*, *i*, *c* (where $\langle w, i\rangle \in c^*$), $\|\mathrm{S}\|^{M,g,w,i,c} = 1$ iff $\langle w, i\rangle \in |\mathrm{S}|(c^*)$.

The idea underlying (68) is that a sentence is true in $\langle w, i\rangle$ relative to a context *c* iff the result of uttering S in *c* leads to a context that keeps $\langle w, i\rangle$ among the live alternatives. The rationale for such a definition can be illustrated in terms of the following example. Suppose we want to know the truth value of a simple sentence ψ in $\langle w, i\rangle$ relative to context *c*. By uttering ψ in *c* we switch to the context set $c^* \cap \psi^{\mathrm{i}}$. Obviously, the worlds in $c^* \cap \psi^{\mathrm{i}}$ are all worlds in which ψ is true (they are essentially the intension of ψ as restricted by the context set c^*). Thus if $\langle w, i\rangle \in c^* \cap \psi^{\mathrm{i}}$, ψ will be true in $\langle w, i\rangle$ (relative to *c*). More complex cases work in pretty much the same way.

Note that if the presuppositions associated with a sentence ψ are not satisfied in c, $\|\psi\|(c)$ will be undefined, and thus for any world w and time i, ψ will fail to have a truth value in $\langle w, i \rangle$ relative to c.

Perhaps it is appropriate at this point to summarize how the recursive specification of context-change potentials and truth conditions work in the model we have been assuming. The first step is the definition of the function $[\![S]\!]^{M,g,w,i,c}$. This gives us what we have called the proto-truth-conditions of S in w, i relative to context c. This characterizes the truth-conditional import of S in a way that abstracts away from presuppositional phenomena. $[\![S]\!]^{M,g,w,i,c}$ is complete; it always assigns a truth value to S (relative to the relevant parameters). In terms of $[\![S]\!]^{M,g,w,i,c}$ we then recursively define the context-change potential of S ($|S|$) for an arbitrary S. This is done as in clauses (65) through (67) above. $|S|(c^*)$ is a partial function defined only if c^* entails the presuppositions associated with S. Finally, in terms of $|S|$ we define the truth conditions for S, namely, $\|S\|^{M,g,w,i,c}$. These truth conditions will be also partial, which reflects both the partiality of $|S|(c^*)$ and our treatment of truth as just truth preservation among the live possibilities in a context.

What we have presented here is a rough first approximation. There are various ways in which the present recursion could and undoubtedly should be extended and modified. One has to spell out the context-change potentials of implication, disjunction, quantifiers of various kinds, modals, etc., and doing so might lead us to revise significantly what we have done above. Our goal here was to illustrate how our truth-conditional approach can be generalized to deal with context dependency and presuppositions in a way that sheds light on the nature of these phenomena. The feature in the approach sketched above that we think is likely to survive further revisions is that one can look at semantics dynamically by considering not just whether a sentence is true or false in a given context but also how such a sentence affects the context in which it is uttered. In particular, the filtering properties of conjunction, as opposed to the behavior of negation, seem to follow naturally from this dynamic view of meaning. By adding the first conjunct to a context c, we automatically add to c the entailments of that conjunct. These create a new context for the second conjunct. The projection properties of conjunction are an immediate consequence of this. In this sense the analysis is sensitive to Gazdar's (1979) observation that the principles that guide presupposition projection are not just arbitrary. The projection properties of connectives are directly linked to how sentences formed with those connectives actually function in discourse.

4.3 Defeasibility

There is an aspect of the treatment we have adopted that deserves some discussion. In chapter 1 and throughout this book we have maintained that the main features of presuppositions are (*a*) their survival in various contexts (the P family), including negation, and (*b*) their defeasibility in certain circumstances. In our formal treatment we have essentially assimilated presuppositions to context-dependent entailments, with the proviso that sentences receive a value only if their presuppositions are entailed by the context set. This feature, which the present approach shares with treatments of presuppositions in terms of supervaluations or three-valued logics, is dictated by the fact that in classical bivalent logic only tautologies are entailed by a sentence and its negation.[11]

This raises the issue of how presuppositions can be defeated. We believe that the extent to which presuppositions are defeasible depends on whether they are triggered conventionally or by means of implicit contextual assumptions. We now turn to a discussion of this distinction.

We suggested in chapter 4 (and above in the present chapter) that the implications of an utterance can in principle be divided into two classes: those that depend only on what is stipulated by the language system (plus a logic) and those that require further nonlinguistic (and defeasible) premises. The first set includes entailments and also what Grice called conventional implicatures. The second set includes conversational implicatures of both the generalized and the particularized variety. This distinction, as pointed out above, also applies to the propositions that an utterance presupposes. Some presuppositions apparently are assigned to a sentence S just by the rules of the language system (together with a logic), whereas others require the addition of certain default pragmatic premises to S.

In fact, as Karttunen and Peters (1979) point out, conventional implicatures generally give rise to conventionally triggered presuppositions and can be essentially assimilated to the latter. Typical conventional presuppositional triggers are cleft sentences or lexical items like *fail to*, *even*, and *manage*. By virtue of meaning alone (69*a*) and (70*a*) presuppose (69*b*) and (70*b*), respectively.

(69) *a.* Even Pavarotti likes Sophia Loren.
b. Pavarotti is the least likely or most surprising member of some contextually salient group to have the property of liking Loren.
c. Pavarotti likes Loren.

(70) *a.* James Bond managed to kiss Sophia Loren.
b. There was some difficulty involved in Bond's bringing about his kissing of Loren.
c. Bond intentionally kissed Loren.

Contexts admitting sentences like (69*a*) must have context sets that entail something along the lines of (69*b*). But this ranking implication depends heavily on such contextual factors as subjective judgments of relative likelihood and the like. Speakers choosing such a mode of expression in some sense thereby announce their own ranking choices in much the same way that modals can be used to express speakers' wishes.

(71) Oh, it can't rain tomorrow: the picnic is planned.

It may seem odd to say that this wish that it will not rain is true or false, but as is clear from the discussion in chapter 5 of modals, an illuminating account of the truth conditions of such sentences is available. What sometimes confuses the issue is that those truth conditions depend heavily on context and furthermore do not generally depend on objective features of the context like who is speaking or when, which means that the truth in question is of more subjective than objective significance. The modals display a much richer abstract semantic structure than *even* and the presuppositional component of *manage*. There are also cases where their truth conditions use much more objective features of context than the speaker's wishes. Nonetheless, the modals are similar in principle to words like *even*, which lends further plausibility to their assimilation to a very context-sensitive component of truth-conditional meaning.

As originally argued in Kempson (1975) and Wilson (1975), typical presuppositional triggers whose presuppositions require not only their meaning but also general conversational implicatures are the factives (*know*, *discover*, *regret*, for example). A general way of making this explicit within the approach we have adopted is as follows.

Let *P* be some set of premises about human actions in general and conversation in particular (and perhaps also including other more specific premises). *P* might include, for example, that speakers generally adhere to Gricean maxims unless there is some good and evident reason not to do so. These assumptions will generally be present in context sets (as taken for granted by the conversationalists) and can be factored out as follows.

(72) S presupposes *p* relative to premise set *P* iff every context *c* such that $c^* \subseteq \bigcap P$ is also such that c^* entails *p*.

The phrase "such that $c^* \subseteq \bigcap P$" represents the relativization of the notion of presupposition to conversational premises. What it says is that a presupposition may be triggered by a sentence S with the aid of certain pragmatic premises *P*. Where the premises in question are general conversational principles, they will be true in most ordinary contexts. Thus language users will tend to think of the sentence itself as bearing the presupposition, failing to notice the role of the ancillary premises.

This leaves open, however, the possibility that in certain cases the premise in the set *P* can be suspended. Consequently, presuppositions that depend on such premises may be defeated when those supporting premises are called into question. This can be illustrated by the presuppositional behavior arising from the indexical character of the sentences in (73), a contrast first discussed in Stalnaker (1974):

(73) *a.* If Pavarotti$_i$ discovers that Loren is now in New York, he$_i$ will be angry. [Relative to context c_a, where sp(c_a) = James Bond]
b. If Pavarotti$_i$ discovers that I am now in New York, he$_i$ will be angry. [Relative to context c_b, where sp(c_b) = Loren]
c. If I discover that Loren is now in New York, I'll be angry. [Relative to context c_c, where sp(c_c) = Pavarotti]
d. Loren is now in New York. [Relative to any of the contexts specified above]

Relative to the three different kinds of contexts we have specified (including also, of course, a fixed time), sentences (73*a–c*) all express exactly the same proposition; their truth-conditional content is identical. Yet (73*a, b*) generally presuppose (73*d*), but (73*c*) does not (an observation that led Stalnaker to conclude that presupposition is pragmatic in the sense of being keyed to contextual factors). On the present approach, an account of this phenomenon might be sought along the following lines. In the case of (73*a*) the potential presupposition (73*d*) will often be actual, for in uttering (73*a*), Bond will usually have no reason to use the factive *discover*, unless he has information concerning Sophia Loren's whereabouts. If Bond does not know where Loren is but knows that Pavarotti is pursuing an investigation that is likely to result in his finding out Loren's present location, (73*a*) can be uttered without presupposing (73*d*); if *New York* carries focal stress, this interpretation is likely. Of course, when Loren utters (73*b*), it is very likely that the common ground includes the proposition that Loren knows her own whereabouts (we can imagine a context in which this assumption fails, but the setting is highly unusual). On the other hand, sentence (73*c*) will generally have the potential presupposition (73*d*) canceled, since Pavarotti's use of the first-person conditional implicates that for all he knows, he himself may not discover that Loren is now in New York, which is not a possibility if he already knows or takes it for granted that she is in New York. Thus the potential presupposition is canceled because it is inconsistent with the context as enriched by implicatures drawn from what Pavarotti has said and the form in which he expressed it. While an actual formalization of this informal line of explanation would require some work, it seems to us that the present approach paves the way for it.

The behavior of presuppositions of the kind exemplified in (73) contrasts with the fact that conventionally triggered presuppositions of the sort exemplified by *even* and *manage* are not really defeasible, because they do not depend on retractable premises.

(74) *a.* Did Michael Jordan manage to catch any passes? [Uttered when M. J. was healthy and was a professional basketball player.]
b. Did even Einstein understand the general theory of relativity?

Sentences like those in (74) are odd precisely because it is exceedingly difficult to think of contexts that might admit them since the presuppositions they trigger are not readily accommodated in a common ground. Thus on the present theory there is an explicit link between defeasibility and triggering mechanisms. Presuppositions are defeasible if they are triggered by defeasible assumptions about human action and conversation.

While presuppositions can arise from either conventional or pragmatic sources, we would expect that their projection properties are the same, since the context-change potential of nonatomic sentences is independent of how the presuppositions of atomic sentences are triggered. In fact in the examples above, we have indifferently used conventionally and conversationally triggered presuppositions.

In sum, conversationally triggered presuppositions can be defeated just as other conversational implicatures can. We have proposed an implicit set of premises, subject to revision, to deal with them. Where instead a trigger is conventional, a presupposition is no more defeasible than an entailment. Of course, just like an ordinary entailment of what is explicitly said, a conventional presupposition of S may be inconsistent with the context set that exists prior to the utterance of S. Recognized inconsistencies demand some revision in the common ground if discourse is to continue. Perhaps a proposition asserted earlier must be withdrawn or a cherished bit of common sense abandoned in the face of evidence. This is what happens, we believe, in the much discussed cases of presupposition cancellation involving negation. If negation is a hole, presupposition cancellation in negative contexts must be regarded as a case of accommodation. Let us see whether this is plausible.

Consider the discourse (75), where the interrogative cleft uttered by *A* conventionally triggers a presupposition that someone opened the door to the porch.

(75) *A, noticing the open door*: Was it you who opened the door to the porch? I closed it at lunchtime.
B: Well, it wasn't me who opened it, because I've been gone all afternoon, and it wasn't Joan who opened it, because she was with me, and it wasn't any of the kids who opened it, because they're on a field trip, and I strongly suspect that nobody opened it—there was a lot of wind this afternoon, you know.

Both *A*'s question and sentences like (76*a*) conventionally presuppose the proposition expressed by (76*b*).

(76) *a*. It was me who opened the door to the porch.
b. Someone opened the door to the porch.

The account of negation in (66) claims that *B*'s denial of (76*a*) and her subsequent denials using cleft sentences all bear presupposition (76*b*). Nonetheless, *B* finally expresses skepticism about that presupposition and thus can hardly be said to be purporting to take it for granted by the time she has finished her reply.

What seems to be happening is that *B* has accommodated the presupposition introduced by *A*'s comment until the final stage, when she proposes that that presupposition be abandoned. Suppose *A* had opened the conversation with (77).

(77) Someone opened the door to the porch. I closed it at lunchtime.

In this case *A*'s utterance has entered proposition (76*b*) into the common ground of the discourse by presenting it as a foregrounded assertion. With no immediate challenge, it simply moves into the background for subsequent talk; it moves in more explicitly but otherwise just as the accommodated presupposition of the query (75*a*) did. *B*'s response can be exactly as before. This time she did not accommodate a presupposition but simply bided her time before challenging a proposition explicitly asserted. The effect, however, is no different. The context set as the discourse proceeds includes the proposition that someone opened the door. She adds further (negative) information: it wasn't *B* herself or Joan or the kids who opened the door. Only when she has eliminated the likely candidates does she propose that *A*'s view of the matter is flawed and should be removed from the common ground—perhaps not completely rejected but no longer treated as if it were mutually believed. Note that if *B* explicitly and immediately challenges *A*'s belief that someone opened the door, she is not very likely to buttress that challenge using negated clefts. She is much more likely to offer something like (78).

(78) *B*: Probably nobody opened it. I've been gone all afternoon, and Joan was with me, and the kids are on a field trip.

Compare this response with the following, which sounds odd:

(79) *B*: Probably nobody opened it. It wasn't me who opened it, it wasn't Joan, . . .

B might of course relent from her immediate challenge and go on with a recounting that presupposes (76*b*), but if she does so, there is generally some signal of a return (perhaps only temporary) to the earlier common ground:

(80) *B*: Well anyway, it wasn't me.

Let us look now to what happens when conversational triggers are involved. Consider the dialogue in (81).

(81) *Speaker 1*: Does Joan regret getting a Ph.D. in linguistics?
Speaker 2: Oh, Joan had thought of getting a Ph.D. in linguistics but decided to study computer science instead.
Speaker 1: So, Joan doesn't regret getting a Ph.D. in linguistics.

Speaker 1 might have rephrased the final comments as in (82*a*) or (82*b*).

(82) *a.* So Joan must not regret getting a Ph.D. in linguistics.
b. Well, if Joan didn't get a Ph.D. in linguistics, then she can't regret having gotten one.

The use of the modals *must* and *can* in (82*a*) and (82*b*) suggests that what is being expressed is something about the effect of removing the proposition that Joan got a Ph.D. in linguistics, presupposed initially by speaker 1, from the common ground, which serves here as the modal base. In uttering (82*a*), speaker 1 makes it explicit that enriching comgrd (c) with the proposition that Joan did not get a Ph.D. in linguistics would make c^* inconsistent with the proposition that she regrets getting a Ph.D. in linguistics. With an utterance of (82*b*) something similar happens: it is acknowledged that a context set enriched by the antecedent of (82*b*)—a context where the original presupposition has to be withdrawn—is inconsistent with an affirmative answer to the original question. Note, however, that if speaker 2 simply says "No, she doesn't," then the presupposition remains intact.

There are many examples like (82) in the literature. It is not always noted, however, that such sentences would be extraordinarily odd if produced as assertive utterances of a negative proposition (requiring, perhaps, an accommodation then immediately rejected), though they are quite fine as denials of an affirmative proposition.

(83) Jim does not know that Ann is unfaithful, because she isn't.

To assert (83) in a context that contains nothing about Ann's fidelity before the utterance occurs is very odd indeed, since it makes the hearer accommodate by adding the proposition that is explicitly denied in the *because* clause. Assertion of a negative sentence is what rule (66) accounts for: the content of that sentence is presented for potential intersection with, and a narrowing down of, the context set. In contrast, denial of an affirmative removes from the existing (and subsequent) common ground an affirmative proposition. Often the affirmative proposition entered the common ground because it was overtly expressed by someone else. In such cases the common ground is not growing monotonically, nor is the context set shrinking monotonically. The common ground may grow, then shrink, and then grow in a different direction.

Finally, Horn's (1985) work on metalinguistic negation, which we mentioned in chapter 4, bears on some cases of apparent defeat of presuppositions. Presuppositions triggered by *manage* and *even* are denied in (84*a*) and (84*b*), respectively.

(84) *a.* I didn't "manage" to break my leg: you might say that it was as easy as falling off a log.
b. We don't "even" like Dorothy Sayers: she's one of the best mystery writers ever.

As the scare quotes informally indicate, what is going on here is not negation of a proposition but criticism of the manner in which someone else has expressed themselves.

In summary, while many problems remain open, an illuminating account of presupposition projection seems promised by further development of the general discourse-theoretic approach illustrated here. Such an approach links in a principled way the projection properties of connectives to their role in discourse, and it links defeasibility (viewed as an adjustment of the context) to how presuppositions are triggered. Presuppositions and presupposition projection per se pose no problem to a truth-conditional semantics. In fact, it would seem reasonable to expect that any theory of these phenomena should aim at preserving the precision and insights of the approach sketched here.

Exercise 7 The basic idea underlying the treatment of conditionals is the following. Uttering a conditional "If S_1, then S_2" in a context c eliminates from c^* all the worlds in which S_1 holds but S_2 does not. This context change can be achieved with either of the following equivalent formulas:

(1) *a.* $|\text{if } S_1 \text{ then } S_2|(c^*) = c^* - [|S_1|(c^*) - |S_2|(|S_1|(c^*))]$
b. $c^* + [\text{if } S_1, \text{then } S_2] = c^* - [[c^* + S_1] - [[c^* + S_1] + S_2]]$

The rule works as follows. We first compute $|S_1|(c^*)$; that is, we increment the context with S_1. We then compute $|S_2|(|S_1|(c^*))$; that is, we increment the context with S_1 and S_2. At this point we subtract $|S_2|(|S_1|(c^*))$ from $|S_1|(c^*)$. This gives us those worlds in c^* where S_1 is true but S_2 is false. Finally, we take the complement of

$|S_1|(c^*) - |S_2|(|S_1|(c^*))$ relative to c^*. This gives us the worlds where either S_1 is false or S_2 is true. Thus we have achieved our goal, which was to eliminate from the context set the worlds in which S_1 is true and S_2 false (which are the worlds ruled out by the assertion of the conditional).

Rule (1) predicts that the projection properties of conditionals are identical to those of conjunctions, as desired. To see this, consider what the first two steps in the application of (1) are. The first step is to compute $c^* + S_1$. This means that the presuppositions of S_1 (the antecedent) must be satisfied by c (and hence by the whole conditional). The second step of the rule requires us to compute the conjunction $[c^* + S_1] + S_2$. This means that, as is generally the case for conjunction, c must satisfy the presuppositions of S_2 *unless* S_1 (plus, perhaps, other propositions already in the common ground in c) entails them. The remaining steps involve only negation, which, as we saw, does not affect presuppositions. It follows that c admits "if S_1 then S_2" iff it admits "S_1 and S_2."

Consider the following case: Let c^* entail the proposition that Kermit was killed and that for all we know, whoever killed Kermit acted alone. Let S_0 be "If it was Ms. Piggy who killed Kermit, it was the butler who helped her." Let S_1 be "It was Ms. Piggy who killed Kermit." Let S_1^p be the proposition that someone killed Kermit. Let S_2 be "It was the butler who helped her." And let S_2^p be the proposition that someone helped Ms. Piggy. As before, S_1^i and S_2^i are the propositions expressed by S_1 and S_2 respectively. Diagram S_1^i, S_1^p, S_2^i, and S_2^p relative to c^*. On the basis of your diagram, is $c^* + S_0$ defined or undefined? Explain.

Consider the following situation: Let c^* entail the proposition that Ms. Piggy killed Kermit. Let S_0 be "If someone doesn't believe that Ms. Piggy killed Kermit, it is the butler who doesn't." Let S_1 be "Someone does not believe that Ms. Piggy killed Kermit." And let S_2 be "It is the butler who doesn't believe that Ms. Piggy killed Kermit." S_1^i and S_2^i are the propositions expressed by S_1 and S_2 respectively. Diagram S_1^i, S_1^p, S_2^i, and S_2^p relative to c^*. Indicate clearly and separately (i) $c^* + S_1$, (ii) $[c^* + S_1] + S_2$, (iii) $[c^* + S_1] - [[c^* + S_1] + S_2]$, and (iv) $c^* + S_0$. Is $c^* + S_0$ defined despite the fact that the presuppositions of S_2 are not satisfied in c? Explain.

7 Lambda Abstraction

In this chapter we are going to study the λ-operator in simplified form. The symbol λ is the Greek letter lambda. We will first consider the logic of the λ-operator abstractly by introducing it in the predicate calculus. We will subsequently discuss several of its applications to natural language semantics. The applications we will consider include coordinated VPs (sec. 3), relative clause formation (sec. 4), and VP ellipsis (sec. 5). These are all cases in which complex predicates of various kinds are being formed. The λ-operator is a formal device to handle the semantics of complex predicates. We will also see how such an operator facilitates the task of arriving at a theory of semantic representation (sec. 2). All this will illustrate its usefulness in semantics.

1 An Elementary Introduction to Lambda Abstraction

For our present purposes we can regard the λ-operator as a way of systematically defining complex predicates in terms of predicates already given. As we will see, the λ-operator is closely related to the set forming operator $\{x : \ldots\}$ and it will help us understand better what is involved in the latter. We will show how the λ-operator works by introducing it first in PC (from chapter 3) and subsequently in the intensional setting of IPC (from chapter 5).

1.1 The λ-operator in an extensional setting

Let us introduce in PC the following syntactic rule.

(1) If ψ is a well-formed formula and x a variable, $\lambda x[\psi]$ is a Pred_1.

The expression $\lambda x[\psi]$ is called a λ-abstract (or λ-expression) and can be read as "the property of being an x such that ψ."[1] We say that x in $\lambda x[\psi]$ is bound by λ and that ψ is the scope of that occurrence of the λ-operator. We will sometimes take the liberty of omitting the square brackets in $\lambda x[\psi]$ and simply write $\lambda x \psi$ if the context makes it clear what the scope of the λ-operator is.

Since an expression of the form $\lambda x[\psi]$ is syntactically a one-place predicate, we can apply it to terms and obtain well-formed formulas. In (2) we give some examples of λ-expressions and in (3) some well-formed formulas derived from them.

(2) *a.* $\lambda x[\neg \text{married}(x) \wedge \text{male}(x) \wedge \text{adult}(x)]$
b. $\lambda x \exists y[\text{love}(y, x)]$

(3) *a.* $\lambda x[\neg \text{married}(x) \wedge \text{male}(x) \wedge \text{adult}(x)](j)$
b. $\lambda x \exists y[\text{love}(y, x)](j)$

If we have in the language of IPC the predicates *married*, *male*, and *adult*, then (2*a*) illustrates how we can define the property of satisfying simultaneously the property of not being married, of being male, and of being an adult. The property defined in (2*a*) can be thought of as the property of being a bachelor. By the same token, if we have in our language the *love* relation, then we can define the property of being loved by someone (the property of being an x such that for some y, y loves x), as illustrated in (2*b*).

These properties can be predicated of individuals. So (3*a*) says that John has the property of being an x such that x is unmarried, x is male, and x is an adult. Under what conditions do we want to say that John has such a property? If and only if he is not married, is male, and is an adult. Similarly, under what conditions will John have the property of being loved by someone? Just in case there is someone who loves John. This means that we want (3*a*, *b*) to have the same truth conditions as (4*a*, *b*), respectively.

(4) *a.* $[\neg \text{married}(j) \wedge \text{male}(j) \wedge \text{adult}(j)]$
b. $\exists y[\text{love}(y, j)]$

The syntactic relations between (3*a*, *b*) and (4*a*, *b*) are fairly obvious. Formulas (4*a*, *b*) are obtained from (3*a*, *b*) by dropping the λx at the beginning, dropping the (j) at the end, and replacing x with j in the body of the λ-expression. This is the syntactic realization of the semantic relation that we want in general to hold between $\lambda x \psi(t)$ and ψ. We can schematize this as in (5).

(5) $\lambda x[\psi](t) \leftrightarrow \psi[t/x]$

Here t is any term (an individual variable or constant) and $\psi[t/x]$ is the result of substituting t for all occurrences of x in ψ.

Rule (5) is a simple generalization of what we did in the above example and states what will come out as a logical equivalence between the result of applying a λ-expression to a term and the result of substituting that term for the variable bound by λ in the formula that the λ-expression is derived from. This rule, which governs the logico-semantic structure of λ-expressions, is usually called *λ-conversion*. The left-to-right part is sometimes referred to as *λ-contraction* or *λ-reduction*, while the right-to-left part is sometimes called *λ-abstraction*.

While the mechanism of λ-conversion is conceptually quite simple, concrete examples can get quite complicated. Consider trying to simplify the following formula:

(6) $\forall x[\lambda z[\lambda w[[Q(w) \wedge B(m)] \leftrightarrow K(x, w)](z)](j)$
$\rightarrow \lambda y[K(y, x) \vee Q(y)](m)]$

To find what the λ-reduced form of (6) is, it is crucial to parse (6) correctly. One must find the scope of each occurrence of the λ-operator and identify the individual term it is predicated of. A tree diagram like the one in (7) might help.

(7)

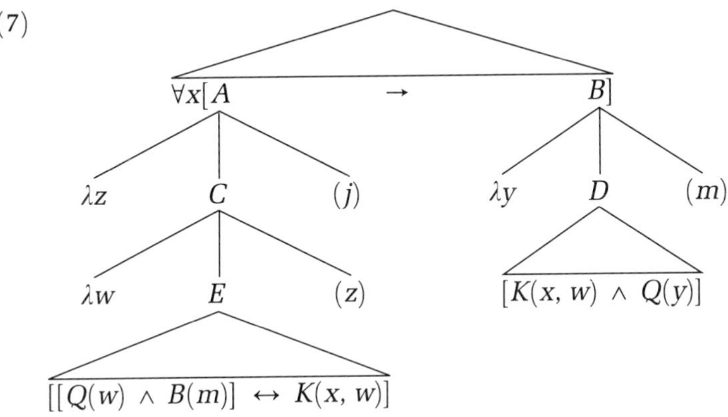

Diagram (7) exhibits the syntactic structure of (6). The topmost node represents the entire formula, and each capital letter represents one of its subformulas. Whenever we find a subtree of the form $[\lambda\alpha\delta(t)]$, we can uniformly substitute t for α in δ. If we start doing this bottom up in (7), after the first step we get the following:

(8)

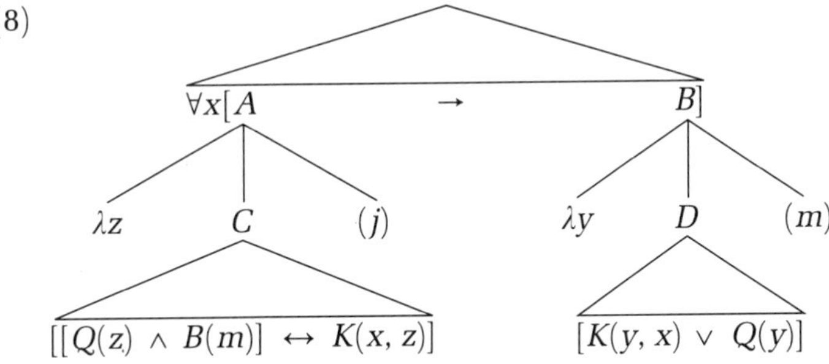

We reduced the subtree rooted in C by substituting z for w in E. If we do the same for the subtree rooted in B, we obtain the following:

(9)

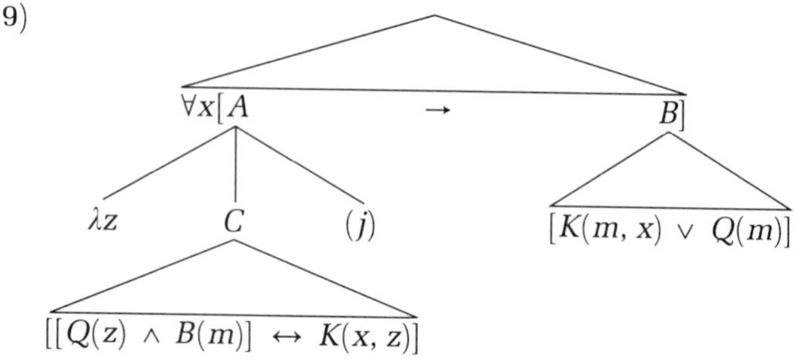

Finally, we repeat again the procedure on the subtree rooted in A, now substituting j for z in C, and we thus obtain the fully reduced form of (6), which is (10):

(10) $\forall x[[[Q(j) \wedge B(m)] \leftrightarrow K(x, j)] \rightarrow [K(m, x) \wedge Q(m)]]$

Exercise 1 Reduce the following formulas as much as you can. Show each step in the derivation.

(1) $\lambda x[\exists z[\lambda y[K(x, y)](z) \wedge R(z, x)]](j)$

(2) $\lambda y[\lambda x[K(x, y)](j)](m)$

(3) $\lambda z[[K(x, z) \wedge R(x, z)] \vee R(z, x)](j)](m)$

(4) $\exists y[\lambda z[\lambda x[B(x) \rightarrow \exists w[R(x, w)]](j) \wedge \lambda x[B(x) \vee Q(x)](z)](y)]$

So far we have considered only the syntax of the λ-operator and stated λ-conversion as a syntactic principle. We must now provide a semantics for λ-terms that makes the principle in (5) valid. This is done in (11).

(11) $[\![\lambda x\psi]\!]^{M,g} = \{u \in U : [\![\psi]\!]^{M,g[u/x]} = 1\}$

In (11) we specify the extension of $\lambda x\psi$ in a model M, with respect to an assignment g. Since we are dealing with a one-place predicate, such an extension will be a set. Which set is determined by successively computing the value of ψ for every u as a value of x. All those individuals that make ψ true in the model will be in the set. Thus the λ-operator in the present setting can be viewed as specifying how to build the set that constitutes the extension of the predicate being defined.

In the box that follows we provide a simple example in which we compute the value of the λ-expression $\lambda x[P(x) \wedge \neg x = m]$ in a model M_8 (also specified below). As the model contains three individuals (Bond, Loren, and Pavarotti), this will involve computing the value of $[P(x) \wedge \neg[x = m]]$ three times.

Exercise 2 Give the extension of the following formulas in M_8 with respect to g_8, where g_8 maps every variable into Bond.

(1) $\lambda x[P(x)]$

(2) $\lambda x[x = m]$

(3) $\lambda x[x = y]$

(4) $\lambda x[P(j)]$

(5) $\lambda x[P(x) \rightarrow [x = m \vee x = j]]$

It turns out that the semantics in (11) validates λ-conversion but only in a restricted form. If a variable clash arises in the process of converting, the result of applying a λ-expression to a term t will not be equivalent to its reduced counterpart. To see what this amounts to, let us consider a specific example. Take a simple model M_9 for IPC such that $U_9 = \{a, b, c\}$, and $V_9(K) = \{\langle a, b\rangle, \langle b, c\rangle\}$. Let us

---

Let M_8 be such that the following hold:

(a) $U_8 = \{\text{Pavarotti, Bond, Loren}\}$
(b) $V_8(P) = \{\text{Pavarotti, Bond}\}$
(c) $V_8(m) = \text{Pavarotti}$
(d) $V_8(j) = \text{Bond}$

And let g be an arbitrary value assignment.

(e) $[\![\lambda x[P(x) \wedge \neg[x = m]]]\!]^{M_8, g} = \{u : [\![P(x) \wedge \neg[x = m]]\!]^{M_8, g[u/x]} = 1\}$ By (11)
(f) $[\![P(x) \wedge \neg[x = m]]\!]^{M_8, g[\text{Pavarotti}/x]} = 0$ By (a) to (d) and the semantics of PC
(g) $[\![P(x) \wedge \neg[x = m]]\!]^{M_8, g[\text{Bond}/x]} = 1$ By (a) to (d) and the semantics of PC
(h) $[\![P(x) \wedge \neg[x = m]]\!]^{M_8, g[\text{Loren}/x]} = 0$ By (a) to (d) and the semantics of PC
(i) $[\![\lambda_x[P(x) \wedge \neg[x = m]]]\!]^{M_8, g} = \{\text{Bond}\}$ By (e) to (h)

furthermore adopt an assignment function g' such that $g'(y) = b$. Under these assumptions the following facts obtain:

(12) a. $[\![y]\!]^{M_9, g'} = b$
b. $[\![\lambda x \exists y[K(y, x)]]\!]^{M_9, g'} = \{b, c\}$

The property of being an x such that something stands in the relation K with x has the set $\{b, c\}$ as its extension in M_9. Moreover, under assignment g', the variable y denotes b. Let us now apply $\lambda x \exists y[K(y, x)]$ to y:

(13) a. $\lambda x \exists y[K(y, x)](y)$
b. $\exists y[K(y, y)]$

Now, formula (13*a*) is true, since something (namely *a*) stands in the K relation to b, which is the individual that y happens to denote. However the contracted form of (13*a*) is (13*b*), and (13*b*) says nothing at all about b; it says that something stands in the K relation with itself, which in M_8 at $\langle w, i\rangle$ is false. Thus (13*a*) is true in M_9 relative to g', while (13*b*) isn't. Hence the two formulas are not equivalent. It is pretty clear what goes wrong in going from (13*a*) to (13*b*): the final y is a free variable in (13*a*), but in the derivation of (13*b*) that occurrence of y gets accidentally bound by the existential quantifier. We can't allow this to happen. This means that the principle of λ-conversion must be qualified accordingly:

(14) $\lambda x \psi(t) \leftrightarrow \psi[t/x]$

Here t is any term and $\psi[t/x]$ is the result of substituting t for all occurrences of x in ψ, *unless* t is a variable that becomes bound as a result of the substitution.

There is an easy way of getting around the problem. As we know from chapter 3, our semantics allows alphabetic changes of bound variables in formulas. That is, if we have a formula ψ that contains n bound occurrences of a variable x and z is a variable not occurring in ψ, the formula that results from substituting z for x in each of its n occurrences in ψ will be equivalent to ψ. Thus, for example, (13*a*) is equivalent to (15*a*).

(15) a. $\lambda x \exists z[K(z, x)](y)$
b. $\exists z[K(z, y)]$

And (15*a*) then reduces unproblematically to (15*b*). Thus whenever the risk of a variable clash arises we can always avoid it by judicious use of alphabetic variants.

We haven't introduced the set forming operator $\{x : \psi\}$ formally, and we have relied on a purely intuitive grasp of its functioning. But it should be clear by now that a full fledged formal syntax and semantics for set abstraction would be very similar to that of the λ-operator. Arguably, the λ-operator is a bit more flexible than set abstraction, in that it generalizes more easily (and this is why we chose to study it here). For example, we will consider shortly how the λ-operator functions in an intensional setting. And in chapter 8 we will introduce multiple abstraction (creating λ-expressions of the form $\lambda y \lambda x[K(y, x)]$). Moreover, in a richer system of types (such as the one considered in chap. 2, sec. 3.4), the λ-operator can be used to define functions of arbitrary complexity using a very simple generalization of the semantics we have adopted. But we will not pursue this here.

1.2 λ-abstraction in an intensional setting

What is involved in using the λ-operator in an intensional setting (such as IPC)? The syntax of such an operator would remain the same. But its semantics would change slightly. In an intensional framework expressions are assigned a value in every world and time under consideration. Thus in particular, given an (intensional) model M for IPC, the semantics in (11) for the λ-operator will be modified simply as follows:

(16) $[\![\lambda x \psi]\!]^{M,w,i,g} = \{u \in U : [\![\psi]\!]^{M,w,i,g[u/x]} = 1\}$

Clearly, other than the reference to worlds and times, nothing much changes.

Exercise 3 Give the values of the following formulas in M_4 (p. 270) at the worlds and times indicated.

(1) $\lambda x[P(x)]$	w', i'''
(2) $\lambda x[x = m]$	$w'', i'; w'', i''; w', i'$
(3) $\lambda x[P(j)]$	$w', i''; w', i'; w'', i''$
(4) $\lambda x[P(x) \rightarrow [x = m \vee x = j]]$	$w', i'; w', i'''$

In spite of the straightforward character of the present extension of the λ-operator to an intensional setting, there are some surprising consequences that stem from it. Consider, for example, the formulas in (17).

(17) *a.* $\square[\lambda x[P(x)](m)]$
b. $\square P(m)$

Let us ask whether these two formulas are equivalent. On the basis of the semantics we have given (17*a*) says that whatever m denotes in the actual world (i.e., in the world we are in) is in the extension of P in every world; (17*b*) instead says that whatever m denotes in a world is P in that world. Suppose now that m is a rigid designator. Then, since m picks out the same entity in every world, clearly (17*a*) and (17*b*) amount to the same. Suppose, on the other hand, that m is not a rigid designator, but something like, say, "Mr. Muscle." Then (17*b*) says that in every world Mr. Muscle, whoever he may be in that world, has property P. But (17*a*) says something quite different. It says that the individual who in fact *happens* to be Mr. Muscle (in the world of evaluation) has property P in every world. Conceivably, (17*a*) might be true, and (17*b*) false, or vice versa. Hence, unless m is a rigid designator, (17*a*) and (17*b*) are not logically equivalent.

Exercise 4 Verify the last claim by (*a*) evaluating (17*a*) and (17*b*) in M_4, in w', at i'' and (*b*) constructing a model where (17*a*) is true and (17*b*) false.

The general moral is that if a formula ψ contains intensional contexts, λ-conversion (14) will be valid only if the term t is a rigid designator. In other words we have the following:

(18) $\exists y[\square[y = t]] \rightarrow [\lambda x[\psi](t) \leftrightarrow \psi[t/x]]$

Here ψ may contain intensional operators and $\psi[t/x]$ is as in (14).

We have thus discovered that, surprisingly, modalities introduce new restrictions on λ-conversion. This further illustrates how model theory can help in bringing logical syntax into sharper focus. We now turn to a discussion of some possible linguistic uses of the λ-operator.

2 Semantics via Translation

In chapter 3, section 3, we discussed the role of semantic representations in a theory of meaning. The conclusion we tentatively arrived at was that while semantics must relate natural language expressions to extralinguistic entities (as on the truth-conditional approach), there might be some advantage in doing so by an intermediate step that links natural language to a logic. In such a view the semantic component of a grammar can be thought of as a map from English onto a logic whose truth-conditional embedding in the world is known. The map onto logic provides us with a convenient representational medium that can perhaps facilitate the specification of semantic generalizations, while providing us with an indirect characterization of truth conditions.

However, it was impossible to come up with a simple compositional map onto (I)PC for the fragments we have considered. To develop such a map, one needs, for example, a way of translating into (I)PC VPs like *loves Pavarotti* in terms of the translations of *loves* and *Pavarotti*. But *loves Pavarotti* is a complex (or derived) property, and we had no systematic way of defining properties. The addition of the λ-operator to (I)PC enables us to do so and thus provides the base for formulating a compositional interpretive procedure that takes the form of a systematic algorithm translating from the relevant level of syntactic representation (in the case at hand, LF) into a suitable logical language (in the case at hand, (I)PC).[2]

In what follows, we will first show how this can be done for the fragment of English developed so far and then discuss some general consequences of this way of proceeding. We repeat here the relevant rules of F_3, for ease of reference.

(19) Syntax of F_3
- *a.* i. TP → NP $\bar{\text{T}}$
  - ii. $\bar{\text{T}}$ → T VP
- *b.* i. TP → TP conj TP
  - ii. TP → NEG TP
- *c.* VP → V_t NP
- *d.* VP → V_i
- *e.* VP → V_dt NP PP[to]
- *f.* T → PAST, PRES, FUT
- *g.* NP → Det N_c
- *h.* $\text{PP}_{[\text{to}]}$ → to NP
- *i.* Det → the, a, every
- *j.* N_P → Pavarotti, Loren, Bond, . . . , he_n, . . .
- *k.* N_c → book, fish, man, woman, . . .
- *l.* V_i → be boring, be hungry, walk, talk, . . .
- *m.* V_t → like, hate, kiss, . . .

n. V_{dt} → give, show, ...
o. conj → and, or
p. NEG → not
q. NP → N_p
r. CP → C TP
s. VP → V_S CP
t. V_s → believe, know, regret, ...
u. C → that

The rules for quantifier raising and T (or NEG) raising are given in (20) and (21).

(20) $[_{TP}\ X\ \text{NP}\ Y] \Rightarrow [_{TP}\ \text{NP}_i\ [_S x\ e_i\ Y]]$

(21) $[_{TP}\ \text{NP}\ X\ \text{VP}] \Rightarrow [_{TP}\ X\ [_S\ \text{NP VP}]]$, where X = T or NEG

The translation map onto IPC is defined recursively. First we state a correspondence between the categories of F_3 and those of IPC. Intuitively, this correspondence determines the logical type of the various expressions (it determines what kind of semantic entity will ultimately correspond to expressions of various syntactic categories).

(22)

F_3	IPC
N_p (proper nouns, traces, and pronouns)	individual terms (constants and variables)
V_i (intransitive verbs)	Pred_1 (one-place predicative expressions)
N_c (common nouns)	Pred_1
V_t (transitive verbs)	Pred_2 (two-place predicative expressions)
V_{dt} (ditransitive verbs)	Pred_3 (three-place predicative expressions)
V_S (believe-type verbs)	relations between individual terms and propositional terms

For any word or phrase α of F_3, α' is going to be its IPC translation. We make the following assumptions concerning lexical entries:

(23) not′ = $\neg$
and′ = $\wedge$
or′ = $\vee$
FUT′ = $\mathbf{F}$
PAST′ = $\mathbf{P}$

that$' = \wedge$

$t_n = x_n$, where t_n is a trace or a pronoun

For lexical entries not listed in (23), we adopt the following convention:[3]

(24) *a.* If α is of lexical category A, α' is a constant of IPC of the appropriate type as defined by (22).

b. In any admissible model M, α' is interpreted as α.

So for example, man$'$ is in Pred_1 (and its denotation is the same as that of the corresponding English word), love$'$ is in Pred_2, and so on.

This forms the basis of the recursion. We come next to the recursive part of the translation map. We design the map so that it assigns a translation to each node of an LF tree in terms of the translation of its daughters. Since the leaves of a well-formed LF tree are lexical entries and we have just assigned a translation to lexical entries, we are guaranteed that the translation map will eventually arrive at a determinate value. Throughout, for any category A, A' denotes the translation of the (sub)tree rooted in A. Essentially there are three types of rules. The first deals with nonbranching (or otherwise semantically vacuous) structures and simply passes up to the mother node the translation of the daughter (e.g., the translation of $[_{\text{NP}}$ Lee$]$ is the same as the translation of *Lee*). The second type of rule deals with predicates and their arguments, or operators and formulas and instructs us to apply the former to the latter. So for example, the translation of $[_{\text{TP}}$ Lee smokes$]$ will be smoke$'$(Lee$'$) and the translation of $[\text{TP}_1$ and $\text{TP}_2]$ will be $\text{TP}_1' \wedge \text{TP}_2'$ (i.e. the result of infixing $\wedge$ between the translations of the two conjuncts). A special instance of this rule is the VP rule. Here we typically have a V (e.g. *give*) and its arguments (for example *War and Peace* and *to Lee*), minus the external one, i.e., the subject. The translation will create a λ-abstract like λx[give$'$(x, War & Peace$'$, Lee$'$)], where we apply the V to its arguments (the preposition *to* is semantically vacuous) and for the subject we put in a variable over which we abstract, creating a predicate that will eventually apply to the external argument. Finally, the third type of rule deals with quantificational structures, introducing the appropriate quantifier.

(25) *a.* i. $[_A\ B]' = B'$

ii. $[_A \text{ to } B] = B'$

example: [to Lee]$'$ = Lee$'$

b. $[_{TP}\ \text{NP}\ \bar{\text{T}}]' = \bar{\text{T}}'(\text{NP}')$
example: $[\text{Lee smokes}]' = \text{smoke}'(\text{Lee}')$

c. $[\text{TP}_1\ \text{conj}\ \text{TP}_2]' = \text{TP}_1'\text{conj}'\ \text{TP}_2'$
example: $[\text{Lee smokes and Kim drinks}]'$
$= \text{smoke}'(\text{Lee}') \wedge \text{drink}'(\text{Kim}')$

d. $[_{VP}\ \text{V NP}]' = \lambda x[\text{V}'(x, \text{NP}')]$
example: $[_{VP}\ \text{like Kim}]' = \lambda x[\text{like}'(x, \text{Kim}')]$

e. $[\text{V NP PP}]' = \lambda x[\text{V}'(x, \text{NP}', \text{PP}')]$
example: $[_{VP}\ \text{introduce him}_j \text{ to Lee }]'$
$= \lambda x[\text{introduce}'(x, x_j, \text{Lee}')]$

f. $[_{CP}\ \text{C TP}]' = \text{C}'\ \text{TP}'$
example: $[\text{that Lee smokes}]' = {}^\wedge\text{smoke}'(\text{Lee}')$

g. $[X\ \text{TP}]' = X'\ \text{TP}'$
examples: $[\text{PAST Lee smoke}]' = \mathbf{P}\ \text{smoke}'(\text{Lee}')$,
$[\text{NEG Lee smoke}]' = \neg\ \text{smoke}'(\text{Lee}')$

h. $[\text{NP}_i\ \text{TP}]$ structures

i. if $\text{NP}_i = [\text{every}\ \beta]_i$, then $[\text{NP}_i\ \text{TP}]' = \forall x_i[\beta'(x_i) \rightarrow \text{TP}']$
example: $[\text{every dog}_i\ [t_i \text{ barks}]]'$
$= \forall x_i[\text{dog}'(x_i) \rightarrow \text{bark}'(x_i)]$

ii. if $\text{NP}_i = [\text{a}\ \beta]_i$, then $[\text{NP}_i\ \text{TP}]' = \exists x_i[\beta'(x_i) \wedge \text{TP}']$
example: $[\text{a dog}_i[t_i \text{ barks}]]' = \exists x_i\ [\text{dog}'(x_i) \wedge \text{bark}'(x_i)]$

iii. if $\text{NP}_i = [\text{the}\ \beta]_i$, then
$[\text{NP}_i\ \text{TP}]' = \exists x_i[\beta'(x_i) \wedge \forall y[\beta'(y) \rightarrow x_i = y] \wedge \text{TP}']$
example: $[\text{the dog}_i\ [t_i \text{ barks}]]'$
$= \exists x_i[\text{dog}'(x_i) \wedge \forall y[\text{dog}'(y) \rightarrow x_i = y] \wedge \text{bark}'(x_i)]$

In the following box we present a complete example. Each node in the given tree is numbered. Below the tree, next to each node number the corresponding compositional translation is given along with an indication of the rule through which it is obtained.[4] The translation schemas in (25) fall in uniform and general patterns, reducing essentially to the application of a predicate or of a sentential operator to its arguments; *application* can be regarded as the core mode of semantic combination. The way in which this happens depends ultimately on the lexical semantic type of the expressions involved. This is much in the spirit of type driven semantics (as discussed in chap. 2, sec. 3.4). The only exceptions are the rules of quantification that have to be specified individually and that do not provide us with translations for quantified NPs as such (only for structures in which those NPs occur). These exceptions derive from the fact that we don't have yet an

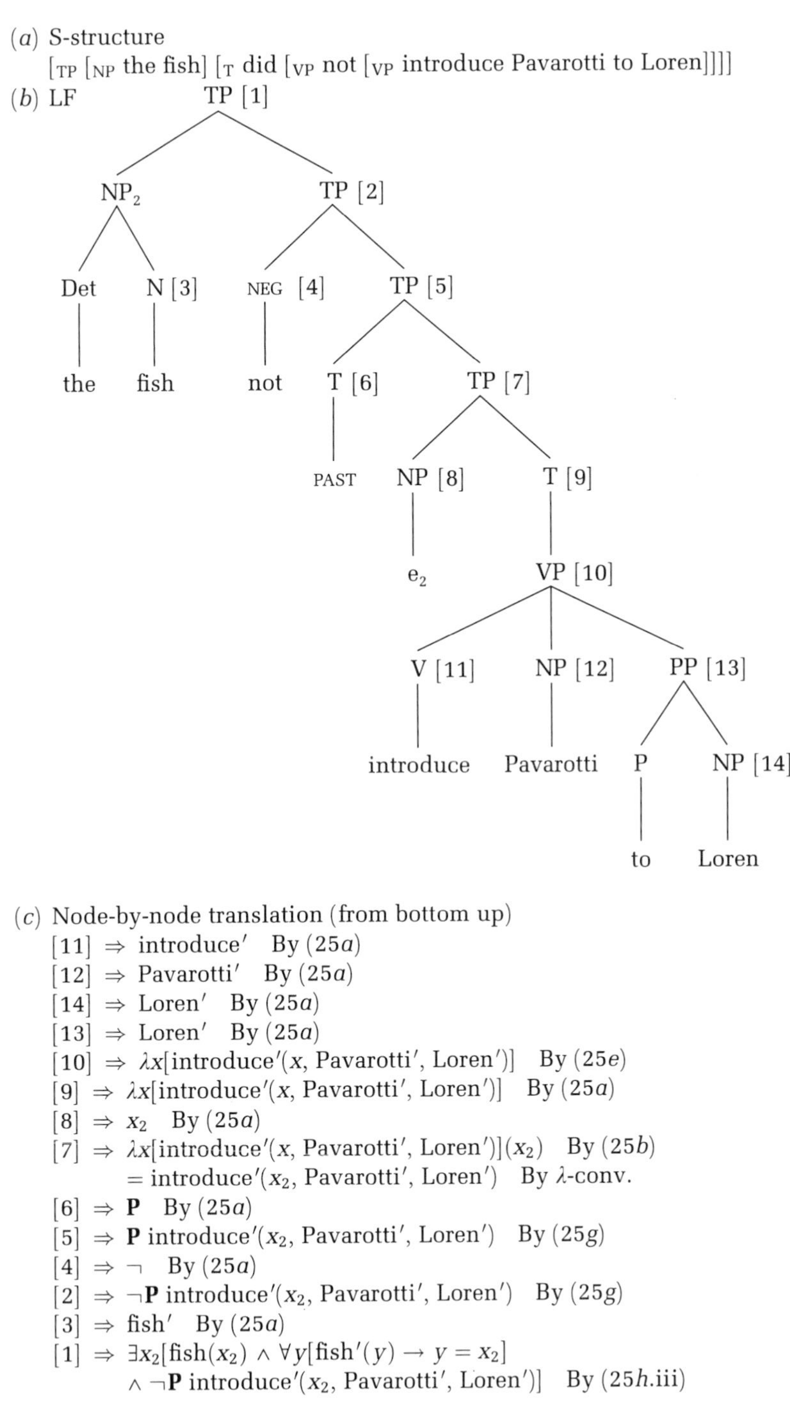

(a) S-structure
$[_{TP}\ [_{NP}$ the fish$]\ [_{T}$ did $[_{VP}$ not $[_{VP}$ introduce Pavarotti to Loren$]]]]$

(b) LF

(c) Node-by-node translation (from bottom up)

$[11] \Rightarrow \text{introduce}'$ By (25a)
$[12] \Rightarrow \text{Pavarotti}'$ By (25a)
$[14] \Rightarrow \text{Loren}'$ By (25a)
$[13] \Rightarrow \text{Loren}'$ By (25a)
$[10] \Rightarrow \lambda x[\text{introduce}'(x, \text{Pavarotti}', \text{Loren}')]$ By (25e)
$[9] \Rightarrow \lambda x[\text{introduce}'(x, \text{Pavarotti}', \text{Loren}')]$ By (25a)
$[8] \Rightarrow x_2$ By (25a)
$[7] \Rightarrow \lambda x[\text{introduce}'(x, \text{Pavarotti}', \text{Loren}')](x_2)$ By (25b)
$= \text{introduce}'(x_2, \text{Pavarotti}', \text{Loren}')$ By λ-conv.
$[6] \Rightarrow \mathbf{P}$ By (25a)
$[5] \Rightarrow \mathbf{P}\ \text{introduce}'(x_2, \text{Pavarotti}', \text{Loren}')$ By (25g)
$[4] \Rightarrow \neg$ By (25a)
$[2] \Rightarrow \neg\mathbf{P}\ \text{introduce}'(x_2, \text{Pavarotti}', \text{Loren}')$ By (25g)
$[3] \Rightarrow \text{fish}'$ By (25a)
$[1] \Rightarrow \exists x_2[\text{fish}(x_2) \wedge \forall y[\text{fish}'(y) \rightarrow y = x_2]$
$\wedge \neg\mathbf{P}\ \text{introduce}'(x_2, \text{Pavarotti}', \text{Loren}')]$ By (25h.iii)

adequate semantics for NPs, something which will be remedied in chapter 9.

Exercise 5 Give the translations of the various LF structures associated with "Every fish will not like a man."

On an approach along the preceding lines, semantics is split into two components. First, a compositional translation into a logical calculus is provided. Second, this logical calculus is equipped with a truth-conditional and model-theoretic semantics. As we have seen, it is possible to provide truth conditions directly for LFs, and in this sense, translation into a logical calculus appears to be dispensable. What such a translation provides us with is an explicit way of representing the truth conditions associated with English sentences. Of course, the calculus must be rich enough to support such an enterprise. The λ-operator is quite useful in this regard, as it enables us to represent compositionally complex VPs in our logical syntax.

In what follows, we will reserve the term *logical form* (with lowercase *l* and lowercase *f*, which we shall abbreviate as *lf*) for the calculus we use to translate LF into. "The logical form of a sentence S, relative to its LF structure *A*" is taken to mean "the translation of *A* into the semantic calculus *lf*."

This kind of two-stage semantics calls for a few general remarks. So far even though we have occasionally found it convenient to translate English into a logical calculus, we had no general procedure for doing so. The "correct" translation had to be decided on a case by case basis. In such a situation there is no way of knowing whether the translation procedure is finitely specifiable, whether it represents a viable tool for characterizing our semantic competence. Now we see that a translation procedure for a fragment of English can be systematically and compositionally specified. We are thus entitled to hope that this method can be extended to larger fragments, that the relation between syntactic structure and logical structure in general is rule-governed.

Is it possible to regard logical form so construed as providing us with a theory of semantic representation, with a theory that characterizes what we grasp in processing a sentence? This question is very controversial. For many the answer is no.[5] We think it is possible, as our logical forms do meet the main requirements that semantic representations are generally expected to meet. What are some such requirements? Minimally, grasping a sentence must involve recovering some representation of its lexical components and some way of amalgamating representations of lexical meanings into representations of the meaning of larger units, until a representation of the meaning of the whole sentence is recovered. Whichever format one eventually chooses for representing lexical meaning, a theory of semantic representation must support this compositional process. Our semantics characterizes precisely that: the compositional process that lexical meanings have to support if they are to do their job of systematically contributing to the meaning of larger units. Moreover, any semantic representations must account for the semantic intuitions of speakers. Given the representations associated with two sentences *A* and *B*, we must be able to tell whether they are contradictory, compatible, or equivalent in terms of their representations at some level. If one uses a logical calculus in the way we are here, equivalence (content synonymy), contradiction, and other semantic relations can be syntactically checked using axioms and rules of inference associated with the calculus (axioms and rules of inference that we are not specifying here).

Furthermore, the particular approach that we are developing, even if it is only a rough first approximation, embodies specific empirical claims about the nature of semantic representation. They can be summarized as follows.

- It has a Boolean core, which simply means the following: one can isolate certain logical words (*and, or, not*) with the logical properties we have discussed. These elements constitute the central devices for gluing together stretches of information. They are related according to the "laws of thought" originally characterized as such by the mathematician George Boole (on which classical logic is based). Much recent work has been devoted to showing that this Boolean core determines the logical structure of every syntactic category (and not just sentences).[6]
- It incorporates a categorization of semantic objects: individuals, properties, and propositions that are related to each other in a certain way and have a certain structure (the structure of propositions is Boolean).

- It has devices to express quantification. Some forms of quantification make use of a variable-binding mechanism; others (like the modals) do not.
- It includes indexical expressions and other context-sensitive features.

The apparatus developed so far is a way of characterizing these properties while meeting the general criteria that any theory of meaning should satisfy. Even though many problems are left open, we think that any adequate theory of semantic representation should incorporate the features we have listed.

Among other things, this shows that the line of inquiry we are pursuing is in principle compatible with an "internalist" or "conceptualist" take on meaning according to which meaning consists solely of mental constructs. A logical calculus of the kind we have arrived at enables us to syntactically check entailments, presuppositions, etc. and can in principle be realized in a finite computational device to which our minds are arguably similar. Under this view, the model theory might be regarded as a way of testing relevant properties of the calculus, such as its soundness (rather than as a reference fixing device).

Although it might conceivably be justified to regard the present theory as a way of characterizing *what* one grasps in processing a sentence, it is not clear that it is equally justified to view the present approach as a characterization of *how* meaning is grasped.[7] But then, the present theory does not make any direct claim as to the specific psychological processes that form the actual mechanisms of comprehension. The relation between semantics and meaning comprehension is just an instance of the relation between grammar, viewed as an abstract rule system, and language processing. Such a relation is not straightforward, although ultimately one would like to see these theories converge to an integrated theory of cognition. What we are trying to do here is to develop a theory of the structural properties that a speaker's representations of meaning must have.

While a logical calculus with the above characteristics might well be the basis of the way meaning is mentally represented, we also believe that this is so only because such a calculus is embeddable in the world. Mental representations represent reality: individuals having properties and standing in relations. Our strategy has been to characterize what such representations are representations of. The logical structure of our calculus is lifted from, and supported by, the denotational structure of the model. As we have pointed out on various occasions, if we didn't have a way of relating our logical syntax to what it represents, we would have simply mapped configurations of symbols (natural language) onto other configurations of symbols (a logical syntax). Accordingly, we don't regard model theory simply as a metatheoretical tool to check that our calculus does what it is supposed to do (i.e., yield a sound relation of equivalence among syntactic representations). We regard it also as a way of anchoring representations to the world.

The program sketched here does not force a particular stance on such difficult foundational issues. But it can help clarify where differences lie.

3 VP Disjunction and Conjunction

Consider sentences like the following:

(26) *a.* Pavarotti is boring and hates Bond.
b. Pavarotti is hungry or is tired.

In (26*a*, *b*) we have what look like conjoined and disjoined VPs. In the present section we are going to discuss briefly their syntax and semantics.

3.1 Generalizing the scope of logical operators

In the early times of transformational grammar it was proposed that sentences like those in (26) be derived from underlying structures that looked like those in (27) via a transformation called conjunction (or disjunction) reduction.

(27) *a.* Pavarotti is boring, and Pavarotti hates Bond.
b. Pavarotti is hungry, or Pavarotti is tired.

It is hard to come across a precise definition of conjunction reduction in the literature, although the intuitive idea behind it is fairly clear.[8] In a coordinated structure of the form [S_1 and S_2] parts of S_2 could be deleted if they were identical in certain ways with parallel parts of S_1. Part of the motivation behind such a proposal was the evident synonymy between (27) and (26). So one could propose that, say, (27*a*) is the S-structure (and LF structure) of (26*a*) and that the deletion of the second occurrence of *Pavarotti* takes place in the phonology and therefore doesn't affect meaning.

This simplistic proposal, however, cannot work. Consider the following:

(28) *a.* A man is boring and hates Bond.
b. Every man is boring or is hungry.

(29) *a.* A man is boring, and a man hates Bond.
b. Every man is boring, or every man is hungry.

Clearly (28*a*, *b*) do not have the same meaning as (29*a*, *b*), their alleged sources. More specifically, (28*a*) entails (29*a*), but not vice versa, and (29*b*) entails (28*b*), but not vice versa. If conjunction reduction were a phonological deletion phenomenon that does not affect meaning, one would not expect this pattern to arise.

These considerations have led various researchers to adopt a syntax for VP conjunction and disjunction of the following kind:[9]

(30) *a.* VP → VP conj VP
b. example

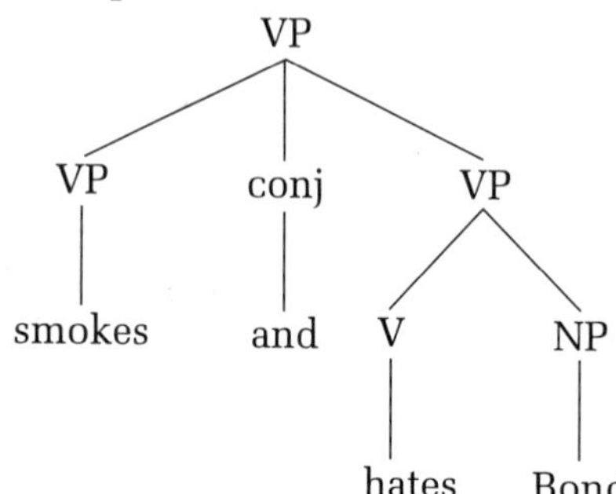

The point then becomes how to interpret conjoined (or disjoined) VPs in such a way that (26*a*, *b*) come out as being equivalent to (27*a*, *b*) but (28*a*, *b*) do not come out as equivalent to (29*a*, *b*), respectively. The λ-operator makes this very easy. We can extend disjunction and conjunction to predicates as follows. For any two predicates P_1 and P_2 of (I)PC we can define a new operator that, when applied to P_1 and P_2, gives us their conjunction or disjunction. One way of doing this is as follows (P_1 and P_2 are in Pred_1):

(31) *a.* $[P_1 \wedge P_2] = \lambda x[P_1(x) \wedge P_2(x)]$
b. $[P_1 \vee P_2] = \lambda x[P_1(x) \vee P_2(x)]$

This kind of definition is usually called a pointwise definition. What it does is take an already defined sentential operator, say $\vee$, and extends it to a predicate operator. In defining how the predicate operator $\vee$ applies to arbitrary predicates P_1 and P_2, we look at the values that $P_1(x) \vee P_2(x)$ gets when we assign to x successively each individual in U. (The domain in U can be regarded as an abstract space in which the individuals contained in U constitute the points, whence the term *pointwise*: we look at the values of $P_1(x) \vee P_2(x)$ point by point, or individual by individual.) The λ-operator makes the job of providing such pointwise definitions extremely straightforward. In this way one can see that the semantic values of predicates (properties) inherit the Boolean structure of propositions. This means, for example, that just as $\neg[\psi \wedge \phi]$ is equivalent to $[\neg\psi \vee \neg\phi]$, the predicate $\lambda x \neg[\psi \wedge \phi]$ will be the same predicate as $\lambda x[\neg\psi \vee \neg\phi]$. Notice that since the extension of one-place predicates is a set, conjunction as applied to predicates amounts to set intersection and disjunction to set union.

The semantics for VP conjunction and disjunction should by now be obvious:

(32) $[\mathrm{VP}_1 \text{ conj } \mathrm{VP}_2]' = \mathrm{VP}' \text{ conj}' \text{ VP}'$

In the box on the following page, we give a more detailed illustration of how the present approach works, by working out example (28*b*). For simplicity, we omit making reference to tense and we revert to using S for sentences. It is easy to see that on the present analysis, (28*b*) does not come out as equivalent to "Every man is hungry or every man is boring."

Exercise 6 Show that (26*a*) and (27*a*) are equivalent but (28*a*) and (29*a*) are not.

Thus an analysis that takes advantage of the λ-operator, as along the present lines, enables one to capture in a very simple way certain scope interactions between quantified subjects and VP-level conjunction and at the same time allows for a rather straightforward syntactic approach to the constructions in question.

Here is a further interesting consequence of the present analysis. Consider the following sentence:

(33) John $[_{\mathrm{VP}}$ $[_{\mathrm{VP}}$ is nice] and $[_{\mathrm{VP}}$ likes everybody]]

One of the coordinated VPs in (33) contains a quantified NP, namely *everybody*. Such an NP cannot be interpreted *in situ*, under

Analysis of (28*b*), "Every man is hungry or is boring"

(*a*) S-structure
$[_S\ [_{NP}$ every man$][_{VP}\ [_{VP}$ is hungry$][_{conj}$ or$][_{VP}$ is boring$]]]$

(*b*) LF

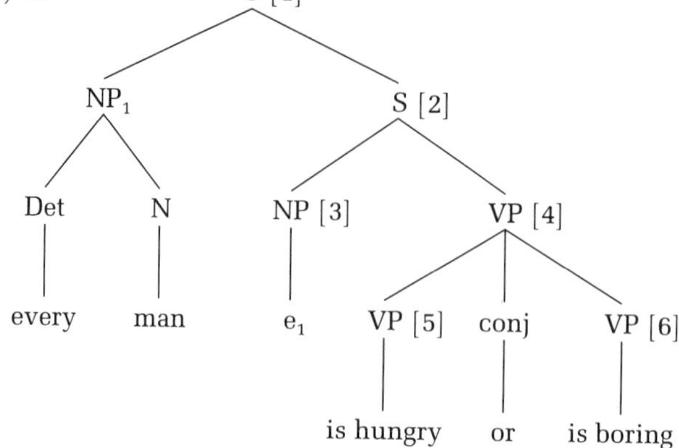

(*c*) Compositional interpretation (each numbered node is associated with its translation)

i. [5] ⇒ hungry′
ii. [6] ⇒ boring′
iii. [3] ⇒ x_1
iv. [4] ⇒ [hungry′ ∨ boring′] By (32)
v. [2] ⇒ [hungry′ ∨ boring′](x_1) By (25*b*)
vi. [1] ⇒ $\forall x_1[\text{man}'(x_1) \rightarrow [\text{hungry}' \vee \text{boring}'](x_1)]$ By (25*h*.i)
$= \forall x_1[\text{man}'(x_1) \rightarrow \lambda y[\text{hungry}'(y) \vee \text{boring}'(y)](x_1)]$ By (31b)
$= \forall x_1[\text{man}'(x_1) \rightarrow [\text{hungry}'(x_1) \vee \text{boring}'(x_1)]]$ By λ-conv.

our current assumptions. It has to be raised. However, it cannot be raised to S (=TP). We know that extraction out of conjoined structures is subject to strong restrictions: it is only possible when an identical constituent is extracted out of the conjuncts across the board, as illustrated in (34).

(34) the boy [[Mary likes who] and [John hates who]]
⇒ the boy who [[Mary likes ____] and [John hates ____]]

Adjoining the NP *everybody* in (34) to S would amount to a violation of the across-the-board constraint on movement. It follows that *everybody* must be adjoined to some lower position, for example, the minimal VP that contains its trace:

(35) *a.* $[_{VP}$ everybody$_1$ $[_{VP}$ likes $e_1]]$
b. $\lambda y \forall x_1[\text{like}(y, x_1)]$

The structure in (35a) can be naturally interpreted as in (35b), i.e. as the property of liking everybody. The general interpretive rule for VP adjoined NPs can be given as follows:

(36) $[[\text{every } \beta]_i \text{ VP}] \Rightarrow \lambda y \forall x_i[\beta'(x_i) \rightarrow \text{VP}'(y)]$

And similarly for other NPs. The idea is this. VPs are predicates while our quantification rules work for formulas. What do we do, then? We apply the VP meanings to a variable, thereby obtaining a formula; we then use our usual quantification rule; finally we abstract over the variable we introduced, thereby creating a suitable VP meaning. This too (like generalized coordination) is a kind of pointwise definition.

Thus, having coordinated VPs leads us to extend our rule for interpreting quantified NPs by adding the category VP as a suitable landing side for raised NPs and extending accordingly our interpretive rule (which turns out to be straightforward). This extension is forced upon us by the necessity of interpreting coordinated VPs that contain quantified NPs, without violating the across-the-board constraint on raising. Such a move, however, is not only theoretically necessary. It has welcome empirical consequences. Consider the sentences in (37).

(37) a. A banner was hanging in front of every window.
b. A banner was hanging in front of every window but was ripped off by the wind.

Sentence (37*a*) admits (in fact, favors) a reading in which *every window* is construed as having scope over a banner (i.e., for every window, there is a banner in front of it). This reading is obtained by adjoining *every window* over the subject to S. However, such a reading disappears in (37*b*). The only interpretation available for this sentence is one in which there was one banner big enough to hang in front of every window, which was ripped off by the wind. This fact is to be expected under the present analysis. The across-the-board constraint on extraction prevents *every window* from being extracted from the VP that contains it in (36*b*), and thus such an NP winds up having narrow scope with respect to the subject.

There are further general consequences of this way of looking at things. It has been noted in a number of recent works that conjunction and disjunction in languages like English are really cross-categorial operators: expressions of virtually any category can be conjoined and disjoined.[10]

(38) *a.* John and every student liked the show. (NP conj NP)
b. Most or every student came. (Det conj Det)
c. John walked in and around the building. (Prep conj Prep)
d. John saw and bought a shirt. (V_t conj V_t)
e. John saw an old and ugly house. (Adj conj Adj)

The kind of conjunction in (38) is sometimes called "constituent conjunction" (as opposed to "sentential or clausal conjunction"). One would like to maintain that whatever the syntactic details, one can come up with a uniform meaning for *and* or *or* across all categories. Such a generalized meaning for *and* or *or* might be a good candidate for the linguistic universal stated as follows:

(39) Operators with the same general logical structure as *and* or *or* are found in all languages; such operators tend to be cross-categorial.

Cross-categorial operators of this kind can indeed be defined by generalizing the pointwise definitions of VP conjunction and disjunction given above. But this goes beyond what can be done here.

The simpleminded version of conjunction reduction given above wasn't able to accommodate the scope phenomena in (28) and (29). This suggests that either one should not analyze them using such a transformation (although perhaps such a transformation might still be needed for other phenomena) or a more elaborate version of conjunction reduction should be developed. Even if the latter hypothesis turns out to be workable, it still seems that its semantics will have to be along the same lines as developed here.

3.2 More on TP

Consider the following sentences:

(40) *a.* Lee came late and will leave early.
b. Lee will come late and will not appreciate the show.

In (35) the coordinated VPs show different tenses. How are they to be generated? In this subsection we will discuss the structure of this type of sentence, which will illustrate once more how λ-

abstraction (or the equivalent) is useful in dealing with complex predicates.

We will consider two strategies to deal with sentences like (40*a*, *b*). The first is to assume that they involve $\bar{\text{T}}$ conjunction:

(41) *a.* $[_{\bar{T}}\ [_{\bar{T}}\ \text{T VP}]\ \text{and}\ [_{\bar{T}}\ \text{T VP}]]$

b.

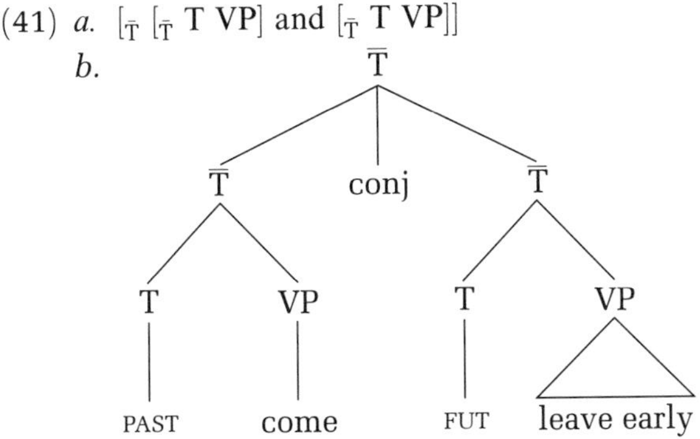

But then what would happen to the two Ts of a conjoined $\bar{\text{T}}$ phrase with respect to our rule of T raising? For one thing, the across-the-board constraint on movement would prevent us from fronting the two distinct Ts in sentences like (40*a*). Moreover, even if we did permit a double T fronting in (40*a*, *b*), the result would not be semantically coherent, for it would mean something like "It was the case that it will be the case that [John came late and John leave early]."

A possible solution would be to provide a way of interpreting T *in situ*, that is, in nonraised position. The λ-operator enables us to do so. By using the same lifting technique introduced in the previous section, we can define a number of predicate-level operators along the following lines:

(42) For any one-place predicate Q,

a. $[\neg Q] = \lambda x[\neg Q(x)]$

b. $[\mathbf{P}Q] = \lambda x[\mathbf{P}Q(x)]$

c. $[\mathbf{F}Q] = \lambda x[\mathbf{F}Q(x)]$

We can then provide a rule for interpreting unraised T or NEG along the following lines:

(43) *a.* $[\text{T VP}]' = \text{T}'\ \text{VP}'$

Example: $[\text{PAST come}]' = \mathbf{P}\ \text{come}' = \lambda x[\mathbf{P}\ \text{come}(x)]$

b. $[\text{NEG VP}]' = \text{NEG}'\ \text{VP}'$

Example: $[\text{not leave}]' = \neg\text{leave}' = \lambda x[\neg\text{leave}'(x)]$

If T is not raised, a sentence like (44*a*) winds up being interpreted as shown in (44*b*):

(44) *a.* Lee will leave.

b. [**F** leave′](Lee′) By (39*a*)

$= \lambda x[\mathbf{F}\ \text{leave}'(x)](\text{Lee}')$ By (38*b*)

$= \mathbf{F}\ \text{leave}'(\text{Lee}')$ By λ-conversion

This is equivalent to what we would get via T raising. The latter rule would still be needed to get all the necessary scope interactions between tense, negation and other scope bearing elements. But the option of interpreting T *in situ* enables us to deal with coordinated structures such as (40).

Exercise 7 Give the S structure and LF for the following sentence (leaving T *in situ*). Then provide a node-by-node translation.

(1) Some man came and will sing.

An alternative approach to the one we have considered relies on the so called VP-internal subject hypothesis (briefly discussed in chapter 5, section 3.1.2). According to this view, the subject is generated within the VP and then raised further up in the clause, as shown:

(45) *a.* Lee will leave.

b. Base structure

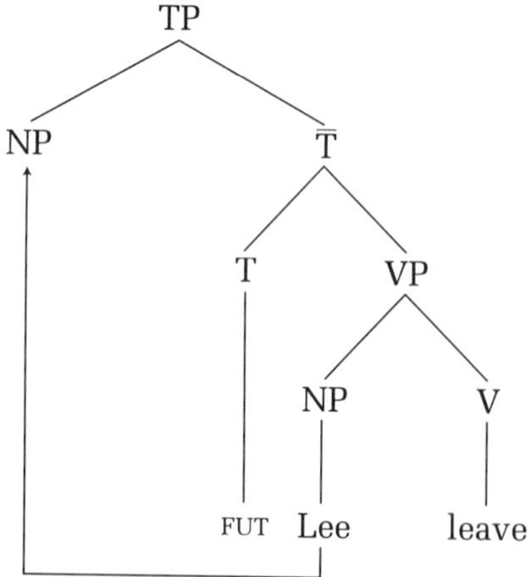

c. S-structure

$[_{\text{TP}}$ Lee$_1$ will $[_{\text{VP}}$ e_1 leave$]]$

The cases in (40) then involve TP conjunction with across-the-board extraction of the VP-internal subject:

(46) *a.* Lee came late and will leave early.
b. $[_{TP}$ PAST $[_{VP}$ Lee come late$]]$ and $[_{TP}$ FUT $[_{VP}$ Lee leave early$]]$
$\Rightarrow$ [Lee$_1$ $[_{TP}$ PAST $[_{VP}$ e_1 come late$]]$
and $[_{TP}$ FUT $[_{VP}$ e_1 leave early$]]]$

The adoption of the VP-internal subject hypothesis entails that VPs are generally going to have a trace in the position of the subject. A natural way to interpret such structures is again by means of the λ-operator. Here are some examples:

(47) *a.* $[_{VP}$ e_2 leave$]$ $\Rightarrow \lambda x_2$ leave$'(x_2)$
b. $[_{VP}$ e_2 love Kim$]$ $\Rightarrow \lambda x_2$ love$(x_2$, Kim$')$[11]

Both the approaches that we have considered predict that wide scope readings for negation are unavailable in conjoined VPs, as NEG raising in these cases is blocked (by the across-the-board constraint on movement). This prediction appears to be correct. Sentence (48*a*) has only the reading represented by (48*b*) and not the one represented by (48*c*).

(48) *a.* Every student is tired and isn't enjoying the show.
b. $\forall x[\text{student}'(x) \rightarrow [\text{tired}'(x) \wedge \neg[\text{enjoy the show}]'(x)]$
c. $\neg\forall x[\text{student}'(x) \rightarrow [\text{tired}'(x) \wedge [\text{enjoy the show}]'(x)]$

In the present section we have discussed coordinated VPs, first without tense and then with tense. The topics that we have just addressed are very complex, and our discussion is too brief to really do justice to them. However, it does illustrate, we think, the usefulness of the λ-operator and more generally how various semantic options interact in interesting ways with theoretical choices in the relevant level of syntax.

4 Relative Clauses

Consider the following italicized phrases:

(49) *a.* a teacher *whom Mary likes* ____
b. the boy *that John believes* ____ *came late*
c. the woman *who* ____ *lives next door*
d. the book *which John thinks he read* ____

Linguists call such phrases *restrictive relative clauses.* In theory-neutral terms relative clauses are predicates derived from sentences; they are often called adjective clauses in traditional school grammars. Typically, such derived predicates are used to modify a head noun (*teacher* and *boy* in (49*a*, *b*)). Strategies for relative clause formation may involve the use of either gaps or resumptive pronouns. English uses the former strategy. In (49*a*–*c*) a dash indicates the position of the gap. English also employs relative pronominals (such as *who*) dislocated to sentence-initial position.

Deriving predicates from sentences is what the λ-operator is expressly designed to do. This strongly suggests that such an operator may be involved in the interpretation of relative clauses.

To see this, we will add a rudimentary form of relativization to F_3. Within the general framework that we are using, relative clauses are transformationally derived. For example, (49*a*) is derived from an underlying D-structure like the one in (50) by fronting the *wh* pronoun:

(50) *a.* a teacher [Mary likes whom]

b.

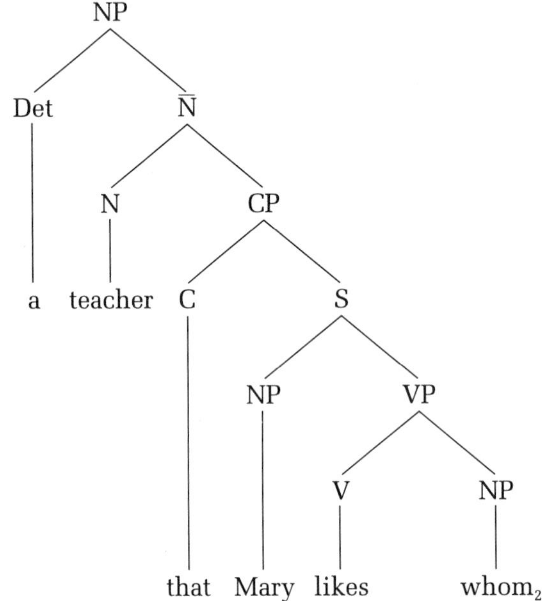

The movement analysis provides a way of capturing the fact that some properties of the dislocated pronoun are inherited from its base position (for example, the case of the *wh* element sometimes depends on its DS position; compare in examples (49*a*) and (49*c*) the distribution of *who* versus *whom*). In (50) we have a clause (a CP) adjoined to a noun and forming with it some kind of intermediate nominal projection N̄ (we are reverting to using S rather than TP, for consideration of tense is irrelevant to the case under consideration). The wh-pronoun is then fronted and adjoined to CP, yielding (51):

(51)

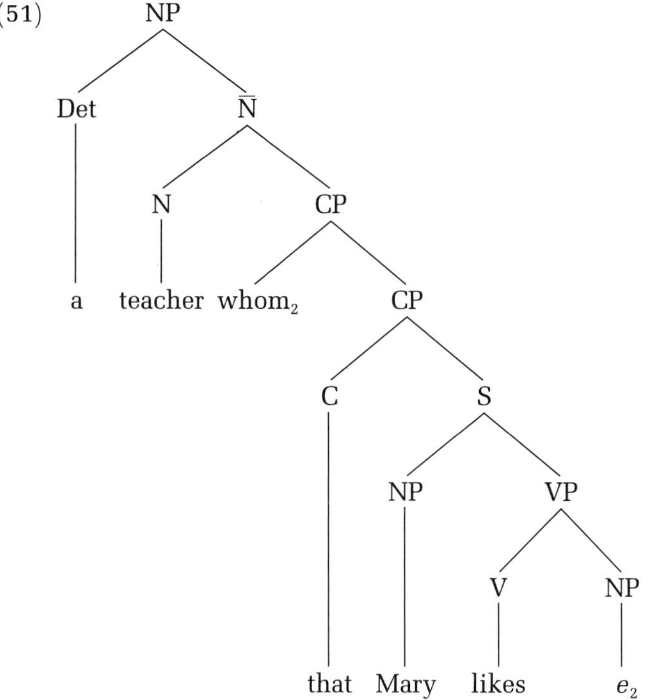

Finally, a constraint, operative in English but not in many other languages, requires the complementizer position to be occupied by a single word. At PF either the complementizer or the wh-pronoun must be deleted, yielding *a teacher that Mary likes* or *a teacher whom Mary likes.* We assume that, since deletion takes place at PF, it does not affect LF. Thus (51) is the structure that actually gets interpreted. The question is how it gets interpreted.

Let us proceed stepwise. The adjoined S will be interpreted by the principles we have already got as follows:

(52) [Mary likes e_2] $\Rightarrow$ like$'$(Mary$'$, x_2)

What is the meaning of *whom Mary likes* (after the complementizer has been elided)? A simple hypothesis is that it denotes the people that Mary likes. This can be obtained by abstracting over the variable associated with the trace:

(53) [whom$_2$ [Mary likes e_2]] $\Rightarrow \lambda x_2$ like$'$(Mary$'$, x_2)

This set can then be used to modify the head noun *teacher*, by intersecting it with its extension (using generalized conjunction):

(54) [teacher [whom$_2$ [Mary likes e_2]]]
$\Rightarrow$ teacher$' \wedge \lambda x_2$ like$'$(Mary$'$, x_2)
$= \lambda y$[teacher$'(y) \wedge \lambda x_2$ like$'$(Mary$'$, x_2)(y)]
By definition of $\wedge$
$= \lambda y$[teacher$'(y) \wedge$ like$'$(Mary$'$, y)] By λ-conversion

Thus the modified noun *teacher whom Mary likes* winds up denoting the set of teachers such that Mary likes those teachers. This seems just right.[12] There are a few glitches to iron out. For example, we are assuming the complementizer in relative clauses (if at all present) makes no semantic contribution. Moreover (53) actually means the *entities* that Mary likes (i.e., we haven't bothered making explicit the restriction to people that *whom* carries along). However, the interpretation principles we have used are fairly general. In particular, we will see in chap. 8, sec. 3.1, that generalized predicate conjunction (i.e., set intersection) is indeed a canonical mode of noun modification. If the present analysis is correct, then fronted relative pronouns are essentially an overt realization of the λ-operator.

In sum, the semantics of relative clauses boils down to the following:

(55) *a.* [who$_n$ CP]$' = \lambda x_n$ CP$'$
b. [$_{\bar{\mathrm{N}}}$ N CP]$'$ = N$' \wedge$ CP$'$

In the box on the next page we provide a more complete example.

Let us reiterate that the syntactic treatment of relative clauses adopted here is a gross oversimplification. The syntax of relative clauses has been studied quite extensively in a variety of frameworks and languages since the inception of generative grammar and of the various more adequate alternative syntactic approaches (transformational and nontransformational) that succeeded classical transformational grammar. The point we wish to emphasize here is that something like λ-abstraction is likely to be necessary on any viable approach for a compositional semantics of relativization. The framework that we are using makes this particularly evident. The gap left behind by a fronted relative pronoun is interpreted in the usual way as a variable, and the fronted relative pronoun coindexed with the gap seems to act precisely like a λ-abstractor over that variable. Thus, dislocated *wh*-pronouns in English appear to be a very direct syntactic manifestation of the λ-operator.

Syntax and semantics of "Pavarotti likes a fish that Loren hates"

(*a*) D-structure
[$_S$ Pavarotti [$_{VP}$ likes [$_{NP}$ a [$_{\bar{N}}$ fish [$_{CP}$ that [$_S$ Loren hates which$_1$]]]]]]

(*b*) S-structure
[$_S$ Pavarotti [$_{VP}$ likes [$_{NP}$ a [$_{\bar{N}}$ fish [$_{CP}$ which$_1$ [$_{CP}$ that [$_S$ Loren hates e_1]]]]]]] From (*a*) via wh-movement

(*c*) LF
[a [$_{\bar{N}}$ fish [$_{CP}$ which$_1$ [$_{CP}$ that [$_S$ Loren hates e_1]]]]]$_2$
[$_S$ Pavarotti [$_{VP}$ likes [$_{NP}$$e_2$]]] From (*b*) via QR

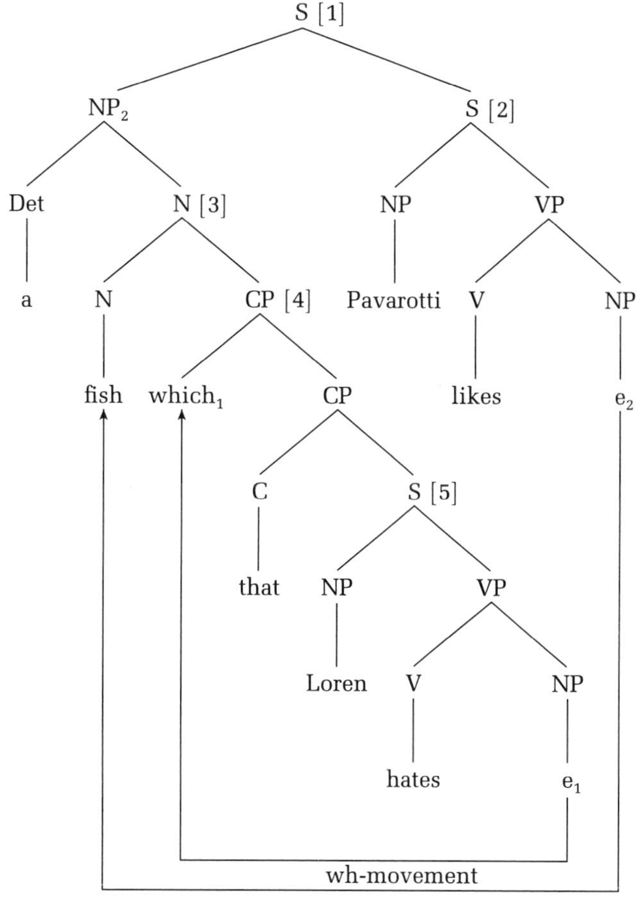

(*d*) Compositional interpretation

i. [5] $\Rightarrow$ hate′(Loren′, x_1) By (25*a*, *b*, *d*)

ii. [4] $\Rightarrow$ λx_1[hate′(Loren′, x_1)] By (55*a*)

iii. [3] $\Rightarrow$ fish′ $\wedge$ λx_1[hate′(Loren′, x_1)] By (55*b*)

$= \lambda y[\text{fish}'(y) \wedge \lambda x_1[\text{hate}'(\text{Loren}', x_1)(y)]$ By (31*a*)

$= \lambda y[\text{fish}'(y) \wedge \text{hate}'(\text{Loren}', y])$ By λ-conversion

iv. [2] $\Rightarrow$ like′(Pavarotti′, x_2) By (25*a*, *b*, *d*)

v. [1] $\Rightarrow$ $\exists x_2\ [\lambda y[\text{fish}'(y) \wedge \text{hate}'(\text{Loren}', y)](x_2)$

$\wedge\ \text{like}'(\text{Pavarotti}', x_2)]$ By (25*h*.ii)

$= \exists x_2\ [\text{fish}'(x_2) \wedge \text{hate}'(\text{Loren}', x_2) \wedge \text{like}'(\text{Pavarotti}', x_2)]$

By λ-conversion

5 VP Anaphora

In the present section we will discuss an anaphoric phenomenon involving VPs, the one illustrated in (56).[13]

(56) *a*. *A*: Does Bill smoke?
B: No. John does ____.
b. John came but Bill didn't ____.
c. John was interested. The others were ____ too.
d. The children asked us to squirt them with the hose, and we did ____.

We will see that this phenomenon (known as VP anaphora, VP ellipsis, or VP deletion in the literature) is governed by interpretive principles that make use, possibly in an essential manner, of something like λ-abstraction.

It should be noted that VP anaphora is sensitive to surface structure. Consider the following paradigm from Hankamer and Sag (1976):

(57) The children asked to be squirted with the hose, and
a. *we did ____.
b. they were ____.
c. we did it.

In contrast to (56*d*), we cannot continue the sentence as in (57*a*); we have to use (57*b*) or (57*c*). The reason is that *do* requires an active verb in its complement, and the only available antecedent in (57*a*) is in the passive. This contrasts with some other forms of anaphora for interpreting VPs that do not appear to be subject to the same restriction: (57*c*) illustrates this with *do it* anaphora.

Considerations such as these might lead one to assume that VP anaphora is a deletion process governed by syntactic identity: one is allowed to delete a VP_1 if there is in the context a VP_2 syntactically identical with VP_1. This was in fact the line taken in early generative work on this topic (see Ross 1966). However, it was later discovered that an approach along these lines runs into serious difficulties. Whether one construes VP anaphora as a deletion process or not, the identity conditions with a contextually specified antecedent cannot be given just in terms of *surface* syntax. They have to be stated at a more abstract level.

Various types of evidence can be used to back up the latter claim. Consider, for example, the following:

(58) Bob left and John will ____.

In (58) the antecedent is in the past, while the missing VP cannot be, as the future auxiliary *will* requires a bare infinitive. The source for the ellipsis in (58), under the identity of surface syntactic forms, would have to be something like *Bob left and John will left too*, which being ungrammatical will not be generated. The the identity conditions licensing VP anaphora must hold at a level where the proper antecedent is present, and surface structure does not seem to be the level. Something like LF (or *lf*) seems to be a better candidate.

The same point can be made by looking at the following example:

(59) *A*: John spoke to Bill about himself.
B: Yes. And Frank did ____ too.

Sentence (59*A*) is ambiguous. It can either mean that John spoke to Bill about John or that John spoke to Bill about Bill. If the former is the case, then (59*B*) must be taken as saying that Frank spoke to Bill about Frank. If the latter is the case, (59*B*) must be interpreted as saying that Frank spoke to Bill about Bill. It is impossible, however, to interpret (59*A*) in one way and (59*B*) in the other. If VP anaphora is a deletion process governed by surface syntactic identity, there is no clear reason why such a restriction should obtain. If, on the other hand, VP anaphora is governed by something like identity of meaning, then the restrictions on the interpretation of (59*B*) are immediately accounted for: the VPs in (59*A*–*B*) must be interpreted in the same way. In the following subsection we will spell this requirement out. Then we will look at how our theory addresses some of the classical puzzles associated with VP anaphora.

5.1 When two VPs have identical meanings

Here is one way in which the phenomenon at hand can be understood. One can maintain the deletion hypothesis but modify what triggers it. An informal characterization of the idea is given in (60).

(60) Delete a VP_1, if in the context there is a VP_2 whose interpretation is identical with that of VP_1.

Since the deletion process takes place at PF, it won't affect LF representations. Thus at LF the copy deleted at PF will be available for interpretive purposes. Condition (60) requires that the deleted copy and its antecedent be interpreted in same way, i.e., they must have the same LF (or the same model theoretic interpretation, represented here by its *lf*-translation).[14]

Let us see how the approach outlined in (60) works by going through examples (58) and (59). Consider (58) first. Its S-structure will be something like (61):

(61) [Bob [PAST leave] and John [FUT *leave*]]

Now, the second occurrence of *leave* can be deleted at PF. At LF, the deleted copy (marked in italics in (61)) will still be there (and will obviously be interpreted in the same way as the first occurrence of *leave*). Hence the sentence is grammatical and receives the correct interpretation. Consider next (59), repeated here as (62).

(62) *A*: John spoke to Bill about himself
B: Yes; and Frank did [*speak to Bill about himself*] too

The VP in italics is the elided one. At the level which feeds into semantic interpretation, namely LF, we have to choose how these VPs are going to be interpreted. These are the options for the unelided VP:

(63) *a.* John_1 [e_1 [$_{\text{VP}}$ spoke to Bill about himself_1]]
b. Bill_1 [John [$_{\text{VP}}$ spoke to e_1 about himself_1]]

Recall that we are assuming that nonpronominal NPs get an index only through QR. Hence to meet the requirement that reflexives be locally bound, the NPs in (62*A*) must be raised, which results in the two LFs in (64*a*–*b*). Now when it comes to interpreting the elided VP, condition (60) forces us to pick whatever options we have picked for the unelided one, i.e., respectively (64) and (65):

(64) Frank_1 [e_1 [spoke to Bill about himself_1]]

(65) Bill_1 [Frank [spoke to e_1 about himself_1]]

This will guarantee that the elided VP is interpreted in the same way as its antecedent.[15]

So far we have understood identity of meaning as a requirement on VP interpretation. However it turns out that this isn't quite enough. Consider the following example (from Reinhart 1983):

(66) Every student saw a snake next to him.

Focus on the reading where *him* is bound by *every student* which would correspond to the following Logical Form:

(67) Every student$_2$ [e_2 PAST [$_{VP}$ see a snake next to him$_2$]]

Now imagine a continuation of the following sort:

(68) Professor Smith did too.

Take (68) on the following LF:

(69) Professor Smith did [$_{VP}$ *see a snake next to him$_2$*] too

The elided VP in (69) is identical to the one in (67) and thus receives the same interpretation, namely (70):

(70) [$_{VP}$ see a snake next to him$_2$] $\Longrightarrow \lambda y \exists z[\text{snake}'(z) \wedge \text{see}'(y, z) \wedge \text{next}'(z, x_2)]$

So on our current understanding of the identity of meaning requirement, (70) would be a legitimate interpretation for (68) as a continuation to (66). However, *him$_2$* in (69) is bound (and hence the sentence says that every student saw a snake next to him, himself). But in (69) it is free, and hence its value would be set to some salient individual. Such an individual could be someone who is prominent in the context of the utterance or recently talked about (say Pavarotti). This erroneously predicts that the discourse constituted by (68) followed by (70) could mean "Every student saw a snake next to himself, and Professor Smith saw a snake next to Pavarotti." What is going wrong here? Evidently, (69) is not an admissible LF in the context at hand. What we want is something like (71):

(71) Professor Smith$_2$ [e_2 did [$_{VP}$ *see a snake next to him$_2$*] too]

In (71) *him$_2$* is bound by *Professor Smith* and the discourse as a whole winds up saying that every student saw a snake next to himself and Professor Smith too saw a snake next to himself, which is an admissible interpretation for such a discourse. The conclusion is that we cannot let a pronoun which is free in one VP be bound in another (in an ellipsis context). This makes sense. If the contrary was allowed, even though the VPs as such may get the same interpretation, once they are embedded into a larger structure they will wind up with different interpretations. Hence the identity condition on meaning won't ultimately be met. What this shows is that in stating the relevant identity condition, we cannot just look at the VPs involved; we must also look at the larger context in which they occur. Such contexts must be "parallel" in terms of their binding relationships, which entails, in particular, that no variable can bound in one of the VPs and free in the other. We will state this requirement in an informal way:

(72) Condition on parallelism
Deletion of VP_1 is allowed in presence of a VP_2 with the same interpretation iff VP_1 and VP_2 are embedded in parallel contexts.

The enterprise of formalizing the relevant concept of parallelism is a complex one, and the success of the present analysis ultimately does depend on it. Such an enterprise cannot be taken up within the limits of the present work (see Rooth 1996 for a very interesting recent approach that relies heavily on his semantics for focus; see also Fiengo and May 1994). We trust that the idea is sufficiently clear for the reader to appreciate what follows.

Having spelled out more fully, if only informally, what it is for two VPs to have identical meanings, we will now turn to an interesting consequence of the approach we have developed so far, having to do with the interpretation of pronouns in a VP anaphora context.[16]

Let us review where we stand. Consider a simple sentence like (73):

(73) John thinks that he is a genius.

Such a sentence has two relevant logical forms:

(74) *a.* John [$_{VP}$ thinks that he_1 is a genius]
b. $John_1$ [e_1 [$_{VP}$ thinks that he_1 is a genius]]

In (74*a*), the pronoun *he*$_1$ is free and its value will be some contextually salient individual (say, again, Pavarotti); in (74*b*) it is bound to *John*. Consider now the possible continuation (75):

(75) And Bill does too.

If we pick the interpretation in (74*a*), the value of the pronoun in the elided VP will stay fixed to the same contextually salient individual. Thus, in the hypothesized context, the discourse as a whole says that John thinks that Pavarotti is a genius and Bill thinks that Pavarotti is a genius. This is known as the *strict* reading of the pronoun. If however, we select the logical form in (74*b*) for the antecedent VP, parallelism will demand that (75) is interpreted as follows:

(76) Bill_1 [e_1 does [$_{\text{VP}}$ *think that* he_1 *is a genius*] too]

Under this construal, the discourse says that John thinks that John is a genius and Bill thinks that Bill is. This is referred to in the literature as the *sloppy* interpretation of the pronoun. This is where we stand so far. Now comes a little surprise. There is a third possible reading that our theory predicts. Consider the interpretation in (74*a*) again, i.e., the one where the pronoun stays free. As we just said, in this case the pronoun will be taken to refer to some individual salient in the context. Now, surely naming John makes him salient. Hence, it cannot be excluded that the pronoun he_1 winds up being coreferential with John (without being bound). This means that if this option is taken in a VP anaphora context, the pronoun he_1 will remain anchored to John. Thus, in particular, the discourse in (73) through (75) is also predicted to have the following interpretation: John thinks that John is a genius and Bill thinks that John is a genius, as an instance of the strict reading. This interpretation is indeed possible.

What is interesting about the previous situation is the following. Our interpretive procedure yields two ways in which in a sentence like *John thinks that he is a genius* the pronoun *he* can be anaphorically dependent on *John*. On the first way, *he* is semantically bound. On the second, it is semantically free, but the context selects John as its value. In simple sentences, these two interpretations just cannot be teased apart. But they can be in VP anaphora contexts. Thus VP anaphora reveals that a seemingly curious consequence of our approach is indeed borne out. This is a point that was forcefully made by Reinhart (1983a, 1983b).

5.2 VP anaphora and scope

In this subsection we are going to discuss briefly some scope phenomena in the context of VP ellipsis. Consider (77):

(77) A student showed the campus to every visitor.

As we know, this sentence is ambiguous, depending on which of the following LFs is selected:

(78) *a.* a student$_1$ [every visitor$_2$ [e_1 showed the campus to e_2]]
b. every visitor$_2$ [a student$_1$ [e_1 showed the campus to e_2]]

Now let us embed sentence (77) and put it in an ellipsis context:

(79) *a.* John thinks that a student showed the campus to every visitor.
b. And Bill does too.

The thing to note here is that the interpretation of the embedded clause in (79*a*), however scope gets resolved, remains constant in (79*b*). It is not possible, for example, to understand one of the two clauses as saying that there is a student that showed every visitor around and the other as saying that every visitor was shown around by a possibly different student. This is just what one would expect on the basis of the hypothesis that VP ellipsis is licensed under semantic identity. Syntactic identity, yet again, would not guarantee this result.

Let us see what happens in unembedded contexts.

(80) *a.* A student showed the campus to every visitor.
b. And a staff member did too.

Here too both readings seem to be available. It seems, in other words, that the elided VP can have either scope construal, depending on how the antecedent clause is understood:

(81) *a.* a staff member$_1$ [every visitor$_2$ [e_1 [*met with* e_2]]
b. every visitor$_2$ [a staff member$_1$ [e_1 [*met with* e_2]]

Any proper formalization of the parallelism condition will guarantee this. Contrast now (80) with (82):

(82) *a.* A professor met with every student.
b. And Mary did too.

The continuation in (82*b*) seems to disambiguate (82*a*) in favor of the subject having wide scope (where one professor meets with every student). The discourse in (82) cannot readily mean "For every student there is a possibly different professor that met with him or her, and Mary met with him or her as well." Such a reading would be obtained by selecting (78*b*) as the interpretation for (82*a*) and by interpreting (82*b*) as follows:

(83) every student$_2$ [Mary$_1$ [e_1 [*met with* e_2]]

Clearly, parallelism is satisfied here. So the question is why is this reading impossible (or at least strongly dispreferred)?[17] Why do proper names contrast with other NPs in having this disambiguating effect in cases such as (82)? The effect appear to be fairly systematic:

(84) *a.* A soldier is guarding every entrance, and an armed civilian is too. [Ambiguous]
b. A soldier is guarding every entrance and Mary is too. [Unambiguous]

(85) *a.* Some secretary admires every professor, and some student does too. [Ambiguous]
b. Some secretary admires every professor, and Lee does too. [Unambiguous]

Such data had been noticed and discussed in the literature on VP anaphora (see especially Hirschbühler 1982). Recently, Fox (1995) has come up with an interesting proposal to explain them. In the remainder of this section, we will sketch Fox's proposal.

Notice, to start, that the possibility of VP adjunction for QR (see sec. 3.1) gives us an alternative way of obtaining a wide scope reading for the subject:

(86) *a.* a student$_1$ [every visitor$_2$ [$_S$ e_1 [$_{VP}$ showed the campus to e_2]]]
b. a student$_1$ [e_1 [$_{VP}$ every visitor$_2$ [showed the campus to e_2]]]

LF (86*b*) is obtained by adjoining the object to VP and it is logically equivalent to (86*a*). Notice that in (86*b*) the object makes a shorter move than in (86*a*)—a fact that will become relevant shortly.

Exercise 8 Show that (86*a*) and (86*b*) are logically equivalent, by providing their node by node (I)PC translations.

Let us consider now the LFs in (78) again (with (78*a*) replaced by the equivalent (86*b*)), and compare them with their correspondents with proper names, namely (87*a*, *b*):

(87) *a.* every student$_2$ [Mary$_1$ [e_1 [*met with* e_2]]]
b. Mary$_1$ [e_1 [$_{VP}$ *every student*$_2$ [*met with* e_2]]]

While the pair in (78) does not yield logically equivalent readings, the one in (87) does. This is a consequence of the semantics of proper names. Intuitively speaking, to say that for every student, Mary met with him or her (i.e., (87*a*)) is just the same as saying that Mary is such that she met with every student (i.e., (87*b*)). Proper names are scopally inert, so to speak. Fox suggests that this might be the key to understanding the unexpected pattern of readings in (82). It is natural enough to maintain that scope shifting operations, like QR apply only to the extent that they make a difference. QR does not apply gratuitously, as it were. This might be viewed as an "economy" principle built into grammar. In the case at hand, such a principle leads to rejecting (87*b*) as a possible LF for "Mary showed the campus to every visitor." The reason for this is that of the two ways of assigning scope to the object VP, (87*b*) clearly is the more economical (as it involves the shortest move). Since the more complex (87*a*) does not result in a semantically distinct interpretation, it is simply not available.[18]

This idea, Fox argues, offers an interesting explanation for the contrast between (80) and (82). In (80), both scope options are available as they result in nonequivalent formulas. Parallelism then forces the scopal choice one makes to remain constant across VP ellipsis contexts. In (82*b*), on the other hand, economy bans the object taking scope over the subject, since we have a proper name. Thus, in a VP ellipsis context parallelism will force us to take the option in which the subject has widest scope. Since in one of the two sentences only one option is available, the other sentence must go along with it, if ellipsis is to be properly licensed. This has the effect of disambiguating the interpretation in (82) (and (84), (85)). Such an effect is due to the interaction of parallelism and economy. (For further data and discussion, see Fox 1995).

We see that the pattern of scope interaction in VP anaphora is quite rich. Pursuing the idea that identity of meaning is the key proves fruitful and leads to a sharpening of our understanding of how grammatically driven interpretive procedures in fact work. The usefulness of λ-abstraction (or interpretive techniques closely related to it) in understanding the working of complex predicates in natural language seems to be confirmed, although it remains to be seen whether the specific proposals presented here will turn out to be ultimately correct.[19]

Exercise 9 Add to F_3 the following rule for possessives:

(1) NP $\rightarrow$ $N_{p,[\text{POSS}]}$ N′

Here [POSS] stands for possessive. Moreover, let us assume (2):

(2) $N_{p,[\text{POSS}]}$ $\rightarrow$ his_n, her_n, Pavarotti's, John's, ...

(For simplicity, we focus here only on proper names and pronouns.) The grammar of F_3 so augmented will generate sentences like the following:

(3) *a.* Sophia Loren likes her mother.
b. Pavarotti gives Sophia Loren's book to Bond.

Give the semantics corresponding to (1) in the form of a translation rule on the model of section 2. Since possessive NPs are semantically similar to definite descriptions (John's book = the book of John's), they will be interpreted in raised position and the relevant translation rule should have the following form:

(4) If NP_i is of the form $[N_{p,[\text{POSS}]}\ N']$, then $[NP_i\ S]' = \ldots$

Such a semantics will involve bringing in something like a possessor relation POS. POS(x, y) is a highly context-dependent relation that can mean, among other things, x belongs to y, x is assigned to y, or x was produced by y.

Illustrate your analysis by giving a node-by-node translation of (3*b*).

6 Conclusions

In the present chapter we have familiarized ourselves with the logical syntax and semantics of the λ-operator, a very powerful device that enables one to define properties of indefinite complexity. One of the things that such an operator makes possible is doing semantics by means of translation into a logical calculus, which raises interesting questions concerning the notions of logical form and semantic representation. We have also seen how the λ-operator appears to be extremely useful in analyzing the structure of complex predicates in English, in particular, relative clauses, conjoined and disjoined VPs, and VP ellipsis. We have considered a number of issues that these phenomena raise for the syntax-semantics interface.

8 Word Meaning

1 Introduction

Often semantics is thought of as the study of what words (or morphemes) mean. Words as significant units have not, however, been our focus so far. In chapter 2 we quoted Frege: "Only in the context of a sentence do words have meaning." This slogan encapsulates the view we have presented in this text: that the central question a linguistic theory of meaning must address is that of how finitely many lexical meanings can be systematically combined to yield indefinitely many sentential meanings. The systematic productivity of linguistic meaning is its most striking feature and distinguishes human languages from many other semiotic systems. What words mean is a matter of the systematic effects they have on the semantic (and pragmatic) properties of (utterances of) sentences containing them, properties like entailments, presuppositions, incompatibility, and perhaps some kinds of implicatures. Word meanings cannot, on our approach, be studied in isolation. The ultimate test of any proposed word meaning must be its contribution to the meaning of sentences containing it and the meaning-relations among such sentences. That is, word meanings must be able to provide an appropriate finite base for an adequate recursive theory of indefinitely many sentential meanings.

In sketching such a theory, we have, of course, said quite a bit already about the meanings of certain words and inflectional morphemes. So-called logical words like *and, or,* and *not* have been directly interpreted by means of set-theoretic operations; tense and modals like *must* and *may* have been partially interpreted, with their precise contribution to propositional content linked to contextual parameters. We have placed some constraints on interpretation of indexical expressions like *I, here,* and *now*; we have also discussed the interpretation of pronouns as context-sensitive expressions and as variable-like elements linked to antecedent NPs. In the next chapter we will introduce a different way of thinking about NP meanings and draw on that to consider in some detail linguistically significant semantic distinctions within the small but very interesting lexical class of quantifying determiners.

We have even said a little bit about the semantic value of words like ordinary Ns and Vs. We have assigned to words in each syntactic category a type of set-theoretic entity that combines with the values associated with other words to yield appropriate values for phrases and sentences. For example, common nouns like *woman* are associated in a model with a function whose value in any circumstance is a set of individuals, and transitive verbs such as *like* with a function from circumstances to sets of ordered pairs of individuals. As we noted in chapter 2, sec. 3.2.4, there are alternative ways to think about the types and semantic combinatorial processes. The important point, however, is that semantic composition requires differentiation of denotation types for lexical items: lexical meanings "fit" together in structured ways. And we also noted that semantic knowledge seems to involve more content-based constraints: we confined our attention to models in which, e.g., the set of individuals picked out by *woman* in a circumstance includes all and only the individuals who are women in that circumstance. In discussing the English fragments described in chapters 3 and 5, we introduced the notion of admissible models for English and used it both to distinguish truth values from truth conditions and to license a richer stock of entailment relations than those recognized in traditional logics. We suggested that speakers' linguistic knowledge allows them to judge not only that sentence (1*a*) entails (1*b*), which depends on the semantic value of the "logical" word *and*, but also that sentence (2*a*) entails (2*b*), which depends on the semantic values of *like* and *hate* as well as on the semantic values of the negative and modal.

(1) *a.* Ophelia likes Hamlet, and Gertrude likes Hamlet's uncle.
    b. Ophelia likes Hamlet.

(2) *a.* Ophelia does not hate Hamlet.
    b. Ophelia may like Hamlet.

One major question for linguistic semantics is which lexically based implications ought to count as entailments based on linguistic knowledge. Here are some more pairs for which analysts have wanted to claim that the (*a*) sentence entails the (*b*) sentence:

(3) *a.* Jules wiped the counter *clean*.
    b. Jules *cleaned* the counter by wiping it.

(4) *a.* Joan *opened* the door.
b. The door *opened.*

(5) *a.* Bond *shaved.*
b. Bond *shaved* himself.

(6) *a.* Pavarotti *ate.*
b. Pavarotti *ate* something.

(7) *a.* Lee is my *uncle*, and Kim is my *aunt.*
b. Lee is *male*, and Kim is *female.*

(8) *a.* Sybilla is a *dog.*
b. Sybilla is an *animate being.*

(9) *a.* Mary gave Bill some *water* to drink.
b. Mary gave Bill some *liquid* to drink.

In (3) through (6), there are formal as well as semantic connections between the *a* and *b* sentences. Moreover, the connections are not confined to sentences with the particular highlighted predicates. We find the same connections manifest in many other verb-adjective or verb-verb pairs. And we find similar kinds of relations in many other languages. It is difficult to avoid the conclusion that in such cases the intuitive judgments of implication reflect speakers' linguistic competence and thus that linguists need to give some account of this competence. Of course, this leaves us with further difficult questions. What is the nature of this competence? How should our grammar incorporate it? In the next section we discuss three different approaches to accounting for such lexically-based linguistic knowledge: lexical decomposition, meaning postulates (or other constraints on models), and abstract syntactic markers.

In (7) through (9), matters are more complicated. The English words *uncle* and *aunt* in (7) are formally quite distinct, but in Italian matters are different.

(10) *a.* Lee è mio zio.
'Lee is my uncle.'
b. Kim è mia zia.
'Kim is my aunt.'

Here the sex distinction is marked by the final vowel. And, of course, there are many other pairs of Italian words with this same formal relationship and the same distinction in sex of referent: still in the kinship domain, for example, Italian distinguishes *cugino* and *cugina*, whereas English has only the sex-neutral *cousin*. Formal markers of sex occur in many of the world's languages: English *-ess*, for example, marks the female member in a number of related pairs: *poet/poetess*, *duke/duchess*, *master/mistress*, *governor/governess*.[1] In cases where there are overt morphological indicators of (presupposed) sex, speakers' linguistic knowledge of their significance seems obvious. Many analysts argue that speakers' linguistic knowledge of sex of referent must also be involved even when no surface forms explicitly indicate anything about sex.

Example (8) raises similar issues. Although the word *dog* carries no overt indicator of the animacy of those included in its denotation, some languages have overt markers that signal something about (presupposed) animacy. Slavic languages provide many examples. In Russian, for example, the accusative form of masculine nouns coincides with the genitive for animates and with the nominative for inanimates.

(11) *a.* Ja vižu èt -ogo kot -a.
I see this ACC = GEN (tom)cat ACC = GEN
'I see this cat.'
(Cf. Ja vižu ètogo studenta. 'I see this student.')
b. Ja vižu èt -ot stol- ∅
I see this ACC = NOM table ACC = NOM
c. *Ja vižu ètot kot. (*Ja vižu ètot student.)
d. *Ja vižu ètogo stola.

In Bantu languages, similar distinctions are made in noun class agreement patterns as the Kiswahili examples in (12) illustrate. Although *kifaru* 'rhino' and *kikombe* 'cup' are in the same noun class, as shown by their plural formation, they select different agreement markers, with *kifaru* patterning with other nouns that refer to people (there are words referring to animals in other noun classes that show similar contrasts to inanimates in agreement patterns).

(12) *a.* Kifaru a-me-anguka. Vifaru wa-me-anguka.
rhino agr-PERF-fall
'The rhino has fallen.' 'The rhinos have fallen.'
(Cf. Mtoto a-me-anguka. 'The child has fallen.')
b. Kikombe ki-me-anguka. vikombe vi-me-anguka
cup agr-PERF-fall
'The cup has fallen.' 'The cups have fallen.'

c. *Kifaru kimeanguka. (Cf. *Mtoto kimeanguka.)
d. *Kikombe ameanguka.

Thus knowing that cats (and students) are animate and that tables are not seems to be necessary for Russian speakers to know that the sentences in (11*a*, *b*) are well-formed whereas those in (11*c*, *d*) are not. Similarly, Kiswahili speakers need to know that rhinos (and children) are animate whereas cups are not in order to distinguish the well-formed (12*a*, *b*) from (12*c*, *d*). So some have argued that knowledge about animacy must be linguistic knowledge for speakers of such languages. In English, animacy is not involved in choosing among otherwise equivalent forms but does seem to be involved in so-called selectional restrictions, which we discussed in chapter 1. Only animate beings, for example, think or sleep or can be frightened; the English sentence (13*a*) seems fine, whereas (13*b*) is odd.

(13) *a.* The thunder frightened my dog.
b. #The thunder frightened my bicycle.

Finally, consider water's being liquid. Liquidity does not have the widespread linguistic significance of distinctions in sex or animacy. There are, however, combinatorial restrictions where it seems to play a role: only liquids seem appropriate as objects of *drink*, for example.

Yet there are also good reasons for thinking that not all of the implications in (3) through (9) are based on linguistic knowledge as such. Suppose, for example, we discover that dogs, that is, the things we now call dogs, are actually exquisite machines that alien beings have deposited here on earth. Would the meaning of the word *dog* change or our understanding of animacy or would the meanings remain constant while our beliefs about the referents change? These are difficult questions that have been mainly addressed by philosophers but may have some empirical dimensions that linguists can explore. And we need to be wary of just what weight we give to linguistic data of the kind cited above. As we saw in our discussion of implicature in chapter four, there are many ways in which extralinguistic beliefs come into play in understanding the import of (utterances of) sentences. Such extralinguistic knowledge can even play a role in mediating morphological relations. The word *womanly*, for example, designates not properties that women have by virtue of the denotational meaning of *woman* but properties that women are normatively expected to have (a quiet voice and pleasant smile, delight in taking care of men and children and a general selflessness, a certain kind of physical appearance, and so on). There are many kinds of knowledge and beliefs that people draw on in using words, only some of which are part of their linguistic competence in the sense of grammatical knowledge.

2 Semantic Analysis of Words

2.1 Some basic concepts characterizing verb meanings

Consider the pair of sentences in (4) above, repeated here in (14), along with an additional sentence. Compare this set with the sets in (15) and (16).

(14) *a.* Joan opened the door.
b. The door opened.
c. The door is open.

(15) *a.* Joan broke the glass.
b. The glass broke.
c. The glass is broken.

(16) *a.* Joan emptied the tub.
b. The tub emptied.
c. The tub is empty.

In each of these sets, the first sentence contains a transitive verb, the second a homophonous intransitive verb, whose subject is the object in the first sentence, and the third a homophonous or morphologically related adjective, whose subject is the same as that of the second sentence. In each case, the (*a*) sentence apparently entails the (*b*) sentence, which in turn entails (with suitable provisos about temporal reference) the (*c*) sentence. But there is more involved: notice that each of (14*a*–16*a*) entails something like (17*a*, *a*′–19*a*, *a*′) respectively and that each of (14*b*–16*b*) entails something like (17–19*b*) respectively.

(17) *a.* Joan caused the door to open.
a′. Joan made the door open.
b. The door became open

(18) *a.* Joan caused the glass to break.
a′. Joan made the glass break.
b. The glass became broken.

(19) *a.* Joan caused the tub to empty.
a′. Joan made the tub empty.
b. The tub became empty.

On the basis of such relations the (*a*) sentences in (14) through (16), which involve making something happen, are often called *causatives*, and the (*b*) sentences, which involve something's becoming the case, are called *inchoatives*. What becomes the case is expressed by the (*c*) sentences. There are many such triples in English (sometimes with less completely transparent morphological relations) and other cases with only two of the three members of the set realized lexically. Such relations occur not only in English. For example, the following two pairs of Italian sentences display the same syntactic and semantic relationships as the (*a*) and (*b*) pairs above.

(20) *a.* Joan ha affondato la barca.
Joan PAST sink the boat
'Joan sank the boat.'
b. La barca e' affondata.
The boat PAST sink
'The boat sank.'

(21) *a.* Joan ha continuato il discorso.
Joan PAST continue the speech
'Joan continued the speech.'
b. Il discorso e' continuato.
The speech PAST continue
'The speech continued.'

And in (22), we have the same relationship between (*a*) and (*b*) as between (*a*) and (*c*) in (14) through (16) (although with a somewhat less transparent morphological connection).

(22) *a.* Joan ha riempito la valigia.
Joan PAST fill the suitcase
'Joan filled the suitcase.'
b. La valigia e' piena.
'The suitcase is full.'

In some languages alternations very similar to these appear to be signaled through specific morphemes. The following is a Chichewa example from Baker (1988, 10–11).

(23) *a.* Mtsuko u-na-gw-a.
Waterpot SP-PAST-fall-ASP
'The waterpot fell.'

b. Mtsikana a-na-u-gw-*ets*-a.
Girl SP-PAST-OP-fall-CAUS-ASP
'The girl made the waterpot fall.'

We see that in (23a) the transitive member of the pair is marked by the italicized morpheme *ets*. As the glosses make clear, this morpheme seems to give rise to a contrast in meaning very similar to the one observed between the (*a*) and (*b*) pairs above. (Many languages, including Chichewa, causativize not only intransitives but also transitives.) English itself has a morpheme that creates contrasts like those between the (*c*) and (*b*) sentences in (14) through (16); sentence (*a*) is essentially equivalent to sentence (*b*), and the *-en*, which forms intransitive verbs from certain adjectives, indicates a change of state, which we have glossed by using *become*.

(24) *a.* The sky reddened.
b. The sky became red(der).

And consider (25). The transitive verb *kill*, although morphologically quite distinct from the intransitive *die* and its morphologically related adjective *dead*, is arguably in the same semantic relation to them as holds for cases like (14) through (16).

(25) *a.* Joan killed Lee.
b. Lee died.
c. Lee was dead.

Meanings involving causation and becoming are not only widespread in the verbal semantics of the world's languages; they are also often expressed by particular morphemes that are regularly incorporated in verbs as in (23) and (24). In addition, such meanings can be implicitly conveyed by syntactic configurations, as in (3*a*) in the preceding section, repeated here in a reduced form as (26*a*), which entails (26*b*) and (26*c*).

(26) *a.* Jules wiped the counter clean.
b. Jules made the counter become clean.
c. The counter was clean.

The conclusion: notions of causation and becoming are central to the semantic architecture of language, part of grammar like tense and modality.

As suggested in (17) through (19), there is a general schema like that in (27) which in some sense underlies (14) through (16) and many other cases. Parts of the schemata apply to lexical relations such as those in (20) to (25), as well as to constructions like the English resultative in (26). In (27), (*a*) corresponds to the transitives, (*b*) to the intransitives, and (*c*) to the adjectives.

(27) *a.* CAUSE(*x*, BECOME($P(b)$))
b. BECOME($P(b)$)
c. $P(b)$

Something like this schema seems widely implicated in the semantics of many of the world's languages and seems to be central to the semantics of verbs and adjectives.

There are now two questions to be answered. The first is what do the capitalized words in schema (27) actually mean? We have characterized them only rather vaguely. What is their exact contribution to truth conditions? The second question is this: How are schemata such as (27) encoded in the grammar? What is their exact status? The rest of this section addresses the first question. In sections 2.2 and 2.3 we will address the second and discuss some general issues that arise in thinking about word meaning.

To give an idea of what is involved in spelling out the meaning of the items capitalized in (27), we draw on the work of Dowty (1979). Let us first introduce BECOME as a sentential operator in IPC (so that for any formula ϕ, BECOME(ϕ) is also a formula. A plausible first approximation to its semantics might be the following:

(28) "BECOME(ϕ)" is true at instant i iff ϕ is true at an i' that immediately follows i and is false at an i'' that immediately precedes i.

So for example BECOME(OPEN(x)) is true at i iff at some i' immediately preceding i, OPEN(x) is false (x is closed at i'), and at some i'' immediately following i, OPEN(x) is true. We have a change of state in the entity denoted by x, which goes from satisfying $\neg$OPEN to satisfying OPEN.

CAUSE, on the other hand, is a two-place operator that relates an individual to a proposition. Intuitively, CAUSE(x, ϕ) holds just in case something that x does (or some property that x has) causes ϕ to be the case. CAUSE is defined in terms of a bisentential operator C. A rough indication of the syntax and semantics of C is given in (29).

(29) *a.* If ϕ, ψ are formulas, then $C(\phi, \psi)$, to be read as "ϕ causes ψ," is also a formula.

b. "$C(\phi, \psi)$" is true at instant *i* in world *w* iff (i) ϕ and ψ are both true at *i* in *w* and (ii) in the worlds that differ minimally from *w*, where ψ is not the case, ϕ is also not the case.

The semantics for *C* is given using the semantics for conditionals developed in Lewis (1973) and Stalnaker (1968); clause (ii) in (29*b*) is essentially their analysis of the semantics of "*if* not ϕ, then not ψ." Let us illustrate the proposal by means of an example. Let *A* stand for "Germany invades Poland" and *B* stand for "Britain enters the war against Germany." Then $C(A, B)$ says that Germany's invasion of Poland caused Britain to enter the war against Germany (tense aside). The truth conditions of $C(A, B)$ are spelled out according to (29) as follows. For $C(A, B)$ to be true, Germany must have invaded Poland, England must have entered the war against Germany, and in the worlds closest to ours (those minimally different from it), where Britain does not enter the war against Germany, Germany must not have invaded Poland. That is, to remove from history Britain's entering the war against Germany, you will have to remove also Germany's attack on Poland. We judge a world in which Germany does not invade Poland and Britain does not enter the war against Germany as more like ours than a world in which Germany invades Poland but Britain does not enter the war. It is this that makes us willing to say that Germany's invasion of Poland caused Britain to enter the war.

Thus (29) tries to make explicit a semantics for causation that uses a resemblance relation among worlds of the kind first proposed for the analysis of conditionals. What we have provided in (29) is only a rough approximation. Several refinements of this type of analysis have been proposed and put to work in studying the logical properties of causation.

The definition of CAUSE is then quite simple:

(30) $\text{CAUSE}(x, \phi) = C(P(x), \phi)$ (for some property *P*)

The definition in (30) says that some property *P* is such that *x* having *P* causes ϕ (where *C* is as defined in (29)).

There are complications. In the (*a*) sentences in (14) to (16), (20) to (23), and (25) to (26), *x* must not only cause ϕ but must do so in some sense directly. In this respect the implicit causatives contrast with the (*a*) and (*a*′) sentences in (17) to (19), and they also contrast with the Chichewa morphological causative in (24). Consider (25*a*), for example. If Joan hires a thug to do the actual deed, she may be legally responsible for causing Lee's death but we refrain from using (25*a*) to describe what she did. Bittner (1998) argues that, cross-linguistically, whenever the causative relation is indicated without an explicit morpheme to signal it, then causation is understood in this special "direct" sense.

While these definitions are far from being problem free, we now have at least a first approximation to the operators we need in order to give some content to the schema in (27) and thus provide some kind of account of the paradigm in (14) through (16). There are various ways to proceed depending on how one chooses to incorporate (27) into the grammar. We will consider three of them in the following subsections.

2.2 Lexical decomposition

One possible hypothesis is that word meanings are constructed from semantic components (like BECOME and CAUSE) that recur in the meanings of different words.[3] So, for example, let $open'_a$ be the state of being open, i.e., (an IPC representation of) the meaning of the English adjective *open* ("a" stands for adjective). Whether $open'_a$ is itself a basic expression of the semantic calculus or is syntactically complex will not concern us here. The interpretation of the intransitive verb meaning $open'_i$ can then be given as in (31).

(31) $\text{open}'_i = \lambda x\ \text{BECOME}(\text{open}'_a(x))$

Now consider the transitive verb *open*. Its meaning can be defined as follows:

(32) $\text{open}'_t = \lambda y \lambda x[\text{CAUSE}(x,\ \text{BECOME}(\text{open}'_a(y)))]$

In (32) we have multiple λ-abstraction, which is a simple extension of abstraction over a single variable. Intuitively, an expression of the form $\lambda x \lambda y[\phi]$ will be a two-place relation that holds of u and u' just in case u and u' satisfy ϕ. More explicitly, we say that relative to a model M, a world w, an instant i, a context c, and an assignment g,

$$[\![\lambda x \lambda y[\phi]]\!]^{M,w,i,c,g} = \{\langle u, u' \rangle : [\![\phi]\!]^{M,w,i,c,g[[u/x]u'/y]} = 1\}.$$

So the λ-expression in (32) will denote a relation that holds between x and y iff some property that x has (or some action that x engages in) causes y to become open. Such a relation is proposed as the analysis of the meaning of the transitive verb *open*.

When the relation between a transitive and intransitive is not morphologically transparent (as in the case of *kill* versus *die*) each member of the pair would be simply listed in the lexicon with its meaning:

(33) *a.* die, V_i, λx BECOME(dead$'(x)$)
b. kill, V_t, $\lambda y \lambda x$[CAUSE(x, BECOME(dead$'(y)$))]

And, of course, we could have the further relations indicated.

(34) *a.* dead, Adj, $\lambda x\ [\neg \text{alive}'(x)]$
b. alive, Adj, $\lambda x[\neg \text{dead}'(x)]$

Other pairs can instead be given by means of various morphological or word-formation rules:

(35) *a.* If α is in Adj, then α or α + en is in V_i.
(If α ends in a nonnasal consonant, then α + en is the verbal form.)
b. $\alpha(+\text{en})'_i = \lambda y[$BECOME$(\alpha'_a(y))]$
α = open, empty, warm, red, black, short, ...

(36) *a.* If α is in V_i, then α is in V_t.
b. $\alpha'_t = \lambda y \lambda x[$CAUSE$(x, \alpha'_i(y))]$
α = sink, drown, open, empty, ...

(37) *a.* If α is in Adj, then α (or α + en) is in V_t.
b. $\alpha'_t = \lambda y \lambda x[$CAUSE$(x,$ BECOME$(\alpha'_a(y))]$
c. α = clean, dirty, smooth, ..., flat, moist, fat, ...

Rule (35) is essentially Dowty's inchoative rule, which forms intransitives from adjectives; rule (36) is the causative rule, forming transitives from intransitives. Unlike syntactic rules, which specify well-formed structures, word formation rules specify possible or potential lexical items. Which actually occur in any speaker's mental lexicon depends on a variety of idiosyncratic factors: we have listed some of the words to which the rule seems actually to apply. Rule (37) is there only because there are cases where an adjective and causative transitive verb are related without any corresponding inchoative intransitive; a more abstract approach to word formation might dispense with this rule. The (*a*) portion of the rules in (35) through (37) specifies morphosyntactic relations between words; the (*b*) part specifies corresponding semantic relations between those words. Such rules are at least a first approximation to what the speaker implicitly knows about the meaning and morphological shape of the pairs involved in the relevant alternations, as well as what is known about possible words that might not have been encountered.

Dowty argues that analyses like those just sketched not only capture the entailment relations that hold in (14) to (16) and (20) to (26). They also, he proposes, account for how predicates distribute across different aspectual classes. An observation that goes as far back as Aristotle (and has been discussed by many[4]) is that VPs can be classified in at least three classes: states, activities, and telic eventualities. Let us consider them briefly in turn.

Examples of states are given in (38).

(38) *a.* John knows Latin.
b. John is on the roof.
c. John is fat.
d. The door is open.

States are like snapshots of the world at a given instant. They lack a natural culmination or end point, and their subject is perceived not as an agent (as doing something) but as an experiencer (as experiencing something). Although judgments are sometimes confounded by semantic and pragmatic factors that we cannot discuss here, states can be identified fairly reliably by examining a number of different grammatical environments. For example, states typically cannot be put in the progressive:

(39) *a.* *John is knowing Latin.
(Cf. John is learning Latin.)
b. *John is being on the roof.
(Cf. John is getting on the roof.)
c. *John is being thin.
(Cf. John is getting thin.)

States are also odd in the imperative:

(40) *a.* *Know Latin!
(Cf. Learn Latin!)
b. *Be on the roof!
(Cf. Go on the roof!)
c. *Be thin!
(Cf. Get thin!)

States are also generally bad in sentences of the form "It look NP an hour (a minute, a year) to VP."

(41) *a.* *It took John a year to know Latin.
(Cf. It took John a year to learn Latin.)
b. *It took John five minutes to be on the roof.
(Cf. It took John five minutes to get on the roof.)
c. *It took John six months to be thin.
(Cf. It took John six months to get thin.)

(The asterisks in (39) through (41) indicate semantic oddness rather than syntactic ill-formedness.)

Activities share with states the property of lacking a natural culmination. Yet they are agentive in that they typically involve a subject doing something. They cannot in general be viewed as instantaneous snapshots of the world. Examples are the following:

(42) *a.* Joan is kicking.
b. Joan is pushing a cart.

Imagine we see a snapshot of Joan with her legs in a certain position. Is she kicking, or is she standing with her legs that way? We can't tell. We need to see Joan for more than an instant to determine whether she is kicking.

The progressive and imperative tests also differentiate activities from states. Unlike states, activities are perfectly natural in the progressive, as (42) illustrates. They are also felicitous in the imperative:

(43) *a.* Kick higher!
b. Push that cart without banging it into the wall!

Activities share with states the property of being infelicitous in the "It took NP an hour to VP" class of environments:

(44) *a.* *It took Joan an hour to kick.
b. *It took Joan an hour to push that cart.

Telic eventualities instead have a natural end point or culmination. Typical examples are the following:

(45) *a.* Joan fell asleep.
b. Michelangelo painted the ceiling of the Sistine Chapel.

They are generally good in the progressive:

(46) *a.* Joan is falling asleep.
b. Michelangelo is painting the ceiling of the Sistine Chapel.

In the imperative they are usually good:

(47) *a.* Fall asleep!
b. Paint the ceiling of the Sistine Chapel!

And unlike states and activities, they are generally good in the "It took NP an hour to VP" environments:

(48) *a.* It took Joan a minute to fall asleep.
b. It took Michelangelo three years to paint the ceiling of the Sistine Chapel.

Note that often the interaction of a predicate with certain phrases shifts the original aspectual class of that predicate. For example, *walk* is basically understood as lacking a natural end point. However, *walk to school* does culminate (when one reaches school). So combining *walk* with the adverbial *to school* bounds the activity of walking, gives it a culmination point, and thereby makes the aspectual class of the entire VP that of telic eventualities, rather than the activity class associated with the verb that heads the VP.

Dowty discusses in detail many further grammatical tests that distinguish these aspectual classes and puts forth a very suggestive hypothesis in this connection. He suggests that all verbs are defined from basic stative predicates in terms of the operators CAUSE and BECOME along with an additional operator DO (which we will briefly discuss in section 3 below), with the semantic properties of the operators determining the properties of the various aspectual classes. Assume that we are endowed with basic stative predicates and the combinatorial apparatus of intensional logic augmented by the operators just mentioned, and then, Dowty argues, predicates will form the three classes discussed above, and we will be able to derive the distribution of various verb phrases with respect to aspectual tests from the semantic properties of the aspectual operators. Consider the causative/inchoative alternations in (14) through (16), and notice that while the adjective is stative, the corresponding verbs express telic eventualities. This follows from the fact that the verbs are defined by means of the change-of-state operator BECOME. So translational decompositions of verbs along the lines just sketched, either specifically specified as in (33) or given more generally by rules like those in (35) to (37), provide an interesting (though not unproblematic) hypothesis concerning both the aspectual properties of these verbs and the entailments associated with them.

Decompositional analysis has been applied to a host of data, including most of that considered in the introduction. For illustration, let us turn from verbs to common noun meanings. In the set below the (*a*) sentences entail the (*b*) and (*c*) sentences, and these entailments seem to depend on the semantic properties of *mother*, *parent*, *female*, *father*, *male*, *wife*, *husband*, and *married*.

(49) *a*. Hilary is a mother.
b. Hilary is a parent.
c. Hilary is female.

(50) *a*. Lee is a father.
b. Lee is a parent.
c. Lee is male.

(51) *a*. Hilary is a wife.
b. Hilary is married.
c. Hilary is female.

(52) *a*. Lee is a husband.
b. Lee is married.
c. Lee is male.

Mother and *wife* differ from *father* and *husband* by licensing application of *female* rather than *male*. *Wife* and *husband* differ from *mother* and *father* in sharing the inference to a sentence with *married* rather than one with *parent*. *Mother* labels a concept that involves femaleness and parenthood; *father* involves maleness and parenthood. The concept designated by *wife* involves femaleness and being married; *husband* involves maleness and being married. This suggests that this class of nouns might also be decomposed into a set of recurrent conceptual features or traits. Within the general setup we are assuming, what we have to do is translate the words designating complex concepts into syntactically complex expressions of our logical calculus, as in (53):

(53) *a*. $\text{mother}' = \lambda x[\text{parent}'(x) \wedge \text{female}'(x)]$
b. $\text{father}' = \lambda x[\text{parent}'(x) \wedge \text{male}'(x)]$
c. $\text{wife}' = \lambda x[\text{married}'(x) \wedge \text{female}'(x)]$
d. $\text{husband}' = \lambda x[\text{married}'(x) \wedge \text{male}'(x)]$

Of course, further decomposition might be proposed, for example, $\text{male}' = \lambda x \neg \text{female}'(x)$ (or vice versa). The point worth making here is that translations like those in (53) allow us to prove the entailments above using standard deductive techniques; the entailments depend only on properties of the logical constants of *lf* (in this case, the λ-operator and logical conjunction). The translations still leave open the semantic value of *parent, female, male*, and *married*, but they provide an explicit representation of the relations of the concepts associated with these words to those associated with the words they are used to translate in (53). The effects of this kind of decomposition appear, however, to be more limited in scope than the adjective and verb decompositions considered above. They involve a limited family of words (e.g., kinship terms), have fewer overt morphological features, interact with a much narrower range of grammatical phenomena. Even in this domain, however, there are recurring abstract concepts like that of animacy that seem to be grammatically relevant in many different languages.

Decomposition has often had a further aim: to identify a stock of universal semantic components from which all languages draw in constructing the concepts their lexicons label. What is sought is a basic language-independent vocabulary for the language of semantic representation, some kind of *interpreted* logic or semantic calculus (a logic whose nonlogical constants are interpreted). It certainly seems plausible that *aiti* (Finnish for *mother*) and *isä* (Finnish for *father*) differ in the same dimension as their English equivalents. The concept of femaleness, for example, is not peculiar to English. We use FEMALE (an English word written in small capital letters) to designate the concept (which might or might not perfectly translate English *female*).

The idea of viewing word meanings as composed from more primitive universal semantic elements was taken up within the framework of transformational grammar by Katz and Fodor (1963) and further developed in work by Katz and Postal (1964), Katz (1966, 1972), and Bierwisch (1969), among others. Some of the most extensive work on word meanings as syntactically structured was done in the late 1960s and early 1970s by generative semanticists: Lakoff (1965), McCawley (1968), and Postal (1970), for example. More recently Jackendoff (1976, 1983) has advanced some interesting proposals about the centrality of spatiotemporal notions in providing a general structural model for the semantic structure of many lexical items. Although this work assumes that primitive semantic elements, the atoms from which word meanings are composed, designate some kind of mental construct or concept, most of it fails to consider how these concepts connect with what we talk about, their role in articulating the objective significance of language.[5]

Let us summarize. Decompositional accounts of lexical meaning have been proposed to elucidate semantic relations among lexical items, apparent semantic universals, aspectual differences, and constraints on possible interactions of conceptually complex words with modifying expressions such as adverbials. Here we have sketched some features of Dowty's decompositional analysis, which tries to accomplish these tasks using the kind of semantic tools studied in this book. Though we have not really been able to do justice to Dowty's analysis within the limits of this work, we have briefly indicated what some of its advantages and disadvantages might be and noted some empirical tests that might bear on the hypothesis of lexical decomposition.

We turn next to ways of achieving similar results that do not decompose lexical items.

2.3 Lexical analysis without decomposition

2.3.1 Meaning postulates Most of the analytical and descriptive work done within decompositional frameworks can be incorporated with only minor modifications within other approaches to the analysis of lexical meaning. Here is an important alternative to the decompositional analysis. The relation between inchoative/causative pairs and their adjectival counterparts can be captured in terms of something like the following "axioms":

(54) *a.* $\Box\forall x[\alpha'_i(x) \leftrightarrow \text{BECOME}(\alpha'_a(x))]$
b. $\Box\forall x\forall y[\alpha'_t(x, y) \leftrightarrow \text{CAUSE}(x, \alpha'_i(y))]$
where $\alpha =$ *open*, *empty*, *break* (*broken*), etc.

Adopting the laws in (30) is tantamount to saying that speakers of English are not willing to use the relevant words in ways that violate them. In any admissible model for English and in any world, something opens just in case it was not open immediately before and becomes open immediately thereafter. Similarly, if someone opens something they cause it to open, i.e., they cause it to become open. Laws of this sort have been dubbed "meaning postulates" by Carnap (1947) and are to be viewed as an integral part of the characterization of the notion of "admissible model for English." Meaning postulates place constraints on admissible models.[6] Meaning postulates can replace decompositional analysis in spelling out the semantic part of morphological rules:

(55) *a.* If α is in Adj, then α (or α + en) is in V_i
b. $\Box\forall y[\alpha'_i(y) \leftrightarrow \text{BECOME}(\alpha'_a(y))]$
where α = open, empty, warm, red, fat, etc.

(56) *a.* If α is in V_i, then α is also in V_t
b. $\Box\forall x\forall y[\alpha'_t(x, y) \leftrightarrow \text{CAUSE}(x, \alpha'_i(y))]$
where α = open, close, empty, sink, redden, fatten, etc.

Meaning postulates such as these are formally equivalent to the decompositional analyses of the preceding section. Given (55) and (56), the following can be shown to hold:

(57) $\text{open}'_t = \lambda x\lambda y[\text{CAUSE}(x, \text{BECOME}(\text{open}'_a(y))]$

We can also posit specific meaning postulates for cases where there is no morphosyntactic relation.

(58) $\Box\forall y\forall x[\text{kill}'(x, y) \leftrightarrow \text{CAUSE}(x, \text{BECOME}(\text{dead}'(y)))]$

However, decompositional translation specifications and meaning postulates are not always formally equivalent. For example, in cases where intuitive judgments do not support the semantic equivalence required by decompositional analyses, meaning postulates allow for partial analyses. As we noted in the preceding section, transitive verbs like *open* and *kill* seem to require a more direct causation than our CAUSE operator, which works more like the English verb *cause* or *make*, requires. One possibility is to replace the causative meaning postulate in (56), which posits equivalence, with (59), which is committed only to one-way entailments.

(59) $\Box\forall x\forall y[\alpha'_t(x, y) \rightarrow \text{CAUSE}(x, \alpha'_i(x, y))]$

Of course, we may ultimately be able to provide a more precise analysis of something like DIRECT CAUSE; if so, then equivalence might still be possible for the causative forming rule.

But there are many cases of word formation rules where the decompositional or any approach that promises full specification of a derived word's meaning seems doomed to failure. Dowty (1979) recognized that actual words are often not interpreted as word formation rules might specify and distinguished semantically transparent from nontransparent derived words; Aronoff (1976), though offering a less fully developed semantic account, suggests something similar. What seems to be missing is the possibility of a middle ground: recognizing that some words have meanings that are only partly determined by their morphological structure.

Consider, e.g., the English word formation rule that forms adjectives from transitive verbs by suffixing *-able*. On the translational approach, such a rule might be formulated as follows:

(60) *a.* If α is in V_t, then $\alpha + able$ is in Adj.
b. $[\alpha + able]' = \lambda x[\Diamond\exists y(\alpha'(y, x))]$
where $\alpha =$ *like*, *hate*, *wash*, etc.

Transparent *-able* formations are those which have this interpretation, and all others are nontransparent. Many, perhaps most, deverbal adjectives with the *-able* suffix have an interpretation that implies something more than (and thus something different from) what (60) specifies, for example, *readable*, *washable*, and probably even *likeable*. If we say that all these English adjectives with *-able* are semantically nontransparent, then this word formation rule does not enter at all into their interpretation.

An alternative is to take more seriously the idea that word formation rules only constrain rather than determine semantic interpretation. Let us revise (60) as follows, using meaning postulates rather than translations for specifying the semantic component.

(61) *a.* If α is in V_t, then $\alpha + able$ is in Adj.
b. $\Box\forall x[[\alpha + able]'(x) \rightarrow \Diamond\exists y(\alpha'(y, x)]$
where $\alpha =$ *like*, *hate*, *wash*, etc.

The syntactic part of (61) is identical to that in (60): it says that affixing *-able* to a transitive verb yields an adjective (albeit potential and not necessarily actualized). The semantic component of the rule, however, simply constrains the interpretation of IPC translations of words so derived. The meaning postulate in (61*b*) says that a person who is likeable can be liked by someone. It does not place any more stringent conditions on being likeable, although the English word *likeable* arguably does. Someone who knows the *-able* rule, hears *likeable* for the first time, and analyzes it as derived by this rule will be guided toward the established interpretation although she will not know the full actual interpretation without further contextual cues. Meaning postulates are well suited for handling meaning relations that are neither completely transparent nor opaque but semantically "translucent." Translucent relations seem to be the norm for word formation rules.[7]

A further important consideration is that even when the meaning postulate approach and the decompositional one are formally equivalent, they may turn out to differ qua theories of semantic competence. In the decompositional approach, no single vocabulary item in the semantic calculus corresponds to English words like *kill* and *die* or the transitive and intransitive verbs *open*. The associated concepts are not basic ones in the semantic calculus; they are assembled from other concepts such as CAUSE, BECOME, and that associated with *dead* (if *dead′* is a basic expression in the semantic calculus and not further reduced to *not′ alive′*). This might suggest that certain concepts are more complex than others, where complexity is determined by the complexity of their decompositions. For example, the semantic representation of *kill* contains that of *die*; *kill* is at least representationally more complex than *die*. In contrast, the meaning postulate approach allows us to hypothesize that concepts like *kill, die,* and *open* are directly labeled by vocabulary items in the semantic calculus; they are not identified with assemblages of more basic concepts. Thus the semantic representation of *kill* on the meaning postulate approach does not contain that of *die*: both are just basic expressions in the semantic calculus, which means neither is translated into a syntactically complex expression. Now this does not mean that there is no cognitive complexity to the concept labeled *kill′*, but it does mean that the translation of *kill* does not itself represent that complexity. It also means that *kill′* designates a conceptual unit. There is no need, on the meaning postulate approach, to think that the same cognitive construct or process is involved in understanding both utterances of *die* and utterances of *kill* and thus that *kill* should be psychologically more complex than *die*.

In fact, experimental evidence suggests that there is no detectable correspondence between complexity at the level of decomposition into features and difficulty in processing. Aitchison (1987, chap. 6) reviews relevant psycholinguistic literature (including Fodor, Fodor, and Garrett 1975, which many linguists found compelling) and concludes that data on comprehension, ease of access, and similar processing phenomena do not support the decompositional view. If representational complexity links to processing complexity, then something like the meaning postulate approach can be taken to be more compatible with psychological evidence on semantic processing and better designed as an abstract characterization of the speaker's knowledge.

Acquisition phenomena also might bear on the issue of lexical decomposition. Children acquire words like *kill* and *die* long before they learn words like *cause* or *become*. Of course, the IPC CAUSE and BECOME predicates need not be equated with English *cause* and *become*; nonetheless, it is striking that what we have analyzed as the relatively more complex items semantically are apparent more directly salient for children. It is often said that young children, while being attuned to causal relations, lack explicit knowledge of abstract notions, like causation, that serve to cross-classify many diverse type of events. But then how can children represent notions like those associated with *kill,* in which causation figures?

Even at a less abstract level we find the order of acquisition is frequently opposite what relative complexity of proposed translations might seem to predict. As Fodor (1987, 161), observes, "Children know about fathers long before they know about males and parents. So either they don't have the concept FATHER when they seem to, or you can have the concept MALE PARENT without having access to its internal structure, namely by having the concept FATHER. Of these alternatives, the last seems best."

The decompositional approach might seem to suggest that the simple concept of *father′* that children first acquire is different from, and perhaps ultimately replaced by, the complex one that they later build from *male′* and *parent′*. In contrast, the meaning postulate approach need only suppose an enrichment of IPC to include basic expressions like *male′* and *parent′* and the concepts they designate along with meaning postulates connecting these later acquired concepts to the earlier ones and also linking earlier concepts to one another. There is a continuity of concepts from one stage to another, although knowledge of the continuing concepts may develop in certain ways. Vocabulary grows along with knowledge of conceptual connections, but the later stages in lexical knowledge generally extend rather than discard the earlier stages. For example, the child who adds *female, male,* and *parent* to a vocabulary that already contains *mother* and *father* might at the same time add meaning postulates like those in (62) to the semantic calculus along with the new basic expressions *female′*, *male′*, and *parent′*.

(62) *a.* $\Box\forall x\forall y[\text{father}'(x, y) \leftrightarrow (\text{male}'(x) \wedge \text{parent}'(x, y))]$
b. $\Box\forall x\forall y[\text{mother}'(x, y) \leftrightarrow (\text{female}'(x) \wedge \text{parent}'(x, y))]$

c. $\Box\forall x[\text{male}'(x) \rightarrow \neg\text{female}'(x)]$
d. $\Box\forall x[\text{female}'(x) \rightarrow \neg\text{male}'(x)]$

The concepts designated by *father′* and *mother′* are still designated by basic expressions in *lf*; those basic expressions are not rendered superfluous when the concepts they designate become analyzable through the introduction of new concepts designated by new basic expressions. The child is at the same time also learning more about the relation of the early concepts *mother′* and *father′* to other concepts (and also, of course, more about what mothers and fathers are like or supposed to be like and so on—the kinds of beliefs that might play a role in generating implicatures and that might be cognitively linked to lexical entries). Lexical analysis by means of meaning postulates is perfectly consistent with diverse (and changing) mental representations of word meanings. Indeed, it implies nothing about how the concepts associated with individual words are structured or how they are processed in comprehension. It does, however, impute a kind of mental integrity to natural language words by associating them with basic units of the semantic calculus stored in a mental lexicon rather than identifying them with complex expressions.

A developmental story like that sketched for kinship terms might be told, mutatis mutandis, about the causative and inchoative verbs we considered earlier. The child enters transitive $\textit{open}'_{t}$, intransitive $\textit{open}'_{i}$, and adjectival $\textit{open}'_{a}$, in her mental lexicon, using them to label concepts that allow her to recognize situations to which sentences like those in (63) apply.

(63) *a.* Joan opened the door.
b. The door opened.
c. The door was open.

At the same time the child presumably adds such meaning postulates as those in (64), which support inferences from (63*a*) to (63*b*) and from (63*b*) to (63*c*) with suitable provisos about time reference.

(64) *a.* $\Box\forall x\forall y[\text{open}'_{t}(x, y) \rightarrow \text{open}'_{i}(y)]$
b. $\Box\forall x[\text{open}'_{i}(x) \rightarrow \text{open}'_{a}(x)]$

But perhaps it is only later that she links constraints like (64) to CAUSE and BECOME by adding to her mental lexicon meaning postulates similar to those in (55) and (56).

Any language user whose mental lexicon includes CAUSE and BECOME can make explicit connections among items that share these abstract components and cross-classify items in the lexicon by means of their shared entailments (the common semantic properties of words) rather than by means of shared components in the sense implied by decompositional approaches. That is, the knowledge that both transitive *open* and transitive *clean* are causatives can be thought of as knowledge that each figures in a meaning postulate specifying a certain kind of connection to the operator CAUSE. We need not require that each contains the operator CAUSE in its translation (or in less compositionally oriented analyses, the feature +CAUSATIVE). We can also investigate cross-linguistic similarities by exploring the possibility that certain directly interpreted constants like CAUSE and BECOME are like the standard logical constants in that they are part of the vocabulary of the semantic calculus for any language. In other words, to adopt the meaning postulate approach is not to ignore data on connections among lexical items or to rule out the possibility of universal elements in semantic representations.

Some decompositional theories are very reductionist: they seek to pare down the vocabulary of the translation language to an absolute minimum (often with the view that this minimal vocabulary will be universal). A thoroughgoing reductionist program requires decisions about which of two closely related words (*male* and *female, child* and *parent*) is to be taken as basic. Such decisions, as Lyons (1977) effectively shows, are ultimately arbitrary. Meaning postulates, on the other hand, can easily link interdefinable words without treating one as more basic than the other.

Meaning postulates and decompositional analyses might, of course, be interpreted as implying different kinds of cognitive models from those we have sketched above, or as we noted earlier, they might be interpreted as themselves having no particular cognitive significance at all. Certainly a decompositionalist does not have to accept the suggestion that more complex representations would be more difficult to process or to acquire. What is associated cognitively with a lexical item will certainly be more than its translation into *lf* and complexity cannot simply be read off from lf representations. Nor is decomposition inconsistent with a certain kind of "integrity" for distinct natural language lexical items. In other words, decompositional programs are by no means defeated by processing and acquisition data of the sort discussed above.[8]

Summing up, meaning postulates are suitable for specifying either necessary or sufficient conditions for applying a word and for specifying other ways in which its interpretation might be constrained by the interpretation of other words in the language. Unlike translational decomposition of a word, semantic analysis of the IPC translation of a word by means of meaning postulates does not require an analysis of the word in terms of a set of conditions individually necessary and jointly sufficient for its applicability. Meaning postulates allow incomplete semantic analysis in that they only constrain the class of admissible models. They are a useful tool in stating empirical generalization on how words are lexically related and, eventually, in working out substantive theories of lexical meaning.

2.3.2 Abstract syntactic elements As we mentioned in chapter one, generative semanticists hypothesized that abstract elements like CAUSE and BECOME were universally available and that languages might lexicalize conceptual units corresponding to syntactic units so that, e.g., the English word *kill* might, at some syntactic level, correspond to the syntactic structure given in (3) of chapter 1, or the slightly simpler (65), which does not directly represent the relation of *dead* to *not alive*.

(65)

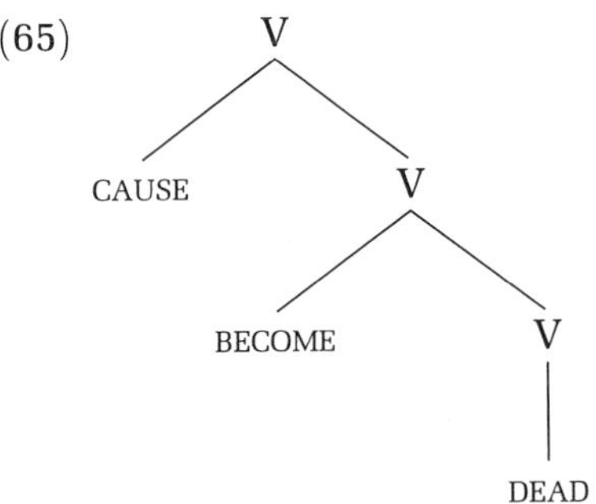

This approach was eventually abandoned in generative linguistics primarily because the syntactic processes involved in lexicalization were unconstrained in problematic ways.

In recent years, however, there has been renewed interest in the idea that abstract elements in syntactic structures might play a role in the specification of the meanings of certain lexical items.[9] Syntax has developed significantly since the days of generative semantics, and thus the current implementation of this idea seems more likely to lead to continued productive linguistic research. So, for example, we might propose that the transitive verb *open* must wind up in the syntactic configuration in (66); in other kinds of structural positions it is filtered out.

(66)

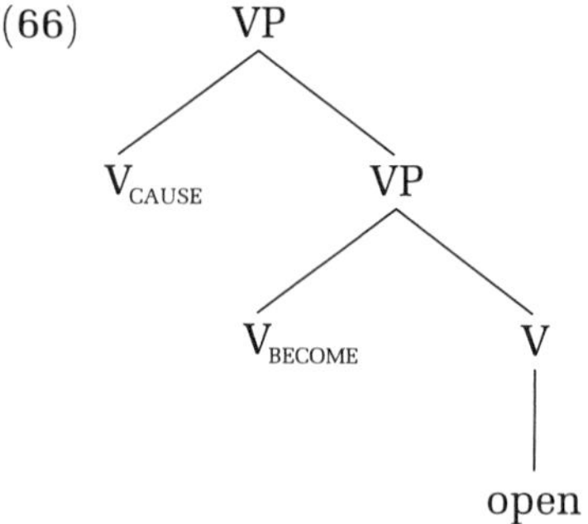

That is, the English transitive verb *open* must be embedded under a phonologically null verb roughly equivalent to Dowty's BECOME operator, which in turn is embedded under a higher phonologically null verb equivalent to Dowty's CAUSE operator (actually, we will want the null CAUSE operator to be equivalent to some more direct notion of causation). Exactly how the semantics is to be spelled out must be filled in, of course, but the basic idea seems to be that what *open* itself contributes semantically is basically something like the state of being open and the change of state and (direct) causation are contributed by the higher null verbs. The lexical item *open* is not decomposed, but some of what we traditionally consider part of its meaning comes from its syntactic relation to other (abstract) elements. In some cases something like the higher verbs in the VP-shell can be overtly realized. Japanese shows a nice contrast with the verb *suru* ('do'). In (67*a*), the word *benkyoo* ('study') is the head noun of the object NP for the full verb *suru*, whereas in (67*b*), *benkyoo* is incorporated into the light verb *suru*, and the object NP is *suugaku* ('mathematics').[10]

(67) *a.* John wa (mai-niti) [$_{NP}$ suugaku no benkyoo]
TOP (every day) mathematics GEN study
o su-ru.
ACC do-IMPERFECT
'John does (engages in) the study of mathematics (every day).'

b. John wa (mai-niti) [$_{NP}$ suugaku] o
TOP (every day) mathematics ACC
benkyoo-su-ru.
study-do-IMPERFECT
'John studies mathematics (every day).'

Another realization of higher abstract verbs is an explicit causativizing morpheme to which the lexical head eventually raises and incorporates, as in the Chichewa example (12) we gave in section 2.1 or the Turkish example from Aissen (1974), cited in Baker (1988), in which the causativizing morpheme is italicized.

(68) O adam-a el aç- *tɨr-* d- ɨm
the man-DAT hand open CAUSE PAST 1sS
'I made the man beg.'

This abstract syntactic approach can be extended to other cases of what prima facie look like purely lexical alternations. Consider for example transitive/intransitive alternations like those exemplified by *shave*, where the intransitive member of the pair is understood reflexively. In the spirit of the line of inquiry we are presently considering, a natural move would be to assume that *shave* (along with many similar verbs) is always transitive: it may, however, occur with a null reflexive object. Thus the structure underlying (69*a*) is hypothesized to be something like (69*b*), where N_{refl} is an unpronounced, i.e., phonologically null, reflexive pronoun, interpreted like all reflexive pronouns, and the interpretation of (69*b*) would be equivalent to that of the formula (69*c*).

(69) *a.* Bond shaved.
b.

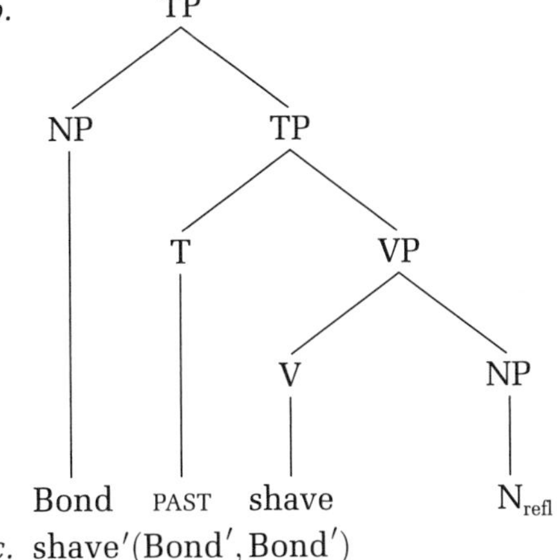

c. shave′(Bond′, Bond′)

Crosslinguistic evidence suggests the presence of some kind of reflexive element. In French and other Romance languages, the corresponding "intransitives" come with a (pronounced) reflexive clitic.

(70) *a.* Marie lave Jacques.
Marie is washing Jacques
b. Marie se lave.
Marie (self) is washing

Abstract elements in the syntax are not new to our semantic project: we have already, e.g., introduced traces to play the same kind of semantic role as pronouns. Thus their use to help elucidate the semantic value of particular lexical items and the semantic relations between (what look like) distinct lexical items seems straightforward. Semantic interpretation is linked in quite systematic ways with syntactic structure, and abstract syntactic analyses have the potential to illuminate these links.

2.4 Summary

We are still a long way from being able to delineate precisely how much semantic analysis of basic content words belongs to the grammar or just how such analysis is actually implemented. We can see, however, that translations, meaning postulates (and probably other constraints on models), and abstract syntactic analyses may all play a role.

3 Modifiers

We have used IPC to translate nouns and verbs and VPs and subject-predicate combinations. We have not yet, however, said much about the semantic analysis of adjectives or adverbs, words whose primary use is as modifiers of nouns and verbs respectively.

3.1 Adjectives

In the present section we will look at how a semantic calculus can help us represent semantic distinctions among words that do not correspond to distinctions in the syntactic category to which those words belong. In this section we show the need for other logical types besides those we already have in IPC and indicate how direct reference to differences in logical types can play a useful role in semantics.

In chapter 1 we noted that within what looks like a single natural language category (adjective) there may be some very general and semantically significant distinctions to be drawn. For example, observe that (71*a*) entails (71*b*) and (71*c*), (72*a*) entails (72*c*) but not (72*b*), and (73*a*) entails neither (73*b*) nor (73*c*), though it does entail (73*d*).

(71) *a.* Pavarotti is a pink tadpole.
b. Pavarotti is pink.
c. Pavarotti is a tadpole.

(72) *a.* Pavarotti is a large tadpole.
b. Pavarotti is large.
c. Pavarotti is a tadpole.

(73) *a.* Pavarotti is a former tadpole.
b. *Pavarotti is former.
c. Pavarotti is a tadpole.
d. Pavarotti was a tadpole.

This suggests that the basic result we want from the semantics of adjectives is something like (74*a*) for adjectives like *pink*, (74*b*) for adjectives like *large*, and nothing of either sort for adjectives like *former*.

(74) *a.* $[\![[\text{pink tadpole}]']\!]^{M,w,i,g} = [\![\text{pink}']\!]^{M,w,i,g} \cap [\![\text{tadpole}']\!]^{M,w,i,g}$
b. $[\![[\text{large tadpole}]']\!]^{M,w,i,g} \subseteq [\![\text{tadpole}']\!]^{M,w,i,g}$

Of course, (74) makes sense only if we suppose that $[\![\text{pink}']\!]^{M,w,i,c,g}$, $[\![[\text{pink tadpole}]']\!]^{M,w,i,g}$, and $[\![[\text{large tadpole}]']\!]^{M,w,i,g}$ are all sets of individuals. Prenominal adjectives like *pink* are sometimes called *intersective*, and those like *large* are called *subsective*; the category exemplified by *former* can be called *nonpredicative*. Let us see how we can understand the pattern in (71) through (73) by looking at these different types of adjectives in turn.

The treatment of intersective adjectives like *pink* appears to be fairly simple. We have already informally treated some such adjectives in predicate position, introduced with the verb *be* "attached" and translated as constants in Pred_1 (as in *Pavarotti is boring*). All we need to do now is treat the *be* as a separate element by adding to F_3 the following rules for adjectives:

(75) VP $\rightarrow$ be Adj
Adj $\rightarrow$ pink, red, hungry, boring, drunk, dead, round, blond, etc.

We can give a semantics for these predicate adjective constructions by means of translation in the style of section 2, chapter 7.

(76) *a.* Members of the syntactic category Adj are translated as constants of category Pred_1 of IPC.
b. $[\text{be Adj}]' = \text{Adj}'$

Together (75) and (76) generate sentences like (77*a*) with syntactic structure (77*b*) and assign to them the reduced translation given in (77*c*).

(77) *a.* Pavarotti is drunk.

b.

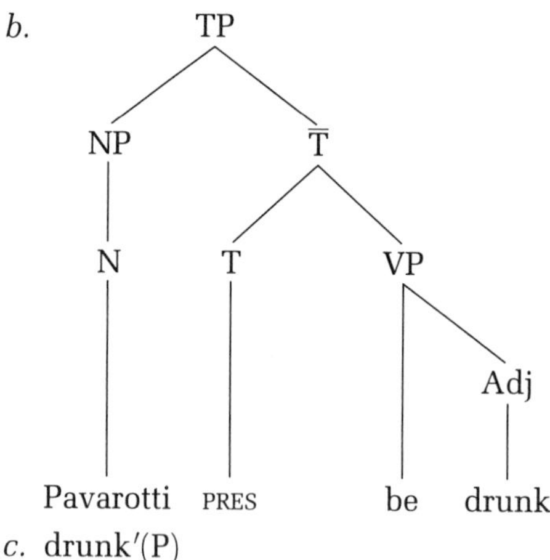

c. drunk′(P)

An intersective adjective like *pink* will receive the same translation in prenominal position as it does in the VP, namely the one-place predicate *pink′*, which has as its extension at every index $\langle w, i \rangle$ the set of things that are pink in world w at time i. The translation of the prenominal adjective *pink* will combine semantically with the translation of the $\bar{\text{N}}$ it modifies by generalized predicate conjunction, which is just set intersection as in (46*a*) above. Prenominal modification of an $\bar{\text{N}}$ by an adjective is thus semantically exactly like postnominal modification of an $\bar{\text{N}}$ by a relative clause. To formulate syntactic and semantic rules that characterize the behavior of intersective adjectives in prenominal and predicative position is a straightforward matter.[11] Prenominal adjectives generally are introduced into the syntax by (78*a*) and intersective adjectives are interpreted by (78*b*).

(78) *a.* $\bar{\text{N}} \rightarrow \text{Adj}\ \bar{\text{N}}$

b. $[_{\bar{\text{N}}}\ \text{Adj}\ \bar{\text{N}}]' = \text{Adj}' \wedge \bar{\text{N}}'$

(The interpretive rule in (78*b*) works only for adjectives whose translation is in Pred_1. Recall that in chap. 7, see, 3.1, we used λ-abstraction to define a generalized conjunction that joins predicates.)

Exercise 1 Give the syntactic tree associated with (*a*) below, along with its node-by-node translation on the model of the example on p. 410.

(1) Every hungry pink pig is cute.

Show that (*b*) is equivalent to (*c*).

(2) The pink pig is hungry.

(3) The pig that is pink is hungry.

Intersective adjectives, then, are simply predicates: they do not require us to expand the basic resources of IPC at all. We also see that the core semantic rule for interpreting noun modification appears to be set intersection. But consider now nonpredicative adjectives like *former*. It is frequently noted that the fact that two $\bar{\text{N}}$s, α and β, have the same extension in given circumstances does not guarantee that *former* α and *former* β will have the same extension. So in the U.S. Senate in the spring of 1988, for example, the set of those who are professional basketball players and those who are astronauts were both empty (and thus equal), but the set of former professional basketball players was nonempty and equal to {Senator Bill Bradley from New Jersey} and the set of former astronauts was the distinct nonempty set equal to {Senator John Glenn from Ohio}. This means that the extension of *former professional basketball player* in given circumstances is not a function of the extension of *professional basketball player*, nor is the extension of *former astronaut* a function of the extension of *astronaut*. This seems to suggest that we should treat these nonpredicative adjectives intensionally. That is, the set of individuals that are now former astronauts depends on the intension of the predicate *astronaut*; more specifically, it depends on who had that property in the past.

A very general way to incorporate this insight is to regard adjectives like *former* as property operators, that is, as functions from properties to properties. For example, *former* can be interpreted as a function that maps the property of being an astronaut to the property of being a former astronaut, the property of being a teacher to the property of being a former teacher, and so on. We can treat similarly other adjectives in this class, like *alleged, false* (as in *false friend*), etc. This means that we need in our semantics a new category, a novel logical type, that of functions from properties to properties.

We continue to do semantics for English by translation into IPC, ensuring that we give an explicit semantics for IPC itself. So our first step is to introduce into IPC the new logico-syntactic category of operators on one-place predicates (which we notate as Op-Pred_1). We assume that an IPC constant in this category is interpreted in a context as a function from properties to properties, which in turn are functions from circumstances (i.e., world-time pairs) to sets. That is, if V is the interpretation function, O a constant of category Op-Pred_1, c a context, w a world, and i a time, then $V(O)(c)(\langle w, i \rangle)$ is a function that maps properties to properties, i.e., to sets relative to each circumstance or world-time pair. We thus add the following rules to IPC:

(79) *a.* If O is in Op-Pred_1 and β is in Pred_1, $O(^\wedge\beta)$ is in Pred_1.
b. If O is in Op-Pred_1 and β is in Pred_1, $[\![O(^\wedge\beta)]\!]^{M,w,i,c,g} = [\![O]\!]^{M,w,i,c,g}([\![^\wedge\beta]\!]^{M,w,i,c,g})$, where $[\![^\wedge\beta]\!]^{M,w,i,c,g}$ is the property r that is the intension of β, that is, for every $\langle w', i' \rangle$, $r(\langle w', i' \rangle) = [\![\beta]\!]^{M,w',i',c,g}$.

In other words, our new IPC operators syntactically combine with one-place predicates to yield new one-place predicates and are semantically interpreted as functions that map input properties onto new output properties.

There is no necessary connection between the extensions of the new output properties and the extensions of the input properties. This provides us with a straightforward way of representing the meaning of $\bar{\text{N}}$s like those in (80*a*) and (81*a*), given in (80*b*) and (80*b*).

(80) *a.* $[_{\bar{\text{N}}}$ former senator$]$
b. former$'(^\wedge$senator$')$

(81) *a.* $[_{\bar{\text{N}}}$ alleged killer$]$
b. alleged$'(^\wedge$killer$')$

The interpretation of various nonpredicative adjectives can be further constrained in terms of meaning postulates like the following for *former*$'$, where Q is any one-place predicate.

(82) $\Box\forall x[\text{former}'(^\wedge Q)(x) \leftrightarrow \mathbf{P}Q(x)]$

Formula (82) is actually a meaning postulate schema: by replacing Q with Pred_1 expressions we get actual meaning postulates. It says that something is a former Q just in case that something was a Q in the past.

Exercise 2 Using the two-place verb *allege*, write a meaning postulate scheme that constrains the meaning of *alleged.*

Notice that an immediate consequence of the present semantics for nonpredicative adjectives is that if, for example, Pavarotti is a former tadpole, it does not follow that he is a tadpole, even though by (82) it follows that he was one. The point is that the inference from (83*a*) to (83*b*) is not in general licensed, which is what we want for this class of adjectives.

(83) *a.* $O(^\wedge\beta)(x)$
b. $\beta(x)$

The failure of such inferences constitutes the main reason for viewing nonpredicative adjectives as members of the logicosyntactic category Op-Pred_1, as functions from properties to properties.

Let us turn now to subsective adjectives. In some ways subsective adjectives are like intersective adjectives: both occur in predicate position (where they express properties), and when they combine prenominally with a nominal, both produce a new nominal whose extension is a subset of the modified nominal. Being pink and being large are both properties (whereas being former isn't a property), and a pink tadpole and a large tadpole are both tadpoles.

Being large, however, is a property that is highly dependent on context: what size something must be to count as large will depend on contextual factors. The size is much smaller if we are looking at tadpoles than if we're looking at elephants; being large is relative to a property (being a tadpole or being an elephant, for example). Subsective adjectives like *large* are often called *relative adjectives* in the linguistics literature. It has sometimes been suggested that their relativity is essentially like that of *former* and *alleged.* It is tempting to propose, for example, that *large tadpole* be interpreted to mean large for being a tadpole and be translated in exactly the same way as *former tadpole* or *alleged tadpole.* An immediate difficulty with such a proposal is that it provides no account of the subsective property of these adjectives or of their being able to occur in predicate position. An even more serious problem for this proposal is that the head nominal does not always set the standard for relative adjectives. For example, consider sentence (84), adapted from an example due to Hans Kamp and Barbara Partee.

(84) Lee built a large snowman.

What counts as large for evaluating a sentence like this one depends not just on standards set by the property of being a snowman but also on other factors: Lee might be a two-year-old in the backyard or a twenty-year-old working on the Dartmouth snow carnival.

In dealing with the subsective adjectives, the contribution of context cannot be ignored. One way of capturing the context-dependent character of adjectives like *large* might be as follows: Let us assume that the context provides us with a set of comparison classes for *large* and similarly for other relative adjectives. We need a set of comparison classes (rather than a single one) to deal with sentences like "A large tadpole is not a large animal," where in the same context the comparison class for the first occurrence of *large* is different from the comparison class for its second occurrence. So let us add to our contextual functions a function $\mathrm{Cl}^n_{\mathrm{A}}$, for each subsective adjective A. Intuitively, $\mathrm{Cl}^n_{\mathrm{large}}(c)$ gives us the set of objects that are large in context c relative to the nth class of objects whose size we are considering. $\mathrm{Cl}^m_{\mathrm{tall}}(c)$ gives us the set of objects that are tall in context c relative to the mth class of objects whose height we are considering, and so on. We then assume that English *large* is associated with a class of predicates of IPC represented as $large_n$, where n is an arbitrary index. $Large_1$, $large_2$, $large_3$, etc., are context-dependent predicates. Their semantics is specified in terms of $\mathrm{Cl}^n_{\mathrm{large}}$ as follows:

(85) For any c, w, and i, $V(\mathrm{large}_n)(c)(\langle w, i \rangle) = \mathrm{Cl}^n_{\mathrm{large}}(c)$.

For each occurrence of *large* in a particular utterance, the context specifies $large' = large_n$.

In (86) we provide an example.

(86) *a.* $[_{\bar{\mathrm{N}}}$ large tadpole$]$
b. $\mathrm{large}_1(x) \wedge \mathrm{tadpole}'(x)]$

The meaning of an $\bar{\mathrm{N}}$ like (85*a*) can be represented as in (85*b*). An individual is going to satisfy the context-dependent property in (85*b*) just in case it is a tadpole and is large relative to the first class of individuals whose size we are considering in the current context. It is of course very plausible to maintain that in a context where we ascribe *large* to a particular $\bar{\mathrm{N}}$, certain properties of entities denoted by that $\bar{\mathrm{N}}$ are going to determine the comparison class. Thus in a context where (85*a*) is used, such a comparison class will very likely be made up of tadpoles.

Notice that an immediate consequence of this analysis is that if something is a large tadpole, it must be a tadpole, which is exactly what we want. Furthermore, we also see why from "*y* is a large tadpole" it does not follow that "*y* is large." To say that *y* is a large tadpole is to apply to *y* a property of the form $[\text{large}_3' \wedge \text{tadpole}']$. From this it does follow that *y* has the property of being large_3 but not that it has the property of being large_n for $n \neq 3$. In other words, from "*y* is a large tadpole" it follows that *y* is large only with respect to a given comparison class. But when we go on to say "*y* is large" we may (and typically will) select a different comparison class. This is why we cannot in general infer (72*b*) from (72*a*) in the way we can infer (71*b*) from (71*a*). The bottom line, however, is that *large* does always translate as a predicate, but exactly which one depends on the context.

So adjectives appear to belong to two different logical types. Intersective and subsective adjectives are properties (subsective adjectives are highly context-dependent ones), whereas nonpredicative adjectives are property modifiers, functions from properties to properties.

By exploiting these semantic differences, we can provide a very simple treatment of adjectives in fragment F_3. Let us summarize the required syntactic rules to introduce both prenominal and postcopular adjectives and the required semantic rules for interpreting them.

(87) *a.* $\bar{\text{N}} \rightarrow \text{Adj}\ \bar{\text{N}}$
a′. If $\Delta = [_{\text{N}}\ \text{Adj}\ \bar{\text{N}}]$, $\Delta' = \text{Adj}' \wedge \text{N}'$, if Adj′ is in Pred_1
$= \text{Adj}'({}^{\wedge}\text{N}')$, if Adj′ is in Op-Pred_1
b. $\text{VP} \rightarrow \text{be Adj}$
b′. If $\Delta = [_{\text{VP}}\ \text{be Adj}]$, $\Delta' = \text{Adj}'$

The semantic rule in (87*a′*) exploits the different logical types that adjectives may have. N̄s are associated with properties. If the adjective we are considering designates a property, we simply conjoin it with the property associated with the head; extensionally, this amounts to set intersection. If it is a property modifier, we apply it to the head.

While in many ways an oversimplification, the approach in (87) has a further interesting consequence. The syntactic rule in (87*b*) licenses well-formed strings like the following:

(88) John is former/alleged/etc.

Yet they are ungrammatical. Why? Consider what their semantics would be on the basis of (87*b*′) and the other semantic rules. It would have to be as in (89).

(89) former′(*j*)

But (89) is semantically incoherent. The expression *former*′ is a property modifier, a function from properties to properties. Consequently, it is undefined for *j*, which is an individual. Hence, (89) is ungrammatical because it is uninterpretable; its translation (89) is incoherent. Its semantics amounts to applying a function to something outside of its domain.

Exercise 3 Give the *lf* of the sentence below relative to one of its LFs.

(*a*) Every large tadpole admires a large former tadpole.

To summarize, we have seen that adjectives display three different patterns of entailments. We have argued that to account for them, they must be classified as belonging to different semantic types. Adjectives like *pink* are properties. Adjectives like *large* are also properties, albeit highly context-dependent ones. Adjectives like *former* are functions from properties to properties. These distinctions not only enable us to capture the different entailments adjectives enter into. They also explain why not every adjective can occur in predicate position. Adjectives like *former* cannot because they are not properties and hence cannot be predicated of individuals.

What we have done is, of course, only a rough first approximation. Much more can be said about adjectives.[12] There are, however, two morals that we think can be drawn from the above discussion. The first is that to do semantics we need to enrich somewhat the standard set of types in IPC: nonpredicative adjectives seem best analyzed as predicate operators. The second is that differences in logical type may actually explain certain distributional properties of classes of expressions and thus constitute a substantive component of the characterization of their behavior. Intersective and subsective adjectives will differ from nonpredicative adjectives by virtue of their being translated as predicates rather than as operators. Subsective adjectives will differ from intersective adjectives by virtue of their heavy dependence on context for fixing values.

3.2 Adverbs

The term *adverb* is used to cover a host of somewhat different kinds of words, only some of which are verb or verb phrase modifiers. It is also sometimes used to include modifiers like prepositional phrases. (We have, of course, already had prepositional phrases inside VPs: we used, e.g., PP[to] for the third argument of verbs like *give* and *introduce*. In this case, the PP is not a modifier but introduces an argument.) In chapter 5 we mentioned modal and temporal adverbials. For example, we analyzed adverbs like *probably* and *necessarily* as modal operators, which apply to sentences. Adverbs like *formerly* and *allegedly*, which are derived from nonpredicative adjectives, are also best analyzed as sentential operators.

In this section, we will limit discussion to adverbs that modify verbs or verb phrases. We will include not only lexical adverbs like *quickly*, *noisily*, and *passionately* but also prepositional phrases like *with a knife*, *to the store*, and *on the mouth*. Our main goal is to illustrate how data about adverbial interpretation can be used as evidence for bringing some new kinds of things, namely events, into our semantic ontology. Right now we have individual entities, truth-values, possible worlds, and times as the basic building blocks from which we construct semantic values. The logic of adverbial modification, however, can be construed as providing evidence that events are also included among the basic kinds of things needed to articulate an adequate theory of natural language semantics. In this section, we draw primarily on Parsons (1990), whose formulation of these arguments is especially lucid. Parsons himself builds on Davidson (1967).

A striking feature of the semantics of adverbs is shown by the entailment pattern in (90).

(90) *a.* Kim kissed Lee passionately on the mouth.
b. Kim kissed Lee passionately and Kim kissed Lee on the mouth.
c. Kim kissed Lee passionately.
d. Kim kissed Lee on the mouth.
e. Kim kissed Lee.

It is intuitively clear that (90*a*) entails (90*b*), which in turn entails both (90*c*) and (90*d*), each of which entails (90*e*); these entailments do not go in the opposite direction. These (one-way) entailment relations are displayed graphically in figure 8.1 and are often

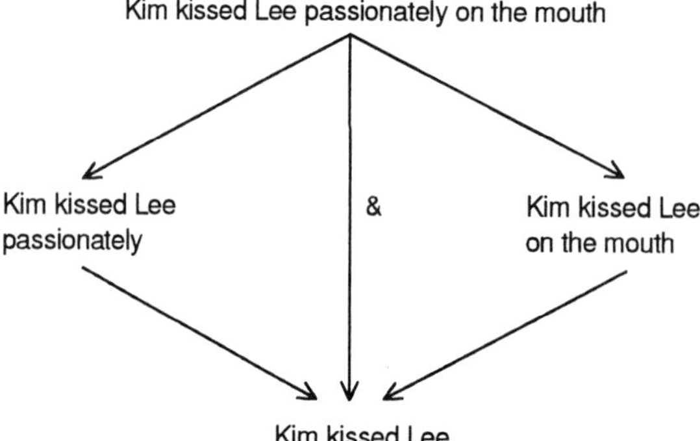

Figure 8.1

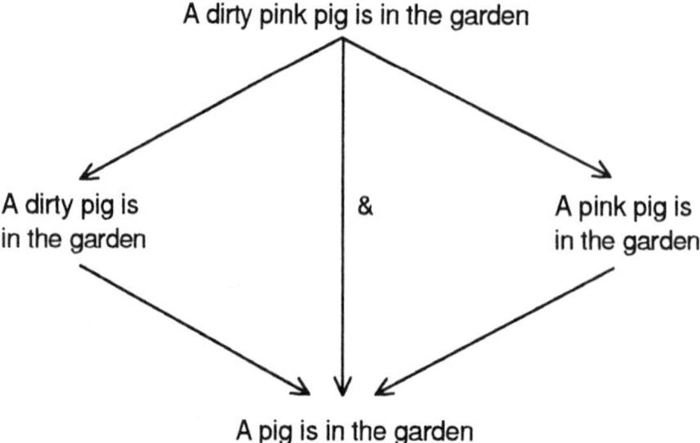

Figure 8.2

dubbed the "diamond pattern." Notice that the implications hold only in the downward direction. Critically, notice that (90*b*), the conjuction at the center of the diamond, does not imply (90*a*), the two-adverb sentence at the top. Perhaps Kim kissed Lee quite dispassionately on the mouth and, on some other occasion, quite passionately on some spot other than the mouth. In such circumstances, (90*b*) would be true but there might well have been no passionate kiss given by Kim to Lee that was also on the mouth, in which case (90*a*) would be false. Notice that we would not have such patterns if we had used such adverbs as *allegedly* or *possibly*.

Now let us compare the pattern in (90) with adjectival modification, considering first predicative and then nonpredicative adjectives. As show in figure 8.2, predicative adjectives show entailment patterns strikingly similar to those in figure 8.1.

Exercise 4 Treating *is-in-the-garden* as translated into $Pred_1$, give the logical form of each of the sentences in figure 8.2 and show why the entailment pattern shown there holds.

Nonpredicative adjectives, on the other hand, behave quite differently.

(91) *a.* An alleged former spy is in the garden.
b. An alleged spy is in the garden and a former spy is in the garden.
c. An alleged spy is in the garden.
d. A former spy is in the garden.
e. A spy is in the garden.

None of the sentences in (91) entails any sentence below it. The contrast between figure 8.2 and (91), as we saw in section 3.1 above, follows from the fact that predicative adjectives translate as predicates whereas nonpredicative adjectives translate as predicate operators. If we treat *pink* and *dirty* as predicates of individuals, the pattern in figure 8.2 follows from familiar logical principles.

Clearly, VP adverbs like those in (90) follow the pattern of the intersective adjectives. If we were to translate them as predicate operators, i.e., functions taking a predicate as input and yielding a predicate as output, then they would be of the same logical type as the non-predicative adjectives. On that approach, the translations we would get would not predict the diamond pattern. There are ways we could achieve this effect (e.g., using meaning postulates), but there would be no insight offered in why the pattern in question holds. On the other hand, translating such modifiers as predicates conjoined with the predicate they modify would allow us to explain the diamond pattern in the same way as we have done for the intersective adjectives. But if adverbs are predicates, of what are they predicated? When *passionately* modifies kiss, one might propose that being passionate is predicated of one of the participants in the kiss; kissing passionately does, after all, entail something about the passionate nature of the kisser. But sentence (90*a*) is not equivalent to sentence (92*a*). We might have Kim being passionate at the time of the kissing yet the passion might not relate directly to the kiss but might have to do with defending her moral principles or be a general disposition not manifested in the particular kiss.

Lee's being passionate, as in (92*b*), is an even less plausible interpretation, and trying to predicate *on the mouth* of the entities explicitly mentioned yields nonsense, as shown in (92*c–d*).

(92) *a.* Kim kissed Lee on the mouth and Kim was passionate.
b. Kim kissed Lee on the mouth and Lee was passionate.
c. # Kim kissed Lee passionately and Kim was on the mouth.
d. #Kim kissed Lee passionately and Lee was on the mouth.

So we have a puzzle. VP adverbs display entailment patterns just like those of predicative adjectives. Adverbs (e.g., *passionately*) are often morphologically derived from adjectives that are predicates of ordinary individual entities (e.g., *passionate*). Yet as VP modifiers, even deadjectival adverbs cannot be analyzed as simply predicating of the entities explicitly mentioned the basic predicate denoted by the adjective.

Here is a sketch of a possible solution. Plausibly, the predicates *passionate* and *on the mouth* in (90*a*) should be understood as applying to the kiss rather than the kisser or kissee. We might hypothesize that verbs have an extra "hidden" argument for events. Suppose, in other words, that the logical form of a sentence like (90*d*) is something like (93).

(93) $\exists e\, \text{kiss}'(\text{Kim}', \text{Lee}', e)$

In (93), e is a variable that ranges over events. We can understand formula (93) as saying that there is an event e, which is a kissing of Lee by Kim. The verb *kiss* is treated as a three-place relation between an event (the kiss), a kisser (in this case, Kim), and a kissee (Lee). The event argument is filled by a variable that is bound by an existential quantifier at some stage. In particular, sentences such as (90*a–d*) above, repeated here as (94*a–d*), will receive translations like those in (94*a′–d′*).

(94) *a.* Kim kissed Lee passionately on the mouth.
a′. $\exists e[\text{kiss}'(\text{Kim}', \text{Lee}', e) \wedge \text{passionate}(e) \wedge \text{on-the-mouth}(e)]$
b. Kim kissed Lee passionately and Kim kissed Lee on the mouth.
b′. $\exists e[\text{kiss}'(\text{Kim}', \text{Lee}', e) \wedge \text{passionate}(e)]$
$\wedge \exists e[\text{kiss}'(\text{Kim}', \text{Lee}', e) \wedge \text{on-the-mouth}(e)]$
c. Kim kissed Lee passionately.
c′. $\exists e[\text{kiss}'(\text{Kim}', \text{Lee}', e) \wedge \text{passionate}(e)]$

d. Kim kissed Lee on the mouth.

d'. $\exists e[\text{kiss}'(\text{Kim}', \text{Lee}', e) \wedge \text{on-the-mouth}(e)]$

Formula (94*a'*) can be understood then as saying that there is a kissing of Lee by Kim and that this kissing was passionate and was on the mouth. We won't give the details of how the translations in (94*a'*–*d'*) are compositionally derived. The basic idea ought to be sufficiently clear: VP adverbs translate as predicates of events and apply to the event argument hypothesized for verbs.

Given this approach, the diamond pattern in figure 8.1 falls out immediately from familiar logical principles. Formula (94*b'*) follows from (94*a'*) by the principle that distributes the existential quantifier across conjunction, (94*c'*) and (94*d'*) each follow from (94*b'*) by conjunction simplification, the same principle that licenses the move from each of (94*c'*) and (94*d'*) to (93). We now see the parallels with respect to adjectives: both (certain) adjectives and (certain) adverbs can be translated as predicates, accounting immediately for their diamond pattern behavior. The difference is that adjectives are predicated of individual entities in the denotation of explicit nominals whereas adverbs are predicated of a distinguished kind of entity, events, hypothesized to be present as "hidden" arguments of verbs.

Let us summarize. In analyzing adjectives, we saw the need to introduce a new logical type, that of predicate operators. In analyzing adverbs, we have considered reasons for introducing a new sort of thing into our ontology, our stock of primitive kinds of things. Event arguments of verbs are not explicitly realized: they have no phonetic substance. But, as with traces, positing this hidden mechanism could give a way to explain much about the behavior of certain kinds of adverbs. There are many further questions about adverbs that we have ignored.[13] There are also many questions about events that we ignore. The analytic usefulness of events is not limited, however, to their utility for explaining entailments involving VP adverbials. Indeed, people now often talk of "event-based semantics." With events in our semantic toolkit, we can shed some light on thematic relations and also on aspectual matters (which we began discussing in section 2.2 above). We turn to these further considerations of verbal semantics in the next section.

4 More on Verbal Semantics

4.1 Thematic relations (θ-roles)

Linguists often talk of *thematic relations* or *roles* (in syntactic discussions, often called *θ-roles*), which have to do with the participants in the events or states sentences describe. Proposed thematic roles or relations often include, for example, *agent* and *experiencer.* Agents are said to do something; experiencers, on the other hand, are said to have certain attitudes or mental states. In (95*a*) Lee is assigned the agent role, but in (95*b*) the role of experiencer.

(95) *a.* Lee kissed Kim.
b. Lee liked Kim.

Which roles Kim is assigned in (95*a*, *b*) is more controversial. In (95*a*) Kim might be classified as a *patient,* the participant most directly affected by the agent's action. In (95*b*) Kim is clearly not a patient but is the trigger of Lee's state, what Lee's state is about. Some linguistics use the term *theme* to indicate this role. In fact, *theme* is often used as a cover label for the role associated with the object in both (95*a*) and (95*b*). Kim is sometimes said to be an *affected* theme in (95*a*) and an *unaffected* theme in (95*b*).

In some form or other, grammarians have appealed to thematic roles since at least the days of Pāṇini, the great Indian linguist who worked on Sanskrit some 2500 years ago. In generative linguistics, they appeared in the late 1960s. Fillmore (1968) spoke of *case relations* and argued that such relations crucially mediate between surface syntax and the way in which verbs and their NP arguments semantically combine in sentences; he also used case relations to say something about semantic relations among verbs. Gruber (1965), who introduced the term *thematic relations*, used them as the basis of a reductionist account of verbal meanings; his ideas have been adopted and extended in a series of discussions of lexical semantics by Jackendoff (see, for example, 1976, 1983). The so-called thematic relations hypothesis associated with this work is that verbs from many different domains have meanings that are somehow patterned on meanings drawn from spatiotemporal domains and articulated in terms of thematic roles most closely associated with notions of motion, location, direction, path, and the like. Many other linguists have in recent years appealed to thematic roles or relations in trying to explain various kinds of morphological and syntactic data. While we cannot survey all the relevant linguistic literature, we would like to discuss briefly some of the issues involved.[14]

The semantic content of thematic roles is notoriously difficult to pin down. Our discussion of adverbial semantics led us to propose that the sentences in (95) might be translated into the formulas in (96).

(96) *a.* $\exists e$ kiss′(Lee′, Kim′, e)
b. $\exists e$ like′(Lee′, Kim′, e)

In each of the sentences in (96), we have a three-place relation and an ordered list of the arguments that relation takes. We have implicitly adopted the convention that the role arguments of *kiss′* will be given in the same order as the overt role arguments of English *kiss.* But of course, languages vary in the way in which different roles (e.g., the kisser and the kissee in (95*a*)) are mapped onto syntactic positions. English uses word order; other languages have freer word order and use case markings. It is important to get clearer on exactly what we are talking about when we talk of thematic roles. Here we will sketch two different ways in which formal semanticists have approached thematic roles. The first is a straightforward extension of the framework already presented in which transitive *kiss* and *like,* for example, map onto two-place logical predicates *kiss′* and *like′*, whose interpretation is constrained by a variety of meaning postulates. The second exploits more radically the idea that verbs have an event argument. Adapting the terminology in Dowty (1989), we call the first an *extended ordered-argument theory;* the second we call an *event-based theory of thematic roles.*

The first approach capitalizes on the fact that each verb licenses certain entailments that help characterize its arguments. (In a more complete treatment we would also consider what verbs presuppose about their arguments, but we will ignore those complications here.)

(97) *a.* Lee kissed Kim.
b. Lee touched (or gestured toward) Kim with her mouth.
c. Lee moved her lips.
d. Lee moved.
e. Lee did something.
f. Lee acted intentionally.
g. A kissing occurred, which was directly caused by Lee.

Similarly, to know what *like* means seems to involve knowing that sentence (95*b*), repeated here as (98*a*) has entailments such as those in (98*b–e*).

(98) *a.* Lee likes Kim.
b. Lee does not hate Kim.
c. Lee has a positive attitude toward Kim.
d. Lee is aware of Kim's existence.
e. Lee is a sentient being.

The kisser role can be thought of as what we can conclude about an entity from its serving as the value of the first argument (x_1) in a formula of the form "kiss′(x_1, x_2, e)." It is the specific role associated with the predicate *kiss′* and its first argument position. Similarly, the liker role is specified by what formulas of the form "like′(x_1, x_2, e)" entail about the entity assigned as the value of x_1; it is the specific role associated with *like′* and its initial argument position. In (99*a*) we provide a general definition of specific roles (what Dowty calls "individual thematic roles"); (99*b*) applies this to defining the role of kisser. (We are assuming, of course, the "hidden" event argument in addition to the arguments that represent participants in the event.)

(99) *a.* For any $(n+1)$-place predicate P and argument position i, the specific role $\langle P, i\rangle$ is the set of properties denoted by the one-place predicates Q that have the semantic property that the formula $P(x_1, \ldots, x_i, \ldots, x_n, e)$ entails the formula $Q(x_i)$.
b. The role of kisser, the specific role $\langle \text{kiss}', 1\rangle$, is the set of all properties denoted by one-place predicates Q that have the semantic property that the formula $\text{kiss}'(x_1, x_2, e)$ entails the formula $Q(x_1)$.

The kisser role, then, includes properties such as those of touching someone with one's mouth, of doing something, of acting intentionally, and so on. Meaning postulates such as (100) will help determine this role.

(100) $\Box\forall x\forall y[\text{kiss}'(x, y) \rightarrow \text{move-}x\text{'s-lips}(x)]$

Exactly the same kind of strategy can be used to define the liker role.

Have we gotten to thematic roles yet? Thematic roles can be thought of as *kinds* of specific roles, so we could define them formally as properties common to sets of specific roles. the specific role $\langle \text{like}', 1 \rangle$, for example, might be intersected with other specific roles, such as $\langle \text{scare}', 2 \rangle$, the specific role our system assigns to the second argument position in formulas translating sentences with the transitive verb *scare.* This latter specific role includes all (and only) the properties attributed to James Bond by virtue of the truth of a sentence like (101).

(101) Something scared James Bond.

Properties that these two specific roles have in common with one another (and with many other specific roles) include those of being aware of something and of being a sentient being, in accord with what is suggested by our informal characterization of an experiencer role.

We want our thematic roles to be characterized by properties common to many specific roles, so such an approach may prove productive. Properties shared by many specific roles will certainly emerge: another example is the property of doing something, which the specific role $\langle \text{kiss}', 1 \rangle$ will share with many other specific roles (like $\langle \text{open}'_t, 1 \rangle$, $\langle \text{give}', 1 \rangle$, $\langle \text{walk}', 1 \rangle$). Doing something is one property often associated with agents.

Thematic roles might then be thought of formally as sets of properties common to many specific roles. We could say that the specific role $\langle P, i \rangle$ is assigned to thematic role θ if all the properties in θ belong to $\langle P, i \rangle$. Thus to say that a kisser is assigned to the AGENT role whereas a liker is not is to say that $\langle \text{kiss}', 1 \rangle$ includes all the properties in AGENT (whatever they might be) and that $\langle \text{like}', 1 \rangle$ does not. So on this approach, thematic roles are simply recurrent entailments associated with argument positions of predicates. This strategy leaves it as an open question whether we could identify a small set of entailments capable of classifying all the argument structures we find in natural language. Perhaps not. Still, there are entailment patterns that recur fairly often, and the approach just sketched provides us with a precise way of thinking about them.

Let us turn now to look at an event-based theory of thematic roles. In the ordered-argument theory, the notion of *n*-place predicates is taken as basic and thematic roles are defined as sets of entailments associated with argument positions. On the event-based theory of thematic roles, thematic roles are taken as primitives and *n*-place predicates are defined in terms of them. Thematic roles are viewed as ways of linking individuals to the events or states described by simple sentences. In particular, thematic relations like AGENT, EXPERIENCER, and THEME can be characterized as (partial) functions from eventualities into their participants. So, for example, "$\text{AGENT}(e) = y$" says that y is the agent of e. This incorporates the view that each eventuality has a unique agent participant (if it has any). (The agent can, of course, be a group, as in "Lee and Robin lifted Kim.") These thematic role functional expressions are not themselves the translations of any natural language expressions but enter into both the specification of the meaning of the predicates corresponding to verbs (for example, in constraints on the interpretation of those predicates) and the specification of the map between the thematic role formulas and syntactic structures of natural language. Thus the translation of the English verb *kiss* will be a complex expression that includes a predicate of events, which we designate as *kiss*″, along with a specification of the various participant roles, in this case, AGENT and THEME.

On this view the English sentences (95*a*, *b*), repeated here as (102*a*) and (103*a*), can be represented as in (102*b*) and (103*b*), respectively, if we ignore tense and the aspectual difference between events like kicking and states like liking. (We will consider these differences in the next subsection.)

(102) *a.* Lee kissed Kim.
b. $\exists e[\text{kiss}''(e) \wedge \text{AGENT}(e) = l \wedge \text{THEME}(e) = k]$

(103) *a.* Lee liked Kim.
b. $\exists e[\text{like}''(e) \wedge \text{EXPERIENCER}(e) = l \wedge \text{THEME}(e) = k]$

Formula (102*b*) can be read as follows: there is an event that is a kissing and the agent of that event is Lee and its theme is Kim.

The thematic role properties of particular verb translations in the calculus could be partly specified by meaning postulates like those in (104).

(104) *a.* $\Box\forall e[\text{kiss}''(e) \rightarrow \exists x(\text{AGENT}(e) = x)]$
b. $\Box\forall e[\text{kiss}''(e) \rightarrow \exists y(\text{THEME}(e) = y)]$

This says that kissing semantically requires an agent and a theme. Similarly, liking requires both an experiencer and a theme.

(105) *a.* $\Box\forall e[\text{like}''(e) \rightarrow \exists x(\text{EXPERIENCER}(e) = x)]$
b. $\Box\forall e[\text{like}''(e) \rightarrow \exists y(\text{THEME}(e) = y)]$

In contrast to *kiss* and *like*, a verb like *swallow* seems to have an optional theme and thus might satisfy something like the following meaning postulate.

(106) $\Box\forall e[\text{swallow}'(e) \rightarrow \Diamond\exists y(\text{THEME}(e) = y)]$

An important difference between these two approaches to thematic relations is the following. On the ordered argument approach, predicates are typed for the number of arguments they take. For example, a transitive verb like *eat* in *John ate an apple*, would correspond to a three-place relation between an eating event, an agent and a theme. This naturally lends itself to a theory of mapping from semantic argument structure into syntactic positions based on the principle that if a predicate has n semantic slots in addition to the event argument, then n corresponding syntactic positions have to be filled. This in turn entails that some kind of operation will be required in order to license, for example, *in*transitive uses of a verb like *eat* (as in *John ate*). On the event based approach, however, verbs are all uniformly analyzed in terms of one-place predicates of events. Hence, something has to determine which of the semantically required thematic roles are going to be syntactically projected (and how). This difference between the two approaches has been put to various linguistic uses.[15]

One thing that emerges, however, is that on either approach the semantic specification of required or allowed thematic roles does not immediately predict what is called the syntactic subcategorization of a verb, whether, for example, the verb requires or permits a direct object. For example, *like* semantically requires both an agent and a theme, and syntactically it requires both subject and object. And with *swallow,* where an agent is semantically obligatory but a theme is optional, the verb is subcategorized for an optional direct object. But matters are not always so straightforward. The verb *eat,* for example, is like *swallow* in that its direct object is syntactically optional but unlike *swallow* in semantically requiring a theme. It satisfies a meaning postulate like (104*b*) rather than (106). Nonetheless, unlike *like, eat* can occur without a direct object. We might even say that *dine* also requires a theme semantically (if one dines, one dines "on" something, dining events being kinds of eating events), but syntactically *dine* neither requires nor even permits a direct object.

In any case, an event-based theory of thematic roles must still address the questions of what functions such roles as agent, experiencer, and theme actually pick out and whether there really are objectively assessable grounds for assigning each subject or direct object NP to some such role. Even if thematic roles are thought of as functions from eventualities to participants in them, we can still ask what properties are attributed to a participant by virtue of being picked out by such a function. What does it tell us about Lee's participation in an event that she is the agent of that event? It has often been observed that different generalizations invoking thematic roles require slightly different conceptions of the properties the bearers of those roles are required to have, of the nature of their participation in the eventuality. For example, being an agent is sometimes said to imply an intentional action and sometimes to imply just activity; intentionality may be relevant for one semantically based generalization, and activity for another.[16] Of course, although they can be manifested independently, activity and intentionality are often linked. In this regard the event-based theory of thematic roles is on a par with the ordered-argument approach.

There are various generalizations whose formulation has been argued to involve thematic roles. One of the most important ones concerns the selection of grammatical relations as it manifests itself in, for example, case-marking patterns. Take a language that has a nominative/accusative contrast in its case system, like Latin, Japanese or (in a morphologically much poorer way) even English. In simple clauses with a transitive verb not marked by passive morphology, the agent argument is marked nominative and the theme argument accusative.

Notice that things could be otherwise. It is perfectly conceivable that the correlation between the nominative case marking and agentivity might be completely random. Yet this does not seem to happen. This suggests that notions such as agent and patient must play a role in the function of language systems.

Of course, the above generalization works only for those verbs whose arguments are clearly classifiable as agents and themes. An interesting case is constituted by psychological verbs such as *like* and *please.* In agent-theme argument structures, the agent is invariably marked nominative. In contrast, experiencer-theme argument structures appear to go either way. With *like* the experiencer is the subject; with *please* the object. This suggests that experiencers are not quite so dominant as agents are.

Furthermore, there are predicates whose argument structures do not naturally lend themselves to classification in terms of the agent/experiencer/theme distinction (consider the verbs *own, weigh, resemble, follow* versus *precede,* etc.), a fact which further limits the scope of the generalization at hand.

There are two main positions that one can take in this connection. One is to look for a quite small set of thematic roles in terms of which each argument of each predicate can be classified. This would indicate that thematic roles are central tools in conceptualizing and lexicalizing events. Moreover, thematic roles could replace arbitrary indexing (ordered arguments) as a way of linking syntactic structure to meaning.

A second position one can take is that though a set of recurrent thematic roles can be individuated and plays a role in stating certain generalizations (like the one above on case marking), such a set is not sufficient to classify each argument of each predicate and thus cannot replace arbitrary indexing in characterizing the link between syntactic positions and meaning. In a sense this would reduce the explanatory power of these notions while still maintaining for them a potentially important role in the grammar. These two positions can be further articulated in various ways.

Thematic roles have also been argued to be important in language acquisition. Suppose a child comes to understand the truth conditions associated with a sentence like "Lee kissed Kim" (however expressed in her language) and is attuned to the notion of an agent and therefore is capable of classifying Lee as the agent. If she has the default expectation that agents are generally subjects, she can then figure out how subjects are encoded in the grammar of her language (she can figure out, for example, whether she is dealing with a subject-verb-object language or an verb-object-subject language). She can then project this information onto cases where thematic information is insufficient to determine grammatical relations (as with psychological predicates perhaps).

Dowty (1989) has proposed a version of this view where notions of thematic roles like agent may be *cluster* or *family resemblance* concepts that are significant primarily in enabling the child to figure out how its language marks grammatical roles. A cluster concept can be thought of as associated not with a single set of properties but with a family of such sets. For the agent concept the union over this family contains all the properties associated with agency; a prototypical bearer of the agent role would exhibit all or almost all of these properties.

The tools we have introduced for semantic analysis do not settle the many difficult questions about thematic roles and their status in linguistic theory. Yet they can help us formulate some of those questions more precisely, one part of being able to explore them productively. The point of interest here is that these notions appear to be amenable to a number of precise truth-conditional analyses. We have briefly considered here two that look particularly promising without trying to choose between them. The possibility of investigating these notions with logical tools should pave the way, we hope, to a better understanding of what their role in linguistic theory should be.

4.2 Aspectual character revisited

In section 2.2 on lexical decomposition, we briefly mentioned the matter of aspectual character (*Aktionsarten*). Verbs and VPs either involve states, on the one hand, or events in the narrow sense of happenings on the other, with events further broken down into those with a natural endpoint—these are called telic—and those lacking such an endpoint—activities or processes. These classifications and their relation to such matters as distribution of the progressive, of imperative forms, of various kinds of temporal adverbials, etc., obviously have something to do with the internal structure of eventualities. Thus bringing events (and states) into verbal semantics may help us articulate a more explicit account of these phenomena.

Again, we'll draw on Parsons (1990) to illustrate. The translations we gave in (102*b*) and (103*b*) of the sentences in (95) ignored the aspectual differences between the eventive verb *kiss* and the stative verb *like*. Parsons posits two basic ways in which eventualities relate to times, culminating and holding. Adding to our calculus the predicates CUL and HOLD and variables ranging over times along with a contextually interpreted term *now′*, we can offer translations like those in (107). (We continue to ignore compositional details such as how tense should be translated; we have also used an event rather than a special state variable for translating the stative.)

(107) *a.* $\exists t \exists e[t < \text{now}' \wedge \text{kiss}''(e) \wedge \textsc{agent}(e) = l$
$\wedge\ \textsc{theme}(e) = k \wedge \textsc{cul}(e, t)]$
b. $\exists t \exists e[t < \text{now}' \wedge \text{like}''(e) \wedge \textsc{experiencer}(e) = l$
$\wedge\ \textsc{theme}(e) = k \wedge \textsc{hold}(e, t)]$

States never culminate but only hold. The progressive form of an event verb like *kiss* is stativelike; sentence (108*a*) might translate something like (108*b*).

(108) *a.* Lee is kissing Kim.
b. $\exists t \exists e[t = \text{now}' \wedge \text{kiss}''(e) \wedge \textsc{agent}(e) = j$
$\wedge\ \textsc{theme}(e) = k \wedge \textsc{hold}(e, t)]$

In addition, once events are in the picture we can talk about their internal structure. So, e.g., events may have development parts, what Parsons calls "in-progress" stages, or target "result" states (the target result state of an event of walking to the store is being at the store). And the semantic structure of causatives and inchoatives, which we discussed in section 2, can be articulated directly in terms of events. So, e.g., (109*a*) can be represented as (109*b*) and (110*a*) as (110*b*), which in turn is equivalent to (112*c*). The event predicate *awaken″* is associated with the intransitive verb *awaken*.

(109) *a.* Joan awakened.
b. $\exists t \exists e[t < \text{now}' \wedge\ \text{awaken}''(e) \wedge \textsc{theme}(e) = j$
$\wedge\ \textsc{become}(\text{awake}')(e) \wedge \textsc{cul}(e, t)]$

(110) *a.* Chris awakened Joan.
b. $\exists t \exists e[t < \text{now}' \wedge \textsc{cul}(e,\ t) \wedge \textsc{agent}(e) = c \wedge \text{awaken}''(e)$
$\wedge\ (\exists t \exists e'[t < \text{t}' < \text{now}' \wedge \textsc{theme}(e') = j \wedge \textsc{become}(\text{awake}')(e')$
$\wedge\ \textsc{cause}(e, e') \wedge \textsc{cul}(e', t')]]$

For the inchoative, we use a predicate operator BECOME that maps predicates of individuals, e.g., *awake′*, into predicates of events; we will need to ensure that, e.g., the theme of an event that satisfies BECOME(*awake′*) will itself satisfy *awake′* at the time the event culminates (that at the time the becoming awake event culminates, Joan, its theme, is awake). The two-event analysis that enters into Dowty's *C* is directly incorporated in the translation in (110), with the subject of the transitive causative being identified as agent of the causing event: this does ensure that in order to awaken someone, the subject has to *do* something to cause the awakening (and not simply, as in Dowty's analysis, to have some property that causes the awakening). But the analysis still does not guarantee immediate or direct causation.

Our point here is not to endorse a particular approach to aspectual character or to the related phenomena of verbal alternations. We just want to illustrate that bringing events into the semantic ontology opens up an interesting range of possible analyses of these matters as well as of such phenomena as adverbial modification and thematic roles. In recent years, events have been widely adopted as fundamental units for semantic analysis.

5 Semantic Imprecision

What do we mean when we say that an expression is semantically imprecise? The basic idea is that its contribution to truth conditions is indeterminate because the criteria we have are just not sharp enough. Consider *red*, for example. Suppose we are looking at color chips in the paint store. Some chips are clearly red, others are clearly orange, and others lie somewhere between a good red and a good orange. Suppose the chip we are looking at is right in the middle of the red-orange range. Then there seems to be no good answer to the question of what truth values to assign to sentences (111*a*) and (111*b*) because there seem to be grounds for saying each is true and grounds for saying each is false: no further facts can help.

(111) *a.* This chip is red.
b. This chip is orange.

To put it another way, ⟦red⟧ and ⟦orange⟧ are not well-defined sets because we may have individuals in our domain of discourse (chips in the paint store) for which it is neither definitely the case that they belong to one or the other set nor definitely the case that they fail to belong to either of them. It is not that our borderline chip is the wrong sort of thing to be classed as red or orange; rather, classification principles simply do not permit a sharp line, as they support both classifications to some extent. We often use sentences like those in (112) in describing such circumstances.

(112) *a.* This chip is kind of red.
b. This chip is somewhat orange.
c. This chip is reddish orange or orangey red.

Or we say of the sentences in (111) that they are "kind of true" or "half true" or something similar. With two chips, 1 and 2, we might use sentences like those in (113).

(113) *a.* No. 1 is redder than no. 2, though both are sort of orange.
b. No. 2 is oranger than no. 1, though both are sort of red.

In such circumstances we might be inclined to say that sentence (114*a*) is more nearly true than (114*b*) and (114*c*) more nearly true than (114*d*).

(114) *a.* No. 1 is red.
b. No. 2 is red.
c. No. 2 is orange.
d. No. 1 is orange.

Kay and McDaniel (1978) proposed that color words and many other lexical items have semantic content that makes reference to a *prototype*, which sets the standard for absolute or full satisfaction of the concept.[17] Thus, they argue, we judge the applicability of color words through similarity to some kind of prototypical exemplars: focal or true red and focal or true orange, for example. What is important is that individuals may be more or less similar to these prototypes. Unlike truth as we have understood it, similarity comes in degrees and thus might seem to provide the basis for understanding noncategorical judgments of "kind of" or "half" true. There is something right about this, but how can such notions of degrees of truth best be understood?

The first thing to see is that not all imprecise concepts are graded in terms of similarity to a prototype. Consider, for example, the sentences in (115).

(115) *a.* Eloise is tall.
b. Peggy is tall.

It seems implausible to propose a prototype associated with *tall* even where we have fixed the relevant contextual property relative to which tallness is to be assessed. Is there a prototype of the tall contemporary American woman? Even if there were, whether or not (115*a*) is true or how "nearly" true it is does not depend on how closely Eloise resembles that prototype. Suppose the prototypical tall American woman is 5 feet 9 inches tall and Eloise is 6 feet 2 inches tall, whereas Peggy is 5 feet 5 inches tall. Peggy's height differs by only 4 inches from that of our prototype, whereas Eloise's differs by 5 inches: Peggy is more similar in height to the prototype than Eloise. But of course (115*a*) should be taken as fully true, whereas (115*b*) is at best "sort of" or "half" true. Appeal to prototypes is thus not always relevant when we are dealing with semantic imprecision.

How can semantic imprecision be handled in a compositional account of truth conditions? The idea we will explore in this section is that imprecision can be dealt with by making our interpretation partial. In chapter 6 we have already introduced the possibility of incomplete or partially undefined dynamic truth conditions. The truth conditions for a sentence were defined only relative to contexts whose common ground entailed the sentence's presuppositions and then only for indices $\langle w, i \rangle$ included in that common ground. The kind of partiality we will need to deal with vagueness, however, is going to be different. The fuzziness of color terminology seems relatively independent of contextual factors. And although measure predicates like *tall* depend on context in their interpretation, relativizing them to contextual parameters does not remove their fuzziness but simply locates the region where fuzziness is found. Even when the context supplies a comparison class for height, whether 5 feet 10 inches or 5 feet 11 inches counts as tall relative to that comparison class may be indeterminate. Finally, the incompleteness of our dynamic definitions of truth is not associated with any notions of "sort of" true or "partly" true or "more" true. To put it another way, there is no structure associated with failure to assign truth values as such: truth value gaps need not in any sense lie between truth and falsity, nor need they be comparable to one another. Partial truth definitions of the kind encountered with presupposition do not result in anything like the "partial" truth associated with borderline cases for imprecise expressions. Although many imprecise expressions also depend on context (like *tall*), the distinctive features of fuzziness do not emerge simply from considerations of contextual and discourse factors leading to incomplete truth definitions.

To keep the discussion that follows relatively simple, we will consider only static truth conditions and ignore both context and discourse. This is just an expository strategy, however. We think that dynamic semantics will ultimately prove useful in the formal analysis of semantic imprecision, although we also think that important features of the approach we adopt below will be part of any successful dynamic account.

As we noted above, the fundamental difference between indeterminacy of truth value assignment due to imprecision or borderline fuzziness of concepts and that arising for other reasons (like presupposition failure) is that in the former but not the latter case there is some intuition about "half" truths and about greater or lesser claims to truth. The question is how these intuitions are to figure in a recursive account of sentential semantics. Some readers may have heard of so-called *fuzzy logics*, which posit a multiplicity of truth values between absolute truth and absolute falsity, indeed non-denumerably many such intermediate values. It is instructive to consider briefly one such fuzzy system, first proposed in Zadeh (1965) and introduced to linguistics in Lakoff (1972), and to explain some of the drawbacks inherent in it and similar approaches to imprecision. We will then introduce the technique of *super-valuation* and show how fuzziness can be more adequately treated using this technique.

We will focus on fuzziness due to imprecise predicates and use color and height terminology as illustrative cases. The strategy in fuzzy semantics for treating such predicates is to suppose that their extensions are what are called *fuzzy sets* rather than sets in the classical sense we have adopted.

As mentioned in our appendix on set theory, each classical set A is associated with a two-valued membership function μ_A (also called the characteristic function of A), which is defined as follows:

(116) Let a be a member of the domain of discourse U. Then
$\mu_A(a) = 1$ iff $a \in A$, and 0 otherwise.

So, for example, let μ_{wom} be the membership function associated with $[\![\text{woman}']\!]$ and suppose that $a \in \mu_{\text{wom}}$ and $b \notin \mu_{\text{wom}}$. Then we will have that $\mu_{\text{wom}}(a) = 1$ and $\mu_{\text{wom}}(b) = 0$. We can then restate the truth conditions of simple monadic predicate formulas as follows.

(117) If μ_{Pred} designates the membership function of $[\![\text{Pred}]\!]$,
$[\![\text{Pred(t)}]\!] = \mu_{\text{Pred}}([\![\text{t}]\!])$.

This is just another way of saying that $[\![\text{Pred(t)}]\!] = 1$ iff the individual $[\![\text{t}]\!]$ is a member of the set $[\![\text{Pred}]\!]$, and otherwise that $[\![\text{Pred(t)}]\!] = 0$.

Fuzzy set theory allows the membership function to assign not only values 1 and 0 but also values that lie between these two. For example, in (113) above we introduced chips 1 and 2, the first redder than the second and the second oranger than the first. Let μ_{red} and μ_{oran} be the fuzzy membership functions. We might then assign membership values as in (118).

(118) *a.* μ_{red} ($[\![$no. 1$']\!]$) = .55 μ_{red}($[\![$no. 2$']\!]$) = .45
b. μ_{oran}($[\![$no. 1$']\!]$) = .45 μ_{oran}($[\![$no. 2$']\!]$) = .55

If we adopt the definition of truth conditions for simple formulas given in (117) but use fuzzy membership functions as in (118), the sentences in (114), repeated in (119) with their *If* translations, will be assigned the intermediate fuzzy truth values indicated.

(119) *a.* No. 1 is red. red′(no. 1′) .55
b. No. 2 is red. red′(no. 2′) .45
c. No. 2 is orange. orange′(no. 2′) .55
d. No. 1 is orange. orange′(no. 1′) .45

Suppose that a third chip, no. 3, lying between no. 1 and no. 2, plugs into the membership functions associated with *red* and *orange* to yield value .5 in both cases; that is, μ_{red}($[\![$no. 3$]\!]$) = .5 = μ_{oran}($[\![$no. 3$]\!]$). Then we will have the following truth values:

(120) *a.* No. 3 is red. red′(no. 3′) .5
b. No. 3 is orange. orange′(no. 3′) .5

How would such intermediate values enter into truth conditions for compound sentences? There are various options here. Zadeh proposed essentially the following account. (We will ignore quantified expressions in what follows and focus only on negation and the logical connectives. We will also continue to omit reference to *M*, *w*, *i*, *c*, and *g*.)

(121) *a.* $[\![[\neg S]]\!] = 1 - [\![S]\!]$
b. $[\![[S_1 \wedge S_2]]\!]$ = the minimum of $[\![S_1]\!]$ and $[\![S_2]\!]$
c. $[\![[S_1 \vee S_2]]\!]$ = the maximum of $[\![S_1]\!]$ and $[\![S_2]\!]$
d. $[\![[S_1 \rightarrow S_2]]\!] = 1$ iff $[\![S_1]\!] \leq [\![S_2]\!]$
Otherwise, $[\![[S_1 \rightarrow S_2]]\!] = [\![S_2]\!]$

Note that if we allow only values 1 and 0, then (121) assigns the same values as the classical approach we have adopted. Although we use Zadeh's valuations for illustrative purposes, the problems we point to arise for any fuzzy logic that shares with Zadeh's the feature of fuzzy truth-conditional definitions for the connectives.[18] We will concretely illustrate the problems of fuzzy truth conditions by discussing some examples.

If we assume the valuations presented in (119) and (120) and standard translations of the kind we have discussed, valuations are assigned to the sentences in (122) as indicated.

(122) *a.* No. 3 is not red. .5 [= 1 − .5]
b. No. 3 is red, or no. 3 is not red. .5 [= max(.5, .5)]
c. No. 3 is red, and no. 3 is not red. .5 [= min(.5, .5)]
d. If no. 3 is not red, then no. 1 is red. 1.0 [because $.5 \leq .55$]
e. If no. 3 is red, then no. 1 is red. 1.0 [because $.5 \leq .55$]

It is easy to calculate values using (121), but the results are hardly intuitive. While it may seem fine to say that (122*a*) is "half" true, one is surprised to find exactly the same intermediate truth value assigned to (122*b*), which has the form of a classical tautology, and (122*c*), which has the form of a classical contradiction. Now people sometimes claim that (122*b*) is of dubious truth in such middling circumstances and that (122*c*) does seem true in some sense. We recognize that (122*b*) can seem more dubious than its tautologous character would seem to warrant and that (122*c*) can, in spite of its contradictory form, function to convey descriptive content. However, for reasons to be detailed shortly, we think that these facts are better explained in a different way. We further note that (122*d*) seems an unlikely candidate for absolute truth in the circumstances we have sketched, since taking no. 3 as not red by no means forces us to take no. 1 as red, since no. 1, although redder than no. 3, is also not red to a significant extent (.45). In contrast, the valuation of (122*e*) as absolutely true seems correct, since no. 1 is indeed redder than no. 3. So there is a contrast between our intuitive judgments of (122*d*) and (122*e*). Yet (122*d*) and (122*e*) cannot be differentiated in this approach.

The following sentences illustrate further problems.

(123) *a.* No. 2 is not red. .55 [= 1 − .45]
b. No. 2 is red, or no. 2 is not red. .55 [= max(.45, 55)]
c. No. 2 is red, and no. 2 is not red. .45 [= min(.45, .55)]
d. If no. 2 is red, then no. 1 is red. 1.0 [because $.45 \leq .55$]
e. If no. 2 is red, then no. 1 is not red. 1.0 [because $.45 \leq .45$]

Here we do find the formal tautology (123*b*) ranked "truer" than the formal contradiction (123*c*), but the tautology fares no better than the monoclausal negative (123*a*), and the contradiction no worse than the simple affirmative (118*b*). It may seem good to have (123*d*) unequivocally true; after all, by hypothesis no. 1 is redder than no. 2. It then seems quite odd that (123*e*) comes out equally (and absolutely) true.

Let us now introduce one more chip and two more sets of fuzzy valuations. Let us suppose we have a chip (no. 4) on the violet side of focal red such that the valuations in (124) hold.

(124) *a.* No. 4 is red. .6
b. No. 4 is orange. 0.0

We can now compare all four chips with respect to the property of being either red or orange.

(125) *a.* No. 1 is red, or no. 1 is orange. .55 [max(.55, .45)]
b. No. 2 is red, or no. 2 is orange. .55 [max(.45, .55)]
c. No. 3 is red, or no. 3 is orange. .5 [max(.5, .5)]
d. No. 4 is red, or no. 4 is orange. .6 [max(.6, 0)]

According to these valuations, the chip lying exactly on the red/orange border (no. 3) is a less good instance of being red or orange than chips lying nearer to red (no. 1) or nearer to orange (no. 2), and all three of these reddish-orangish chips are less good instances of being red or orange than the somewhat violet and not at all orange chip (no. 4), which happens to be a bit redder. We have no clear intuitions as to whether in these circumstances (125*a*) and (125*b*) should count as "truer" than (125*c*); our own inclination is to judge all three as equally and absolutely true. But we do have sharp intuitions that any of the three has at least as much claim to being true as (125*d*) and indeed that their claim is greater (and thus that they are in some sense "truer"), in light of the iffiness of the judgment that no. 4 is red and the unequivocal nature of the judgment that no. 4 is not orange. The supervaluational analysis of borderline cases introduced below accords with these intuitive judgments more closely than the fuzzy logic approach, as we will shortly see.

Finally, note also there is no real intuitive basis for comparing middling values of simple sentences that are semantically unrelated. Suppose, for example, that we return to the sentences in (115) and assign them valuations in (126).

(126) *a.* Eloise is tall. 1.0 [height = 6 feet 2 inches]
b. Peggy is tall. .5 [height = 5 feet 5 inches]

We then get results such as those in (127).

(127) *a.* If Peggy is tall, then no. 1 is red. 1.0
b. If Peggy is tall, then no. 2 is red. .45
c. Peggy is tall, and no. 3 is red. .5
d. Peggy is tall, and no. 1 is red. .5
e. Peggy is not tall, or no. 1 is red. .55

Comparing Peggy's height to the redness of the chips seems at best puzzling. Note also that (127*a*) and (127*e*), which are truth-conditionally equivalent in standard bivalent semantics, are assigned quite different fuzzy values.

We could continue to adduce problematic examples, but the moral seems clear. Although there is initially some intuitive plausibility in treating borderline cases as taking intermediate truth values, serious difficulties arise if we treat the values of compound sentences as functions of the intermediate values assigned to simple sentences, which is what any fuzzy semantics requires.[19] It seems clear that we need an alternative approach to characterizing the middleness of borderline cases for imprecise expressions. We next discuss the method of supervaluations, which seems to provide a promising alternative for the treatment of imprecision.

Exercise 5 A. Justify the values assigned in (127).
B. Assign values to the following sentences.

(1) No. 2 is not red.

(2) No. 2 is not orange.

(3) If no. 2 is not orange, then no. 3 is orange and not orange.

(4) If no. 2 is not orange, then no. 1 is red.

(5) No. 1 is red, or no. 2 is not red.

(6) No. 1 is not red, and no. 2 is not red.

Supervaluations were introduced by van Fraassen (1966) and then applied to the analysis of semantic imprecision in Fine (1975) and in Kamp (1975).[20] Our account here is just a first approximation, but it does show the distinctive features of the approach.

The general strategy of supervaluations is to assign truth values in three stages. The initial valuation, which we will notate as $[\![\ ]\!]^{\mathrm{P}}$, is partial; that is, $[\![S]\!]^p$ may be 1, 0, or undefined. The intuitive idea is that borderline cases of the sort we have discussed above will give rise to truth value gaps where $[\![S]\!]^p$ is undefined. We will ignore the details of the recursive definition of $[\![S]\!]^p$ for the moment and just note that atomic sentences get the value 0, or get the value 1, or are undefined. A compound sentence that contains an atomic sentence whose value is undefined will itself be undefined at this initial stage; otherwise, the recursive definition of initial truth conditions proceeds just as in our earlier fragments.

If we stopped there, the approach at the sentence level would be essentially equivalent to the three-valued logic proposed in Bochvar (1939), where *undefined* functions as a third truth value. For us, however, the partial function $[\![\ ]\!]^p$ is only a step on the way to defining the partial supervaluation $[\![\ ]\!]^*$ and is not itself the final analysis.

In the second stage we look at a family Σ of total valuations $[\![\ ]\!]^t$ of the standard bivalent sort; that is, for every atomic sentence S, $[\![S]\!]^t = 0$ or 1, and connectives receive their standard truth-functional definitions. The total valuations in Σ *extend* the partial valuation $[\![\ ]\!]^p$ in the sense that they do not change the values assigned by $[\![\ ]\!]^p$ but only fill in the truth value gaps with 1s or 0s. In other words, if $[\![S]\!]^p$ is defined, then $[\![S]\!]^p = [\![S]\!]^t$. So we move from an initial partial interpretation function $[\![\ ]\!]^p$ to a family Σ of complete interpretations, which contains different ways of completing $[\![\ ]\!]^p$.

In the third and final stage of supervaluation, we generalize over the values assigned by the complete valuations in Σ and define a partial supervaluation $[\![\ ]\!]^*$ as follows.

(128) *a.* $[\![S]\!]^* = 1$ iff for all $[\![\ ]\!]^t \in \Sigma$, $[\![S]\!]^t = 1$.
b. $[\![S]\!]^* = 0$ iff for all $[\![\ ]\!]^t \in \Sigma$, $[\![S]\!]^t = 0$.
c. $[\![S]\!]^*$ is otherwise undefined.

It is easy to see that classical formal tautologies and classical formal contradictions will emerge as tautologies and contradictions for the final partial supervaluation $[\![\ ]\!]^*$. An example will show how this works. Consider the tautology in (129*a*) and the contradiction in (129*b*).

(129) *a.* No. 3 is red, or no. 3 is not red.
b. No. 3 is red, and no. 3 is not red.

As before, we will suppose that no. 3 is a borderline case of redness. That is, our initial partial valuation $[\![\ ]\!]^{\mathrm{p}}$ is undefined for the sentences in (130).

(130) *a.* No. 3 is red.
b. No. 3 is not red.

Now any of the complete valuations $[\![\ ]\!]^{\mathrm{t}}$ by definition assigns values to each of the sentences in (130). If $[\![(130a)]\!]^{\mathrm{t}} = 1$, then it must be the case that $[\![(130b)]\!]^{\mathrm{t}} = 0$ (since $[\![\ ]\!]^{\mathrm{t}}$ is classical), and thus we will have that $[\![(129a)]\!]^{\mathrm{t}} = 1$ and $[\![(129b)]\!]^{\mathrm{t}} = 0$. If, on the other hand, $[\![(130a)]\!]^{\mathrm{t}} = 0$, then $[\![(130b)]\!]^{\mathrm{t}} = 1$, and thus once again we will have that $[\![(129a)]\!]^{\mathrm{t}} = 1$ and $[\![(129b)]\!]^{\mathrm{t}} = 0$. It therefore follows that $[\![(129a)]\!]^{*} = 1$ and $[\![(129b)]\!]^{*} = 0$, since all the complete valuations in Σ assign these sentences the same values.

Note that for supervaluations it makes little sense to think of *undefined* as a third truth value. The reason is that we cannot define $[\![\ ]\!]^{*}$ for a compound sentence simply by considering what $[\![\ ]\!]^{*}$ assigns to its constituents. For example, two sentences S_1 and S_2 may have the same structure, and $[\![\ ]\!]^{*}$ may assign to the components of S_1 and S_2 the same values, and yet we may find that $[\![S_1]\!]^{*}$ is undefined, but $[\![S_2]\!]^{*}$ receives a value. Consider, for example, sentence (115*b*), repeated here as (131*a*):

(131) *a.* Peggy is tall.
b. Peggy is tall, or no. 3 is red.
c. No. 3 is red, or no. 3 is not red.

Assume as above that (131*a*) is borderline and thus that $[\![(131a)]\!]^{\mathrm{p}}$ and $[\![(131a)]\!]^{*}$ are both undefined. Now how we close gaps for tallness has no connection to how we close gaps for redness. Thus for some $[\![\ ]\!]^{\mathrm{t}}$, $[\![(130a)]\!]^{\mathrm{t}} = [\![(131a)]\!]^{\mathrm{t}} = 1$, and for some other $[\![\ ]\!]^{\mathrm{t}'}$, $[\![(130a)]\!]^{\mathrm{t}'} = [\![(131a)]\!]^{\mathrm{t}'}0$. It follows then that in some completions of our original $[\![\ ]\!]^{P}$, the disjunction of (131*a*) and (130*a*), given in (131*b*), will be false, and in other it will be true. But then $[\![(131b)]\!]^{*}$ is undefined because it does not receive the same value for every member of Σ. Notice, however, that $[\![(131c)]\!]^{*} = [\![(129a)]\!]^{*} = 1$. Now (131*b*) and (131*c*) are both disjunctions with the property that $[\![\ ]\!]^{*}$ is equally undefined for each disjunct. If $[\![\ ]\!]^{*}$ assigned values to disjunctions on the basis of what it assigns to each disjunct, then we would have $[\![(131b)]\!]^{*} = [\![(131c)]\!]^{*}$. But we have just seen that $[\![(131b)]\!]^{*}$ is undefined, while $[\![(131c)]\!]^{*} = 1$. This means that in supervaluational approaches we cannot regard *undefined* as an intermediate truth value that enters compositionally in the valuation of larger formulas.

We now flesh out the supervaluation approach to imprecision. First, we have to say something about how the initial partial valuation $[\![\ ]\!]^{\mathrm{p}}$ is to be defined. Second, we need to say more about the family Σ in order to see how the supervaluation technique can figure in an account of the perceived middleness of truth value gaps arising from fuzziness and of the notion of degrees of truth. Finally, we will look at how the supervaluational approach we propose fares with the problematic cases for fuzzy logic approaches.

In defining $[\![\ ]\!]^{\mathrm{p}}$, we need to say something only about how imprecise expressions contribute to these initial partial truth conditions. For example, relative to a model *M*, a context *c*, a world *w*, and a time *i*, predicates like *red′* and *tall′* can be thought of as dividing the domain of individuals into three nonintersecting sets: the set of things of which the predicate is definitely true, the set of things of which it is definitely false, and the set of things of which it is indeterminate whether the predicate holds or not. We will call the set of individuals to which the predicate definitely applies in the given circumstances its *positive extension*, and we will denote it by $[\![\mathrm{Pred}]\!]^{+}$. The set of things of which the predicate is definitely false will be called its *negative extension*, and we will denote it as $[\![\mathrm{Pred}]\!]^{-}$. In other words, instead of having the model's interpretation function assign to each predicate a set of individuals, we have it assign two sets as in (132*a*) and use these sets in defining truth conditions as in (132*b*).[21]

(132) *a.* Where $[\![\mathrm{Pred}]\!]^{+} \cap [\![\mathrm{Pred}]\!]^{-} = \varnothing$,
$[\![\mathrm{Pred}]\!]^{\mathrm{p}} = \langle [\![\mathrm{Pred}]\!]^{+}, [\![\mathrm{Pred}]\!]^{-} \rangle$.
b. $[\![\mathrm{Pred(t)}]\!]^{\mathrm{p}} = 1$ iff $[\![\mathrm{t}]\!] \in [\![\mathrm{Pred}]\!]^{+}$,
$= 0$ iff $[\![\mathrm{t}]\!] \in [\![\mathrm{Pred}]\!]^{-}$,
is otherwise undefined.

Truth conditions for negation and the binary connectives are defined as in (133). These are just the classical definitions except that if a constituent receives no value, the compound sentence also lacks a value.

(133) *a.* $[\![\neg \mathrm{S}]\!]^{\mathrm{p}} = 1$ if $[\![\mathrm{S}]\!]^{\mathrm{p}} = 0$,
$= 0$ if $[\![\mathrm{S}]\!]^{\mathrm{p}} = 1$,
is otherwise undefined.

b. $[\![S_1 \wedge S_2]\!]^p = 1$ if $[\![S_1]\!]^p = [\![S_2]\!]^p = 1$,
$= 0$ if (i) $[\![S_1]\!]^p = [\![S_2]\!]^p = 0$ or (ii) $[\![S_1]\!]^p = 0$ and $[\![S_2]\!]^p = 1$ or (iii) $[\![S_1]\!]^p = 1$ and $[\![S_2]\!]^p = 0$,
is otherwise undefined.

c. $[\![S_1 \vee S_2]\!]^p = 1$ if (i) $[\![S_1]\!]^p = [\![S_2]\!]^p = 1$ or (ii) $[\![S_1]\!]^p = 0$ and $[\![S_2]\!]^p = 1$ or (iii) $[\![S_1]\!]^p = 1$ and $[\![S_2]\!]^p = 0$,
$= 0$ if $[\![S_1]\!]^p = [\![S_2]\!]^p = 0$,
is otherwise undefined.

d. $[\![S_1 \rightarrow S_2]\!]^p = 1$ if (i) $[\![S_1]\!]^p = [\![S_2]\!]^p = 1$ or (ii) $[\![S_1]\!]^p = [\![S_2]\!]^p = 0$ or (iii) $[\![S_1]\!]^p = 0$ and $[\![S_2]\!]^p = 1$,
$= 0$ if $[\![S_1]\!]^p = 1$ and $[\![S_2]\!]^p = 0$,
is otherwise undefined.

Next we want to consider the family Σ and the possible total valuations that extend an initial partial valuation. Let us begin by considering what additional constraints we want to place on possible initial interpretations of imprecise adjectives, since such constraints may affect permitted complete extensions of those interpretations. At present all we have done is to divide the extension of certain predicates into a positive part, a negative part, and a possibly nonempty middle ground. But we have not actually said anything about the relation between the positive and negative extensions that might give content to the notion that what remains is somehow *between* them. Nor, of course, do we have any analogue of the infinite range of degrees of membership in the extension of a predicate, which was used to structure the middle ground in fuzzy theory.

The reason fuzzy theory initially seems so appealing is that we do have some kind of *ordering* associated with each imprecise predicate of the individuals in its domain. Middleness and grades thereof derive from this ordering. In the case of color words, the ordering seems to be mediated by comparisons to something like a prototype, perhaps a distinguished individual that serves as a focal exemplar of the color in question. Individual *a* is redder than individual *b*, for example, if the color of *a* is more similar to prototype *r*, which exemplifies focal red, than is the color of *b*. For words like *tall* and *short*, individuals can be compared directly in terms of their heights. For some imprecise expressions the ordering may be partial. Expressions like *beautiful* and *intelligent* fall in this category. Perhaps Joan is more intelligent than Bill, and Leslie is more intelligent than Chris, but neither Joan nor Bill can be compared in intelligence to Leslie or Chris; one pair might exemplify some sort of mathematical intelligence and the other practical wisdom.

We can capture these intuitions by resorting to a (possibly partial) order relation as a component of the interpretation of our imprecise predicates. (Where appropriate, we could have that order mediated by similarity to a prototype, but we will ignore that complication here.) We implement this idea by having $[\![\ ]\!]^{\mathrm{p}}$ assign not only negative and positive extensions to each imprecise expression but also a relation that orders individuals with respect to the degree to which they satisfy the predicate. This relation might depend on context, just like the comparison class, but we will continue to ignore contextual effects here. The important feature of the ordering relations is that it constrains possible positive and negative extensions as well as possible completions of the initial imprecise interpretation. We use $\prec_{\mathrm{Pred}}$ to indicate this ordering relation: $x \prec_{\mathrm{Pred}} y$ is read "x is ranked lower than y on the ordering associated with Pred." Suppose that the predicate is *tall′*. Then read the intended order relation $\prec_{\mathrm{tall}}$ as follows: $x \prec_{\mathrm{tall}} y$ iff x is less tall than y. So we modify (132*a*) as follows:

(134) $[\![\mathrm{Pred}]\!]^{\mathrm{p}} = \langle [\![\mathrm{Pred}]\!]^{+}, [\![\mathrm{Pred}]\!]^{-}, \prec_{\mathrm{Pred}} \rangle$
Conditions:
a. $[\![\mathrm{Pred}]\!]^{+} \cap [\![\mathrm{Pred}]\!]^{-} = \varnothing$
b. If $x \in [\![\mathrm{Pred}]\!]^{+}$ and $x \prec_{\mathrm{Pred}} z$, then $z \in [\![\mathrm{Pred}]\!]^{+}$.
c. If $x \in [\![\mathrm{Pred}]\!]^{-}$ and $z \prec_{\mathrm{Pred}} x$, then $z \in [\![\mathrm{Pred}]\!]^{-}$.

What (134) does is to ensure that if an individual is in the positive extension of *tall′* then so are all taller individuals, and if an individual is in the negative extension, then so are all the less tall individuals.

Now we are ready to say what constraints we place on total extensions $[\![\ ]\!]^{\mathrm{t}}$.

(135) For every $[\![\ ]\!]^{\mathrm{t}}$, $[\![\mathrm{Pred}]\!]^{\mathrm{t}} = \langle [\![\mathrm{Pred}]\!]^{\mathrm{t}+}, [\![\mathrm{Pred}]\!]^{\mathrm{t}-}, \prec_{\mathrm{Pred}} \rangle$.
Conditions:
a. $[\![\mathrm{Pred}]\!]^{\mathrm{t}+} \cap [\![\mathrm{Pred}]\!]^{\mathrm{t}-} = \varnothing$
b. If $x \in [\![\mathrm{Pred}]\!]^{\mathrm{t}+}$ and $x \prec_{\mathrm{Pred}} z$, then $z \in [\![\mathrm{Pred}]\!]^{\mathrm{t}+}$.
c. If $x \in [\![\mathrm{Pred}]\!]^{\mathrm{t}-}$ and $z \prec_{\mathrm{Pred}} x$, then $z \in [\![\mathrm{Pred}]\!]^{\mathrm{t}-}$.
d. $[\![\mathrm{Pred}]\!]^{\mathrm{t}+} \cup [\![\mathrm{Pred}]\!]^{\mathrm{t}-} = U$ (the domain of individuals)
e. $[\![\mathrm{Pred}]\!]^{+} \subseteq [\![\mathrm{Pred}]\!]^{\mathrm{t}+}$
f. $[\![\mathrm{Pred}]\!]^{-} \subseteq [\![\mathrm{Pred}]\!]^{\mathrm{t}-}$

Clause (d) ensures that the interpretation is total, and clauses (e) and (f) ensure that we don't change values assigned by the initial partial valuation.

That are, of course, additional kinds of constraints placed by the language on the initial model and its possible completions. These constraints are of the sort we captured earlier through meaning postulates. For example, we will want to place constraints like those in (136) through (139) on possible initial interpretations and their completions. The constraints in (136) require that *tall′* and *short′* be incompatible predicates.

(136) a. $[\![\text{tall}]\!]^{+} \subseteq [\![\text{short}]\!]^{-}$ $\quad [\![\text{tall}]\!]^{t+} \subseteq [\![\text{short}]\!]^{t-}$
b. $[\![\text{short}]\!]^{+} \subseteq [\![\text{tall}]\!]^{-}$ $\quad [\![\text{short}]\!]^{t+} \subseteq [\![\text{tall}]\!]^{t-}$

In (137) we state the incompatibility of instances of focal colors: things that are definitely orange are not definitely red, etc.

(137) a. $[\![\text{orange}]\!]^{+} \cap [\![\text{red}]\!]^{+} = \varnothing$ $\quad [\![\text{orange}]\!]^{t+} \cap [\![\text{red}]\!]^{t+} = \varnothing$
b. $[\![\text{violet}]\!]^{+} \cap [\![\text{red}]\!]^{+} = \varnothing$ $\quad [\![\text{violet}]\!]^{t+} \cap [\![\text{red}]\!]^{t+} = \varnothing$

In (138) we ensure that what is red is oranger than what is violet and more violet than what is orange, thus positioning what is red between what is violet and what is orange.

(138) a. If $x \in [\![\text{red}]\!]^{+}$ and $y \in [\![\text{violet}]\!]^{+}$, then $y \prec_{\text{orange}} x$.
If $x \in [\![\text{red}]\!]^{t+}$ and $y \in [\![\text{violet}]\!]^{t+}$ then $y \prec_{\text{orange}} x$.
b. If $x \in [\![\text{red}]\!]^{+}$ and $y \in [\![\text{orange}]\!]^{+}$, then $y \prec_{\text{violet}} x$.
If $x \in [\![\text{red}]\!]^{t+}$ and $y \in [\![\text{orange}]\!]^{t+}$, then $y \prec_{\text{violet}} x$.

Finally, (139) guarantees that an individual in the middle ground between what is red and what is orange will be classed as either red or orange by each complete model.

(139) If $x \notin [\![\text{red}]\!]^{+}$, $x \notin [\![\text{orange}]\!]^{+}$, and there exist $y \in [\![\text{orange}]\!]^{+}$ and $z \in [\![\text{red}]\!]^{+}$ such that $y \prec_{\text{red}} x$ and $z \prec_{\text{orange}} x$, then for all $[\![\ ]\!]^{t}$, either $x \in [\![\text{red}]\!]^{t+}$ or $x \in [\![\text{orange}]\!]^{t+}$.

The notion of completeness requires that each individual in the domain of color terminology be assigned to the positive extension of one of the color words, which reflects the idea that the colors are adjacent to one another. We would not want something analogous for *tall′* and *short′*, since they are not thought of as necessarily adjacent to one another, being only incompatible but not contradictory.

Supervaluations then will be defined with respect to the largest family Σ that satisfies the general constraints in (135) and specific lexical constraints of the sort exemplified in (136) through (139).

We can now compare the supervaluational approach to that of fuzzy logic. Let us start by considering how tautologies and contradictions are handled. We have seen that supervaluations assign truth to formal tautologies and falsity to formal contradictions. How, then, can we explain the fact that someone may apparently want to dissent from (129*a*), yet seem to assent to (129*b*) (repeated here for convenience)?

(129) *a.* No. 3 is red, or no. 3 is not red.
b. No. 3 is red, and no. 3 is not red.

Consider first dissenting from a formal tautology. People do describe borderline cases by uttering sentences like those in (140).

(140) *a.* It's not true that no. 3 is red or that no. 3 is not red.
b. No. 3 is neither red nor not red.

One plausible explanation is that we understand such utterances by appeal to an unpronounced *definitely* operator. Thus we might say that sentence S is [definitely] true only if $[\![S]\!]^{p} = 1$. The idea is that definite truth is truth with respect to the initial partial valuation; whatever is initially either false or undefined will fail to be [definitely] true. Similarly, an individual is [definitely] red only if that individual belongs to $[\![\text{red}]\!]^{+}$, the positive extension of *red*. Thus dissent from the formal tautology seems to involve denying definite truth. Since no. 3 is a borderline case, although (129*a*) is supertrue ($[\![(129a)]\!]^{*} = 1$), it fails to be [definitely] true ($[\![(129a)]\!]^{p}$ is undefined).

It is interesting that assertive utterance of a formal contradiction like (129*b*) is used in a much narrower range of contexts than denial of a formal tautology like (129*a*), where the denial may be signalled by uttering one of the sentences in (140). This seems quite inexplicable on the fuzzy logic account, since the negative of the formal tautology will always take the same fuzzy truth value as the formal contradiction (neither can be greater than .5). We have noted that truth conditions may be partial for reasons other than imprecision. In these cases, just as with indeterminacy due to imprecision, speakers use the device of dissenting from the formal tautology in order to deny definite or determinate truth.

(141) *a.* It's neither true that I've stopped drinking wine for breakfast nor true that I haven't stopped drinking wine for breakfast: I've never drunk wine before five in the evening!
b. The square root of five is neither red nor not red.
c. It's not the case that the present queen of France is fat, nor is it the case that the present queen of France is not fat: France no longer has a queen.

Presumably we can explain such utterances just as we explained how sentences like those in (139) work: they are interpreted as if they contained an unpronounced operator essentially equivalent to *definitely*. But conversationalists don't in these cases utter formal contradictions:

(142) *a.* ?I've stopped drinking wine for breakfast, and I haven't.
b. ?The square root of five is red, and it isn't red.
c. ?The present queen of France is fat and not fat.

This contrasts with their tendency to assent to formally contradictory sentences like (129*b*). In thus using a formal contradiction, we seem explicitly to signal that we are speaking of middling circumstances. The characteristic feature of fuzzy borderlines is that they in some sense license assertion of both the affirmative and the negative, which is why in such circumstances assertion of either affirmative or negative by itself is problematic. It has often been suggested that we interpret the formal contradictions by supposing that the speaker is equivocating, using an ambiguous expression in two different senses. We said something like this ourselves in chapter 1, and some expansions of the formally contradictory sentences do suggest such an analysis. The expression *in a sense*, which might seem to suggest disambiguation, does occur often in such expansions. So we find sentences like those in (143).

(143) *a.* Monks are poor [in the sense of not having individual possessions, wearing fine clothing, or living in elegantly furnished surroundings], yet they are not poor [in the sense that they need have no worries about adequate nutrition and health care and they are well educated and have access to books, music, and art].
b. Susan is smart [in the mathematical sense], and yet she is not smart [in the sense of knowing how to make her way in the world].

Yet further reflection shows that such utterances typically differentiate straightforward disambiguation from indication of jointly available though conflicting ways to remove imprecision. The sentences in (143) are cases of the latter, indicating imprecision, and not of the former, indicating ambiguity. Take the word *smart*, which (especially in British varieties of English) may indicate stylishness rather than any kind of intelligence. Sentence (144) is quite odd with its genuinely disambiguating expansions.

(144) ?Susan is smart [in the sense of being highly intelligent], but she is not smart [in the sense of adhering to canons of style].

Nor do formal contradictions work to indicate different context-sensitive parameters of the kind we saw with the modals. Sentence (145), indicating different kinds of modal base for establishing the truth-conditions for *can*, is as bizarre as (144).

(145) ?Jeremy can drive [in the sense that he knows how to do it], but he can't drive [in the sense that he has been forbidden to do so by his parents].

The sentences in (144) and (145) have an air of (ineffective) puns. They contrast sharply with the readily usable formal contradictions for borderline cases.

The assertion of a sentence jointly with its negation is the hallmark of semantic imprecision and not of ambiguity or contextual setting of parameters. The reason is that the semantics of the imprecise predicate brings with it the potential in the middle ground for the truth of both the affirmative and the negative by licensing the Σ family for admissible complete interpretations of the predicate. A middling chip on the orange-red border, for example, may rank higher in redness than some other chip that is not [definitely] orange, and thus it may have to be classed as red on some completion. At the same time it ranks higher in orangeness than some other chip that is not [definitely] red, and thus it must be classed as not red (and indeed, on our assumptions above, as orange) on some other completion. Both completions, unlike two different senses of a genuinely ambiguous expression or two distinct values for a single contextual parameter, may be used in a single context. So we may utter sentences like (146) of the middling chip, even though both emerge in these circumstances as superfalse.

(146) *a.* No. 3 is both red and not red.
b. No. 3 is both red and orange.

An utterance of sentence (146*a*) essentially asserts that no. 3 is a borderline case of red, and (146*b*) asserts more specifically that no. 3 lies on the red-orange border. The conflicting potential completions of an imprecise predicate are a part of its "global" semantic value and are tied to the order relation and the constraints linking both partial and complete interpretations of the predicate to those of other semantically related predicates (linking, for example, interpretations of *red* and *orange*).

We can now also give substance to the intuitive judgment that chips 1, 2, and 3 are all much better instances of red or orange than is the rather red but somewhat violet chip 4. Since no. 3 is in the middle of the red-orange continuum, (147*a*) will emerge as supertrue, whereas (147*b*) remains indeterminate on the supervaluation, being true in those completions that put no. 4 in the positive extension $[\![\text{red}]\!]^{t+}$ and false in those that put it in the negative extension $[\![\text{red}]\!]^{t-}$.

(147) *a.* No. 3 is red, or no. 3 is orange.
b. No. 4 is red, or no. 4 is orange.

But what about one sentence's being "truer" than another? Here too the supervaluational approach to imprecision offers something interesting and more satisfactory than the fuzzy degrees of truth. By hypothesis, no. 1, no. 2, and no. 3 each lies in the borderline between red and orange, but no. 1 is redder than both no. 2 and no. 3, and no. 2 is also less red than no. 3, our central borderline case. We also have no. 4, which is redder than any of these but on the violet side of focal red. These chips are ordered by $\prec_{\text{red}}$ as follows:

(148) no. 2 $\prec_{\text{red}}$ no. 3 $\prec_{\text{red}}$ no. 1 $\prec_{\text{red}}$ no. 4

All the sentences in (149) emerge as indefinite in the supervaluation.

(149) *a.* No. 1 is red.
b. No. 2 is red.
c. No. 3 is red.
d. No. 4 is red.

Consider, however, Σ_1, Σ_2, Σ_3, and Σ_4, the subfamilies of complete interpretations that put no. 1, no. 2, no. 3, and no. 4, respectively, in the positive extension of *red′* and thus make sentences (149*a*–*d*) respectively, true. From the constraints on completions in (135*b*, *c*), we obtain that $\Sigma_2 \subset \Sigma_3 \subset \Sigma_1 \subset \Sigma_4$ (which matches exactly the ordering in (148)). The family of interpretations that make (149*a*) true must be larger than that which make (149*c*) true because no. 1 is redder than no. 3, and thus every interpretation that makes no. 3 red must make no. 1 red. Yet there will be completions that make no. 1 red without making no. 3 red. For the same reason, both Σ_3 and Σ_1 are larger than the class of interpretations making (149*b*) true, and of course the largest family of all is that making (149*d*) true. We could define a measure on these subfamilies that yielded values like .55 as the size of Σ_1, .45 as the size of Σ_2, .5 as the size of Σ_3, and .6 as the size of Σ_4. Such a measure would mimic fuzzy values.

We should also point out that there is no reason to take the numbers assigned to the subfamilies associated with interpretations of *red′* as comparable with those associated with interpretations of *tall′*. The two sets of subfamilies do not stand in inclusion relations to one another, since how we complete a partial interpretation of *red′* is independent of how we complete a partial interpretation of *tall′*. This explains why (in contrast to what happens for the sentences in (149) there is little intuitive content to a degree of partial truth for sentences like those in (150), which are like the sentences in (149) in remaining indefinite in the supervaluation.

(150) *a.* Eloise is tall, and no. 3 is red.
b. If Peggy is tall, then no. 4 is red.

To summarize, we have presented here two formal approaches to vagueness and have argued that the supervaluation approach takes us closer to a genuine understanding of the phenomena involved than the fuzzy logic approach. To be sure, there is much more to be said about the analysis of semantic imprecision, and there are many outstanding problems that we have ignored. Yet what we have done suffices to illustrated, we think, a very important general issue raised at the outset of the present work. The fact that meanings are vague is no obstacle to the use of truth-conditional techniques in semantics. Indeed, such techniques might be our best tool for understanding imprecision.

9 Generalized Quantifiers

One of the problems left over from previous chapters is the interpretation of NPs. The kind of semantics for NPs that we have been able to develop so far is not fully compositional, which gives rise to a number of problems (see, for example, chapter 3, section 2.2). In the present chapter we will address the issue of how this situation might be improved, and this will give us an occasion to become acquainted with some interesting current results in semantics. To simplify things, we will formulate our approach in an extensional setting. Recasting it in an intensional framework is straightforward.

1 The Semantic Value of NPs

The problem of interpreting NPs may be put as follows. Take an arbitrary NP, say *every student*. It forms a syntactic unit, and compositionality demands that it also form a semantic unit. The problem is what such a semantic unit could be.

To answer this question, we have to reassess the role of NPs in channeling truth conditions. Consider simple subject-predicate sentences like the following:

(1) *a.* Every student smokes.
    b. Every student snores.
    c. Every student likes Loren.

Sentence (1*a*) is true iff every student belongs to the set of people who smoke; sentence (1*b*) iff every student belongs to the set of people who snores; (1*c*) iff every student belongs to the set of people who like Loren. The pattern is clear. The semantic contribution of *every student* in these sentences seems to depend only on which set every student belongs to. This suggests that we might interpret *every student* as a set of sets: the set of sets to which every student blongs. We can picture this roughly as follows, where A_i is a set to which every student belongs.

(2) $[\![\text{every student}]\!] = \{A_1, A_2, \ldots, A_i, \ldots\}$

In general, a sentence of the form "Every student *Q*s" will be true just in case the extension of the predicate *Q* (i.e., the set of *Qs*) is in the set of sets associated with *every student*. Sentence (1*a*) is true iff the extension of the predicate *smokes* is a member of ⟦every student⟧, and so on.

A set of sets may seem a curious kind of object to serve as the semantic value of an NP. An analogy with logical connectives might be helpful. It certainly is not obvious how to specify the semantic value of words like *and* and *or*. To approximate such a goal, our strategy has been to look at the contribution of those words to the truth conditions of the sentences in which they occur. On this basis it becomes possible to construct abstract objects (such as functions from ordered pairs of truth values to truth values) that can reasonably be maintained to represent the meaning of words like *and* and *or*, that is, their contribution to truth conditions. The game we are playing here with NPs is similar. Our reason for looking at the contributions of NPs to truth conditions is to define an abstract object that can be said to represent their meaning. Sets of sets look promising.

Other NPs can be analyzed along fully parallel lines. Consider the following, for example.

(3) Some student smokes.

We can assume that ⟦some student⟧ is the set of sets that some student or other belongs to. Suppose, for example, that some student likes bananas. Then we will put the set of people who like bananas in the set ⟦some student⟧. Further suppose that some other student has the property of not liking bananas. Then we will also want the set of people not liking bananas to be in ⟦some student⟧. There is nothing paradoxical about that. Suppose, on the other hand, that no student has the property of smoking, then the set of people who smoke will not belong to the set ⟦some student⟧. On these assumptions we can say that a sentence of the form "Some student *Q*s" is true iff the extension of the predicate *Q* belongs to ⟦some student⟧ and be sure that this will get us exactly the same truth conditions that we get by the standard PC semantics for (3).

What we just said can be pictorially represented as in the following diagram from Dowty, Wall and Peters (1981, 122).

(4) $[\![\text{every student}]\!] =$

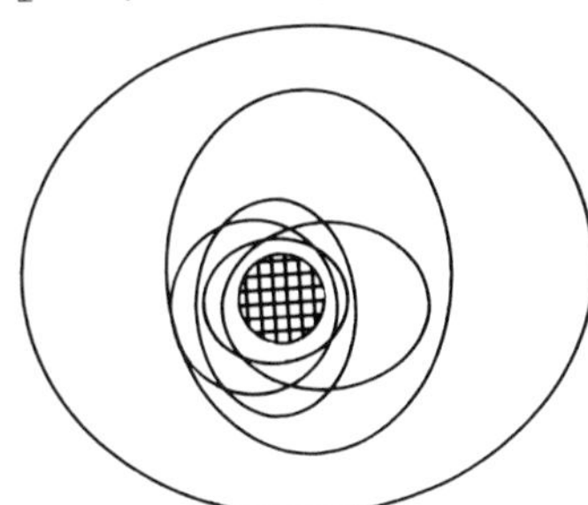

The checkered circle represents the set of students, and the other circles are the other sets to which those students all belong.

Similarly, we can interpret $[\![\text{some student}]\!]$ as the set that contains all the sets to which some student or other belongs. This can be pictured as follows:

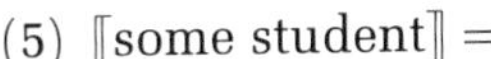

(5) $[\![\text{some student}]\!] =$

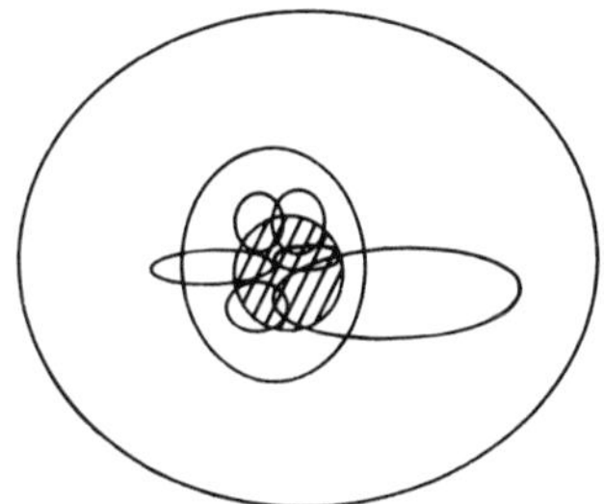

The circle with the hatching represents the set of students, and the other circles are the other sets to which some student belongs.

Using set-theoretic notation, we can give the semantic values of the NPs in question as follows:

(6) *a.* $[\![\text{every student}]\!] = \{X \subseteq U : [\![\text{student}]\!] \subseteq X\}$
  b. $[\![\text{some student}]\!] = \{X \subseteq U : [\![\text{student}]\!] \cap X \neq \varnothing\}$

Hence, $[\![\text{every student}]\!]$ is the set of subsets of the domain U of which the students are a subset, and $[\![\text{some student}]\!]$ is the set of all subsets of U whose intersection with the set of students is nonempty.

We can give a similar characterization for all the NPs that we have encountered. In what follows we list a few:

(7) $[\![\text{the } A]\!] = \{X \subseteq U : \text{for some } u \in U, [\![A]\!] = \{u\} \text{ and } u \in X\}$

This is the set of those Xs such that $[\![A]\!]$ is a singleton and X contains the only member of $[\![A]\!]$.

(8) $[\![\text{two } A]\!] = \{X \subseteq U : X \cap [\![A]\!] \text{ contains two or more members}\}$ or $\{X \subseteq U : X \cap [\![A]\!] \text{ contains exactly two members}\}$

(9) $[\![\text{no } A]\!] = \{X \subseteq U : [\![A]\!] \cap X = \varnothing\}$

This is the set of those *X*s whose intersection with the set $[\![A]\!]$ is empty.

(10) $[\![\text{most A}]\!] = \{X \subseteq U : X \cap [\![A]\!] \text{ is bigger than } X^- \cap [\![A]\!]\}$

This is the set of those *X*s whose intersection with the set of *A*s is bigger than the intersection of their complements with the set of *A*s.

In general, where α is any NP and β any predicate, we will say that $\alpha\beta$s is true iff $[\![\beta]\!] \in [\![\alpha]\!]$. To see how this gives us the right truth conditions, let us work through a couple of examples.

(11) The student smokes.

This is true iff $[\![\text{smokes}]\!] \in [\![\text{the student}]\!]$. By (7), this is equivalent to $[\![\text{smokes}]\!] \in \{X \subseteq U : \text{for some } u \in U, [\![\text{student}]\!] = \{u\} \text{ and } u \in X\}$. Thus there has to be exactly one student and that student must be a smoker. These are exactly the truth conditions that our Russellian analysis of definite descriptions associates with (11) (see chapter 3, section 1.2).

Consider (12) next:

(12) No student smokes.

Sentence (12) is true iff $[\![\text{smokes}]\!] \in \{X \subseteq U : [\![\text{student}]\!] \cap X = \varnothing\}$. If the latter condition obtains, the set of students and the set of smokers must have no member in common. This is the case iff no student smokes.

The reader can verify that the other proposed NP meanings will also give us the right truth conditions. For example, a sentence like "Most students smoke" comes out true iff the number of smoking students is bigger than the number of students that don't smoke.

Thus it seems that we have found the right kind of abstract object to represent the contribution of NPs to the truth conditions of the sentences in which they occur. NPs can be interpreted as sets of sets. We will call these objects *generalized quantifiers.* It should be borne in mind that we are taking generalized quantifiers as the semantic value of full NPs ([Det $\bar{\text{N}}$] structures) and not as the semantic values of determiners (like *every* or *some*).[1] This use of the term generalized quantifier is a slight departure from standard practice in elementary logic, where quantifiers are associated only with determiners.

How can we represent the contribution of determiners to meaning? Well, determiners combine with nominals to yield NPs. Given our hypothesis about the semantics of NPs, and given that nominals denote sets, what do we need? Apparently, a determiner should be something that combines with a set (the semantic value of a nominal) to produce a set of sets (the semantic value of an NP). So determiners can be analyzed as functions from sets of individuals to generalized quantifiers. This means that the meaning of the determiners considered so far can be given in the following terms:

(13) For every $Y \subseteq U$,
  a. $[\![\text{every}]\!](Y) = \{X \subseteq U : Y \subseteq X\}$
  b. $[\![\text{some}]\!](Y) = \{X \subseteq U : X \cap Y \neq \varnothing\}$
  c. $[\![\text{the}]\!](Y) = \{X \subseteq U : \text{for some } u \in U, Y = \{u\} \text{ and } u \in X\}$
  d. $[\![\text{two}]\!](Y) = \{X \subseteq U : X \cap Y$ contains two or more *members*$\}$ or $\{X \subseteq U : X \cap Y$ contains exactly *two members*$\}$
  e. $[\![\text{no}]\!](Y) = \{X \subseteq U : Y \cap X = \varnothing\}$
  f. $[\![\text{most}]\!](Y) = \{X \subseteq U : X \cap Y \text{ is bigger than } X^{-} \cap Y\}$

It is possible, then, to say that the meaning of, say, *some student* can be compositionally specified in terms of the meanings of *some* and *student* as $[\![\text{some}]\!]([\![\text{student}]\!])$. By (13*b*), $[\![\text{some}]\!]([\![\text{student}]\!])$ yields the generalized quantifier $\{X \subseteq U : X \cap [\![\text{student}]\!] \neq \varnothing\}$, which is what we want.

Thus we now have a way of representing directly the meanings of determiners and NPs (that is, their contribution to truth conditions). But we have so far looked just at subject-predicate sentences. Can we generalize the present analysis to more complex sentences? It turns out to be quite simple to do so by combining the present treatment with standard variable-binding mechanisms. We will first describe our strategy informally by looking at particular examples. Then we will illustrate the approach more precisely by developing a fragment that incorporates the present semantic analysis of NPs.

Consider (14).

(14) John likes every student.

According to our analysis, the semantic value of *every student* is the generalized quantifier $[\![\text{every}]\!]([\![\text{student}]\!]) = \{X \subseteq U : [\![\text{student}]\!] \subseteq X\}$. We can say that (14) is true iff the set of people that John likes belongs to $\{X \subseteq U : [\![\text{student}]\!] \subseteq X\}$. In symbols, (14) is true iff $\{x : \text{John likes } x\} \in \{X \subseteq U : [\![\textit{student}]\!] \subseteq X\}$. This reduces cases like (14) to ones like (12), which means checking whether a certain set belongs to a certain NP denotation. We can get at the right set in a less ad hoc way by raising the NP in (14) and obtaining the following structure:

(15) [every student]$_i$ [John likes e_i]

The relevant set, $\{x : \text{John likes } x\}$, can be compositionally recovered from the structure [John likes e_i].

The same idea can be applied to more complicated structures. Here is an example. (Keep in mind that this is just a preview of an explicit formal treatment of generalized quantifiers, which will be introduced shortly.)

(16) *a.* Every student likes some professor.

b.

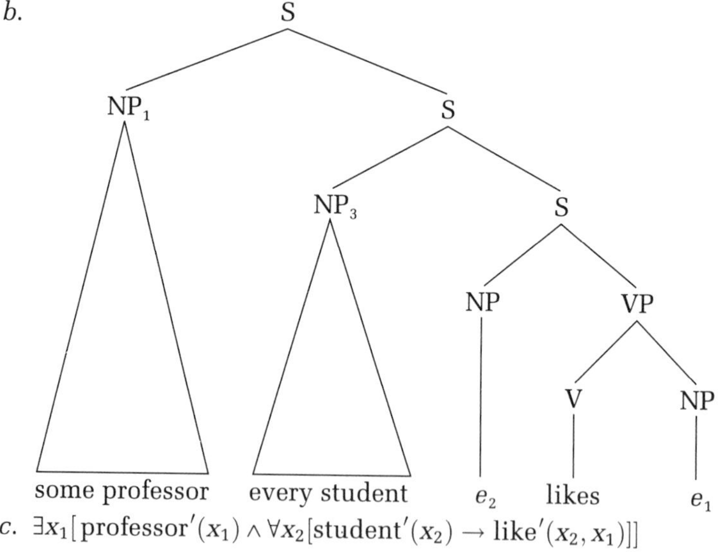

c. $\exists x_1[\text{professor}'(x_1) \wedge \forall x_2[\text{student}'(x_2) \rightarrow \text{like}'(x_2, x_1)]]$

Structure (16*b*) is one of the familiar LFs that our grammar associates with sentence (16*a*), irrelevant details aside. However, the interpretation of NPs has now changed. *Every student* and *some professor* are now interpreted as $\{X \subseteq U : [\![\text{student}]\!] \subseteq X\}$ and $\{X \subseteq U : X \cap [\![\text{professor}]\!] \neq \varnothing\}$, respectively. This is the information we want to use in giving the truth conditions for (16*b*). So to find out whether (16*a*) is true on analysis (16*b*), proceeding, as usual, from the bottom up, we assign to the most embedded S node in (16*b*) the meaning expressed by the IPC formula "like$'(x_2, x_1)$." Thus far there is nothing new. Here is where the novelty comes in. From "like$'(x_2, x_1)$" we can construct the set $\{x_2 : \text{like}'(x_2, x_1)\}$ and check whether it is in $\{X \subseteq U : [\![\text{student}]\!] \subseteq X\}$. This is going to depend on the individual assigned to x_1. For each particular individual assigned to x_1 we can determine whether the set of things that like that individual belong to $\{X \subseteq U : [\![\text{student}]\!] \subseteq X\}$. Such a condition holds iff every student likes x_1. We can then move up and check whether the set of people that every student likes (that is, $\{x_1 : \text{every student likes } x_1\}$) belongs to $\{X \subseteq U : X \cap [\![\text{professor}]\!] \neq \varnothing\}$. Intuitively, we find the individuals that every student likes and then we check to see whether one of these individuals is a professor. As a result of this process (16*b*) will get exactly the same truth conditions as (16*c*).

What all this amounts to is that our analysis of NPs as generalized quantifiers extends to any sentence whatsoever once it is coupled with a variable-binding mechanism of the familiar kind. All this will become clearer as we work through our next fragment. But first let us summarize what our proposal amounts to.

It is possible to provide a semantic category that corresponds to the syntactic category NP. The semantic category that we need is that of generalized quantifiers (sets of sets). Such objects encode precisely the information that NPs contribute to the truth conditions of sentences (much as functions from truth values into truth values encode the information that logical connectives contribute).

2 PC_{GQ} and F_4

We will first extend PC to incorporate generalized quantifiers. The resulting logic will be called PC_{GQ}. We will then specify a new fragment F_4. The syntax of F_4 is going to be identical to that of F_3. The semantics, however, will be specified in the form of a compositional translation map onto PC_{GQ}, which will enable us to see how our new semantics for quantification works for English.

Let us start by adding two new categories to the logical syntax of PC, namely, D (for determiner) and Q (for quantifier). We further assume that *every'*, *the'*, *some'*, *no'*, and *most'* are constants in D. (We are here following the convention initiated in chapter 7 whereby α' denotes the translation of α into our logic.) We thus add two more syntactic rules:

(17) *a.* If α is in D and β is in Pred$_1$, $\alpha(\beta)$ is in Q.
b. If α is in Q and β is in Pred$_1$, $\alpha(\beta)$ is a well-formed formula.

This means that PC$_{GQ}$ will contain all the well-formed formulas of PC but will additionally contain well-formed formulas like those in (18*a*–*c*):

(18) *a.* some′(man′)(run′)
b. $\text{most}'(\lambda x[\text{man}'(x) \wedge \text{sing}'(x)])(\text{smoke}')$
c. $\text{some}'(\text{professor}')(\lambda x_1[\text{every}'(\text{student}')(\lambda x_2[\text{like}'(x_2, x_1)])])$
d. $\exists x_1[\text{professor}'(x_1) \wedge \forall x_2[\text{student}'(x_2) \rightarrow [\text{like}'(x_2, x_1)]]]$

Formula (18*b*) says most men that sing smoke. The semantics for PC$_{GQ}$ will make (18*c*) equivalent to (18*d*).

Such a semantics can be specified as follows. A model M for PC$_{GQ}$ is a pair $\langle U, V\rangle$ such that (19) holds:

(19) If α is a D, $V(\alpha)$ is a function that maps any subset of U onto a set of sets of members of U (that is, for any $Y \in \mathscr{P}(U)$, $V(\alpha)(Y) \subseteq \mathscr{P}(U)$). In particular,
$V(\text{every}')(Y) = \{X \subseteq U : Y \subseteq X\}$
$V(\text{some}')(Y) = \{X \subseteq U : Y \cap X \neq \varnothing\}$
$V(\text{the}')(Y) = \{X \subseteq U : \text{for some } u \in U, Y = \{u\} \text{ and } u \in X\}$
$V(\text{no}')(Y) = \{X \subseteq U : Y \cap X = \varnothing\}$
$V(\text{most}')(Y) = \{X \subseteq U : \text{ card}(Y \cap X) > \text{card}(Y \cap X^-)\}$

(The function card(X), the cardinality of set X, gives the number of elements in X.)

Given a model M and an arbitrary assignment to the variables g, the semantics rules corresponding to (17*a*, *b*) are as follows:

(20) *a.* If α is a D and β is a Pred$_1$, $[\![\alpha(\beta)]\!]^{M,g} = [\![\alpha]\!]^{M,g}([\![\beta]\!]^{M,g})$.
b. If α is a Q and β is a Pred$_1$, $[\![\alpha(\beta)]\!]^{M,g} = 1$ iff $[\![\beta]\!]^{M,g} \in [\![\alpha]\!]^{M,g}$.

In the following box, we verify that the semantics so specified assigns identical truth conditions to (18*c*) and (18*d*). We proceed as follows. First we assume that (18*a*) is true; then we work out under what conditions this holds applying our semantic rules. This involves computing the truth conditions for the subformula $\text{every}'(\text{student}')(\lambda x_2[\text{like}'(x_2, x_1)])$; this is done in a separate subbox. Looking at the above computation, we see that we first form the set of those u' that every student likes. Then we check whether the intersection of this set with the set of professors is nonempty

(a) $[[(18a)]]^{M,g} = 1$ Assumption
(b) $[\![\lambda x_1[\text{every}'(\text{student}')(\lambda x_2[\text{like}'(x_2, x_1)])]\!]^{M,g} \in [\![\text{some}']\!]^{M,g}([\![\text{professor}']\!]^{M,g})$ From (a), by (20a, b)
(c) $[\![\lambda x_1[\text{every}'(\text{student}')(\lambda x_2[\text{like}'(x_2, x_1)])]]\!]^{M,g} \in \{X \subseteq U : [\![\text{professor}']\!]^{M,g} \cap X \neq \varnothing\}$ From (b) by (19)
(d) $\{u : [\![\text{every}'(\text{student}')(\lambda x_2[\text{like}'(x_2, x_1)])]\!]^{M,g[u/x_1]} = 1\} \in \{X \subseteq U : [\![\text{professor}']\!]^{M,g} \cap X \neq \varnothing\}$ From (c), by the semantics of λ
(e) $[\![\text{professor}']\!]^{M,g} \cap \{u : [\![\text{every}'(\text{student}')(\lambda x_2[\text{like}'(x_2, x_1)])]\!]^{M,g[u/x_1]} = 1\} \neq \varnothing$ From (d), by def. of $\in$

Computation of every′(student′)(λx₂[like′(x₂, x₁)])]

(f) $[\![\text{every}'(\text{student}')(\lambda x_2[\text{like}'(x_2, x_1)])]]\!]^{M,g[u/x_1]} = 1$ Assumption
(g) $[\![\lambda x_2[\text{like}'(x_2, x_1)])]\!]^{M,g[u/x_1]} \in \{X \subseteq U : [\![\text{student}']\!]^{M,g[u/x_1]} \subseteq X\}$ From (f) by (20a, b) and (19)
(h) $\{u' : [\![\text{like}'(x_2, x_1)])]]\!]^{M,g[[u/x_1]u'/x_2]} = 1\} \in \{X \subseteq U : [\![\text{student}']\!]^{M,g} \subseteq X\}$ From (g), by the semantics of λ
(i) $[\![\text{student}']\!]^{M,g} \subseteq \{u' : [\![\text{like}'(x_2, x_1)])]]\!]^{M,g[[u/x_1]u'/x_2]} = 1\}$ From (h) by def. of $\in$
(j) $[\![\text{student}']\!]^{M,g} \subseteq \{u' : u' \text{ likes } u\}$ From (i), by def. of modified assignment

(k) $[\![\text{professor}']\!]^{M,g} \cap \{u : [\![\text{student}']\!]^{M,g} \subseteq \{u' : u' \text{ likes } u\}\} \neq \varnothing$ From (e), by (j)

(whether some professor is liked by every student). But these are precisely the truth conditions associated with (18d). These results are perfectly general and apply to all pairs that have the same structure as (18c) and (18d).

Let us now turn to fragment F_4. As mentioned above, its syntax is identical to the syntax of F_3, and its semantics is given by a translation map essentially identical to the one specified in chapter 7, section 2. The only difference concerns the rules for interpreting quantifiers. They are replaced by the following translation rules (ignoring tense, for simplicity):

(21) a. $[\text{Det } \overline{\text{N}}]' = \text{Det}'(\overline{\text{N}}')$
b. $[_{\text{S}} \text{ NP}_i \text{ S}]' = \text{NP}_i'(\lambda x_i \text{S}')$

Let us give a couple of examples that illustrate how the translation procedure for F_4 works.

(22) *a.* Some student runs.

b. LF and translation

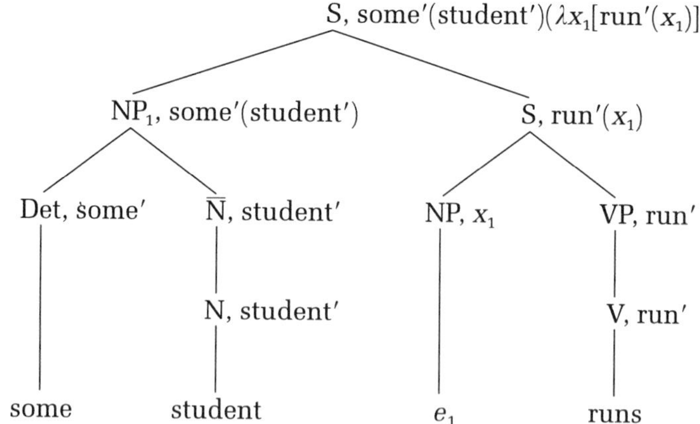

(23) *a.* Every student likes some professor.

b. LF and translation

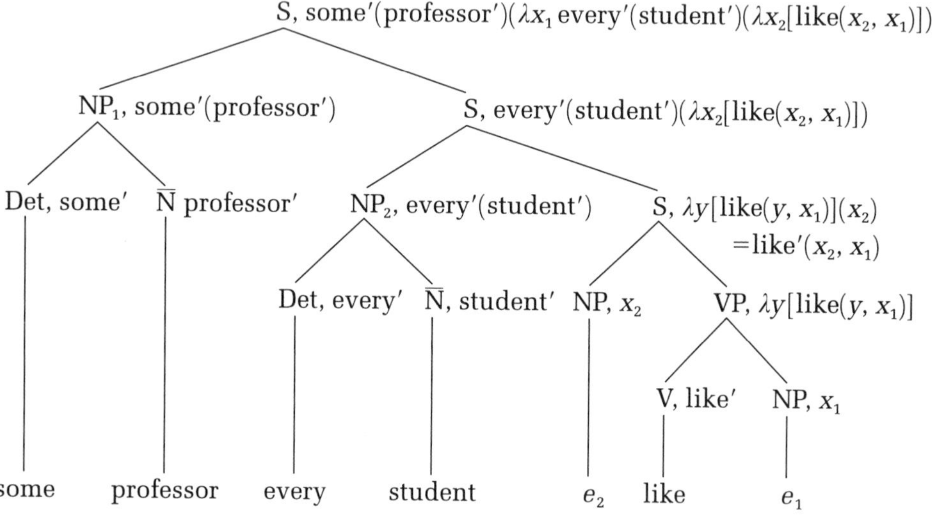

Exercise 1 Give the LFs and PC_{GQ} translations of the following sentences:

(1) Some fish likes the man.

(2) The man that smokes loves Loren.

(3) Every man runs and smokes.

(4) Every man gave a book to the woman.

The category NP now receives a translation and an interpretation, which were lacking in F_3. By introducing a more abstract semantic category (the category of generalized quantifiers), it seems possible to achieve a more principled overall relation between syntax and semantics.

3 Generalized Conjunction

The new semantics for NPs developed in the preceding section has been motivated so far by a desire for compositionality. We are now going to see that it enables us to generalize further our semantic analysis of conjunction and disjunction in a way not possible on the previous approach to NP interpretation.

We have already noted that conjunction and disjunction (and to a more limited extent negation) are cross-categorical operators: they operate on elements of the same syntactic categories, no matter what the category is. This applies also to the categories *Det* and *NP*, as the following examples illustrate:

(24) NP
- *a.* *Every student* and *some professor* came.
- *b.* *Not every student* came.
- *c.* John likes *every dog* or *some fish*.
- *d.* *John* and *every woman* left early.

(25) Det
- *a.* *Some* but *not all* students came.
- *b.* *Some* or *most* or *all* students came.
- *c.* *Many* but *less than 100* students were there.

We have also pointed out how non-S-level operators appear to inherit their Boolean properties from their S-level counterparts, at least in a number of core cases. We proposed a partial account for this behavior by generalizing conjunction, disjunction, and other operators from the S level to the VP level (see chapter 7, section 4). The semantic apparatus we had before did not allow us to extend our approach to other categories, most prominently, to the category NP. Under the approach developed in the present chapter, however, NPs have a richer structure, which might enable us to define conjunction, disjunction, and possibly other logical operators for them as well. In particular, NPs are interpreted as sets of sets. Sets can be intersected and unified with other sets, or they can be complemented. We can exploit this structure to analyze NP-level operators.

To see what happens when we intersect or unify NP interpretations, it might be best to start with some concrete examples. Consider (26):

(26) Every woman and some man smoke.

The NP *every woman* denotes the set $\{X \subseteq U : [\![\text{woman}']\!] \subseteq X\}$, and *some man* the set $\{X \subseteq U : [\![\text{man}']\!] \cap X \neq \varnothing\}$. The intersection of these two sets is the set $\{X \subseteq U : [\![\text{woman}']\!] \subseteq X \text{ and } [\![\text{man}']\!] \cap X \neq \varnothing\}$. If the extension of a property, say the property of being a smoker, is in $\{X \subseteq U : [\![\text{woman}']\!] \subseteq X \text{ and } [\![\text{man}']\!] \cap X \neq \varnothing\}$, it must be the case that every woman smokes and some man smokes. This suggests that we can indeed interpret NP-level conjunction simply as set intersection.

It is not hard to see that similar considerations apply to disjunction and negation. Consider, for example, (27):

(27) *a.* Not every woman smokes.
b. $\mathscr{P}(U) - \{X \subseteq U : [\![\text{woman}']\!] \subseteq X\}$
$= \{X \subseteq U : [\![\text{woman}']\!] \not\subseteq X\}$

In (27*b*) we give the set-theoretic complement of the set associated with the NP *every woman* (relative to $\mathscr{P}(U)$). Suppose that the extension of the property of smoking, $[\![\text{smoke}']\!]$, belongs to that set. It must then be the case that some woman is not a smoker, for otherwise the condition that $[\![\text{woman}']\!] \not\subseteq [\![\text{smoke}']\!]$ would not be satisfied. This suggests that it is correct to interpret NP negation as set-theoretic complementation.

Consider (28) next:

(28) *a.* Some woman or some man smokes.
b. $\{X \subseteq U : [\![\text{woman}']\!] \cap X \neq \varnothing\} \cup \{X \subseteq U : [\![\text{man}']\!] \cap X \neq \varnothing\}$
$= \{X \subseteq U : [\![\text{woman}']\!] \cap X \neq \varnothing \text{ or } [\![\text{man}']\!] \cap X \neq \varnothing\}$

In (28*b*) we provide the union of the semantic values of the NPs *some woman* and *some man*. For $[\![\text{smoke}']\!]$ to be in that set, it must be the case that either some man smokes or some woman smokes, which again suggests that we can analyze NP disjunction as set-theoretic union.

What about cases where a proper name is conjoined or disjoined with a quantified NP, as in (24*d*)? If a proper name is interpreted as an individual, then we cannot unify or intersect it with anything, for individuals don't have the right structure. However, it turns out to be easy enough to interpret proper names as generalized quantifiers. Proper names can be lifted in an information-preserving way to the category of generalized quantifiers. For example, the proper name *Pavarotti* can be interpreted as the set of sets to which Pavarotti belongs.

(29) *a.* $[\![\text{Pavarotti}]\!] = \{X \subseteq U : \text{Pavarotti} \in X\}$
b.

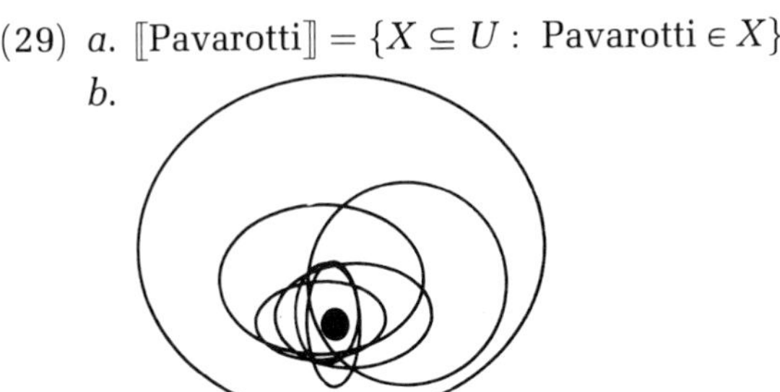

In (29*b*), where the black circle represents Pavarotti, we have this idea represented pictorially.

Interpreting proper names in this fashion leaves the truth conditions of simple sentences like "Pavarotti smokes" unaltered. We simply say that the sentence is true iff the extension of the property of smoking belongs to the generalized quantifier associated with *Pavarotti*. This yields the following chain of equivalences:

(30) *a.* "Pavarotti smokes" is true iff
b. $[\![\text{smoke}']\!] \in [\![\text{Pavarotti}]\!]$ iff
c. $\text{P} \in [\![\text{smoke}']\!]$

Formula (30*c*) gives us back the way of interpreting sentences with proper names we had before.

In terms of the above analysis of proper names it is straightforward to extend our theory of NP-level operators to cases involving conjunction with proper names, for now we can define set-theoretic operations on the denotations of proper names. Here is an example:

(31) *a.* Pavarotti and every woman smoke.
b. $[\![\text{smoke}']\!] \in [\![\text{Pavarotti}]\!] \cap [\![\text{every woman}]\!]$ iff
c. $[\![\text{smoke}']\!] \in \{X \subseteq U : \text{Pavarotti} \in X\}$
$\cap \{X \subseteq U : [\![\text{woman}']\!] \subseteq X\}$ iff
d. $[\![\text{smoke}']\!] \in \{X \subseteq U : \text{Pavarotti} \in X \text{ and } [\![\text{woman}']\!] \subseteq X\}$

For (31*d*) to be the case we must have that Pavarotti $\in [\![\text{smoke}']\!]$ and $[\![\text{woman}']\!] \subseteq [\![\text{smoke}']\!]$. So this appears to be the right analysis for (31*a*).

Exercise 2 On the model of (31), compute the denotation for the NPs in the sentences below, and make sure that the analysis we have given assigns the right truth conditions in every case. (In doing this exercise, assume that plural nouns denote the same set as their singular counterparts. Assume as usual that *and* and *but* are truth-conditionally identical.)

(1) Most men, but not Pavarotti, smoke.

(2) Some men and every woman but no children smoke.

(3) Pavarotti or Loren or Bond smokes.

Does the analysis above predict that (2) and (3) are equivalent to (4) and (5), respectively?

(4) Every woman and some men but no children smoke.

(5) Bond or Loren or Pavarotti smokes.

The above remarks can be sharpened by introducing quantifier-level conjunction, negation, and disjunction into PC_{GQ} along the following lines:

(32) *a.* If α, β are in Q, then $[\alpha \wedge \beta]$, $[\alpha \vee \beta]$, and $[\neg\alpha]$ are also in Q.
b. If α, β are in Q, then
$[\![[\alpha \wedge \beta]]\!]^{M,g} = [\![\alpha]\!]^{M,g} \cap [\![\beta]\!]^{M,g}$
$[\![[\alpha \vee \beta]]\!]^{M,g} = [\![\alpha]\!]^{M,g} \cup [\![\beta]\!]^{M,g}$
$[\![[\neg\alpha]]\!]^{M,g} = \mathscr{P}(U) - [\![\alpha]\!]^{M,g}$

The extension above of PC_{GQ} can be regarded as a simple generalization of our pointwise definition of VP-level conjunction, disjunction, and negation developed in chapter 7. To see what these additions to PC_{GQ} amount to, let us consider a few examples. In what follows, the (*b*) formulas are the PC_{GQ} representations of the (*a*) sentences. The (*c*) formulas are the first-order counterparts of (and provably equivalent to) the (*b*) formulas.

(33) *a.* Every man and every woman run.
b. $[\text{every}'(\text{man}') \wedge \text{every}'(\text{woman}')](\text{run}')$
c. $\forall x[\text{man}'(x) \rightarrow \text{run}'(x)] \wedge \forall x[\text{woman}'(x) \rightarrow \text{run}'(x)]$

(34) *a.* Some man or every woman smokes.
b. $[\text{some}'(\text{man}') \vee \text{every}'(\text{woman}')](\text{smoke}')$
c. $[\exists x[\text{man}'(x) \wedge \text{smoke}'(x)] \vee \forall x[\text{woman}'(x) \rightarrow \text{smoke}'(x)]]$

(35) *a.* Every woman or John runs.
b. [every′(woman′) ∨ John′](run′)
c. $[\forall x[\text{woman}'(x) \rightarrow \text{run}'(x)] \vee \text{run}'(j)]$

In fact, we can carry this program further and introduce determiner-level logical operators along the following lines:

(36) *a.* If α, β are in D, then $[\alpha \wedge \beta]$, $[\alpha \vee \beta]$, and $[\neg\alpha]$ are also in D.
b. If α, β are in D, for any $Y \subseteq U$,
$[\![[\alpha \wedge \beta]]\!]^{M,g}(Y) = [\![\alpha]\!]^{M,g}(Y) \cap [\![\beta]\!]^{M,g}(Y)$
$[\![[\alpha \vee \beta]]\!]^{M,g}(Y) = [\![\alpha]\!]^{M,g}(Y) \cup [\![\beta]\!]^{M,g}(Y)$
$[\![[\neg\alpha]]\!]^{M,g}(Y) = \mathscr{P}(U) - [\![\alpha]\!]^{M,g}(Y)$

The technique we are employing here should by now be familiar. Determiners denote functions from sets to generalized quantifiers. We have already defined conjunction, disjunction, and negation over generalized quantifiers. We can lift this structure up to the domain of determiners. Take, for example, a determiner of the form $[\mathrm{D} \wedge \mathrm{D}']$. This must denote a function from sets to generalized quantifiers. For any set Y, what is the value of $[\mathrm{D} \wedge \mathrm{D}'](Y)$ going to be? We can define it as $\mathrm{D}(Y) \cap \mathrm{D}'(Y)$, whose components have already been defined. All of the definitions in (36) are instances of this simple schema.

With this in mind, let us now look at some concrete examples.

(37) *a.* Not all but some men smoke.
b. [[¬every′] ∧ some′](man′)(smoke′)

Formula (37*b*) constitutes the $\mathrm{PC_{GQ}}$ representation of (37*a*). The complex determiner "[¬every′] ∧ some′" is licensed by (36*a*). By the corresponding semantic clauses in (36*b*) in interaction with (32*b*), we get the following equivalences:

(38) *a.* [[¬every′] ∧ some′](man′)(smoke′) iff
b. [[¬every′(man′)] ∧ some′(man′)](smoke′) iff
c. $[\![\text{smoke}']\!] \in \{X \subseteq U : [\![\text{man}']\!] \not\subseteq X\}$
$\cap \{X \subseteq U : [\![\text{man}']\!] \cap X \neq \varnothing\}$ iff
d. $[\![\text{smoke}']\!] \in \{X \subseteq U : [\![\text{man}']\!] \not\subseteq X\}$
and $[\![\text{smoke}']\!] \in \{X \subseteq U : [\![\text{man}']\!] \cap X \neq \varnothing\}$ iff
e. $[\![\text{man}']\!] \not\subseteq [\![\text{smoke}']\!]$ and $[\![\text{man}']\!] \cap X \neq \varnothing$ iff
f. $\neg\forall x[\text{man}'(x) \rightarrow \text{smoke}'(x)] \wedge \exists x(\text{man}'(x) \wedge \text{smoke}'(x)]$

Thus the generalization of logical operators to determiners seems to give us the right results.

Exercise 3 Work out the PC_{GQ} renderings of the following sentences on the model of (38). Assume that *all* has the same meaning as *every.*

(1) Most but not all men smoke.

(2) Most or all men smoke.

(3) Some or most but not all men smoke.

The above results enable us to move toward an analysis of conjoined and disjoined structures along the following lines. One can have conjunction schemata that directly generate structures such as the following:

(39)

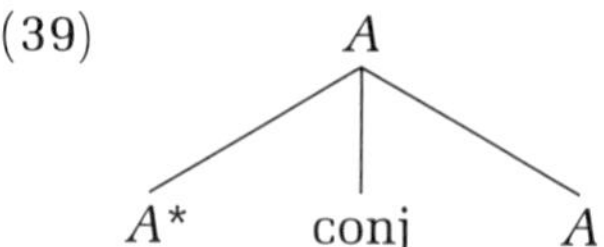

Here A is any category, and A^* indicates a sequence of one or more As. The scheme in (39) generates phrase structures like the following:

(40)

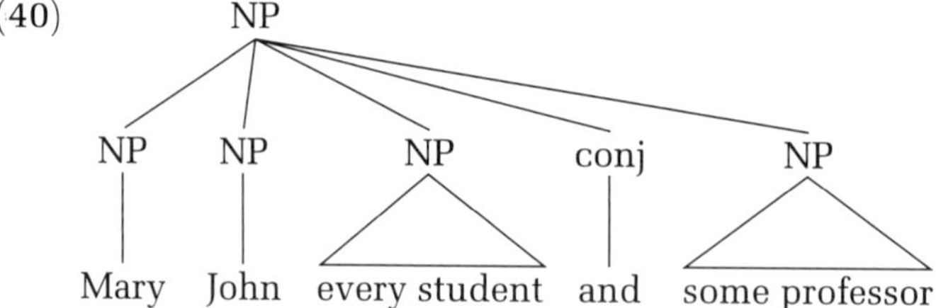

Complex NPs such as the one in (40) can then be straightforwardly interpreted in terms of the semantics we have developed. In particular, (40) is interpreted as in (41).

(41) $[\text{Mary}' \wedge \text{John}' \wedge \text{every}'(\text{student}') \wedge \text{some}'(\text{professor}')]$

The interpretation of (41) contributes the right truth conditions to the sentences where such an NP occurs.

Of course, the syntax in (39) is a very rough first approximation that leaves many problems open. To mention a simple one, conjoined NPs trigger plural agreement, which we haven't discussed. Despite this and other limitations, however, we think that some refinement of the approach we have developed is ultimately necessary for the reasons detailed below.

There is a clear tendency for such operatorlike words as *and* and *or* to be cross-categorial. This tendency appears to be universal, as a matter of fact. For example, in most languages it is possible to conjoin members of virtually every category, and this usually, though certainly not always, happens with the same morpheme (*and*, in English). Moreover, the meaning of the NP-level *and* appears to be closely and systematically related to the meaning of *and* at the VP and S levels. This can be no accident. All the different varieties of *and* obviously have a common meaning, and we would like our theory to account for that. There must be a way to regard the meanings of these seemingly distinct varieties of *and* as instances of the same logical operation. Whatever that operation is, it is presumably universal.

The approach presented here goes some way toward explaining the pattern just described and identifying a common meaning for the various instances of conjunction. According to such an approach, we have an underlying Boolean structure (roughly, the Boolean structure of propositions) that can be systematically lifted to other semantic domains by means of a general and straightforward mathematical technique, namely, pointwise definitions. This is the basis of cross-categorial generalizations of logical operators. Such a Boolean structure, one might speculate, is a powerful module for concept formation that humans appear to be endowed with.

Viewing NP denotations as generalized quantifiers is thus not just a way to get a more elegant (more compositional) semantics. It is also a crucial step toward a full-fledged characterization of cross-categorial Boolean operators.

4 Generalized Quantifiers and Empirical Properties of Language

The generalized quantifier approach turns out to shed some new light on a wide variety of properties of language. Here we will consider a few of them.

4.1 Negative polarity items

In English as well as in many other languages there are such items as *ever*, *any*, and *give a damn* that appear to be somehow restricted to occurring in negative contexts, as the following examples illustrate.[2]

(42) *a.* *John saw any bird.
b. John did not see any bird.

(43) *a.* *Some student gives a damn about Pavarotti.
b. No student gives a damn about Pavarotti.

(44) *a.* *Many students ever read a book about Pavarotti.
b. Few students ever read a book about Pavarotti.

Expressions with these distributional characteristics are often called negative polarity items. There are several issues that their behavior raises, many of which remain open. One of the problems that they pose is how to make precise the notion of a negative context. What exactly do (42*b*), (43*b*), and (44*b*) have in common? This is the question that we briefly address here.

The characterization of a negative context for polarity items is further complicated by examples such as the following:

(45) *a.* *Some student who ever read a book about Pavarotti would want to meet him.
b. Every student who ever read a book about Pavarotti would want to meet him.

The context in (45*b*) does not seem intrinsically more negative than the one in (45*a*). Yet our judgments concerning the contrast between (45*a*) and (45*b*) are quite sharp.

It turns out that the informal notion of a negative context can be made precise in semantic terms along the following lines. Let us say that a determiner D is right upward entailing/monotone iff for any set X, Y, and Z, if $(Z \cap X) \in \mathrm{D}(Y)$, then $X \in \mathrm{D}(Y)$.[3] Essentially, according to this definition, right upward monotone determiners are those that validate the following inference pattern:

(46) $\delta(\alpha)(\beta \wedge \gamma) \rightarrow \delta(\alpha)(\beta)$

So, for example, *some*, *many*, and *every* are right upward monotone, while *no*, *few*, and *two* (in the sense of exactly two) are not, as the following examples illustrate for *some* and *no*:

(47) *a.* Some student is Italian and blond $\rightarrow$ some student is blond
b. No students are Italian and blond $\nrightarrow$ no students are blond

We are assuming that predicates like *is Italian* and *is blond* are associated with the sets of Italians and blond people respectively. The term *upward* indicates that the entailment is from a set to its supersets ($[\![\beta \wedge \gamma]\!]$ is a subset of $[\![\beta]\!]$). The term *right* tells us that this entailment concerns the right argument of the determiner ($\beta \wedge \gamma$ and β in (46)).

In a similar vein we can say that a determiner is right *downward* monotone iff for every set X, Y, and Z, if $X \in \mathrm{D}(Y)$, then $X \cap Z \in \mathrm{D}(Y)$. The relevant entailment here is from a set to one of its subsets, as schematically illustrated in (48).

(48) $\delta(\alpha)(\beta) \rightarrow \delta(\alpha)(\beta \wedge \gamma)$

According to this definition, *every*, *some*, and (*exactly*) *two* are not right downward monotone, while *no* and *few* are, as is illustrated by the following pattern of entailment:

(49) *a.* Every student is Italian $\nrightarrow$ every student is Italian and blond

b. Few students are Italian $\rightarrow$ few students are Italian and blond.

Thus from this classification, numeral determiners (in the *exactly* sense) are neither upward nor downward monotone on their right argument.

A parallel criterion can be applied to the left argument of a determiner. The definitions should at this point be straightforward. We say that a determiner D is left upward entailing/monotone iff for any set X, Y, Z, if $X \in \mathrm{D}(Y \cap Z)$ then $X \in \mathrm{D}(Y)$.[4] The entailments that need to be checked are thus of the following form:

(50) $\delta(\alpha \wedge \gamma)(\beta) \rightarrow \delta(\alpha)(\beta)$

It can be seen that *some* and (*at least*) *two* are left upward monotone, while *every*, (*exactly*) *two*, *no*, and *few* are not:

(51) *a.* Some Italian students smoke $\rightarrow$ some students smoke

b. Every Italian student smokes $\nrightarrow$ every student smokes

The set of Italian students is the intersection of the set of students with the set of Italians.

Furthermore, we say that a determiner D is left downward monotone iff for every set X, Y, Z if $X \in \mathrm{D}(Y)$, then $X \in \mathrm{D}(Y \cap Z)$. The relevant class of entailments can be schematized as follows:

(52) $\delta(\alpha)(\beta) \rightarrow \delta(\alpha \wedge \gamma)(\beta)$

Accordingly, *every*, *no*, and *few* are left downward monotone, while *some* and *two* (in either the *at least* or the *exactly* sense) are not.

Table 9.1 Determiners classified by entailment patterns

	LEFT	RIGHT
Upward	some/a at least *n*	some/a every at least *n* many most
Downward	no few (?) every	no few

(53) *a.* Few students smoke → few Italian students smoke
b. Some students smoke ↛ some Italian students smoke

In conclusion, it is possible to classify natural language determiners on the basis of the entailment patterns that they give rise to. The resulting classification can be summarized as in table 9.1 (see Barwise and Cooper 1981, 219).

The classificatory criteria extend naturally to other operators. In particular, there is a clear sense in which negation is downward monotone. Perhaps the best way to see this is as follows. Think of propositions as sets of worlds. As we saw in chapter 5, section 2, negation can be thought of as set-theoretic complementation, and entailment as set inclusion. Consequently, the following holds:

(54) If p^- and $q \subseteq p$, then q^- follows.

This inference pattern is familiar from elementary logic as *modus tollens*. From the complement of p and the premise that q is a subset of p, it follows by set theory that the complement of p is a subset of the complement of q (if $q \subseteq p$ then $p^- \subseteq q^-$). Therefore, if we interpret the subset relation as entailment in possible world semantics, the proposition represented by the complement of p will entail the proposition represented by the complement of q. So negation preserves information when we go from a set of worlds to one of its subsets; that is, it is downward entailing. The information represented by the complement of a set of worlds p must be contained in the information associated with the complement of any subset of p.

It should be clear by now where the above considerations are leading. What lies behind the intuitive notion of a negative context is the model-theoretic property of downward monotonicity. In (55) we state constraints on negative polarity items.

(55) In a structure of the form $\delta(\alpha)$, where δ is a quantifier, a determiner, or in general a functor of some kind, a negative polarity item can occur within α iff δ is downward entailing with respect to α.

Let us consider some examples:

(56) *a.* John doesn't ever smoke.
b. $\neg([\text{ever smoke}]'(j))$

Ever in (56*a*) is licensed because it occurs within the scope of negation, which is downward entailing, as the schematic logical form in (56*b*) illustrates.

(57) *a.* No man ever smokes.
b. no′(man′)([ever smoke]′)

Here *ever* is licensed because it occurs within the right argument of *no*, which is right downward entailing. Equivalently, we can say that *ever* occurs within the argument of "no′(man′)," which is a downward entailing generalized quantifier.

(58) *a.* No man who ever heard about Pavarotti will want to miss his concert.
b. no′([man who ever heard about *Pavarotti*′])([will want to miss his concert]′)

(59) *a.* *Some man who ever heard about Pavarotti will want to miss his concert.
b. Some′([man who ever heard about Pavarotti]′)([will want to miss his concert]′)

In (58*a*) *ever* is licensed because it occurs within the left argument of *no*, which is left downward entailing. In (59*a*) *ever* is not licensed, because *some* is not left downward entailing; the resulting sentence is ungrammatical.

It is easy for the reader to check by looking at table 9.1 that the pattern of grammaticality pointed out in (42) through (45) is completely accounted for on the basis of (55). Particularly interesting is how the rather puzzling contrast in (45) follows from (55):

every, like *no* and unlike *some*, is downward monotone on its left argument.

In fact, the above considerations are by no means limited to the determiners we have considered. Take for example a more complex determiner, say *at most three*. By our classification, such a determiner is right downward monotone, as shown by the validity of the following:

(60) At most three students smoke → at most three students smoke cigars

Therefore, *at most three* should license negative polarity items within its scope. And indeed this is so:

(61) At most three students give a damn about Pavarotti.

Also, negation can be seen to reverse the (right) upward monotonicity of determiners:

(62) Not every student smokes → not every student smokes cigars

Hence, *not every* should be a negative polarity trigger, which is indeed the case:

(63) Not every student gives a damn about Pavarotti.

Examples of this sort can be multiplied and have been extensively discussed in the literature. Of interest to us is the following. The distribution of negative polarity items has long been an intriguing puzzle for linguists. Our semantics seems able to provide and interesting angle from which these phenomena can be studied. In particular, it provides us with criteria that enable us to see why those particular contexts should be singled out by negative polarity items, to see what it is that makes that class of contexts natural.

4.2 Conservativity

Let us say that a determiner is conservative iff for every X and every Y, $X \in \mathrm{D}(Y)$ iff $X \cap Y \in \mathrm{D}(Y)$. From this definition it follows that conservative determiners will validate the following equivalence:

(64) $\delta(\alpha)(\beta) \leftrightarrow \delta(\alpha)(\alpha \wedge \beta)$

Here are some examples of determiners that, on the basis of this criterion, appear to be conservative:

(65) *a.* Every man smokes iff every man is a man who smokes.
b. Some man smokes iff some man is a man who smokes.
c. No man smokes iff no man is a man who smokes.
d. Fewer than five but more than two men smoke iff fewer than five but more than two men are men who smoke.

The list could go on an on. In fact, there seems to be no determiner that fails to have the property of being conservative. This leads us to hypothesize the following universal:

(66) Every determiner in every language is conservative.

One might suspect that perhaps every logically conceivable determiner (or every pragmatically plausible one) is conservative. This would make conservativity, whatever it is, a rather uninteresting property. This suspicion, however, is easy to dissipate. It is easy to come up with abstract examples of nonconservative determiners. Here are a couple:

(67) *a.* Let D_1 be a function such that for every set Y, $\mathrm{D}_1(Y) = \{X \subseteq U : Y^- \subseteq X\}$.
b. Let D_2 be a function such that for every set Y, $\mathrm{D}_2(Y) = \{X \subseteq U : Y^- \nsubseteq X\}$.

Let us show that D_1 is not conservative by constructing a model with respect to which "$\delta(\alpha)(\beta)$" is true that "$\delta(\alpha)(\alpha \wedge \beta)$" is not, where δ is interpreted as D_1. Let the domain U of this model be the set $\{a, b, c\}$. Let α denote $\{a, b\}$ and β denote $\{a, c\}$. The denotation of $\delta(\alpha)$ in this model will be $\mathrm{D}_1(\{a, b\}) = \{X \subseteq U : \{a, b\}^- \subseteq X\} = \{X \subseteq U : \{c\} \subseteq X\} = \{\{c\}, \{a, c\}, \{b, c\}, \{a, b, c\}\}$. Thus "$\delta(\alpha)(\beta)$" will be true in this model, for $\{a, c\} \in \mathrm{D}_1(\{a, b\})$. But "$\delta(\alpha)(\alpha \wedge \beta)$" will be false, for the denotation of "$\alpha \wedge \beta$" will be $\{a, b\} \cap \{a, c\} = \{a\}$, and $\{a\} \notin \mathrm{D}_1(\{a, b\})$. This suffices to show that D_1 is not conservative. (The nonconservativity of D_2 can be shown similarly. We leave it as an exercise for the reader.)

So there are nonconservative functions of the same semantic type as determiner meanings (indeed, it can be shown that there are lots of them). There is no *logical* reason why such functions cannot constitute determiner meanings.

How about the pragmatic plausibility of these potential determiners? Consider, for example, what a determiner δ_1 that has D_1 as its denotation expresses. The formula $\delta_1(\alpha)(\beta)$ says that all the things that are not α have property β. For instance, δ_1

(student′)(smoke′) says that all nonstudents smoke. The latter makes perfect sense. Intuitively, the meaning of δ_1 does not appear to be different in quality from, say, the meaning of *no* (as in "No student smokes"). There is nothing intrinsically odd about trying to convey the information that all non αs are β. In fact, we can convey it as we just did. But we cannot convey it by means of a determiner. There is no lexically simple determiner that means *all non*. Furthermore, such a sequence does not form a constituent. Prefixing *non-* is a syntactic operation that affects nominals. The bracketing in *all nonstudents* is uncontroversially taken to be $[_{\text{Det}}$ all $[_{\text{N}}$ nonstudents$]]$. Thus, *all non-* cannot plausibly be regarded as a complex determiner.

Here is another example of a nonconservative potential determiner:

(68) $\text{D}_3(Y) = \{X \subseteq U : X \subseteq Y\}$

It is easy to see that D_3 is not conservative. By the definition of D_3, $X \cap Y \in \text{D}_3(Y)$ is the case iff $X \cap Y \subseteq Y$. By the logic of set theory, this is always true, and it by no means entails that $X \subseteq Y$ (which is contingent). Since in general $X \cap Y \subseteq Y$ holds whether or not $X \subseteq Y$ holds, $X \cap Y \in \text{D}_3(Y)$ can obtain without $X \in \text{D}_3(Y)$ obtaining. Thus conservativity fails in the right-to-left direction in terms of (64). Now the interesting thing about D_3 is that English has a word that expresses exactly what D_3 does. The word is *only*. The truth conditions of (69*a*), for example, appear to be just the truth conditions given in (69*b*) and informally in (69*c*):

(69) *a.* Only students smoke.
b. $[\![\text{smoke}']\!] \in \text{D}_3([\![\text{student}']\!])$ iff $[\![\text{smoke}']\!] \subseteq [\![\text{student}']\!]$
c. The set of smokers is a subset of the set of students.

If the meaning of *only* as it occurs in structures like (69*a*) is characterized by the nonconservative function D_3, then the proposed universal in (66) makes a sharp prediction: *only* cannot be a determiner, it cannot belong to the category Det. And in fact it does not appear to belong to this category. For example, determiners cannot cooccur with pronouns or proper names, while *only* can:

(70) *a.* *Every/some/the/many Pavarotti smokes.
b. Only he/Pavarotti smokes.

Moreover, *only*, unlike determiners, is able to modify a wide variety of syntactic categories, as illustrated below:

(71) *a.* Pavarotti only sleeps. (VP)
b. Pavarotti sleeps only with his teddy bear. (PP)
c. Pavarotti sings only loudly. (Adv)
d. Pavarotti is the only singer that I admire. ($\bar{\text{N}}$)

In fact, *only* appears to be basically an adverbial that can be semantically construed as a cross-categorial operator (in the same sense in which *and* is cross-categorial).[5]

This state of affairs is interesting, we think. There is a wide variety of logically conceivable nonconservative determiner meanings. Some of these potential determiner meanings are so natural that human languages have specific ways of expressing them. But human languages do *not* appear able to express them *as* determiners, as members of the syntactic category Det. Thus the universal in (66) seems to constitute a substantive, empirically falsifiable claim about the structure of natural language. Such a claim could not even be stated properly if we didn't have the notion of a generalized quantifier and the truth-conditional and model-theoretic apparatus within which such a notion can be construed. If we lacked such an apparatus, we could not identify a nontrivial empirical property of natural language.

One might wonder why things should be this way. Why does the universal in (66) hold? Why are there only conservative determiners? As it turns out, a rather interesting answer to these questions stems directly from the general perspective that we are adopting. Imagine starting out with just *every* and *some* as basic determiners. Then imagine building complex determiners out of the basic ones using essentially just negation, conjunction, and disjunction (the Boolean operations defined on the set of determiners as in (36)). What set of determiners do we obtain? A theorem has been proved that shows that we obtain *exactly* the set of conservative determiners.[6]

Let us restate this in slightly more precise terms. Let CONS be the set of conservative determiners, the set that contains all and only the determiners that satisfy conservativity. Now let us recursively define another set, call it D*, as follows:

(72) *a.* some′, every′ $\in \mathrm{D}^*$
b. If A, B are in D*, then $[\neg A], [A \wedge B], [A \vee B], A_B \in \mathrm{D}^*$.

Here $\neg$, $\wedge$, $\vee$ are defined as in (36), and for any C, $C' \subseteq U$, $C' \in A_B(C)$ iff $C' \in A(B \cap C)$. The notation A_B thus simply introduces adjectival restrictions in determiners. For example, "$\text{some}'_{\text{blond}'}(\text{student}')(\text{smoke}')$" means that some blond student smokes. It can be proved that for finite universes, $D^* = \textsc{cons}$.

So by means of Boolean operations we can define only conservative determiners. Furthermore, *any* conservative determiner can be defined out of *every* and *some* in terms of iterated applications of Boolean operations. This suggests that the conservativity universal (66) must be linked in nonaccidental ways to the Boolean structure that permeates semantics.

Here is one way in which such a link might be realized. The category Det is the category that mostly expresses quantification. That is, it is a "logical" category (what, perhaps inappropriately, traditional grammarians would call a "closed-class" or "functional" category). Natural language expresses as determiners only functions that have a Boolean structure. If we are mentally endowed with cross-categorial Boolean functors as the basic combinatorial tool of our capacity for concept formation, it makes sense that we find in the category Det (a logical category par excellence) only those functions that such a capacity delivers to us. This, it should be noted, does not constrain *what* we can express but only *how* we can express it.

Even if this speculation turns out ultimately to be wrong, the result described above still provides a strong connection between conservativity and Boolean structure. The fact that we find in Det only conservative determiners must correlate in some fundamental way with the Boolean character of natural language semantics.

Exercise 4 For each of the following sentences, give its LF, its PC_{GQ} translation, and its model-theoretic interpretation. In (1) we give an example.

(1) *a.* John eats every fish.

b. LF

$[_S\ [\text{every fish}]_1 [_S\ \text{John eats}\ e_1]]$

c. PC_{GQ} translation

$\text{every}'(\text{fish}')(\lambda x_1[\text{eat}'(j, x_1)])$

d. Model-theoretic interpretation

$\{u \in U : [\![\text{eat}'(j, x_1)]\!]^{M,g[u/x_1]} = 1\} \in \{X \subseteq U : [\![\text{fish}']\!]^{M,g} \subseteq X\}$

(2) John pets a cat.

(3) John likes the cat that he pets.

Consider next the following example:

(4) *a.* Every man and a woman smoke.
b. PC_{GQ} translation
$[\text{every}'(\text{man}') \wedge \text{a}'(\text{woman}')](\text{smoke}')$
c. Model-theoretic interpretation
$[\![\text{smoke}']\!]^{M,g} \in \{X \subseteq U : [\![\text{man}']\!]^{M,g} \subseteq X\}$
$\cap \{X \subseteq U : [\![\text{woman}']\!]^{M,g} \cap X \neq \emptyset\}$
d. Reduction steps
$[\![\text{smoke}']\!]^{M,g} \in \{X \subseteq U : [\![\text{man}']\!]^{M,g} \subseteq X$ and
$[\![\text{woman}']\!]^{M,g} \cap X \neq \emptyset\}$
$[\![\text{man}']\!]^{M,g} \subseteq [\![\text{smoke}']\!]^{M,g}$
$[\![\text{woman}']\!]^{M,g} \cap [\![\text{smoke}']\!]^{M,g} \neq \emptyset$

For the following sentences give their translations into PC_{GQ}, their model-theoretic interpretations, and their reduction steps, as above.

(5) John and the woman smoke.

(6) John likes a cat or a dog that sings.

---

5 Concluding Remarks

In the present chapter we have introduced a new way of dealing with quantified expressions. The key to this new approach is the introduction of a more complex semantic category, the category of generalized quantifiers (sets of sets). This approach enables us to do a number of things. First, it provides us with a compositional semantics for NPs, which appears to be impossible on a standard first-order approach (such as the one we have in PC). Second, it allows us to bring out the truly cross-categorial nature of logical words, such as *and* or *or*. Third, it enables us to come up with simple and precise classificatory criteria for NPs that allow us to characterize, perhaps optimally, the distribution of negative polarity items. And fourth, it enables us to offer an explanation for a substantive universal characteristic of natural language determiners. All of the above results are only a small sample of the work currently being pursued in this area of semantics.

We are interested here more in a general point that stems from the considerations above than in this or that specific result. The truth-conditional and model-theoretic approach to meaning we have presented is not just an exercise in applied logic. It has real empirical bite and a profound relevance for linguistic theory. Without it, it would seem, there are nontrivial properties of language that we would just miss. The present kind of semantics thus seems capable of contributing in a fundamental way to the attempt to characterize what a human language is. Such a semantics might well be limited in its scope. It might well need to be put in a broader perspective and perhaps changed in fundamental ways. But it has empirical payoffs that linguistic theory cannot disregard. Truth-conditional semantics is here to stay.[7]

Appendix Set-Theoretic Notation and Concepts

This appendix provides a brief and highly selective introduction to the basic set-theoretic concepts, terminology, and notation assumed in the text.

1 Sets and Set Membership

A *set* is a collection of entities of any kind. The *members* of a set need not share any properties.

A set can be finite: the set of people in room 220, Morrill Hall, Cornell University, at 2 P.M. on Tuesday, April 20, 1999. A set can be infinite: the set of integers greater than one million.

A finite set can in principle be specified by *enumerating* or *listing* its members, for example, the set consisting of Orwell's *1984*, the square root of 2, Noam Chomsky, and the muffin Sally McConnell-Ginet ate for breakfast on Sunday, September 4, 1988. This set can be designated as in (1):

(1) {*1984*, Noam Chomsky, $\sqrt{2}$, Sally's breakfast muffin for 9/4/88}

When we use the notation in (1), the order in which things are listed inside the curly brackets makes no difference. So (1), (2*a*), and (2*b*) all refer to the same set.

(2) *a.* {Noam Chomsky, *1984*, $\sqrt{2}$, Sally's breakfast muffin for 9/4/88}
b. {*1984*, $\sqrt{2}$, Noam Chomsky, Sally's breakfast muffin for 9/4/88}

Some sets can be specified by *description:* the set of all redwood trees chopped down in California during 1984. This set can be designated as in (3):

(3) $\{x : x$ is a redwood tree chopped down in California during 1984}

A minor notational variant is to use a vertical bar instead of a colon when designating a set descriptively. Hence, we can designate the set in (3) as in (4):

(4) $\{x \mid x$ is a redwood tree chopped down in California during 1984$\}$

A set is completely defined by its members, the entities that belong to it. Different descriptions that happen to specify the same entities thus specify the same set. For example, as the authors of this book were the only semanticists at Cornell during 1986/1987, each of the three expressions in (5) designates the same set.

(5) *a.* {Gennaro Chierchia, Sally McConnell-Ginet}
b. $\{x : x$ is one of the authors of *Meaning and Grammar*$\}$
c. $\{x : x$ was a semanticist at Cornell during 1986/1987$\}$

This notion of set is *extensional:* only the members of a set matter and not how they are chosen or identified. If two sets have the same members they are the same entity. *Properties*, on the other hand, are intensional: two properties can well be true of the very same objects and yet be distinct; consider the properties of being bought and being sold. We sometimes, however, identify properties with extensional sets.

A set may contain other sets as its members. For example, $\{\{a, b\}, c\}$ has two members: c and the set $\{a, b\}$.

Below are some notations and their definitions:

$a \in P$ The element a is a *member* of set P or *belongs* to P. For example, $j \in \{x : x$ is a linguist$\} = j$ belongs to the set of linguists; $j \in \{j, a\} = j$ belongs to the set consisting of j and a.

$a \notin P$ The element a is *not* a member of set P or does not belong to P. For example, $m \notin \{x : x$ is an actor$\} = m$ does not belong to the set of actors, and $m \notin \{a, m\} = m$ does not belong to the set consisting of m and a (which is false).

$A = B$ Where A and B both designate sets, this says that they are *identical*. This happens just in case whenever $a \in A$, then $a \in B$ and whenever $b \in B$, then $b \in A$. This is the basic *identity condition* for sets. Two sets are said to be *disjoint* if they have no members in common.

$\{a\}$ *A unit set* or *singleton set* to which only a belongs. For example, $\{x : x$ has resigned the U.S. presidency while in office$\} =$ {Nixon}, and $\{1\} =$ the set that contains just the number 1. Note that $\{a\} \neq a$. Nixon is different from the set of those who have resigned; he simply happens to be the sole member of that set at the time of writing.

$\varnothing$ The *empty set* or *null set*. The set containing no elements. Note that there is only one such set. The set of female United States presidents (as of 1999) is the same as the set of males who have won two Nobel prizes in the sciences (as of 1999). Each has the same members, namely none.

$P \subseteq R$ The set P is a *subset* of R or is *included in* R. This means that every member of P is also a member of R. For example, the set of U.S. Senators (P) is a subset of the U.S. population over 30 (R); $\{a, b, c\} \subseteq \{a, b, c, l, m\}$ = the set that contains a, b, and c is a subset of the set that contains a, b, c, l, and m; $\{a, b\} \subseteq \{a, b\}$ = the set that contains a and b is a subset of itself.

$P \subset R$ The set P is a *proper subset* of R or is *properly included* in R. This means that $P \subseteq R$ and $P \neq R$, that is, that all members of P also belong to R but R has at least one member that does not belong to P. The last subset example in the previous definition is not a proper subset; the other are.

$P \not\subseteq R$ The set P is *not included* in R; there is at least one member of P that does not belong to R. For example, the set of mathematicians (P) is not included in the set of men (R), because some mathematicians are not men, and $\{a, b\} \not\subseteq \{a, c, d\}$ = the set that contains a and b is not included in the set that contains a, c, and d, because b is in the former but not the latter set.

$P \cup R$ The *union* of P and R (also read "P union R") or the *join* of P and R. The union of P and R is a set that contains all the elements of P and all the elements of R. If something is either a member of P or a member of R, then it is a member of $P \cup R$. The set consisting of the union of Italians (P) and syntacticians (R) consists of those belonging to either group. Pavarotti is an Italian, so he is included, and Chomsky is a syntactician, so he is included. To give a further example, $\{a, b\} \cup \{a, c, d\} = \{a, b, c, d\}$. Note that $P \cup R = R$ if and only if $P \subseteq R$. (Convince yourself of this by using the definitions.)

$\bigcup P$ Where P is a set of sets, $\bigcup P$, the *generalized union over* P, is the set that contains all the elements of each member of P. That is, $\bigcup P = \{x\text{: for some } B \in P, x \in B\}$. For example, $\bigcup\{\{a, b\}, \{c\}, \{b, d\}\} = \{a, b, c, d\}$, and $\bigcup\{\{a\}, \{b\}, \varnothing\} = \{a, b\}$.

$P \cap R$ The *intersection* of P and R (also read "P intersection R") or the *meet* of P and R. The intersection of P and R is a set whose members contains all and only the elements shared by P and R. If something is a member of P and also a member of R, then it is a member of $P \cap R$. For example, the set consisting of Italians (P)

who are also syntacticians (R). Pavarotti is not in the set, because he is not a syntactician. Chomsky is not a member, because he is not an Italian. But Luigi Rizzi does belong because he is both Italian and a syntactician. To give two further examples, $\{a, b, c\} \cap \{f, g, c\} = \{c\}$, and $\{a, b\} \cap \{c\} = \varnothing$. Note that $P \cap R = P$ if and only if $P \subseteq R$, and that $P \cap R = \varnothing$ if and only if P and R are disjoint. (Again, use the definitions to show this.)

$\bigcap P$ Where P is a set of sets, $\bigcap P$, the *generalized intersection over* P, is the set that contains the elements that belong to every member of P. That is, $\bigcap P = \{x\text{: for every } A \in P, x \in A\}$. Here are two examples: $\bigcap\{\{a, b, c, d\}, \{a, b, d\}, \{a, d\}\} = \{a, d\}$, and $\bigcap\{\{a, b\}, \{c, d\}\} = \varnothing$.

$P - R$ The *difference* of P and R or the *complement* of R relative to P. This set consists of those members of P that are not also members of R. For example, the set of linguists (P) who are not French (R). This set contains Luigi Burzio, who belongs to the set of linguists, but not N. Ruwet, who belongs to the set of French linguists. Here are some other examples: $\{a, b, c\} - \{a, b\} = \{c\}$, and $\{a, b, c\} - \{a, d\} = \{b, c\}$, and $\{a, b, c\} - \{d\} = \{a, b, c\}$. Note that $P - R = \varnothing$ if and only if $P \subseteq R$. (See the appropriate definitions.)

R^- The *complement* of R consists of everything that does not belong to R relative to some understood *domain* or *universe of discourse* D; that is, $R^- = D - R$. For example, if the domain D is the set of dogs and R is the set of spaniels, then $D - R =$ all non-spaniel dogs (highland terriers, golden retrievers, mongrels, etc.). Again, relative to the set of integers N, $\{x : x \text{ is odd}\}^- = \{x : x \text{ is even}\}$.

Union, intersection, and complementation are all *operations* that take two sets and form a third set. Generalized union and generalized intersection take a family of sets and form a set.

2 Power Sets and Cartesian Products

The notion of power set is defined as follows.

$\mathscr{P}(A)$ The *power set* of A is the set of all subsets of A. If A contains n elements, then $\mathscr{P}(A)$ contains 2^n elements. The set A itself and the null set are always members of $\mathscr{P}(A)$. For example, let $A = \{\text{Chris}, 1\}$. Then $\mathscr{P}(A)$ is $\{\{\text{Chris}, 1\}, \{\text{Chris}\}, \{1\}, \varnothing\}$. Also, $\mathscr{P}(\{a, b, c\}) = \{\{a, b, c\}, \{a, b\}, \{a, c\}, \{b, c\}, \{a\}, \{b\}, \{c\}, \varnothing\}$.

From the definition of power set it follows that $A \subseteq B$ iff $A \in \mathscr{P}(B)$.

Let us now distinguish sets from ordered structures.

$\{a_1, \ldots, a_n\}$ This designates a *set* of n elements if each of $a_1, \ldots, a_n$ is different. If some elements appear more than once in the designation of the set, then the set has fewer than n elements: what matters for set identity is not how the elements are listed but which individual elements are listed. For example, $\{a, b, c\} = \{a, a, b, b, b, c, c, c, c\}$. Repetition is redundant, since the identity of a set depends only on which elements belong to it. For the same reason, it does not matter in what order the elements are enumerated: $\{a, b, c\} = \{b, c, a\}$.

$\langle a_1, \ldots, a_n \rangle$ This designates an *ordered n-tuple*. Here the same element may recur nonredundantly, for order is critical. The identity of an n-tuple depends on the identity of elements in each of the distinct n positions. This means that $\langle a_1, \ldots, a_n \rangle = \langle b_1, \ldots, b_n \rangle$ if and only if $a_1 = b_1$ and $a_2 = b_2$ and ... and $a_n = b_n$. This is the identity condition for ordered n-tuples. For instance, $\langle a, b \rangle \neq \langle b, a \rangle$, and $\langle a, a \rangle \neq \langle a, a, a \rangle$.

Although intuitively we can think of distinct positions and elements that fill each position (with the same element in principle able to fill more than one position), it is possible to define ordered n-tuples with only set-theoretic notions and without introducing order directly. If, for example, we identify $\langle a, b \rangle$ with $\{\{a\}, \{a, b\}\}$ and $\langle a, b, c \rangle$ with $\{\{a\}, \{a, b\}, \{a, b, c\}\}$ and so on, then we can use our identity conditions for sets to show that we have reproduced the identity conditions for ordered pairs and triples and so on. We mention the possibility of this reduction just to indicate why ordered n-tuples are considered set-theoretic objects. It is because they can be regarded as sets of a special kind.

Let us now turn to the notion of a Cartesian product.

$A \times B$ The *Cartesian product* of A and B is the set of all ordered pairs whose first member belongs to A and whose second member belongs to B. Thus, $A \times B = \{\langle x, y \rangle : x \in A \text{ and } y \in B\}$. The Cartesian product of the set of real numbers with itself is used to define points on a plane; the first number usually represents the horizontal axis, and the second the vertical. As an example of a Cartesian product we have $\{a, b\} \times \{1, 2\} = \{\langle a, 1 \rangle, \langle a, 2 \rangle, \langle b, 1 \rangle, \langle b, 2 \rangle\}$.

More generally, if $A_1, \ldots, A_n$ are sets, $A_1 \times \cdots \times A_n$ (the Cartesian product of $A_1, \ldots, A_n$) is the set that contains all the ordered n-tuples $\langle a_1, \ldots, a_n \rangle$ such that $a_1 \in A_1$ and ... and $a_n \in A_n$.

The power set of a Cartesian product $A \times B$ will be the set containing all the sets of ordered pairs that one can build out of A and B. In symbols, $a \in \mathscr{P}(A \times B)$ iff $a \subseteq A \times B$.

3 Relations

Sets of ordered n-tuples and Cartesian products are useful in characterizing relations from a set-theoretic perspective. In set theory a two-place or binary extensional *relation* is a set of ordered pairs, a three-place or ternary relation is a set of ordered triples, and in general an n-place or n-ary relation is a set of ordered n-tuples. A one-place or unary relation is just a set of individuals.

Let A and B be two sets. A binary relation R between members of A and members of B will be a subset of the Cartesian product $A \times B$. In symbols, $R \subseteq A \times B$. Another way of expressing this is to say that a binary relation R between members of A and members of B is a member of the power set of $A \times B$. In symbols, $R \in \mathscr{P}(A \times B)$.

The definition above can be extended to n-place relations. If $A_1, \ldots, A_n$ are sets, an n-place relation K among $A_1, \ldots, A_n$ will be a subset of $A_1 \times \cdots \times A_n$ (that is, $K \subseteq A_1 \times \cdots \times A_n$).

Two-place or binary relations are particularly important. If R is a two-place relation between sets A and B, the set of elements from which the first members of the pairs in relation R are drawn is the *domain* of R, and the second members are drawn from the *range* or *codomain* of R. Relations are often notated as follows: aRb. This is just another notation that says the pair $\langle a, b\rangle$ belongs to relation R; that is, $\langle a, b\rangle \in R$. We often read this as "a stands in relation R to b." We can think of the incomplete VP *is the author of* as designating a binary relation that holds between an author and something she or he wrote, as designating the set of ordered pairs whose first member is an author and whose second is something the author wrote. Call this set A. Then $A = \{\langle$Chomsky, *Aspects*$\rangle$, $\langle$Alcott, *Little Women*$\rangle$, $\langle$Hollander, "The Coiled Alizarine"$\rangle$, $\langle$Chomsky, "Remarks on Nominalization"$\rangle, \ldots\}$. Hence, $\langle$Austen, *Emma*$\rangle \in A$ means that Austen is the author of *Emma*; $\langle$Shakespeare, *Syntactic Structures*$\rangle \notin A$ means that Shakespeare is not the author of *Syntactic Structures*. Generally, $\langle a, b\rangle \in A$ means that a is the author of b. We can think of the incomplete VP *was written by* as designating the set of ordered pairs whose first member is a piece of writing and whose second member is the person who wrote the work in question. Call this set B.

Then $B = \{\langle$*Aspects*, Chomsky$\rangle$, $\langle$*Little Women*, Alcott$\rangle$, $\langle$"The Coiled Alizarine," Hollander$\rangle$, $\langle$"Remarks on Nominalization," Chomsky$\rangle, \ldots\}$. Hence, $\langle$*On Raising*, Postal$\rangle \in B$ means that *On Raising* was written by Postal. More generally, $\langle a, b\rangle \in B$ means that a was written by b.

A binary relation R is the *converse* of another such relation S if whenever $\langle a, b\rangle$ belongs to R (whenever aRb), then $\langle b, a\rangle$ belongs to S (bSa). As defined above, *is the author of* (relation A) is the converse of *was written by* (relation B).

A relation R is *reflexive* iff every element in the domain bears the relation to itself, that is, iff for all a in the domain, $\langle a, a\rangle \in R$ (aRa). For example, *being the same age as* designates a reflexive relation. Set inclusion is a reflexive relation between sets (for every set $A, A \subseteq A$), whereas proper set inclusion is not (for every set A, it is not the case that $A \subset A$). A relation that is not reflexive is *nonreflexive*. The transitive verb *like* is associated with a *nonreflexive* relation, since individuals do not always like themselves (though some do). A relation is *irreflexive* if nothing stands in that relation to itself. Proper inclusion is irreflexive since no set is properly included in itself. In most set theories, membership is irreflexive (no set belongs to itself).

A relation R is *transitive* iff whenever aRb and bRc (or $\langle a, b\rangle \in R$ and $\langle b, c\rangle \in R$), then aRc (or $\langle a, c\rangle \in R$). Both ordinary set inclusion and proper set inclusion are transitive relations; *being older than* also designates a transitive relation. A relation that is not transitive is *nontransitive*. The membership relation between elements and the sets to which they belong is nontransitive. For example, Mary might belong to the Task Force for Battered Women (TFBW), and the TFBW might belong to the United Way, but it does not follow that Mary belongs to the United Way. Again, the transitive verb *like* designates a relation that is nontransitive. Joan may like Linda, and Linda may like Bill, but we may find that Joan does not like Bill. If R is a relation such that whenever aRb and bRc, it is not the case that aRc ($\langle a, c\rangle \notin R$), then R is said to be *intransitive*. For example, *being the mother of* is associated with an intransitive relation (if we confine our attention to biological motherhood). (Note that a transitive verb need not designate a transitive relation, nor is intransitivity of relations associated with intransitive verbs. Grammatical and mathematical terminology must be kept distinct here.)

A relation R is *symmetric* if whenever aRb ($\langle a, b\rangle \in R$), then bRa ($\langle b, a\rangle \in R$). The relation *being five miles from* is symmetric. A relation that is not symmetric is *nonsymmetric. Being the sister of* is a nonsymmetric relation, since Joan may be the sister of Lee and Lee may be the brother (not sister) of Joan. A relation is *asymmetric* if it is never the case both that aRb and bRa. *Being the mother of* is an asymmetric relation, unless we go beyond standard biological parenthood (which allows all sorts of more complex scenarios: my (step) daughter might marry my father and then become my (step) mother, making me my own grandmother). Proper set inclusion and set membership are asymmetric.

An *equivalence relation* is a relation that is reflexive, transitive, and symmetric. An equivalence relation R *partitions* a set A into *equivalence classes*, which are *disjoint* and whose union is identical with A. For each a in the domain of R, let $S(a) = \{b \in A : aRb\}$. Then $S(a)$ is the equivalence class to which a belongs. *Being the same age as* is an equivalence relation, and each equivalence class consists of a *cohort:* those who are some particular age.

Relation R is *one-one* if each element in the domain is paired with exactly one element in the range and vice versa. The relation between individuals and their fingerprints is thought to be one-one. Relation R is *one-many* if some members of the domain are paired with more than one member of the range. *Being the mother of* is associated with a one-many relation, since some mothers have several children. Relation R is *many-one* if different members of the domain can be paired with the same member of the range. *Being the child of* is associated with a many-one relation, since sometimes several children have the same parent. A relation is *many-many* if it is both many-one and one-many. *Has visited* designates a many-many relation between people and cities, since a person may visit many cities and a particular city may be visited by many people.

4 Functions

A two-place relation R is a *function* just in case any element a in the domain of R is the first member of only one ordered pair, that is, just in case if aRb and aRc, then $b = c$. A function is a relation that is not one-many but either one-one or many-one. The relation *is the author of* that we discussed in the last section is not a function: it holds between Chomsky and *Syntactic Structures* and also between Chomsky and "Remarks on Nominalization." That is putting Chomsky in the first slot of "____ is the author of ____" does not uniquely determine a value to fill in the second slot. Contrast this with its converse, *is written by* (we restrict our attention to single-authored works). Here once the first slot is filled in, there is a single value for the second slot. In other words, *was written by* can be associated with a function that assigns books, essays, poems, etc., to the individual who wrote them. The expression *was born in* designates a function that assigns a unique year to each person, the year in which the person was born. (Of course, the same year will occur as second member of different ordered pairs, since many different people are born in a single year.)

The first member of an ordered pair in a function is its *argument*; arguments belong to the domain of the function. The second member of an ordered pair in a function is its *value*; values belong to the function's range.

To indicate that $\langle x, y \rangle$ belongs to the function f, we often write $f(x) = y$. A function of this type is a one-place function, for it takes only one argument. Thus a one-place function is a one-one or a many-one two-place relation. Examples of such functions are the following:

was-born-in(Alan) = 1962
was-born-in(Blanche) = 1897
the-height-of(Sally) = 5 feet, 4 inches
the-senior-senator-from(N.Y.) = Patrick Moynihan (as of spring 1999)

When a function has a small domain we often represent it in tabular form. So, for example, if the domain is {Alan, Lisa, Greg} and the function is that expressed by x's *spouse*, we might display the pairings in an array:

$$\begin{bmatrix} \text{Alan} & \rightarrow & \text{Nancy} \\ \text{Lisa} & \rightarrow & \text{Bob} \\ \text{Greg} & \rightarrow & \text{Jill} \end{bmatrix}$$

This is just an alternative way of representing x's spouse(Alan) = Alan's spouse = Nancy, etc.

By means of our definitions, we can designate the same function in different ways; the notion of function is extensional like the notion of set that helps define it. Suppose that $f_1(x) = x^2 - 1$ and $f_2(x) = (x - 1)(x + 1)$. We have specified f_1 and f_2 using different rules for determing the value of the function, but the rules yield exactly the same value for any numerical argument. Thus $f_1 = f_2$; that is, we have not two functions but only one.

Some helpful notation is the following:

$f : A \to B$ In words, *f maps A*, its domain, *onto B*, its range.
B^A The set of functions with domain A and range B; that is, the set of functions from A to B.

From the above definition it follows that $(C^B)^A$ is the set of all functions from A onto C^B. Thus a member g of $(C^B)^A$ is a function-valued function. For any $a \in A, g(a)$ is a function from B onto C, or for any $b \in B, g(a)(b) \in C$. This should not be confused with $C^{(B^A)}$, which is the set of all functions from B^A to C. That is, a function h in $C^{(B^A)}$ will map each function $d \in B^A$ onto a member of C; that is, $h(d) \in C$.

A *complete function* assigns values to every member of its domain; every member of the domain is a first member of an ordered pair belonging to the function. A function that fails to assign values to some members of its domain is a *partial function*. Generally, when reference is made simply to functions, it is complete functions that are meant.

Any set can be associated with a particular distinguished function called its *characteristic function* or its *membership function* relative to a given universe or domain D. The characteristic function of A relative to D is the function μ_A with domain D such that $\mu_A(x) = 1$ iff $x \in A$ and $\mu_A(x) = 0$ iff $x \notin A$.

It is conventional to choose $\{0, 1\}$ as the range of characteristic functions, although any two-membered set will do the job. What is crucial is that the specification of a set defines a unique characteristic function and the specification of a complete function from universe D to $\{0, 1\}$ defines a unique subset of D. The characteristic function sorts the members of D into those that belong to A and those that do not. The fact that we can go from a set to a unique function and from a function to a unique set allows us for certain purposes to identify sets with their characteristic functions.

The characteristic functions associated with the members of $\mathscr{P}(A)$, the power set of set A, are just the family $\{0, 1\}^A$. Any characteristic function of a subset of A belongs to this family, and any member of this family is the characteristic function of some subset of A.

So far we have considered only one-place (unary) functions. However, we can extend our approach to n-place functions (functions that take n arguments). An n-place function g from $A_1, \ldots, A_n$ to B is an $(n+1)$-place relation such that for any $a_1 \in A_1, \ldots, a_n \in A_n$ and any $b, b' \in B$, if $\langle a_1, \ldots, a_n, b\rangle \in g$ and $\langle a_1, \ldots, a_n, b'\rangle \in g$, then $b = b'$. We write $g(a_1, \ldots, a_n) = b$ for $\langle a_1, \ldots, a_n, b \rangle \in g$. For example, addition over the positive integers is a two-place function mapping two numbers onto their sum. It is the infinite set $\{\langle x, y, z \rangle : x$ and y are positive integers and $z = x + y\} = \{\langle 1, 1, 2 \rangle, \langle 1, 2, 3 \rangle, \langle 2, 1, 3 \rangle, \ldots\}$.

It turns out that n-place functions can always be reduced to the successive application of one-place functions. The reduction is often called *currying* a function, in recognition of logician H. B. Curry, who adapted the technique from M. Schönfinkel, in whose honor Kratzer and Heim (1998) speak of *schönfinkelization*. The basic idea is simple, and we will illustrate it using the addition function that maps any two integers onto their sum. That is, we begin with $f(x, y) = x + y$. The trick is to let functions assign other functions as values. So for any x, let $f'(x)$ be the function that when applied to y yields $f(x, y) = x + y$. In other words $f'(x)(y) = f(x, y) = x + y$. Exactly which function is assigned as $f'(x)$ depends, of course, on the argument x. So if $x = 2$, $f'(2)$ is the function that when applied to argument y yields the value $2 + y$; i.e., $f'(2)(y) = 2 + y$ and thus $f'(2)(3) = [2 + y](3) = 2 + 3 = f(2, 3)$. If $x = 4$ then $f'(4)$ is the function that when applied to argument y yields the value $4 + y$; i.e., $f'(4)(y) = 4 + y$ and thus $f'(4)(2) = [4 + y](2) = 4 + 2$. Or we can take the second argument first and let $f''(y)$ be the function that when applied to x yields $f(x, y) = x + y$. In this case, we have $f''(y)(x) = x + y = f(x, y)$. So $f''(2)(x) = x + 2$ and $f''(2)(3) = [x + 2](3) = 3 + 2 = f(3, 2)$. And so on.

5 Boolean Algebras

Finally, we need to define the algebraic notion of a *Boolean algebra*, which we mention at several points in the text. An algebra is just a set together with operations that map an element or elements of the set onto some unique element of the same set. Boolean algebras have three operations: two binary operations (which we will denote with $\cap$ and $\cup$) and a unary operation (denoted by $^-$). There are also two distinguished elements of the set (denoted by 1 and 0). Call the set **B**.

Then the elements of the algebra satisfy the following axioms:

(1) For any $A, B \in \mathbf{B}$,
  a. $A \cup B = B \cup A$
  b. $B \cap A = A \cap B$

This axiom says that both the binary operations are *commutative*.

(2) For any $A, B, C \in \mathbf{B}$,
   a. $A \cup (B \cup C) = (A \cup B) \cup C$
   b. $A \cap (B \cap C) = (A \cap B) \cap C$

This says that both binary operations are *associative*.

(3) For any $A, B, C \in \mathbf{B}$,
   a. $A \cup (B \cap C) = (A \cup B) \cap (A \cup C)$
   b. $A \cap (B \cup C) = (A \cap B) \cup (A \cap C)$

This says that each binary operation is *distributive* over the other.

(4) For any $A \in \mathbf{B}$, A^- is the unique element satisfying the conditions $A \cup A^- = 1$ and $A \cap A^- = 0$.

Our choice of symbols for the operations is motivated by the fact that the set-theoretic operations in a particular domain form a Boolean algebra. A nonempty set D generates a Boolean algebra as follows. Let $\mathbf{B} = \mathscr{P}(D)$, the power set of D or the set whose members are all the subsets of D. Interpret the operations as ordinary set union ($\cup$), intersection ($\cap$), and complementation ($^-$), and let $1 = D$ and $0 = \varnothing$ (the null set). The resulting structure is then a Boolean algebra. Propositional logic also forms a Boolean algebra under a suitable interpretation if we identify $\vee$ with $\cup$, $\wedge$ with $\cap$, and $\neg$ with $^-$. Intuitively, 0 and 1 correspond to falsity and truth, respectively. A bit more has to be said to make this precise, but the point is that the axioms above are indeed theorems of propositional logic.

Further easy-to-read resources for linguists with little or no formal background are Wall (1972) and Allwood, Andersson, and Dahl (1971). Partee, ter Meulen, and Wall (1990) cover a much wider range of basic mathematical material relevant for work in formal linguistics. The reader might also find it useful to consult an elementary introduction to set theory like Halmos (1960) or Stoll (1963).

Notes

Chapter 1

1. See for example, work in generalized phrase-structure grammar (GPSG) as described in Gazdar, Klein, Pullum, and Sag (1985) and related approaches, such as those outlined in Pollard and Sag (1988).
2. See van Riemsdijk and Williams (1986) for an introduction to the "principles and parameters" framework in current Chomskyan syntactic theory. Chomsky (1986), especially 3.4, discusses how parametric approaches shed new light on the structure of the human language faculty. (Chomsky 1995 and other recent work in the minimalist framework does not really use the "parameter" idea directly.) Within semantics, explicitly comparative work is more recent. Although still not very extensive, research on crosslinguistic semantics is rapidly increasing. Chierchia (1998a, 1998b) argues that parameters belong in semantic theory, whereas other recent work on crosslinguistic semantics takes a somewhat different approach to the question of universals; see, e.g., Bach et al (1995) and Bittner (1995).
3. See Chomsky (1965) for the distinction between formal and material universals of language and J. D. Fodor (1977) for an excellent account of the contributions of McCawley and others in generative semantics and more generally of semantic research in the generative tradition into the early seventies.
4. The illustration comes from Cresswell (1985, 3).
5. See esp. Grice (1975, 1978), both of which are reprinted in Grice (1989). Grice also suggested that some inferences are licensed by virtue of noninformational aspects of linguistic meaning rather than by either entailment or conversational principles; we defer discussion of these so-called *conventional implicatures* until chapter 4.
6. See Evans (1980) for detailed discussion of this issue.
7. See, for example, Higginbotham (1983).
8. See J. D. Fodor (1977) for a discussion of this essentially syntactic account of anomaly and of the observations that led linguists to explore more semantic approaches.
9. Hollander's poem, "Coiled Alizarine: For Noam Chomsky," is reprinted from John Hollander, *The Night Mirror* (Atheneum Publishers, 1971) on page 1 of Harman (1974).

Chapter 2

1. See J. A. Fodor (1975) for a discussion of the notion of a "language of thought" and its semantic relevance.
2. A clear and more extensive formulation of these criticisms can be found in Lewis (1972).
3. A problem that clearly shows the direct semantic relevance of these questions is the mass/count distinction, the semantic (and syntactic) differences between nouns like *gold, furniture, equipment*, etc. versus *boy, cat, chair*, etc. See, for example, Pelletier (1979).
4. This argument is already implicit in Frege (1892). More recent versions of it can be found in Church (1956) and Davidson (1967a). Barwise and Perry (1983) dub it "the slingshot." The argument might be a little hard to grasp at first. A full understanding of it is not a necessary prerequisite for subsequent material.

5. In contemporary philosophy of language one of the most influential proponents of this view is Donald Davidson. See, for example, Davidson (1967a, 1977).
6. A rule of the form "$A \rightarrow BC$" is to be read as "A rewrites as B followed by C." Its intuitive interpretation is roughly the following: an expression of category A can be composed of an expression of category B followed by an expression of category C.
7. The branch of logic known as proof theory can be viewed as an attempt to characterize entailment in syntactic terms. Yet proof theory is linked in several ways to *semantic* characterizations of entailment (such as the ones studied in this book). We will come back to the relation between proof theory and semantics in chapter 3.
8. On the semantics of orders and imperatives from a truth-conditional point of view, see, for example, Huntley (1984) and references therein.
9. On the semantics of questions from a truth-conditional point of view, see, for example, Karttunen (1977) and Groenendijk and Stokhof (1984) and references therein.
10. On this, see Stalnaker (1984), chapter 2.

Chapter 3

1. The notion of alphabetic variant will play a role in our discussion of VP anaphora in chapter 7. The basic idea is that when variables are bound, it will not matter which variable we happen to have chosen; thus, e.g., $\forall x_7 \exists x_3 [P(x_7) \rightarrow Q(x_3)]$ will turn out to be equivalent to $\forall x_2 \exists x_7 [P(x_2) \rightarrow Q(x_7)]$. If you can get from one formula ϕ to another formula ψ simply by changing $\forall x_n$ (or $\exists x_n$) to $\forall x_m$ ($\exists x_m$), and also changing all and only occurrences of x_n that are bound by $\forall x_n$ (or $\exists x_n$) to x_m, then ϕ and ψ are sometimes said to be immediate alphabetic variants. If you can get from ϕ to ψ by a finite series of moves, each of which takes you from a formula to an immediate alphabetic variant of that formula, then ϕ and ψ are alphabetic variants.
2. Strictly speaking, for each i, t_i is a metavariable, that is, a variable in the metalanguage that ranges over terms (individual variables and constants) of the object language. In fact, we generally use category symbols with systematic ambiguity as names of linguistic objects and as names of categories.
3. Quantificational semantics is sometimes given in terms of *sequences* of elements in the domain that specify the values of variables; the nth element of a sequence is the value assigned to the nth variable. An assignment function g determines the sequence $\langle g(x_1), g(x_2), \ldots, g(x_n), \ldots \rangle$, and given a sequence for interpreting variables, we can define an assignment function whose value for the nth variable is the nth member of the sequence.
4. There is an exception, however. A formula like $Q(x_3) \vee \neg Q(x_3)$ will be true no matter what value is assigned to x_3, since the same value must be assigned to a single variable in all its occurrences and thus the formula in question will always express a tautology.
5. Russell's (1905) quantificational approach contrasts with Frege's (1892) view of singular definite descriptions as referring expressions that presuppose the existence of a unique referent; Strawson (1950) was an influential criticism of the Russellian position and defense of the Fregean. Some authors, e.g., Peacocke (1975) and Hornsby (1977), have maintained that there is an ambiguity between referring and quantificational definite NPs. Kadmon (1987) and Neale (1990) contain extensive discussions of the issues involved.
6. Adopting a notation with restricted quantifiers does not suffice to make *most* first-order definable. To interpret *most*, we can no longer quantify just over individuals but must essentially quantify over higher-order entities like sets. On this, see, for example, Barwise and Cooper (1981) and our chapter 9.
7. This example is from Hirschbühler (1982).
8. The labels *deep* (D) and *surface* (S) are kept in current transformational theories mostly for historical reasons; their role in the theory has changed significantly since their original appearance on the linguistic scene.
9. We are using the prescriptively "incorrect" *them* as a gender-neutral singular pronoun. As Matossian (1997) showed, *they/them* is the overwhelming preference in spoken American

English, even from well educated speakers. It has also been used by such writers as William Shakespeare, Jane Austen, and George Eliot.

10. According to some, for example, May (1985), LF does not disambiguate scope completely but merely constrains admissible scope configurations.
11. Our thanks to Fred Landman for pointing this example out to us. The relation of pronouns to antecedents in disjunctions raises many complicated issues (see Simons 1998 for discussion).
12. Universal quantifiers can bind across conjuncts only under quite special circumstances. See Roberts (1987) for a discussion.
13. Influential work on this topic includes Cooper (1979), Evans (1980), Kamp (1981), and Heim (1982).
14. These phenomena have been widely discussed in the transformational literature. A classic paper is Lasnik (1976). Also see Bach and Partee (1980), Chomsky (1981), and Reinhart (1983a, 1983b).
15. See also Reinhart and Reuland (1993).

Chapter 4

1. Frege (1918), p. 5 in the English translation.
2. But see also Huntley (1984), where an analysis of imperatives within a truth-conditional framework is presented.
3. Austin's thumbnail characterizations here and below can be found in Austin (1962) at the beginning of lecture 9, 2nd ed., p. 109.
4. Searle noted this in a lecture at the 1987 Summer Institute of the Linguistic Society of America, Stanford University.
5. See also chapter 3 of Searle (1969).
6. Searle (1965) in Martinich (1985, 128).
7. Grice's theory of conversational implicature was first presented in the William James Lectures at Harvard in 1967. Although much of the material has been in print for some time (see Grice 1968, 1969, 1975, 1978), the complete lectures did not appeared until 1989, along with an introduction written some twenty years later. This volume also includes related papers by Grice and an epilogue that gives a retrospective view of his overall philosophical program.
8. Horn and Levinson made their endorsement in their course on pragmatics at the 1987 Summer Institute of the Linguistic Society of America, Stanford University.

Chapter 5

1. Henceforth we will often use *world* instead of *world-time pair or circumstance* when no confusion results.
2. Kamp (1971) and Dowty (1979) are among the early applications of possible world semantics to questions of temporal semantics; many others have built on Kamp's and Dowty's work.
3. Chap. 8, sec. 2, briefly discusses some manifestations of aspect in English, but a substantial treatment of this topic is beyond the scope of our text.
4. Actually, it has been argued that heads can only move to higher *head* positions (see, e.g., Travis 1984). In this case, the head of T would wind up in, say, the complementizer position (much like what happens with so called subject-auxiliary inversion in English yes-no questions).
5. Strictly speaking (32c) should be something like $[_{TP}\ \text{NP T VP}] \Rightarrow [\text{T}\ [_{TP}\ \text{NP}\ [_{\bar{T}}\ \text{VP}]]]$
6. Hornstein (1990) introduced the Reichenbach framework to many linguists; Dowty (1982), Hinrichs (1986), Kamp and Reyle (1993), and others develop explicit truth-conditional instantiations of the general reference-time idea.

7. See Zucchi (forthcoming) for a general overview and critical discussion of this literature.
8. This section is based mainly on Kratzer (1981). The version of her theory that we present here is highly simplified and doesn't convey the coverage and depth of her analysis.
9. Strictly speaking, this takes us beyond first-order logic. There are a number of options in this connection, but we cannot get into a discussion of them here.
10. This argument in favour of the predicative view was formulated originally in Chierchia (1984), where it was construed as an argument that IGs are syntactically VPs, rather than clauses. Further arguments in favor of the predicative view of IGs (based on so called "de se" phenomena) were put forth in Chierchia (1989). For a different view of these phenomena, see, e.g., Higginbotham (1992). On control structures in general, see Dowty (1985) and the papers in Larson et al. (1992) and the references therein.
11. A classical point of reference in connection with this line of thought is Davidson (1969). We should add, however, that the positions we outline here are just pedagogical fictions (they are not held, in the simplistic form we provide, by anyone in particular).
12. See J. A. Fodor (1978, 1981). But see also the caveat in note 6.
13. See Thomason (1977).
14. Recent semantic approaches developed within discourse representation theory could be taken as following the general strategy illustrated in (101). See Asher and Kamp (1989) and Zeevat (1984). See also Larson and Segal (1995, chap. 11).
15. See also Lewis (1972), Bigelow (1978), and Cresswell (1985).

Chapter 6

1. This example is modeled on one used in Stalnaker (1974).
2. There is interesting work in model-theoretic semantics on such point-of-view expressions, for example, Cresswell (1978).
3. Many such examples are discussed in Fillmore (1975) and Bennett (1978).
4. A number of Montague's papers are collected in Montague (1974), which also contains Thomason (1974), a useful introduction to Montague's program. Classics in tense logic include Reichenbach (1947) and Prior (1967).
5. Barwise and Perry (1983) discuss this point in terms of what they call the efficiency of language, which lies in the possibility of using the same linguistic form to express different propositional contents in different contexts.
6. What *but* does is much more complex than the simple notion of contrast suggests. For more detailed analyses that make explicit links to the discourse functions of *but*, see L. Carlson (1983) and Blakemore (1989).
7. In the linguistics literature, Kempson (1975) and Wilson (1975) presented important arguments that the presupposed status of factive complements was not a matter of conventional meaning; we consider below some arguments from Stalnaker (1974) about the status of presuppositions associated with factives.
8. See Sag and Prince (1979) for an extensive bibliography of the early work. In addition to more recent works cited in the text, see also Beaver (1995, 1997), Geurts (1994), Heim (1992), and van der Sandt (1988, 1992).
9. See Stalnaker (1974) for arguments that presupposition is a fundamentally pragmatic notion in the sense of being what conversationalists take for granted.
10. Keenan (1969) is an example from the linguistics literature of a three-valued logic for accommodating presupposition failure. Supervaluations were applied to the treatment of presupposition in van Fraassen (1969). Neither kind of logic has anything to say about the way in which presupposition projection depends on discourse, which is the theme we pursue here. The approach presented below could be supplemented by either a three-valued or a supervaluational logic.
11. Assume that S and not S each entails S′. Then in every model in which S is true, S′ must be true, and in every model in which not S is true, S′ must be true. It follows, then, that S′ must be true in every model, for in every classical model either S or its negation will be true. Thus S′ must be a tautology.

Chapter 7

1. Strictly speaking, properties are intensional and we are here proceeding extensionally; the extension of a λ-term in the simplest case will be a set of entities or the characteristic function of such a set. However, the dominant practise is to use the term "property" for λ-terms and, having hereby warned the reader, we think it innocent enough to stick to that practise even in the present extensional context. We also note that it is, of course, the semantic value of the λ-abstract and not the syntactic expression itself that is a property (or the extensional equivalent thereof).
2. This only applies to (I)PC. In the framework sketched in chap. 2, sec. 3.4 (which is based on Montague's version of functional type theory) it is possible to represent VPs like *love Pavarotti* directly, without resorting to the λ-operator. Even in that framework, however, more complex VPs (such as those to be discussed in the following sections) would require something like the λ-operator.
3. The present tense under our current assumptions makes no contribution, and thus we are going to assume that PRES′ is just the identity map, that is, for any ϕ, PRES′ $\phi = \phi$.
4. In the version of F_3 we have given, we are omitting, for simplicity, modals, infinitives and gerunds. Notice, however, that in our treatment of infinitives and gerunds we relied on having abstraction in our semantics (using our informal grasp of set abstraction); we now see how that approach can be made explicit. The translation of infinitives can be set up so as to yield the following results: [PRO$_n$ to smoke]′ $= \lambda x_n[\text{smoke}'(x_n)]$
5. Relevant discussion can be found in Dowty (1979) and Thomason (1980), among other works.
6. See, for example, Partee and Rooth (1983), Keenan and Faltz (1985), and Link (1983). See the appendix for a definition of Boolean algebras.
7. This important distinction is discussed in Johnson-Laird (1983).
8. See Chomsky (1957, chap. 5), for the first discussion of the phenomenon in transformational terms and an explicit formulation of the process as he then saw it.
9. See Partee and Rooth (1983); Sag, Wasow, Gazdar, and Weisler (1985); and references therein.
10. See Partee and Rooth (1983) and references therein.
11. Alternatively, one can interpret structures of the form [John$_i$ [$_{VP}$ e_i smokes]] on a par with quantificational structures, as we did at the end of section 2.4, chapter 3. On this approach, $[\![[\text{John}_i\ [_{VP}\ e_i \text{ smokes}]]]\!]^{M,g} = 1$ iff $[\![[e_i \text{ smokes}]]\!]^{M,g[j/e_i]} = 1$, where $j = [\![\text{John}]\!]^{M,g}$.
12. The basic idea of analyzing the semantics of relative clauses this way goes back to Quine (1960).
13. The main sources for this section are Sag (1976) and Williams (1977).
14. An interpretive alternative, whereby some empty place holders are generated and then a procedure to interpret them is provided, is also viable (see, e.g., Williams 1977). We wish to stay neutral on these two alternatives and our adoption here of the deletion hypothesis is just an expository convenience.
15. Actually things wouldn't change in the elided VP if we were to pick another set of indices. For example, instead of (64*a*) we could have (i):
    (i) Frank$_3$ [e_3 [spoke to Bill about himself$_3$]]
    LF (i) amounts to an alphabetic variant of (64*a*) and is logically equivalent to it. So, in fact, the relevant LFs have to be identical up to alphabetic change of bound variables. The definition of alphabetic variance for LF mimics the one for logical languages. See Sag (1976, 101 ff.) for a discussion of the issues involved.
16. On this, see Kratzer and Heim (1998, chap. 9), by which the following subsection is inspired.
17. In some contexts, some speakers do seem to allow such an interpretation. Suppose, for example, that every student needs to consult with some professor or other about course registration and also needs to get the signature of Mary, who is the registrar.
18. If such interpretations are not impossible but only dispreferred, as suggested in the preceding note, then perhaps Fox's economy principle ought to be conceived as part of a module that establishes the relative markedness or accessibility of interpretations.
19. See Heim (1997) for an argument that VP ellipsis requires VPs to denote open formulas rather than properties.

Chapter 8

1. The *-ess* affix is not very productive in contemporary English but only a century or so ago, as women began to teach at American institutions of higher learning (especially those for women students), some suggested they should be called *professoresses*. As was pointed out in Lakoff (1975) and has been widely discussed since, such pairs are seldom distinguished only by sex of referent.
2. We are grateful to Wayles Browne and to Vicki Carstens for the Russian and the Kiswahili examples respectively.
3. Lyons (1977, vol. 1, chaps. 8–9) contains much excellent discussion of traditional work of this kind. See also Lehrer (1974) and Cruse (1986).
4. See, for example, Vendler (1967), Kenny (1963), Dowty (1979), and Verkuyl (1972, 1989), among others. We will briefly discuss below Parsons (1990), which in certain ways builds on Dowty's work.
5. Again we recommend J. D. Fodor (1977) for a thoughtful overview of both generative semantics and the work of Katz and his colleagues. Bolinger (1965) is an incisive critique of Katz and Fodor (1963). Katz's more recent work, like (1981), abandons the psychologistic perspective and proposes that the designated concepts are extramental abstract objects. Yet Katz is still uninterested in the questions about reference and truth that we have argued constitute the most powerful tool to test semantic theories. Pustejovsky (1995), which proposes a quite elaborate scheme of multi-leveled semantic representations for words, is among the most recent generativist accounts of word meaning.
6. Not all constraints on models for a language can be formulated as meaning postulates, i.e., within the language itself. Our requirement that, e.g., *woman'* should denote in any circumstance all and only those who are women in that circumstance is not a meaning postulate of IPC because it links the interpretation of IPC to that of another language, namely, English. Barwise and Perry (1983) talk generally of "constraints", and Higginbotham (1989) discusses elucidations of meaning.
7. The question of how word formation rules figure in a grammar is a complex one, which we cannot really address here. Bauer (1983) gives an introductory overview. Theoretical treatments of such issues include Lieber (1980), Selkirk (1982), Kiparsky (1988), Di Sciullo and Williams (1987), and Baker (1988). Some very illuminating work on semantic properties of English verbs appears in Levin (1993) and Levin and Rappaport Hovav (1995).
8. Wierzbicka (1996) objects to our discussion of these issues in the first edition, pointing out that *because* is acquired very early and suggesting that a basic concept of causation figures in the inventory of semantic primitives. As we say, neither acquisition nor processing data settle the issue of whether lexical items are decomposed, but such data do suggest that the relation between lexical items and concepts may be rather more complex than standard accounts envisage.
9. Hale and Keyser (1993) emphasizes the semantic relevance of the syntactic configurations in which words occur.
10. Hoshi and Saito (1993) discuss this phenomenon; we thank Takashi Toyoshima for the example. There is also considerable discussion in Baker (1996, chap. 8) of the whole issue of complex predicates.
11. Adjectives like *pink* are also vague or imprecise. We will discuss this issue in section 5.
12. See, for example, McConnell-Ginet (1973), Kamp (1975), Siegel (1976), and Klein (1980).
13. See, e.g., Jackendoff (1972, chap. 3), McConnell-Ginet (1982), Ernst (1984), and Wyner (1994) for more discussion of adverbial semantics.
14. Sometimes thematic roles are used only to develop a theory of how arguments are fed into relations. For example, van Riemsdijk and Williams (1986, 241), say that "θ-theory, as outlined here, is not committed to ... a system of argument *types* ... such as *agent*." Thematic roles in this sense have no semantic import. Here we will be concerned primarily with approaches to thematic roles according to which thematic roles like agent or experiencer are not arbitrary labels of argument slots but are viewed as having substantive semantic content. Analysis of thematic roles in formal semantic frameworks did not begin until the 1980s. See, e.g., G. Carlson (1984), Chierchia (1984, 1989), Parsons (1990, 1995), Dowty (1989), and Krifka (1987) for relevant discussion.

15. See, e.g., Dowty (1979) or Parsons (1990, 1995) for discussion. See also Kratzer (1995), which argues that objects are fed in via the ordered argument method, while subjects are fed in via thematic roles, so that, e.g., the logical form of (*a*) would be something like (*b*):
(*a*) Lee kissed Kim
(*b*) $\exists e\,[\text{kiss}'(e, \text{Kim}') \wedge \text{AGENT}\ (e) = \text{Lee}']$
Kartzer links these ideas to the semantics of voice.
16. See, for example, Rosen (1984) and Dowty (1989) for discussions of problems in arriving at semantic content of thematic roles adequate for all the different generalizations that invoke them. Jackendoff (1987) informally characterizes a particular set of thematic roles that he argues underlie the syntax-semantics correspondence, whereas Levin and Rappaport (1986) use somewhat differently conceived thematic roles in their interesting account of a word formation rule.
17. Coleman and Kay (1981) apply the prototype idea to analysis of a more abstract part of the vocabulary. More recently Lakoff (1987) has argued that prototypes are central to basic word meanings and more generally play a critical role in structuring basic conceptual categories. For all we know, some version of this view may prove right, but we disagree sharply with Lakoff's conclusion that truth-conditional theories of semantics are thereby ruled out. As the rest of this section shows, it is quite possible to hold that prototypes and similarity relations of some kind organize conceptual categories associated with individual words and still maintain a truth-conditional approach to semantics.
18. There are many different fuzzy logics, and there is especially great variation in definitions of the fuzzy conditional. Zadeh's system is essentially like Łukasiewicz's (1930) infinite-valued calculus.
19. See Morgan and Pelletier (1977) for a discussion of technical problems with fuzzy logics.
20. The general approach has been extended and further developed by Kamp (1981), Pinkal (1983, 1984, 1987), Klein (1980), and McConnell-Ginet (1989). Williamson (1994) argues that supervaluationist approaches, although in some ways superior to fuzzy logics, ultimately fail; he proposes instead a view of vagueness as not semantic but epistemic. Williamson's basic idea, which we cannot really consider here, is that we do not and cannot *know* where the line is drawn between the tall and the not tall but, given a context, there is a determinate line.
21. This definition does not do justice to the context dependency of these expressions. However, it is easy to modify it along the lines of our treatment of adjectives in section 3, for example. We will ignore these complications here, as they do not affect our main point.

Chapter 9

1. What we have been calling NP corresponds in recent syntactic work to DP (as the determiner seems to be the head of the construction). Under this analysis, it is DP that corresponds to generalized quantifiers. The literature on generalized quantifiers is quite extensive. See Barwise and Cooper (1981), Keenan and Stavi (1986), and van Benthem (1983), among others.
2. The main source of this section is Ladusaw (1979). Also see Linebarger (1987).
3. *Right upward entailing/monotone* corresponds to *monotone increasing* in the terminology of Barwise and Cooper (1981).
4. *Left upward entailing/monotone* corresponds to *persistent* in the terminology of Barwise and Cooper (1981).
5. For an analysis of *only*, see Rooth (1985) and references therein.
6. Two different versions of the proof can be found in Keenan and Stavi (1986) and van Benthem (1983). The formulation of the theorem adopted here is van Benthem's.
7. This statement is a free paraphrase of Williams (1984, 406).

References

Abusch, D. (1997). "Sequence of Tense and Temporal *De Re*." *Linguistics and Philosophy* 20: 1–50.

Aissen, J. (1974). "The Syntax of Causative Constructions." Ph.D. dissertation, Harvard University. Republished in 1979 by Garland Press, New York.

Aitchison, J. (1987). *Words in the Mind: An Introduction to the Mental Lexicon.* Oxford: Blackwell.

Allwood, J., L.-G. Andersson, and Ö. Dahl (1977). *Logic in Linguistics.* Cambridge: Cambridge University Press.

Anderson, S. R. (1972). "How to Get *Even*." *Language* 48: 893–906.

Aronoff, M. (1976). *Word Formation in Generative Grammar.* Cambridge: MIT Press.

Asher, N., and H. Kamp (1989). "Self-Reference, Attitudes, and Paradox." In G. Chierchia, B. H. Partee, and R. Turner, eds., *Properties, Types, and Meaning*, vol. 1. Dordrecht: Kluwer.

Austin, J. L. (1962). *How to Do Things with Words.* Oxford: Oxford University Press. Revised second edition, 1975.

Bach, E., E. Jelinek, A. Kratzer, and B. H. Partee, eds. (1995). *Quantification in Natural Languages.* Dordrecht: Kluwer.

Bach, E., and B. H. Partee (1980). "Anaphora and Semantic Structure." In K. J. Kreiman and A. Ojeda, eds., *Papers from the Parasession on Pronouns and Anaphora.* Chicago Linguistics Society.

Bach, K., and R. M. Harnish (1979). *Linguistic Communication and Speech Acts.* Cambridge: MIT Press.

Baker, M. (1988). *Incorporation: A Theory of Grammatical Function Changing.* Chicago: University of Chicago Press.

Baker, M. (1996). *The Polysynthesis Parameter.* New York: Oxford University Press.

Bar-Hillel, Y. (1954). "Indexical Expressions." *Mind* 63: 359–379.

Barwise, J., and R. Cooper (1981). "Generalized Quantifiers and Natural Language." *Linguistics and Philosophy* 4: 159–219.

Barwise, Jon, and John Perry (1983). *Situations and Attitudes.* Cambridge: MIT Press.

Bauer, L. (1983). *English Word-Formation.* Cambridge: Cambridge University Press.

Beaver, D. (1995). "Presupposition and Assertion in Dynamic Semantics." Ph.D. dissertation, University of Edinburgh.

Beaver, D. (1997). "Presupposition." In J. van Bentham and A. ter Meulen, eds., *The Handbook of Logic and Language.* Amsterdam: Elsevier and Cambridge: MIT Press.

Belletti, A. (1990). *Generalized Verb Movement.* Turin: Rosenberg and Sellier.

Bennett, D. C. (1975). *Spatial and Temporal Uses of English Prepositions.* London: Longman.

Bennett, M. (1978). "Demonstratives and Indexicals in Montague Grammar." *Synthese* 39: 1–80.

Bennett, M., and B. H. Partee (1978). *Towards the Logic of Tense and Aspect in English.* Bloomington: Indiana University Linguistics Club.

Benthem, J. van (1983). "Determiners and Logic." *Linguistics and Philosophy* 6: 47–88.

Bierwisch, M. (1969). "On Certain Problems of Semantic Representation." *Foundations of Language* 5: 153–184.

Bigelow, J. C. (1978). "Believing in Semantics." *Linguistics and Philosophy* 2: 101–144.

Bittner, M. (1995). "Crosslinguistic Semantics." *Linguistics and Philosophy* 17: 53–108.

Bittner, M. (1999). "Concealed Causatives." *Natural Language Semantics* 7, no. 1: 1–78.

Blakemore, D. L. (1987). *Semantic Constraints on Relevance.* Oxford: Blackwell.

Blakemore, D. L. (1989). "Denial and Contrast: A Relevance-Theoretic Analysis of BUT." *Linguistics and Philosophy* 12: 15–38.

Bochvar, D. A. (1939). "On a Three-Valued Logical Calculus and Its Application to the Analysis of Contradictories." *Matematicheskii Sbornik* 4: 287–308.

Bolinger, D. L. (1965). "The Atomization of Meaning." *Language* 41: 555–573.

Brown, P., and S. C. Levinson (1978). "Politeness: Some Universals in Language Usage." In E. Goody, ed., *Questions and Politeness.* Cambridge: Cambridge University Press. Reissued in 1987 with corrections, a new introduction, and a new bibliography as *Politeness: Some Universals in Language Usage.* Cambridge: Cambridge University Press.

Carlson, G. (1984). "On the Role of Thematic Roles in Linguistic Theory." *Linguistics* 22: 259–279.

Carlson, L. (1983). *Dialogue Games: An Approach to Discourse Analysis.* Dordrecht: D. Reidel.

Carnap, R. (1947). *Meaning and Necessity.* Chicago: Chicago University Press.

Carston, R. (1988). "Explicature, Implicature, and Truth-Theoretic Semantics." In R. Kempson, ed., *Mental Representations: The Interface between Language and Reality.* Cambridge: Cambridge University Press.

Chierchia, G. (1984). "Topics in the Syntax and Semantics of Infinitives and Gerunds." Ph.D. dissertation, University of Massachusetts at Amherst. Republished in 1989 by Garland Press, New York.

Chierchia, G. (1989). "Structured Meanings, Thematic Roles, and Control." In G. Chierchia, B. H. Partee, and R. Turner, eds., *Properties, Types, and Meaning,* vol. 2, *Semantic Issues.* Dordrecht: Kluwer.

Chierchia, G. (1998a). "Plurality of Mass Nouns and the Notion of Semantic Parameter." In S. Rothstein, ed., *Events in Grammar.* Dordrecht: Kluwer.

Chierchia, G. (1998b). "Reference to Kinds across Languages." *Natural Language Semantics* 6, no. 4: 339–345.

Chomsky, N. (1957). *Syntactic Structures.* The Hague: Mouton.

Chomsky, N. (1965). *Aspects of the Theory of Syntax.* Cambridge: MIT Press.

Chomsky, N. (1981). *Lectures on Government and Binding.* Dordrecht: Foris.

Chomsky, N. (1986). *Knowledge of Language: Its Nature, Origin, and Use.* New York: Praeger.

Chomsky, N. (1995). *The Minimalist Program.* Cambridge: MIT Press.

Church, A. (1956). *Introduction to Mathematical Logic.* Princeton: Princeton University Press.

Coleman, L., and P. Kay (1981). "Prototype Semantics: The English Verb *Lie.*" *Language* 57: 26–44.

Cooper, R. (1979). "The Interpretation of Pronouns." In F. Heny and H. Schnelle, eds., *Selections from the Third Groningen Roundtable,* Syntax and Semantics, no. 10. New York: Academic Press.

Cooper, R. (1983). *Quantification and Syntactic Theory.* Dordrecht: D. Reidel.

Cresswell, M. J. (1973). *Logics and Languages.* London: Methuen.

Cresswell, M. J. (1978). "Prepositions and Points of View." *Linguistics and Philosophy* 2: 1–42.

Cresswell, M. J. (1985). *Structured Meanings.* Cambridge: MIT Press.

Cresswell, M., and A. von Stechow (1982). "*De Re* Belief Generalized." *Linguistics and Philosophy* 5: 503–535.

Cruse, D. A. (1986). *Lexical Semantics.* Cambridge: Cambridge University Press.

Curry, H. B. (1930). "Grundlagen der kombinatorischen Logik." *American Journal of Mathematics* 52: 509–536, 789–834.

Davidson, D. (1967a). "Truth and Meaning." *Synthese* 17: 304–323. Reprinted in A. P. Martinich, ed., *The Philosophy of Language.* Oxford: Oxford University Press, 1985.

Davidson, D. (1967b). "The Logical Form of Action Sentences." In N. Rescher, ed., *The Logic of Decision and Action.* Pittsburgh: Pittsburgh University Press.

Davidson, D. (1969). "On Saying That." In D. Davidson and J. Hintikka, eds., *Words and Objections: Essays on the Work of W. V. O. Quine.* Dordrecht: D. Reidel. Reprinted in A. P. Martinich, ed., *The Philosophy of Language.* Oxford: Oxford University Press, 1985.

Davidson, D. (1977). "The Method of Truth in Metaphysics." In P. French, T. Uehling, and H. Wettstein, eds., *Contemporary Perspectives in the Philosophy of Language.* Minneapolis: University of Minnesota Press.

Di Sciullo, A. M., and E. Williams (1987). *On the Definition of Word.* Cambridge: MIT Press.

Donnellan, K. (1966). "Reference and Definite Descriptions." *Philosophical Review* 75: 281–304. Reprinted in A. P. Martinich, ed., *The Philosophy of Language.* Oxford: Oxford University Press, 1985.

Dowty, D. (1979). *Word Meaning and Montague Grammar.* Dordrecht: D. Reidel.

Dowty, D. (1982). "Tense, Time Adverbials, and Compositional Semantic Theory." *Linguistics and Philosophy* 5: 23–58.

Dowty, D. (1985). "On Recent Analyses of the Semantics of Control." *Linguistics and Philosophy* 8: 291–331.

Dowty, D. (1989). "On the Semantic Content of the Notion of 'Thematic Role'." In G. Chierchia, B. H. Partee, and R. Turner, eds., *Properties, Types, and Meaning,* vol. 2, *Semantic Issues.* Dordrecht: Kluwer.

Dowty, D., R. Wall, and S. Peters (1981). *Introduction to Montague Semantics.* Dordrecht: D. Reidel.

Enç, M. (1981). "Tense without Scope: An Analysis of Nouns as Indexicals." Ph.D. dissertation, University of Wisconsin.

Engdahl, E. (1986). *Constituent Questions.* Dordrecht: D. Reidel.

Ernst, T. B. (1984). "Towards an Integrated Theory of Adverb Position in English." Ph.D. dissertation, Indiana University. Distributed by the Indiana University Linguistics Club, Bloomington.

Evans, G. (1980). "Pronouns." *Linguistic Inquiry* 11: 337–362.

Fiengo, R., and R. May (1994). *Indices and Identity.* Cambridge: MIT Press.

Fillmore, C. J. (1968). "The Case for Case." In E. Bach and R. T. Harms. eds., *Universals in Linguistic Theory.* New York: Holt, Rinehart and Winston.

Fillmore, C. J. (1975). *Santa Cruz Lectures on Deixis, 1971.* Bloomington: Indiana University Linguistics Club. Reissued as *Lectures on Deixis.* Stanford: CSLI Publications, 1997.

Fine, K. (1975). "Vagueness, Truth, and Logic." *Synthese* 30: 265–300.

Fodor, J. A. (1975). *The Language of Thought.* New York: Thomas Y. Crowell.

Fodor, J. A. (1978). "Propositional Attitudes." *Monist* 61: 501–523.

Fodor, J. A. (1981). *Representations.* Cambridge: MIT Press.

Fodor, J. A. (1987). *Psychosemantics.* Cambridge: MIT Press.

Fodor, J. D. (1970). "The Linguistic Description of Opaque Contexts." Ph.D. dissertation, MIT. Republished in 1979 by Garland Press, New York.

Fodor, J. D. (1977). *Semantics: Theories of Meaning in Generative Grammar.* New York: Thomas Y. Crowell.

Fodor, J. D., J. A. Fodor, and M. F. Garrett (1975). "The Psychological Unreality of Semantic Representations." *Linguistic Inquiry* 6: 515–531.

Fox, D. (1995). "Economy and Scope." *Natural Language Semantics* 3: 283–341.

Fraassen, B. van (1966). "Singular Terms, Truth-Value Gaps, and Free Logics." *Journal of Philosophy* 63: 481–495.

Fraassen, B. van (1969). "Presuppositions, Supervaluations, and Free Logics." In K. Lambert, ed., *The Logical Way of Doing Things.* New Haven: Yale University Press.

Frege, G. (1892). "Über Sinn und Bedeutung." *Zeitschrift für Philosophie und philosophische Kritik,* new series 100: 22–50. English translation in P. Geach and M. Black, eds., *Translations from the Philosophical Writings of Gottlob Frege.* Oxford: Blackwell, 1980. Reprinted in A. P. Martinich, ed., *The Philosophy of Language.* Oxford: Oxford University Press, 1985.

Frege, G. (1918). "Der Gedanke." *Beitrage zur Philosophie des deutschen Idealismus* 2: 58–77. English translation in G. Frege, *Logical Investigations,* ed. by P. T. Geach. New Haven: Yale University Press, 1977.

Freidin, R., ed. (1991). *Principles and Parameters in Comparative Grammar.* Cambridge: MIT Press.

Gazdar, G. (1979). *Pragmatics: Implicature, Presupposition, and Logical Form.* New York: Academic Press.

Gazdar, G., E. Klein, G. Pullum, and I. Sag (1985). *Generalized Phrase Structure Grammar.* Oxford: Blackwell.

Geach, P. (1962). *Reference and Generality.* Ithaca: Cornell University Press.

Geurts, B. (1994). "Presupposing." Ph.D. dissertation, Universität Osnabrück, Germany.

Ginet, C. (1979). "Performativity." *Linguistics and Philosophy* 3: 245–265.

Grice, H. P. (1957). "Meaning." *Philosophical Review* 67: 377–388. Also in Grice (1989).

Grice, H. P. (1968). "Utterer's Meaning, Sentence-Meaning, and Word-Meaning." *Foundations of Language* 4: 225–242. Also in Grice (1989).

Grice, H. P. (1969). "Utterer's Meaning and Intentions." *Philosophical Review* 78: 147–177. Reprinted in A. P. Martinich, ed., *The Philosophy of Language* (Oxford: Oxford University Press, 1985) and in Grice (1989).

Grice, H. P. (1975). "Logic and Conversation." In P. Cole and J. Morgan, eds., *Speech Acts,* Syntax and Semantics, no. 3. Reprinted in A. P. Martinich, ed., *The Philosophy of Language* (Oxford: Oxford University Press, 1985) and in Grice (1989).

Grice, H. P. (1978). "More on Logic and Conversation." In P. Cole, ed., *Pragmatics,* Syntax and Semantics, no. 9. Reprinted in Grice (1989).

Grice, H. P. (1982). "Meaning Revisited." In N. V. Smith, ed., *Mutual Knowledge.* New York: Academic Press. Reprinted in Grice (1989).

Grice, H. P. (1989). *Studies in the Way of Words.* Cambridge: Harvard University Press.

Groenendijk, J., and M. Stokhof (1984). *Studies on the Semantics of Questions and the Pragmatics of Answers.* Amsterdam: Juriaans.

Gruber, J. (1965). "Studies in Lexical Relations." Ph.D. dissertation, MIT. Distributed by the Indiana University Linguistics Club, Bloomington. Reprinted in Gruber, *Lexical Structures in Syntax and Semantics.* Amsterdam: North Holland, 1976.

Haegeman, L. (1990). *Introduction to Government and Binding Theory.* Oxford: Blackwell.

Hale, K., and S. J. Keyser (1993). "On Argument Structure and the Lexical Expression of Syntactic Relations." In K. Hale and S. J. Keyser, eds., *The View from Building 20: Essays in Linguistics in Honor of Sylvain Bromberger.* Cambridge: MIT Press.

Halmos, P. R. (1960). *Naive Set Theory.* Princeton, N.J.: D. Van Nostrand.

Hankamer, J., and I. Sag (1976). "Deep and Surface Anaphora." *Linguistic Inquiry* 7: 391–426.

Harman, G., ed., (1974). *On Noam Chomsky: Critical Essays.* Garden City, N.Y.: Doubleday.

Heim, I. (1982). "The Semantics of Definite and Indefinite NPs." Ph.D. dissertation, University of Massachusetts at Amherst. Republished in 1989 by Garland Press, New York.

Heim, I. (1983). "On the Projection Problem for Presuppositions." In M. Barlow, D. P. Flickinger, and M. T. Westcoat, eds., *Proceedings of the West Coast Conference on Formal Linguistics,* vol. 2. Stanford Linguistics Association, Stanford University.

Heim, I. (1992). "Presupposition Projection and the Semantics of Attitude Verbs." *Journal of Semantics* 9: 183–221.

Heim, I. (1997). "Predicates or Formulas? Evidence from VP Ellipsis." In A. Lawson, ed., *Proceedings of SALT VII.* CLC Publications, Cornell University.

Higginbotham, J. (1983). "Logical Form, Binding, and Nominals." *Linguistic Inquiry* 14: 395–420.

Higginbotham, J. (1989). "Elucidations of Meaning." *Linguistics and Philosophy* 12: 465–518.

Higginbotham, J. (1992). "Reference and Control." In Larson et al. (1992).

Hinrichs, E. (1986). "Temporal Anaphora in Discourses of English." *Linguistics and Philosophy* 9: 63–82.

Hirschbühler, P. (1982). "VP Deletion and Across the Board Quantifier Scope." In J. Pustejovsky and P. Sells, eds., *Proceedings of NELS*, vol. 12. GLSA, Amherst, Mass.

Horn, L. R. (1972). "On the Semantic Properties of Logical Operators in English." Ph.D. dissertation, UCLA. Distributed by the Indiana University Linguistics Club, Bloomington.

Horn, L. R. (1985). "Metalinguistic Negation and Pragmatic Ambiguity." *Language* 61: 121–174. A revised and expanded version appears as chapter 6 of Horn (1989).

Horn, L. R. (1989). *A Natural History of Negation*. Chicago: University of Chicago Press.

Hornsby, J. (1977). "Singular Terms in Contexts of Propositional Attitude." *Mind* 86: 31–48.

Hornstein, N. (1990). *As Time Goes By*. Cambridge: MIT Press.

Hoshi, H., and M. Saito (1993). "The Japanese Light Verb Construction: A Case of LF Theta Marking." In J. Abe, H. Hoshi, Y. Miyamoto, and M. Saito, eds., *A Formal Grammar of Japanese II*, Second Annual Research Report submitted to BBN Systems and Technologies. University of Connecticut, Storrs.

Huntley, M. (1984). "The Semantics of English Imperatives." *Linguistics and Philosophy* 7: 103–133.

Jackendoff, R. (1972). *Semantic Interpretation in Generative Grammar*. Cambridge: MIT Press.

Jackendoff, R. (1976). "Towards an Explanatory Semantic Representation." *Linguistic Inquiry* 7: 89–150.

Jackendoff, R. (1983). *Semantics and Cognition*. Cambridge: MIT Press.

Jackendoff, R. (1987). "The Status of Thematic Relations in Grammatical Theory." *Linguistic Inquiry* 18: 369–411.

Jacobson, P. (1992). "Flexible Categorial Grammar: Questions and Prospects." In R. Levine, ed., *Formal Grammar: Theory and Implementation*, pp. 168–142. Oxford: Oxford University Press.

Jaeggli, O., and K. Safir, eds. (1989). *The Null Subject Parameter*. Dordrecht: Kluwer.

Johnson-Laird, P. (1983). *Mental Models*. Cambridge: Harvard University Press.

Kadmon, N. (1987). "On Unique and Non-unique Reference and Asymmetric Quantification." Ph.D. dissertation, University of Massachusetts.

Kamp, H. (1971). "Formal Properties of 'Now'." *Theoria* 37: 227–273.

Kamp, H. (1975). "Two Theories about Adjectives." In E. Keenan, ed., *Formal Semantics of Natural Language*. Cambridge: Cambridge University Press.

Kamp, H. (1981). "A Theory of Truth and Discourse Representation." In J. Groenendijk, T. Janssen, and M. Stokhof, eds., *Formal Methods in the Study of Language*. Mathematical Centre Tracts, no. 135. Amsterdam: Mathematisch Centrum.

Kamp, H., and U. Reyle (1993). *From Discourse to Logic*. Dordrecht: Kluwer.

Kaplan, D. (1969). "Quantifying In." In D. Davidson and J. Hintikka, eds., *Words and Objections: Essays on the Work of W. V. O. Quine*. Dordrecht: Reidel.

Kaplan, D. (1977). "Demonstratives." Reprinted in J. Almog, J. Perry, and H. Wettstein, eds., *Themes from Kaplan*, New York: Oxford University Press, 1989.

Karttunen, L. (1973). "Presuppositions of Compound Sentences." *Linguistic Inquiry* 4: 169–193.

Karttunen, L. (1977). "The Syntax and Semantics of Questions." *Linguistics and Philosophy* 1: 3–44.

Karttunen, L., and S. Peters (1979). "Conventional Implicature." In C.-K. Oh and D. A. Dineen, eds., *Presupposition*, Syntax and Semantics, no. 11. New York: Academic Press.

Katz, J. J. (1966). *The Philosophy of Language*. New York: Harper and Row.

Katz, J. J. (1972). *Semantic Theory*. New York: Harper and Row.

Katz, J. J. (1981). *Language and Other Abstract Objects*. Totowa, N.J.: Rowman and Littlefield.

Katz, J. J., and J. A. Fodor (1963). "The Structure of a Semantic Theory." *Language* 39: 170–210.

Katz, J. J., and P. M. Postal (1964). *An Integrated Theory of Linguistic Descriptions*. Cambridge: MIT Press.

Kay, P., and C. K. McDaniel (1978). "The Linguistic Significance of the Meanings of Basic Color Terms." *Language* 54: 610–646.

Keenan, E. L. (1969). "A Logical Base for English." Ph.D. dissertation, University of Pennsylvania.

Keenan, E. L., and L. M. Faltz (1985). *Boolean Semantics for Natural Language.* Dordrecht: D. Reidel.

Keenan, E. L., and J. Stavi (1986). "A Semantic Characterization of Natural Language Determiners." *Linguistics and Philosophy* 9: 253–326.

Kempson, R. M. (1975). *Presupposition and the Delimitation of Semantics.* Cambridge: Cambridge University Press.

Kenny, A. (1963). *Actions, Emotions, and Will.* New York: Humanities Press.

Kiparsky, P. (1988). "Morphology and Grammatical Relations." Manuscript, Department of Linguistics, Stanford University.

Klein, E. (1978). "On Sentences Which Report Beliefs, Desires, and Other Mental States." Ph.D. dissertation, University of Cambridge.

Klein, E. (1980). "A Semantics for Positive and Comparative Adjectives." *Linguistics and Philosophy* 4: 1–45.

Klein, E., and I. Sag (1985). "Type-Driven Translation." *Linguistics and Philosophy* 8: 163–201.

Kratzer, A. (1981). "The Notional Category of Modality." In H. Eikmeyer and H. Rieser, eds., *Words, Worlds, and Contexts.* Berlin: de Gruyter.

Kratzer, A. (1995). "The Semantics of Voice." *Proceedings of the 13th West Coast Conference on Formal Linguistics.*

Kratzer, A. (1998). "Scope or Pseudoscope? Are There Widescope Indefinites?" In S. Rothstein, ed., *Events in Grammar.* Dordrecht: Kluwer.

Kratzer, A., and I. Heim (1998). *Semantics in Generative Grammar.* Oxford: Blackwell.

Krifka, M. (1987). "Nominal Reference and Temporal Constitution: Towards a Semantics of Quantity." In J. Groenendijk, M. Stokhof, and F. Veltman, eds., *Proceedings of the Sixth Amsterdam Colloquium.* Instituut voor Taal, Logica en Informatie, University of Amsterdam, Amsterdam.

Kripke, S. (1959). "A Completeness Theorem in Modal Logic." *Journal of Symbolic Logic* 24: 1–14.

Kripke, S. (1963). "Semantical Considerations on Modal Logic." *Acta Philosophica Fennica* 16: 83–89.

Kripke, S. (1972). "Naming and Necessity." In D. Davidson and G. Harman, eds., *Semantics for Natural Language.* Dordrecht: D. Reidel. Revised edition published as S. Kripke, *Naming and Necessity.* Oxford: Blackwell, 1980. Selections reprinted in A. P. Martinich, ed., *The Philosophy of Language.* Oxford: Oxford University Press, 1985.

Kripke, S. (1977). "Speaker's Reference and Semantic Reference." In P. A. French, T. E. Uehling, and H. K. Wettstein, eds., *Contemporary Perspectives in the Philosophy of Language.* Minneapolis: University of Minnesota Press. Reprinted in A. P. Martinich, ed., *The Philosophy of Language.* Oxford: Oxford University Press, 1985.

Ladusaw, W. (1979). "Polarity Sensitivity as Inherent Scope Relations." Ph.D. dissertation, University of Texas at Austin. Distributed by the Indiana University Linguistics Club, Bloomington.

Ladusaw, W., and D. Dowty (1988). "Towards a Non-grammatical Account of Thematic Roles." In W. Wilkins, ed., *Thematic Relations.* New York: Academic Press.

Laka, I. (1990). "Negation in Syntax: On the Nature of Functional Categories and Projections." Ph.D. dissertation, MIT.

Lakoff, G. (1965). *On the Nature of Syntactic Irregularity.* Report NSF-16, The Computation Laboratory of Harvard University. Reprinted as G. Lakoff, *Irregularity in Syntax.* New York: Holt, Rinehart and Winston, 1970.

Lakoff, G. (1972). "Hedges: A Study in Meaning Criteria and the Logic of Fuzzy Concepts." In P. M. Peranteau, J. N. Levi, and G. C. Phares, eds., *Papers from the Eighth Regional Meeting of the Chicago Linguistics Society.* Chicago. Reprinted in *Journal of Philosophical Logic* 2 (1973): 458–508.

Lakoff, G. (1987). *Women, Fire, and Dangerous Things: What Categories Reveal about the Mind.* Chicago: University of Chicago Press.

Lakoff, R. (1975). *Language and Woman's Place.* New York: Harper and Row.

Langendoen, D. T., and H. B. Savin (1971). "The Projection Problem for Presuppositions." In C. J. Fillmore and D. T. Langendoen, eds., *Studies in Linguistic Semantics.* New York: Holt, Rinehart and Winston.

Lappin, S., ed. (1996). *The Handbook of Contemporary Semantic Theory.* Oxford: Blackwell Reference.

Larson, R., S. Iatridou, U. Lahiri, and J. Higginbotham (1992). *Control and Grammar.* Dordrecht: Kluwer.

Larson, R., and G. Segal (1995). *Knowledge of Meaning.* Cambridge: MIT Press.

Lasnik, H. (1976). "Remarks on Coreference." *Linguistic Analysis* 2: 1–22.

Lehrer, A. (1974). *Semantic Fields and Lexical Structure.* Amsterdam: North-Holland.

Levin, B. (1993). *Towards a Lexical Organization of English Verbs.* Chicago: University of Chicago Press.

Levin, B., and M. Rappaport (1986). "The Formation of Adjectival Passives." *Linguistic Inquiry* 17: 623–661.

Levin, B., and M. Rappaport Hovav (1995). *Unaccusatives: At the Syntax-Lexical Semantics Interface.* Cambridge: MIT Press.

Levinson, S. C. (1983). *Pragmatics.* Cambridge: Cambridge University Press.

Levinson, S. C. (forthcoming). *Presumptive Meanings: The Theory of Generalized Conversational Implicature.* Cambridge: MIT Press.

Lewis, D. (1969). *Convention.* Cambridge: Harvard University Press.

Lewis, D. (1972). "General Semantics." In D. Davidson and G. Harman, eds., *Semantics for Natural Language.* Dordrecht: D. Reidel. Reprinted in B. H. Partee, ed., *Montague Grammar.* New York: Academic Press, 1976.

Lewis, D. (1973). *Counterfactuals.* Oxford: Blackwell.

Lewis, D. (1979). "Scorekeeping in a Language Game." In R. Bäuerle, U. Egli, and A. von Stechow, eds., *Semantics from Different Points of View.* Berlin: Springer Verlag.

Lieber, R. (1980). "On the Organization of the Lexicon." Ph.D. dissertation, MIT. Distributed by the Indiana University Linguistics Club, Bloomington.

Linebarger, M. (1987). "Negative Polarity and Grammatical Representation." *Linguistics and Philosophy* 10: 325–387.

Link, G. (1983). "The Logical Analysis of Plural and Mass Terms: A Lattice-Theoretic Approach." In R. Bäuerle, C. Schwarze, and A. von Stechow, eds., *Meaning, Use, and Interpretation of Language.* Berlin: de Gruyter.

Łukasiewicz, J. (1930). "Many-Valued Systems of Propositional Logic." In S. McCall, ed., *Polish Logic.* Oxford: Oxford University Press, 1967.

Lyons, J. (1977). *Semantics.* Vols. 1 and 2. Cambridge: Cambridge University Press.

Matossian, L. A. (1997). "Burglars, Babysitters, and Persons: A Sociolinguistic Study of Generic Pronoun Usage in Philadelphia and Minneapolis." Ph.D. dissertation, University of Pennsylvania.

May, R. (1977). "The Grammar of Quantification." Ph.D. dissertation, MIT. Distributed by the Indiana University Linguistics Club, Bloomington.

May, R. (1985). *Logical Form: Its Structure and Derivation.* Cambridge: MIT Press.

McCawley, J. D. (1968). "Lexical Insertion in a Grammar without Deep Structure." In B. J. Darden, C.-J. N. Bailey, and A. Davison, eds., *Papers from the Fourth Regional Meeting of the Chicago Linguistics Society.* Chicago.

McCawley, J. D. (1971). "Prelexical Syntax." In R. S. O'Brien, ed., *Report of the Twenty-Second Annual Round Table Meeting on Linguistics and Language Studies,* Monograph Series on Languages and Linguistics, no. 24. Washington: Georgetown University Press.

McConnell-Ginet, S. (1973). "The Syntax and Semantics of Comparative Constructions in English." Ph.D. dissertation, University of Rochester.

McConnell-Ginet, S. (1982). "Toward a Linguistically Realistic Theory of Adverbs." *Language* 58: 144–184.

McConnell-Ginet, S. (1989). "The Construction of Meaning: Formal Semantics and Vagueness." Manuscript, Department of Modern Languages and Linguistics, Cornell University.

Montague, R. (1968). "Pragmatics." In R. Klibansky, ed., *Contemporary Philosophy: A Survey.* Florence: La Nuova Italia Editrice. Reprinted in Montague (1974).

Montague, R. (1973). "The Proper Treatment of Quantification in Ordinary English." In J. Hintikka, J. Moravcsik, and P. Suppes, eds., *Approaches to Natural Language.* Dordrecht: D. Reidel. Reprinted in Montague (1974).

Montague, R. (1974). *Formal Philosophy: Selected Papers of Richard Montague.* Ed. by R. H. Thomason. New Haven: Yale University Press.

Morgan, C. J., and F. J. Pelletier (1977). "Some Notes Concerning Fuzzy Logics." *Linguistics and Philosophy* 1: 79–98.

Morgan, J. L. (1969). "On the Treatment of Presuppositions in Transformational Grammar." In R. I. Binnick, A. Davison, G. Green, and J. Morgan. eds., *Papers from the Fifth Regional Meeting of the Chicago Linguistics Society.* Chicago.

Neale, S. (1990). *Descriptions.* Cambridge: MIT Press.

Parsons, T. (1990). *Events in the Semantics of English.* Cambridge: MIT Press.

Parsons, T. (1995). "Thematic Relations and Arguments." *Linguistic Inquiry* 26: 635–662.

Partee, B. H. (1973). "Some Structural Analogies between Tenses and Pronouns in English." *Journal of Philosophy* 70: 601–609.

Partee, B. H. (1979). "Semantics: Mathematics or Psychology?" In R. Bäuerle, U. Egli, and A. von Stechow, eds., *Semantics from Different Points of View.* Berlin: Springer Verlag.

Partee, B. H., and M. Rooth (1983). "Generalized Conjunction and Type Ambiguity." In R. Bäuerle, C. Schwarze, and A. von Stechow, eds., *Meaning, Use, and Interpretation of Language.* Berlin: de Gruyter.

Partee, B. H., A. ter Meulen, and R. Wall (1990). *Mathematical Methods in Linguistics.* Dordrecht: Kluwer.

Peacocke, C. (1975). "Proper Names, Reference, and Rigid Designation." In S. Blackburn, ed., *Meaning, Reference, and Necessity,* pp. 109–132. Cambridge: Cambridge University Press.

Peirce, C. S. (1902). "Logic as Semiotic: The Theory of Signs." Reprinted in C. S. Peirce, *Philosophical Writings,* ed. J. Buchler. New York: Dover, 1935.

Pelletier, F. J., ed. (1979). *Mass Terms: Some Philosophical Problems.* Dordrecht: D. Reidel.

Perrault, C. R. (1987). "An Application of Default Logic to Speech Act Theory." Report no. CSLI-87-90, Center for the Study of Language and Information, Stanford University.

Pinkal, M. (1983). "Towards a Semantics of Precisification." In T. Ballmer and M. Pinkal, eds., *Approaching Vagueness.* Amsterdam: North-Holland.

Pinkal, M. (1984). "Consistency and Context Change: The Sorites Paradox." In F. Landman and F. Veltman, eds., *Varieties of Formal Semantics.* Dordrecht: Foris.

Pinkal, M. (1987). "Imprecise Concepts and Quantification." Manuscript, Institute of Linguistics, University of Stuttgart.

Pollard, C., and I. Sag (1988). *Information-Based Syntax and Semantics,* vol. 1, *Fundamentals.* Chicago: University of Chicago Press.

Pollock, J.-Y. (1989). "Verb Movement, Universal Grammar, and the Structure of IP." *Linguistic Inquiry* 20: 365–424.

Postal, P. M. (1970). "On the Surface Verb 'Remind'." *Linguistic Inquiry* 1: 37–120. Also in C. J. Fillmore and D. T. Langendoen, eds., *Studies in Linguistic Semantics.* New York: Holt, Rinehart and Winston, 1971.

Postal, P. M. (1971). *Cross-Over Phenomena.* New York: Holt, Rinehart and Winston.

Prior, A. N. (1967). *Past, Present, and Future.* Oxford: Oxford University Press.

Pustejovsky, J. (1995). *The Generative Lexicon.* Cambridge: MIT Press

Putnam, H. (1975). "The Meaning of 'Meaning'." In K. Gunderson, ed., *Language, Mind, and Knowledge.* Minneapolis: University of Minnesota Press.

Quine, W. V. O. (1960). *Word and Object.* Cambridge: MIT Press.

Radford, A. (1988). *Transformational Grammar.* Cambridge: Cambridge University Press.
Reichenbach, H. (1947). *Elements of Symbolic Logic.* New York: Free Press.
Reinhart, T. (1979). "Syntactic Domains for Semantic Rules." In F. Guenthner and S. J. Schmidt, eds., *Formal Semantics and Pragmatics for Natural Language.* Dordrecht: D. Reidel.
Reinhart, T. (1983a). "Coreference and Bound Anaphora: A Restatement of the Anaphora Question." *Linguistics and Philosophy* 6: 47–88.
Reinhart, T. (1983b). *Anaphora and Semantic Interpretation.* Sidney: Croom Helm.
Reinhart, T. (1997). "Quantifier Scope: How Labor Is Divided between QR and Choice Functions." *Linguistics and Philosophy* 20: 335–397.
Reinhart, T., and E. Reuland (1993). "Reflexivity." *Linguistic Inquiry* 24: 657–720.
Roberts, C. (1987). "Modal Subordination, Anaphora, and Distributivity." Ph.D. dissertation, University of Massachusetts at Amherst.
Rodman, R. (1976). "Scope Phenomena, 'Movement Transformation,' and Relative Clauses." In B. H. Partee, ed., *Montague Grammar.* New York: Academic Press.
Rooth, M. (1985). "Association with Focus." Ph.D. dissertation, University of Massachusetts at Amherst.
Rooth, M. (1996). "Focus." In S. Lappin, ed., *The Handbook of Contemporary Semantic Theory.* Oxford: Blackwell.
Rosen, C. (1984). "The Interface between Semantic Roles and Initial Grammatical Relations." In D. M. Perlmutter and C. Rosen, eds., *Studies in Relational Grammar,* vol. 2. Chicago: University of Chicago Press.
Rosenbaum, P. (1967). *The Grammar of English Predicate Complement Constructions.* Cambridge: MIT Press.
Ross, J. R. (1966). "Constraints on Variables in Syntax." Ph.D. dissertation, MIT. Distributed by the Indiana University Linguistics Club, Bloomington.
Ross, J. R. (1970). "On Declarative Sentences." In R. A. Jacobs and P. S. Rosenbaum, eds., *Readings in English Transformational Grammar.* Waltham, Mass.: Ginn.
Russell, Bertrand. (1905). "On Denoting." *Mind* 14: 479–493.
Sadock, J. (1974). *Toward a Linguistic Theory of Speech Acts.* New York: Academic Press.
Sag, I. (1976). "Deletion and Logical Form." Ph.D. dissertation, MIT. Republished in 1980 by Garland Press, New York.
Sag, I., and E. Prince (1979). "Bibliography of Works Dealing with Presupposition." In C.-K. Oh and D. A. Dinneen, eds., *Presupposition,* Syntax and Semantics, no. 11. New York: Academic Press.
Sag, I., T. Wasow, G. Gazdar, and S. Weisler (1985). "Coordination and How to Distinguish Categories." *Natural Language and Linguistic Theory* 3: 117–171.
Saussure, F. de (1916). *Cours de linguistique generale.* Paris: Payot. English translation published as *A Course in General Linguistics.* New York: Philosophical Library, 1959.
Schiffer, S. (1972). *Meaning.* Oxford: Oxford University Press.
Schönfinkel, Moses (1924). "Über die Bausteine der mathematischen Logik." *Mathematischen Annalen* 92: 305–316.
Searle, J. (1965). "What Is a Speech Act?" In M. Black, ed., *Philosophy in America.* Ithaca: Cornell University Press. Reprinted in A. P. Martinich, ed., *The Philosophy of Language.* Oxford: Oxford University Press, 1985.
Searle, J. (1969). *Speech Acts.* Cambridge: Cambridge University Press.
Selkirk, E. O. (1982). *The Syntax of Words.* Cambridge: MIT Press.
Siegel, M. (1976). "Capturing the Russian Adjective." In B. H. Partee, ed., *Montague Grammar.* New York: Academic Press.
Simons, M. (1998). "'Or': The Semantics and Pragmatics of Disjunction." Ph.D. dissertation, Cornell University.
Soames, S. (1979). "A Projection Problem for Speaker Presupposition." *Linguistic Inquiry* 10: 623–666.
Sperber, D., and D. Wilson (1986). *Relevance: Communication and Cognition.* Cambridge: Harvard University Press.
Stalnaker, R. (1968). "A Theory of Conditionals." In N. Rescher, ed., *Studies in Logical Theory.* Oxford: Blackwell.

Stalnaker, R. (1974). "Pragmatic Presuppositions." In M. Munitz and P. Unger, eds., *Semantics and Philosophy*. New York: New York University Press.

Stalnaker, R. (1978). "Assertion." In P. Cole, ed., *Pragmatics*, Syntax and Semantics, no. 9. New York: Academic Press.

Stalnaker, R. (1984). *Inquiry*. Cambridge: MIT Press.

Stockwell, R. P., P. Schachter, and B. H. Partee (1973). *The Major Syntactic Structures of English*. New York: Holt, Rinehart and Winston.

Stoll, R. R. (1963). *Set Theory and Logic*. San Francisco: W. H. Freeman and Co.

Strawson, P. F. (1950). "On Referring." *Mind* 59: 320–344.

Tarski, A. (1935). "Der Warheitsbegriff in den formalizierten Sprachen." *Studia Philosphica* 1: 261–405. English translation in A. Tarski, *Logic, Semantics, and Metamathematics*. Oxford: Oxford University Press, 1956.

Tarski, A. (1944). "The Semantic Conception of Truth." In *Philosophy and Phenomenological Research* 4: 341–375. Reprinted in A. P. Martinich, ed., *The Philosophy of Language*. Oxford: Oxford University Press, 1985.

Thomason, R. H. (1974). "Introduction." In R. Montague (1974).

Thomason, R. H. (1977). "Indirect Discourse Is Not Quotational." *Monist* 60: 340–354.

Thomason, R. H. (1980). "A Note on the Syntactical Treatment of Modalities." *Synthese* 44: 391–395.

Travis, L. (1984). "Parameters and Effects of Word Order Variation." Ph.D. dissertation, MIT.

Van der Sandt, R. (1988). *Context and Presupposition*. London: Croom Helm.

Van der Sandt, R. (1992). "Presupposition Projection as Anaphora Resolution. *Journal of Semantics* 9: 333–377.

Van Riemsdijk, H., and E. Williams (1986). *Introduction to the Theory of Grammar*. Cambridge: MIT Press.

Vendler, Z. (1967). *Linguistics in Philosophy*. Ithaca: Cornell University Press.

Verkuyl, H. J. (1972). *On the Compositional Nature of the Aspects*. Dordrecht: D. Reidel.

Verkuyl, H. J. (1989). "Aspectual Classes and Aspectual Composition." *Linguistics and Philosophy* 12: 39–94.

Wall, R. (1972). Introduction to Mathematical Linguistics. Englewood Cliffs, N.J.: Prentice-Hall.

Wierzbicka, A. (1996). *Semantics: Primes and Universals*. Oxford and New York: Oxford University Press.

Williams, E. (1977). "Discourse and Logical Form." *Linguistic Inquiry* 15: 131–153.

Williams, E. (1984). Review of N. Chomsky, *Lectures on Government and Binding and Some Concepts and Consequences of the Theory of Government and Binding*. *Language* 60: 400–408.

Williamson, T. (1994). Vagueness. London and New York: Routledge.

Wilson, D. (1975). *Presuppositions and Non-truth-conditional Semantics*. New York: Academic Press.

Wyner, A. Z. (1994). "Boolean Event Lattices and Thematic Roles in the Syntax and Semantics of Adverbial Modification." Ph.D. dissertation, Cornell University.

Zadeh, L. (1965). "Fuzzy Sets." *Information and Control* 8: 338–353.

Zeevat, H. (1984). "Belief." In F. Landman and F. Veltman, eds., *Varieties of Formal Semantics*. Dordrecht: Foris.

Zucchi, S. (forthcoming). *Lectures on Tense and Aspect*. Center for the Study of Language and Information, Stanford University.

Index